THE OXFORD HAND

ABRAHAMIC RELIGIONS

THE OXFORD HANDBOOK OF THE

ABRAHAMIC RELIGIONS

Edited by

ADAM J. SILVERSTEIN

and

GUY G. STROUMSA

Associate Editor

MOSHE BLIDSTEIN

OXFORD

UNIVERSITY PRESS

OXFORD
UNIVERSITY PRESS

Great Clarendon Street, Oxford, OX2 6DP,
United Kingdom

Oxford University Press is a department of the University of Oxford.
It furthers the University's objective of excellence in research, scholarship,
and education by publishing worldwide. Oxford is a registered trade mark of
Oxford University Press in the UK and in certain other countries

First published 2015
First published in paperback 2018

Published in the United States of America by Oxford University Press
198 Madison Avenue, New York, NY 10016, United States of America

British Library Cataloguing in Publication Data
Data available

Library of Congress Cataloging in Publication Data
Data available

ISBN 978–0–19–969776–2 (Hbk.)
ISBN 978–0–19–878301–5 (Pbk.)

The editors wish to dedicate this Handbook to two towering scholars
in recognition of their pioneering work
in deciphering the roots of the Abrahamic religions
and fostering relations between children of Abraham

Patricia Crone (1945–2015)

R. J. Zwi Werblowsky (1924–2015)

In memoriam

TABLE OF CONTENTS

PART I. THE CONCEPT OF THE ABRAHAMIC RELIGIONS

PART II. COMMUNITIES

PART V. RITUALS AND ETHICS

PART VI. EPILOGUES

List of Contributors

David Abulafia, Professor of Mediterranean History at the University of Cambridge and Papathomas Professorial Fellow at Gonville and Caius College, Cambridge.

Gil Anidjar, Professor in the Department of Religion, the Department of Middle Eastern, South Asian, and African Studies, and the Institute for Comparative Literature and Society, Columbia University.

Carol Bakhos, Professor in the Department of Near Eastern Languages and Cultures, University of California, Los Angeles.

Antony Black, Professor Emeritus, Department of Politics, University of Dundee.

Moshe Blidstein, Postdoctoral Fellow at the Martin Buber Society of Fellows, Hebrew University of Jerusalem.

Rémi Brague, Professor Emeritus of Medieval and Arabic Philosophy, University of Paris I.

Richard W. Bulliet, Professor of History, Columbia University.

Leonardo Capezzone, Associate Professor, Italian Institute of Oriental Studies, Sapienza University of Rome.

William E. Carroll, Thomas Aquinas Fellow in Theology and Science at Blackfriars and a member of the Faculty of Theology and Religion of the University of Oxford.

Reuven Firestone, Regenstein Professor in Medieval Judaism and Islam, Hebrew Union College.

David F. Ford, Regius Professor of Divinity, University of Cambridge, and Director of the Cambridge Interfaith Programme.

Carlos Fraenkel, Associate Professor, Departments of Philosophy and Jewish Studies, McGill University, Montreal.

David M. Freidenreich, Pulver Family Associate Professor of Jewish Studies, Colby College, Waterville, Maine.

Harvey E. Goldberg, Professor Emeritus, Sarah Allen Shaine Chair in Sociology and Anthropology, Hebrew University of Jerusalem.

Lutz Greisiger, Postdoctoral Fellow at the Martin Buber Society of Fellows, Hebrew University of Jerusalem.

Sidney H. Griffith, Professor of Early Christian Studies, Catholic University of America.

Moshe Idel, Max Cooper Professor Emeritus of Jewish Thought, Hebrew University of Jerusalem.

Clemens Leonhard, Professor of Liturgical Studies, University of Münster.

Martin Lüstraeten, Lecturer in Liturgical Studies, University of Münster.

Yousef Meri, Visiting Professor, Department of Studies of Contemporary Islam, Faculty of Shari'a, University of Jordan (2014–15).

David Nirenberg, Deborah R. and Edgar D. Jannotta Professor of Medieval History and Social Thought, University of Chicago.

Peter Ochs, Edgar Bronfman Professor of Modern Judaic Studies, University of Virginia.

Peter E. Pormann, Professor of Classics and Graeco-Arabic Studies, University of Manchester, and Director of the John Rylands Research Institute.

David S. Powers, Professor of Islamic History, Cornell University.

Tariq Ramadan, Professor of Contemporary Islamic Studies, Faculty of Oriental Studies, University of Oxford.

Malise Ruthven, author of *Islam in the World* (1984, revised and updated 2015), *The Divine Supermarket* (1990), *A Fury for God* (2002), *Fundamentalism: A Very Short Introduction* (2004, 2007) and other books. He lives in London.

Mark Silk, Professor of Religion in Public Life and Director of the Leonard E. Greenberg Center for the Study of Religion in Public Life at Trinity College in Hartford, Connecticut.

Adam J. Silverstein, Associate Professor of Middle Eastern Studies, Bar Ilan University.

Uriel Simonsohn, Lecturer in the Department of Middle Eastern History, University of Haifa.

Nicolai Sinai, Associate Professor of Islamic Studies, University of Oxford, and Fellow of Pembroke College.

Yuri Stoyanov, Research Associate, Department of Languages and Cultures of the Near and Middle East, SOAS, University of London.

Guy G. Stroumsa, Martin Buber Professor Emeritus of Comparative Religion, Hebrew University of Jerusalem and Professor Emeritus of the Study of the Abrahamic Religions, University of Oxford.

John Tolan, Professor of History, University of Nantes.

Dorothea Weltecke, Chair for the History of Religions, Center of Excellence 'Cultural Foundations of Social Integration', University of Konstanz.

INTRODUCTION

ADAM J. SILVERSTEIN, GUY G. STROUMSA, AND MOSHE BLIDSTEIN

THE primary aim of this book is to contribute to the emergence and development of the comparative study of the Abrahamic religions. The Handbook thus includes authoritative yet accessible studies on a variety of topics dealing comparatively with Judaism, Christianity, and Islam, as well as with the interactions between the adherents of these religions throughout history. Underpinning this is the assumption that there is something to be gained from studying these religious traditions together, an assumption to which we will devote some attention in what follows.[1]

In a sense, the comparative study of the Abrahamic religions has been undertaken for many centuries, first by adherents of the respective religions who sought to make sense of their neighbours and competitors (and, in many cases, to refute their claims about religious truth), later by European scholars, Catholics and Protestants alike, in the early modern period, for whom adopting a comparative approach to the monotheistic religions was obvious. More often than not, these studies reflected a polemical rather than an ecumenical approach to the topic, a fact also emphasized by the Enlightenment pamphlet about 'The Three Impostors' (Moses, Jesus, and Muhammad), who deceived humankind with their false claims to prophecy.

Since the nineteenth century and the development of the scholarly, non-theological study of religions, the comparative study of the Abrahamic religions has not been pursued either intensively or systematically, and it is only very recently that the comparative study of Judaism, Christianity, and Islam has picked up in earnest. It should be noted that despite its recent use in interfaith dialogue, the concept of the Abrahamic religions reflects the fundamental 'family resemblances', to use a Wittgensteinian metaphor, between these religions. Hence the concept is useful for the

[1] There are, of course, a number of traditions originating within these three main Abrahamic Religions that might also be considered 'Abrahamic', such as those of the Samaritans, the Mormons, and the Bahais. However, in order not to further complicate what is an already complex picture, we have asked our contributors to focus on Judaism, Christianity, and Islam.

comparative study of these religions, which seeks to identify differences and distinctions between them at least as much as similarities.

Over the past few decades, a handful of scholars have been instrumental in creating the modern, academic groundwork for the study of the Abrahamic religions. It is perhaps to Francis E. Peters, more than to anyone else, that this emerging field is indebted: Peters has both authored introductory surveys on this topic—as *The Children of Abraham* (Princeton, 1986) and *The Monotheists: Jews, Christians, and Muslims in Conflict and Cooperation* (Princeton, 1994)—and has usefully collected primary sources from each of the three traditions, published in the three-volume set *Judaism, Christianity, and Islam: The Classical Texts and their Interpretation* (Princeton, 1990), amongst other contributions to specific sub-topics within the field.[2]

With the field's growth came the almost inevitable scholarly dissensions. Objections to the comparative study of religions are in some ways understandable and to be expected. After all, the implication of comparative studies is that religions and their adherents influence one another, while scholars of a religious tradition often accept, at least implicitly, the internal narrative of these religions, which emphasizes their autonomous development. Similarly, since Islam is the youngest of the three Abrahamic religions, studies of Islam in the context of Judaism and Christianity often amount to investigations into the 'origins' of things Islamic, which can have the effect—even if unintended—of downplaying the originality and contribution of Islam and Muslims to history. Moreover, some voices have recently been heard, which raise a caveat about the relevance of 'Abraham' to the comparative study of these religions, or against the heuristic value of the concept of Abrahamic religions outside interfaith dialogue.[3]

Traditionally, what has been more common than the comparative study of the Abrahamic religions has been the study of two of these religions together, to the exclusion of the third one. Studies of Judaism and Christianity, of Christianity and Islam, and of Judaism and Islam, have contributed greatly to our understanding of the beliefs, practices, and interactions between these respective communities. However, in excluding the third side of the triangle, as it were, these studies are necessarily limited and provide only a partial picture of a complex and dynamic interface between the beliefs and practices of these communities throughout the ages.

Be all that as it may, the study of Abrahamic religions is as much about encounters between traditions as it is about encounters between peoples. Abrahamic studies of

[2] E.g. *The Voice, the Word, the Books: The Sacred Scriptures of the Jews, Christians, and Muslims* (Princeton: Princeton University Press, 2007); and *Jerusalem and Mecca: The Typology of the Holy City in the Near East* (New York: New York University Press, 1986). Other scholars, including in Continental Europe, have also contributed significant studies to this field, e.g. H. Busse, *Islam, Judaism, and Christianity: Theological and Historical Affiliations* (Princeton: Wiener Markus, 1998); and Karl-Josepf Kuschel, *Abraham: A Symbol of Hope for Jews, Christians and Muslims* (London: SCM, 1995).

[3] On Abraham: J. D. Levenson, *Inheriting Abraham: The Legacy of the Patriarch in Judaism, Christianity, and Islam* (Princeton: Princeton University Press, 2012); on the concept itself: A. W. Hughes, *Abrahamic Religions: On the Uses and Abuses of History* (Oxford: Oxford University Press, 2012).

such topics as 'Mysticism', 'Prophethood', 'Messianism', 'Theology', 'the Hereafter', amongst many others, concern not the individual traditions or communities but rather the topics themselves as they have been interpreted and developed by the various Jews, Christians, and Muslims who have applied themselves to these topics. Put another way, what brings the Abrahamic religions together is a common set of questions about God and his world; what distinguishes the Abrahamic religions from each other are their respective answers to these questions.

We should stress that the point of the comparative study of the Abrahamic religions is not, contrary to a common misconception, to stress how much the relevant religions have in common—though, it is admitted that this is often an element of 'Abrahamic' initiatives of many sorts—but to illuminate our understanding of *each* individual religion by situating it appropriately in its spiritual, social, and historical context(s). As Max Müller memorably put it: 'He who knows only one religion knows none.' Accordingly, even those who choose not to engage in the comparative study of religions must accept that in order to appreciate the unique stance of their chosen religion on a given topic they must know what alternative stances were tellingly rejected.

The Handbook is divided into six parts. Part I is dedicated to histories, examinations, and criticisms of the very concept of the Abrahamic religions, providing various perspectives on its contexts, functions, and viability. Reuven Firestone and Gil Anidjar discuss the figure of Abraham, the former as reflected in the Abrahamic traditions themselves and the latter as seen through the prism of continental philosophy. The historical manifestations of the idea of the Abrahamic religions as sharing essential attributes, whether the figure of Abraham or more general principles, are examined by Adam J. Silverstein. Guy G. Stroumsa explores the place of the study of the Abrahamic religions in the development of the discipline of comparative religion in the eighteenth to twentieth centuries, while Mark Silk traces the concepts of 'Abrahamic' and 'Judaeo-Christian' in English and American discourse of same period. Finally, Rémi Brague warns about the dangers inherent in such terms as 'the three monotheisms', the 'three religions of Abraham', or the 'three religions of the book'.

From this foundation, Part II moves to historical perspectives on the interactions between Jewish, Christian, and Islamic communities. Richard Bulliet presents the essential similarities between the theology, practice, and social realities of Islam and Christianity, and argues that an 'Islamo-Christian' civilization is a more valid concept than a tripartite, 'Abrahamic' one. David Abulafia proposes to see the shores of the Mediterranean as a central stage for interactions between the three religions, whether negative or positive. The place of law in the interactions between Abrahamic communities is studied by Uriel Simonsohn and John Tolan, the former investigating especially the legal institutions of Christian and Jewish communities under the aegis of the Islamic caliphate and the latter focusing on the perceptions of Jews and Muslims in Christian law and historical consciousness throughout history. Dorothea Weltecke closes this section with an analysis of various medieval discourses of religious multiplicity in the Abrahamic religions, which showed 'different levels of ethical and religious respect towards the other.'

The next three parts discuss substantial issues central to the practice and thought of all three religions. Part III includes chapters on scripture and its interpretation throughout history, as well as conceptions of religious history. Nicolai Sinai traces the history of modern historical-critical interpretation of both the Bible and the Quran, and its significance for the development of the Abrahamic religions in the modern period. Carol Bakhos surveys classical scriptural exegesis of the three religions—Jewish ancient exegesis and midrashic literature, Christian patristic exegesis, and Islamic interpretation of the Quran up to the twelfth century. David Powers discusses the Islamic doctrine of Muhammad as the final prophet, and its ramifications for Islamic understanding of the other Abrahamic religions. Lutz Greisiger analyses the varieties of Abrahamic eschatological vision and practice, their common and diverging nature and dynamics.

Part IV turns to issues of religious thought and philosophy central to all three traditions, focusing especially on the common questions discussed by the great thinkers of the Abrahamic religions in the Middle Ages. Observing that 'one of the defining features of the Abrahamic religions that ties them closely together is undoubtedly their constant recourse to the classical tradition', Peter Pormann proceeds to survey the engagement of philosophers and theologians of the Abrahamic traditions with Greco-Roman thought and literature. The next three chapters discuss central aspects of philosophical discourse among Abrahamic thinkers. Sidney H. Griffith focuses on the philosophical discourse on the concept of the 'oneness' of the one God, which developed in ninth-century Baghdad among thinkers of the three religions; Carlos Fraenkel investigates models for the relationship between theology and philosophy developed by Muslim, Jewish, and Christian thinkers of the eleventh and twelfth centuries in Islamic-ruled lands; and William E. Carroll discusses the problematic of accommodating the doctrine of creation *ex nihilo* with scientific and philosophical understanding in the Middle Ages. Yuri Stoyanov explores the relationships of the monotheistic Abrahamic religions with heretical traditions, ideas, and practices of religious dualism. This part closes with two chapters on major issues in the intersections between thought and practice: Moshe Idel presents an overview of mystical thought, traditions, and practices in the Abrahamic religions, and Anthony Black charts currents of political thought over the centuries.

Part V explores interactions and comparisons in the realm of practice and ethics. Prayer, the most pervasive ritual of all Abrahamic religions, is the subject of the first chapter by Clemens Leonhard and Martin Lüstraeten. The two next chapters, by Moshe Blidstein and David Freidenreich, analyse practices and discourses of purity, defilement, and dietary prohibition, both as important dimensions of each religion and as central aspects of their interrelations throughout history. Harvey E. Goldberg discusses the significance of life-cycle rituals in the Abrahamic religions, historically as well as in contemporary societies, and the value comparative analysis brings to their understanding. Yousef Meri surveys practices and concepts of sainthood in the three religions and the associated practice of pilgrimage, focusing on interactions in medieval Syria. David Nirenberg and Leonardo Capezzone discuss the place of love—towards

God, fellow humans, or the self, as well as by God towards humans—in the self-perception of the Abrahamic religions. Lastly, Malise Ruthven analyses historical and contemporary manifestations of fundamentalism in the Abrahamic religions.

Part VI comprises three Epilogues, intended to provide a broader perspective on the comparative study of the Abrahamic religions from the viewpoint of each of the religions and to complement the individual foci of the various chapters. These Epilogues, accordingly, are penned by writers who are at once eminent scholars and influential voices in their respective religious communities.

Although the chapters in this volume deal with a wide variety of topics, almost inevitably, some subjects have benefited from more attention within the chapters than others. This is partly a function of each contributor's own specialization and interests, partly a ramification of the complexity of a field that draws on primary sources in over a dozen languages, and partly a reflection of the fact that this field is still very much in its formative stages and few are the scholars expert in the comparative study of all three religions in relation to their topic of choice, or daring enough to rise to the challenge of the comparative approach. Unfortunately, certain topics that might be deemed central to this emerging field have not been covered in dedicated chapters: fundamental topics such as women and gender, the family, education, religious law, ethics, Satan, a phenomenological approach to the Abrahamic religions, martyrdom, and the impact of modern science on these religions, have been treated only in passing, and not systematically in chapters of their own. Ideally, it would also have been preferable to have more women and Muslims among the chapters' authors. This proved impossible and this too reflects the fact that the field is still in its infancy.

Such regrettable omissions serve to remind us that there is still much work to be done in establishing the comparative study of Abrahamic religions on firm academic foundations. It is our hope that this volume will introduce scholars, students, and other readers to the challenges and rewards of studying these three religions together. Although our approach is by no means shaped by interfaith concerns, we believe that inasmuch as ignorance is the mother of prejudice this handbook might play a role in fighting religious intolerance in all its forms.

PART I

THE CONCEPT OF THE ABRAHAMIC RELIGIONS

CHAPTER 1

ABRAHAM AND AUTHENTICITY

REUVEN FIRESTONE

It is clear, of course, that the Abrahamic religions are designated as such because they identify deeply with Abraham, recognizing him as the first to arrive at the truth of monotheism and live out the ideal relationship with God. Whether known as Abraham, Avraham, or Ibrāhīm, he is the archetype of the stalwart religious individual willing even to abandon family and community in the journey to realize the truth of God. Yet while the Abrahamic religions all recognize his key role, each understands his nature differently. In Judaism Abraham is a Jew who represents unfailing obedience to divine law, while in Christianity he is the epitome of Christian faith. And in Islam Abraham was the first Muslim who submits fully and without reservation to the divine will. Abraham is known uniquely—and differently—in other religions as well. For Bahais he is the direct ancestor of Bahá'u'lláh confirming his prophetic authenticity. For the Latter Day Saint movement (Mormonism) he serves as the authority for believers' exaltation to return as joint-heirs with God. And in the Yazidi holy book, The *Kitêba Cilwe* or 'Book of Illumination', Abraham is steadfast even when thrown into a great fire by the evil Nemrud for insisting on the Yazidi vision of divine truth.

To all these and other religions as well, Abraham serves as an archetype or model, the ideal individual in communion with God and a vital symbol around which religious ideologies are constructed. But because the religions that revere Abraham differ, so do their Abrahams, and this has caused the meaning and significance of Abraham to be disputed between rival religions that contest their authority through his symbolism. Thus, not only does Abraham serve as a symbol of the common aspirations of the Abrahamic religions by his centrality in their sacred writings, he is also a source of disagreement and interreligious polemic, and a fulcrum for leveraging spiritual difference and claims to religious superiority.

Abraham as *Homo Religiosus*

Abraham's persona has come to assume cosmic proportions as the first and hence ideal representation of humanity in authentic and ongoing relationship with the divine. His story is that of the ideal religious person, the *homo religiosus*. Abraham is the first patriarch, the *av* in the Hebrew Bible (Gen. 17: 5; Deut. 1: 8, 6: 10; Josh. 24: 3; Isa. 51: 2, etc.), and his role as forefather is affirmed in all the Abrahamic religions. His very name *Avraham*, explains Gen. 17: 5, means that he will be 'the father of many nations' (*av hamon goyim*).

Key aspects of his nature are passed down to his progeny, that chosen sector of humanity in ongoing relationship with God through prophecy and divine teachings. According to the Hebrew Bible, those outside the Abrahamic genealogy who do not voluntarily join up with the community cannot be a part of its intimate association with God. Yet the notion of Abraham's cherished bond with God was so powerful and influential that it became a prototype for other, even competing communities by way of different lines of genealogical or spiritual descent, and his traits depicted in the Hebrew Bible became recurring topoi in subsequent sacred writings, sometimes in contradistinction to the biblical representations. All three post-biblical sacred writings of the New Testament, Quran, and Talmud contest the meaning of the Hebrew Bible Abraham and reconstruct his persona in the image of their ideal religious person. Subsequent contention over his spiritual inheritance became such a vital source of bitter religious polemic that the great medieval Jewish polymath, Moses Maimonides (d. 1204), could observe 'the consensus of the greater part of the population of the earth glorifying him and considering themselves as blessed through his memory, so that even those who do not belong to his progeny pretend to descend from him' (*Guide for the Perplexed* (Maimonides 1956) 3: 29).

Abraham in the Hebrew Bible

The earliest known source for the character of Abraham is the Hebrew Bible, which portrays him as the first to live in enduring relationship with God. Earlier figures such as Adam and Eve or Noah act within narratives that appear as specific landmarks in the unfolding of human history, but their relationship with God does not continue beyond a single narrative encounter. Abraham, in contrast, is the first biblical personage whose life extends beyond any individual incident in sacred history. He serves as the pivot upon which the divine focus turns from humanity as a whole to a specific group of people within the larger flow of history. God calls Abraham to go forth and follow his guidance; Abraham responds fully and without hesitation (Gen. 12). At that point the unfolding universal history of humanity with which the Bible begins actually comes to an end. From that moment onward, human history is expressed only through its interaction with one particular sector of humankind, the family and progeny of the patriarch who recognizes God.

Exactly why Abraham is chosen for his pivotal role is not explicitly indicated in the Hebrew Bible, and that question later became an issue around which were formed competing claims for Abraham's persona by successive religious communities. For the Hebrew Bible, however, the issue is not what precipitated God's call but what came afterwards. Abraham always responded appropriately to the divine imperative. He was obedient. Even if not always convinced of the purpose or reasoning behind God's demands (Gen. 12: 11–20; 17: 12–17; 21: 10–14), Abraham chose to obey, and it is by virtue of this dogged obedience that he demonstrates his loyalty and trust in God and the divine promise. The biblical accounting of Abraham's loyalty is structured around a number of motifs or topoi, and these became contested among the religious communities that counted him as spiritual or genealogical forefather and progenitor.

Abraham as Founder of Sacred Sites

Abraham is the first biblical personage to establish sacred sites that become identified and revered by subsequent generations of believers. In Eliadian terms, Abraham is associated with hierophany, eruption of the sacred, by building altars in response to or in preparation for divine revelation. Thus Bethel ('The House of God') becomes identified via Abraham's altars (Gen. 12: 8; 13: 3), and the sanctity of Jerusalem itself originated, according to the Bible, through God's communication to Abraham at Moriah (Gen. 22: 2–9/2 Chron. 3: 1).

Abraham's Community and the Divine Promise

Already in Haran, Abraham is chosen by God to become a great nation (Gen. 11: 31–12: 2), and the motif of special relationship between his family and progeny is repeated throughout the Bible. God blesses him, promises innumerable offspring that will inherit the Land of Canaan as an everlasting legacy, protection from the predation of foreign peoples, and assures him that he will be a 'father of many nations' from whose loins will spring kings (Gen. 12: 1–3; 13: 12–17; 17: 1–8, 15–21; 22: 17–18).

Abraham as Obedient Servant of God

Abraham is the faithful servant who responds unswervingly to God's charge. When God commands him to leave his community for an unknown land he obeys, as he does in response to all divine directives. The nature of their relationship is epitomized by God's pronouncement initiating the eternal covenant, 'I am God Almighty. [If you] walk before me you will be blameless' (Gen. 17: 1). The conditional nature of this declaration is often lost in translation. The pronouncement means that Abraham will be protected by God from the dangers of life if he responds to the divine imperative.[1] He is tested throughout the remainder of his life in the Bible for his obedience, yet he passes every trial. Finally and in response to fulfilling the greatest trial to sacrifice his future and the future of his family and clan with the offering of his last son, God proclaims, 'Because you have done this and have not withheld your son, your favoured one, I will bestow my blessing upon you and make your descendants as numerous as the stars of heaven and the sands on the seashore; and your descendants shall seize the gates of their foes. All the nations of the earth shall bless themselves by your descendants, because you have obeyed my command' (Gen. 22: 16–18).

Abraham as Covenantal Partner

The institution of covenant (Heb. *brit*) in the Hebrew Bible is complex and occurs in a variety of forms (Weinfeld 1971). In its most significant form it defines an eternal bond between God and Israel against which is characterized God's relationship with humanity in general. God first establishes an eternal covenant with Abraham and God promises him innumerable offspring and a specific land in which they will settle and thrive. It is subsequently ratified with the giving of the Law to the entire community of Israel at Mt Sinai and remains a referent throughout the Hebrew Bible.

The covenant first appears in relationship to Abraham in the enigmatic 'covenant between the pieces' of Gen. 15 when God promises him unlimited progeny. The covenant is 'cut' with Abraham using a play on words associated with his cutting of the sacrifice, and God promises his offspring the Land of Canaan. It appears again in chapter 17 along with a name change from Abram to Abraham, 'father of many nations' (verse 5) and a promise of great fertility and future royalty (verse 6). God declares its eternality with the words, 'I will maintain my covenant between me and you and your offspring to come as an everlasting covenant throughout the ages, to be God to you and to your offspring to come' (verses 7–8). The sign of this agreement is ritual circumcision, another form of cutting and a kind of fleshy sacrifice (Eilberg-Schwartz 1990: 175) that is required among all of Abraham's male posterity forever. Not all of his progeny are included in the covenant, however, for God mysteriously limits it only to the line of Isaac: 'As for Ishmael . . . I hereby bless him. I will make him fertile and exceedingly numerous . . . But My covenant I will maintain with Isaac' (Gen. 17: 20–1).

This *promissory* covenant obtains within the small Abrahamic family as God remains in ongoing personal relationship with the leaders of each patriarchal generation. Centuries later, with God's redemption of hundreds of thousands of Abraham's

[1] This translation reflects the ancient Near Eastern notion that one is protected by one's god(s) by supporting it through offerings and engaging in certain prescribed behaviours.

progeny from Egyptian bondage into an expanded tribal nation, the divine promise is reaffirmed (or extended) as an *obligatory* covenant with the entire People of Israel at Mt Sinai through the revelation of God's word (Weinfeld 1971: 1018). Submission to the personal intervention of God is thus succeeded by submission to the divine will through obedience to God's Law. Like the Abrahamic covenant, the Sinaitic covenant is affirmed ('signed') in the blood of sacrifice (Exod. 24: 3–8), and like Abraham, his heirs who uphold that covenant are God's 'treasured possession among all the peoples' (Exod. 19: 5). If they fail to live out the covenantal obligation, 'Yet even then . . . I will not reject them or spurn them so as to destroy them, annulling my covenant with them: for I the Lord am their God' (Lev. 26: 44). The Abrahamic covenant is thus reaffirmed and expanded at Sinai. It never expires (2 Kings 13: 23; Ps. 105: 8–9, 42; 1 Chron. 16: 16–17).

Abraham as the Friend of God

In light of this special and ongoing relationship with the divine, it is not surprising that Abraham is referred to with special reverence in the Hebrew Bible. Like Moses and David, he is called on occasion God's servant (Gen. 26: 24; Ps. 105: 6, 42). Only Abraham, however, is God's 'love' or 'friend' (*ohavi*—Isa. 41: 8, 2 Chron. 20: 7).

Abraham in the New Testament

The New Testament emerges from within the paradigmatic sacred history of the Hebrew Bible and extends that history while simultaneously interpreting it to confirm its own particular sense of being with the divine. Regarding a similar relationship between the Written and Oral Torahs of Judaism, Susan Handelman (1982: 39) has observed that 'interpretation is not essentially separate from the text itself—an external act intruded upon it—but rather the *extension* of the text . . . a part of the continuous revelation of the text itself'. Abraham appears over seventy times in the New Testament, where the familiar motifs associated with him in the Hebrew Bible are extended to take on new meaning.

The Abraham of the Gospels

The Abraham of the Gospels (including Acts) seems not to differ significantly from the Hebrew Bible's representation. A new association is presented with the image of Abraham sitting in the heavenly Paradise (Matt. 8: 11–12; Luke 16: 19–31), a motif occurring also in other post-Hebrew biblical Jewish literatures (*4 Macc.* 13: 17; *b. Kiddushin* 72b; *Pesikta Rabbati* 43: 4). Luke 1: 70–3 supports the continued veracity of the Abrahamic covenant and God's promise to Abraham's progeny.

John's understanding of Abraham as father (*av*), however, does not accept the biological relationship to be a sign of merit. Jews technically may be Abraham's descendants (*sperma Abraam*), but they are not necessarily true to him merely by claiming to be his children or because he is their progenitor. John 8: 39b: 'If you were Abraham's children, you would do as Abraham did... (*ei tekna tou Abraam este, ta erga tou Abraam epoieite*)' (Siker 1991: 136). Abrahamic ancestry becomes irrelevant in light of the Jews' purported desire to kill Jesus, for evil intention belies any value to genealogical status. On the other hand, Abraham's status as *av* remains important when Jesus' intimacy with the patriarch is referenced to win an argument: 'Your father Abraham was overjoyed to see my day; he saw it and was glad' (John 8: 56).

Acts 7 presents a recapitulation of Israelite history, including the covenant of circumcision and the divine promise of the land as an everlasting possession, which does not alter the image of Abraham as presented in the Hebrew Bible. It also refers to Jews as the 'stock of Abraham' (13: 26) and not in a disparaging manner, all part of the view of Luke-Acts that the mission of the church evolved from a limited group centred in Jerusalem into a worldwide and universal movement.

Matthew 3: 7–9 critiques Jewish claims that Abrahamic ancestry is a privilege when a group of Pharisees and Sadducees come to John the Baptist for ritual immersion: 'Vipers' brood! Who warned you to escape from the wrath that is to come? Prove your repentance by the fruit you bear; and do not imagine you can say, "We have Abraham for our father." I tell you that God can make children for Abraham out of these stones!' This likely reflects an internal Jewish argument over the merit that may accrue from one's righteous forebears, a notion in Judaism called *zekhut avot* ('merit of the fathers'), suggested already in the Hebrew Bible (Deut. 4: 37; 2 Chron. 6: 41–2) and developed in detail in rabbinic literature (Marmorstein 1920). Some Jews believed that descendants of the righteous patriarchs could be protected from the punishment that would normally result from sin (*b. Sotah* 10b; *b. Yoma* 87a; *b. Yevamot* 64a) while others believed that such merit had limited efficacy or was destined to come to an end (*b. Sanhedrin* 104a; *b. Shabbat* 55a: *me'ematay tamah zekhut avot?*).

The Abraham of the Epistles: Faith Trumps Obedience and Spirit Trumps Law

Abraham's persona and significance change markedly in the Epistles. In Romans 4, Abraham proves his merit not through his unwavering obedience but through his unwavering faith, and here we also discern a Christian response to the question of why God chose Abraham. Whereas in Genesis his faith is determined by steadfast obedience (Gen. 12; 15: 6; 22), Romans purposely sets forth faith as independent of acts. Romans also removes Abraham's intrinsic importance from the covenant of circumcision and the ensuing promise to Abraham's progeny.

> We have just been saying: 'Abraham's faith was counted as righteousness.' In what circumstances was it so counted? Was he circumcised at the time, or not? He was not yet circumcised, but uncircumcised; he received circumcision later as the sign and hallmark of that righteousness which faith had given him while he was still uncircumcised. It follows that he is the father of all who have faith when uncircumcised, and so have righteousness 'counted' to them; and at the same time he is the father of the circumcised, provided they are not merely circumcised, but also follow that path of faith which our father Abraham trod while he was still uncircumcised. (Rom. 4: 9–12)

Because Abraham's excellence in faith was proven before his circumcision and even before his first act of obedience, obedience to God's law cannot be the source of his merit (cf. Rom. 2: 25–31, 4: 1–22, etc.). His patriarchal role, therefore, obtains in relation to all who share his faith, whether or not they belong to the community of Israel that was identified through obedience to the divine command for circumcision (Collins 1985). Romans thus considers the Jewish claim of exclusive relationship with Abraham irrelevant, for anyone with faith—whether Jew or Gentile—may now claim a form of descent from father Abraham.

This leads to a major point of the Pauline writings, namely, that faith and spirit supersede the law, at least for Gentiles (Parkes 1979: 50–7). 'It was not through law that Abraham and his descendants were given the promise that the world should be their inheritance, but through righteousness that came from faith . . . The promise was made on the ground of faith in order that it might be valid for all Abraham's descendants, not only for those who hold by the law, but also for those who have Abraham's faith . . .' (Rom. 4: 13–16).

The passage goes on to equate Abraham's generic trust in God depicted in Genesis with the very specific Christian faith in the saving power of Christ:

> . . . no distrust made him doubt God's promise, but, strong in faith, he gave glory to God, convinced that what he had promised he was able to do. And that is why Abraham's faith was 'counted to him as righteousness' (Gen. 15: 6). The words 'counted to him' were meant to apply not only to Abraham but to us; our faith too is to be 'counted', the faith in the God who raised Jesus our Lord from the dead; for he was given up to death for our misdeeds, and raised to life for our justification. (Rom. 4: 22–5)

Spiritual Lineage Trumps Genealogy

The Pauline writings argue against the Hebrew biblical notion of tribal religion. In the ancient Near East, communities were organized around kinship, and every nation had its own national deity (1 Kings 11: 5; 2 Kings 11: 13, etc.). Anyone born into a community worshipped its national god and could no easier change her religion than change her family identity (Firestone 2008: 11–33). The notion of 'conversion' or switching from one religious belief system to another was unknown in the ancient Near East until the coming of Hellenism (Nock 1933), but by the time of Christianity's emergence the old notion of tribal religion was waning. Graeco-Romans were seeking new forms of spiritual fulfilment and were joining with Jews of various sects including early Christianity, as well as developing other religious expressions (Gager 1985; Valantasis 2000; Burkert 1987).

Pauline writings critique the traditional markers of religious identity through a novel view of the constraint articulated within the divine promise expressed in Genesis 17. In Genesis 17: 15–20 God announces that Abraham will have a son through Sarah and pledges an everlasting covenant with this promised child, while rejecting Abraham's son born naturally (without divine promise) through Hagar. Romans comments, 'Not all the offspring of Israel are truly Israel' (9: 7). It is not Abraham's 'son born of nature' who is blessed, but rather the son 'born through God's promise' (9: 8). Romans 9 then identifies the 'natural born son' of Genesis with the Jewish people who claim genealogical kinship to Abraham, while the son of the promise represents the faithful who will benefit from the promise of everlasting life through Christ. As stated in Galatians 3: 7: 'You may take it, then, that it is those who have faith who are Abraham's sons.'

A similar notion is articulated in Galatians 4: 21–5: 1 where the 'natural born' son of Romans is the slave's son Ishmael 'born in the ordinary course of nature'. The freeborn son Isaac, on the other hand, was born through God's promise. The former's slavery represents the old covenant of Sinai epitomized by the law while the latter's freedom represents the new covenant of the heavenly Jerusalem that represents the freedom of the spirit. The innovation of this interpretation is, like that of Romans, in the reversal of positions. The biblical Isaac no longer symbolizes the Jewish people but rather those 'born of promise' and representative of a new freedom. The rejected Ishmael on the other hand, the slave's son, represents the Jews. The discourse ends with an assurance directed to Gentiles: 'Now you, my friends, like Isaac, are children of God's promise, but just as in those days the natural-born son persecuted the spiritual son, so it is today. Yet what does scripture say? "Drive out the slave and her son, for the son of the slave shall not share the inheritance with the son of the free woman"... It is for freedom that Christ set us free' (Gal. 4: 28–5: 1). In Galatians 3: 16 the promise is narrowed to only one of Abraham's offspring, that being Christ, and concludes that believers in Christ receive the Abrahamic blessing: 'So if you belong to Christ, you are the seed of Abraham and heirs by virtue of the promise' (Gal. 3: 29).

While these Romans and Galatians texts carry the general sentiment of the New Testament, a different opinion is offered in James, which calls for faith in conjunction with acts.

> Was it not by his action, in offering his son Isaac upon the altar, that our father Abraham was justified? Surely you can see faith was at work in his actions, and by these actions his faith was perfected? Here was fulfilment of the words of Scripture: 'Abraham put his faith in God, and that faith was counted to him as righteousness', and he was called 'God's friend'. You see then it is by action and not by faith alone that a man is justified. (Jas. 2: 21–4)

The Covenant of the New Testament

The Galatians 4 passage examined previously associates Abraham's two sons with the two covenants of Sinai and heavenly Jerusalem and argues that the latter surpasses the former. The most complete articulation of this theme is found in Hebrews 8: 6–9: 26, where the new covenant (*brit ḥadashah*) of Jeremiah 31: 30–3 is identified as that of Jesus' ministry: 'But in fact the ministry which Jesus has been given is superior to theirs, for he is the mediator of a better covenant, established on better promises' (Heb. 8: 6). Jesus replaces the high priest in this thematic extension and offers himself in place of the old Temple sacrifices as the more efficacious in removing the stain of sin (Heb. 9: 11–14, 23–8): 'That is why the new covenant or testament of which he is mediator took effect once a death had occurred, to bring liberation from sins committed under the former covenant; its purpose is to enable those whom God has called to receive the eternal inheritance he has promised them' (Heb. 9: 15).

As with the promissory and obligatory forms of covenant 'cut' with Abraham and the Israelite nation in the Hebrew Bible, the new covenant of the heavenly Jerusalem is ratified in blood: '[Y]ou have come to Mount Zion, the city of the living God, the heavenly Jerusalem, to myriads of angels, to the full concourse and assembly of the firstborn who are enrolled in heaven, and to God the judge of all, and to the spirits of good men made perfect, and to Jesus the mediator of a new covenant, whose sprinkled blood has better things to say than the blood of Abel' (Heb. 12: 18–24).

The new covenant is eternal just as the old had claimed to be (Heb. 13: 20) and was inaugurated with blood like the other (Heb. 9: 15–22), but the sacrifice of Jesus is far more efficacious than the animal sacrifices of the old covenant (Heb. 9: 12–14). Jesus' atoning sacrifice on the cross parallels Abraham's near-sacrifice of Isaac, but while Abraham's merit is found in his willing obedience to God's command even to destroy his own future through the sacrifice of his only remaining son, Jesus' merit lies in the atoning sacrifice fulfilled (cf. Gen. 22: 2/John 1: 18, 34, 3: 16; Gen. 22: 8/John 1: 36; Gen. 22: 13/John 1: 29, etc.). And while Abraham's merit in Jewish tradition could be drawn upon by his progeny when in need of divine grace, the even greater merit in Jesus' self-sacrifice accrues to all the true spiritual descendants of Abraham—those who believe in the saving power of Christ.

As in the Hebrew Bible, the Abraham of the New Testament is the first to know God, the recipient of the divine promise, the covenantal partner, and the unique 'friend of God' (Jas. 2: 23), but through a subtle manoeuvring of the Genesis paradigms he is separated from the Hebrew biblical trope of obedience and becomes the epitome of Christian faith. He remains the patriarch (*av*), but the relationship is defined spiritually rather than genealogically. This allows the founder of monotheism to represent Gentiles rather than Jews and argues that his merit (and that of Jesus who represents the fulfilled sacrifice) passes only to his true inheritors, those with faith in Christ.

Abraham in the Quran

The Quran lays out its messages with no obvious chronology and without discrete parts that can be identified as legal, narrative, homiletic, and so forth. Units within and between chapters tend to be more compact than those of the Hebrew Bible or New Testament, and motifs may appear in seemingly disparate loci (Neuwirth 2006; Watt and Bell 1970). The Quran, therefore must be treated as a single unit. Second only to Moses in number of appearances, Abraham is one of the more familiar biblical figures to be found in the Quran and appears more than one hundred times in some twenty-five chapters. He is often included in formalized lists of monotheistic prophets (2: 136, 140; 3: 33, 84; 4: 163; 12: 38; 19: 58; 33: 7; 38: 45; 57: 26, etc.), but his role as the first person to realize the truth of monotheism and to live in relationship with God finds particular significance, perhaps because it serves as a prototype for Muhammad's religious conversion and leadership.

The quranic Abraham discovers the unity of God through the power of his own thinking. He is the first to realize monotheism through reason. References to his reasoning out monotheism are organized around three themes. In one he proves the futility of celestial worship and the necessary existence of a primary cause (Q. 6: 74–83). In another he demonstrates the ineffectuality of idol worship by personally destroying his people's graven images (Q. 19: 41–50; 21: 51–71; 37: 83–99). And in the third he either argues against the pointlessness of idolatry or publicly refuses to take part in the folly (Q. 26: 70–104; 29: 16–17; 43: 26–8; 60: 4; cf. Ginzberg 1937: I. 191–8, V. 211–12).

Abraham Reasons God's Unity

As with the New Testament, the Quran offers a rationale for God's choice of Abraham, but rather than absolute faith we find rational arguments supporting the unity of God (citations in paragraph above). Abraham is steadfast and unwavering in the face of argument, imprisonment, and even attempts on his life. A true monotheist, he is faithful while resolute in his reasoning that deduces the existence of God through rational thought. These aetiologies, like virtually all narratives or narrative references in the Quran, are not placed within a particular chronology in relation to other stories, yet they are considered by Islamic tradition as having occurred prior to God's dealings with Abraham. The quranic Abraham stories are thus read with an eye to the biblical chronology, and this chronologizing became formalized through genres of scriptural interpretation that are read in conjunction with the text of Islamic scripture.

Abraham Builds the Meccan Sanctuary

To this Islamic image of Abraham as the first monotheist is added a parallel to his biblical role as the founder of sacred sites. In the Quran, however, Abraham is associated with Arabian rather than Israelite geography, thereby expanding his biblical function by bringing him into an Arabian context (Firestone 1991; 1992). In Q. 2: 125–7, Abraham establishes the sacred Kaʿba in Mecca in response to God's command. He purifies it, prays that it become an area of safety, raises up its foundations with his son Ishmael, ensures that it be a shrine dedicated to the one God, and proclaims the requirement to make pilgrimage to it (Q. 3: 95–7; 14: 35–7; 22: 26–7).

Ishmael's involvement in erecting the foundations of the Kaʿba is connected with a prayer that their descendants become a Muslim nation.

> We covenanted Abraham and Ishmael [saying]: Purify My house for those who circumambulate, are engaged [with it], and bow and prostrate themselves. . . . And when Abraham and Ishmael were raising up the foundations of the House [they prayed]: Our Lord, accept [this] from us, for You are the Hearer, the Knower. Our Lord, make us submitters to You (*muslimayn laka*) and our progeny a nation submissive to You (*umma muslima laka*) . . . . (2: 125–8)

This reflection on Abraham's Ishmaelite descendants exhibits a sentiment similar to the Hebrew Bible in establishing a biological genealogy of relationship with Abraham. But this rendering privileges Ishmael over Isaac and pre-dates later attempts in Arabic literature to focus the merit of Abraham in the line of Ishmael, the progenitor of the Arab tribes from which Islam would spring (Firestone 1990: 61–79, 135–51).

Abraham as Muslim

Abraham's role as original monotheist is expressed through the use of the terms 'religion of Abraham' (*millat ibrahīm*), 'pre-Islamic monotheist' (*ḥanīf*), and the qualifier that 'he was not an idolater' (*wamā kāna min al-mushrikīn*) (Watt 1979; Rubin 1990; Rippin 1991). These three expressions tend to be strung together, as in Q. 3: 95 when revelation is directed to Muhammad with the words, 'Say: God speaks the truth, so follow the religion of Abraham, the pre-Islamic monotheist. He was not an idolater' (see also Q. 16: 120, 123; 22: 78). This description may be found also in contexts which are defensive of Islam or outright polemical. In Q. 6: 161, for example, Muhammad is directed by God in the following way: 'Say: My Lord has guided me on a straight path, a right religion, the religion of Abraham the pre-Islamic monotheist. He was not an idolater' (cf. 12: 38) (Bell 1960: I. 133). More obvious polemical uses of this description may be found in 2: 130: 'Who dislikes the religion of Abraham other than those who fool themselves?' or 2: 135: 'They say: Be Jews or Christians [to be] rightly guided. Say: But rather, the religion of Abraham the pre-Islamic monotheist. He was not an idolater.'

The latter example is striking in that it sets up the religion of Abraham against the claims of Jews and Christians. Abraham is established in the Quran as the original and pure monotheist, steadfast and upright. He is also associated with a divine covenant (Michel 1983). His heirs, however, do not automatically reflect Abraham's monotheistic perfection. In 2: 124, for example, God appoints Abraham to be a leader for the people after he passes the divine test, but when Abraham asks about the status of his progeny he is answered: 'My covenant does not include sinners.' In a similar passage, God says: 'We have given the Book and the Wisdom to the family of Abraham, and We have given them a great kingdom. Some of them believed in it and some turned away from it. Hell is sufficient for their burning' (Q. 4: 54–5).

As noted above in relation to Q. 2: 128, Abraham and Ishmael pray that they and their progeny be 'submitters' to God. The biblical patriarchs are neither Jews nor Christians according to the Quran but, rather, 'small-m *muslims*'—not modern Muslims of today, of course, but nevertheless individuals who submit to God. They represent a kind of pure and primordial, uncorrupted monotheism that is distinct from the inadequate institutionalized forms of religion known to the Jews and Christians: 'Do you say that Abraham, Ishmael, Isaac, Jacob and the tribes were Jews or Christians? Say: Do you know, or God? And who is worse than one who hides the testimony that he has from God. God is not ignorant of what you do' (2: 140).

In an even more striking passage the Quran argues:

> O People of the Book, why do you argue about Abraham when the Torah and Gospel were not revealed until after him? Have you no sense? Are you not those who argue about what you know? So why do you argue about what you do not know? God knows, but you know not. Abraham was not a Jew nor a Christian, but rather a pre-Islamic monotheist (*ḥanīf*), a *muslim*, and not an idolater. (3: 65–7)

Here as in the previous examples, 'small-m *muslim*' does not refer directly to the institutional religion of Islam that would arise later, for it is clear that Abraham preceded the revelation and the last and quintessential prophet of Islam by millennia. But the use of that term is nevertheless significant because it makes him a primordial monotheist and separates him from the less than adequate religiosity and piety of Jews and Christians who claim Abraham as their patriarch and progenitor. The passage continues: 'The best of humankind with regard to Abraham are those who have followed him and this prophet, and those who believe. God is the Guardian of the believers. Some of the People of the Book would love to lead you astray, but they only lead themselves astray though they are not aware' (3: 68–9).

Abraham and Covenant

The issue of covenant in the Quran is complex and merits independent treatment (Firestone 2011). Two words are generally used, *mithaq* and *ʿahd*, and they are in some cases used interchangeably. There is mention of a *mithaq* with the prophets (3: 81; 33: 7), with the People of the Book denoting the Jews of Muhammad's own day (3: 187; 7: 169), with Christians (5: 14), and with unspecified people (13: 20, 25), but the overwhelming majority of references are to the ancient divine covenant with the Children of Israel (2: 27 [?], 2: 63, 83, 93; 4: 154; 5: 7, 12, 70). The Children of Israel as a collective break the covenant, however, and only a few remain true to the divine command. The covenant referred to here is that of Mount Sinai and the context as provided in the Quran occasionally parallels a formulation found also in Jewish midrash: 'And We made your covenant and We raised up above you the mountain [saying]: Take hold firmly of what We have given you and hear/obey' (2: 93; see also 4: 154, and cf. Ginzberg 1937: III. 92 and VI. 36).

The other common term for covenant is *ʿahd*, which is used when God directs Abraham and Ishmael to purify God's House (2: 125). In the preceding verse, God informs Abraham, 'My covenant (*ʿahdi*) does not apply to wrongdoers, an oblique reference to the Abrahamic covenant (*brit*) known from Genesis 17. As with this example, quranic references to prior covenants may note how they were invalidated by the sins of those who had been a part of the covenant, a position that we have observed above was also expressed in the New Testament (Heb. 8: 6–9: 26) and which is at variance with the standard Hebrew Bible depiction in which the covenant will not be broken despite the sins of Israel (Lev. 26: 42–5; Isa. 54: 9–10, 59: 21). The Quran includes Christians among the sinners: 'And those who say: "We are Christians", We made their covenant but they forgot a part of what they were reminded [through revelation]. So We incited enmity and hatred between them until the Day of Resurrection, when God will tell them what they have done' (Q. 5: 14). The quranic position holds that, because neither the Children of Israel nor the Christians kept proper faith with God, the prior covenants are no longer valid except among a small remnant of believers identified as those few Arabian Jews and Christians contemporary with Muhammad who accepted the message of the Quran that he brought. A parallel occurs in Romans 11: 1–7, where it is proclaimed that only a remnant among Israel remains 'chosen by the grace of God' (Rom. 11: 5)—that is, those who do not reject the new message of Christianity.

Similar to emerging Christianity, emerging Islam establishes its position in the contemporary religious economy through the use of familiar authenticating religious topoi. By managing or exploiting the classic motifs of Abraham and covenant established by earlier scripture, emerging Islam claims authenticity and legitimacy while simultaneously critiquing the practice if not the essence of the establishment traditions. Notwithstanding the blanket critique of prior monotheisms, the quranic Abraham bears a greater resemblance to his namesake in the Hebrew Bible than in the New Testament. Abraham tends toward obedience, law, and ritual as he prays to be shown the requisite ritual obligations (2: 128, 14: 40), announces others (22: 27), and is associated with four of the five required pillars of Islam (witnessing the one God and the prophethood of Muhammad (2: 129), prayer (2: 125–9), giving alms (22: 78), and the pilgrimage (22: 26–7)). He submits entirely to the will of God—the meaning of the term *muslim* that is so closely associated with the patriarch (2: 128–32, 136; 3: 67; 37: 103, etc.).

The quranic Abraham also appears in narratives familiar from the Hebrew Bible. He is the original monotheist covenanted with God (2: 124–5) founder of sacred sites, and as in both the Hebrew Bible and the New Testament, he is God's friend (4: 125). But while the Quran establishes Abraham's piety and monotheism, it also disengages him from Jews and Christians. The quranic Abraham warns his people to be pious and true to God (29: 16–17), charges his children to be *muslims* (2: 132) and prays that his heirs will pray to God as he does (14: 40), but the impiety of most of his descendants and followers invalidated their membership in previous covenants (37: 113, 2: 27, 2: 93, 4: 155, 5: 13–14, etc.).

The new divine revelation thus enables both pagans and the People of the Book to return to the pristine monotheism of Abraham (as well as other great prophetic personages): 'We have inspired you [Muhammad] with revelation just as we inspired Noah and the prophets after him. We gave divine inspiration to Abraham, Ishmael, Isaac, Jacob and the tribes, Jesus, Job, Jonah, Aaron and Solomon, and we gave David psalms' (4: 163). 'Who is better in religion than those who surrender themselves to God while being good and following the religion of Abraham the pre-Islamic monotheist? For God took Abraham as a friend' (4: 125).

Abraham in the Oral Torah

Judaism, like Christianity, emerged out of the cultural and religious mélange of late antique Palestine (Boyarin 1999; Schwartz 2001; Cohen 1999; Schafer 2012). A number of forms and expressions of Judaism competed for dominance during this period, and rabbinic Judaism only became truly ascendant around the sixth or seventh centuries CE. Of particular interest here is its claim to a revelation in the Oral Torah that is distinct from the Hebrew Bible but read in conjunction with it. Like Christianity and Islam, Judaism's theology, ritual practice, organizational structure, and leadership differs fundamentally from that of biblical religion.

Unlike Christianity and Islam, however, rabbinic Judaism never officially declared its Oral Torah a new revelation. On the contrary, it placed the origin of this revelation in exactly the same time and place as that of the Written Torah of the Hebrew Bible. In place of a new revelation, it developed the retroflective idea of a spoken revelation given simultaneously with the written revelation at Mount Sinai. Unlike the revelation rendered into a written scripture, this part of the divine message remained in oral form for many centuries, only to be recorded hundreds of years after the redaction and canonization of the Hebrew Bible.

According to the Oral Torah itself, it was passed down orally by Moses to his successor Joshua, who in turn passed it to the tribal elders, the prophets, and eventually the rabbis (*Mishnah Avot* 1.1). When it was finally reduced to writing, it became known collectively as 'Talmud', meaning literally, learning or study. The term may apply to a specific collection known as the Talmud or it may also apply to a larger library of rabbinic literature including a collection called 'midrash', and it is the latter sense of Talmud or Oral Torah that is used here.

The Oral Torah is not unlike the New Testament and Quran in that it derives much of its authority from an intimate topical and literary association with the Hebrew Bible. The Oral Torah's retrovision characterizes the nature and self-concept of Judaism, for unlike Christianity and Islam, Judaism did not view itself as a new movement but as the authentic continuing expression of biblical religion. It nevertheless appropriates the Abraham and covenant motifs and infuses them with new meaning. A number of other roughly contemporary Jewish texts do the same, but they fell out of the Jewish canon and cannot be considered here despite the fact that they include important material on Abraham (Sandmel 1956; Moxnes 1980; Stone 1972; Siker 1991: 17–27).

Abraham's Merit Passes to his Children

As in the Quran, the rabbinic Abraham was the first to recognize God (*Gen. Rabbah* 38.13; 39.1, 3; 64.4; *b. Nedarim* 32a, etc. Cf. Josephus *Jewish Antiquities* 1.156, 7.8; *Jubilees* 21.3; *Apocalypse of Abraham* 4.6). Appearing in a variety of narratives as a true monotheist even before his divine call to leave the land of his birth, he shows the futility and emptiness of idolatry while proving the reality of the true Creator-God of history, and his merit devolves upon his children: 'Happy are the righteous. Not only do they acquire merit, but they bestow merit upon their children and children's children to the end of all generations' (*Yoma* 87a). Abraham's progeny are royalty because they inherit the royal status of their princely father Abraham for his intimate relationship with God (*b. Sukkah* 49b, interpreting Song 7: 2 and Ps. 47: 10).

Potential counter-claims by Christians or Muslims to be spiritual or genealogical inheritors of Abraham are disqualified by condemnation of Abraham's other son Ishmael and his grandson Esau, the progenitors according to later rabbinic Judaism of the religious communities of Islam and Christianity.[2] Christian and Muslim claims to have inherited the mantle of monotheist exemplar from biblical monotheism are countered repeatedly through an exegetical process that parallels the scriptural arguments put forth in the New Testament and Quran. A classic representation of this schema may be found in *Sifrei Devarim* (*Ha'azinu* 7), which responds to Deut. 32: 9: *For the Lord's portion is His people*:

> This is comparable to the case of a king who had a field which he leased to tenant farmers. The tenant farmers began to take and steal from it, so he took it back from them and gave it to their children. But they became worse than the first [tenant farmers]. [When] a son was born to the king, he said to them: Get out from my [land]. You cannot stay in it. Give me back my portion so that I may declare it [to be mine]. In the same way, when our father Abraham came into the world, there issued from him the refuse of Ishmael and the sons of Qeturah. When our father Isaac came into the world, there issued from him the refuse of Esau, the chiefs of

[2] On Ishmael's evil ways, see *Gen. Rabbah* 53.11, *Exod. Rabbah* 1.1; *PRE* 30 (66b), 31 (70b), etc. On Esau's evil ways, see *Gen. Rabbah* 61.7, 63.8, 11–14; *Exod. Rabbah* 1.1; *PRE* 29 (66a–b), 39 (93b–94a). The traditions condemning Ishmael and Esau emerged certainly before the emergence of Islam and may have developed also before emerging Christianity when Esau was associated with the pagan Roman Empire, but the Hebrew legends remained a convenient internal means for Jews to counter the claims of their monotheistic competitors.

> Edom who were worse than the first. When Jacob came, however, no refuse issued from him. Rather, all of his sons were fit like him, as it is said (Gen. 25: 27): *And Jacob was a perfect man* (ish tam), *dwelling in tents*. From where [do we learn] that [God] declares Jacob [and all his progeny] to be His? As it is said (Psalm 135: 4): *For the Lord has chosen Jacob for Himself, Israel.*

Abraham was a Jew

The Abraham of the Talmud epitomizes the rabbinic Jew by acting entirely in conformity with the Judaism of the Oral Torah by observing rabbinic customs found explicitly in the Talmud but not clearly articulated in the Hebrew Bible. 'Abraham knew even the laws of the *'eruv* of courtyards' (*Gen. Rabbah* 64.4). 'No one ever occupied himself with [the observance of] commandments as did Abraham our father' (*b. Nedarim* 32.2). He instituted the morning prayer as well as the laws of wearing fringes (*tzitzit*) and the daily donning of phylacteries (Ta-Shma 1973). 'We have found that Abraham our father fulfilled the entire Torah [that is, both Written and Oral] even before it was given, as it is said (Gen. 26: 5): *because Abraham obeyed Me and kept My charge: My commandments, My laws, and My teachings*' (*m. Kedushin* 4.14).

The Covenant with Jews Endures Forever

Countering the claims of the New Testament and later the Quran, the Oral Torah repeatedly expresses the notion that the biblical covenant endures through the Jewish people. *Deut. Rabbah* 8.6, for example, interprets Deut. 30: 11 to claim that Abraham's descendants remain the sole recipients of the divine promise. '[*Surely this commandment which I enjoin upon you this day* . . .] *is not in the heavens* . . . Moses said to Israel: Do not say: Another Moses will arise and bring us another Torah from heaven.'

In the following passage, a parable is offered in relation to Deut. 7: 12 [*And if you obey these rules and observe them carefully*] *the Lord your God will maintain the covenant and the love*. Despite the tragedy of the destruction of the Temple the biblical covenant with the Jewish people was never broken. A crown will yet be placed on the head of Israel, who will be returned to intimate relationship with God epitomized by the Abrahamic covenant. Abraham bequeathed precious stones to Israel that were gladly matched with God's own. The future will bring a redemption that will confirm and vindicate Judaism.

> Rabbi Shim'on ben Halafta said: To what may [the message of] this [verse] be compared? To a king who married a noble woman who brought for him [into the marriage] two precious stones. So too, the king matched her with two precious stones. The noble woman lost hers, so the king took back his. After some time, she was able to set herself straight and brought back the two precious stones, whereupon the king brought back his. The king said: all of these will be set into a crown that will be laid unto the head of the noble woman. Thus you find that Abraham gave his children two precious stones, as it is said (Gen. 18: 19): [*Abraham*] *will*

command his children and his household after him to keep the way of the Lord by doing righteousness and justice (tzedakah umishpat). So too, did God match them with two precious stones: love and mercy (*hesed verahamim*), as it is said (Deut. 7: 12) *the Lord your God will maintain the covenant and the love* . . . [But] Israel lost its own [contribution], as it is said (Amos 6: 12): . . . *for you have turned justice into poison weed and the fruit of righteousness into wormwood.* So too did God take His back, as it is said (Jer. 16: 5): *For I have taken away My peace . . . mercy and compassion.* Israel was able to set itself straight and bring back the precious stones. From where [do we know this]? Thus is it written (Isa. 1: 27): *Zion will be redeemed with justice and her repentant ones in righteousness.* God too brought His back. From where [do we know this]? Thus is it written (Isa. 54: 10): *For the mountains may move and the hills be shaken, but My kindness shall never move from you nor My covenant of friendship be shaken—said the Lord who takes you back in love.* When [Israel] restores its own, and the Holy One gives His own, the Holy One will say: All of these will be set into a crown that will be laid onto the head of Israel, as it is said (Hos. 2: 21–2): *And I will betroth you to Me forever, I will betroth you to me with righteousness and justice, and with goodness and mercy, and I will betroth you with faithfulness; then shall you know the Lord.* (*Deut. Rabbah* 3.7)

Conclusion

Rabbinic Judaism, Christianity, and Islam each engaged in a re-envisioning of the biblical Abraham in order to demonstrate the validity of its religious expression against the claims of others. The biblical Abraham was 'Christianized', 'Islamized', and 'Judaized' because of his importance as *homo religiosus* in popular religious discourse. He is the quintessential monotheist, religious founder, and human in unique personal and ongoing relationship with God. He epitomizes human partnership with God through covenant. He represents the religious ideal. It is no surprise that he becomes a contested symbol claimed by Jews, Christians, and Muslims as representative exemplar of each religion. To Christians he is the epitome of faith in God, to Muslims he exemplifies submission to God, and to Jews he fully lives out God's commandments. But these Abrahams are different from one another, and the claims for exclusive representation became polemical and elitist, inviting counter-claims that naturally develop into tense relationships of contention and strife. A comparative analytical reading of the sources reveals the great power of symbols and the human and institutional desire to claim ownership of them.

References

Bell, R. 1937/1960. *The Quran: Translated, with a critical re-arrangement of the Surahs.* 2 vols. Edinburgh: T&T Clark.

Boyarin, D. 1999. *Dying for God: Martyrdom and the Making of Christianity and Judaism.* Stanford, CA: Stanford University Press.

Burkert, W. 1987. *Ancient Mystery Cults.* Cambridge, MA: Harvard University.

Cohen, S. 1999. *The Beginnings of Jewishness*. Berkeley and Los Angeles: University of California.

Collins, J. 1985. 'A Symbol of Otherness: Circumcision and Salvation in the First Century'. In J. Neusner and E. S. Frerichs, eds, *To See Ourselves as Others See Us: Christians, Jews, 'Others' in Late Antiquity*. Chico, CA: Scholars Press, 163–86.

Eilberg-Schwartz, H. 1990. *The Savage in Judaism*. Bloomington and Indianapolis: Indiana University Press.

Firestone, R. 1990. *Journeys in Holy Lands: The Evolution of the Abraham-Ishmael Legends in Islamic Exegesis*. Albany, NY: SUNY Press.

Firestone, R. 1991. 'Abraham's Association with the Meccan Sanctuary and the Pilgrimage in the Pre-Islamic and Early Islamic Periods'. *Le Museon Revue d'études orientales* 104: 365–93.

Firestone, R. 1992. 'Abraham's Journey to Mecca in Islamic Exegesis: A Form-Critical Study of a Tradition'. *Studia Islamica* 76: 5–24.

Firestone, R. 2008. *Who are the* Real *Chosen People: The Meaning of Chosenness in Judaism, Christianity and Islam*. Woodstock, VT: Skylight Paths.

Firestone, R. 2011. 'Is there a Notion of "Divine Election" in the Quran?' In G. Reynolds, ed., *New Perspectives on the Quran: The Quran in its Historical Context 2*. London: Routledge, 393–410.

Gager, J. 1985. *The Origins of Anti-Semitism: Attitudes toward Judaism in Pagan and Christian Antiquity*. New York: Oxford University Press.

Ginzberg, L. 1937/1968. *The Legends of the Jews*. 7 vols. Philadelphia: Jewish Publication Society of America.

Handelman, S. 1982. *The Slayers of Moses: The Emergence of Rabbinic Interpretation in Modern Literary Theory*. Albany, NY: State University of New York.

Josephus, F. 1960. *Complete Works*, trans. W. Whiston. Grand Rapids, MI: Kregel Publications.

Maimonides. 1956. *Guide for the Perplexed*, trans. M. Friedländer. New York: Dover.

Marmorstein, A. 1920. *The Doctrine of Merits in Old Rabbinical Literature*. London: Jews' College.

Michel, T. 1983. 'God's Covenant with Mankind According to the Quran'. *Secretariatus pro Non-Christianis Bulletin* 52: 31–43.

Moxnes, H. 1980. 'God and his Promise to Abraham: First Century Appropriations'. In H. Moxnes, ed., *Theology in Conflict*. Leiden: Brill, 117–69.

Neuwirth, A. 2006. 'Structural, Linguistic and Literary Features'. In J. D. MacAuliffe, ed., *The Cambridge Companion to the Quran*. Cambridge: Cambridge University Press, 97–113.

Nock, A. D. 1933. *Conversion*. Oxford: Clarendon Press.

Parkes, J. 1979. *The Conflict of the Church and the Synagogue*. New York: Atheneum.

Rippin, A. 1991. 'Raḥmān and the Ḥanīfs'. In W. Hallaq and D. Little, eds, *Islamic Studies Presented to Charles Adams*. Leiden: Brill, 153–68.

Rubin, U. 1990. 'Ḥanīfiyya and Ka'ba: An inquiry into the Arabian pre-Islamic Background of *dīn Ibrāhīm*'. *Jerusalem Studies in Arabic and Islam* 13: 85–112.

Sandmel, S. 1956. *Philo's Place in Judaism: A Study of Conceptions of Abraham in Jewish Literature*. Cincinnati: Hebrew Union College.

Schafer, P. 2012. *The Jewish Jesus: How Judaism and Christianity Shaped Each Other*. Princeton: Princeton University Press.

Schwartz, S. 2001. *Imperialism and Jewish Society*. Princeton: Princeton University Press.

Siker, J. S. 1991. *Disinheriting the Jews: Abraham in Early Christian Controversy.* Louisville, KY: Westminster/John Knox Press.

Stone, M. 1972. *The Testament of Abraham: The Greek Recensions.* Missoula, MT: Society of Biblical Literature.

Ta-Shma, I. 1973. 'Abraham'. *Encyclopaedia Judaica.* Jerusalem: Encyclopaedia Judaica, I. 115–17.

Valantasis, R. ed. 2000. *Religions of Late Antiquity in Practice.* Princeton: Princeton University Press.

Watt, W. M. 1979. 'Ḥanīf'. *The Encyclopaedia of Islam,* 2nd edn. Leiden: Brill, III. 165–6.

Watt, W. M. and Bell, R. 1970. *Introduction to the Quran.* Edinburgh: Edinburgh University Press, 57–85.

Weinfeld, M. 1971. 'Covenant'. *Enyclopaedia Judaica.* Jerusalem: Encyclopaedia Judaica, V. 1012–22.

CHAPTER 2

YET ANOTHER ABRAHAM

GIL ANIDJAR

> God Himself is the ultimate Abraham.
>
> Slavoj Žižek

WAS Abraham religious? Was he, I don't know, very religious? Was he more religious on a particular day of the week, or was it only when the angels dropped by? More so when he bargained with God or did battle for his nephew? Was his religion more visible, more ostentatious, when he migrated—twice—to labour in Canaan, cursed or blessed himself and his descendants with a life of aliens, when he built or arranged a house (or the Kaʿba), or when he realized all on his own and no thanks to the king of Sodom (Sodom!) his version of the American dream (livestock, silver, and gold, and a private mausoleum too—a lasting investment there)? Was it visible when he denied Sarah—twice, again (not thrice, like Peter with Jesus)—or banished Hagar and their son to the wilderness? Did he perhaps affirm and demonstrate his religiosity better when he circumcised himself and his son, later walked with his son, the same or the other, to the mountain, or had his servant swear with his hand on his genitals? Was that because he was against mixed marriages, by the way? Was Keturah? And did Abraham have a take on abortion as well, a religious take? What was his religion anyway? Can we be sure he had one? And if so one only? I mean, Abraham did undergo a conversion, right? Right? Does that mean, then, that he had, or that he acquired, a religion the way one might say that he had his sons, as it were, in possession? But according to what notion of property or belonging? Following which separation of spheres (economy, law, religion)? And with what understanding, what definition, what institution, or science of religion? If Abraham really had a religion, was it temporally or spatially, better yet, administratively, demarcated, as it were, on the side, done while he otherwise attended to more practical or urgent economic matters (again, the livestock, the gold), to science (land survey, well drilling), to politics (tribal those, with a touch of diplomatic acumen), or to law (contracts, definitely contracts)? Was he distinctly preoccupied as well with the sphere of aesthetics (Sarah was beautiful, was she not, and Abraham said so too)? Seriously though, 'was Abraham a political accommodationist or a metaphysical believer?' (Halbertal and Margalit 1992: 138). No doubt Abraham, if such is his name (recall that it was not), surrendered himself to God. He was, as Hobbes puts it, 'first in the Kingdome of God by Covenant' (Hobbes 1996: ch. XL, 249). But what exactly does that mean? Was Abraham religious (see Ruprecht 2002)?

The problem of meaning here begins and ends, perhaps, with translation—if such is possible, if a 'technique of translation' is, that is, available.[1] As he refers to the prophet, Muhammad Asad underscores this difficulty and writes (with a measure of ethnolinguistic enthusiasm) that

> when his contemporaries heard the words islam and muslim, they understood them as denoting man's 'self-surrender to God' and 'one who surrenders himself to God', without limiting these terms to any specific community or denomination—e.g., in [Quran] 3: 67, where Abraham is spoken of as having 'surrendered himself unto God' (kana musliman), or in 3: 52, where the disciples of Jesus say, 'Bear thou witness that we have surrendered ourselves unto God (bi-anna muslimun)'. In Arabic, this original meaning has remained unimpaired, and no Arab scholar has ever become oblivious of the wide connotation of these terms. Not so, however, the non-Arab of our day, believer and non-believer alike: to him, islam and muslim usually bear a restricted, historically circumscribed significance, and apply exclusively to the followers of the Prophet Muhammad. (Asad 1980: xi)

Provincializing Religion

The notion of the Abrahamic, of Abrahamic religions, does not simply find its historical origin in Abraham.[2] Nor did the citational, rhetorical, or exegetical references to Abraham in the sources serve in any obvious manner a religious purpose. They may—I repeat: they may—have served a Jewish, Christian, or Muslim purpose (more likely, purposes), but it was not a religious one. There was no general rule under which

[1] Derrida (2001: 183) insists on the constant and simultaneous necessity and impossibility of translation ('At every moment, translation is as necessary as it is impossible. It is the law; it even speaks the language of the law beyond the law, of the impossible law'). Assmann (2010: 23–4) separates a 'hermeneutics of translation' from a 'hermeneutics of difference', whereby the latter, by virtue of its uncompromising exclusivity, appears devoid of 'translational technique'.

[2] See J. Boyarin (1997), and see van Seters (1975); Firestone (1990); Hendel (2005). Massad (2009) criticizes the received notion of the Abrahamic as an Islamic construct, and see Hawting (2010) for a different argument (which more or less equates the words *dīn* and *milla* as 'religion'); and see Guy G. Stroumsa, 'From Abraham's Religion to the Abrahamic Religions', Inaugural Lecture delivered before the University of Oxford on 12 May 2010, Abrahamic Religions Chair (published in Stroumsa (2011)). I thank Professor Stroumsa for allowing me to read the text of his lecture.

the particular events or emergences that Abraham's name marks operated as mere instances or indeed particulars.[3] Not for a very long time. Whether theologico-genealogical ('the God of Abraham'), metaphorico-spiritual ('the father of circumcision to them who are not of the circumcision only'), or politico-prophetic ('Behold I shall make you a leader of men!'), Abraham does not found one religion (or many) among others, nor is his multifarious memory exhausted by the category of religion (Gen. 26: 24; Rom. 4: 12; Q. 2: 124). Neither he nor his legacy can be confined, nor are they reducible, to religion. Could the Axial Age (see Eisenstadt 1986)? What Abraham started (his inheritance and world-historical significance) is in no way intended to be diminished here, nor could it be. Was it, however, religious? Was it not equally (or, as it were, unequally) civilizational or theologico-socio-political, philosophical or even ethno-cultural? Is it not still? Although Abraham was not necessarily the very first who walked with God, he may well have been the most important, that is, among the earliest and perhaps the first prophet indeed. But what that has to do with religion is hardly clarified thereby.

None of what is said here amounts to another intervention in the debate on the historicity of religion, on the category of religion. Nor is it a version of the claim that 'anything that counts as a "way of living" or a "mode of social life" can only be understood and criticized on its own terms' (MacIntyre 1964: 120). The consensus is now well established that the Latin word *religio* underwent massive transformations, indeed, a re-creation, within the Christian context, and spread outward from there (its translations are another, later development in which missionaries, philologists, administrators, and other imperial secretaries and potentates played a part that is only beginning to be understood) (W. C. Smith 1991; Asad 1993; Balagangadhara 1994; McCutcheon 1997; J. Z. Smith 1998; Derrida 2002; Margel 2005; Masuzawa 2005; Stroumsa 2010). It is a strange consensus, to be sure, which acknowledges the particularity of a word or concept only to maintain it as a universal ground of comparative study. 'History is supposed to exist in the same way as the earth' (Chakrabarty 2000: 74). And so, still, religion. Invented, reinvented, or discovered, religion continues to be invoked, its very name spreading even now, precisely there where its very pertinence has come under pointed interrogation (Vries 2008). Accordingly, there are those among us who teach the modern invention of religion, or its Christian genealogy, and nevertheless insist on, or persist in, using the term with regard to periods and places in which its usage or meaning is—often by their very own account—questionable, metaphorical, anachronistic, or even imperialistic. Does all this testify to a better, more expansive, understanding of religion or religions? To religion as a proper object? To a religious imperative in scholarship and in science? The narrative of science's progress seems not to sit easily with the matter of religion—or its alleged returns. There are, furthermore, those who advocate the dismissal of the word

[3] 'Thus sceptic and believer do not share a common grasp of the relevant concepts any more than anthropologist and Azande do', which does not imply, as MacIntyre (1964: 132–3) makes clear, that agreement is contingent on understanding, nor understanding contingent on agreement.

altogether, as if it were possible (King 1999; Dubuisson 2003). Far from me to recommend that we should simply refrain from speaking of religion and bid, after Trouillot, 'Adieu, Religion' (Trouillot 2002, and see Sheehan 2005). Besides, religion has all too often been an unacknowledged, albeit paradoxical, beneficiary of another 'repressive hypothesis' (Foucault 1978; Assmann 1997)—but there are other ways in which one could practice incitement (to discourse, to hatred, or to the war on terror). One could acknowledge this and other 'returns', though, the return of science even, of the comparative science of race or, better yet, of phrenology. And what about alchemy? What about the unfinished projects of pre-modernity? The way I want to propose going about the matter here is, I think, more agnostic. I wish to ask about and imagine Abraham, away from 'a restricted, historically circumscribed significance' that would 'apply exclusively to the followers' of this or that prophet, as per Asad (1980: xi). I too want to think of another Abraham, an Abrahamic other.[4]

There are already plenty of Abrahams of course. From Abram to Abraham and Ibrāhīm, from the Bible to the Quran, from Paul to Feuerbach and Auerbach, from Kierkegaard to Kafka or Derrida, there is much more than one Abraham (is there not more than one Abrahamic?). There are humble Abrahams and prophetic Abrahams; genealogical Abrahams and ridiculous Abrahams; religious Abrahams and literary Abrahams. And consider that 'in the case of Abraham, the Muslim and Jewish accounts are so intertwined, each influencing the other, that in charting the development of their motifs one can not treat them as truly separate entities' (Lowin 2006: 2). How do we—should we—bring them together, compare them or differentiate between them? Along similar lines, how do we gather, compare, distinguish, and ultimately isolate, religion? Or religions? How do we translate, finally, religion? What does it mean, what could it mean, to imagine yet another Abraham?

To be sure, to deny a religion the man whom it praises as the greatest of its fathers is not a deed to be undertaken lightheartedly.[5] But I am not thinking of a 'secular' (or Egyptian?) Abraham. God forbid. I wish instead to reflect along the lines of Shapin and Schaffer (1989), who have taught us about the emergence of a new 'art of separation', the separation of politics from science (Walzer 1984). Think of this as 'Leviathan and the God Pump' (lately, we have been hearing of the God gene, so this should be relatively easy). Not necessarily religion and science, an issue that is probably overdone and overrated these days. Consider instead the possibility that, as Bruno Latour might phrase it, 'we have never been religious'. Or, after the fashion of Franz Rosenzweig's famous quip: if you want to distinguish the German from the Jew, put him on the operating table. Cut him (them?) open. See what survives the procedure. Put Abraham

[4] The phrase 'I can think of another Abraham' is Kafka's phrase in a letter to Robert Klopstock, dated June 1921, which Ronell (2002: 280ff.) reads; Derrida (2007) follows up; and see Hammerschlag (2008) and Julien and Nault (2011).

[5] I cite and alter Freud's famous opening sentence to his *Moses and Monotheism*: 'To deny a people the man whom it praises as the greatest of its sons is not a deed to be undertaken lightheartedly' (Freud 1939: 3).

under the knife (for a change) and find—or lose—your religion. After a similar fashion, we might register the separation between science and politics that Shapin and Schaffer document, at the same time as we recognize that the separation was never quite accomplished, never quite established, and above all never actually successful. What was constantly at stake was rather a strange and ongoing endeavour, closer even to an attempt to part the sea (but Abraham was no Moses). Politics and science, like religion and politics, did not quite manage to cleanse themselves of the other. They were never quite 'other' to each other. And though we have the rudiments of an account with regard to the trials and failures that trace their shared history, we do not have, to my knowledge, an account of what led us (us?) to divide being, and how, not just into regions and religions, but into these specific, and strangely ossified ones: science, politics, economy, religion, and so forth.

Some will object that the (historical) distinction between science and politics that was achieved, or at least initiated, in the seventeenth century is an advance, a sign of progress. And the same will no doubt be said about religion and politics in the nineteenth (or was it in fact in the first century—God, Caesar, and all?). Secularization as specialization. The rhetoric of progress, or of supersession, notwithstanding, it may well be the case. But this does not amount to a demonstration that the spheres of existence thereby designated are objective—or universally normative—regions of being. Unlike the earth, these would not always have existed after all. Recall, in this context, Borges's encyclopedia, as described by Michel Foucault. 'The monstrous quality that runs through Borges's enumeration consists . . . in the fact that the common ground on which such meetings are possible has itself been destroyed. What is impossible is not the propinquity of the things listed, but the very site on which their propinquity would be possible' (Foucault 2002: xviii). What if the things we now easily list were in fact monstrous? What if our encyclopedias, now enriched by way of the novel designator 'Abrahamic religions', were equally so? And what if we were to acknowledge that the 'common ground' on which 'religions' allegedly meet has also been destroyed, if it ever were there? Their propinquity impossible? Once again, their existence can most certainly be projected onto earlier historical periods, and translated anew into other cultural spheres. They can even be produced or propped up as 'reality-effects'. But precisely therein lies their monstrosity, for 'the quality of monstrosity here does not affect any real body, nor does it produce modifications of any kind in the bestiary of the imagination; it does not lurk in the depths of any strange power. It would not even be present at all in this classification had it not insinuated itself into the empty space, the interstitial blanks separating all these entities from one another' (xvii). The question that remains is therefore not so much whether we understand life, labour, and language (or politics, science, and religion) better than our ancestors or disadvantaged contemporaries, but rather what does the division of being which has insinuated itself between these regions serve? What do the 'empty space, the interstitial blanks separating all these entities', and the distribution of our existence into these particular spheres tell us about ourselves? What do they do for us? By proposing to think of another Abraham, I ask about the uses and abuses of the notion of religion, its monstrosity, however historicized and particularized. I also wonder about the reduction of Abraham to a religious figure.

Try telling a prophet about the separation of powers.

We understand, for instance, that *homo oeconomicus* is a recent invention, a discovery. At the same time, we (we economists, that is, and those similarly inclined) happily project this construct backward and outward. 'Economics', one eager advocate writes, 'enables us to examine behavior within the framework of capitalist societies, but also of socialist societies, and not only of today's societies, but of societies in both the past and a potential (post-industrial) future as well' (Kirchgässner 2007: 8).[6] And the desert grows. But what is at stake in this instance should be obvious. Exchange and accumulation may or may not be all there is to human beings, but by isolating—or expanding—our economic being, our understanding too may increase (or indeed diminish). Our sense of an alternative economic existence, of 'rational choice', indeed, the very meaning of 'economy', may reveal itself as contingent—or not. Whatever the case may be, economic thinking of this sort, hegemonic as it is, cannot adjudicate on whether existence is or should be grounded on, or lived according to, economic principles, nor can it demonstrate, with the psychologists in tow, that motivation has taken, that it should have taken, the form it now appears to have, if it in fact does. Some normative intervention (as to the verification and validity of explanatory models), some translation, at the very least, has to happen (Asad 1993; Chakrabarty 2000), minimally some efforts in global and historical marketing, if we are to recast, say, the basic social unit as primarily a function of economic accumulation, as the effect of emotional (read: neuro-chemical, right?) dispositions, or as the main instrument of biological or genetic survival. Not that 'the proper of man' has to be one—or all—of the above. The point is that these are not equivalent, nor are they necessarily primary or even distinct, even if they can be isolated. By means of an air-pump, for instance, that is, in a vacuum. As if it were possible.

Not quite a devotee of some universal *homo religiosus*, Soren Kierkegaard famously opposed (on Abraham's behalf, as it were) the ethical and the religious. This particular distinction too must be interrogated, though not in order to revive the familiar equation of religion with morality. My purpose is rather to ask whether Abraham does not become a more pertinent, and uncanny, figure if we understand him, and ourselves, as never having been religious. It might extend his reach, suit better his dominion. Now, to be perfectly clear about my intentions here, I will repeat that the distribution of being not just into regions, but into the very regions we have instituted and continue to uphold, the division of the world into distinct spheres such as religion

[6] I find inspiration in the forthcoming work of Dotan Leshem on 'the Pre-Modern Origins of the Economy', where the ancient separation of 'three spheres of existence (the economic, the political, and the philosophical)' is brought under interrogation in its contingency and diachronic persistence. Interestingly, Leshem does not isolate a 'religious' sphere, though he later attends to the further division, brought about in and by early Christianity, between the economical and the theological, or, as Giorgio Agamben puts it, 'between power as government and effective management, and power as ceremonial and liturgical reality' (Agamben 2011: xii).

and politics (or genealogy), law and economics, arts and science—these are not universal distributions and divisions. And the specific role and function that religion plays in this context is to naturalize them, to buttress the legitimacy of the modern age (Cole and Smith 2010). It is at once important and true, of course, that religion is 'a science left aside, or forgotten, by Michel Foucault's "archaeology of knowledge in the age of reason"' (Stroumsa 2010: 38). But more than that, the isolation of religion (or its dismissal) generally occludes the enduring force of one particular 'religion'—in which these divisions and distributions find their source and power—by maintaining its status, quite precisely, as religion, one among many, as it were, and thereby diminishing its significance and accurate limits. Consider then that we have never been religious—not unless we have always already been Christians.[7] Otherwise put, Christianity is the only religion. Or it is no religion at all.[8] Christianity is at any rate better understood as the particular distributive system, a network if you will, which has slowly devised a division of the world, a distribution of being into spheres, and key among these is religion. By casting itself as 'only' a religion (although its own practical understanding—indeed, understandings—has always been much more expansive, involving the world as a whole, and the next world too), Christianity occludes its inheritance (Abrahamic or not) from itself, and from us. Accordingly, it recasts its difference from Judaism, Islam and, for that matter, capitalism by placing them in categories that either level the difference among them (all religions, 'monotheistic religions') or increase its distance from them (economics, as in 'capitalism and religion') (Anidjar 2009). But one can think, still, of another Abraham.

Phrases in Dispute

It is after all no mere foreshadowing that Abraham appears to us as a migrant and an immigrant, burdened with ostentatious signs, which may or may not be recognizable as religious (Bernstein 1994; Asad 2006; Fernando 2010). First down, way down in Egypt land, Abraham is an exile, himself the threat of exodus and displacement and the promise of liberation. And although Hobbes may have gone too far when he attempted

[7] Boyarin (2007) makes the persuasive argument that Christianity produced the Jewish-Christian difference as a 'religious' difference (strangely enough, Boyarin does not think that Hinduism was the recipient of a similar benevolence). He also explains that Christianity produced itself as a religion, which leads me to a different conclusion than his. In my view, what he calls 'the subject of Christianity' is not quite a religious subject, though it does fashion itself as such, as it were, diminutively. Christianity does dis-embed religion, in other words, but first of all, from itself, from a more expansive self or subject. In a sense that is fundamentally different from Judaism in Boyarin's description, Christianity is and is not a religion; and see Barber (2011).

[8] In Taubes's concise 1953 formulation, 'Christian history can have no religious significance of any kind for the Jewish creed; nor can the division of historical time into "BC." and "AD." be recognized by the synagogue' (Taubes 2010: 48).

'to reduce the authority of the canon to [his] conception of political authority' (Halbertal 1997: 140), it does not mean he had no ground for conceiving of Abraham as a political figure, a civil sovereign, and indeed a leader of men. An improbable character at the wellspring of literature, simultaneously aggrandized and diminished father, yet another among Kafka's countrymen who pray for admittance to the law, Abraham is an actor of unfathomable depth in a foundational narrative. He is the subject of the absolute, the absolute subject, as it were, one who, sovereign no more, only submits, to his spouse and to his God, embraces an ethics of passivity or does what he is told, merely following orders perhaps. Does Abraham thereby ascend to a higher ethical order, an order higher than ethics, or does he figure our 'social legacy', the quintessence of patriarchy (Delaney 1998)? Between law and society, Abraham does not comfort us either in our translations of law (Hallaq 2009). Nor is clarity gained, in his case, by dividing law from, say, narrative in the Bible, as if God were a storyteller one day and a legislator the next. Much like light and darkness (and a few other things), the two can of course be distinguished, and they have been indeed (there were days when Moses had to judge the people, and days when he had to supervise the building of the Tabernacle, but what this conveys is that law and architecture were as religious, as political, as negotiations with God on the future of the people). But little is added, in fact, by casting them as religious except perhaps to reduce the challenge they pose to our current existence. For there is a dispute here at work. At least there has been one.[9] 'O followers of earlier revelation! Why do you argue about Abraham?' (Q. 3: 65). If only they did really! And this is not merely the challenge posed by the religious to the ethical, but in excess of it. This requires a different measure. It is also, to repeat, a challenge of translation, the possibility and impossibility of translation.

I am not saying that Abraham was sublimely ridiculous (as Kafka further suggested), or that he was a 'primitive' for whom being appeared as an undifferentiated chaos. I am merely suggesting the possibility that neither Abraham, nor his heirs, divided the world according to the same categories, let alone according to ours. This should hardly constitute an abrupt or revolutionary newsflash. But recall that much as Moses could hardly have been a microbiologist (not that this prevented people from saying that he was (Hart 2007)), there is little to be gained—or is there now?—by suggesting that Abraham was the local equivalent of a scientologist, you know, just another religious guy—or spy—on an impossible mission. If Abraham were otherwise than religious, if we have never been religious, then Abraham may have a different lesson to teach us. More broadly, if the Abrahamic is not about religion, it may be because it sends us back to a division whereby Judaism, Christianity, and Islam (not to mention—I shall

[9] I refer to the dispute—the 'unresolvable difference' as Taubes referred to it—that opposed Judaism (and Islam) to Christianity (see note 8 above). After Taubes and Funkenstein (1993), Raz-Krakotzkin (2007) has been elaborating a history of the transformations of the Jewish-Christian dispute and an account of how it was defused. Dispute, should this need to be said, does not refer to some purported 'clash of civilizations'. Dispute means proximity and discord, not necessarily comparability or translatability.

continue to invoke 'religious' monikers—Hinduism and Buddhism, but the list is longer than, and different from, the usual suspects) are not confronting each other on an even or level plane, much less a religious one (however explosive or tame), not even on a civilizational plane. For what, again, of 'capitalism and religion'? What of 'markets and punishment' (Harcourt 2011)? And would someone seriously claim, for instance, that 'Marxism' (or 'Liberalism') and 'Capitalism' are just two modes of 'economic' existence? That they can be effectively compared according to narrowly conceived parameters such as work and money? The 'dispute' between them is of a different order, of different orders, and it must be conducted on wider grounds, with different divisions of being at stake. As with 'feudalism', that other 'pre-modern' construct (Davis 2008), there are different social, political and symbolic arrangements, and other divisions of being at stake.[10] Here too, there is no equivalence, therefore, no general rule to warrant or justify the comparison between them, to restrict it to a matter of mere economics. Minimally, such rule remains to be found. And if it is the case, the dispute, the challenge, however threatening or tamed, can hardly be seen as having been resolved.

Consider Lyotard's warning (1988: 106): 'One does not dare think out Nazism because it has been beaten down like a mad dog, by a police action, and not in conformity with the rules accepted by its adversaries' genres of discourse (argumentation for liberalism, contradiction for Marxism). It has not been refuted.' At least we know, the wisdom goes, who the bad guy was in this case. But have we dared think out religion? The question is not simply whether religion has been refuted (has it?), although it is also that. It is whether it has ever existed. The critique of Christianity, at any rate, has always been conducted while subsumed under a general and generalized critique of religion, pre-emptively extending the benevolence of critique to all, newly and grudgingly acknowledged, religions. Which is why the question remains whether religion has been properly thought out in conformity with rules accepted by its adversaries' genres of discourse. I propose therefore that the dispute between (and therefore beyond) so-called religions must be seen as exceeding any shared category or established rules and genres, the result of a coup de force whereby different modes of collective existence were levelled and tamed for comparative purposes (Olender 1992). For now, the dispute has been and continues to be managed and defused, in fact contained and confined to a diminutive sphere, namely, religion. Religion, that old-new science, is a strategy of containment; it is an art of separation.

[10] As Chakrabarty puts it, '"precapitalist" speaks of a particular relationship to capital marked by the tension of difference in the horizons of time. The "precapitalist," on the basis of this argument, can only be imagined as something that exists within the temporal horizon of capital and that at the same time disrupts the continuity of this time by suggesting another time that is not on the same, secular, homogeneous calendar (which is why what is precapital is not chronologically prior to capital, that is to say, one cannot assign it to a point on the same continuous time line). This is another time that, theoretically, could be entirely immeasurable in terms of the units of the godless, spiritless time of what we call "history," an idea already assumed in the secular concepts of "capital" and "abstract labor"' (Chakrabarty 2000: 93).

The dispute, should there be one, cannot always and at all times be conducted on all fronts, of course. Kierkegaard was right. Abraham also raises an unprecedented challenge to ethics. But also to much else. For why stop at ethics? Who would fail to recognize that Abraham interrogates and unsettles what today passes for law and for politics, and indeed, for religion? A non-religious Abraham—an Abrahamic that is not about religion, religious accommodation, or comparative religion—potentially loosens the very premises upon which modern society is organized as a whole (as Delaney [1998: 5] poignantly asks, 'why is the willingness to sacrifice one's child the quintessential mode of faith, why not the passionate protection of the child?'), from market capitalism (God didn't say 'buy my book' in every language, nor did he proceed to trademark it with a copyright sign), to medical experimentation (self-circumcision anyone?), carceral or burial practices (do you know what it means today to be buried for all eternity?). We may accept or refuse that challenge; we may participate still in defusing the dispute, but by claiming that it is a religious one we hardly begin to contend with it.

Constructive Criticism

According to Assmann (2010), the dispute started much earlier, if not as early as Abraham. It is the nature of this dispute, the art of separation it implies or sustains, that I want to explore in the remainder of this chapter. For what Assmann calls 'the Mosaic distinction' ('the shift from "polytheistic" to "monotheistic" religions, from cult religions to religions of the book, from culturally specific religions to world religions, in short, from "primary" to "secondary" religions', p. 1) is indeed a dispute, though it is not quite about god or gods. It later came to be identified as 'monotheism' (a term Assmann acknowledges as a modern invention), but it is not about a divine economy either, the number or organization of divine entities. 'God's oneness is not the salient criterion here but the negation of "other" gods. This negation', Assmann continues, 'is a theological rather than religious matter' (31). Strictly speaking then, monotheism is not quite a religion. It should even be questionable to what extent it is more aptly described as a 'counterreligion', but it is certainly a dispute, the original dispute and the revolt that rises against 'the cult of the dead and that of the ruler' (28). The 'Mosaic distinction', at any rate, institutes a new relation to the world and to the divine by separating between them. It establishes the two terms—God and world—as distinct (hence Assmann proposes 'cosmotheism' as the opposite of 'monotheism'). More generally, and as its name clearly indicates, the Mosaic distinction is the making of a decisive separation and a strict division (between true and false, for example, or between god and the world). It is ultimately about difference and 'translatability', rather than about religiosity (18–20). It constitutes a new carving of the world, linguistic and otherwise, and the policing of its borders (within the world, but also between the world and its divine other). Thus, 'for Judaism, it is utterly self-evident that monotheism draws a border and that the Jews are responsible for policing this border' (17). At its starkest, the Mosaic distinction and these borders it establishes bring about 'a new form of hatred into the world: hatred for pagans, heretics, idolaters and their temples, rites, and gods' (16). That is why, for Assmann, what must be acknowledged as important, even foundational, 'is the fact that the gods and cults of the traditional religion were abolished and persecuted in accordance with the Mosaic distinction' (32).

At this point of my argument, the question to reiterate is: what is it that makes the Mosaic distinction a 'religious' distinction, the violence and hatred it harbours, unleashes, or simply brings about, 'religious' violence and hatred? Who is it, what kind of subject is it, that 'makes' the distinction and over what? What is the nature and the extent of the Mosaic claim? If it implicates the entire cosmos, the claim neither emerges from, nor applies to, a separate sphere called 'religion'. The second question that must be raised has to do with the exclusive character of the 'monotheistic' art of separation as it is characterized by Assmann. I do want to underscore that, although I see him as part of a larger, and puzzling, movement that has tended to place on religion, and particularly monotheistic (or 'Semitic') religion, the burden of blame for violence and intolerance in human history, I do think Assmann is right to emphasize difference and distinction as a crucial dimension of understanding. We are indeed talking of an art of separation—of one among many. Yet, in insisting on using the word 'religion' and in presenting us with what can only be described as a Solomonic paradigm, Assmann evokes only one, narrow facet of this 'monotheistic religion' (as Freud had already called it after the German fashion), one circumscribed and limited aspect. Let me reiterate that I am convinced by Assmann's claim that the important issue is not the matter of numbers, from the many to the one. Biblical monolatry, many have pointed out, was not about the one and only God but about the exclusive God. This is precisely why I wish to recall the Solomonic trial here, because it indicates something significant with regard to both numbers and exclusivity.

In the famous illustration of the wisdom of King Solomon, there are two mothers, one of whom will be revealed (as well she must) a false mother. This seems to agree with Assmann's argument and with what he describes of the Mosaic distinction: an exclusive assertion of truth and falsity operates by way of exclusivity and even exclusion. Accordingly, Solomon demonstrates that there is a true mother and a false one, excluding and expelling the latter. Now, much earlier, and before she, like Job, demanded to have her day in court ('Let the LORD decide who is right, you or me', Gen. 16: 5); before the dispute that is, Sarah (then called Sarai still) had asked to be 'built up'. She had asked for something constructive, a construction in the form of a son (16: 2). The Hebrew phrasing, which famously leaves the request ambiguous between construction and reproduction, is quite limpid with regard to Sarah's future claim. Whatever happens, it will be her belonging, her property. She will be the mother and owner. Sarah, in other words, stakes her legal, property claim as a mother. It is with regard to and against that very claim that Hagar in fact asserts herself, and it is with regard to that claim as well that Sarah asks for a trial, one that prefigures another trial of and between mothers, the famous trial of Solomon. 'It becomes obvious that the story . . . is Hagar's as well as

Sarah's and that the issue addressed to YHWH was a question concerning motherhood between Hagar and Sarah and not that of the birth of a son to an aged patriarch—particularly since the name of the future child reflects incidents in the life of the Matriarch' (Teubal 1997: 111). The difference between two trials, somehow on a par with the difference between two mothers, perhaps pales when compared to the unsettling fact that, within the bounds of the narrative sequence, Ishmael will have had two mothers, both of whom are in fact recognized by a divine judgement that challenges our sense of truth, along with the conduct of exclusivity and indeed violence.

What has not been adequately remarked, then, or measured in its full significance, is that one finds in the Solomonic narrative a later instantiation of a prior, much more famous narrative of two mothers, a repetition with a difference that suggests an alternative understanding, indeed, a distinct art of separation. One could refer to this, somehow inadequately but for our purposes here pertinently, as the Abrahamic moment. I would do so at the very least because I see Assmann's insistence on Moses (here again not only his own, of course) as symptomatic of a strange displacement of Abraham, the marginalization—as it were in plain sight—of the Abrahamic by way of a recasting of the foundations of 'monotheism' in Moses (Moses the Egyptian, one could say, recasts Abraham the Chaldean, not to speak, but this is a different story, of Jesus the Jew). Yet, foundational as it is, this Abrahamic moment does not simply stand in opposition to the Mosaic distinction (after all, Moses too had two mothers).[11] Rather, it broadens and expands the field of its operations. It too establishes distinctions, and initiates disputes, but it does so without adjudicating absolutely—that is to say, by absolving or dissolving, by absolution—on ultimate validity. In my reading, then, the Abrahamic is hardly about 'religion' nor does it make its intervention—the institution of a new art of separation—by attending merely to God and world. Rather, the Abrahamic comes into the world by attending to the presence, or rather co-presence of translation and difference, with regard, in this case, to mothers, and more precisely to two mothers who stand in a relation of complex temporality (both untimeliness and contemporaneity, even simultaneity). The Abrahamic is what ultimately reduces the number of mothers, but it does so locally only, that is to say, without subtraction. Moreover, and crucially so, the Abrahamic does not pronounce on the true mother, nor even on the true son. It cares little for true and false. Instead, the Abrahamic separates mothers and distributes blessings. Put another way, the Abrahamic establishes motherhood as locally exclusive (you will have no other mother before me), but not globally or cosmically so. It states that there are other gods, that there is another mother. There is indeed a dispute then, but—*pace* Assmann—there is no absolute invalidation. This paradoxically means, that, as with the gods and as with the world, motherhood was multiple in the first place (ultimately oneness will be God's alone). Like the world and the gods, motherhood is there to be divided, divided and distributed anew by way of

[11] 'One of the most uncanny attractions of Egypt', writes Barbara Johnson in her discussion of 'Moses the Egyptian' (2010: 50) 'is thus the idea that European culture might have a double origin. It might have two mothers, in effect.' And see 'The Theme of the Two Mothers' in Vitz 1993: 26–9.

translation and difference. The Abrahamic institutes a dispute alright. It constitutes itself as dispute over the regions and divisions of the world, which includes difference and/as untranslatability.[12]

References

Agamben, G. 2011. *The Kingdom and the Glory: For a Theological Genealogy of Economy and Government (Homo Sacer II, 2)*, ed. L. Chiesa and M. Mandarini. Stanford, CA: Stanford University Press.

Anidjar, G. 2009. 'The Idea of an Anthropology of Christianity'. *Interventions: International Journal of Postcolonial Studies* 11 (3): 367–93.

Asad, M. 1980. *The Message of the Qurān*. Gibraltar: Dar al-Andalus.

Asad, T. 1993. *Genealogies of Religion: Discipline and Reasons of Power in Christianity and Islam*. Baltimore: Johns Hopkins University Press.

Asad, T. 2006. 'Trying to Understand French Secularism'. In H. D. Vries and L. E. Sullivan, eds, *Political Theologies: Public Religions in a Post-Secular World*. 1st edn. New York: Fordham University Press, 494–526.

Assmann, J. 1997. *Moses the Egyptian: The Memory of Egypt in Western Monotheism*. Cambridge, MA: Harvard University Press.

Assmann, J. 2010. *The Price of Monotheism*, trans. R. Savage. Stanford, CA: Stanford University Press.

Balagangadhara, S. N. 1994. *'The Heathen in His Blindness...': Asia, the West, and the Dynamic of Religion*. Leiden: Brill.

Barber, D. C. 2011. *On Diaspora: Christianity, Religion and Secularity*. Eugene, OR: Cascade Books.

Bernstein, M. A. 1994. *Foregone Conclusions: Against Apocalyptic History*. Berkeley: University of California Press.

Boyarin, D. 2007. *Border Lines: The Partition of Judaeo-Christianity*. 1st pbk edn. Philadelphia, PA: University of Pennsylvania Press.

Boyarin, J. 1997. 'Another Abraham: Jewishness and the Law of the Father'. *Yale Journal of Law and the Humanities* 9: 345–94.

Chakrabarty, D. 2000. *Provincializing Europe: Postcolonial Thought and Historical Difference*. Princeton: Princeton University Press.

Cole, A. and Smith, D. V., eds. 2010. *The Legitimacy of the Middle Ages: On the Unwritten History of Theory*. Durham, NC: Duke University Press.

Davis, K. 2008. *Periodization and Sovereignty: How Ideas of Feudalism and Secularization Govern the Politics of Time*. Philadelphia: University of Pennsylvania Press.

Delaney, C. L. 1998. *Abraham on Trial: The Social Legacy of Biblical Myth*. Princeton: Princeton University Press.

[12] For their questions and comments on earlier versions of this chapter, I am grateful to the participants of the MESAAS Colloquium at Columbia University and to the audience at the Seventh International Conference on Unity and Plurality in Europe, convened in Mostar by the International Forum Bosnia in July 2012. I particularly wish to thank Professor Rusmir Mahmutćehajić for his kind engagement and hospitality.

Derrida, J. 2001. 'What is a "Relevant" Translation?', trans. L. Venuti. *Critical Inquiry* 27 (2): 174–200.

Derrida, J. 2002. 'Faith and Knowledge: The Two Sources of "Religion at the Limits of Reason Alone"', trans. S. Weber. In G. Anidjar, ed., *Acts of Religion*. New York: Routledge, 42–101.

Derrida, J. 2007. 'Abraham, the Other', trans. G. Anidjar. In B. Bergo, J. D. Cohen, and R. Zagury-Orly, eds, *Judeities: Questions for Jacques Derrida*. 1st edn. New York: Fordham University Press, 1–35.

Dubuisson, D. 2003. *The Western Construction of Religion: Myths, Knowledge, and Ideology*, trans. W. Sayers. Baltimore: Johns Hopkins University Press.

Eisenstadt, S. N., ed. 1986. *The Origins and Diversity of Axial Age Civilizations*. Albany, NY: State University of New York Press.

Fernando, M. L. 2010. 'Reconfiguring Freedom: Muslim Piety and the Limits of Secular Law and Public Discourse in France'. *American Ethnologist* 37 (1): 19–35.

Firestone, R. 1990. *Journeys in Holy Lands: The Evolution of the Abraham-Ishmael Legends in Islamic Exegesis*. Albany, NY: State University of New York Press.

Foucault, M. 1978. *The History of Sexuality*. 1st American edn. New York: Pantheon Books.

Foucault, M. 2002. *The Order of Things: An Archaeology of the Human Sciences*. London: Routledge.

Freud, S. 1939. *Moses and Monotheism*, trans. K. Jones. New York: Vintage Books.

Funkenstein, A. 1993. *Perceptions of Jewish History*. Los Angeles: University of California Press.

Halbertal, M. 1997. *People of the Book: Canon, Meaning, and Authority*. Cambridge, MA: Harvard University Press.

Halbertal, M. and Margalit, A. 1992. *Idolatry*. Cambridge, MA: Harvard University Press.

Hallaq, W. B. 2009. *Sharīʿa: Theory, Practice, Transformations*. Cambridge: Cambridge University Press.

Hammerschlag, S. 2008. 'Another, Other Abraham: Derrida's Figuring of Levinas's Judaism'. *Shofar: An Interdisciplinary Journal of Jewish Studies* 26 (4): 74–96.

Harcourt, B. E. 2011. *The Illusion of Free Markets: Punishment and the Myth of Natural Order*. Cambridge, MA: Harvard University Press.

Hart, M. B. 2007. *The Healthy Jew: The Symbiosis of Judaism and Modern Medicine*. New York: Cambridge University Press.

Hawting, G. 2010. 'The Religion of Abraham and Islam'. In M. Goodman, G. H. V. Kooten, and J. V. Ruiten, eds, *Abraham, the Nations, and the Hagarites: Jewish, Christian, and Islamic Perspectives on Kinship with Abraham*. Leiden: Brill, 477–501.

Hendel, R. S. 2005. *Remembering Abraham: Culture, Memory, and History in the Hebrew Bible*. Oxford: Oxford University Press.

Hobbes, T. 1996. *Leviathan*, ed. R. Tuck, revised student edn. Cambridge: Cambridge University Press.

Johnson, B. 2010. *Moses and Multiculturalism*. Berkeley: University of California Press.

Julien, J. and Nault, F. 2011. *Plus d'une voix: Jacques Derrida et la question théologico-politique...* Paris: Cerf.

King, R. 1999. *Orientalism and Religion: Post-Colonial Theory, India and the Mystic East*. London: Routledge.

Kirchgässner, G. 2007. *Homo Oeconomicus: The Economic Model of Individual Behavior and its Applications in Economics and Other Social Sciences*. New York: Springer.

Lowin, S. L. 2006. *The Making of a Forefather: Abraham in Islamic and Jewish Exegetical Narratives*. Leiden: Brill.

Lyotard, J. 1988. *The Differend: Phrases in Dispute*, trans. G. van den Abbeele. Minneapolis: University of Minnesota Press.

McCutcheon, R. T. 1997. *Manufacturing Religion: The Discourse on Sui Generis Religion and the Politics of Nostalgia*. New York: Oxford University Press.

MacIntyre, A. 1964. 'Is Understanding Religion Compatible with Believing?' In J. Hick, ed., *Faith and the Philosophers*. Princeton Theological Seminary. New York: St Martin's Press, 115–33.

Margel, S. 2005. *Superstition: l'anthropologie du religieux en terre de chrétienté*. Paris: Galilée.

Massad, J. A. 2009. *La Persistance de la question palestinienne*, trans. J. Marelli. Paris: La Fabrique.

Masuzawa, T. 2005. *The Invention of World Religions, Or, how European Universalism was Preserved in the Language of Pluralism*. Chicago: University of Chicago Press.

Olender, M. 1992. *The Languages of Paradise: Race, Religion, and Philology in the Nineteenth Century*, trans. A. Goldhammer. Cambridge, MA: Harvard University Press.

Raz-Krakotzkin, A. 2007. *The Censor, the Editor, and the Text: The Catholic Church and the Shaping of the Jewish Canon in the Sixteenth Century*, trans. J. Feldman. Philadelphia: University of Pennsylvania Press.

Ronell, A. 2002. *Stupidity*. Urbana, IL: University of Illinois Press.

Ruprecht, L. A. 2002. *Was Greek Thought Religious: On the Use and Abuse of Hellenism, from Rome to Romanticism*. 1st edn. New York: Palgrave.

Shapin, S. and Schaffer, S. 1989. *Leviathan and the Air-Pump: Hobbes, Boyle, and the Experimental Life: Including a Translation of Thomas Hobbes, Dialogus Physicus De Natura Aeris by Simon Schaffer*. Princeton: Princeton University Press.

Sheehan, J. 2005. *The Enlightenment Bible: Translation, Scholarship, Culture*. Princeton: Princeton University Press.

Smith, J. Z. 1998. 'Religion, Religions, Religious'. In M. C. Taylor, ed., *Critical Terms for Religious Studies*. Chicago: University of Chicago Press, 269–84.

Smith, W. C. 1991. *The Meaning and End of Religion*. Minneapolis: Fortress Press.

Stroumsa, G. G. 2010. *A New Science: The Discovery of Religion in the Age of Reason*. Cambridge, MA: Harvard University Press.

Stroumsa, G. G. 2011. 'From Abraham's Religion to the Abrahamic Religions'. Historia Religionum 3: 11–22.

Taubes, J. 2010. *From Cult to Culture: Fragments toward a Critique of Historical Reason*, ed. C. E. Fonrobert and A. Engel. Stanford, CA: Stanford University Press.

Teubal, S. J. 1997. *Ancient Sisterhood: The Lost Traditions of Hagar and Sarah*. Athens: Ohio University Press.

Trouillot, M.-R. 2002. 'Adieu, Culture: A New Duty Arises'. In R. G. Fox, ed., *Anthropology Beyond Culture*. Oxford: Berg, 37–60.

Van Seters, J. 1975. *Abraham in History and Tradition*. New Haven: Yale University Press.

Vitz, P. C. 1993. *Sigmund Freud's Christian Unconscious*. Grand Rapids, MI: Eerdmans.

Vries, H. D., ed. 2008. *Religion: Beyond a Concept*. New York: Fordham University Press.

Walzer, M. 1984. 'Liberalism and the Art of Separation'. *Political Theory* 12 (3): 315–30.

CHAPTER 3

ABRAHAMIC EXPERIMENTS IN HISTORY

ADAM J. SILVERSTEIN

THAT Jews, Christians, and Muslims should unite in some way under the banner of their common ancestor Abraham is essentially a modern idea. After all, in the past, those belonging to these religions mostly lived under the rule of one another (usually Jews under Christianity or Jews and Christians under Islam) and there was no pretence to the fact that the three communities and their religions bear comparison, unification, or inclusiveness. Political Correctness is a modern predicament and, with few exceptions, triumphalism dictated relations between the three religions and their adherents. Thus, it would be unreasonable to expect that anything resembling a modern 'Abrahamic' initiative was proposed in pre-modern times. With this in mind, in what follows I will merely seek to demonstrate that the two principles on which such initiatives are based sprung up from time to time. The two principles are: (1) A focus on Abraham as a unifier of distinct (even rival) religious communities; and (2) a recognition that Judaism, Christianity, and Islam are comparable to each other while different from other religions; their adherents should therefore afford each other preferential treatment of sorts. It will thus be argued that, in a sense, modern Abrahamic initiatives are new recipes using old ingredients.

ABRAHAM AS A UNIFYING FIGURE

Already the Hebrew Bible tells us that Abraham would be seen as an ancestor for more than one nation. In Gen. 12: 3 God tells Abram (as he was still known): 'And I will bless them that bless you, and he who curses you I shall curse; and in you shall be blessed all the families of the earth', suggesting that Abraham will come to have some sort of universal relevance. In a later passage we hear, moreover, that God changed Abram's name to 'Abraham' to reflect his future association with many peoples. Gen. 17: 3–6 reads: 'Abram fell on his face, and God talked with him, saying: "As for me, behold my covenant is with you and you shall be the father of a multitude of nations. And your name shall no longer be called 'Abram' but your name shall be 'Abraham', for I have made you the father of a multitude of nations. And I will make you exceedingly fruitful and I will make of you nations."'

That Abraham would be important to numerous nations is thus one of the things that God promises him and in a curious way the modern recognition that Abraham is a forefather of sorts for all three religions serves both a social and also a theological purpose as it is proof that this aspect of the promise has been fulfilled. What Jews, Christians, and Muslims have debated over the millennia is thus not whether Abraham's legacy is important—for to this they all signed up—but rather which religious community is the real heir to his legacy. Though it goes against the grain of modern Abrahamic initiatives to put things this way, Abraham unifies the adherents of these religions not in agreement but in debate.

It is precisely this competition over the claim to Abraham's legacy that often led Jews, Christians, and Muslims to sharpen and highlight their unique stance on Abraham's importance to them, meaning that in periods of interfaith debate Abraham would feature heavily in these exchanges, or even—more subtly—in one religion's descriptions of itself. For while Jews usually refer to themselves as the children of 'Abraham, Isaac, and Jacob' (and to their God as the God of all three), at times the phrase is collapsed into the single name of 'Abraham', as in the central prayer in the Jewish prayerbook, the Eighteen Benedictions, where the first benedictions, which focuses on the 'Patriarchs' (*avot*), reads:

> Blessed are you, God, our God and *the God of our forefathers, God of Abraham, God of Isaac, and God of Jacob*, the great, heroic, awesome God, the supreme God, who bestows kindnesses and creates all, who remembers the kindnesses of the Patriarchs and brings a Redeemer to their descendants, with love, for the sake of His Name. O King, Helper, Saviour and Shield. *Blessed are you, God, the Shield of Abraham.* [Emphasis mine.]

In other cases, the usual 'Abraham, Isaac, and Jacob' as forefathers is simply replaced by 'Abraham', as in the following passage from the Babylonian Talmud: 'R. Yochanan b. Zakkai said of his student, R. Elazar b. Arach: "Blessed is the Lord, God of Israel, who has given a son to our Forefather Abraham, who knows how to comprehend, research, and expound upon the issue of Maaseh Merkavah ... How fortunate are you, our Forefather Abraham, that Elazar b. Arach emerged from your loins!"' (*Ḥagiga* 14b).

Similarly, although the Quran refers to 'Abraham, Isaac, and Jacob' (Q. 29: 26) and Muslim Tradition places great theological focus on Abraham's other line through Ishmael, it appears that the early Muslim community focused specifically on Abraham himself. This is attested to not only by the repeated reference to 'the religion of Abraham' throughout the Quran but also by the dozens of religious inscriptions from Arabia and the Negev in the pre- and early Islamic period that focus on Abraham alone and on a religion centred on him (Pines 1984: *passim*; Nevo and Koren 2003: 186–90, 195). This focus on Abraham persisted well into the Islamic period and there is a Muslim inscription from as late as 735 CE that refers to 'the Lord of Muhammad and Abraham' (Donner 2010: 255), demonstrating that this focus on Abraham was not meant in an ecumenical vain (as the reference to Muhammad in this inscription proves) but rather it uses Abraham as an identifier of Islam almost on a par with Muhammad himself. That Muslims were claiming Abraham for themselves, rather than attempting to use his broad appeal to include others, is hardly surprising as the Quran itself is clear on this:

> O People of the Book! Why do you argue about Abraham, when the Torah and the Gospel were not revealed until after him? Have you no sense? You are those who argue about that of which you have some knowledge but why then do you argue about that of which you have no knowledge? God knows. You do not know. Abraham was not a Jew, nor yet a Christian; but he was a *ḥanīf muslim*, and he was not of the idolaters. (Q. 3: 65–8)

While Jews and Muslims in late antiquity were consciously associating themselves with Abraham, it does not appear to be the case that Christians did so to a comparable extent. The New Testament opens with a genealogy of Jesus that takes him back to Abraham (but not further; Matt. 1: 1–17), and Romans 4 is a clear statement of Christianity's exclusive claim to Abraham, while the church fathers also stressed the centrality of Abraham and his legacy to Christian theology (Siker 1991). And yet, there was a surprising willingness on the part of some Christians to assign Abrahamic credentials to non-Christians. In one case, a Christian author refers indifferently to the Jewish convert to Islam, Kaʿab al-Aḥbār as 'a scribe from the seed of Abraham' (Lassner 2000: 374). Moreover, the 'religion of Abraham' (*millat Ibrāhīm*) that the Quran cites so approvingly was something that for Christians smacked of obsolescence. Consider, for instance, the following exchange between an early Muslim and a Christian, which dates from the first half of the eighth century: 'The Arab: "Why do you not believe in Abraham and his commandments, when he is the father of prophets and kings, and scripture testifies to his righteousness?" The Monk: "What sort of belief in Abraham do you expect from us, and what are these commandments which you want us to observe?" The Arab: "Circumcision and sacrifice, because he received them from God."' (Crone and Cook 1977: 12–13; Hoyland 1997: 470–1.)[1] Whatever reverence the Christian interlocutor in this exchange reserved for the Patriarch Abraham, it is clear that the latter was not deemed to be a role-model for him in any practical way. The reason for this is illuminated by the numerous Christian texts from the early Islamic period that associated 'Abrahamic' religion with a primitive form of monotheism that had yet to benefit from the updates introduced by Jesus' career (Hoyland 1997: 535–41).

[1] It is a curious fact that the Monk in this exchange, despite being circumspect about this Abramo-centric religion, was called 'Abraham' himself (Crone and Cook 1977: 163 n. 23).

For Muslims, by contrast, Abraham was the architect (with Ishmael) of God's House in Mecca, thereby setting the groundwork and precedent for the all-important ḥajj, while combining biographical details that in the Judaeo-Christian tradition are split between the biblical Abraham and the Temple-building Solomon.

Interesting though the foregoing points may be, they appear to depict Abraham as a divisive character in interfaith relations. We shall now see that Abraham could also play the role of a unifier.

First, as Jews and Christians continued to read and interpret the Bible, the idea that Abraham would be the father of many (even competing) nations was one that would be revisited. Already in a later passage from the Hebrew Bible (Ps. 47) we hear of an enthronement ceremony that will involve all nations of the world recognizing God, including a specific reference to 'the people of the God of Abraham'. Whom the phrase 'people of the God of Abraham' referred to was, as everything else in the Bible, open to interpretation and Christians and Jews debated the issue.[2]

In late antiquity, when rabbinic activity was arguably at its height, the idea of Abraham as a unifier was expressed in rabbinical exegesis not on Gen. 15–17 or on Ps. 47, but on the Song of Songs, where 8: 8–9 begins 'We have a little sister...' A tantalizing reading of this verse, recorded in the midrashic collections of *Tanḥuma* (ad loc.) and *Genesis Rabba* (39.3), focuses on the identity of this 'sister' (*aḥot*) and rather boldly states that she is none other than Abraham, since he 'united (*iḥā*) all of humankind before God, just as one who tears a garment apart and then sews it together. Hence, he was called 'sister' (= unifier).' This is hardly the most obvious reading of the word 'sister' in this context and, had they wanted to, the authors of this interpretation could easily have done away with it. And yet, Abraham's bridge-building qualities were (seemingly) forcibly read into the verse.

It may well be the case that Jews living under Christian rule, where Abraham's relevance to more than one nation was manifest, better appreciated Abraham's role as a unifier of peoples. In the Mishna (*Bikkurim* 1: 4), we are told that when delivering the first fruits to the Temple a convert to Judaism may not use the liturgical phrase 'God of our forefathers' that Jews would use in this context since the convert was not, strictly speaking, a descendant of the Israelite forefathers. While the Babylonian Talmud agrees with this verdict, the Jerusalem Talmud (*y. Bikkurim* 64a (1: 4)) offers a different perspective, according to which even a convert adduces the forefathers since 'God made Abraham the forefather of a multitude of nations so that Abraham becomes the father of everyone in the world who enters under the wings of the Divine Presence.'

Second, it would appear that Jews from different regions and periods actually sought to build bridges with rival nations by appealing to their common descent from Abraham. Already in the Second Temple period, the Jews and the people of Sparta are described as seeking common purpose by referring to their respective Abrahamic

[2] We will see below how Judah Halevi interprets this phrase. Interestingly, already in the ancient Greek (LXX) and Syriac versions of the Psalm the word 'nation' (*ʿam*) is read as though it says 'with' (*ʿim*), thereby neutralizing the phrase somewhat.

credentials. The First Book of Maccabees (12: 20–3) provides us with the following text of a letter from the Spartans to the Jews: 'Arius, king of the Spartans, sends greetings to Onias, the chief priest. It has been found in a writing concerning the Spartans and Jews, that they are kinsmen, and that they are descended from Abraham. Now since we have learned this, please write us about your welfare. We for our part write you that your cattle and property are ours and ours are yours. So we command them to report to you to this effect.' Josephus is also aware of this letter, including the notion that the Spartans ('Lacedaemonians') and Jews are both descended from Abraham (*Jewish Antiquities* 12.4.10). Although the initiative in uniting the two peoples with reference to Abraham appears in this case to have been that of the Spartans, the mere fact that it is a biblical unifier who is appealed to here suggests that the idea originated with the Jews themselves.[3]

This is supported by the fact that Jews are known to have made use of this diplomatic ruse on other occasions, two of which involve the inhabitants of Arabia, albeit in very different periods. In the first instance, a mid-fifth-century Christian author tells us the following about the 'Saracens':

> This is the tribe which took its origin and had its name from Ishmael, the son of Abraham; and the ancients called them Ishmaelites after their progenitor. As their mother Hagar was a slave, they afterwards, to conceal the opprobrium of their origin, assumed the name of Saracens, as if they were descended from Sara, the wife of Abraham. Such being their origin, they practise circumcision like the Jews, refrain from the use of pork, and observe many other Jewish rites and customs. If, indeed, they deviate in any respect from the observances of that nation, it must be ascribed to the lapse of time, and to their intercourse with the neighbouring nations. Moses, who lived many centuries after Abraham, only legislated for those whom he led out of Egypt. The inhabitants of the neighbouring countries, being strongly addicted to superstition, probably soon corrupted the laws imposed upon them by their forefather Ishmael. The ancient Hebrews had their community life under this law only, using therefore unwritten customs, before the Mosaic legislation. These people certainly served the same gods as the neighbouring nations, honouring and naming them similarly, so that by this likeness with their forefathers in religion, there is evidenced their departure from the laws of their forefathers. As is usual, in the lapse of time, their ancient customs fell into oblivion, and other practices gradually got the precedence among them. *Some of their tribe afterwards, happening to come in contact with the Jews, gathered from them the facts of their true origin, returned to their kinsmen, and inclined to the Hebrew customs and laws.* From that time on, until now, many of them regulate their lives according to the Jewish precepts. (Sozomen ch. 38, emphasis mine.)

[3] There is evidence of pagans revering Abraham too, and the annual festival of Abraham near Hebron that Sozomen describes for the fourth century CE, was attended not only by the expected Jews and Christians but also by pagan 'Palestinians, Phoenecians, and Arabs' (in Stroumsa 2011: 17–18; and Stroumsa 2013: 163–4).

In this passage, it seems that the Jews who reminded the fifth-century Arabians of their common, Abrahamic heritage did so not necessarily for diplomatic purposes but perhaps in the interests of proselytizing them. For a more explicit case of 'Abrahamic diplomacy' we turn to our second text from Arabia, which was written some two centuries later, referring to events from the eve of Islam:

> Twelve peoples [representing] all the tribes of the Jews assembled at the city of Edessa. When they saw that the Iranian troops had departed and left the city in peace, they closed the gates and fortified themselves . . . They departed, taking the road through the desert . . . to the sons of Ishmael. *[The Jews] called [the Arabs] to their aid and familiarized them with the relationship they had through the books of the [Old] Testament.* Although [the Arabs] were convinced of their close relationship, they were unable to get a consensus from their multitude, for they were divided from each other by religion. In that period a certain one of them, a man of the sons of Ishmael named Muhammad, a merchant, became prominent. A sermon about the Way of Truth, supposedly at God's command, was revealed to them, *and [Muhammad] taught them to recognize the God of Abraham, especially since he was informed and knowledgeable about Mosaic history. Because the command had come from On High, he ordered them all to assemble together and to unite in faith. Abandoning the reverence of vain things, they turned toward the living God, who had appeared to their father—Abraham.* Muhammad legislated that they were not to eat carrion, not to drink wine, not to speak falsehoods, and not to commit adultery. He said: 'God promised that country to Abraham and to his son after him, for eternity. And what had been promised was fulfilled during that time when [God] loved Israel. *Now, however, you are the sons of Abraham, and God shall fulfil the promise made to Abraham and his son on you. Only love the God of Abraham, and go and take the country which God gave to your father, Abraham.* No one can successfully resist you in war, since God is with you' . . . All the remnants of the sons of Israel then assembled and united, becoming a large force. After this they dispatched a message to the Byzantine emperor, saying: *'God gave that country as the inherited property of Abraham and of his sons after him. We are the sons of Abraham. It is too much that you hold our country.* Leave in peace, and we shall demand from you what you have seized, plus interest.' The emperor rejected this. He did not provide a fitting response to the message but rather said: 'The country is mine. Your inheritance is the desert. So go in peace to your country.' (Sebeos, ch. 30; emphasis mine.)

By the Middle Ages, Abraham's shared legacy was recognized by some of the leading scholars of the relevant religions. In some cases this was grudgingly so: the great Maimonides (d. 1204)—who experienced violent persecution at the hands of his co-Abrahamists—states that Abraham's activity 'has resulted, as we see today, in the consensus of the greater part of the population of the earth in glorifying him and considering themselves as blessed through his memory, so that even those who do not belong to his progeny pretend to derive from him' (in Maimonides 1963: II. 515). It appears that in this statement Maimonides was both settling theological scores with his Christian and Muslim rivals while also attempting to show that the biblical promise that Abraham would be 'blessed through him' has been fulfilled. Similarly, Judah Halevi (d. 1141), in his pro-Jewish polemical work *Sefer ha-Kuzari*, makes it clear that he is aware of the rival (Christian and Muslim) claims to Abraham's legacy. In one instance he simply states that 'The essence of Abraham passed over to Isaac, to the exclusion of the other sons who were all removed from the land, the special inheritance of Isaac...' (Halevi 1946: 58). In another he is even more direct: 'For there exists no connection between God and any other creed, as He pours out His light only on the select people. They [the Jews] are accepted by Him, and He by them. He is called "the God of Israel" and they [the Jews] are "the people of the God of Abraham"' (p. 177). Elsewhere too (p. 103) Judah Halevi stresses that the 'people of the God of Abraham' whom we encountered in Psalm 47, are the Jews—perhaps indicating that he was aware of counter-claims lodged by Christians in his day. Interestingly, in the correspondence between Hasdai ibn Shaprut (d. *c*.975) and the Khazar king of his day, the latter explains that his ancestor chose Judaism because 'the Israelite religion is the best and truest. I have chosen it, as it is the religion of Abraham' (p. 276), once again scoring points for the Jewish claim to Abraham's legacy, even though the Khazar king also mentioned in his letter that he was a descendant of Noah's son Japheth, and hence not genealogically related to Abraham at all (as the latter was from Noah's son Shem). We shall return to Judah Halevi's work below.

Somewhat less territorial over Abraham's legacy was the quranic exegete Fakhr al-Dīn al-Rāzī (d. 1210), who—writing on the other side of the Muslim world from the Mediterranean of Judah Halevi and Maimonides—described Abraham as 'An individual whose merit is recognized by all religious groups and sects... among the People of the Book the Jews and Christians acknowledge his merit and are honoured that they are among his children' (al-Rāzī 1981: IV. 36).

In summary, from biblical times to the Middle Ages, Abraham's role and legacy were debated amongst Jews, Christians, and Muslims, who could not but recognize his centrality not only to their own religious tradition but to those of others. Occasionally, perhaps influenced by the Bible's own prophecy about Abraham's shared legacy, some scholars came to appreciate Abraham's role in bringing rivals together, such as the rabbis who described Abraham as one who 'united mankind before God'. At least to some degree the 'Abrahamic' aspect of modern Abrahamic initiatives has forerunners in pre-modern history.

Recognition of Shared Attributes amongst Abrahamic Religions

It could be argued that 'Abraham' is not actually what the idea of 'Abrahamic Religions' is about: rather, it is about the comparability of the three (or more) religions whose adherents have sought in recent decades to bridge the divides that separate their respective communities by appealing to the shared attributes of their religions. What we are dealing with, then, is a quest for commonalities, only one of which (and a minor one at that) is the figure of Abraham himself. In the preceding pages I have attempted to show that from time to time these communities could be brought together—in agreement or in debate—with reference to the figure of Abraham. In what follows, I will attempt to show that they also did so without reference to Abraham, demonstrating that there were Jews, Christians, and Muslims through the ages who, in both theory and in practice, sought to acknowledge that their religions belonged to a single, preferred group of religions, which distinguished them from other, inferior groups. In other words, it will be shown that the *idea* of considering these religions together is one that has arisen before, at various times and in a variety of places.

Perhaps unsurprisingly Jews have been more likely than Christians or Muslims to look for common ground or cause with the other religions, for two reasons: first, Jews from the first to the twentieth centuries have almost always lived under the rule of others and they had neither the inclination nor the political muscle to impose inflexible interpretations of interfaith relations on themselves or on others. It was in their interest that Christians and Muslims deem them to be familiar rather than alien. Second, perhaps under the influence of the historical circumstances just mentioned, Jewish theology came to include concepts and frameworks that would allow certain types of non-Jews to be recognized as righteous or even deserving of a portion in the Hereafter. The central concept in this context is the idea of 'Noachide Law', this being a set of seven largely moral laws (prohibiting theft, murder, adultery, and the like) that are intended for all but the Jews. There are thus two 'Torahs': one for the Jews, the other for the other 'Children of Noah' and those who follow the rules stipulated for them (be they Jews following the Torah or Noachides following the code devised for them) will be rewarded accordingly (Novak 1983: *passim*). Crucially, in addition to the 'moral' laws prescribed for non-Jews are prohibitions against blasphemy and idolatry. Thus, although in theory Noachide Law should be universal, it only really applied to non-idolatrous theists, and in actual fact Jews almost always had Christians and/or Muslims in mind when considering the concept.

An interesting historical implication of the idea that the non-Jewish descendants of Noah should have a monotheistic system of moral laws is that Jews could, on occasion, be seen to take a favourable view on the emergence of Christianity or Islam in areas that were hitherto pagan. In some cases, in fact, Jesus or Muhammad were deemed to have been 'true' prophets who were simply sent by God to 'the Gentiles', as part of the process of spreading Noachide religion where it did not yet exist. Precisely this message was spread by the various messianic pretenders who emerged in the eastern Islamic world, from the mid-eighth century and for 200 years thereafter, characters such as Abū 'Isā al-Iṣfahānī, Yūdghān of Hamadan, and Mushkā of Qum (al-Shahrastāni 1961: 215–18). Regarding Abu 'Isa, the karaite scholar al-Qirqisānī (d. 937) writes:

> Abu 'Isa confessed the prophetic nature of Jesus b. Miriam and that of [Muhammad] and said that each of them was sent [by God] to his people. He ordered [his

> own disciples] to read the Gospels and the Quran and to gain an understanding of their meanings. He said that the Christians and Muslims are required to observe their faiths just as the Jews are required to observe the one they claim. (In Nemoy 1930.)

That Jewish theology could support such a position, and that there were those who adopted it does not mean that such ideas were, in practice, accepted widely: when, in 2002, Chief Rabbi Jonathan Sacks published his *The Dignity of Difference*, in which he argued that, 'God has spoken to mankind in many languages: through Judaism to Jews, Christianity to Christians, Islam to Muslims... *God is God of all humanity, but no single faith is or should be the faith of all humanity*' (Sacks 2002: 55), there was an outcry of such force (amongst certain ultra-orthodox Jews) that Rabbi Sacks was compelled to remove the offending passages from a subsequent edition of the book.

Perhaps a better received discussion of Judaism's relation to other religions is that of Judah Halevi in his *Sefer ha-Kuzari*, which we have encountered above. The book was produced in early medieval Spain, where a 'Golden Age' of interfaith tolerance is said to have been enjoyed by local Jews, Christians, and Muslims; and as it is written in Judaeo-Arabic, the book itself exemplifies the hybrid Jewish-Muslim culture of the time. And yet, *Sefer ha-Kuzari* is a polemical work, aimed not at showing that all three religions are equally valid pathways to God/Heaven/Salvation but rather that only [rabbinic] Judaism is God's religion. Interestingly, in making his case Judah Halevi provides us with some of the most tantalizing evidence for the existence of an Abrahamic 'idea' some 900 years ago. Of particular significance to us are those discussions in the text where Halevi attempts to show that despite getting close to Judaism, both Christianity and Islam have fallen short. The first passage is a (fictitious) exchange between the Khazar king and the rabbi representing Judaism in the debate, concerning the Jewish Sabbath:

> KING: Other nations desire to imitate you, but they only have the pain without the joy, which can only be felt by him who remembers the cause for which he bears the pain.
>
> RABBI: Even in other instances of imitation no people can equal us at all. Look at the others who appointed a day of rest (*yawm li 'l-rāḥa*) in the place of Sabbath. Could they contrive anything which resembles it more than statues resemble living human bodies? (Halevi 1946: 125).

Many modern Abrahamic initiatives would similarly focus on the shared idea of a weekly Day of Rest, but presumably with a more conciliatory tone than that adopted by Halevi here. A second passage from this work that deserves our attention is one in which the Khazar king and the rabbi discuss the validity of other religions and their practices:

> KING: Certainly if later religions admit the truth, and do not dispute it, then they all respect the place [viz. the Holy Land—AS] and call it the stepping stone of the prophets, the gate of heaven, the place of gathering of the souls. They, further, admit the existence of prophecy among Israel, whose forefathers were

distinguished in a like manner. Finally, they believe in the work of creation, the flood, and nearly all that is contained in the Torah. They also perform pilgrimages to this hallowed place.

RABBI: Their veneration of the land of prophecy consists chiefly in words, and at the same time they also revere places sacred to idols . . . Retaining the relics of ancient idolatry and feast days, they changed nothing but the forms. These were, indeed, demolished but the relics were not removed. I must also say that the verse in the Bible, occurring repeatedly, 'Thou shalt not serve strange gods, wood and stone' (Deut. 28: 36, 64), contains an allusion to those who worship the wood, and those who worship the stone . . . The leader of each of these parties maintained that he had found the divine light at its source, viz. in the Holy Land, and that there he ascended to heaven, and commanded that all the inhabitants of the globe should be guided in the right path. They turned their faces towards the land in prayer, but before long they changed and turned towards the place where the greatest number of their people lived. (Halevi 1946: 190ff.)

There is a lot going on here, not least of which is the Khazar king's question. Presumably Halevi placed this question in the king's mouth because he deemed the idea to be worthy of refutation. Were there in fact Jews at the time who challenged the rabbis with questions about the validity of Christianity and Islam? The answer that Halevi has provided (via the rabbi, of course) is complex and not at all straightforward. He argues both that other religions are insincere in their religious beliefs (re: the Holy Land), that they retain pagan traditions (clearly referring here to the ḥajj), that the Bible itself prophesied that these religions will emerge and should not be followed (quoting Deuteronomy), and that although a religion might have started off the right path (referring here to the early Muslim practice of facing Jerusalem in prayer) they quickly strayed from this path for frivolous reasons. Halevi appears to be trying everything here but try as he may, the Khazar king's question itself (as well as aspects of the rabbi's reply) are clear indicators that people were thinking 'Abrahamically' in twelfth-century Andalusia.

As stated, Andalusia is often associated with a 'Golden Age' of interfaith cooperation and tolerance. One of the convincers for this argument is the literary productivity of Jews writing under Muslim rule in Spain and Portugal, who not only produced works of great quality and quantity but who also created literary styles unique to the region. Most famously, Jewish poets created Hebrew verse using a fusion style based on Arabo-Islamic paradigms. Judah Halevi (himself a poet) makes an interesting statement amidst all his pro-Jewish polemicizing that indicates yet another layer of Abrahamic consciousness: language. With regard to the Hebrew language the rabbi of the work says:

It is the language of [Abraham's grandfather] Eber after whom it was called Hebrew, because after the confusion of tongues it was he who retained it. Abraham was an Aramaean of Ur Kasdim, because the language of the Chaldaeans was Aramaic. He employed Hebrew as an especially holy language and Aramaic for everyday use. For this reason, Ishmael brought it to the Arabic speaking nations, and the consequence was that Arabic, Aramaic, and Hebrew are similar to each other in their vocabulary, grammatical rules, and formations. (Halevi 1946: 109)

Now, as an educated Jew Halevi will have been schooled in the Hebrew and Aramaic of the Bible and of the rabbis, and as a product of Andalusian society he learnt Arabic too. It is therefore conceivable that he is simply making a linguistic point about languages that he knows. But it is also possible that—bearing in mind the many comparisons he draws (albeit reluctantly) between the three Abrahamic religions—what Halevi has in mind here are the languages of Moses, Jesus, and Muhammad respectively.

The caveat remains, of course, that Judah Halevi was not arguing in favour of comparisons between the Abrahamic religions but against them. What is interesting to us is that in doing so he inadvertently demonstrated that such comparisons were current where and when he lived.

One scholar who was heavily influenced by the *Sefer ha-Kuzari* was Saʿad Ibn Kammūna (d. 1285). Unlike Judah Halevi, however, Ibn Kammūna's *Examination of the Three Faiths*, which describes and actually defends against criticism each of the three Abrahamic religions, is not an overtly polemical work. In the words of one scholar, it is 'dispassionate, claims to be and tries to appear unprejudiced and objective, treating all parties with equal detachment... The *Examination* is indeed a piece of comparative religious study by a thirteenth-century author' (Perlmann 1967: xi). In fact, the work was so fair in its coverage of each religion that initially it was unclear precisely to which community the author belonged and it was not uncommon to assume that it was the work of a Muslim author (Pourjavadi and Schmidtke 2006: 19). Writing in Iraq under Mongol rule, Ibn Kammūna began his work with an excursus on the idea of Prophecy, which all three religions share, thereby giving his work a theoretical framework of sorts. One imagines that Ibn Kammūna would not have spoken about 'Abrahamic' religions as much as about 'Prophetic' ones. (That other religions, e.g. Zoroastrianism, have prophets too does not seem to have troubled the author.) Eventually Ibn Kammūna was outed as a Jew and although no single question about Islam raised in the book is not to be found in Muslim sources too, 'the cumulative sting of their array was no doubt resented by some people as malevolent and arrogant' (Perlmann 1967: x). To us, Ibn Kammūna's treatment of the three religions might seem even-handed; to a majority Muslim population in Iraq, considering the three religions with such equilibrium is itself an insult to Islam's superiority and Ibn Kammūna was given a death-sentence in absentia. The point remains, however, that his work would not be out of place on any modern 'Abrahamic' bookshelf.

It should be noted that both Judah Halevi and Ibn Kammūna were active during periods of interfaith strife: the Reconquista, the Crusades, and then the Mongol conquests of the Near East each had a traumatic impact on relations between Jews, Christians, and Muslims (and, in some cases, within each religion). It is thus not necessarily the case that scholars adopted an 'Abrahamic attitude' only when social and political circumstances were favourable. And it is not only from the medieval Muslim world that Jewish scholars emerged who argued for a comparative and cooperative approach to Christianity and Islam.

Jacob Emden, a German rabbi of the eighteenth century (d. 1776), was probably more concerned with theological developments within Judaism in his time (especially the influence of Sabbatean movement) than he was with Judaism's relations with other religions. And yet, his enormously influential works display an unequivocal acknowledgement of the validity of other Abrahamic religions (though of course he does not use such terms), and the following statement of his implies that such ideas were widespread at the time: 'That which we have mentioned several times in our works is well-known, that all those who believe in the Torah of Moses (be they from whatever nation) are not in the category of idol worshippers and the like even though they do not observe it [the Torah] fully because they are not commanded to do so. Our Rabbis have already taught: "The pious of the nations of the world have a share in the World to Come"' (Elman 2011: 370). Emden was influenced by the Enlightment's ideas of tolerance and wove them into the Noachide framework that rabbinic Judaism afforded him.

Centuries before either Emden or the Enlightenment another Jewish authority was fashioning the Noachide framework in ways that are of great interest for our purposes. The French rabbi Menaḥem ha-Meiri (d. 1309) focused on the category of 'Ones Possessed of Religion' (*ba'al dat*) or 'Nations Ordered by the Ways of Religions' (*ummot ha-gedurot be-darkhei ha-datot*), a category that basically comprised Christians and Muslims. In the Meiri's view, those belonging to this category are exempted from the limitations imposed by the Talmudic rabbis on Jews' interactions with 'Gentiles'. A particularly striking example of the Meiri's boldness in redefining the relationship between Jews and others comes from his exegesis on the Talmudic saying 'Israel is not subject to the stars' (*eyn mazal le-yisra'el*; *b. Shabbat* 156a). This statement is, quite naturally, taken to be a Jewish rejection of astrological determinism. The Meiri accepts that the saying is anti-astrological but insists that by 'Israel' the rabbis meant all 'those who are restricted by the ways of religion' (Halbertal 2000: 16), thereby including Christians and Muslims too. Moshe Halbertal interprets the Meiri's attitude towards 'ones possessed of religion' as being the ideological descendant of philosophical attitudes held by Jewish philosophers emanating from the Muslim world in the preceding century (Halbertal 2000: 18–19). In particular, it has recently been shown (Ben-Simon 2012) that the Meiri's approach towards other monotheists was shaped by the works of the philosopher Jacob Anatoli (d. 1256) who spoke in a similarly conciliatory tone about 'Nations that Resemble [Judaism]' (*ummot ha-mitdammot*). Anatoli, for his part, was an enthusiastic student of Maimonides' works (his father-in-law was Samuel Ibn Tibbon (d. 1230), who translated Maimonides' works from Arabic into Hebrew, and who greatly influenced Anatoli's formation). One little-known statement of Maimonides himself is of particular relevance to us, for reasons that will be immediately apparent. In a passage from the Mishneh Torah that appears to have been excised from numerous editions of this work, Maimonides says:

> Man does not have the power to grasp the thoughts of the Creator, for our ways are not His ways and our thoughts are not His thoughts. [Hence, for example] All the preaching of Jesus the Christian and of that Ishmaelite who came after him were

> only [effected] in order to pave the way for the Messiah and to heal the entire world [through] worshipping God together. As it is stated [in Zeph. 3: 9] 'For at that time I will change the language of all peoples to a clear speech, that all of them may call upon the name of God and serve him together.' (Maimonides 1998: 12: 289)

Maimonides is echoing (albeit, probably inadvertently) the Noachide ideas that the false Judaeo-Persian messiahs discussed above espoused, namely that Jesus and Muhammad were agents of God, sent to bring pagans to monotheism. But he was also reflecting the sort of thinking that was apparently common amongst Jewish 'Philosophers' of his day in the western provinces of the Muslim world. A glimpse into their mindset, with particular reference to their views on Jewish/Gentile relations, comes from a statement in the *Sefer ha-Kuzari*. No great fan of (Aristotelian) Philosophy himself, Judah Halevi puts into the Khazar king's mouth the following statement: 'In the opinion of the Philosophers ... he becomes a pious man who does not mind in which way he approaches God, whether as a Jew or a Christian or anything else he chooses' (Halevi 1946: 98). This statement, while associated in Halevi's mind with the derided Philosophers, may well reflect the sort of flexible, cooperationist thinking that influenced the Meiri, Anatoli, Maimonides, and their sources. It sounds remarkably like something one would find in the manifesto of a modern Abrahamic initiative and, taken together, the materials surveyed above demonstrate that Jews from ancient to early modern times devised conceptual categories within which Judaism, Christianity, and Islam were accommodated, compared, and distinguished from all other religious systems.

Both the 'Noachide' framework and the categories of 'Nations that Resemble [Judaism]' and 'Nations Ordered by the Ways of Religions' have an equivalent of sorts in Muslim ideas about other religions, particularly that of 'the People of the Book' (*ahl al-kitāb*). Just as Jews used 'Noachide' to denote non-Jews—though they too were descendants of Noah—Muslims used the phrase 'People of the Book' to denote certain non-Muslims—though Muslims too had a 'Book'. Before exploring the idea of 'People of the Book' it is worth bearing in mind that according to a recent theory (Donner 2010), Islam itself began as an ecumenical 'Believers' movement aimed at bringing together strict monotheists—be they Arabians, Jews, or Christians—who subscribed to a set of beliefs about God and Salvation (monotheism, prophecy, scripture, reward and punishment, the Hereafter, amongst other things). This movement, moreover, made Abraham a headlining figure and should Donner's mildly revisionist reconstruction of early Islam be accepted it will be possible to see this period as the best candidate for a historical 'Abrahamic experiment' along modern lines.

Be this as it may, within a century Muslims clearly differentiated between their religion and the religions of others. The category of 'others' included both those who did not have a scripture (or 'Book', *kitāb*) and those who did, the *ahl al-kitāb*.[4]

[4] This latter category largely overlaps with, but is still entirely distinct from, the category of protected peoples, *ahl al-dhimma*. The main difference for our purposes is that whereas the People of the Book is a label which places Jews, Christians, and Muslims on equal footing (though each would argue that his

The distinction is quranic, as is the acceptance of those who possess scripture as legitimate religious communities. As the Quran (3: 199) puts it:

> And there are, certainly, among the People of the Book, those who believe in God and in that which has been revealed to you, and in that which has been revealed to them, humbling themselves before God. They do not sell the Verses of God for a little price, for them is a reward with their Lord. Surely God is Swift in account.

Elsewhere, the Quran (2: 62) identifies these communities as being Jews, Christians, and the elusive 'Sabians', and suggests that the righteous amongst these communities will be rewarded by God. Both the practical questions arising from a Muslim's dealings with non-Muslim neighbours (mostly Zoroastrians in the east and Christians in the west) and the fact that the Quran itself mentions these communities in such interesting terms, led Muslim scholars to consider their relationship to members of other communities and the category of 'People of the Book' was continually reinterpreted to accommodate other religions as realities dictated. Hence, Zoroastrians and even Hindus could—in the eyes of some scholars—qualify for inclusion.

In the twelfth century, the Persian scholar al-Shahrastānī (d. 1153) sought to make analytical sense of the differences between the various religions and sects known to him.[5] In his chapter on the People of the Book he distinguishes between those who have an 'authentic Scripture' (*kitāb muḥaqqaq*) such as the Jews and Christians, and those who have a pseudo-scripture, such as the Zoroastrians and Manichaeans (Shahrastānī 1961: 208ff.). In his view, the Quran only has the former in mind when referring to the People of the Book.[6] He also recognizes that both Jews and Christians on the one hand, and Muslims on the other, have a 'direction of prayer' (*qibla*), with the latter facing Mecca the former Jerusalem (p. 209).

Not only did Muslims accept that Jews and Christians also had scriptures (and *qiblas*) but—obvious though it may sound—they also recognized that each of the three religions had a pivotal character bearing that religion's message.[7] An anecdote preserved in a tenth-century Arabic geographical work describes some ninth-century travellers discovering a sarcophagus in a chamber of one of the smaller pyramids in Egypt:

'Book' is superior to the other ones), the idea of Protected Peoples places Muslims above Jews, Christians, and others who came to benefit from Muslim protection.

[5] It should be pointed out that his book on this topic is remarkably balanced in its coverage of other religions.

[6] The practical distinction between the two groups is that although one can have routine relationships with the pseudo- *ahl al-kitāb* and they are protected communities, one cannot marry them or eat meat that they have prepared (whereas this is permitted with those possessing an 'authentic' Book).

[7] Interestingly, Muslim scholars recognized yet another commonality shared by Jews, Christians, and Muslims, namely their splintering into scores of sects. As a famous *ḥadīth* attributed to the prophet Muhammad has it: 'The Jews divided into seventy-one sects, the Christians into seventy-two sects, and my community will divide into seventy-three sects' (in Mottahedeh 2006: 156ff.). The dubious one-upmanship aside, this statement (and the many variations on it found in *ḥadīth* collections) presupposes that the three religions are to be compared to each other.

> We found in the sarcophagus the corpse of a ruler (*shaykh*); under his head was a tablet of white onyx that had cracked from the fire we had set . . . we took the tablet, and joining it together, found on one side two images of gold. One of the images was of a man, in his hand was a serpent, the other was the image of a man on a donkey, holding a staff, on the other side of the tablet was a third image of a man mounted on a camel bearing a rod. So we took all of this to Ahmad ibn Tulun (d. 884—AS), who called for an artisan to join together the tablet. We collectively came to the consensus that the three images corresponded to Moses, Jesus, and Muhammad. (Muhallabi 2006: 160)

Associating each religion with a founding-figure is hinted at in Judah Halevi's statement concerning the similarity between Hebrew, Aramaic, and Arabic (as mentioned above) and is overtly indicated by the author of the medieval anti-religious work 'The Treatise of the Three Imposters' (*De tribus impostoribus*), which sought to discredit Judaism, Christianity, and Islam by attacking the credibility of Moses, Jesus, and Muhammad respectively (Minois 2012). Similarly, defending the credibility of these three could serve to establish the legitimacy of their religions in general. In the words of Ibn Kammūna (Perlmann 1971: 39):

> As it is impossible to mention every claimant to prophethood and to mention the arguments for his prophethood, let us confine ourselves to the most important claimants widely known in our time and place, the arguments of the Jews, Christians, and Muslims about the prophethood of Moses, Jesus, and Muhammad, may they all be blessed.

It is not only philosophers who could be seen to think 'Abrahamically' but also, perhaps predictably, mystics. Maimonides' son, Abraham, invested considerable energies (and at a considerable personal price) towards the advancement of what is commonly called 'Jewish-Sufism', which aimed to meld Jewish theology and practice with Islamic patterns of spirituality. And of course one finds that Sufis themselves—who are often (in)famous for blurring the details of orthodoxy in favour of the big picture (as they see it)—also made tolerant noises about members of other (monotheistic) religions. In the words of perhaps their most famous proponent, Jalāl al-Dīn Rūmī (d. 1273):

> The love for the Creator is latent in all the world and in all men, be they Magians, Jews or Christians, indeed in all things that have being. How indeed should any man not love Him that gave him being? Love indeed is latent in every man, but impediments veil that love; when those impediments are removed that love becomes manifest. (Arberry 1961: 214f.)

Although Rūmī includes Zoroastrians alongside the expected Jews and Christians, it is clear that he restricts his judgement to monotheists (and considers the Magians to be monotheists, rather than dualists), both from his assumption that they love 'the Creator' (singular) and from the following statement of his: 'After all, everyone acknowledges the Oneness of God, that He is Creator and Provider, that He controls everything, that to Him all things shall return, and that it is He who punishes and forgives' (Arberry 1961: 108). It is as though Rūmī is unaware of the existence of pagans and polytheists and in this case, and others like it, it may be that when we find Muslim authors making tolerant statements about Jews and Christians they are not being specifically 'Abrahamic' but more generally ecumenical; their worldview was merely restricted to the monotheistic world. Accordingly, scholars whose worldview was suitably broad might be deemed to have been 'ecumenical' rather than 'Abrahamic'. Hence, when al-Bīrūnī (d. 1048) sought to make conciliatory comments about other religions he adopted a fair and sophisticated approach to Judaism and Christianity (as expected) but also included the obviously polytheistic, idolatrous Hinduism within the category of religions who worship a single God, devoting an in-depth and respectful monograph to the religion (Jeffrey 1951). Others, such as Shahrastānī, chose specifically to distinguish Judaism and Christianity from other religions (such as Hinduism, of which he was well aware), and group them together with Islam as being Scriptural religions. The point here is that not all Muslim scholars who were tolerant of other religions were specifically 'Abrahamic', though some clearly were.

In many ways, the 'Abrahamic' idea makes good political sense, as can be seen from the political support that modern Abrahamic initiatives enjoy, especially in countries where Jews, Christians, and Muslims exist in significant numbers and interact (e.g. the USA, the UK, France, and elsewhere). Such considerations also applied in pre-modern times and there are cases in which political leaders created or sponsored interfaith institutions and related initiatives. Perhaps most striking is the case of the Mughal Emperor Akbar the Great (r. 1556–61), who created what he called the *Dīn-i Ilāhī* ('Divine Religion'; Roy Choudhury 1985). He built a multi-faith 'House of Worship' (*'Ibādat khāna*), where interfaith discussions were held, and he further eroded the distinction between Islam and other religions by repealing the poll-tax (*jizya*) that non-Muslims are expected to pay. Generally speaking, his initiative aimed at reconciling Islam with Hinduism, Christianity, Jainism, and Zoroastrianism and, as such, while it was ecumenical it was not, strictly speaking, Abrahamic.

Akbar's religious innovations influenced the Persian ruler Nader Shah Afshar (r. 1736–47), who is quoted as having said: 'If God is one, religion must be one!' (Fischel 1952: 31). He thus ordered the heads of the Jewish and Christian communities to translate their scriptures into Persian, but the Abrahamic initiative did not go much further than that. Both Akbar the Great and Nader Shah were, at least to some extent, motivated by political realities: Akbar was a Muslim ruling over a largely Hindu population and Nader Shah was a Sunni ruling over a largely Shi'ite one; blurring the differences between the competing sects and religions in one's realm could serve to blunt any religious basis for objecting to their rule.

Little attention has been paid to Christian ideas about the commonalities shared with Judaism and Islam. This is for the most part because Christianity did not develop in any meaningful way categories such as 'Noachide' peoples, 'Nations Ordered by Religions' or 'Peoples of the Book' and examples of inter-Abrahamic cooperation led by

Christians tend to consist of individual actions or statements on the part of individual Christians rather than wide-ranging theoretical categories within which to embrace Judaism and Islam as comparable religious traditions.[8] As with Judaism and Islam, it is within the circles of medieval philosophers that we find Christian acknowledgement of the value of other Abrahamic religions: Thomas Aquinas (d. 1274) could cite the works of the Jew Maimonides and the Muslim Averroes in support of his own religion's arguments, just as Michael Scott (d. 1232) read the works of Muslim philosophers such as Avicenna and Averroes in their original Arabic, while having interacted with and influenced the Jewish Jacob Anatoli, whose ideas about other religions we have encountered above.

A tantalizing example of Christian acknowledgement of theological commonalities with other Abrahamic traditions comes not from the circles of philosophers but from the travelogue of William of Rubruck, which describes the latter's mission to the Mongol court in the thirteenth century, where he partook in an interfaith debate between Christians, Muslims, and Buddhists. We are told that on the eve of this disputation, 'Rubruck dissuaded the Nestorian priests from engaging first with the Muslims as they had intended, pointing out that as fellow monotheists the Muslims were their allies against the "idolators"; and when the Nestorians proved unable to prove the existence of God but could only quote the Scriptures, he induced them to allow him to open for the Christian cause' (*Itinerarium*, ed. Jackson 2013: 17; and see Kedar 1999).

While certain mystics, philosophers, and (Jewish) messianic pretenders encountered above seemed able to accept other monotheistic religions as equally valid paths to God, Heaven, or Salvation, most of the examples cited concern those who merely reserved a higher level of interreligious tolerance for members of other Abrahamic religions, while still maintaining that their own religion was superior to the others. Although many modern Abrahamic initiatives adopt a tone or manifesto that implies parity between the religions, it is surely the case that many participants still hold exclusivist beliefs: would participating Christians really not prefer the Jews and Muslims around the table accept Jesus? Would the Muslim participants not want the Jews or Christians to embrace Islam? Similarly, it is important to stress that proponents—both past and present—of the Abrahamic idea do not seek and have not sought to argue that the three religions are 'the same', as that would challenge the integrity, individuality, and *raison d'être* of each religion. It is, moreover, the logic of racists and other bigots to take a group of individuals who share certain attributes and judge them to be 'all the same'.

Rather, Abrahamic initiatives then and now seek to underline the fact that the three religions can reasonably be grouped together on account of their common attributes,

[8] It is hard to reconcile ecumenical, interfaith ideas with Paul's clear statement 'If you confess with your mouth, "Jesus is Lord", and believe in your heart that God raised him from the dead, you will be saved' (Romans 10: 9). The implication is that one cannot 'be saved' without signing up to these ideas. Similarly, Jesus himself is quoted as having said 'No one comes to the Father but by me' (John 14: 6), which again categorically excludes non-Christians from Salvation.

that there is more that unites them than divides them, and that they belong to a discrete group of religions, which are—for whatever reason—preferred to those religious or irreligious communities that are outside the Abrahamic fold. This is not to say that the history of relations between adherents of these three religions has been dominated by fuzzy feelings of 'Abrahamic' camaraderie. Quite to the contrary, it is arguable that there have been more low points in the history of Abrahamic interfaith relations than high points, and for every even-handed coverage of the three religions that we find on medieval bookshelves there are many more polemical works written by Jewish, Christian, or Muslim scholars against each other. The point of this chapter has merely been to show that both the focus on Abraham as a unifying figure and the idea that Judaism, Christianity, and Islam are comparable and familiar (in the literal sense of the word), have important precedents in the history of these religions.

References

Arberry, A. J. 1961. *Discourses of Rumi*. London: John Murray.

Ben-Simon, Y. 2012. 'On the Sources of the Meiri's Commentary on Proverbs and of the Phrase "Nations Ordered by Religion"'. *JSIJ* 11: 1–19.

Carlebach, E. and Schachter, J. J., eds. 2011. *New Perspectives on Jewish-Christian Relations*. Leiden: Brill.

Crone, P. and Cook, M. A. 1997. *Hagarism: The Making of the Islamic World*. Cambridge: Cambridge University Press.

Donner, F. M. 2010. *Muhammad and the Believers at the Origins of Islam*. Cambridge, MA: Harvard University Press.

Elman, Y. 2011. 'Meiri and the Non-Jew: A Comparative Investigation'. In Carlebach and Schachter 2011: 263–96.

Fischel, W. J. 1952. 'The Bible in Persian Translation: A Contribution to the History of Bible Translations in Persia and India'. *The Harvard Theological Review* 45 (1): 3–45.

Halbertal, M. 2000. '"Ones Possessed of Religion: Religious Tolerance in the Teachings of the Me'iri"'. *The Edah Journal* 1: 1.

Halevi, Judah. 1946. *The Book of Kuzari*, trans. H. Hirschfeld. New York: Pardes.

Hoyland, R. G. 1997. *Seeing Islam as Others Saw It: A Survey and Evaluation of Christian, Jewish, and Zoroastrian Writings on Early Islam*. Princeton: Darwin Press.

Jackson, P. 2013. *The Itinerarium of Friar William of Rubruck*. In the Commentary Project of the Center for Central Eurasian 'Civilization Archive'. Available at: <http://cces.snu.ac.kr/com/205iof.pdf> (accessed 19 August 2013).

Jeffrey, A. J. 1951. 'Al-Biruni's Contribution to Comparative Religion'. In *Al-Biruni Commemoration Volume*. Calcutta: Iran Society.

Kedar, B. Z. 1999. 'The Multilateral Disputation at the Court of the Grand Qan Mongke, 1254'. In H. Lazarus-Yafeh, M. R. Cohen, S. Somekh, and S. H. Griffith, eds, *The Majlis: Interreligious Encounters in Medieval Islam*. Wiesbaden: Harrassowitz, 162–83.

Lassner, J. 2000. *The Middle East Remembered*. Ann Arbor: University of Michigan Press.

Maimonides. 1963. *The Guide of the Perplexed*, trans. S. Pines. Chicago: University of Chicago Press.

Maimonides. 1998. *Mishneh Torah by Moses Maimonides: Book of Shoftim*, ed. S. Frankel. Jerusalem and Bnei Brak: Shabse Frankel.

Minois, G. 2012. *The Atheist's Bible: The Most Dangerous Book that Never Existed*. London: University of Chicago Press.

Mottahedeh, R. 2006. 'Pluralism and Islamic Traditions of Sectarian Divisions'. *Svensk Teologisk Kvartzalskrift*. Årg. 82: 155–61.

al-Muhallabī, al-Ḥasan ibn Aḥmad. 2006. *Al-Kitāb al-ʿAzīzī, aw, al-Masālik wa-al-mamālik*. Damascus: al-Takwīn lil-Ṭibāʿah wa-al-Nashr wa-al-Tawzīʿ.

Nemoy, L. 1930. 'Al-Qirqisani's Account of the Jewish Sects and Christianity'. *Hebrew Union College Annual* 7: 317–97.

Nevo, Y. D. and Koren, J. 2003. *Crossroads to Islam: The Origins of the Arab Religion and the Arab State*. Amherst, NY: Prometheus.

Novak, D. 1983. *The Image of the Non-Jew in Judaism: An Historical and Constructive Study of the Noahide Laws*. Lewiston, ME: E. Mellen Press.

Perlmann, M., ed. 1967. *Examination of the Inquiries into the Three Faiths*. Berkeley: University of California Press.

Perlmann, M., trans. 1971. *Ibn Kammunah's Examination of Three Faiths: A Thirteenth Century Essay in the Comparative Study of Religion*. Berkeley: University of California Press.

Pines, S. 1984. 'Notes on Islam and on Arabic Christianity and Judaeo-Christianity'. *Jerusalem Studies in Arabic and Islam* 4: 135–52.

Pourjavadi, R. and Schmidtke, S. 2006. *A Jewish Philosopher of Baghdad: ʿIzz al-Dawla ibn Kammūna (d. 683/1284) and his Writings*. Leiden: E. J. Brill.

al-Rāzī, Fakhr al-Dīn. 1981. *al-Tafsīr al-Kabīr*. Beirut: Dār al-Fikr.

Roy Choudhury, M. L. 1985. *The Din-I-Ilahi or The Religion of Akbar*. 3rd edn. New Delhi: Oriental Reprint.

Sacks, J. 2002. *The Dignity of Difference: How to Avoid the Clash of Civilizations*. London: Continuum.

al-Shahrastānī, Abū al-Fatḥ b. ʿAbd al-Karīm. 1961. *Kitāb al-Milal wa al-Niḥal*. Cairo: Muṣṭafá al-Bābī al-Ḥalabī.

Siker, J. S. 1991. *Disinheriting the Jews: Abraham in Early Christian Controversy*. Louisville, KY: Westminster/John Knox Press.

Stroumsa, G. G. 2011. 'From Abraham's Religion to the Abrahamic Religions'. *Historia Religionum* 3: 11–22.

Stroumsa, G. G. 2013. 'Athens, Jerusalem, and Mecca: The Patristic Crucible of the Abrahamic Religions'. In M. Vinzent, ed., *Studia Patristica* 62: 153–68.

CHAPTER 4

THREE RINGS OR THREE IMPOSTORS? THE COMPARATIVE APPROACH TO THE ABRAHAMIC RELIGIONS AND ITS ORIGINS

GUY G. STROUMSA

Comparative Religion in The Nineteenth and Twentieth Centuries

In a book entitled *Comparative Religion, its Genesis and Growth*, published in 1905, Louis Henry Jordan (1855–1923), analysed the genesis and growth of a then new and blooming approach—especially in England—to the study of religious phenomena, an approach of which he was the great herald. More than a hundred years later, 'Comparative Religion' would appear at first sight to be a moribund discipline, now replaced by Departments of 'Religious Studies' whose existence depends on whether enough students are attracted for the topic to be deemed worthy of existence by the ruthless laws of market imposed upon universities in the twenty-first century. These departments look all too often like amorphous patchworks and spineless entities, in which 'anything goes'. 'Comparative Religion', by contrast, had at least the advantage of a clear method: religious phenomena from various historical and cultural milieux could and should be compared. Their differences as well as their similarities were to be highlighted, as they alone would offer the key not only to the nature, but also to the syntax of religion in its different manifestations. In many ways, the phenomenology of religion, *en vogue* mainly between the two World Wars, and immediately after the Second World War, should be seen as the sequel of Comparative Religion. As we shall see, however, this method (as all methods in the Humanities) was hardly value free (*wertfrei* in Weberian parlance), and reflected both explicit theologies and implicit ideologies (or explicit ideologies and implicit theologies) of the imperial and colonial age. It remains obvious, nonetheless, that, like languages and cultures, religions could and should be compared, families of religions identified, and taxonomies established.

The field of 'comparative religion' reflects the state of the art in the late nineteenth century. The expression itself points to the intellectual milieu in which it was conceived: the Victorian age, when the British Empire was at its zenith, encouraged the comparison of cultures in all fields: linguistics, history, archaeology, law, political and economic systems, as well as religion. The last three decades of the nineteenth century, which saw the birth of 'comparative religion', also witnessed the emergence of 'world religions'. These 'big' religions in terms of numbers of believers or practitioners were also deemed 'great' and comparable, *mutatis mutandis*, to Christianity in their theological riches, geographical spread, historical span, and impact on a number of civilizations.

Islam, obviously, belonged to this 'club', but it was eclipsed, to a great extent, by the great religious traditions of India, which all in all attracted more immediate interest and deeper sympathy. As we now know, 'Hinduism', a term which has no Sanskrit equivalent, is a recent western scholarly invention, which represents the 'consolidation' of the many and varied religious traditions of India. Buddhism, on its side, a religion to a great extent discovered by the West in the nineteenth century, fascinated the minds as a godless religion, and also as some kind of eastern parallel to Christianity, stemming from the archaic rituals and beliefs of India just as Christianity had emerged from those of ancient Israel. In contradistinction with Islam, Hinduism and Buddhism were considered to be rich and complex religions, at once exotic and fascinating.

In order to understand this deep difference in European attitudes to Islam and to what would be called, following Friedrich Max Müller (1824–1900) and his major translation project of 'The Sacred Books of the East', 'the religions of the East', we must recall the nineteenth-century classification of languages into families: the Aryan or Indo-European languages versus the Semitic ones. This linguistic classification had a deep impact on the taxonomy of religions: it was usually assumed to be paralleled by ethnic and religious classifications: hence, the categories of Semitic peoples and of Semitic religions, and the postulated existence of a single, original Semitic people, and of a single, original Semitic religion. On the other hand, just as Sanskrit, Greek, and Latin (and other European languages) shared many traits, so the cultural and religious traditions of India were perceived as retaining some kind of family resemblance to those of Europe. This was a major scholarly fallacy. To be sure, it was not the cause for the mounting racial anti-Semitism and feelings of spite or strong distaste for Islam among European intellectuals. It remains beyond doubt, however, that the fallacy would strengthen such attitudes and offer them scholarly support.

I shall deal here with a major puzzle in the history of modern scholarship. The obvious 'family resemblances', to follow Wittgenstein's usage of the term, between Judaism, Christianity, and Islam had been clearly recognized throughout the centuries and up to the Enlightenment. The modern scholarly study of these religions, however, has shown a remarkable lack of interest in thinking and studying the three religions together, in comparative fashion. The historical and comparative study of religions, which developed as a discipline in the second half of the nineteenth century, has rarely discussed Judaism, Christianity, and Islam in the same framework, and thus has remained to a great extent unable to perceive clearly, from a structural as well as from a genetic perspective, either their close similarities or their deep differences. It is only very recently that the locution 'Abrahamic religions' has become fashionable among scholars and that the comparative scholarly study of these religions seems to have picked up momentum. Established four years ago, the Chair that I had the honour to inaugurate at Oxford has now been followed by one at Cambridge (with the more theologically coloured name 'Abrahamic Faiths and Shared Values'), and by various similar positions or programmes in other academic institutions, at least in Great Britain. Moreover, a plethora of books, certainly not all of them scholarly, are being published these days on topics such as 'Abraham, our common father' and the Abrahamic religions. Hence, it is from various angles that one should study the intellectual, cultural, and religious context of the late emergence and slow, erratic development of the comparative study of the Abrahamic religions, in a number of European countries, during the last two centuries.

Focusing on *Wissenschaftsgeschichte* in a peculiar way, the present inquiry is to a great extent the study of an absence. Why is it, it asks, that nineteenth-century scholarship neglected the comparative study of Judaism, Christianity, and Islam? This inquiry also stands at the confluence of a number of disciplines: Orientalism (more particularly the study of Islam, as well as Arabic, Turkic, and Iranian philology, all disciplines blooming in the period under study), and Jewish Studies (*Wissenschaft des Judentums*), the multi-disciplinary study of post-biblical Judaism, Jewish history, and Jewish languages and literatures, a field more or less created *ab ovo* by Jewish scholars in the nineteenth century, and the scholarly study of Christianity (in particular early and late antique Christianity), as it slowly sought to disengage itself from theology—without ever fully succeeding in achieving this goal. These different fields of study were special cases in the emerging comparative and historical study of religions (or *Religionswissenschaft, Histoire des religions*). They are also related to the invention and early development of the concept of 'world religions' in the last three decades of the nineteenth century.

In a sense, this inquiry offers a sequel, dealing with a later period, and more sharply focused, to my study of the modern science of religion, *A New Science: The Discovery of Religion in the Age of Reason*. In this book, I argued that the modern science of religion started in the period between Reformation and Enlightenment rather than, as is usually claimed, in the late nineteenth century, when the first Chairs devoted to the study of religion were established. In her excellent book, *The Invention of World Religions*,

Tomoko Masuzawa calls attention to the fact that the nineteenth-century scholarly discovery and study of the religions of South and East Asia, principally Buddhism and Hinduism, as well as Confucianism and Shintoism—all terms forged by European scholars—entailed (or reflected) a weakened interest in the religions born in the Near East, first and foremost Islam, but also Judaism. In a previous period, the Near East, usually simply referred to as 'the East', had been considered to be the soil of all human religious origins. Now relegated to the East of the West, but belonging to the West of the 'true' East, as it were, Islam and Judaism thus fell between Europe and India, between the two poles of Indo-European cultural and religious creativity. To be sure, no one could deny the quality of 'world religion' to Islam, and the 'Semitic mind' was endowed, most famously by Ernest Renan, with the unique insight of the unity of God, but all in all, the attraction of the 'true' East, coupled with the combination of growing anti-Semitism and Islamophobia, meant a strong devaluation of both Islam and Judaism, and a clear preference for Indo-European religious systems and cultural traditions over Semitic religions and cultures. Christianity, perceived as essentially a European religion, was thus managing to escape its Jewish, Near Eastern origins.

Throughout the centuries, there was a close family relationship of sorts between Judaism, Christianity, and Islam, although it always remained quite a problematic one, engendering, more often than brotherly love, vicious arguments over primacy. This family relationship was now bound to become seriously weakened. From the days of the Romantic movement in the early nineteenth century on, a remarkable and widespread, although certainly not universally shared, lack of deep interest in Islam and Judaism, seems to break the spell of what we now call the Abrahamic religions. For a full millennium, roughly from the eighth to the eighteenth century, Christian thinkers had perceived the world as divided between four main religious families: Christianity, Judaism, Islam, and 'the rest', also known as 'paganism'. This fourfold taxonomy did not as a rule entail the existence of a 'Triple Alliance' between the monotheistic traditions. Polemics remained the usual medium of communication between them. But one should note that a 'theological triangle' (to use the expression coined by the Swiss historian of religion Philippe Borgeaud) has one major advantage over a dual or polar relationship: it permits a more complex relationship, not necessarily centred upon 'zero-sum-game polemics'.

A Theological Triangle

Judaism, Christianity, and Islam do not represent the first such 'theological triangle'. Antiquity had already witnessed that between Greece, Egypt, and Israel, and then that between pagans, Christians, and Jews. One could also refer to the San Jiao of Medieval China, in which Confucian, Buddhist, and Taoist traditions and rituals created a remarkable syncretism and symbiosis of constant exchanges. But the Abrahamic triangle certainly represents the major such complex interface of religions in western history. As proof of its remarkable duration, let us mention only the deep popularity in the days of the Enlightenment, of the anonymous *Liber de Tribus Impostoribus*, probably the most popular *samizdat* of the eighteenth century, at least in its French version, *Le Livre des trois imposteurs*. The other obvious witness of the presence of the similarity between the three monotheistic religions in the Enlightenment is the 'parable of the three rings' in Lessing's *Nathan der Weise* (the play, written in 1779, was first produced in 1784)—a parable which has been shown to have a very long history, starting with a Syriac text of the eighth century, and undergoing through the ages a number of reformulations, including, famously, in Boccaccio's *Decameron*.

In order to identify the vectors of the transmission and transformations of knowledge, we must probe the reasons for the odd disappearance of the natural relationship between the three Abrahamic religions, through the study, in the period lasting approximately from the mid-nineteenth to the mid-twentieth century, of a number of exceptional individuals, coming mainly from three intellectual cultures of Western Europe: German, French, and English. One can analyse the comparative approaches of three great scholars, the French Ernest Renan, the German Julius Wellhausen, and the Scotsman William Robertson Smith. While these three very different but equally towering scholars were well equipped to launch the modern comparative study of Judaism, Christianity, and Islam, they did not quite do so, and we shall inquire into the reasons for this odd fact. It should be noted that all three scholars, owing to their ambivalence towards the orthodoxies of the various churches into which they were born and in which they were educated, ran into some serious conflict with the religious and academic authorities of their respective countries, in each case with dramatic impact on their career. The history of scholarship, it should be pointed out, is obviously more than the list of the achievements of individual scholars; it is also a record of the scholarly institutions and the frames they offer which permit or prevent free research and intellectual breakthroughs. Such scholarly institutions include universities, of course, but also theological seminaries, scientific academies, scholarly journals, conferences, and publishing companies. Although it will not be possible to deal here with these scholarly institutions, one should not forget the crucial role they played in our story. In contradistinction with early modernity, when scholarship remained essentially the personal adventure of highly gifted and idiosyncratic individuals, from the nineteenth century on research has mainly been carried on within universities. It is, indeed, the dialectical interaction between individual thinking and institutionalized systems of knowledge that transforms disciplines. Moreover, although we do not deal directly with Christian theology and modern ideologies, one cannot really understand intellectual discourse and scholarly practices without constant reference to their cultural, religious, and ideological background.

Some major vectors highlight the leading role of Jewish scholars in the study of Islam as an Abrahamic religion. In the nineteenth century, Romanticism, national movements, and the emergence of modern universities, with their division into Faculties (due to which the study of religion became split between the faculties of theology, philosophy, and classical philology and oriental studies) all contributed to the break-up of the integrative reflection on the Abrahamic religions. This break-up was finalized by the combined impact of growing Islamophobia, which reflected a condescending and denigrating attitude to Islamic societies, an aversion to rather than a fear of Islam, together with rising racial anti-Semitism (a term coined by one of its protagonists, Wilhelm Marr, in the 1870s, which reflects the mutation of traditional Christian anti-Judaism in an age of secularization). The cultures to which Muslims belonged were usually perceived as deeply foreign to those of Europe, and at once strikingly and irremediably inferior to them. At the time, the Jews of Europe were starting to go out of the ghettos—and discovering, painfully, that this was not enough to get them what Heine called an 'entrance ticket' to European society, a ticket which still only baptism could fully provide. The Jews were identified as stemming from the Orient, and often considered as still belonging to it in many ways. It should be noted that Jews often embraced these oriental roots with pride. This self-identification is reflected in the orientalizing architecture of many nineteenth century synagogues, a style often meant to allude to the mythical symbiosis, or *convivencia*, between Muslims, Jews, and Christians in al-Andalus, medieval Islamic Spain, and it would also be echoed in the Zionist urge to return to the East, to Palestine. At the turn of the century, art in Jewish Palestine, too, would embrace the orientalizing trend. The Jewish chapter in the history of the comparative study of the Abrahamic religions, moreover, is endowed with a particular importance, as Jewish scholars offered some major contributions to the comparative study of Christianity and Judaism as well as of Islam and Judaism. Indeed, some particularly gifted Jewish scholars, from Abraham Geiger to Ignaz Goldziher transformed the European approach of Islam.

In the twentieth century, major events such as the globalization processes, the genocide of the European Jews, and the immigration waves of varied Muslim populations to Western Europe would offer both the immediate context and the necessary conditions for lowering the artificial, ideological boundaries erected between the different fields of study under discussion. The rise of the concept of the 'Judaeo-Christian tradition', mainly after the Second World War, and then of the concept of the 'Abrahamic religions' (starting in the 1970s) offered intellectual justification for accepting, first, the remnants of the now-defunct Jewish communities, and then the fast-growing Muslim communities, into the European family, as it were, a family now recognized as being a family of religions as much as of nations, although until very recently it could only conceive of itself in Christian terms. Although the concept of the Abrahamic religions is first rooted in the perceived need for new interfaith approaches, it is now more and more widely adopted in reference to the scholarly study of Judaism, Christianity, and Islam. Its adoption is borne out by recent attempts to both enhance and question its heuristic value. One might ask whether this use of the term is legitimate, and whether it is helpful for the critical and comparative study of Judaism, Christianity, and Islam. I think, however, that ways can be found through which the scholarly, comparative study of the Abrahamic religions should be approached in order to avoid pitfalls.

We can detect, then, some paradigm shifts in systems of knowledge and on the reconstruction of central cognitive structures, throughout the trajectory of modern scholarship on religion. The formation and restructuring of concepts and methods modifies fields of study, sometimes deeply transforming them. It should be obvious, I repeat, that such fields are never innocent productions of knowledge. They are ultimately related to the construction of the self through the understanding of the other, in particular when they deal directly with religious identities. In a sense, this historical and comparative study of religions, a particularly delicate, interdisciplinary field of scholarship, should also have an impact on the conditions of transformation of European identities. I shall now review a number of medieval and pre-modern comparative approaches to Judaism, Christianity, and Islam, in order to describe the state of affairs in the early nineteenth century.

'Abrahamic Religions' in Pre-Modern Times

Although the expression 'Abrahamic religions' is quite recent, its gestation has been a very long one. While the term 'comparative religion' reflects the modern, non-theological approach to the study of religious phenomena, it would be naive to conceive it as representing a clear break from a non-scientific past, and to oppose a wholly scholarly present to a totally theological past. In the pre-modern world, religious interaction between members of different religious communities was mainly polemical, but religious polemics also included cognitive elements. Beyond the obvious fact that it was useful to know the opponent's position in order to refute it, one must remember that already in late antiquity, both Greek philosophers and Christian theologians had recognized the existence of a single, deep truth, disguised by the various mythological and religious traditions, but shared by the sages of all camps. What needs emphasizing in our present context is the fact that since antiquity, religious polemics were never devoid of an effort, at times a serious one, to understand other religions, as well as of real hermeneutical contacts between religious intellectuals from all sides. Far from being a completely modern phenomenon, the comparison of religions thus has a very long pedigree, hailing back, at least, to Herodotus. In antiquity, comparing religions was a common exercise in cultural relativity. To give only one instance, in the *interpretatio graeca* Herakles was identified with both the Roman Hercules and the Phoenician Melqart.

This deep belief in the fundamental closeness between the elites of the different religious and cultural traditions, pagans, Jews, and Christians, was at once reinforced and complicated in the 'Abrahamic triangle'. The idea of a 'family resemblance' between Judaism, Christianity, and Islam is as old as the appearance of the third of these religions. The close genetic relationship between Judaism and Christianity had been obvious since at least Justin Martyr's *Dialogue with Trypho the Jew* in the mid-second century, and patristic literature makes it very clear that Christians, as well as Jews, conceived of themselves as being the true children of Abraham. Nascent Islam sought to reiterate the same argument of the true fidelity to Abraham's pure religion, original monotheism, in front of its perversion by earlier communities, this time not only Jews, but also Christians. And John of Damascus, the first Christian polemic writer against Islam, makes it clear in the early eighth century that for him Islam was more a Christian heresy than a fully fledged religion.

As soon as Islam appears on the scene, the idea of comparing the three cognate monotheisms becomes at once possible and imperative. In a sense, the assumption is that there was only one divine revelation, and hence only one true message of God, while similarities in other religious traditions are conceived as proofs of their origin as falsifications of the original message. The devil, God's main imitator, is held responsible for the striking similarities between falsehood and truth. Hence, the two ideas of a shared truth and of religious imposture are as in fact two sides of the same coin.

Like the comparison of religions, religious imposture has a long history. In the biblical tradition, it is identical with the idea of false prophecy. As is well known, Livy tells us in the tenth book of his *History* how Numa Pompilius, Rome's first mythical king, forged the story of the nymph Egeria's nightly revelation of the religion he wanted to impose on the Romans. He did so in order to assuage his barbarian nation, which otherwise would not have accepted his religious laws willingly, thus putting religious imposture in the service of political leadership. Religion, indeed, is usually perceived in Rome as a political invention, as noted by Cicero in his *De natura deorum* (1.118). For Livy, Numa's lie is a pious one, and it is a legitimate one—a lesson which Macchiavelli will learn very well. Lucian of Samosata, in the second century CE, gives us a classical example of religious imposture, in the case of Alexander, the false prophet from Abonoteichos. In monotheistic climate, since the Hebrew Bible, religious imposture is usually perceived as false prophecy. Prophecy usually ignores established forms of religious authority, and establishes a direct link to the deity. In early Christianity, the Second, glorious Coming of Christ, the *parousia*, was to be preceded by the appearance of the Antichrist, a devilish imitator of Jesus Christ. This is the background of the nexus between heresy and false prophecy in early Christianity, for instance in the case of Montanus in the second century, or in that of Mani in the third. The Jewish perception of Jesus as a false prophet, or the Christian (as well as the Jewish) perception of Muhammad as a false prophet, should be seen in the same perspective.

Throughout the Middle Ages, a vast and complex web of interreligious intellectual exchanges developed, for the most part expressed in polemical literature: Jewish–Christian, Christian–Muslim, or Jewish–Muslim. Although much knowledge of the religious other is reflected in those texts, such knowledge usually remains embedded in the polemical framework. The triadic approach, involving not only two disputing sides, but a third party, offers the promise (not always kept) of a less direct polemical attitude, as well as that of a more balanced, comparative approach—hence the crucial importance of such texts, which can be seen as the prehistory of the modern, comparative study of the Abrahamic religions. I shall therefore refer here, very briefly, to a number of authors who, throughout the long Middle Ages, offered particularly interesting developments on the comparison of the three Abrahamic religions.

Obviously, the parable of the three similar, or even identical rings, which we now know mainly through Lessing's play *Nathan the Wise* (*Nathan der Weise*), cannot antedate the appearance of Islam. It appears for the first time, it would seems, in an eighth-century Syriac text which purports to preserve a debate supposedly held in 782 between Timothy, the Nestorian Patriarch from 780 to 823, and al-Mahdī, the third Abbasid caliph. A rather similar story occurs in *The Proof of the Christian Religion*, a theological tract in Arabic written by Abu Raita al-Takriti, who died no later than 830.

In the early twelfth century, the Andalusian Jewish thinker and poet Judah Halevi (1075–1141) authored the *Book of Kuzar*, or *Kuzari*, an apology of Judaism, the 'despised religion'. In the *Kuzari*, written in Judeao-Arabic, he describes how the Khazar king, in his search for religious truth, hears a Christian and a Muslim sage before moving to a Jewish sage—who alone will provide satisfactory answers to his intellectual queries and spiritual quest. It may be worth noticing that Halevi's almost exact contemporary, the French Pierre Abelard (1079–1142), has a philosopher instead of a Muslim argue with a Jew and a Christian in his *Dialogue of a Philosopher with a Jew and a Christian*, a text redacted between 1136 and 1139. To some extent, the philosopher takes the place of the Muslim, since for medieval thinkers such as Abelard, the only Muslims with whom one could possibly have an intellectual discussion were philosophers. The expected identity of the winner in such texts (the Christian for Abelard, the Jew for Halevi) is less important than the fact that the discussion is presented as a rational one, where the characters of the three religions (or of Christianity, Judaism, and philosophy for Abelard) all seek to present rational arguments in support of their faith.

In the following century, Saʿad Ibn Manṣūr Ibn Kammūna (d. 1284?) would pen what is perhaps the most remarkable comparative study of Judaism, Christianity, and Islam in the Middle Ages, his *Examination of the Three Faiths* (*Tanqīḥ al-abḥāth lil-milal al-thalāth*). Ibn Kammūna was a Jew, but it is as a philosopher that he approaches the comparative study of the three monotheistic faiths, starting with a general study of prophecy before moving to a critical examination of and reflections on each of the three religions. Ibn Kammūna is obviously familiar with Halevi's *Kuzari*. Despite his essentially critical attitude, he shows sympathy for both Jesus and Muhammad. (In contradistinction to his philosophical works, it would seem that the *Tanqīḥ* did not attract much attention on the part of Muslim or Jewish intellectuals, neither at the time nor later). As Ibn Kammūna's works survived only in Arabic (rather than Judaeo-Arabic) manuscripts, persistent rumours circulated about his conversion to Islam, late in life. The truth of these rumours, however, has been recently questioned and refuted. A biographical detail which may be less doubtful is his having barely survived an attempted lynch in 1284, about four years after the completion of his comparative work, and close to his death. This attempted lynch reflects the violence of the reaction within the Muslim community to Ibn Kammūna's critical view of religion.

More or less in the same years that Ibn Kammūna wrote his *Examination of the Three Faiths*, Ramon Llull (*c*.1232–*c*.1315), the inspired Franciscan mystical thinker from Majorca who has often been called *Arabicus Christianus*, published in Catalan his *Book of the Gentile and of the Three Wise Men* (1274–6). The book presents (in an elaborate literary frame) a pagan asking a Jew, a Christian, and a Muslim to describe their religion for him. The three sages, each in his turn, present the case for the unity of God and for other central tenets of their different religions. The work reflects a rather good knowledge of Judaism and Islam, a rare occurrence at the time. Most noteworthy and unusual is the fact that the author does not tell us which of the three religions the pagan chose.

Giovanni Boccaccio (1313–75) wrote his *Decameron* around 1353. As is well known, this work offers (in Day 1, Tale 3) the classical version of the parable of the three rings, more or less as it will appear in Lessing's play. Sultan Saladin had asked the Jew Melchizedek which one of the three religions was the true one, and Melchizedek answered the Sultan by telling the story of the three rings (two of which are perfect copies of the original one) given by a merchant to his three deserving sons, so that none of them would become his sole inheritor. *Lis dou di vrai aniel*, a French poem from the thirteenth century, seems to have been the proximate channel through which the legend reached Boccaccio. From then on, in any case, the parable would become very widespread during the Renaissance. Carlo Ginzburg (1980) has shown in a seminal study how the story appears again in the mouth of the sixteenth-century heretical Italian miller Menocchio.

Renaissance Christian thinkers also dealt with the comparison of the three Abrahamic religions in another register. In his *De pace fidei* (XIX), a book written shortly after the Ottoman conquest of Constantinople in 1453, Nicolas of Cusa (1401–64) imagines an interreligious dialogue taking place in heaven, the only rational region. There, a religious concordat is agreed upon by wise Christians, Jews, and Muslims. Given full powers, they then meet in Jerusalem, their common religious centre, to receive, in the name of all, the single faith (*una religio in rituum varietate*), and they establish perpetual peace within the city, 'in order that in this peace, the Creator of all things be glorified in all *saecula*. Amen.'

A century later, at the dawn of modernity, the two French thinkers Guillaume Postel (1510–81) and Jean Bodin (1530–96) would also offer various reflections which can be described as 'Abrahamic'. For Postel, a visionary Jesuit who became the first Professor of Hebrew at the newly established Collège de France, God had revealed himself essentially not through one but rather through two chains of tradition: in parallel to Abraham, the Indian Brahmans represented the second transmission of divine wisdom to humankind. Although Postel is usually perceived as a rare 'illuminé', it should be noted that people as different as Isaac Newton and the Catholic theologian Pierre-Daniel Huet supported the same view. In his *Absconditorum clavis* (1547), Postel describes how Jews, Christians, and Muslims, all successors of the law of nature, will equally be saved if they observe the law of Abraham. For him, both Moses and Muhammad had received a part of the divine spirit, fully revealed in Jesus.

Jean Bodin seems to have harboured a particular sympathy for Judaism, which he considered to be, among the different religions, closest to the law of nature. In his *Heptaplomeres* (assuming the work is indeed truly his), the Jew Solomon draws a parallel between Jesus, Simon Magus, and Apollonius of Tyana, all three of whom he considered religious impostors. In the same work, Senamy, the religiously indifferent, states that the great number of religions may indicate that they are all equally true.

In 1570, the French Franciscan Melchior de Flavin (d. 1580?) travelled to the Holy Land, where he preached the union between Christians, Jews, and Muslims in order to counter growing atheism. From now on, the comparison of religions in the West would happen within the framework of a religiously complex pluralism, as Jews and Muslims start appearing there as real protagonists.

In the Ottoman Empire, of course, things remained much more traditional. Abd al-Ghani ibn Isma'il al-Nabulsi (1641–1731), a scholar stemming from a Palestinian family, wrote a polemical treatise on the religious status of the *dhimmīs* (i.e. the religious minorities, essentially Jews and Christians) which reflected a remarkably liberal attitude. Just like Guillaume Postel for Jews and Muslims, al-Nabulsi argues that Jews and Christians can be saved in the hereafter even without converting to Islam. Suffice it for them to have faith (*iman*) in their hearts. Such a tolerant attitude to religious minorities may well be less striking on the part of a Muslim than on that of a Christian, and yet it seems to have been rare enough to be worthy of notation.

Perhaps the most interesting work of comparative study of the Abrahamic religions during the Enlightenment is that of the Irishman John Toland (1668–1722), *Nazarenus, or Jewish, Gentile and Mahometan Christianity*. The book, published in 1718, developed ideas already expressed by Toland in a French manuscript of 1710, *Christianisme judaïque et mahométan*. Toland established his argument upon the *Gospel of Barnabas*, an apocryphal text of which a single Italian manuscript was the only testimony. His goal was to offer a historical argument on the Jewish roots of Christianity in order to promote the status of the Jews in contemporary European societies. Similarly, in *Les Lettres persannes* (Lettre 60; 1721), Montesquieu refers to Christianity and Islam as to the two branches from the old Jewish stem.

Around the same time, an anonymous treatise started to circulate in Europe, the *Traité des trois imposteurs, ou l'esprit de M. de Spinoza*. This was a very curious book, rather different from the earlier Latin *De tribus impostoribus*, in which Moses, Jesus, and Muhammad were presented as three religious impostors who had sought to keep humankind under the yoke of false religions. Despite the fact that the book has elicited a very great number of studies, much remains mysterious about its contents, its sources, and the circumstances of its appearance. The idea of the three impostors incarnates the revolt against monotheism. In his *Treatise on the Immortality of the Soul* (1516), Pietro Pomponazzi (1462–1525) had stated that the three monotheistic religions affirmed the immortality of the soul only in order to ensure the people's obedience. The idea of imposture was at the core of religious polemics in the second half of the seventeenth century, mainly in England and Holland. In the eighteenth century, however, the idea of the three impostors would also be used as a foil, barely covering an essentially anti-Christian attitude. For the radical Enlightenment, the fight against the church (see Voltaire's famous expression: 'Ecrasez l'infâme!') was immediate and concrete, while the presence of Moses and Muhammad was mainly meant to camouflage the perception of Jesus as a religious impostor.

Like the parable of the three rings, the story of the three impostors goes back, at least, to the Middle Ages. Although, as we have seen, the concept of religious imposture has its roots in antiquity, the idea of the three impostors appears of necessity later than the parable of the three rings. For Renan, the three impostors were originally a medieval chimera, 'born in the mind of theologians shocked by the cohabitation of the three worlds at the courts of Palermo and Toledo'. Muhammad, of course, had always been considered by Christian and Jewish thinkers alike to have been an impostor. This view was repeated at the turn of the eighteenth century in Pierre Bayle's *Dictionnaire historique et critique* (1697; 2nd edn 1802; English translation 1709). In the early Muslim world, the idea of religious imposture was also present, for instance among a number of freethinkers, Ismaili dissidents, and Qarmatians. But for medieval Christian authors, it is Averroes (the Latinized name of the twelfth-century philosopher and legal scholar Ibn Rushd) who stood at the root of the idea of a religious imposture shared by Jews, Christians, and Muslims. According to the Italian theologian Gilles of Rome (1247–1316), Averroes had stated that the religion of the Christians was impossible, that of the Jews infantile, and that of the Muslims made for pigs. According to Gilles, Averroes had claimed: 'Quod nulla lex est vera, licet possit esse utilis' (in free translation: 'since no religion is true, religion may at best be useful'), a return to the Roman conception of religion as the cement of civil society, with no truth value.

In Lessing's *Nathan the Wise*, Saladin's three sons, who possess each a ring apparently identical to the other two, are called *Betrüger*, impostors. Indeed, the role of the parable in the play is to respond to the story of the three impostors. Similarly, Lessing intended in *The Education of the Human Race* (*Die Erziehung des Menschengeschlechts*), a text from 1780, to offer a revision of the thesis that humankind had been successively deceived by Moses, Jesus, and Muhammad. Rather than a series of deceptions, one read the history of the monotheistic religions as a series of steps in the progressive religious education of humankind. While the origins of the idea of the three impostors must remain in the dark, what counts for us here is the clear thematic affinity between it and the parable of the three rings. In a remarkable and idiosyncratic book, *Veritas sive Varietas, Lessings Toleranzparabel und das Buch von den drei Betrügern*, Friedrich Niewöhner has shown that 'the two traditions were closely associated with the doctrine of religious tolerance'. As Niewöhner has shown, Lessing, who was at heart a Spinozist, was deeply influenced by the twelfth-century Jewish thinker Maimonides in his comparative approach to religion.

At the time of the French revolution, therefore, European intellectuals knew, in one way or another, that Judaism, Christianity, and Islam were cognate religions, and that the religious history of humankind had to be approached, to a great extent, as the interface of these three religions and their intertwined history. The birth of the Abrahamic religions as a field of study, then, should have started in the early nineteenth century, with the development of philology and orientalism in the German universities. We must ask, then, why this did not happen?

The Abrahamic Eclipse

Instead of a provisory conclusion, I shall offer here some reflections on the cognitive shift which happened in the nineteenth century and in the first half of the twentieth century. In the nineteenth century, which has been deemed by some German historians the *Gründungsjahrhundert*, the foundational century, the major categories used to understand the contemporary world took shape. A number of phenomena, which happened more or less simultaneously, are at the root of what we can call *the Abrahamic eclipse* of the nineteenth century.

Herder, who had been Kant's student in Königsberg, wrote moving pages on the spirit of the Orient in general, and of Hebrew poetry in particular. Herder also supported granting full citizen rights to the Jews. A free spirit like Schoppenhauer was able to speak of 'the Jewish faith and its two branches, Christianity and Islam' (Marchand 2009: 301), but he belonged here to a minority. Such voices would soon be muffled by very different sounds. For most German Romantic thinkers, Judaism was a fossil religion: 'Judaism is long since a dead religion', claimed Schleiermacher in his fifth speech *On Religion* (1996: 113–15; the text was first published in 1799). On his side, Hegel had no use for Islam in his historical taxonomy of religions. For him, Islam was characterized by its 'fanatic religiosity', although it had the advantage of having been purged from the nationalist character of Judaism. For most European intellectuals in the Romantic age, Islam was indeed perceived as a 'regression' in the historical progress of world consciousness. Such a perception of Islam would long remain prevalent among many historians of religions. In this respect, one could refer to the Dutch Old Testament scholar and orientalist Abraham Kuenen.

In the first decades of the nineteenth century, the mental world of European intellectuals was changing rapidly. The Enlightenment *Republic of Letters* was fast being replaced by the competing nationalism of intellectuals in the Europe of nations. These nations, establishing different educational systems and scientific institutions, developed at the same time national traditions of scholarship in general, and of orientalism in particular. The new growth of national patterns and traditions of scholarship was rendered even more complex by the religious fault lines between Protestant and Catholic societies.

At the institutional level, the creation of different faculties in German universities meant that students of Graeco-Roman antiquity worked in isolation from both theologians and Orientalists (as a rule, Hebraists taught in Theological rather than Oriental faculties). According to the recent discovery of the families of languages, Sanskrit and ancient Iranian belonged to the same family as Greek, Latin, and almost all other European languages. This linguistic taxonomy offered an easy step to identifying the peoples speaking those languages as related to one another, and, moreover, to their religions belonging to similarly large families. Hence, one started speaking about Semitic and Aryan religions. Now this move happened at a time of secularization. As Christianity was more and more conceived as the cultural capital of Europe, intellectuals and scholars alike became deeply ambivalent to its genetic relations with Judaism, a Semitic religion of the ancient Near East. Jesus was now perceived more as a European Christian than as a Palestinian Jew. The conundrum of growing secularization and nationalism thus left less and less room for the Jews in Europe. Precisely then, as they were starting to exit the ghettos, they sought to integrate the ambient societies, in which they were clearly made to feel unwelcome. These were the times of the transformation of traditional Christian anti-Judaism into a new form of racial hatred, anti-Semitism. In such conditions, both Judaism and Islam were felt to belong to an East too close to Europe for not being perceived as a threat, rather than to a distant, exotic, and attractive Far East. In a sense, one could say that both Judaism and Islam became the victims of the European mechanism of boundary building. Regrettably, the close relationship between the study of Judaism and that of Islam (and the Jewish study of Islam) in the nineteenth century does not seem to have interested Edward Said. Yet, it is in this context that we can justify his description of Orientalism as that 'strange, secret sharer of Western Anti-Semitism' (Said 1978: 28).

Perhaps the most decisive element that prevented the development of the triple-faced study of monotheist religion was the more and more common use of the concept of 'world religions', which can be found already in 1864 (Nongbri 2012: 128). While Judaism, a national rather than a universal religion, clearly did not belong to that exclusive club, Islam remained marginal in it, despite both the huge numbers of its practitioners and its worldwide geographical spread, remaining much less attractive to students of religion than Buddhism, for instance, the religion of the East which one liked to compare to Christianity in the West. We are entitled, then, to claim, together with Jürgen Osterhammel (2009: 1240–4), that the discovery of the 'World religions' disrupted the 'Abrahamic family'. Much before the end of the nineteenth century, the three rings had disappeared, together with the three impostors. For the great majority of scholars, Judaism, Christianity, and Islam had so little in common that their comparative study was not deemed significant. Our question, then, should be rephrased: How was the idea of a family relationship, of a *suggeneia*, between Judaism, Christianity, and Islam reclaimed by scholarship? This would be an arduous and tortuous way.

Suggested Reading

For a history of the modern study of religion, see Kippenberg 2002 and Masuzawa 2003, with further bibliography for further reading. It is to be noted that little deals specifically with the Abrahamic religions in most studies of comparative religion. A contemporary theory of religion (Riesebrodt 2010) offers interesting suggestions on the Abrahamic religions. For a recent criticism of the usefulness of the concept of Abrahamic religions, see Hughes 2012. The very rich study of Marchand 2009 focuses on Germany, but offers many insights of general interest for our topic. Massignon (1997, but the different texts were published starting in the 1920s) was seminal for the recent use of 'Abrahamic religions', on which cf. Stroumsa 2011.

References

Ginzburg, C. 1980. *The Cheese and the Worms: The Cosmos of a Sixteenth-Century Miller.* London: Routledge & Kegan Paul.

Hughes, A. W. 2012. *Abrahamic Religions: On the Use and Abuse of History.* Oxford: Oxford University Press.

Jordan, L. H. 1905. *Comparative Religion: Its Genesis and Growth.* Edinburgh.

Kippenberg, H. G. 2002. *Discovering Religious History in the Modern Age.* Princeton: Princeton University Press.

Marchand, S. L. 2009. *German Orientalism in the Age of Empire: Religion, Race and Scholarship.* Cambridge: German Historical Institute and Cambridge University Press.

Massignon, L. 1997. *Les trois prières d'Abraham.* Paris: Cerf.

Masuzawa, T. 2003. *The Invention of World Religions, or How European Universalism was Preserved in the Language of Pluralism.* Chicago: Chicago University Press.

Nongbri, B. 2012. *Before Religion: A History of a Modern Concept.* New Haven: Yale University Press.

Osterhammel, J. 2009. *Die Verwandlung der Welt: Eine Geschichte des 19. Jahrhunderts.* Munich: Beck.

Riesebrodt, M. 2010. *The Promise of Salvation: A Theory of Religion.* Chicago: Chicago University Press.

Said, E. 1978. *Orientalism.* New York: Vintage.

Schleiermacher, F. 1996. *On Religion: Speeches to its Cultured Despisers.* Cambridge: Cambridge University Press.

Sloterdijk, P. 2007. *Gottes Eifer: Vom Kampf der drei Monotheismen.* Frankfurt, Leipzig: Insel Verlag.

Stroumsa, G. G. 2011. 'From Abraham's Religion to the Abrahamic Religions'. *Historia Religionum* 3: 11–22.

Toland, J. 1718. *Nazarenus, or Jewish, Gentile, and Mahometan Christianity.* London: Brown.

CHAPTER 5

THE ABRAHAMIC RELIGIONS AS A MODERN CONCEPT

MARK SILK

In the last decades of the twentieth century, the term 'Abrahamic' began to be used with increasing frequency as a way of associating Judaism, Christianity, and Islam as related faiths, and as an indicator of religious values shared by members of these religious traditions. The term itself was more than two centuries old, however, and its history bears importantly on contemporary usage. That history is intertwined with the history of the term 'Judaeo-Christian', which earlier in the twentieth century came to be used in a comparable way to associate Judaism and Christianity and to indicate a common system of values. This chapter on the modern evolution of the idea of the Abrahamic will therefore make reference to the related idea of the Judaeo-Christian.

'Abrahamic' first appears in the 1730s as the adjectival form of the patriarch. The English deist Thomas Morgan, for example, refers to 'the Abrahamic Family', 'Abrahamic Righteousness', and 'the Abrahamic Covenant' in his popular work, *The Moral Philosopher*. It is noteworthy that, in one of the earliest uses of the word, Morgan interprets God's covenant with Abraham in universal terms: whereas the Mosaic Law applied merely to the Israelite nation, the Abrahamic Covenant possessed, according to him, 'the only true justifying Faith and Righteousness, by which all Nations, and every Man, must be accepted and rewarded of God' (Morgan 1739: 53, 70, and *passim*; 105). By contrast, contemporary Anglicans embraced the traditional Christological view of the Abrahamic covenant. Thus, at the end of the eighteenth century, Sir Richard Joseph Sullivan contended that 'the whole design of Christ's mission was to restore the old religion, and the true Abrahamic righteousness, by which Abraham, Noah, Enoch, and all good men, from the beginning of the world, had been justified and accepted of God' (Sullivan 1794: 176).

That such 'Abrahamic faith' was intended for all humanity was advanced by John Murray, the English preacher who brought Christian Universalism (the belief that all people are saved through Jesus) to America in the late eighteenth century. According to historian George Huntston Williams, Murray conceived of Abrahamic faith as belonging to all those who recognized the 'revolutionary implications' of the gospel preached to Abraham (Williams 2002: xiii). In antebellum America, the Universalist George Rogers saw Christ as enabling every creature to return to the Abrahamic covenant. A hymn entitled 'Abrahamic Covenant', which Rogers published in 1838, begins, 'The Abrahamic Covenant all people embraced | By it all who fell in Adam are in Jesus embraced' (Rogers 1837: 130). Universalists also used the concept to refer to their own community. 'Brethren of the Abrahamic faith!' wrote the Universalist pastor Thomas J. Whitcomb in 1844. 'Let ours be faith in the great cause of human emancipation, remembering that the foundation of God standeth sure—and his promises are no more Yea and Nay, but Yea and Amen!' (Whitcomb 1945: 54).

The universalist Abrahamic faithful were, of course, building on St Paul's formulation of Jesus' mission as involving a restoration of God's covenant with Abraham. In eighteenth- and nineteenth-century writing, 'Abrahamic' appears most frequently conjoined with 'covenant', very often in order to draw an invidious distinction between this earlier compact between God and man and the subsequent one with the Israelites at Mt Sinai. The point, as the authors of a late eighteenth-century Bible commentary put it, was that Romans 11: 17 provided 'incontestable proof that we Gentile Christians are taken into the Abrahamic covenant, (for the Sinai covenant is abolished) as truly and fully, as the nation of the Jews was' (Dodd et al. 1770: 193). The Abrahamic covenant was, in the words of the Anglican divine Edward Stopford in 1837, 'the true and everlasting covenant' (Stopford 1837: 87).

Within Anglo-American Protestantism, conflict did arise over how this covenant was passed on to the next generation. In 1807, the Massachusetts pastor Samuel Worcester argued that Romans 11 showed that 'the Abrahamic church was continued in its true character; and that the Gentile believers were brought into the same church, and admitted to a participation in the same privileges and blessings' (Worcester 1807: 26; Worcester 1820: 65). Admission to the 'Abrahamic church' had been through circumcision, which God ordered Abraham to perform on his son Isaac when Isaac was eight days old. For Worcester and many other Congregational, Episcopalian, Lutheran, Methodist, and Presbyterian clergy in antebellum America, this constituted a powerful argument on behalf of infant baptism, against the growing numbers of Baptists and others who, following the Anabaptists of the sixteenth century, vigorously asserted that baptism, the rite of passage into the covenant of grace, could only be undertaken by professed believers. In a debate with the Baptist Alexander Campbell in Ohio in 1820, the Presbyterian minister John Walker said, 'My opponent has endeavored to lead, to coax, and to drive me from the Abrahamic Covenant, but I will not give it up. It is the main pillar upon which I stand, and I will not relinquish it.' On the other side, in 1842, the Georgia Baptist clergyman J. H. T. Kilpatrick went so far as to preach against the belief that the Abrahamic covenant was the 'real proper covenant of grace' (Kilpatrick 1847: 139). The contest over the relevance of circumcision to baptism dominated discussions of the Abrahamic covenant in America in the first half of the nineteenth century.

During this period, 'Judaeo-Christian' also came to be used to sort out connections between Christianity and Judaism. Initially, the adjectival 'Judaeo-' was employed in different ways to signify a hybrid Jewish phenomenon, such as by calling Yiddish 'Judaeo-German' or 'Judaeo-Polish'. In 1829, a missionary to the Jews named Joseph Wolff described being advised 'to establish a Judeo-christian church', by which he meant one that permitted Jews to maintain such practices as circumcision and Saturday worship (Wolff 1829: 314). In 1841, an article on the Jews of Poland in the *Foreign Quarterly Review* identified as 'Judeo-Christians' the followers of the self-proclaimed messiah Jacob Frank, whose teachings combined elements of Judaism and Christianity' (*Foreign Quarterly Review* 1841: 249). But 'Judaeo-' was most widely used (in French as well as English) to refer to the early followers of Jesus who opposed Paul in wishing to restrict the Christian message to Jews and who insisted on maintaining Jewish law and ritual. These were the Judaeo-Christians par excellence, and they were commonly referred to as such, in both academic and more popular writing. The famous British physicist John Tyndall, addressing the Glasgow Sunday Society in 1880, thus noted that 'James was the head of the Church at Jerusalem, and Judeo-Christians held that the ordination of James was alone valid', while Peter 'ate with the Gentiles, when no Judeo-Christian was present to observe him; but when such appeared he withdrew himself, fearing those which were of the circumcision.' So far as the interpretation of the New Testament was concerned, 'Judaeo-Christian' pointed to a restriction of the divine promise to the Jews, even as 'Abrahamic' indicated an extension of that promise to the Christians.

At the same time, Judaeo-Christian terminology began to be used to identify a tradition set apart from other religious traditions as well as from more secular outlooks. In the 1870s, the German philosopher Eduard von Hartmann predicted that the religion of the future would combine Hindu and Judaeo-Christian elements—as the Belgian academic Eugène Goblet d'Alviella characterized it, one that would 'borrow the conception of the Divine immanence from India, and the idea of the Divine unity from the Judeo-Christian tradition' (d'Alviella 1885: 310).[1] Von Hartmann likewise contrasted the 'Hindu idea' with the 'Judeo-Mahometano-Christian idea of the world' (Hartmann 1876: 163). At the end of the century, the French novelist Anatole France had one of his characters contrast the world system of Laplace with 'the old Judeo-Christian cosmogony'. Altogether, 'Judaeo-Christian' usage was more descriptive and analytical, less theologically loaded than 'Abrahamic.'

Yet the late eighteenth and nineteenth centuries also saw the development of less theological Abrahamic language, pointing not to the covenantal relationship with God but to ethno-religious lineages that included Jews, Christians, and others as well. In 1778, for example, a review of an Arabic grammar in the English *Monthly Review* used biblical genealogy to argue that the posterity of Ishmael could be considered 'pure Arab' because both the 'Abrahamic family' and the Arabians had a common

[1] Alviella cites the French edition of Hartmann's work (Hartmann 1876).

progenitor. In 1812, William Magee, of the Church of Ireland, referred to Abrahamic manners, 'such as were common to all the seed of Abraham, Israelites, Ishmaelites, and Idumaeans' (Magee 1812: 103). In his *Manual of Comparative Philology* (1838: 229), the Bedfordshire divine William Balfour Winning identified three 'Abrahamic races' linked, respectively, to Jacob, Ishmael, and Esau. From Jacob came the Israelites, or Jews; from Ishmael, the Arabians and thence the Mahometans; and from Esau, the Edomites, whom Winning, relying on rabbinic sources, identified with the Romans/Christians. A few years later, the Essex divine Charles Forster discussed the identical three 'Abrahamic stocks' in his two-volume *Historical Geography of Arabia; or, the Patriarchal Evidences of Revealed Religion* (1844: 2). In this way, Judaism, Christianity, and Islam made their appearance as the three Abrahamic religions on the strength of biblical genealogy, with an assist from the rabbis.

To be sure, the genealogical approach could be apologetic and polemical as well as descriptive. In his two-volume *Mahometanism Unveiled* (1829: 417, 423), Forster had concluded—from his 'establishment of the descent of the chief Arab tribes from Ishmael, and from other members of the Abrahamic family'—that the religion of pre-Islamic Arabia 'must have emanated originally from the patriarchal revelation'.[2] Indeed, drawing on a phrase of the eighteenth-century Bishop of London, Thomas Sherlock, Forster found 'clearer understanding of the divine truth among the ancient Arabians, than among the privileged descendants of Abraham', i.e. the Jews. It was no doubt the privileging of the Abrahamic covenant in Christian theology that made such ethnographic imagining possible. In the right hands, it could lead to outright appreciation of the third Abrahamic faith. In an 1849 work titled *The Hand of God in History*, the Presbyterian minister Hollis Read went so far as to portray Muhammad's establishment of Islam as God's fulfilment of 'his promise [in Gen. 17: 20] to a great branch of the Abrahamic family, the posterity of Ishmael', as well as a way 'to check effectually the power and progress of idolatry, and to scourge a corrupt Christianity; to rebuke and humble an apostate church by making her enemy a fairer example of God's truth than she was herself' (Read 1849: 256).

It is thus simply not the case, as University of Rochester religion professor Aaron Hughes argues in *Abrahamic Religions: On the Uses and Abuses of History*, that prior to the twentieth century 'Abraham' and 'Abrahamic' were used solely as 'vehicles of exclusion based on the ideology of superiority', and that 'Abrahamic' is 'never invoked objectively, but always religiously' (Hughes 2012: 55). That is not to say that Hughes is wrong to call attention to the supersessionist character of much nineteenth-century usage: the Abrahamic covenant was the means by which Christians understood themselves to have supplanted the Jews as the 'true' Israel. Even so eccentric a belief as Anglo-Israelism held that the English became the true Israel through the Abrahamic covenant (Cooper 1893: 514). But it is important to understand that supersessionism is not, as Hughes suggests, the antithesis of ecumenical acceptance of another religious

[2] Sherlock's use of the phrase may be found in Sherlock (1812: 169).

tradition. It is an ambivalent doctrinal stance—one that acknowledges the truth of an antecedent religion even as it declares its superiority over it. This ambivalence provided a range of options—from the claim to have entirely replaced an antecedent Abrahamic faith all the way to acceptance of its continued validity.

For that reason, it is significant that the Abrahamic covenant was understood as coming in the middle of a sequence of arrangements between God and man, all of which were legitimate. The eighteenth-century English hymnodist and theologian Isaac Watts, for example, distinguished among patriarchal (Noachite), Abrahamic, Jewish, and Christian religions (Watts 1753: 511). Schemas of this sort made it possible for later writers to recognize the Abrahamic family of faiths as set apart from the other religions of the world. In 1888, the Irish Protestant evangelist Henry Grattan Guinness and his wife set out seven eras from the Adamic to the Christian in *The Divine Programme of The World's History*. The Abrahamic era came third; it featured God's promise that all the nations of the earth would be blessed by Abraham's seed.

> How are we to decide which of the earth's nations have been influenced by Abraham's seed and which have not? The question is easily answered. *All the monotheism in the world is traceable to Abraham.* Wherever we find a nation which worships the one and true God, there we find a nation and a family that has been blessed through the patriarch and his seed. Hence not the Jews only, but all the professing Christian nations and the Mohammedan one as well, must form our first group of nations; while the second will consist of those nations professing polytheistic, pantheistic, and other forms of religion, as well as those which have none; including thus *all* idolators and all the fetish and devil worshippers of every kind.

As far as the Guinnesses were concerned, the Abrahamic portion of the divine programme was going well, with some 600 million people subscribing to Abrahamic monotheism and 800 million not (Guinness 1888: 156–7). While no one would accuse them of putting Judaism and Islam on the same footing as Christianity, their presentation of the three Abrahamic religions as joined in a common divinely sanctioned project represents what might be called a moderated or ecumenical supersessionism. It also testifies to the rise of the idea of monotheism in western thought. As measured by Google's N-gram Viewer, 'monotheism' barely existed in English writing until the late 1820s, but in the half-century from the mid-1840s until the mid-1890s its usage increased fifteen-fold.[3] While this is not the place to examine the history of that concept, suffice to say that it resulted from increased experience of the religions of the world in the age of imperialism and the growth in the academic study of those religions. There can be little question that the acceptance of monotheism as a basic category of religious civilization contributed greatly to the readiness of western

[3] The N-gram Viewer graphs the frequency of a given word over time in the books and periodicals digitized by Google through 2008. The program can be utilized on-line at <http://books.google.com/ngrams/>.

Christians to acknowledge that Judaism, Christianity, and Islam occupied contiguous spiritual territory.

In the United States, the foremost proponent of Abrahamic monotheism may have been Joseph Pomeroy Widney, a Midwestern Methodist who shaped metaphysical religion in California in the early twentieth century. Born in Ohio in 1841, Widney emigrated to the Golden State for his health after briefly serving in the Civil War. Becoming a doctor, he spent two years as a surgeon in the Indian wars, during which he had a profound spiritual experience of the oneness of God in the Arizona desert. He went on to a distinguished career as a physician, helping to establish and serving as dean of the University of Southern California Medical School, and taking an active role in boosting Southern California's civic and commercial culture generally. Above all, he cared about his adopted home's religious life. An early enthusiast of the Holiness movement, he was instrumental in founding the Church of the Nazarene in Los Angeles in 1895. He then returned to the Methodist church, ministering to thousands as a member of its City Mission. But he was most committed to the mission of creating a 'wider faith' than Methodism, for which he built his own chapel, called Beth-El and dedicated to the 'All-Father'. There he conducted Sunday services in the latter decades of a very long life (Frankiel 1988: 95–100).

Because of his early experience in Arizona, Widney was convinced that monotheism was a creation of the desert, and that it pre-existed Abraham—indeed, that Abraham was called out of Ur of the Chaldees in order to save this pure faith. 'The Unity of God is the heirloom of the desert peoples, and it is their message to humanity', he wrote in *The Genesis and Evolution of Islam and Judaeo-Christianity*, a volume he published in 1932 with the aim of promoting the 'evolution of one general world-faith out of many'. Although, in Widney's view, Judaism, Christianity, and Islam were all desert religions, Islam 'most nearly represents the primitive generating faith'. By contrast, Christianity had been corrupted by contact with 'the polytheism of the West' (Widney 1932a: xiii, 19, 20, 27). This, he wrote in *The Faith That Has Come to Me* (also published in 1932), placed it 'at a disadvantage in the contest with the simple monotheism of Judaism and Islam, those other great Abrahamic religions of the world' (Widney 1932b: 241). This is the first appearance in print of the expression 'Abrahamic religions' recorded in Google's book digitization project. Notably, it is not used in a way to indicate the superiority of the writer's religious tradition over the others. Indeed, it does the opposite.

Widney was at the furthest liberal extreme of the Protestantism of his day, but a readiness to recognize the authenticity of the other Abrahamic monotheisms can be found at the opposite end of the spectrum as well, thanks to the dispensational understanding of history that captured evangelical imaginations in the late nineteenth century. The idea that history unfolded in a series of divinely determined epochs culminating in the millennial age dates back at least to the writings of the Calabrian monk Joachim of Fiore in the late twelfth century. In Anglo-American Protestantism, these epochs, or dispensations, were closely tied to the covenantal concept. The eighteenth-century dissenter Micaiah Towgood (1751: 31), for example, merged the two, referring to 'the Abrahamic and Mosaic dispensations'. '[T]he evangelical covenant is the same as the Abrahamic covenant, and', wrote the American Methodist Peter P. Sandford (1832: 450), 'the Abrahamic Church is the same as the Christian Church, only under a different dispensation'. Not surprisingly, the followers of the millenarian preacher William Miller saw the imminent Second Coming as the fulfilment of the Abrahamic covenant, as was explained in an 1843 tract by Richard Hutchinson titled, *The Abrahamic covenant: the grand heir, coming in his kingdom, now to be expected at every moment.*

In the latter part of the century, as the war over infant Baptism lost its intensity, American Baptists no longer felt the need to steer clear of the Abrahamic covenant, so long as it was rightly understood (Palmer 1871: 314–44). It remained 'the fundamental church covenant in every subsequent time', with '*a world-wide missionary import*', wrote Thomas C. Johnson (1899: 123), a professor of church history at the (Baptist) Union Theological Seminary in Richmond. Like other conservative evangelicals, Baptists increasingly turned to premillennialism, the belief that Christ would return to reign for a thousand years prior to the Final Judgement. The Scofield Reference Bible, first published in 1909, became the pre-eminent source of dispensationalist doctrine for premillenialists, laying out a sequence of seven dispensations from 'Man Innocent' (before the Fall) to 'Man under the Personal Reign of Christ' (the millennial age). The Abrahamic dispensation ('Man under Promise') came fourth.

Similarly, in his widely used (to this day) fundamentalist textbook, *Principles of Biblical Hermeneutics* (1947), J. E. Hartill—for four decades a professor of Bible at Northwestern College in Minnesota—identifies the Abrahamic Covenant as coming fourth in line after Edenic, Adamic, and Noachic covenants. Unlike the first three, which he considers applicable to all human beings, Hartill sees the Abrahamic covenant as involving only the patriarch and his heirs, fleshly and spiritual. He therefore divides the nations of the world into 'those who have come in contact with Abraham and his seed' and those who have not, and likewise the religions of the world. 'Abrahamic' is his term for the 'Monotheistic group', which includes 'Jews, Mohammedans, and professed Christians'. The non-Abrahamic are those attached to 'Pantheism and Idolatry'. Hartill ties the covenantal principle of biblical interpretation closely to dispensationalist theology, providing (in line with the Scofield Bible) a Dispensation of Promise that corresponds almost exactly to the period covered by the Abrahamic Covenant: from Abraham's 'call' until the Exodus. To be sure, the premillennialist schema presents the Abrahamic dispensation as a way station on the road to the Second Coming, but by associating Judaism and Islam with Christianity as manifestations of God's promise, it puts the three Abrahamic religions on the same footing relative to the other religions of the world. Among millenarians, an institutionalized expression of this point of view can be found in two small Adventist denominations, both of which call themselves the 'Church of God of the Abrahamic Faith'. In 1965, the *Restitution Herald*, one of their official publications, included Judaism and Islam with Christianity as manifestations of 'Abrahamic Faith' and identified Abraham as 'the physical or spiritual ancestor of peoples who alone in a polytheistic or atheistic world teach the worship of the one and only God'.

If Christians learned early on to see themselves as the heirs to God's covenant with Abraham, even more did Muslims recognize themselves as restorers of what the Quran calls the *millat ibrāhīm*—the way or religion of Abraham. Following such self-understanding, non-Muslim students of Islam in the nineteenth century created a separate current of Abrahamic discourse by calling attention to Islam's relationship to Judaism and Christianity. In his book, Aaron Hughes dismisses this identification as part of an orientalist reductionism that invoked the Abrahamic merely 'to show that a particular Islamic custom, belief, or practice is unoriginal and derives its ultimate origin from another religion, be it Judaism or Christianity' (Hughes 2012: 48). Again, however, Hughes overstates his case. Nineteenth-century French Islamicists regularly identified Muslims as belonging to 'the great Abrahamic family' without drawing invidious distinctions between Islam and other religions. Indeed, in *Mahomet* (Fontane 1898: 362), the tenth volume of his popular *Universal History*, the prolific Marius Fontane writes that the 'genius of the Prophet' was to create 'a Judeo-Christianity purged of complications'; and, in what was hardly meant to be a negative assessment, goes on to say that Muhammad 'does away with the priest, rejects mythology, and suppresses the supernatural'.

The Islamicist who did the most to advance the concept of the Abrahamic religions was Louis Massignon, who began teaching Muslim sociology at the Collège de France in Paris in 1919. As a student, Massignon had been profoundly affected by the Muslim spirituality of a family he lived with while doing archaeology in Baghdad. He later converted to Christianity, became a lay Franciscan (adopting the spiritual name Ibrāhīm), and ultimately was allowed to become a priest as part of the Melkite Greek Catholic Church, which uses Arabic as its official language and permits priests to marry. Deeply committed to enhancing Christian–Muslim relations, and politically involved on behalf of Muslims in the French colonies, Massignon lifted up the figure of Abraham as a way to bring Jews, Christians, and Muslims together. In 1935, his book *The Three Prayers of Abraham: Second Prayer* connected Abraham's blessing of Ishmael to Islam. In 1949, an abbreviated version, titled *The Three Prayers of Abraham, Father of All Believers*, called Islam 'a mysterious response of grace to Abraham's prayer for Ishmael and the Arabs' (Massignon 1989: 14).

At a time when the Catholic church took a dim view of ecumenical outreach of any sort, Massignon was attacked by co-religionists for being overly committed to Islam and to Abrahamic dialogue generally. He died on 31 October 1962, just as the Second Vatican Council was getting under way, but it would turn out that, in its new-found ecumenism, Vatican II's change of attitude towards Islam would owe much to his emphasis on the figure of Abraham. In *Lumen gentium*, approved in November, 1964, the Council declared that God's 'plan of salvation' included the Muslims, 'who, professing to hold the faith of Abraham, along with us adore the one and merciful God, who on the last day will judge mankind'.[4] In *Nostra aetate*, approved in October,

[4] <http://www.vatican.va/archive/hist_councils/ii_vatican_council/documents/vat-ii_const_19641121_lumen-gentium_en.html>.

1965, the Council proclaimed its 'esteem' for the Muslims, who 'adore the one God, living and subsisting in Himself; merciful and all-powerful, the Creator of heaven and earth, who has spoken to men; they take pains to submit wholeheartedly to even His inscrutable decrees, just as Abraham, with whom the faith of Islam takes pleasure in linking itself, submitted to God.' *Nostra aetate* went on to say that the church 'remembers the bond that spiritually ties the people of the New Covenant to Abraham's stock', i.e. the Jews.[5] The Council did not, to be sure, place Islam or Judaism on the same level as Christianity. But the two other Abrahamic faiths were singled out for special status as worshipping the same God the Christians worshipped.

Massignon's work at the intersection of scholarship and interfaith promotion was carried on by his student James Kritzeck, a professor of Oriental Studies at Princeton and a devout Catholic as well. Kritzeck had written an article on Christian–Muslim relations for *The Bridge*, the yearbook of the Institute of Judaeo-Christian Studies at Seton Hall University, and in 1965 he expanded it into a slim volume titled *Sons of Abraham: Jews, Christians and Moslems*. The book reviewed the history of the relations among the three faiths, culminating with the author's translations of passages from *Nostra aetate*. Kritzeck concluded:

> There will be further efforts among Jews, Christians, and Moslems to understand one another better, and to realize more fully both their common tradition and their common debts. This realization will enable them the better to know, to love, and to serve the God of Abraham, Isaac, and Jacob.
>
> Peace to all the sons of Abraham: *shalom*, *salām*, and, in God's mercy, *salus*. (Kritzeck 1965: 95)

Salus means 'salvation' rather than peace (*shalom*, *salām*); behind the punning equivalence of his final sentence Kritzeck hints at his belief in his own faith's superiority.

Other Christian Islamicists were prepared to go a bit farther. In a study published the following year, William Montgomery Watt, a priest in the Episcopal Church of Scotland as well as a professor in Arabic and Islamic studies at the University of Edinburgh, read God's promise to raise up a prophet in Deuteronomy 18 as referring to Muhammad.

> With a little stretching of the sense here and there, Muhammad might perhaps be said to be one fulfilment of this prophecy. He cannot be said to have guided the people of God as a whole, but, insofar as the Arabs were on the fringe of the Abrahamic tradition, he may be said to have given guidance to a part of the people of God.

Watt goes on to say that while Christians and Jews would vigorously deny the claim of 'Muslim polemic writers' that 'only Muhammad properly fulfills that prophecy', he nonetheless 'belongs to the Abrahamic tradition, and that tradition had envisioned advances through charismatic religious leaders'. This identification of the Abrahamic

[5] <http://www.vatican.va/archive/hist_councils/ii_vatican_council/documents/vat-ii_decl_19651028_nostra-aetate_en.html>.

tradition with the prophetic figure closely tracks the neo-orthodox view that Hebraic prophetism was at the core of the Judaeo-Christian tradition. Watt himself says as much, identifying Muhammad as 'a charismatic religious leader within the Abrahamic (or Judaeo-Christian) tradition' (Watt 1961: 270). In a subsequent book, he portrays Islam itself as an equal partner with the earlier faiths, writing that it 'stands within this Biblical or Judaeo-Christian tradition, or, to use a phrase which avoids any suggestion of inferiority, within the Abrahamic tradition' (Watt 1974: 55).

Whatever their own religious commitments, by the late 1960s academics were increasingly making use of the concept of the Abrahamic religions. In *The Myth of Asia* (1969: 72), for example, Emory University English professor John M. Steadman argued that there was a need to 'recognize a third category of faiths, distinct from the "Nirvana religions" and the Abrahamic "religions of Law"'. In 1970, the *Cambridge History of Islam* effectively canonized the concept when it declared that Islam had 'strode forth from its homeland with the essential determinations and decisions already made. It had placed itself in the line of the *Abrahamic* religions' (von Grunebaum 1970: 474). But another decade would be needed for the concept to begin to establish itself in the larger public sphere. During the middle decades of the twentieth century, it was the Judaeo-Christian concept that held sway.

In the 1930s, when anti-Semitism was on the rise on both sides of the Atlantic, Judaeo-Christian language began to be used by interfaith organizations such as the National Conference of Christians and Jews to indicate a common religious cause (Schultz 2011). It also served to signal opposition to fascism, whose adherents and fellow-travellers were increasingly using 'Christian' as a signature term, giving their organizations names such as the Christian American Crusade, the Christian Aryan Syndicate, and the Christian Mobilizers. In its 1941 handbook, *Protestants Answer Anti-Semitism*, the left-liberal *Protestant Digest* described itself as 'a periodical serving the democratic ideal which is implicit in the Judeo-Christian tradition'. During the Second World War, the term and a host of related ones—Hebraic-Christian, Hebrew-Christian, Jewish-Christian, even Judaistic-Christian—were widely employed in a series of annual convocations held in New York City by the Conference on Science, Philosophy and Religion in their Relation to the Democratic Way of Life, Inc. Organized by Lyman Bryson of the Columbia Teachers College and Louis Finkelstein of the Jewish Theological Seminary, the Conference originated, in the words of the political scientist Carl Friedrich, 'essentially as a rallying point for Judeo-Christian forces in America against the threat presented to them by the Axis ideology and actions' (Friedrich 1944: 620).

After the war, 'Judaeo-Christian' gained nationwide popularity, as pastors, politicians, and pundits seized on the term to mobilize the spiritual forces of America against 'godless communism'. As Daniel Poling, president of the Military Chaplains Association of the United States, asserted at the association's 1951 convention, 'We meet at a time when the Judeo-Christian faith is challenged as never before in all the years since Abraham left Ur of the Chaldees.'[6] The following year, in a speech before the Freedoms

[6] *New York Times*, 23 July 1952.

Foundation, President-elect Dwight D. Eisenhower declared, 'Our form of government has no sense unless it is founded in a deeply felt religious faith, and I don't care what it is. With us of course it is the Judeo-Christian concept but it must be a religion that all men are created equal' (Henry 1981: 41). Judaeo-Christian language was also employed theologically, by neo-orthodox Protestants interested in emphasizing the 'Hebraic' over the 'Hellenic' dimension of Christianity. Led by Reinhold Niebuhr, they identified what was shared by Judaism and Christianity less in terms of articles of faith or moral ordinances than in a common understanding of the flawed nature of humankind and in a commitment to the prophetic critique of human institutions. Some were prepared to abandon Christian supersessionism altogether and acknowledge the spiritual sufficiency of Judaism via a 'dual covenant' theology.

Notwithstanding the inclusionary political and theological impulse behind it, Judaeo-Christian terminology provoked significant Jewish ambivalence. As early as 1943, a well-known publicist named Trude Weiss-Rosmarin (1943: 11) called it 'a totalitarian aberration' to tie Jewish-Christian goodwill to a shared religious identity. In 1970, the writer and publisher Arthur A. Cohen published *The Myth of the Judeo-Christian Tradition*, a collection of articles in which he denounced the Judaeo-Christian tradition as the invention of German Protestant higher critics interested in promoting a 'de-Judaizing of Christian theology' that 'could not be more evident than in the pitiful inability of the Protestant (and to a slightly—but only slightly—lesser extent, Catholic) Church to oppose German National Socialism' (Cohen 1970: xviii, 199). That, of course, turned the history of the term's use upside down. Cohen's book nevertheless received a warm reception that signalled a general fatigue with the 'Judaeo-Christian tradition', which an enthusiastic reviewer for the liberal Catholic magazine *Commonweal* called 'the catch-all of textbook writers, Western Civ. Lectures, Brotherhood Week toastmasters, and Jews and Christians who cannot think of anything else to speak of to one another when it comes to religious convictions' (Arnold 1970: 96–7). As America left its cold war consciousness behind, 'Judaeo-Christian' began to take on some outright negative connotations as well. In 'The Historical Roots of Our Ecologic Crisis', a widely read article published in *Science* magazine in 1967, the medievalist Lynn White (1967: 1206) blamed 'the Judeo-Christian dogma of creation' for instilling in western society an ethic of exploitation of the natural world.[7] In *Facing West: The Metaphysics of Indian-Hating and Empire Building*, the radical American historian Richard Drinnon (1980: xiii) dismissed 'Judeo-Christian teleology with its reified time, which had and has little or nothing to do with the cycles of organisms'.

The sense among progressives that 'Judaeo-Christian' had outlived its usefulness opened the door to using 'Abrahamic' as a substitute, especially after 1979, when the Iranian Revolution thrust political Islam onto the world stage. In 1980, John Howard

[7] Perhaps not coincidently, White's blaming of the Judaeo-Christian harked back to Aldo Leopold's blaming of the Abrahamic in the foreword of his environmentalist classic, *A Sand County Almanac* (1948): 'Conservation is getting nowhere because it is incompatible with our Abrahamic concept of land. We abuse land because we regard it as a commodity belonging to us.' (Leopold 2013: 4.)

Griffin, the author of *Black Like Me*, told Studs Terkel, 'The world has always been saved by an Abrahamic minority.'[8] A decade later, the liberal Protestant theologian Harvey Cox gave a talk in which he called for a return to 'Abrahamic faith'.[9] After the attacks of 11 September 2001, Roland Homet, an Episcopal layman and international lawyer, described attending an interfaith forum that came to the conclusion that coercing others to adopt our values 'does not represent the best of the Abrahamic tradition'.[10] 'Abrahamic' was, however, much less frequently used to point to a common value system than to designate what Judaism, Christianity, and Islam had (or did not have) to share. In 1990, for example, *New York Times* religion columnist Peter Steinfels noted 'the strong refusal of the Abrahamic faiths—Judaism, Christianity and Islam—to identify God with the world' (Steinfels 1990). On the presidential front, Jimmy Carter titled his 1985 book on the Middle East, *The Blood of Abraham*—blood that, according to Carter, 'still flows in the veins of Arab, Jew, and Christian' (Carter 1985: 208). In 2009, Barack Obama issued a proclamation noting that the 'rituals of Hajj and Eid-ul-Adha both serve as reminders of the shared Abrahamic roots of three of the world's major religions'.[11]

Where Abrahamic language came into its own was through a range of conferences, interfaith 'trialogues', academic centres, and books designed to enhance understanding among members of the three faiths in the late twentieth and early twenty-first centuries. In 1995, the Library of Congress created an 'Abrahamic' subject heading that by the end of the century had accumulated three dozen titles. The best-seller of the genre has been *Abraham: A Journey to the Heart of the Three Faiths*, by Bruce Feiler, a popular writer on various religious and lifestyle subjects. Published in 2002, the book perfectly caught the post-9/11 wave of interest in helping American Christians and Jews better understand Muslims. In it, Feiler described travelling through time and space in search of Abraham and discovering the 'Great Abrahamic Hope' not in 'an oasis somewhere in the deepest deserts of antiquity' but rather in 'a vast, underground aquifer' stretching around the world (Feiler 2002: 215). On the strength of the book's success, Feiler set about organizing public forums called 'Abraham summits' and small group meetings called 'Abraham salons'—interfaith gatherings for 'The Descendants of Abraham' that were intended to 'trace us back to Abraham and the love of one God'.[12] Meanwhile, on the academic front, Jewish, Christian, and Muslim theologians and religious thinkers came together, in conferences and between hard covers, to identify similarities and points of contact among the three faiths. Historians of religion undertook comparative studies of their intellectual and cultural relationships. As in the days of Massignon, these scholarly efforts were connected to a strong commitment to interfaith understanding.

[8] *Washington Post*, 16 October 1980.

[9] *St Petersburg Times*, 20 April 1991.

[10] <http://divinity.uchicago.edu/sightings/wisdom-serpents-religion-and-american-foreign-policy-roland-homet>.

[11] <http://www.whitehouse.gov/the-press-office/statement-president-hajj-and-eid-ul-adha>.

[12] Abraham Salon website: <http://abrahamsalon.org/node/5>.

But the Abrahamic project was far more politically fraught than Jewish-Christian dialogue had been. Judaeo-Christian language was deployed in the mid-twentieth century against a common foe, be it fascist or communist. Abrahamic language was intended to include the very 'other' that was popularly perceived, particularly in the wake of 9/11, as the principal ideological opponent of western values. Ironically, resistance to the new inclusiveness often turned up in Judaeo-Christian garb. For even as enthusiasm for 'Judaeo-Christian' waned on the left, it was embraced by the Christian right, which burst onto the American scene at the end of the 1970s.

In his best-selling manifesto, *Listen America!* (1980: 134), Jerry Falwell, the founder of the Moral Majority, described the refusal of the state of Alabama to participate 'in any conference that did not establish traditional Judeo-Christian values concerning the family'. In 1983, the Moral Majority's publication denounced a 'systematic pattern of discrimination against . . . [books] which display philosophical positions rooted in the Judeo-Christian tradition'.[13] In this way, 'Judaeo-Christian' came to be deployed as a kind of rhetorical talisman against what was perceived as a rising tide of secularism—and, in due course, of alien religious forces as well. In 1992, when Pat Robertson's Christian Coalition had succeeded the Moral Majority as the Christian's right's marquee organization, Robertson rhetorically asked himself, 'How dare you maintain that those who believe in Judeo-Christian values are better qualified to govern America than Hindus and Muslims? My simple answer is, "Yes, they are"' (Robertson 1992: 319). After the midterm elections of 2006, Rep. Virgil Goode, a Virginia Republican, achieved some notoriety by publicly criticizing the decision of the first Muslim elected to Congress to take his oath of office by placing his hand on a Quran. In an op-ed titled 'Save Judeo-Christian Values' published in *USA Today* on 2 January 2007, Goode explained:

> Let us remember that we were not attacked by a nation on 9/11; we were attacked by extremists who acted in the name of the Islamic religion. I believe that if we do not stop illegal immigration totally, reduce legal immigration and end diversity visas, we are leaving ourselves vulnerable to infiltration by those who want to mold the United States into the image of their religion, rather than working within the Judeo-Christian principles that have made us a beacon for freedom-loving persons around the world.

In sum, just as progressives had once adopted Judaeo-Christian language to include Jews under an umbrella of shared values, so they employed 'Abrahamic' to make sure that Muslims were similarly included. And just as 'Christian' had served as a fascist cue for hostility to Jews in the 1930s, so did 'Judaeo-Christian' become an emblem of evangelical hostility to Muslims in the post-cold war era.

In contrast to Jewish ambivalence about 'Judaeo-Christian', Muslim interfaith partners showed no reluctance to be considered Abrahamic. Not only was this because of their traditional identification with Abraham, but also, as the most recent of the

[13] *Moral Majority Report* (May 1983), 8.

Abrahamic faiths, they did not have to worry about being subjected to supersessionism on the part of their Abrahamic partners. The Abrahamic project did run into liberal criticism on the left for its exclusivity in a society increasingly conscious of the existence of non-Abrahamic religious communities in its midst. Writing in the *Washington Post* in 2006, Stephen Prothero, a religion professor at Boston University, criticized the use of the Abrahamic concept to define American values.

> What intrigues me about this new notion of a Judeo-Christian-Islamic (aka Abrahamic) America is how it manages to be both inclusive and exclusive at the same time. Obviously, it admits Muslims in what had once been a Protestant-Catholic-Jewish club. But by stressing such Western religious staples as monotheism, it obviously excludes religions that affirm no God (Buddhism) and those that affirm many (Hinduism).
>
> I see both the Judeo-Christian and the new Judeo-Christian Islamic one as rearguard efforts to keep the Christian America model alive—efforts that will likely fail. We live in a country where Buddhists and Hindus are now asking for a place at the table of American faiths . . .

Other religion scholars took issue with 'Abrahamic' on more scholarly grounds. In 2012, Jewish Studies professor Jon Levenson published *Inheriting Abraham: The Legacy of the Patriarch in Judaism, Christianity & Islam*, which picked apart the competing understandings of Abraham in the textual traditions of the three religions. Levenson, who teaches at the Harvard Divinity School, singled out for criticism an initiative of Harvard's Global Negotiation Project called Abraham's Path. Dismissing its use of the figure of Abraham to forge interfaith understanding, he undertook a close reading of the several Abrahamic scriptures to show how each faith's understanding of the patriarch differed in significant ways. 'There is no neutral Abraham to whom appeal can be made to set aside the authoritative documents and traditions of the separate Abrahamic religions', he wrote (Levenson 2012: 204). Hughes's *Abrahamic Religions* dismisses the Abrahamic project on broader grounds, identifying the problem not so much through competing textual understandings of the patriarch as in the failure of contemporary ecumenists to understand the long history of sectarian interpretations of their connection to Abraham. Hughes, a nominalist in his view of religious phenomena, was above all critical of the readiness of religion scholars to lump Judaism, Christianity, and Islam into a universal category, contending that the very idea of each tradition as a singular entity with essential features was problematic.

Both Levenson and Hughes harked back to the kind of Judaeo-Christian fatigue that began to afflict intellectuals in the 1960s, when that term began to seem like, at best, an empty signifier of goodwill and, at worst, a bar to understanding the realities of mutually hostile and problematic religious worldviews. Yet 'Judaeo-Christian' survived, and not only among the ideologists on the conservative side of the American culture wars. The linkages and interactions—historical, liturgical, theological—between Judaism and Christianity were too evident, and too much worth investigating—to keep the term from enjoying a vigorous life in print. According to Google N-gram, in the first decade of the twenty-first century 'Judaeo-Christian' occurred between four and five times more frequently in English books and periodicals than it did in the 1950s, and more than twice as frequently as 'Abrahamic'.

'Abrahamic' too is on the rise; its English usage doubled between 1980 and 1995, and doubled again by 2005. There is every reason to expect that, like 'Judaeo-Christian', it will continue to enjoy favour in academic as well as popular usage. For the religiously committed, whatever their sense of their own privileged position, and however differently they understand the figure of Abraham, the idea that all three religions trace their origins to the patriarch provides a powerful reason for considering them members of the same spiritual family. For more secular scholars of religion, it is hard to deny the importance of studying the mutual influences of the three traditions, especially between the formative period of Islam in late antiquity and the fertile era of intellectual exchange in the high Middle Ages.

From its origins in the eighteenth century, the term 'Abrahamic' has carried with it an important dimension of inclusion—of reaching beyond one's immediate religious community even when that community is understood as having a superior claim on religious truth. That dimension has persisted even among those less than enthusiastic about the Abrahamic project in the post-9/11 world. In 2007, Richard Land, the head of the Southern Baptist Convention's Ethics and Religious Liberty Commission, was faced with considerable opposition among his co-religionists to the presidential candidacy of Mitt Romney. Baptists were suspicious of Mormons, whom they particularly objected to calling Christian. 'Judaeo-Christian' had likewise become too close for comfort for American evangelicals to bestow on Mormonism. So Land proposed calling it 'the fourth Abrahamic religion'.[14] Whether that was a promotion or a demotion wasn't clear to *Time* magazine, and the Mormons themselves showed no interest in signing on. But it demonstrated, if further demonstration were needed, how easily the Abrahamic covenant could once again be made to extend even to bitter rivals.

References

Arnold, W. 1970. *Commonweal* 96, 2 April.

Carter, J. 1985. *The Blood of Abraham*. Boston: Houghton Mifflin.

Cohen, A. A. 1970. *The Myth of the Judeo-Christian Tradition*. New York: Harper & Row.

Cooper, C. F. 1893. 'The Discussion in Yarmouth, Nova Scotia; Number IX—Anglo-Israelism'. *The Banner of Israel* 17.

d'Alviella, E. G. 1885. *The Contemporary Evolution of Religious Thought in England, America and India*, trans. J. Moden. London: Williams & Norgate.

Dodd, W. et al. 1770. *A Commentary on the Books of the Old and New Testament, Vol. III*. London.

[14] *Time*, 24 October 2007.

Drinnon, R. 1980. *Facing West: The Metaphysics of Indian-Hating and Empire Building.* Minneapolis: University of Minnesota Press.

Falwell, J. 1980. *Listen America!.* Garden City, NY: Doubleday.

Feiler, B. 2002. *Abraham: A Journey to the Heart of Three Faiths.* New York: Morrow.

The Foreign Quarterly Review. 1841. London: Black & Armstrong.

Fontane, M. 1898. *Mahomet: Histoire universelle.* Vol X. Paris: Lemerre.

Forster, C. 1829. *Mahometanism Unveiled,* Vol. II. London.

Forster, C. 1844. *Historical Geography of Arabia; or, the Patriarchal Evidences of Revealed Religion,* Vol. II. London: Duncan & Malcolm.

Frankiel, S. S. 1988. *California's Spiritual Frontiers: Religious Alternatives in Anglo-Protestantism, 1850–1910.* Berkeley: University of California Press.

Friedrich, C. J. 1944. 'Problems of Communication'. In L. Bryson, L. Finkelstein, and R. M. MacIver, eds, *Science, Philosophy and Religion,* Vol. IV, *Approaches to World Peace.* New York: Harper.

von Grunebaum, G. E. 1970. 'The Sources of Islamic Civilization'. In P. M. Holt et al., eds, *The Cambridge History of Islam,* Vol. IIB. Cambridge: Cambridge University Press, 469–510.

Guinness, H. G. 1888. *The Divine Programme of The World's History.* London: Hodder & Stoughton.

Hartmann, E. 1876. *La Religion de l'avenir.* Paris: Baillière.

Henry, P. 1981. '"And I Don't Care What It Is": The Tradition-History of a Civil Religion Proof Text'. *The Journal of the American Academy of Religion* 49 (1): 35–49.

Hughes, A. 2012. *Abrahamic Religions: On the Uses and Abuses of History.* Oxford: Oxford University Press.

Johnson, T. C. 1899. 'God's Ordained Missionary Society'. *The Union Seminary Magazine* 11.

Kilpatrick, J. H. T. 1847. 'The Commission'. In R. Fleming, ed., *The Georgia Pulpit; or, Ministers' Yearly Offering.* Richmond: Ellyson, I. 132–50.

Kritzeck, J. 1965. *Sons of Abraham: Jews, Christians and Moslems.* Baltimore: Helicon.

Leopold, A. 2013. *A Sand County Almanac & Other Writings on Ecology and Conservation,* ed. C. Meine. New York: The Library of America.

Levenson, J. D. 2012. *Inheriting Abraham: The Legacy of the Patriarch in Judaism, Christianity and Islam.* Princeton: Princeton University Press.

Magee, W. 1812. *Discourses and Dissertations on the Scriptural Doctrines of Atonement and Sacrifice,* Vol. II. London: Hudson.

Massignon, L. 1989. *Testimonies and Reflections.* Notre Dame, IN: University of Notre Dame Press.

Morgan, T. 1739. *The Moral Philosopher,* Vol. II. London.

Palmer, T. R. 1871. 'The Abrahamic Covenants'. *The Baptist Quarterly* 5: 314.

Read, H. 1849. *The Hand of God in History.* Hartford, CT: H. Huntington.

Robertson, P. 1992. *The New World Order.* Boston: G. K. Hall.

Rogers, G. 1837. *The Pro and Con of Universalism,* Vol. I. Cincinnati: R. P. Brooks.

Sandford, P. P. 1832. 'Nature and Constitution of the Visible Church'. *The Methodist Magazine and Quarterly Review* 14: 438–49.

Schultz, K. M. 2011. *Tri-Faith America: How Catholics and Jews Held Postwar America to its Protestant Promise.* New York: Oxford University Press.

Sherlock, T. 1812. *Discourses Preached at Temple Church,* Vol. IV. Oxford: Clarendon Press.

Steadman, J. M. 1969. *The Myth of Asia.* New York: Simon & Schuster.

Steinfels, P. 1990. 'Beliefs'. *New York Times,* 20 January.

Stopford, E. 1837. *The Scripture Account of the Sabbath.* London: J. Hatchard.

Sullivan, R. J. 1794. *A View of Nature, A View of Nature in Letters to a Traveler among the Alps*, Vol VI. London: T. Becket.

Towgood, M. 1751. *Dipping Not the only Scriptural and Primitive Manner of Baptizing.* London.

Watt, W. M. 1961. *Islam and the Integration of Society.* London: Routledge & Kegan Paul.

Watt, W. M. 1974. *Muhammad: Prophet and Statesman.* Oxford: Oxford University Press.

Watts, I. 1753. 'A Caveat against Infidelity'. In *Sermons, Discourses, and Essays.* London.

Weiss-Rosmarin, T. 1943. *Judaism and Christianity: The Differences.* New York: Jonathan David.

Whitcomb, T. J. 1945. 'Visit to 'Good Luck;' Murray's First Landing Place—Potter's Field'. *The Universalist Union* 10.

White, L., Jr. 1967. 'The Historical Roots of Our Ecologic Crisis'. *Science* 155 (3767): 1203–7.

Widney, J. P. 1932a. *The Genesis and Evolution of Islam and Judaeo-Christianity.* Los Angeles: Pacific Publishing.

Widney, J. P. 1932b. *The Faith That Has Come to Me.* Los Angeles: Pacific Publishing.

Williams, G. H. 2002. *American Universalism.* 4th edn. Boston: Skinner House Books.

Winning, W. B. 1838. *A Manual of Comparative Philology.* London.

Wolff, J. 1829. *Missionary Journal*, Vol. III. London.

Worcester, S. 1807. *Two Discourses on the Perpetuity and Provision of God's Gracious Covenant with Abraham and His Seed.* 2nd edn rev. Salem.

Worcester, S. 1820. *Infant Sprinkling Proved to Be a Human Tradition; Being the Substance of a Debate on Christian Baptism.* Steubenville, OH.

CHAPTER 6

THE CONCEPT OF THE ABRAHAMIC RELIGIONS, PROBLEMS AND PITFALLS

RÉMI BRAGUE

In the past several years, three expressions have entered the media when it comes to talking about religion. Every time, it is a question of three things: 'the three monotheisms'; 'the three religions of Abraham'; 'the three religions of the book'. It is difficult to come across an organ of the press or to pick up a newspaper (be it religious or secular) without having one or another of these formulations put forth as self-evident. At a higher level, books that have one of them as titles, or which contain them (some of which are of high quality), have multiplied since the 1980s.[1]

It would be interesting to study the history of these expressions—something I have not had the courage to do. I would be tempted to venture, in lieu of an inventory, that the genealogy of these expressions could very well go back to the Middle Ages; and, more exactly, that the idea of associating Judaism, Christianity, and Islam comes from a desire to condemn them all rather than embracing them in a common sympathy! In this way, what are called today 'the three religions' would simply be the latest version of what was applied long ago to 'the three impostors', Moses, Jesus, and Muhammad, deemed to have deceived humanity.

[1] The first book that bore the express title *Les trois monothéismes* was a work by the psychoanalyst D. Sibony, which had as its subtitle *Juifs, Chrétiens et Musulmans entre leurs sources et leurs destins* (Paris: Le Seuil, 1992). The philosopher and scholar of Islam R. Arnaldez published *Trois messagers pour un seul Dieu* (Paris: Albin Michel, 1983), and *À la croisée des trois monothéismes: une communauté de pensée au Moyen Age* (Paris: Albin Michel, 1993).

In any event, one can believe that these expressions were more recently conceived, and continue to be used, out of noble motives. These would indicate a point in common for the religions in question, eventually some common ground in practice.

My immediate purpose is to show that these three expressions are at once false and dangerous. They are *false* because each masks a serious error concerning the nature of the three religions that one claims to bring together under a common roof. They are *dangerous* because they encourage an intellectual sloth that relieves one of closely examining reality. I will examine them in order, starting with the idea of 'monotheism'.

Three monotheisms?

The term 'monotheism' comes from outside, not within, religions. The 'monotheisms' do not speak of themselves this way. To be sure, certain expressions they use allow themselves to be translated in this way, such as the Arab *tawḥīd*, 'affirmation that God is one'—a word that, by extension, took on a meaning close to 'theology'. Speaking very precisely, among some Jews there is a characterization of Judaism as 'ethical monotheism', a phrase that, perhaps, is attributable to the German rabbi Leo Baeck (1873–1956).

The term 'monotheism' was born rather late, in the seventeenth century, from the pen of Henry More, one of the Christian Platonists of Cambridge, who used it in English in 1660 (see the *Oxford English Dictionary*, 'monotheism'). Its subsequent career saw it occur much more among the philosophers than the theologians, and almost never was it used as an expression of piety by simple believers.

Monotheism is not Essentially Religious

Let us begin with a synthetic statement: monotheism—and, moreover, polytheism—has nothing specifically religious in its meaning; it primarily comes from philosophy.

There are non-monotheistic religions that exist. But, conversely, there are non-religious monotheisms, in which one finds a philosophical affirmation of a God who is not the object of a religion. This is the case with the deism of certain Enlightenment thinkers. Here, though, we can always ask if this does not involve a certain weakened version of Christianity, in which only an answer to the question of the number of gods was retained. The best examples, therefore, should be sought among the Greek philosophers who never heard of Judaism and, even less, of Christianity. Thus, the pre-Socratic Xenophanes of Colophon (who lived in the sixth to fifth century before Christ) opposed to the various imaginings of the nations, each of whom represented the deity in their image, 'a sole god, the greatest among the gods and men, who resembles mortals neither in appearance nor in thought' (fragment 21 B 23, ed. Diels and Kranz). After him, Aristotle called the unchanging first mover of his natural philosophy by the name of 'god'. It appears that this god knows nothing outside of itself (*Metaphysics* 12.7, 1072b25, 29–30).

In contrast, Epicurus admitted the existence of several gods. They live in the interstices separating the innumerable worlds postulated by his cosmology. They enjoyed a perfect beatitude and took no thought, and had no concern, for those worlds and their inhabitants (Brague 1999: 54–5). The philosopher publicly acknowledged the gods of the city and rendered them appropriate worship, but did not consider them to be true gods.

The affirmation of a sole God is therefore not necessarily a religious phenomenon. One can have a God without religion. Conversely, one can have a religion without God, as was the case with primitive Buddhism.

There are not Only Three Monotheisms

When one says 'the three monotheisms', the use of the definite article assumes that there are only three. However, these purported 'three monotheisms' were not the first. The first was, perhaps, the invention of the Pharaoh Amenophis IV, who took the name Akhnaton (1250 BCE). The underlying idea is that a sole God is the true one, the others only being subordinate delegates. In its case, Israel began with a national God, to whom alone worship should be given, but the other gods were the legitimate gods of the neighbouring nations. It was only after the return from exile that the idea emerged that there is but one God, the other gods being false, that is, 'idols' (Isa. 44: 8; 47: 21).

These 'three monotheisms' were also not the last. Religious fecundity did not dry up, especially among the colonized peoples of the Third World (Voodoo and Pentecostalism among African blacks) or who had had contact with the West (the Cargo cult in New Guinea). In contrast, almost no one invented new polytheisms. Religions emerge most often from a pre-existing religion that they claim to reform. And these 'maternal' religions are monotheistic. Thus, in the nineteenth century religions such as Mormonism were born from Christianity and the Bahai religion from Islam. The religion of the Sikhs, born in the seventeenth century from Hinduism, borrowed monotheism from Islam.

The new religions of today understand themselves as adjuncts to pre-existing religions, for example, Kimbanguism, born in the 1930s in the Republic of Congo (then the Belgian Congo) from the preaching of Simon Kimbangu, which succeeded in being admitted into the ecumenical Council of Churches. This is rare, since the older religions most often find it hard to admit that the new religions can claim to represent a legitimate version of themselves. Thus, Judaism does not accept Christianity, Christianity does not accept Islam, and the latter in turn does not accept Bahaism.

Do Monotheism and Polytheism Simply Oppose One Another?

The real question is not the quantity of gods. It is never a matter of merely determining their number by counting. In fact, one can wonder if a veritable polytheism has ever existed outside of the polemics of those who attack it. Aristotle (*Metaphysics* 5.6, 1016b31–5) distinguishes different sorts of unity or, more concretely, different cases when one says 'it is the same thing'. He therefore distinguishes unity by number (the same thing, which 'does not constitute number'), by species (you and I are members of the human race), by genus (my dog and I are living beings), and by analogy (scales and feathers are the same thing, because scales are to fish what feathers are to birds). One can say that every religion attributes to the divine one or another of these different levels of unity. The divine can present itself as an individual, a family, a teeming race, a level of being. In each case, though, it is distinguished from what it is not, i.e. the 'profane', by characteristics that constitute it as a unity. As a consequence, the proper question is to ask what the monotheism makes of plurality, and what the polytheism makes of unity.[2]

Ancient paganism knew the idea of a 'world' of the divine, a pantheon that made all the gods members of a single, and unique, collectivity. This is what Homer said so magnificently: 'The gods are not unknown to one another, even if they live in separate dwellings' (*Odyssey* 5.79–80). And above the family of the Olympians hovered Destiny (*Moira*), which regulated the succession of the generations constituting the family. Fathers were dethroned in favour of their sons. Perhaps it was this impersonal power that, for the Greeks, was the veritable cause of the unity of the divine.

The Real Question

The real question, therefore, is to ask *how* God is one, what is the mode of unity that relates the divine to itself. Here I will simply sketch a point that I will develop below. 'To be one': that can mean to affirm that God is unique. There is only one. The set 'gods' only contains one member. Here, however, one encounters a paradox that arises from rather simple logic. Unity, like every number, is not the property of the thing, but of the class to which it belongs. To say that God is one, is to suppose that he belongs to a higher class, that of 'unities'. Thus, while one thinks that by affirming God's unity one is making him something supreme, in reality one is devaluing him, because he is subordinated to the class of unities.

This is why religions do not content themselves with affirming that God only exists as a single exemplar (his 'uniqueness'). They also say something about the way in which he is one with himself (his 'unity').

[2] This is the question posed by Gisel 2006: 13.

God can be one by way of continuity with himself, because he is, as it were, of a single piece. The Quran offers a representation of this sort when, in a famous sura which was often invoked against the Christian idea of the Trinity, it calls God 'the Impenetrable' (*aṣ-ṣamad*) (112: 2). Even the most ancient commentators did not understand the meaning of the adjective, and they had to venture conjectures. They sometimes explained that God is wholly continuous or homogeneous, without imperfection, without defect, like a piece of forged metal (Gimaret 1988: 320–3).

God can be one by way of fidelity to himself in the context of a design of salvation being worked out in history. This, perhaps, is what is expressed by the famous formula in the Book of Exodus by which the God of Israel presented himself to Moses, calling himself 'I will be He whom I will be' (Exod. 3: 14).

God can be one by way of the total accord, in love, of the three hypostases of the divine substance. For Christianity, the Trinity is *not* a way of attenuating the rigour of monotheism. To the contrary, it is a way of thinking to a conclusion *how* God is one. If 'God is love' (1 John 4: 16), it is love that must constitute the internal law of his being, and thus of his unity with himself (as I said, I will develop these thoughts later in the work).

I do not like it therefore when, as often happens, it is said (whether to credit or discredit them makes no difference) that Islam or Judaism profess a 'strict monotheism'. This is as though there could be 'less strict' monotheisms, Christianity, for example. It is enough simply to try to imagine what a relaxed monotheism—one that is accommodating, easy-going—to see the absurdity of this sort of formulation. God is not *more or less* one . . . The difference is not in the harder or softer character of the monotheism, but in the way in which the unity is conceived.

Islamic Monotheism

It was not Islam that discovered the unique God, 'The-God', Allah. He was already known to the Arabs. 'If you ask them: "Who created heaven and earth, who subjected the sun and the moon?", they answer: "God!". . .' (Q. 29: 61, 31: 25, 39: 38; cf. 43: 9 ('the Powerful, the Knowing'); 43: 87 (' . . . who created them . . . ')). The Allah before Muhammad was, perhaps, what the historians of religion call an 'idle god' (*deus otiosus*). Such a God creates the world, then retires, letting lesser divinities administer the created order and share the prayers and sacrifices of men. Islam, therefore, would be a sort of short-circuit, passing by the divinities tasked with interceding, in order to arrive directly at the creator God.

We however are not very clear about the religion of the Arabs at the time of Muhammad. The traditional history supposes that they, in the main, were pagans, polytheists therefore, with a few Christian tribes, some Jewish ones, and a small number of isolated individuals given the mysterious name of *ḥanīf*, we could say: monotheists without any particular denomination. Arab historians have collected the data pertaining to the idols worshipped in ancient Araby.[3] It seems, however, that they attributed to the epoch of Muhammad a religious situation that had already disappeared for several centuries, and that the Araby of the time was much more Christianized than was generally thought. The Quran speaks often of the 'associators' (*mushrikūn*), those who associate one, or several other beings, with the unique God. And it does so in rather harsh terms. Who were they, though? Pagans? Or rather Christians, adherents of Trinitarian doctrine as it had been interpreted by those who rejected the dogma defined at the Council of Nicaea concerning Christ, that he is 'of one substance with the Father'? Some have thought so, with arguments that do not lack in value (Hawting 1999; Gallez 2005).

A Mutual Recognition of the Monotheisms?

It is at least paradoxical to see monotheism as an element common to the three religions, since it historically functioned as a golden apple, that is, an apple of discord. In fact, these three religions only recognize the others as monotheistic with great difficulty.

Christianity does recognize the monotheism of Judaism. Judaism finds it harder to return the favour. Employing a phrase from the Quran (5: 73), Maimonides reproached Christians with making God 'the third of three'.[4] It was not until the Rabbi of Perpignan Menaḥem ha-Meiri (d. 1315) that the dominant opinion (although not unanimous) became that Christians are not 'idolators'.[5]

Judaism recognized the monotheism of Muslims, once the misunderstanding was cleared up concerning the worship offered to the Kaʿba.[6] Islam would without difficulty recognize the monotheism of Jews, if the Quran did not reproach them for associating a mysterious personage named ʿUzayr (9: 30) with God. Perhaps this is the Esdras of the Bible, unless it is the garbled name of an angel.

Christianity today considers the monotheistic character of Islam to be obvious. It was not always thus, however. John of Damascus, one of the first Christians to write on the religion of the 'Ismaelites', turns the charge that Christians adore the cross to the countercharge of worshipping the Black Rock of Kaʿba. And the popular literature of the Middle Ages saw Muslims as pagans, adoring Muhammad and two other idols![7] For their part, many Muslims admit that Christians are not polytheists. But what to make of the formulas in the Quran which formally accuse them of associating 'monks', or even Jesus and his Mother, with God (9: 31; 5: 116)?

[3] See, for instance, Ibn al-Kalbî (1969).

[4] Maimonides 1972: 69, 'First Tractate on the Resurrection'; trans. Fradkin 2000: 154.

[5] Menahem ha-Meiri, *Beth ha-Bḥira*, on 'Avoda Zara 53 [*non vidi*].

[6] Maimonides 1972: 112, 'Letter on the Persecution', ch. 2; Maimonides 1989: II. 726, 'Answer to Ovadia the Proselyte'.

[7] John of Damascus, *Heresy* 100.5 (ed. Le Coz 1992: 218–20); *La Chanson de Roland* 1.8, 32.416–17, 47.611, etc. (ed. Jenkins 1924: 4, 40, 53, respectively).

Thus, to speak of the religions as 'monotheistic' does not get us very far in understanding them. One still has to ask, what model of divine unity is at work, and what are the consequences of the application of the model? In other words, what is the meaning of this-or-that affirmation of divine unity?

Three religions of Abraham?

By the phrases 'the three religions of Abraham' or 'the three Abrahamic religions', people believe they establish common ground, by appealing to a common ancestor. In truth, however, this is another golden apple.

The Common Personages

All three, Judaism, Christianity, and Islam, have books in which the name of a person named Abraham appears. (The Arabic of the Quran writes with a slight variation: Ibrahīm. This, perhaps, is due to a later incorrect reading of an obsolete form of writing (Luxenberg 2004: 102–3).) Abraham, however, is not the only biblical personage whose name is common to all the religions. This is also the case for Adam, Noah, Joseph, Moses, and Jonah, who appear in the Old and New Testament as well as the Quran. In its turn, the Quran knows Jesus and his mother, the Virgin Mary, while the foundational writings of Judaism obviously do not mention them.

Islam, though, gives to the one that Christians name Jesus a very different name than the one by which he was known to the Jews (*Yeshu*), as well as by Christian Arabs (*Yeshūʿ*). The Quran calls him *ʿĪsā*, a name that recalls in a surprising way that of Esau (*ʿĪsū*). In this, should one see the trace of an implicit comparison of the three religions? That of the Jews coming from Jacob (Israel), the Arabs from Ishmael, and Christians from Esau? It is well known that Jewish texts often identified Christians in a symbolic way with Esau.

At a more general level a problem arises, that of the presence in the three religions of literary figures bearing the same name. Simply because the names are the same does not mean that the personages are. Their personal traits are embedded and revealed in the particular narratives of the different writings. And what is recounted in the holy books of the three religions with respect to these figures is not uniform, far from it. The history of Joseph is the only one that the Quran recounts in an integral, orderly way, in sura 12, entitled 'Joseph' (*Yūsuf*). It reprises the grand features of the biblical account (Gen. 37–50), and adds some details drawn from the Jewish legends found in the midrash (de Prémare 1989). The same thing can be said, *grosso modo*, of the figure of Moses.

Moreover, the meaning of the biblical figures does not solely depend upon these individual narratives looked at in isolation. It also depends in large part upon the connections among them which shed reciprocal light. The meaning of the figure of

Mary in Christianity is hardly conceivable without the 'typological' connection between her and Eve, which is not found in Islam (Gisel 2006: 134).

But it is with respect to Jesus that the Quran and the New Testament most differ. The miracles reported in the Quran are healings, which are not specified. The Quran adds spectacular miracles, in which the embellishing of the apocryphal Gospels makes itself seen: Jesus speaking as an infant, or creating birds of bronze, animating them, then destroying them (3: 49; 5: 110). Jesus' teaching is not reported. Finally, Jesus was not crucified by the Jews, it only 'seemed to them' (*shubbiha lahum*) that he had been (4: 157). Taken up to heaven, he had not died and therefore did not need to be resurrected.

The Same Abraham?

As for the figure of Abraham, it is rather a source of disagreement than of concord. In truth, for Judaism and for Christianity, Islam is not Abrahamic. It is not in its conception of prophecy, nor in its conception of history. Jesus, the Twelve, Paul, and the first Christians were all Jews. They thus linked themselves to an Abrahamic genealogy that no one contested. The problem only surfaced when Paul had believers of Gentile origin admitted into the Christian community. He justified this enlargement by interpreting the story of the two sons of Abraham, the son of the slave Agar and the son of Sarah, the free woman, with the first representing 'the flesh', the second 'the spirit' (Gal. 4: 21–31).

Muhammad and the first Muslims were not of Jewish stock and did not live in the Holy Land. They, therefore, had to attach themselves to the biblical history by inventing a genealogy. They constructed one by also representing the history of two of Abraham's sons. In the Bible, Ishmael was the ancestor of the desert nomads (Gen. 16: 12). One only had to see in them the Arabs for the equation to be made. It does not appear that the idea of connecting themselves to Ishmael came to the Arabs before Muhammad. No previous genealogy of biblical inspiration existed before the Islamic enterprise (Dagorn 1981).

The history of Abraham is not interpreted in the same way in Judaism and in Christianity. Both underscore the extraordinary faith of the patriarch, who was ready to sacrifice the son that God had promised him. Judaism prefers to put the accent upon the non-sacrifice of Isaac. In fact, it does not talk about the *sacrifice* of the son, but his 'binding' (*ʿaqedah*), with the child having been bound, as one did with the animals of the Temple. The central event is God's intervention, as He restrains the hand of Abraham and substitutes a goat for the human victim. Christianity adds to the example of Abraham's faith an allegorical reading of his sacrifice as a prefiguration of the cross of Christ. Everything is turned upside down: it is God himself who sacrifices his beloved Son. The situation of Islam is more complex. The Quran leaves vague the identity of the son who was to be sacrificed. Was it to have been Isaac, as in the Bible? Or Ishmael?

Moreover, the Quran places Abraham in a series of prophets who would have received a book, projecting backwards the model of Muhammad. Abraham is therefore deemed to have received, like Moses, pages or 'leaves' (Q. 53: 37; 87: 19; see 20: 133), which neither the Old nor the New Testament mentions. Above all, the Quran makes use of the figure of Abraham to recount a history that neither Judaism nor Christianity knows anything about, and for good reason: that of the foundation of a house by the patriarch (Q. 2: 125–7). The word (*bayt*) can mean 'temple', and the purpose of the edifice clearly shows that this is the case: one had to bow and prostrate oneself therein (Q. 22: 26). The Quran does not say anything about the particular location of this building, but the subsequent Islamic tradition placed it in the 'sterile valley', that of Mecca, and saw in the house, the cubic temple of the Kaʿba. This furnished the pilgrimage to them with a legitimacy that went back to the oldest antiquity.

Three Religions of Abraham, or Only One?

In the West, one has the habit of speaking of the 'religions of Abraham' in the plural. This, above all, is a Christian locution. For Islam there is *only one* 'religion of Abraham', which is Islam itself. For the Christian, to speak of the 'religion of Abraham' is to include Judaism and Islam, and to associate them with Christianity in a vague sort of fraternity. For Islam, on the other hand, it means to exclude Judaism and Christianity: 'Abraham was neither a Jew nor a Christian, but a true believer (*ḥanīf*) and Muslim (*muslim*), and he was not one of the polytheists (*mushrik*)' (Q. 3: 67).[8] This exclusion operates by a series of retrenchments. The operation is already found in the Quran: 'They have said: "Be Jews or Christians, you will be well advised". Say: "But no! . . . Follow the religion of Abraham, a true believer who was not numbered among the polytheists"' (2: 135). For the Muslim religion, Islam already was the religion of Abraham. This religion of Abraham, anterior to Judaism as well as Christianity, was moreover already that of Moses, Noah, and even Adam, as it was later the religion of Jesus. It was the religion of all of the humanity which was to come from the loins of Adam. This was a humanity which even before the creation of the world, miraculously drawn from its first ancestor, confessed the lordship of God, in a scene described in the Quran (7: 72).

What, then, is the status of the two other religions, apparently chronologically anterior to the religion preached by Muhammad? The main current of Islam sees in them deformations, betrayals of the message originally addressed to Abraham. This derives logically from the fundamental teaching of the deformation (*taḥrīf*) of the previous scriptures.[9] It is derived from the interpretation of the verses of the Quran:

[8] I give these three key terms the meaning that they have in traditional Muslim exegesis. These words are obscure and their interpretation, especially the word *muslim*, anachronistic.

[9] See my work, Brague 2005: 117–19, and above all, Lazarus-Yafeh 1992. The Indian reformer Ahmad Khan (1817–98)—against whom Jamâl ed-Dîn el-Afghanî wrote the *Refutation of Materialists*—seems to have been the first to propose the abandonment of this teaching. See Gisel 2006: 124.

'certain Jews altered [the meaning] of the [revealed] words' (4: 46 and 5: 13; 5: 41; 2: 75). The meaning of these quranic verses is not totally clear, but the passages most often were interpreted as signifying that the sacred texts were tampered with. The common view is the following: the Jews imagine that they have in their hands the Torah revealed to Moses, the Christians believe they possess 'the Gospel' (in the singular) which was revealed to the prophet Jesus. But the two books, the Torah and the Gospel, were corrupted, the first by the Jews, the second by the Christians, which deprives both of the genuineness they claim. Those guilty for these deformations are sometimes identified: Esdras for the Torah, St Paul for the Gospel. Happily, the authentic content of the revelations made to Moses and to Jesus was preserved, precisely in the Quran.

Thanks to its invocation of Abraham, Islam effects a paradoxical operation according to which, on one hand, it is the last of the religions, on the other, the first of all of them.

Thus, the 'Abraham' that the three religions would have in common is a vague abstraction. This smallest of common denominators coincides with none of the concrete figures revered by them and in which they recognize themselves. To accept such an Abraham would be for each religion to renounce a dimension of its faith.

Three religions of the book?

A Deceptive Expression

Among Christians and Jews, but also among certain Muslims, one speaks of 'three religions of the book'. The expression is deceptive. First of all, because it already has a meaning in one of the religions, Islam. Islamic law has the concept of 'people of the book' (*ahl al-kitāb*). In the Islamic city, there is no place for pagans, who, in principle, only have the choice between conversion and death. In contrast, the members of the religions that already had a sacred text when Muhammad came on the scene, i.e. Judaism and Christianity, as well as Zoroastrianism, do have a juridically defined place by rules that fix the rights and duties of the 'protected' communities (*ahl al-dhimma*). Islam, however, clearly does not consider itself as being a part of these 'peoples of the book'.

The second defect of this expression is its imprecision. Does a 'religion of the book' signify a religion in which there is found a sacred book or books? In this sense, every religion coming from a people that knows writing has one or several written texts. These can be narratives, what are called myths, legends concerning the god or the gods of this religion. They can equally be instruments of worship, for example, collections of hymns, of religious songs. They can also be cultic 'recipes', as it were, concerning the art and manner of sacrifice, of how to offer gifts to the divinity. One can find in them rules of conduct, of morality, counsels concerning how to please the divinity. Finally, one can find collections of the teachings of the founder of the religion.

It is fitting, therefore, not to identify the religions of a book with the three religions of Judaism, Christianity, and Islam. Moreover, a religion in which there is a book is not, by that fact, a 'religion *of the book*'. And finally, even if one limits oneself to Judaism, Christianity, and Islam, one has to make distinctions because, as we will see, the relation of each of these religions to its own book is not the same in each case.

Three Very Different Books

This is explained, first of all, by the difference in the nature of these three books. They were redacted according to different rhythms, accelerating as one progressed. The period of redaction for the Old Testament was approximately eight centuries, for the New Testament about seventy years, for the Quran, about twenty years. Moreover, they were not composed with the same aim in mind. The texts brought together in the Old and New Testaments, composed by different authors, in different contexts, and for different reasons, only formed a sacred book once they were assembled and deemed canonical. In contrast, the Quran seems to have been composed in order to serve as the sacred book of a community. It situates itself in this way in a series of works that probably began in the third century CE, with the book of Mani, the founder of Manichaeism, and which continued as late as the nineteenth century with the book of the Bahais, the Book of Mormon, and many others.[10]

The Old Testament

The Old Testament is less a book than a library, a collection of books that belong to all the literary genres. There you find history, whether actual or mythic, legislation, poetry, including erotic poetry such as the Song of Songs, quasi-philosophic writing, e.g. Ecclesiastes, prophetic exhortations, and the so-called 'Wisdom' literature. Its oldest texts probably date back to 1200 BCE, while the most recent differ somewhat between Jews and Christians. The Jews only accept the texts written in Hebrew and in Aramaic, while Christians add texts translated into Greek (Sirach) or written directly in that language (Wisdom), which include some that emerged in the first century before Christ.

During the course of these thousands of years of redaction, later texts contained reflections upon the previous texts, commenting on them, pointing back to them. The fifth book of the first five books of the Bible, which Christians call Deuteronomy (in Greek: 'the second law') and the Jews call 'the repetition of the Torah' (*Mishneh Torah*), is a reflection upon the laws contained in the three previous books.

The danger for the reader of the Old Testament is to place all these texts on the same plane, to consider them as if they had the same status, while one must pay the closest attention to the literary genre of each book: historical narrative, poem, parables . . .

[10] See the excellent little book of A. Jeffery (1952).

The New Testament

The New Testament also contains different literary genres: the four Gospels, the narratives of the life, teachings, and passion of Jesus; the Acts of the Apostles, the history of the beginnings of the spread of Christianity; the Epistles, letters written by the principal apostles to the communities for which they felt responsible; finally, the Apocalypse, a book of revelations. Their authors differ; one can even discern different schools of interpretation of the life of Jesus. Nonetheless, the New Testament presents a greater unity than the Old, it is written in one language, a popular Greek (*koiné*), and its redaction only occurred over a few decades.

The Quran

The Quran, at least on the surface, has a greater unity: it is the work of one hand, in which intertextuality abounds (repetitions, citations, allusions). The main difficulty in reading it resides in its very obscure vocabulary, for the very simple reason that the Quran itself is the oldest work in the Arab language that we possess, with the exception of a few inscriptions and, perhaps, certain poems (the so-called 'anteislamic poetry') which could have been rewritten at a later date, and adapted to a more recent state of the language for better understanding.[11] We therefore lack a context, a base-line, which allows us to interpret it.

Three Relations to the Book

With Judaism, Christianity, and Islam we have three religions, each of which has its book, but which has a different relationship with the book. At the risk of oversimplifying, I would express these relations in three formulas that I will develop shortly. The religion of Israel is a history that led to a book; Christianity is a history recounted in a book; Islam is a book that leads to a history.

Judaism

Let us begin chronologically with Judaism, taken in a large sense. The religion of ancient Israel did not rest exclusively on the existence of a book. It was during the course of its history that the library that we call the Old Testament was composed, and it was composed in circumstances closely connected with the political development of the people.

The religion of ancient Israel is a national religion, a worship offered to its god by a people, in the same way that neighbouring peoples offered their worship, hymns, and sacrifices to their gods. This religion had sacrifices, feasts, and places of worship which,

[11] This is the hypothesis of the Egyptian Ṭaha Ḥusayn (1926), in a work which rendered him quite suspect, *Fī 'shi'ir al-jāhilī* [*On Pre-Islamic Poetry*] (re-edn, Cairo: Dâr al-Nahâr, 1995) [*non vidi*].

at a certain period, were reduced to one: the Temple at Jerusalem, the clergy of which exercised a sort of monopoly.

In the course of this history, a certain number of documents were produced, such as chronicles of kings. A people loves to sing of its glorious ancestors, the patriarchs; this, in part, is the subject of Genesis. Israel also codified the civil and penal code the king imposed on his people. Priests wrote down the ritual of the Temple at Jerusalem, as well as its collection of hymns.

Judaism properly speaking, Judaism in the narrow sense, was constituted by a series of tragic events in the history of Israel. Around 70 CE, to be a Jew could no longer mean being the subject of the king of Israel, nor inhabiting the land since the majority of the Jewish people did not live there; the Romans ended matters by forbidding the Jews to live in Palestine. Nor could it consist in offering sacrifices in the Temple, which had been destroyed. The people no longer had a principle of identity. What remained was a way of life, whose political, moral, and domestic rules had been formulated by the Torah. This is the meaning of the suffix '-ism' in Judaism. Judaism consists in conducting oneself as if in the land of Judah (the region of Jerusalem), by focusing upon the Torah, by following its rules. The Torah itself was interpreted as a rule of life; this is the meaning of the Hebrew word *halakha* which signifies the path to follow, the 'way to conduct one's life'.

Judaism is therefore a religion of a book in an entirely different sense from the religion of ancient Israel, which rested on the political, economic, and cultural life of a nation, a nation which produced a book. Judaism is almost entirely different: it is the book which produced the nation. According to the expression of Heinrich Heine, the Bible is the 'portable homeland' of every Jew.[12] To be a Jew is to follow the rules of the Torah, which constitute the deepest identity of a people and which, therefore, require to be more and more precisely specified. To it were added discussions concerning the manner of precisely interpreting the commandments and the prohibitions given by God; this formed the Talmud.

Christianity

Christianity is first of all a fact, a movement, an event tied to the specific person of Jesus of Nazareth; the book was posterior. When the evangelists recounted the history of Jesus, their aim was not to write a biography but to show that the life of Jesus of Nazareth completed the meaning of the history of Israel, and even of human life as such. The beginning of Christianity was therefore first of all an event: the preaching of Jesus and the proclamation of his disciples who said that he was resurrected, that he appeared to a certain number of witnesses, and that he would return in glory.

The first Christians may have thought that the return of Jesus was near, that Jesus was going to manifest himself soon. They had neither the time nor the need to write

[12] Heine 1968: 511.

this message. At most, one could write to the community to whom one had preached this extraordinary event, to ask it to wait patiently, not to lose hope. This is the content of the oldest texts of the New Testament, the two letters of St Paul to the Christians of Thessalonica. It was only in a second stage that they began to collect the sayings of Jesus, which contained rather remarkable expressions. It seems that they established lists of sayings, as well as of miracles, to which the four evangelists had access, and that these were combined with a historical framework, in order to produce the Gospels from these two sources.

We, therefore, have an event which is recounted afterwards in a book, but the essential was the event, not the book.

Islam

Islam is also an event: the first fact of Islamic history that we know by independent, identifiable sources is the seventh-century conquest by Arab tribes of the southern Mediterranean and of the Middle East to Iran. The origin of this expansion seems to be the preaching of an exceptional leader who succeeded in allying these tribes by inaugurating a conquest, perhaps of the entire world, of a vast territory in any event. The sayings of this preacher were collected at a date that can hardly be determined. According to Muslim tradition, Muhammad would have begun receiving messages from above towards 610 or 615. After having preached to his compatriots of Mecca without great success, around 622 he went to Medina, where he received a better welcome. He then would have returned with a force to Mecca a short while before his death in 632.

We do not know exactly when the Quran was brought together.[13] According to the dominant tradition, it would have been the third successor of Muhammad, Osman (ʿUthmān), caliph from 644 to 656, who established a unified text. He would have had a certain number of copies made in order to send to the principal centres of the Arab army; he would have had other texts burned, which explains why there is only one, the deviant sources having been destroyed. Western scholars do not accept this version of the facts for various reasons, including contradictions in the narratives. They themselves, however, have arrived at contradictory conclusions.

The book plays in Islam, as a mode of life producing a civilization, a special place. It was necessary to give rules of life to all these conquerors of an immense territory, so that they could distinguish themselves from others. These rules were sought in the Quran. There they found certain rules attributed to God himself, for example, concerning questions of inheritance, marriage, of penal law. This however amounted to very little. They, therefore, were completed by declarations of the prophet, real or supposed, which became the source of law. What Muhammad, the perfect man, did,

[13] See de Prémare 2002 and his excellent little book, de Prémare 2004.

the Muslim ought to be able to do also, unless the text specifies that something was a privilege of the prophet (e.g. Q. 33: 50).

The Idea of Revelation

The concept of 'revealed religion' is also deceptive, because 'revelation' does not have the same meaning in the three religions.

What is revealed in Judaism is the history of the people of Israel. This history is more than the indifferent context within which something of God would have been revealed. The events themselves are at once the means of revelation and its object. The commands contained in the Torah were given by God at a certain moment in this history. Among them, which were directly revealed? The rabbis discussed the question: The entire Torah? The ten commandments? Solely the Name of God, all the rest having been uttered by Moses?

For Christianity, the revealed object is not the New Testament, but the person of Christ himself; the book only recounts the history, reports the teaching, of this person.

In Islam, the revealed object is truly the book; the person of Muhammad, at least in primitive Islam, had little importance. This is why one can consider Islam to be the sole religion of the book in the strict sense. For Islam, the Quran has for its author not Muhammad but God who dictated it to him; Muhammad was merely the scribe. In the same way, the author of *Paradise Lost* was Milton, not the daughter to whom, having become blind, he dictated his poem.

In Judaism and Christianity, the holy book is an inspired book, that is to say, written and composed by men who are 'aided' by God, in such a way that they do not teach any errors concerning his nature or his will. But nothing prevents the Bible from containing errors of fact, for example, in matters of chronology, nor from containing a vision of the physical universe that today is completely passé. For Islam, the Quran *cannot* contain error, contradiction, or supersedable content. What seems to be so is rectified in passages that are assumed to have been subsequently revealed. It is necessary that everything in the Quran be true, even definitive. That is why an abundant, and regularly revised, literature attempts to show, with each new scientific discovery, that it was contained in the Quran.

If the revealed *objects* differ, the revealed *content* of these objects differs as well. For Judaism and Christianity, revelation is a self-manifestation of God by himself. A manifestation of God which, because it is personal, necessarily remains mysterious. For Islam, God does not manifest himself as he is in himself, but only expresses his will in uttering commands. And there is no question of him entering into human history by contracting an alliance with man.

Thus, the presence of a book, a fact common to all three religions, masks three different ways of relating to that book. These, in turn, flow from the three different ideas of the way in which these sacred books were communicated to men.

Three religions?

One can extend these observations with an even more provocative question. Is it the case that *three* religions really exist?

How do the Three Religions Distinguish Themselves from Each Other?

Let us begin with Christianity. It is a form of Judaism. Jesus of Nazareth was a Jew, the twelve apostles as well, as was St Paul and the other authors of the New Testament. Christianity began as a sort of Jewish history, then it gradually, and painfully, separated itself from Judaism. On one hand, because Christians—those who followed St Paul—turned to the pagans to announce the good news of the resurrection. On the other hand, because the Jews considered the Christians to be heretics, and excluded them from the community. A tension emerged which ended with the gradual separation of the two religions, but from an initial unity.

Islam in contrast was born independently of Israel, far from the Holy Land, and among a people that was not Jewish. Muhammad was neither Jewish nor Christian. According to traditional history, he was rebuffed by the rabbis of Medina who refused to recognize his message. This is why he 'theorized' this difference, by claiming, as we saw, a connection with Abraham prior to the law of Moses and the life of Jesus.

Three religions therefore, or two? In a certain way, one can consider that we are in the presence of two 'demi-religions', on one hand, Judaism and the Christian rending of Jewish unity, and on the other, a religion, Islam, which one can consider, depending upon one's view, as a second, or third, religion.

Three Books?

The answer to this question is not simple because Christianity has a 'double' holy book which includes the holy book of Judaism. The expression 'the Bible' merits attention. To say 'the Old and the New Testament' seems obvious. However, to retain the Old Testament was not obvious; during the second century CE primitive Christianity was tempted to discard the Old Testament. This was the endeavour of Marcion. For him, the God of the Old Alliance was a God of wrath, who was supplanted by the God of love of the gospel.[14] The church did not follow this path, however, considering Marcion to

[14] See the great book—finally available in French (even though it was published in 1924)—of A. von Harnack, *Marcion: l'évangile du Dieu étranger. Une monographie sur l'histoire de la fondation de l'Église catholique*, trad. B. Lauret et al. (Paris: Le Cerf, 2003).

be a heretic; it retained the paradox of a double holy book. Judaism and Christianity therefore have in common the Old Testament. The New Testament constitutes the way in which Christians interpret the events of the life of Jesus in the light of what had been announced, at least according to them, in the Old Testament.

Islam in contrast has a holy book that is proper to it. It is not understood as a sort of 'Third Testament'. In fact, as we have seen, it is a fundamental teaching of Islam, without which it probably could not exist, that the books appealed to currently by the other two religions are not genuine. Islam, therefore, has no need of either the Old or the New Testament. In practice, it does not read them, sometimes it even forbids their being read.

We have already observed that two-and-a half religions, rather than three, exist. In the same way we have two-and-a half books rather than three, with the difference between Judaism and Christianity residing, rather naturally, in the reading given of the Old Testament, quite different in the two religions.

Conclusion

The use of the three expressions I just studied arises, to be sure, from the best will in the world. People seek to discern the common elements upon which they are all agreed, in order to make possible a productive dialogue. However, we know where good intentions often lead. In fact, the vocabulary I criticized gives rise to confusions rather than clarity. It masks real differences underneath a surface harmony. As a result, it produces the opposite of what it desires. If one wants to have a real dialogue, one must begin by respecting the other. This implies that one understand him as he understands himself, taking the words he uses with the meaning he gives them, and accepting the initial situation of disagreement, in order to move forward toward better understanding.

References

Arnaldez, R. 1983. *Trois messagers pour un seul Dieu.* Paris: Albin Michel.

Arnaldez, R. 1993. *À la croisée des trois monothéismes: une communauté de pensée au Moyen Âge.* Paris: Albin Michel.

Brague, Rémi. 1999. *La Sagesse du monde: histoire de l'expérience humaine de l'univers.* Paris: Fayard.

Brague, Rémi. 2005. *La Loi de Dieu: histoire philosophique d'une alliance.* Paris: Gallimard.

Dagorn, R. 1981. *La Geste d'Ismaël d'après l'onomastique et la tradition arabes.* Geneva: Droz.

de Prémare, A.-L. 1989. *Joseph et Muhammad: le chapitre 12 du Coran.* Aix-en-Provence: Université de Provence.

de Prémare, A.-L. 2002. *Les Fondations de l'islam: entre écriture et histoire.* Paris: Le Seuil.

de Prémare, A.-L. 2004. *Aux origines du Coran: questions d'hier, approches d'aujourd'hui*. Paris: Téraèdre.

Diels, H. and W. Kranz. 1922. *Die Fragmente der Vorsokratiker: griechisch und deutsch*. Berlin: Weidmannsche Buchhandlung.

Fradkin, H., trans. 2000. 'Moses Maimonides: Treatise on the Resurrection'. In R. Lerner, *Maimonides' Empire of Light: Popular Enlightenment in an Age of Belief*. Chicago: University of Chicago Press, 154–77.

Gallez, E. M. 2005. *Le Messie et son prophète: aux origins de l'Islam*. Versailles: Éditions de Paris.

Gimaret, D. 1988. *Les Noms divins en Islam: exégèse lexico-graphique et théologique*. Paris: Le Cerf.

Gisel, P. 2006. *Les Monothéismes: judaïsme, christianisme, islam, 145 Propositions*. Geneva: Labor et Fides.

von Harnack, A. 2003. *Marcion: l'évangile du Dieu étranger. Une monographie sur l'histoire de la foundation de l'Église catholique*, trans. B. Lauret et al. Paris: Le Cerf.

Hawting, G. R. 1999. *The Idea of Idolatry and the Emergence of Islam: From Polemic to History*. Cambridge: Cambridge University Press.

Heine, H. 1968. *Geständnisse*. In *Werke*, Vol. IV: *Schriften über Deutschland*, ed. H. Schanze. Frankfurt am Main: Insel.

Ḥusayn, Ṭaha. 1926. *Fî 'sh-shi'r al-jâhilî* [*Sur la poésie antéislamique*]. re-edn. Cairo: Dâr al-Nahâr, 1995.

Ibn al-Kalbî, Hicham. 1969. *Les Idoles* [*Kitâb al-Asnâm*], ed. and trans. W. Atallah. Paris: Klinck-sieck.

Jeffery, A. 1952. *The Qur'ân as Scripture*. New York: Russell F. Moore.

Jenkins, T. A., ed. 1924. *La Chanson de Roland*. Boston: Heath.

Lazarus-Yafeh, H. 1992. *Intertwined Worlds: Medieval Islam and Bible Criticism*. Princeton: Princeton University Press.

Le Coz, R., ed. 1992. *John Damascene: écrits sur l'Islam. Sources chrétiennes*. Paris: Cerf.

Luxenberg, C. 2004. *Die syro-aramäische Lesart des Koran: Ein Beitrag zur Entschlüsselung der Koransprache*. 2nd edn. Berlin: Schiler.

Maimonides. 1972. *Igrot (Letters)*, ed. J. Kafih. Jerusalem: Mosad ha-Rav Kook.

Maimonides. 1989. *Responsa (Tshuvot HaRambam)*, ed. J. Blau. Jerusalem: MA.

Sibony, D. 1992. *Les trois monothéismes: Juifs, Chrétiens et Musulmans entre leurs sources et leurs destins*. Paris: Le Seuil.

PART II

COMMUNITIES

CHAPTER 7

ISLAMO-CHRISTIAN CIVILIZATION

RICHARD W. BULLIET

THE phrase 'Islamo-Christian civilization' first appeared in 2004 in the book *The Case for Islamo-Christian Civilization* by historian Richard W. Bulliet. It was coined with a twofold purpose. First, in the aftermath of the terrorist attacks of 9/11, it was proposed as a way of focusing on the shared history and characteristics of the Islamic and Christian religious communities, rather than on past and current episodes of enmity between them. It followed the pattern of 'Judaeo-Christian civilization', a phrase that came into vogue in the 1950s as an oblique avowal of the post-Holocaust mood of interfaith reconciliation in Europe and America. Secondly, it was proposed as a way of encouraging historical and conceptual investigation of the great extent of overlap and parallel growth between the two religions that manifested itself in myriad ways over many centuries. It took as an axiom this notion: the greater the recognition of a sibling relationship between Islam and Christianity, the better the prospects for peaceful coexistence in future years.

Half of the people in the world profess either Christianity or Islam. Within each of these vast communities there are variant interpretations that stray far from the earliest versions of the faith. As a rule, believers who define their faith by adherence to what they understand those earliest versions to be exhibit hostility toward, or at most grudging toleration of, interpretations that came into being at a later point in time. Within Christianity, Catholics went through centuries of militant opposition to Protestants, and many Protestants and Catholics find it difficult to grant full acceptance to Mormonism, Christian Science, and other comparatively recent interpretations of Christianity. Within Islam, it is difficult to assign chronological priority to either Sunnism or Shiʿism, but Sufi organizations and branches of Shiʿism that emerged at comparatively late dates, such as the Nuṣairīs and the Druze, initially encountered hostility from the older versions of the faith. Interpretations that have emerged even more recently, such as the Bahais and the Aḥmadis, still face widespread rejection as versions of Islam.

For later versions of a faith to encounter difficulty in establishing their legitimacy in the eyes of those who adhere to earlier versions is normal in religious history, but this does not generally prevent the sundry versions being gathered under a single umbrella for purposes of identification. That is to say, when people speak of Christianity today, they group Catholics, eastern Orthodox, and Protestants together despite the undeniable histories of enmity within Christendom, just as estimates of the world Muslim population group Sunnis and Shiʿis together despite their manifest differences, and in some contexts, murderous hostility. This being the case, how difficult can it be to look beyond the historical episodes of Muslim–Christian warfare and vilification, which were no greater in dogmatic intensity or bloodthirstiness than those between Catholics and Protestants or between Sunnis and Shiʿites, and group Christianity and Islam together as a single Islamo-Christian civilization encompassing half the world?

If we go back to the early days of Islam, it is apparent that the first Muslims were no more certain that they were pioneers of a new religion than were the first followers of Jesus. Scholars sometimes use the term 'believers', *muʾminun* in Arabic, for Muhammad's earliest followers and refer to the early community that formed around Jesus' disciples after the crucifixion as 'the Jesus movement' in order to account for the time that elapsed before the words Muslim and Christian became fixed as the signifiers of new faith communities. When the distinctiveness of Islam became universally recognized remains a matter of debate, but medieval sources reflecting Christian viewpoints on the matter express ambivalence for several centuries. To medieval Christians, it seemed quite possible that Islam was a Christian heresy, just as Protestantism would seem to be to Roman Catholics a millennium later. After all, many Germanic peoples followed the Egyptian bishop Arius in his Unitarian teaching that Jesus was not truly or fully God, but rather a man who became divinized at the time of his baptism. Yet the Arians are always classified as Christians, albeit of heretical belief.

The *Gospel of Barnabas*, an account of the life of Jesus dating in the extant Italian and Spanish versions to the sixteenth century, provides evidence that some Christians and/or Muslims—the actual author is unknown—never gave up the idea that the two religions were one. Not only does the 'gospel' mirror the details about Jesus' life contained in the Quran while including the substance of the New Testament Gospels, but it explicitly 'predicts' the coming of Muhammad, as when God says: '"When I shall send thee into the world I shall send thee as my messenger of salvation, and thy word shall be true, insomuch that heaven and earth shall fail, but thy faith shall never fail." Mohammed is his blessed name' (*Barnabas* 97.10).

Was it political and military success that reified Islam's position as a separate faith? Or was it perhaps the bewilderment and fear of the Christians who saw the majority of their brothers and sisters in faith absorbed within the Muslim caliphate, ultimately to convert in large numbers to Islam over a period of some four centuries? There is no way of telling. If one looks, however, at the earliest widespread public avowal of Islam accessible to people of all faiths, namely, the gold and silver coinage in Arabic script that began to be issued in year seventy-six of the hijra, it is easier to see the caliphate as an economic power focused on the Arab people than as the institutional embodiment of a new religion. There was no iconic equivalent of the cross to symbolize doctrinal difference, and the words of the Quran that appeared on the coins would have conveyed very little to most people in an era when fewer than 5 per cent of the population of the caliphate could actually read the Arabic script.

What would have made Islam seem like a branch of Christianity rather than an absolutely separate religion? First and foremost, quranic revelation portrayed Jesus as a divine messenger who brought a sacred book to the Israelites and predicted the coming of Muhammad: 'Jesus, the son of Mary, said: "O children of Israel! Behold, I am an apostle of God unto you, [sent] to confirm the truth of whatever there still remains of the Torah, and to give [you] glad tidings of an apostle who shall come after me, whose name shall be Ahmad [i.e. Muhammad]"' (Q. 61: 6). The virginity of Mary was similarly affirmed. Jesus' death on the cross was denied, but that was not an unheard-of view among early Christians who followed the so-called Docetist heresy.

Close Muslim readers of the New Testament further pointed to passages that could be taken to imply that Jesus would send another 'Comforter' or 'Intercessor'—Greek *paraklētos*, sometimes taken as a misspelling of *periklytos* meaning 'praised one', i.e. Muhammad—to care for people after his own departure. 'Nevertheless I tell you the truth: it is to your advantage that I go away, for if I do not go away, the Paraclete will not come to you; but if I go, I will send him to you. And when he comes, he will prove the world wrong about sin and righteousness and judgement' (John 16: 7–8). And again: 'If you love Me, keep My commandments. Then I will ask the Father, and He will give you another Paraclete to be with you forever. He is the Spirit of Truth whom the world cannot receive, for it does not see Him nor know Him, but you know Him, for He is ever with you and will be in you' (John 14: 16–17).

Eminent Muslim scholars repeatedly interpreted these passages as predictions of the coming of Muhammad, or as intimations of the End Times of the world when a Messiah ('anointed one'), known to both Sunni and Shiʿite Muslims as the *Mahdī* ('the right guide'), would come to redeem a sinful world. In that eschatological context, which was elaborated extensively in the collections of Muhammad's sayings, or *ḥadīth*, Muslim tradition strongly affirmed that Jesus would return in the End Times to combat and defeat the demonic Antichrist, known to Muslims as the *Dajjāl*, and thus pave the way for the arrival of the *Mahdī*, who would preside over a millennium of peace and justice.

Christian theologians, naturally, did not share these Muslim interpretations. They saw John's verses dealing with the Paraclete as references to the Holy Spirit, one of the three components of the Trinity, despite the implication in the cited verses that the Paraclete had not yet arrived while the Holy Spirit figured in Jesus' baptism. But the effort of the Muslims to see Muhammad's coming predicted in the Bible, both in the Old and the New Testaments, was parallel to the systematic Christian effort to interpret the Old Testament as a prediction of the coming of Jesus Christ and his church. Both Muslims and Christians, in other words, sought to portray their spiritual founders as fulfilling prophecies found in earlier scripture.

In hindsight, it seems apparent that Islam was not just a new version of Christianity. Rather, they did indeed become separate religions regardless of any ambiguity, or efforts at doctrinal reconciliation, that may have existed in the first centuries after Muhammad. Yet hindsight changes depending on how far past the history is that one is scrutinizing. It is easy to find Protestant and Catholic leaders around the year 1600 who denied the validity of one another's faith, just as it is easy to find Catholic and Orthodox leaders in 1100 who rejected one another's version of Christianity, or Protestant preachers today who cannot accept the Mormon brand of Christianity. Eventually, however, once many battles had been fought, Protestant, Catholic, and Orthodox Christians came grudgingly to accept one another as Christians. And they may all eventually agree to accept under the Christian umbrella the Church of Jesus Christ of Latter Day Saints (the Mormons) and Korea's Unification Church, established by Sun Myung Moon, who represents himself as the Messiah and the Second Coming of Jesus Christ.

By some measures, Islam is closer to Christianity doctrinally than either the Mormons or the Unification Church. To be sure, Islam denies the Trinity, as have various Christian sects over the centuries from the Arians to the Unitarians. But the revelations contained in the Quran and the traditions preserved in the *ḥadīth* echo and reiterate the traditions of the Jews and Christians who were living at the time of Muhammad and contain almost none of the extra-biblical content that pervades the Book of Mormon, especially in its account of Jesus appearing in the Americas after his resurrection and his establishment there of a community of believers. Nor is there any quranic parallel to Sun Myung Moon's claim that he is the Messiah who has come to complete the unfinished mission of Jesus. Muhammad is one of God's Messengers, not a Messiah. If a sufficient degree of hindsight someday allows the Mormons and the Unification Church to be fully accepted as parts of the world Christian community, then it would be absurd to deny the possibility of a similar reconceptualization of Islam.

Except that Muslims would thereby lose their independent identity and history as a separate and remarkably successful religion. There are Muslims who do, in fact, consider themselves Christians by virtue of the reverence they feel for Jesus as a Messenger of God, but they subordinate this sort of affiliation to their primary identity as Muslims. Are there Christians who feel that they are also Muslims? Perhaps, particularly among those individuals who are attracted to Sufism. But no amount of hindsight is likely to see the concept of Christianity engrossed into the concept of Islam, if only because the former is six centuries older than the latter.

The term Islamo-Christian recommends itself as an epithet signifying the vast degree of overlap between the two faiths, a degree of overlap that is significantly greater than the overlap suggested by the commonplace term Judaeo-Christian. Use of this term encourages a comparison between Islam and Christianity that can yield valuable insights into each religion's history and institutional structure. What follows outlines some of the lessons that can be learned by exploring the common characteristics of Islamo-Christian civilization.

Hellenism

Both Christianity and Islam emerged from the philosophical, institutional, and cultural milieu of Hellenism. Over time, the major Latin and Greek writings of the Hellenistic era became available to people of both faiths in their own languages. The learned elite valued these works as essential underpinnings of their culture and worked diligently to refine and augment them, and to harmonize them with their scriptures. When Christians became aware of the trove of Hellenistic lore available in Arabic translations of classical texts, they eagerly rendered those works into Latin. By contrast, when Muslims with a knowledge of these texts travelled to India and China, they found no special interest in what they contained. Practitioners of Chinese or Ayurvedic medicine were not eager for the insights of Galen, nor did Confucian and Hindu philosophers seek enlightenment in the works of Aristotle, Avicenna, and Averroes. This Hellenistic substrate accounts for many of the shared cultural traits of Islamo-Christian civilization, as well as for the great dissimilarity among Muslim and Christian cultural traits in the lands outside the ambit of Hellenism that the two religions spread to from the fourteenth century, mostly in Asia, sub-Saharan Africa, and the western hemisphere.

Abrahamic Scripture

Islam and Christianity obviously share certain scriptural elements present in the Old Testament. Does this make it plausible to conceive of a Judaeo-Islamo-Christian civilization? Not easily. Islam recognizes parts of the Torah, particularly the accounts of the creation, some patriarchal stories from Noah to Moses, and a few tales from the era of David and Solomon, but not the books of prophecy. Of the New Testament, the four Gospels make a limited contribution to Muslim belief, but the later books virtually none. In addition, Islamic law bears similarities to Jewish law, particularly in the techniques by which the law is derived from sacred sources. As for Christianity, the Old Testament is accepted *in toto*, but not Jewish law. Judaism, of course, makes no recognition of non-Judaic elements in the New Testament and the Quran. What the three faiths share, therefore, is mostly cosmology and whatever lessons can be read into the tales of the patriarchs and kings. The absence of common scripture-based engagement with Christology, salvation, proselytization, and apocalypse, which arise in Christianity and Islam but only minimally, if at all, in Judaism, provides a narrow base on which to postulate a tripartite civilizational identity. The social reality of Judaism being restricted to a small, kinship defined, population after the destruction of the Second Temple in 70 CE, and of Christianity and Islam becoming enormous, multi-ethnic, world-spanning religious systems in the subsequent centuries, underlines this limitation.

Sin and Salvation

Most versions of Islam and Christianity incorporate an expectation that individual believers will be awarded the pleasures of Paradise or the torments of Hellfire in a last judgement that will bring earthly history to an end. Islamo-Christian imaginings of the End Times anticipate a Messiah, known to Muslims as the Mahdī; an alluring demonic figure, the Antichrist for Christians and the *Dajjāl* for Muslims, whom the naive will follow to their doom; and the reappearance of Jesus, as the Messiah for Christians and as the heroic slayer of the *Dajjāl* for Muslims.

Both components of Islamo-Christian civilization have experienced repeated episodes of millenarian expectations, often accompanied by social or political turmoil, and repeated anxieties about God punishing the community for moral wrongdoing. Christians and Muslims alike saw the Mongol invasions of the thirteenth century as punishments for sin. Some Christians felt the same way about the Arab conquests of the seventh century, the Black Death of 1348, the Ottoman conquests of the fifteenth century, and even the terrorist attacks of 9/11. Some Muslims similarly saw the Crusades as a divine punishment.

Though both religions have differing and complex, but generally parallel, ideas about what will determine a believer's fate in the hereafter, punishing sin in the here and now can inspire wide support. In Islam, the phrase 'commanding the right and forbidding the wrong' has a long history of warranting intrusive action to correct wayward groups or individuals. Destroying wine jars and breaking musical instruments constituted a theme for this kind of corrective behaviour. Though it has been argued that this is a uniquely Muslim behaviour pattern, it has in fact been extremely common in American Protestantism. Twentieth-century Muslim leaders sometimes praised America's prohibition movement, including physical attacks on saloons, as a highpoint of Christian culture. Moreover, Protestants and Catholics alike participated in crazed witch-hunts that tortured and killed tens of thousands of women who were regarded by their neighbours as social deviates.

Hyper-awareness of the imminence of divine judgement and the wages of sin has recurred repeatedly among both Christians and Muslims. Islamic tradition maintains that a renewer or revivifier of the faith, called a *mujaddid*, will appear at the beginning of each century. Calls upon Christians to repent of their sins and live every day as Jesus would have them live have again and again found receptive audiences. Polling has revealed that over half of America's evangelical Protestants expect the End Times to occur before the year 2050. Messianic expectations, with parallel emphases on forswearing sinful behaviours, excite many Muslims as well.

It may well be that these forceful and recurrent expectations contribute to some elements of Islamo-Christian civilization being inclined to expect change rather than embrace unchanging tradition. The idea of 'progress' is not without theological underpinnings.

Spirituality and Mysticism

Both branches of Islamo-Christian civilization accepted spiritual and mystic otherworldliness even as they elaborated clerical, legal, and governmental structures that focused on the mundane world. In Christianity, otherworldliness first took the form of individuals and groups living apart from society as monks and nuns, and later became manifest in the doctrines and lifestyles of certain groups of Protestants, like the Quakers. In Islam, an early proliferation of non-communal ascetics and mystics (Sufis) evolved into an ever-growing network of Sufi brotherhoods after the thirteenth century. Individual Sufis in the early centuries were ecstatic mystics seeking union with God. Within the brotherhood structure, ecstasy was routinized. A *shaikh* could guide a devotee toward divine union, but most brethren never attained such a level.

Several concerns that contributed to the eventual emergence of Protestantism simultaneously, that is, in the twelfth to fifteenth centuries, contributed to the coalescence of Islamic spirituality into brotherhoods (*turuq*). The languages of common people became spiritual vehicles alongside Latin and Arabic. Expressions of Islamic mysticism filled volumes of poetry in Persian, Turkish, and Urdu. Christian mystics produced parallel works in Provençal, German, and other languages. Christians and Muslims alike attributed charisma to local saintly figures who were not always credentialled as clergy or *ʿulamā*. Movements led by people like Peter Waldo and John Wycliffe stirred Christians. In Islam, Sufi *shaikhs* and descendants of the prophet received local allegiance and, after their deaths, shrine visitations. Collective religious expression grew alongside a more passive witnessing of church pageantry, or a similarly passive reverence for the strictures of Islamic law. Sufi brotherhoods instituted *dhikrs*, or vocal or performance remembrances of God, in which all brethren took part. Protestants instituted congregational singing. Christians who were poor in worldly goods but spiritually rich formed communes of Beguines and Beghards outside the framework of monastic institutions, while in Islam a proliferation of Sufi convents and rules of behaviour manifested a parallel devotion to poverty in the name of God. Overall, the monopoly on religious authority claimed by Christian clergy and Muslim legists (*fuqahā*) came into question.

Why these changes in the popular attitudes of Christians and Muslims toward their respective faiths took place simultaneously in Islam and Christianity is uncertain. But their eventual resolution in the growth of Protestantism and the proliferation of Sufi brotherhoods strongly affected the religious environments of the two faiths after 1500. Conflict with the Catholic hierarchy led Protestants to emphasize militancy more than otherworldliness. In Islam the emphasis was reversed, though some Sufi orders did become militarized.

Conversion

Seeking and welcoming converts has characterized both Islam and Christianity throughout their histories. Requirements for 'membership' have generally been low, often amounting to little more than a willingness of proselytes to self-identify as Muslims or Christians. This has made possible a large array of sects, pietistic groups, and syncretic movements catering to individuals who take comfort in retaining some elements of their old religious traditions after formal or nominal adoption of a Christian or Muslim identity. Conversion rituals and traditions explicitly exclude membership qualifications based on language, colour, ethnicity, or previous religious identity.

State and Law

Throughout history, Islamo-Christian civilization has been inextricably intertwined with governing and legal institutions. Though modern Christians living in secular societies often cite Jesus' command to render unto Caesar that which is Caesar's as a basis for a strict separation of church and state, Christianity has a consistent history of maximal involvement with governing structures from the time of the Emperor Constantine (*c.*320) down to the nineteenth century. Many Christians continue today to believe that their religious and moral views should be taken into account by the state. For its part, Islam has a governing tradition that goes back to the prophet Muhammad, develops in a series of avowedly religious caliphates, sultanates, and emirates, and continues to appeal to many Muslims today despite a general turn toward secular governance in the nineteenth century.

As a legal system, the elaboration of canon law by the Roman Catholic church lost much of its relevance in the course of the Wars of Religion between Protestants and Catholics in the sixteenth century. Protestantism and Orthodox Christianity never adumbrated law codes comparable to those of the Catholic church. Islamic law, or *sharīʿa*, a much more extensive and elaborate phenomenon, suffered considerable shrinkage in the nineteenth century as civil, commercial, and criminal codes derived from European sources were adopted by secularizing governments. Unlike canon law, however, it remains a touchstone of Muslim identity and thus a significant factor in political affairs. Inasmuch as the *sharīʿa* never encountered a delegitimizing force as substantial as the Peace of Westphalia that confined Europe's legal systems within national boundaries and thus made law a matter of kings and parliaments rather than of popes and church councils claiming universal jurisdiction, Islamic law still retains a claim to supra-national authority that puts it at odds to some degree with the modern nation-state system.

Violence and Toleration

Islamo-Christian civilization is steeped in religiously sanctioned violence, but it can also embrace toleration. At its outset Christianity suffered persecution; but once in power, it eventually extirpated virtually every pagan cult in Europe. In some instances, the violence took the form of warfare followed by forced baptism of the defeated survivors. Charlemagne's wars against the Saxons are a case in point. During his first campaign he destroyed Irminsul, the pillar or tree trunk the Saxons believed sustained the world; and after his last he ruled that anyone persisting in their pagan belief should be killed. Later the Teutonic Knights in the Baltic region exercised a similar degree of warlike violence against the pagan Prussians. More often, however, bans on pagan beliefs and traditions were ordered and enforced by the Christian clergy without extensive bloodshed—unless one includes the witch-hunting craze. Zero tolerance of paganism was nevertheless assumed.

Ironically, despite explicit quranic condemnations of idol-worship, the Arab conquests that established the Muslim caliphate involved little or no forced conversion or slaughter of unbelievers. This is because the prior spread of Christianity through the Middle East and North Africa had already eliminated paganism from most areas outside the Arabian peninsula proper, and even there modern scholars have cast doubt on its extent. The Quran mandated tolerance for the Christian and Jewish populations that predominated in the conquest areas west of Iran, and the Arabs extended similar tolerance de facto to the Zoroastrians of Iran and Buddhists of Central Asia.

Contemporary Muslim and Christian spiritual leaders often renounce past violence and embrace, to a greater or lesser degree, some form of ecumenism. Yet each religion reserves the right to defend itself, as a religious community, when it feels it is under attack by the other. For an Osama bin Laden, this has meant portraying 'Crusaders and Jews' as groups that have been killing and injuring Muslims for decades. For President George W. Bush and President Barack Obama, this has meant recognizing what are called militant jihadist groups as a worldwide enemy. As leaders of a secular republic, both presidents have explicitly eschewed making a connection between these groups and the religion of Islam per se. However, many Christians in the United States and Europe do make such a connection. The degree of mutual distrust vividly recalls centuries of enmity between Catholics and Protestants, Catholics and Orthodox Christians, and Sunnis and Shiʿites.

Word and Language

Drawing on their Hellenistic philosophical substrate, both religions attribute great importance to words and language. Philosophically, this takes the form of identifying Jesus with a Neoplatonic *logos* and ascribing (co-)eternal status to the Quran as God's word. Muslims further consider the Arabic language the chosen vehicle of God's utterance to the extent of relegating all translations into other languages to a distinctly lower level of truth and reliability. Christians accepted the fact that the Bible was composed in Hebrew and Greek, but they place great reliance on translations, first into Latin and later into vernacular languages. Many regard the words of the Bible as literally true and divinely inspired regardless of the language they encounter them in. Memorization of the Quran in Arabic became a hallmark of Islam at a very early point. Memorization of the Mass, the psalter, and favourite hymns has played an important role in some Christian communities, but has often been confined to the clergy.

Writing systems stand in for religious identity. Texts in the Arabic, Roman, Greek, Cyrillic, Armenian, or Ethiopian scripts are typically taken as visual religious signifiers regardless of the actual language or the import of the words. Calligraphy became a medium of artistic expression in all of these sacred scripts.

Clergy

Religious specialists form a core element of both Muslim and Christian societies though they do not have a monopoly on scriptural knowledge. Catholic and Orthodox priests do exercise a monopoly over certain sacred rituals that is more clearly delineated in doctrine than are the ritual roles of mosque leaders (imams) and religious judges (*qāḍīs*) in Islam. This is less the case in Protestantism. Over the past two centuries it has become increasingly common for Christian laypeople and Muslims without formal religious credentials to play active roles in debating, interpreting, and innovating matters of faith.

The movement away from seeing clergy as the moral core of society contributed strongly to the emergence of currents of secular modernity in European Christianity from the seventeenth century onward, and from the nineteenth century onward in Islam, where the equivalent of the clergy are known as *ʿulamā*. This temporal difference explains many of the discordant views Muslims and Christians have entertained of one other in recent times, but overall, Islamo-Christian civilization shares a fairly consistent tradition of ordinary believers respecting or deferring to clergy/*ʿulamā* on matters of faith and morals. Clerical roles in, and in remonstrance against, government have recurred in both faiths.

Education and Mission

Though Christianity and Islam have not been unique as religions developing high-level educational institutions, they have expanded their institutional structures beyond those of any other faith. The common Hellenistic substrate of Islamo-Christian civilization partly accounts for this, though religious concerns long outpaced scientific or secular ones. Similarities in the organization of Muslim *madrasas* (higher Islamic colleges) and Christian universities, both of which proliferated from the fourteenth century onward, have suggested direct influences across confessional boundaries. This cannot be proven, but it is entirely plausible.

Law played a more important role in Islamic institutions than in Christian ones, where theology predominated. Both focused on training young men to address the concerns of their societies, unlike pre-university monastic practices that kept Christian scholars isolated from secular society. The Muslim focus on law fed graduates into legal and teaching careers while Christian theology entertained metaphysical discussions that paved the way for scientific enquiry. In the absence of a hereditary aristocracy, Muslim military and administrative elites often received specialized education within their respective institutions leading in modern times to a sharp divide between religious and governmental educational practices.

In the absence of the Roman Catholic commitment to clerical celibacy, whole families of Muslim scholars worked to advance various intellectual programmes. Family networks gave the *ʿulamā* a partial structural independence from state authority parallel to that which was secured in Christian society by the ecclesiastical hierarchy headed by the pope. Though the rise of Protestantism fractured the unity of the Roman church, the nascent Protestant denominations held fast to their doctrinal independence, and families of Protestant clerics sometimes came to resemble those of leading Muslim *ʿulamā*.

Missionary outreach became an important area of activity for educated clerics. Sufi *shaikhs*, who were often highly educated, gained particular prominence in forging syncretic relations with peoples in new lands who were in the process of shifting their identities to Islam. More normative, *madrasa*-trained, scholars played a missionary role in bringing heterodox communities, many of them originally inspired by Sufism, closer to the views of the Muslim mainstream. Christian missionaries played a similar dual role. Many devoted their careers to improving the lives and morals of other Christians. Others focused on bringing unbelievers into the fold.

At the present day, the United States and Saudi Arabia stand out in the commitment of some of their most devout citizens to missionary activity around the world. As at earlier points in history, some of this activity is doctrinally fundamentalist and revivalist in character while other movements operate through good works and personal witness for the faith in a spirit of ecumenical cooperation.

The Future of Islamo-Christian Civilization

The life or death of a catchphrase is inconsequential. However, Muslims and Christians will continue to interact far into a seemingly indefinite future. Whether their interaction will incline toward growing conflict or mutual tolerance cannot be predicted, but people who hope for the latter need tools to help their cause along. Viewing the two religions as estranged siblings that have the potential to rediscover, or reinvent, their family ties, and in so doing discover a peaceful *modus vivendi*, can be such a tool. Hysterical diatribes attributing the vilest of motives or the most sordid and deceitful origins to one side or the other can lead in the opposite direction.

As a matter of history, there is no denying the intimacy of contact and closeness of relationships between Islam and Christianity, just as there is no denying their eras of interfaith warfare and of constructive cultural borrowing. Judaism, the religion with the closest claim to being a third partner in faith, has, at least since 70 CE, lacked the numbers, the zeal for converts, the agency of state power, and the apocalyptic dreams of the other two. Despite the profundity of Judaism's contributions to both of its offshoots in the scriptural, legal, ethical, and philosophical arenas, its historical interactions with them have taken the form of discrimination, persecution, exclusion, and grudging tolerance rather than crusades, jihads, conquests, reconquests, and imperial domination. The details of the relations among the three, and separately between Jews and Christians and between Jews and Muslims, warrant close attention, both historically and today. But the bigger challenge is to understand the past, and prepare for the future, of relations between Islam and Christianity. The concept of Islamo-Christian civilization can be of value in that enterprise.

Suggested Reading

Aslan, R. 2011. *No God but God: The Origins, Evolution, and Future of Islam*, updated edition. New York: Random House.

Bulliet, R. W. 2004. *The Case for Islamo-Christian Civilization*. New York: Columbia University Press.

Cook, M. 2001. *Commanding Right and Forbidding Wrong in Islamic Thought*. Cambridge: Cambridge University Press.

Donner, F. M. 2010. *Muhammad and the Believers: At the Origins of Islam*. Cambridge, MA: Harvard University Press.

Makdisi, G. 1984. *The Rise of Colleges: Institutions of Learning in Islam and the West*. Edinburgh: Edinburgh University Press.

Toland, J. V. 2002. *Saracens*. New York: Columbia University Press.

CHAPTER 8

THE ABRAHAMIC RELIGIONS IN THE MEDITERRANEAN

DAVID ABULAFIA

I A Meeting-Point for the Three Religions

The Mediterranean has been a significant meeting-point for the three Abrahamic religions, while at the same time each of those religions identified as its place of origin lands a little away from the shores of the *Yam haGadol*, or 'Great Sea', which lay just over the horizon of the Jews and early Christians of Jerusalem, and further over the horizon of the early Muslims of Mecca and Medina. At certain points in the history of Judaism, lands to the east, notably Babylonia, were of far greater importance than the Mediterranean lands in the development of religious ideas and practices, and much the same can be said of early Islam. Adherents of the three religions jostled with one another in Iraq and Iran over many centuries. And yet the Mediterranean has been an exceptionally important place of interaction, competition, and, at times, of conflict among Jews, Christians, and Muslims, throughout the centuries since the rise of Islam. It has been a space in which members of these religions have defined their identity ever more sharply in relation to one another, in which sectarian divisions characterized all three religions, and in which there has existed a constant flow of population, as Jews migrated (or were deported, or expelled), as Muslims arrived as conquerors, and as the ethnic composition and sectarian identity of the Christian lands around the Mediterranean constantly mutated. One cannot, then, argue that these religions are in some fundamental way 'Mediterranean'; but it is impossible to deny that the Mediterranean provided a stage on which they were able to interact in positive and negative ways. In this chapter, the emphasis will be upon the themes of crystallization of identity and dispersion, though some attention will also need to be paid to the bloodier forms of interaction, epitomized by the Crusades and by the Ottoman confrontation with imperial Spain. Relations between sects within the three religions will not be treated here, except where they are relevant to the relationship to one of the other religions.

II Fuzzy Boundaries

There are still many open questions concerning the origins and permanence of Jewish dispersion across the Mediterranean. Cicero bears witness to the presence of Jews in Sicily during the latter days of republican Rome, while Roman Jews, who have preserved their distinctive liturgy, like to see themselves as a 2,000-year-old community. The slave trade apparently brought Jews into Etruscan lands even earlier. The continuities are impossible to prove, but one feature of the dispersion needs to be emphasized. It was the Judaean Jews rather than the Samaritans, their rivals in the Holy Land, who were mobile. The Samaritans ranged little further westwards than Egypt, although they experienced deportation eastwards, away from the Mediterranean; this exposed them in the early Byzantine period to mass extermination by imperial troops campaigning in Palestine. The Jews of Palestine had already undergone massive slaughter under Vespasian and Hadrian; but the presence of Jews much further afield provided a demographic reserve that rendered possible their survival through the calamities and persecutions of late antiquity and the early Middle Ages. Rome itself became home to many thousands of Jews, whose presence is documented both in the Jewish catacombs in the north-east of the modern city and in the synagogue of Ostia, which may have functioned for 400 years, and apparently contained a bake-house and classrooms.

It is uncertain how recognizable the Judaism practised by these people would have been to later generations of rabbinic Jews. The poet Juvenal wrote satirically about the Jews, and he shared general incomprehension about Sabbath observance. Although avoidance of pork was a well-known feature of Jewish life, it is probably impossible to establish whether an elaborate code of *kashrut* (Jewish dietary law) existed, or how widespread were conversion and intermarriage with non-Jews. In particular, the presence of 'God-fearers' who had not actually become Jews and were constrained only by the much simpler code of Noachide laws makes it hard to distinguish Jews of Palestinian descent from those who were gradually brought into the community. Among the latter, we certainly have to include circumcised slaves, who might continue to live a Jewish life (whatever that meant) after many became freedmen. Even if DNA evidence appears to show that a high proportion of Jews, right up to modern times, are descended from ancient inhabitants of Palestine, the argument that the Mediterranean world was a major theatre of conversion to Judaism in late antiquity and right up to the seventh or eighth century carries weight. This is a theme that has been heavily emphasized by some modern writers, although the claim (by Shlomo Sand) that the dispersal of the Jews is in effect a later myth cannot be seriously sustained.[1]

Patristic theologians such as John Chrysostom might inveigh against the Jews; stallholders in the bazaar in Constantinople might refuse to sell their produce to those who disagreed about the relationship between Father, Son, and Holy Ghost, but the boundaries between the faiths were much fuzzier than those examples might indicate. The vituperation expressed towards Judaism derived from a sense of bitter competition, not a wish to kick those who were already down. The wider public was attracted by ethical codes and religious aspirations that were not vastly different—love for one's neighbour, the hope that God would offer rewards in the next world if not in this one. The Christian martyr Pionius, who died at Smyrna in 250 during the Decian persecutions, refused to take part in the pagan cult at a time when both Jews and pagans were celebrating their festivals (possibly the Jewish festival of Purim and the pagan Dionysia—both times when drunkenness was more than tolerated). On such occasions the celebrations of Jews and Gentiles merged imperceptibly.[2] In the early fifth century, there is evidence that Jews and Christians coexisted peacefully in Minorca, in what the bishop described as 'easy acquaintance' (rather too easy for his liking), until, inspired by the arrival of the bones of the Protomartyr Stephen, the Christians marched on the major centre of Jewish settlement, Magona, and attacked the synagogue, after which they engaged in debate with the Jews, partly on these lines: 'if you truly wish to be safe and honoured and wealthy, believe in Christ.' In the end the Jews of Minorca were browbeaten into accepting Christianity, but it is impossible to escape the conclusion not just that Jews and Christians had been on good terms until St Stephen arrived, but that the boundaries between Judaism and Christianity had been very permeable, which was exactly what bishops disliked. Violence prompted the Jews of Minorca to convert; but mutual familiarity lessened the shock of conversion.[3]

To say that the boundaries between faiths were fuzzy is not to say that religion was a thin veneer and that belief was half-hearted—rather, the opposite: the existence of several layers of religious belief, including a thick pagan residue in some areas, gave religious life more, not less, intensity. A similar mistake is often made when looking at religion in Japan or China: there, a single individual can worship in many ways, just as ancient Mediterranean travellers might invoke the gods of the Phoenicians or Etruscans when far from home in Greece. These attitudes long persisted in the Mediterranean, and it is said that peasants in the countryside near Naples were sacrificing to pagan gods as late as the nineteenth century, 'just to be sure'. Many modern scholars emphasize that it was in a heavily laden atmosphere of religious interaction and competition that Islam was born: the Quran is full of references to Jews, Christians, and 'Sabeans'; and the Samaritans already proclaimed that 'there is no God but God and Moses is his prophet'. Nor is it clear that Muhammad's 'Jews', to whom the Quran

[1] Goldstein 2009; Sand 2009; also Wexler 2009.

[2] Lane Fox 1986: 481–2.

[3] Severus of Minorca 1996.

makes repeated reference, were rabbinic Jews, rather than Judaizing pagan tribes, or breakaway sects.[4] These characteristics of early Arabia were even more marked in the Mediterranean. Alongside religious syncretism we observe ethnic mixing, as Berbers, in particular, wandered in and out of Judaism, Christianity, and Islam. Whether Kahina, the Berber prophetess who resisted the Arab armies, was in some way Jewish is far from certain, but the arguments that the conquering armies that eventually ended up in Spain included Jews, Christians, and indeed pagans makes sense; the Islamization of the Berbers of the Maghrib was a slow process that was only completed in the twelfth century. One Berber tribe is said to have converted to Islam twelve times, as new waves of conquerors entered its territory from the east time and again, making their demands for submission (*Islam*), which were quickly obeyed and then as quickly forgotten. The existence of syncretic groups such as the Barghawata in western Morocco between the eighth and the twelfth centuries further reveals the interpenetration between the Abrahamic religions not very far from the Mediterranean, though more needs to be known about the apparently Jewish and Christian elements in their beliefs, and the extent to which they were attempting to create a Berber parallel to Islam using their own Berber alternative to the Quran; it is possible that the information we have concerning their beliefs and practices was doctored to make them appear less faithful to Islam than was actually the case.[5] The Islamization of Morocco was effected with the coming of the Almoravids in the eleventh century and the Almohads in the twelfth, but these movements too had a strong sense of tribal Berber identity, as will be seen shortly.

The Barghawata emphasized their identity as Masmuda Berbers. But ethnic mixing also characterized the early medieval Mediterranean, and left its mark on the relationship between the three religions. The Jewish example deserves particular attention, in view of the traditional assumption that this religious group sealed itself off from its neighbours by discouraging conversion and intermarriage. It is possible that Visigothic legislation forbidding circumcision was directed not at the children of professing Jews but at the practice of circumcising slaves, which had the convenient result that they could then count as Jews and handle wine for their Jewish masters. (It is also possible that much of this legislation was the result of confusion between one circumcised people, already present in Spain, the Jews, and another, the Arabs, of whose successful military campaigns, tending ever westwards, there was increasing awareness.) Later, in Muslim-ruled Spain (al-Andalus), Slav captives were brought into Jewish households, alongside the thousands of *Ṣaqāliba* who served Muslim and Christian masters; and again some, many, or maybe even most were made into proselytes.[6]

This ethnic mixing had parallels among the much larger Christian and Muslim communities. Just looking at al-Andalus, we can detect the arrival of Coptic Christians, Yemenite Arabs, and many other easterners during the eighth and ninth centuries. A protest movement among Córdoban Christians in the 840s, generated by the

[4] Newby 1986; Bowersock 2013.

[5] *Encyclopedia of Islam* (2nd edn), 'Barghawata'; cf. Iskander 2007.

[6] On this see Wexler 2009.

awareness that their culture was becoming Arabized and even Islamized, was stimulated by contact with the Christian monasteries of the Holy Land. Forty Christians denounced Islam in public and were put to death, which was exactly what they hoped to happen. Intermarriage between Muslim men and Christian women drew the children of these families away from Christianity towards Islam, though some of the martyrs were the product of such mixed marriages. Christians of high status, and probably others too, avoided pork, had their children circumcised in grand ceremonies, and thus assimilated into the dominant religion by a process of religious osmosis that at a certain point left them or their children with an Islamic identity, even if they had never formally converted.[7] The erosion of Christianity in al-Andalus has to be understood as part of a wider set of relationships, one that left the boundaries between the Abrahamic religions much more open than was to become the case after the tenth century. The status of the Christians and Jews as *dhimmīs* (protected peoples), paying additional taxes, sometimes the target of abuse, and, at least in theory, denied political office meant that Islam could be a lure, especially for those who hoped for a career at court (something similar is visible among the Jews and Samaritans at the Fatimid court in Egypt). Interestingly, though, the Jews did not assimilate on a similar scale to the Christians, and developed a different, but also intimate, relationship with Islam, borrowing religious ideas, poetic techniques, and attitudes to law and their sacred texts. The presence of Islam reinforced Spanish Judaism, while it weakened Spanish Christianity. The Judaism of al-Andalus became a mirror image of Islam, as the Jews adapted Arabic rhyming verse to Hebrew, as they assimilated Islamic ideas about the nature of God, and as they immersed themselves in Talmudic studies with the same vigour as Muslim students of *ḥadīth*.

The era of ill-defined boundaries came to an end at different times in different areas of the Mediterranean. Indeed, it lingered longest in the eastern Mediterranean. It was a phenomenon of frontier regions, above all. The Byzantine–Seljuq frontier region saw much crossing of boundaries, not just military, as raiding parties of *ghāzīs* and *akritai* roamed the open spaces of Anatolia, but religious crossing occurred too, well represented by the Gabras family; this was a noble Greek family, several of whose members reappear as Muslims under Turkish dominion.[8] In what are now Syria and Lebanon, the shading between communities remained grey, at least within the different religions: the Maronites and some Armenians accepted the pope's authority, even though their theological differences from Rome might have made a papal courtier uneasy. And in Syria sundry religious groups persisted that retained elements of pre-Islamic beliefs; some, like the Alawites and Druze, saw and still see themselves as true Muslims, but others, deeper into the interior, owed more to Zoroastrian and pagan beliefs, notably the Mandaeans, the Yazidis, and the elusive, and very possibly mythical, planet-worshipping Sabeans, who may simply be a misrepresentation of one of these groups.[9] In eleventh- and twelfth-century Egypt, the political ascendancy of the Shīʿah Fatimids could only be

[7] Coope 1985; Wolf 1988. [8] Bryer 1970.
[9] Chwolson 1856; cf. Hjärpe 1972.

sustained by tolerance towards the Sunni majority, not to mention the substantial Coptic and Jewish population. Rome too was a frontier region in that period, since to the south there lay extensive areas inhabited by Christians owing religious allegiance to Constantinople, even if in parts of Apulia and across the water in Dalmatia they followed a Latin liturgy. Southern Italy became the home to a Uniate liturgy, using Greek but acknowledging papal supremacy, that still survives in the monastery of Grottaferrata, at the very gates of Rome, founded by Nilus of Rossano at the start of the eleventh century. For the city of the popes lay not at the centre of the Catholic world but at its southern edge, even though it also lay at the centre of the greatly fragmented Christian *oikoumené* if one counted in Byzantium and the Christians of the Islamic Mediterranean.[10]

III Solid Boundaries

The important question is how this changed—how the indeterminate boundaries turned into walls. Here we are talking not just of lines on the map (as places such as Sicily became predominantly Latin Christian rather than Greek Christian) but of walls between the different communities in places where they coexisted side by side, as they did in *reconquista* Spain and in Norman Sicily. We can observe the crystallization of the religious groups into self-confident communities led by literate elites and wedded to codes of law embodied in the Talmud, in the evolving system of canon law, and in Muslim *ḥadīths* and fatwas. Among the Spanish Jews, for instance, the study of the Talmud seems to have developed in the tenth and eleventh centuries, thanks to the patronage of Ḥasdai ibn Shaprut, the courtier of the caliph of Córdoba, and Samuel ibn Naghrīla (Shemuel ha-Nagid), the vizier of the Berber king of Granada. The great revival of legal studies at Bologna and other Italian centres brought into existence codes of canon law built upon the *Decretum* of Gratian.[11] Increasing self-confidence was reflected in the explicit antagonism between and within the three religions: Latin Christian critiques of not just Judaism but of Greek Orthodoxy; Greek Orthodox critiques of Latin and Armenian Christianity (sometimes for being too 'Jewish'—as shown by the use of unleavened bread in the Mass!); sharp words from the eleventh-century Spanish Muslim ibn Ḥazm about Judaism, including accusations that Jews were secretly condemning Islamic beliefs; and, by the late twelfth century, heresy-hunting within the Latin Christian communities of the Mediterranean, particularly against the Cathars of Languedoc and Italy, who were themselves influenced by Byzantine heretical groups such as the Bogomils and beyond that by pre-Islamic religions of the Middle East. (The recently revived argument that the Cathars were a fantasy of the Catholic imagination, and particularly of the early Inquisition, ignores

[10] Llewellyn 1970. [11] Winroth 2000.

the survival of Cathar and Bogomil texts in Western Europe, in the former case strongly dualistic).[12]

In the Islamic world the increasingly sharp boundaries can be seen most clearly in the Maghrib and al-Andalus. The imposition of strict Sunni orthodoxy by the Almoravids in the eleventh century marks the final stage in the Islamization of the Berbers of Morocco, and an important stage in the Islamization of Berber tribes in the western Sahara. But the tribal nature of this process is revealed by the arrival of a radical challenge from the Almohad movement, encompassing Morocco, Algeria, Tunisia and parts of southern Spain, which seized control of the Almoravid capital at Marrakesh in the mid-twelfth century and imposed a Berber form of Islam (with prayers in Berber, as among the Barghawata), with a prophetic leader (establishing a new caliphate), and with a radical theology that proclaimed a return to the pristine purity of early Islam. Significantly, the Almohads had some difficulty with the concept of toleration for the Peoples of the Book, which has been maintained by their Almoravid predecessors, though with far greater strictness concerning the subordination of Christians and Jews. Although Almohad policy towards Jews and Christians varied from place to place and decade to decade, the Almohads presided over the extinction of Latin Christianity in the Maghrib and over the suppression of Jewish communities in parts of Spain and North Africa. In essence, they saw their system of beliefs as universal, and there was no room in them for the other Abrahamic faiths, nor indeed for Sunni Muslims.[13] Practical politics and underground resistance, especially in al-Andalus, rendered these ideals impossible to achieve; but the battle lines had been drawn. Already with the coming of the Almoravids, and the deportation of many Andalusi Christians to Fez (or the flight of Christians and Jews northwards to Toledo and Burgos), the struggle for control of the Iberian peninsula had mutated from a contest among many petty kings, Muslim and Christian, who were skilled at making alliances across the religious boundaries, into a Christian crusade against a Muslim jihad.

The boundaries also became more visible in the eastern Mediterranean as the crusading movement absorbed the energies of western Christendom from the late eleventh century onwards. While the establishment of Christian crusader states in what are now parts of Turkey, Syria, Lebanon, Israel, the Palestinian territories, and Jordan was initially seen from Cairo, and to some extent from Constantinople, as another irritating barbarian invasion, the crusader occupation of Jerusalem gradually generated an Islamic response, particularly under the late twelfth-century Kurdish leader Saladin. His unification of Syria with Egypt meant that the Latin kings of Jerusalem could no longer play off one Muslim neighbour against another. The shaykh of Shayzar, Usāmah ibn Munqidh, had hobnobbed with Frankish nobles, wryly observed the primitive medicine of his Christian neighbours, and was allowed to worship on the Temple Mount/Ḥaram ash-Sharīf. He saw the Franks as brave but

[12] I thus reject Moore 2012, and other works in that vein; see instead Barber 2013.

[13] Fromherz 2010; for a nuanced view of Almohad relations with Jews and Christians, see 'Religious Minorities under the Almohads', special issue of *The Journal of Medieval Iberian Studies*, 2 (2) (2010).

crude neighbours, a source of amusement more than hostility. By the time of Saladin the Haram mosques, converted into churches following the crusader conquest in 1099, had become the focus of a holy war for the recovery of what Muslims were reminded was their third holiest site.[14]

Two characteristics of this confrontation need to be emphasized. The Christian west was profoundly ignorant about Muslim beliefs; the translation of the Quran commissioned by Abbot Peter of Cluny in the middle of the twelfth century went under the unflattering title 'Law of Mahumet the pseudo-prophet', and was intended as a denunciation of Islamic beliefs. In many ways this ignorance persisted well into the eighteenth century. This did not, of course, preclude an interest in Arabic scientific works, or Greek works that were accessible (in Toledo and elsewhere) in Arabic translation, and this interest could extend to works of philosophy that had important religious implications, by Avicenna, Averroes, or the unidentified Avicebron (in fact the Spanish Jew ibn Gabirol). A meeting of minds was possible when contemplating questions such as how to prove the existence of God, where Thomas Aquinas could draw on Averroes and Maimonides, or in mystical circles where Ramon Llull could make use of Sufi contemplatives and where Abraham Abulafia's Kabbalah reveals a knowledge of Christianity and Islam that one might expect from someone born in Zaragoza in 1240.[15] On the ground, though, confusion persisted as to the status of Islam: a pagan cult built around the worship of Apollo and other gods (as in *The Song of Roland*)? Or a wild heresy, given the reverence shown to Jesus and Mary, ʿĪsā and Maryam? The general lack of curiosity also pervaded the merchant communities from Genoa, Pisa, Venice, and eventually Barcelona that gained a foothold in ports along the coasts of the Levant and the Maghrib.

There were, of course, some exceptions. A disputation recorded in 1286 between the Genoese merchant Ingheto Contardo and a Jew, which took place in Majorca, reveals a friendliness and sympathy between the two sides that was almost certainly far more widespread than hostile tracts denouncing the religious beliefs of the other side would suggest.[16] Tolerant attitudes are also visible in the works of Ramon Llull (1232–1316). Llull was unusually well informed and mild-mannered about Islam and Judaism; he was born in Majorca in 1232, very soon after the Christian conquest, and died in 1316, by which time the Muslim population of the island had fallen considerably. But he was regarded in his day as an enthusiastic eccentric, and even investigated for wrong belief. However, Llull's handbook on how merchants could engage in conversations about religion with Muslims, with a view to converting them, had no known users—and just as well, because public condemnation of Islam would only lead to expulsion or even execution. In his *Book of the Gentile and the Three Wise Men* he made plain his belief that Jews, Christians, and Muslims all worshipped the same God.[17] But he was insisting on this at a time when this was an unfamiliar idea—even

[14] Sivan 1968; Hitti 2000.
[15] Urvoy 1980; Hames 2000; Hames 2007.
[16] Limor 1994.
[17] Ramon Llull, *Book of the Gentile and the Three Wise Men*, in Bonner 1993.

Jews could find themselves branded as devil-worshippers, though this, admittedly, was not a general view. The hardening of attitudes in the late Middle Ages can also be observed in his native Majorca. There, at the end of the thirteenth century, the king of Aragon set aside an area of the capital city as a walled reserve in which Jews would be compelled to live. Although it was quite a spacious area, this segregation—the first example in a Mediterranean Christian kingdom—enhanced the view of the Jews as alien others whose presence, unless carefully controlled, might contaminate society.[18] No such act was performed for the Majorcan Muslims, but as far as is known they were not permitted a mosque and their numbers were in steep decline; and a few years earlier, in 1287, the entire population of Minorca, inhabited solely by Muslims, was sold into slavery by the Aragonese king. A hardening of attitudes can also be observed in Sicily and southern Italy. Conflict between Christians, including newly arrived 'Lombards' from mainland Italy, and Sicilian Muslims had been ignited following the death of King Roger II in 1154; he had tried hard to keep the peace between the Muslim and Greek communities who still constituted the vast majority of the island's population a hundred years after the Norman conquest of Sicily had begun.[19] By the early thirteenth century the Muslims had established an autonomous enclave in western Sicily and were in rebellion against the Crown. Frederick II crushed the rebellion and deported the entire Muslim population of Sicily to Lucera in southern Italy, over a period of years. Far from seeking to establish a Muslim foothold in southern Italy, Frederick sought to isolate the Lucerans from the Islamic world and, while his relations with the papacy remained equable, he encouraged Christian missions to persuade them to turn Christian. But he also valued them as soldiers and took pleasure in their dances and music; it was an ambiguous relationship, and they came to be treated as the ruler's *servi*, a term that (as when it was applied to Jews) varied in its meaning, but could be interpreted to mean 'slaves' when it was convenient to do so. In 1300 all the Luceran Saracens were sold as slaves to private buyers. The current king, Charles II of Naples, needed the money to finance his war for the reconquest of Sicily, which he had lost to the Aragonese; and he also detested the practices of 'Belial' that his courtiers had detected among the Muslims of Lucera. Religious identity and personal freedom or unfreedom were closely tied together. It is no surprise to find that the same king also unleashed a vigorous campaign against the Jews, apparently on the basis of the blood libel alleging that Jews used the blood of Christian boys in their Passover unleavened bread. During the 1290s it was difficult to live as a Jew in southern Italy, particularly in Apulia, and groups of *neofiti* came into being, converts to Christianity who maintained Jewish practices in secret. Not just people underwent conversion: synagogues, such as the one in Trani now known as Santa Maria Scolanova (i.e. 'the new synagogue'), were converted into churches.[20]

The stiffening of the boundaries can also be observed in Iberia, even though this was a region in which all three religions continued to coexist until the end of the fifteenth

[18] Abulafia 1994: 75–99. [19] Abulafia 1990; Abulafia 2004a.

[20] Abulafia 1996.

century, and in the case of Islam even into the sixteenth century. Rulers in Aragon, Castile, and the kingdoms of Navarre and Portugal adopted a pragmatic view of the presence of non-Christians, but also perpetuated a policy of toleration that was deeply rooted in Iberian history (and no doubt owed its existence to the toleration practised in al-Andalus). The Jews and Christians of al-Andalus had been treated as *dhimmīs*, but not, until the coming of the Almoravids, according to the strictest interpretation of dhimmitude; by comparison, the Jews and *mudéjars* (subject Muslims) of the Christian kingdoms were treated as the king's *servi*, as a literal part of the 'Royal Treasure', and like *dhimmīs* they paid a tax (that of the Muslims of Aragon was known as the *peyta*) and were in theory denied the chance to exercise authority over Christians.[21] Muslims played a significant role in the armies of Castile and Aragon, while Jews, some of whom also served as soldiers (though more rarely), functioned as royal tax collectors—members of families such as ibn Yaḥya and Benveniste in Aragon-Catalonia, and Abulafia in Castile. The rewards could even include permission to build a substantial synagogue, as can be seen in the surviving case of Don Samuel Abulafia's sumptuous Tránsito synagogue built in the 1350s, probably to compensate the Jews for damage to their synagogues from riots that took place during the Black Death. But it was a precarious existence: Don Samuel was accused of peculation by his possibly psychotic boss King Pedro the Cruel and put to death in 1360. The same Don Pedro was keen to support allies in the faction-ridden Muslim kingdom of Granada, of which more in a moment, and was criticized both for appearing in public in Arab robes and, inevitably, for his reliance on a Jewish treasurer. What the Tránsito synagogue reveals is that the relationship between the religions was triangular: the stucco decoration, contemporary with that of Pedro's Alcázar in Seville and parts of the Alhambra, is the work of *mudéjar* craftsmen, and it is adorned with inscriptions both in Hebrew and in Arabic.[22] As late as 1400 Jews continued to favour Islamic styles of architecture, as in the synagogue at Segovia (which also survives); this style apparently became a badge of identity, as did the continuing knowledge of Arabic, which could be harnessed in translation work. Alongside these still quite Arabized Jews we can count the Mozarabs of Toledo, an extraordinary community of Arabic-speaking Christians, who retained a separate identity and their own parish structure following the conquest of the city by the Christians in 1085, and whose distinctive liturgy and music survives to this day in Toledo cathedral.[23] Further evidence for the survival of some degree of mutual toleration can be found in the persistence of the *mudéjar* communities that could be found across Iberia—by the late fifteenth century this even applied to parts of northern Spain remote from the Mediterranean, as they dispersed northwards out of the conquered south.

One Iberian kingdom has barely been mentioned so far, contrary to the romantic view disseminated by tour guides in the Alhambra; Nasrid Granada, the Muslim kingdom that survived from 1250 to 1492, was not a haven of toleration for the three

[21] Abulafia, 2004b; Abulafia 2000.
[22] Dodds 1992: 124–8.
[23] Hitchcock 2008.

Abrahamic religions. Its Christian population was very small, as a result of the suppression of Christianity in the Almohad realms out of which the Nasrids carved their dominion. They were not Almohads at all, but strict Sunni Muslims following the Malikite interpretation of Islamic law. They did rule over a Jewish population, but that was much smaller than it had been in the eleventh-century kingdom of Granada, under the rule of the Berber Zirid dynasty; at that time Lucena and Granada itself had had large Jewish populations. As home to many Andalusian Muslims who had been displaced by the Christian conquest of other parts of southern Spain, Granada was marked by a strong sense of its Islamic identity, amply recorded on the walls of the Alhambra palaces.[24] Thus a sharp line divided Christian Spain, even while it contained a large Jewish and Muslim population, from the almost exclusively Muslim kingdom of Granada. This line became sharper after the conquest of Granada by Ferdinand and Isabella at the start of 1492: although they tolerated the practice of Islam for several years, rebellion led to its suppression in 1502–3, throughout the lands ruled by Castile (but in Aragon not until 1525).[25] And this coincided with the decision by these monarchs to expel all professing Jews from Castile, Aragon, Sicily, and Sardinia in 1492.

Here again the lines lie not exactly where one might expect. This decision, which had such implications for the religious map of the Mediterranean, was the result of the breaking down of barriers between Judaism and Christianity, as much as it was the result of the insistence on creating a new barrier. For in the aftermath of the anti-Jewish pogroms that broke out across Spain in 1391, large numbers of New Christians (*conversos*, Marranos) found themselves suspended between their old and their new religion, often ignorant about Christianity and unable for emotional reasons, or because they were indeed secret Jews, to abandon Jewish norms—dietary laws, the observance of festivals, circumcision, and so on.[26] Some *conversos* took comfort in the advice of Maimonides, itself based on the Muslim doctrine of *taqiyya*, that concealment of one's religion in time of adversity was acceptable. The expulsion of 1492 was an attempt, encouraged by the Inquisition, to remove professing Jews from society so that the converts and their descendants would not be drawn back to Judaism, as indeed happened, and continued to happen for centuries—there was something of a revival of crypto-Judaism in seventeenth-century Majorca, for instance.[27]

Yet one effect of the expulsion was to scatter the Sephardim across the Mediterranean (the Hebrew term *Sephardim*, 'Spaniards', is used here in its proper sense: Jews of Iberian origin or descent).[28] They coexisted with Andalusi Muslims in Fez and Tunis, often sharing the use of Spanish and remembering the words of long ballads about Moors and Christians. They became so dominant in the Jewish communities of Italy,

[24] Arié 1990; Harvey 1991. [25] Harris 2007; Coleman 2003.

[26] Yovel 2009. [27] Selke 1986.

[28] The regrettable and ignorant practice in modern Israel and elsewhere of calling all Mizraḥi, i.e. 'eastern', Jews *Sephardim* derives in part from the similarities between the liturgy of the Spanish Jews and those of Babylonia and other eastern lands. There were many true Sephardim in the Levant and even further east, with a strong sense of their identity, but that does not make all eastern Jews Sephardim; unfortunately it has not stopped them assuming Spanish descent.

Greece, and Turkey that in many communities the Sephardim imposed their rituals as well as their language. One feature that they preserved from Spain was their multiple identity: Jewish merchants might move between the ports of the Ottoman world or Italy as Jews, especially after the duke of Tuscany gave them special privileges in his new commercial centre at Livorno; when they set foot in Iberia they were 'Portuguese', wary of the Inquisition but also well aware of how to pass themselves off as good Catholics. By comparison, the position of the Muslims who remained in Spain (very many in the kingdom of Valencia) seemed less difficult: in some areas no effort was made to ensure that the Moriscos, as they came to be known, actually practised or knew about Christianity, even though their contact with the Muslim world became weaker and their knowledge of Islamic law was in steep decline by 1500. Their expulsion in 1609–14, following suspicions about their allegiance at a time of Spanish–Turkish conflict, made no allowance for the fact that one could not generalize: some Moriscos, not least those who became priests, were indeed convinced Christians, and even without government orders to prohibit 'Moorish dancing' and Muslim dress, many had assimilated quite readily into the dominant Christian culture. So, not surprisingly, they, like the Sephardim and earlier Andalusi refugees, led a life somewhat apart from the indigenous inhabitants of the north African towns where they settled.[29] They, like the Sephardim, insisted on their superior culture and breeding. Spain had seeded the Mediterranean with its own inhabitants, even if it was not until very modern times that the mother land thought of taking them back (the Spanish government issued a decree permitting all true Sephardim to claim Spanish citizenship in 2012; unsurprisingly it has not issued a similar invitation to those of Morisco descent).

IV A Fractured Mediterranean

A political boundary divided Christendom and Islam through the middle of the Mediterranean by the end of the sixteenth century, as Turks and Spaniards established their areas of influence. The Ottoman reach extended as far as the Barbary states along the coast of north Africa, even if their rulers adopted decidedly independent policies; but along the coasts of the eastern Mediterranean the Ottomans ruled over Christians and Jews, and interpreted the *dhimmī* regulations lightly enough to permit these communities to flourish, especially in the major trading cities such as Salonika and Izmir (Smyrna). Following the expulsion of the Jews from Spain, the Ottomans congratulated themselves on their acquisition of a large number of Jewish artisans and merchants, even if they declined to make use of one of the most impressive skills the Sephardim brought to Turkey: the art of printing. Muslims were a familiar sight on the streets of Marseilles, Naples, Palermo, and other cities in the Christian

[29] García-Arenal 2003; Harvey 2003.

Mediterranean, but mainly as slaves—an exception must be made for the Muslim occupation of Toulon, fully countenanced by Francis I of France, as an enthusiastic ally of the Ottomans, in 1543–4.[30] Raiding the coast for slaves became a profitable sport enjoyed by Barbary corsairs and by Christian pirates such as the Knights of St John (the Hospitallers), based in Malta; the great hope was to capture people of consequence or wealth, who could afford a big ransom. What we do not see is an engagement of cultures. In the sixteenth century some fragments of al-Idrisi's world geography, written in Arabic for Roger II of Sicily in 1154, were at last published in Latin translation. But curiosity about Islam remained muted in Western Europe, even at a time when great swathes of Eastern Europe lay under the domination of Muslim emperors. In the Islamic world, there were some moments when religious interactions occurred: the bizarre career of the self-proclaimed Messiah Shabbetai Ẓevi, beginning in seventeenth-century Izmir, reveals interesting interaction between Zevi and Protestant merchants with whom he had contact as a young man.[31] We hear of a lively disputation in eighteenth-century Tiberias between Rabbi Ḥaim Abulafia, who helped refound the city, and a Christian respondent.[32] All this does not add up to much: the various communities inhabited their distinct worlds, and the *millet* system encouraged that. Western European curiosity about eastern religions (in the plural) was a phenomenon of the eighteenth century and after, and was more closely linked to the extension of British influence in India than to the Mediterranean. Napoleon was much more interested in the Egypt of the Pharaohs than in the Egypt of the caliphs, sultans, and Mamluks, both for geopolitical reasons and as a way of promoting his own imperial vision.

Yet what was created in this period was a series of port cities where different communities did manage to coexist; and in the nineteenth century, following the opening of the Suez Canal, this coexistence reached its most impressive scale in Alexandria, a city that had almost always been host to a mixed population, first of Greeks, Jews, and Egyptians, and now of Greeks, Jews, Copts, Italians, Turks, Lebanese, Maltese, and much else. Much the same can be said of Beirut, Izmir, Salonika, and a number of other key points on the Mediterranean shores of the Ottoman Empire; and of Trieste, the sole Mediterranean port of the Austro-Hungarian Empire. This is not the place to describe the disintegration of this world of coexistence—a long, slow, painful process, marked by savagery (at Izmir in 1922, at Salonika in 1943) or at least dispossession (at Jaffa in 1948, at Alexandria in 1956).[33] One of the most remarkable features of the Mediterranean since the mid-twentieth century has been the disappearance of Jewish communities from almost the entire Mediterranean apart from the place where they have become concentrated, the State of Israel (and, increasingly, and very controversially, the Palestinian territories next door); the only other area of dense Jewish population around the sea is southern France. One should not underestimate the significance of the conflict between Israel and its Arab neighbours within the wider

[30] Isom-Verhaaren 2011.
[31] Scholem 1973; Goffman 1990.
[32] Wasserstein 1994.
[33] Abulafia 2011: 583–600.

confrontation that took place between the western world and the allies of the Soviet Union; equally one should not overestimate the religious dimension, despite some ugly words about Jews and Judaism (as in the works of Quṭb and other revolutionary figures, or anti-Semitic cartoons in the Arab press). But the terms of engagement have changed: secular Arab governments in Gaza and Libya have been swept aside; the future of Syria is uncertain, but once again it may not lie in the hands of the nationalist secularists—the substantial Christian population of Syria is ebbing away, sometimes under brutal assault by a self-proclaimed caliphate; and Christianity has already declined steeply in the lands that may or may not some day become the State of Palestine. Even in Turkey and Morocco moderate Islamic parties have taken power, while Algeria, whose military had resisted Islamist rivals, faces a deadly threat from al-Qaeda. Tunisia, on the other hand, has achieved greater stability, with the election of a non-Islamist government and a reduction in political tension. The Mediterranean looks more fragmented than ever, and religion has become a more important factor in its politics than it was throughout the twentieth century, when nationalist and pan-Arab slogans were proclaimed throughout the Arab world, and when Marxism rather than Islam was the creed of Arab political leaders, even if it was sometimes transmuted into a strange potpourri (as with Colonel Ghaddafi's 'Green Book' in Libya).

And yet—the ultimate irony—on the facing shores Christianity has lost its hold over more and more of the European population, while many Jews declare their Jewish identity to be cultural (whatever that means) rather than religious. The Mediterranean has ceased to be a place of encounter, sometimes peaceful, sometimes violent, between adherents of the three Abrahamic faiths; it is now one of several meeting-points between modern secular society and a revived and assertive Islam.

References

Abulafia, D. 1990. 'The end of Muslim Sicily'. In J. Powell, ed., *Muslims under Latin Rule 1100–1300*. Princeton: Princeton University Press, 103–33.

Abulafia, D. 1994. *A Mediterranean Emporium: The Catalan kingdom of Majorca*. Cambridge: Cambridge University Press.

Abulafia, D. 1996. 'Monarchs and Minorities in the Late Medieval Western Mediterranean: Lucera and its Analogues'. In S. Waugh and P. Diehl, eds, *Christendom and its Discontents: Exclusion, Persecution and Rebellion, 1000–1500*. Cambridge: Cambridge University Press, 234–63.

Abulafia, D. 2000. 'The Servitude of Jews and Muslims in the Medieval Mediterranean', *La Servitude dans les pays de la Méditerranée occidentale chrétienne au XIIe siècle et au-delà: déclinante ou renouvelée?* In *Mélanges de l'École française de Rome: Moyen Âge–Temps Modernes*, 112: 687–714.

Abulafia, D. 2004a. 'The Italian Other'. In D. Abulafia, ed., *Italy in the Central Middle Ages*. Oxford: Oxford University Press, 215–36.

Abulafia, D. 2004b. '*Nam iudei servi regis sunt*: The Jews in the Municipal *fuero* of Teruel (1176–7)'. In H. Hames, ed., *Jews, Muslims and Christians in and around the Crown of Aragon: Essays in Honour of Professor Elena Lourie*. Leiden: Brill, 97–123.

Abulafia, D. 2011. *The Great Sea: A Human History of the Mediterranean*. London: Penguin and New York: Oxford University Press.

Arié, R. 1990. *L'Espagne musulmane au temps des Naṣrides, 1250–1492*. Paris: Éditions de Boccard.

Barber, R. 2013. *The Cathars: Dualist Heretics in Languedoc in the High Middle Ages*. 2nd edn. Harlow: Longman.

Bonner, A. 1993. *Doctor Illuminatus: A Ramon Llull Reader*. Princeton: Princeton University Press.

Bowersock, G. 2013. *The Throne of Adulis: Red Sea Wars on the Eve of Islam*. New York: Oxford University Press.

Bryer, A. 1970. 'A Byzantine Family: The Gabrades *c*.979–*c*.1653'. *University of Birmingham Historical Journal* 12: 164–87.

Chwolson, D. A. 1856. *Die Ssabier und die Ssabismus*. 2 vols. St Petersburg: Kaiserl. Akad. Wis.

Coleman, D. 2003. *Creating Christian Granada: Society and Religious Culture in an Old-World Frontier City 1492–1600*. Ithaca, NY: Cornell University Press.

Coope, J. 1985. *The Martyrs of Córdoba: Community and Family Conflict in an Age of Mass Conversion*. Lincoln, NE: University of Nebraska Press.

Dodds, J. 1992. 'Mudejar Tradition and the Synagogues of Medieval Spain: Cultural Identity and Cultural Hegemony'. In V. Mann, T. Glick, and J. Dodds, eds, *Convivencia: Jews, Muslims and Christians in Medieval Spain*. New York: George Brazillier, 113–31.

Fromherz, A. 2010. *The Almohads: The Rise of an Islamic Empire*. London: I. B. Tauris.

García-Arenal, M. 2003. *La Diaspora des Andalousiens*. Aix-en-Provence: Edisud.

Goffman, D. 1990. *Izmir and the Levantine World, 1550–1650*. Seattle: University of Washington Press.

Goldstein, D. 2009. *Jacob's Legacy: A Genetic View of Jewish History*. New Haven: Yale University Press.

Hames, H. 2000. *The Art of Conversion: Christianity and Kabbalah in the Thirteenth Century*. Leiden: Brill.

Hames, H. 2007. *Like Angels on Jacob's Ladder: Abraham Abulafia, the Franciscans, and Joachimism*. Albany, NY: SUNY Press.

Harris, A. K. 2007. *From Muslim to Christian Granada: Inventing a City's Past in Early Modern Spain*. Baltimore: Johns Hopkins University Press.

Harvey, L. P. 1991. *Islamic Spain, 1250–1500*. Chicago: University of Chicago Press.

Harvey, L. P. 2003. *Muslims in Spain, 1500 to 1614*. Chicago: University of Chicago Press.

Hitchcock, R. 2008. *Mozarabs in Medieval and Early Modern Spain: Identities and Influences*. Aldershot: Ashgate.

Hitti, P., trans. 2000. *An Arab-Syrian Gentleman and Warrior in the Period of the Crusades: The Memoirs of Usāmah ibn Munqidh*. First published 1929; new edn with introduction by R. Bulliet. New York: Columbia University Press.

Hjärpe, A. 1972. *Analyse critique des traditions arabes sur les Sabéens ḥarraniens*. Uppsala: Skriv Service.

Iskander, J. 2007. 'Devout Heretics: The Barghawata in Maghribi Historiography'. *Journal of North African Studies* 12: 37–53.

Isom-Verhaaren, C. 2011. *Allies with the Infidel: The Ottoman and French Alliance in the Sixteenth Century*. London: Tauris Academic Studies.

Lane Fox, R. 1986. *Pagans and Christians in the Mediterranean World from the Second Century AD to the Conversion of Constantine*. London: Viking.

Limor, O. 1994. *Die Disputationen zu Ceuta (1179) und Mallorca (1286): Zwei antijüdische Schriften aus dem mittelalterlichen Genua*. Munich: Monumenta Germaniae Historica.

Llewellyn, P. 1970. *Rome in the Dark Ages*. London: Faber & Faber.

Moore, R. I. 2012. *The War on Heresy: The Battle for Faith and Power in Medieval Europe*. London: Profile Books.

Newby, G. D. 1986. *A History of the Jews of Arabia from Ancient Times to their Eclipse under Islam*. Columbia, SC: University of South Carolina Press.

Sand, S. 2009. *The Invention of the Jewish People*. London: Verso.

Scholem, G. 1973. *Sabbatai Ṣevi, the Mystical Messiah 1626–1676*. London: Routledge & Kegan Paul.

Selke, A. 1986. *The Conversos of Majorca: Life and Death in a Crypto-Jewish Community in Seventeenth-Century Spain*. Jerusalem: Magnes Press.

Severus of Minorca. 1996. *Letter on the Conversion of the Jews*, ed. S. Bradbury. Oxford: Oxford University Press.

Sivan, E. 1968. *Islam et la Croisade: idéologie et propagande dans les réactions musulmanes aux croisades*. Paris: Librairie d'Amérique et d'Orient.

Urvoy, D. 1980. *Penser l'Islam: les présupposés islamiques de l'Art de Lull*. Paris: J. Vrin.

Wasserstein, D. 1994. 'Jewish-Christian Relations in Eighteenth-Century Tiberias'. In A. Levy, ed., *The Jews of the Ottoman Empire*. Princeton: Princeton University Press, 301–14.

Wexler, P. 2009. *The Non-Jewish Origins of the Sephardic Jews*. Albany, NY; SUNY Press.

Winroth, A. 2000. *The Making of Gratian's Decretum*. Cambridge: Cambridge University Press.

Wolf, K. B. 1988. *Christian Martyrs in Muslim Spain*. Cambridge: Cambridge University Press.

Yovel, Y. 2009. *The Other Within: The Marranos, Split Identity and Emerging Modernity*. Princeton: Princeton University Press.

CHAPTER 9

JUSTICE

URIEL SIMONSOHN

FROM the moment of revelation, the most explicit manifestation of God's will and accord with temporal beings has been seen in the implementation of his law. Full compliance with the latter is considered a sign of religious conviction, an expression of unconditional devoutness. It is in this context that we find the judge functioning as an intermediary between God and his people, an executer of divine providence and the supreme overseer of social order. The present discussion offers a comparative analysis of the application of justice in Near Eastern Jewish, Christian, and Muslim communities in the first few centuries after the Islamic conquest. Justice is a very broad topic, bearing relevance to scholars of diverse disciplines, including theology, law, and ethics, among numerous others, but the perspective offered here is strictly that of social history, with particular emphasis on the interplay between law and society. It is my premise that the application of justice was perceived as a form of mediation between God and his believers carried out through the central role of the judge. Given this premise, I attempt to unfold some of the social aspects of that role by reviewing its diverse forms and modes of practice within the lives of communities that belonged to the three monotheistic traditions under discussion.

The Muslims, Jews, and Christians of the early Islamic period were settled across a vast territory stretching from Mesopotamia in the east and along the coasts of the Mediterranean in the west. Despite the highly local nature of confessional communal arrangements, both Jewish and Christian communities maintained firm relations with distant centres of authority from which they drew guidance and leadership in matters of a social, spiritual, and quotidian nature. In general terms and to varying degrees, the Rabbanite Jewish congregations, such as those of Iraq, Syria, Palestine, Yemen, Egypt, and North Africa, are known to have submitted to the authority of the exilarch (*resh galuta*), the gaonic academies of Sura and Pumbedita (based in Baghdad by the late ninth century), and to the gaonic academy in Palestine. At the same time, having congregated around communal institutions, Jews owed allegiance to regional (as opposed to central) leaders as well. These men were not only former disciples of the gaonic academies but also individuals who had acquired their offices thanks to their erudition, their affiliation with local rabbinic schools, their mercantile activities, or their membership in prominent households.[1]

The Christian communities at the centre of this discussion were affiliated with the East Syrian and West Syrian Churches, also known, respectively, as Nestorians and Jacobites. Like the Rabbanite communities, eastern Christian communities were scattered throughout congregations that submitted to the authority of ecclesiastical centres lacking any precise geographical boundaries. Predominantly, the East Syrian patriarch, the catholicos, held sway from his seat in Ctesiphon (and later from Baghdad) over an ecclesiastical setting that extended throughout Mesopotamia, eastern Arabia, and the Iranian plateau, with missionary posts as far east as India and China. His West Syrian counterparts sat in Antioch, holding jurisdiction over a region previously under Roman sovereignty, and in Takrīt, the West Syrian centre that had dominated the region under Sasanian rule.[2]

Despite some notable differences between the Jewish and Christian communities, on the one hand, and their Muslim overlords, on the other, the Muslim communities were similarly headed by caliphs and scholars whose powers were sanctioned by their religious authority. Here, lineage, prodigy, piety, and scripture were invariably recruited for the sake of leadership and spiritual guidance. While the Muslims did possess a clear political centre—the caliphal court and its subordinate governors—in practice, the prominence of local aristocracies suggests a relatively loose setting of administrative commitments.[3]

The authority of the geʾonim rested on a relatively informal set of arrangements. Whereas caliphs and patriarchs drew their authority from a highly formalized and structured administrative hierarchy, the gaʾon was often forced to rely on a set of social contracts underpinned largely by interpersonal ties and master–disciple bonds. In all three religious communities, however, the heavy reliance of central confessional authorities on regional agents attests to the delicate position of the former. Although the geʾonim, patriarchs, and caliphs tended to present their authority in exclusive terms, significant evidence suggests that their social and spiritual patronage was often contested by individuals of diverse backgrounds. Gaonic authority was regularly compromised by regional Rabbanite leaders, ecclesiastical leaders expressed their discomfort with the influence exerted by Christian lay figures, monks, and holy men, and the caliphs are recorded as frequently vying for authority with scholars and political adversaries. Thus, in all three cases we find central confessional leaders working hard to maintain relations with regional agents in order to fortify their position atop a hierarchical setting designed to secure their control and their office.

[1] For general surveys on the history of Jewish communities under early Muslim rule, see Mann 1920–2; Goitein 1967–93; Gil 1992; Ben-Sasson 1996; Gil 2004; Bareket 1999.

[2] For general surveys on the history of Christian communities under early Muslim rule, see Morony 1984; Dagron et al. 1993; Ducellier 1996; Eddé et al. 1997; Baum and Winkler 2003.

[3] A very useful survey of Islamic history in the early period is Berkey 2003.

The social picture that emerges is highly complex, involving a variety of players who possess diverse forms of social capital and seem to have been in constant negotiation or competition over power. This image is confirmed and further enhanced when observed through the attitudes of religious elites to judicial power. The latter's demands for judicial exclusiveness in various contexts highlight the prominent role of judicial institutions as a means of asserting and sustaining social control. Their outlook stemmed from the principal premise that a key mechanism for maintaining religious, political, and social powers was a legal apparatus that would preserve the confessional and social commitments of communal members.

Scriptural Models

Jewish, Christian, and Islamic conceptions of justice were formulated against the background of their respective scriptural traditions. Scripture constituted the primary source of reference for confessional laws, which governed every aspect of life, including the principles of judicial practices (Crone and Hinds 1986: 44; Elon 1994: I. 4; Hallaq 2005: 21, 33). For the adherents of Judaism, Christianity, and Islam, it was the biblical past that was to legitimize and set a precedent for later practices and institutions (Walzer et al. 2000: xl). The legal orders underlying the lives of these communities were founded upon a divine covenant between the biblical primordial forefathers and God, the one and only true judge (See *Pirkei Avot* 4: 8; 2 Tim. 4: 1; Rebstock 1999: 2). According to this covenant, the community was established 'as a sacral fellowship under God' (Walzer et al. 2000: xxxix). As such, it relied on the services of mediators, whose duty it was not only to convey divine messages but also to ensure their implementation through judicial sanction. The images of Moses, David, Solomon, Paul, and Muhammad as lawmakers and judges are only some of the better-known examples of leaders who had set down principles for future generations of judges, and whose careers provided exemplary models for these later judges.

The Bible calls for the appointment of judges over every tribe and in every town, exhorting the Israelites' judge to pursue 'justice, and only justice' as part of the fulfilment of God's promise to his people (Deut. 16: 18–20). Justice is to be upheld in the most rigorous fashion by those chosen qualified individuals, first the tribal judges and later the Levites and priests (Deut. 17: 8–9). At the same time, the general public was not released from the obligation to enforce justice as well: 'The congregation shall judge between the slayer and the avenger of blood, in accordance with these ordinances' (Num. 35: 24). Whereas the biblical narrative reflects a society that was regulated by a well-defined judicial apparatus, the principal approach presented in the Gospels exhorts believers to resolve their disputes quietly (Matt. 18: 15–17). Within the broader exhortation to refrain from dispute and retaliation, the Christian believer is also encouraged to refrain from condemning his neighbour and even to overlook his sins (Gould 1993: 123–32). Only as a final resort, if a dispute is inevitable, is it to be brought before the church for arbitration (*The Apostolic Constitutions*, 2: 6). Those who are to sit in judgement are the saints (1 Cor. 6: 1–2), the shepherds of the flock, the bishops. At this early stage of Christianity, however, the bishop's jurisdiction was limited to matters considered holy, leaving unto the temporal leader what was his (Matt. 22: 21; Mark 12: 17).

The Quran calls for the dispensation of justice in accordance with God's revelation. Thus, for example, sura 4: 105 reads: 'Surely we have sent down to thee the Book with the truth, so that thou mayest judge between the people by that God has shown thee.' The image of the judge is modelled here on that of Muhammad, whose mission as a messenger of truth was to uphold the ideals put forth by God and his Book (Hallaq 2005: 43). It was Muhammad who laid the foundations of an Islamic judiciary, setting an example for future Muslim judges (Tyan 1938: I. 19). However, despite the close association between polity and judiciary, it has been noted that the Quran refers to Muhammad's judicial authority only once as an ordinance of sovereignty (Schacht 1966: 10). His judicial authority was first and foremost religious. It follows (much as it does from the principles expressed in the Christian tradition) that, had Islamic ethics been fully implemented, an Islamic legal system would have been entirely redundant. Hence the recurring insistence on forgiveness found in the Quran, as in sura 2: 263: 'Honourable words, and forgiveness, are better than a freewill offering followed by injury; and God is All-sufficient, All-clement'; or sura 4: 149: 'If you do good openly or in secret or pardon an evil, surely God is All-pardoning, All-powerful' (Schacht 1966: 11).

Principles of Praxis

Rabbinic Justice

Jewish rabbinic judicial practices of the early Islamic period trace their immediate origins to historical precedents and legal deliberations of the period following the destruction of the Second Temple (*c.*70 CE). While modern scholars have been inclined to view Talmudic law as 'the guide of the Jewish judges in the dispensation of justice' (Mann 1919–20: 342), they have also come to recognize the difficulty of obtaining an 'accurate description of the judicial institutions and their infrastructure' through early rabbinic sources (Hecht et al. 1996: 124; see also Baer 1950: 7). Thus, any attempt to reconstruct the foundations on which early medieval rabbinic institutions of justice operated must be qualified by this vagueness. Nonetheless, what emerges clearly from the Mishnah and the Talmud is the image of a Jewish leadership bereft of the political prerogatives of sovereign agents (Walzer et al. 2000: xxi).

In general terms, early rabbinic sources speak of permanent judicial bodies before which Jews were to settle their disputes and regulate their legal affairs. Yet these same sources also refer to individuals who assumed judicial authority on an ad hoc basis without the formal appointment of central institutions. Within this relatively fluid definition of judicial authority, rabbinic law provides rules and definitions that placed certain limits on the array of choice between various authorities and regulated the manner in which judicial procedures were to take place.

A judge's authority was heavily dependent on his reputation as a *gamir*, a learned individual well immersed in the law. In other words, the authority of judicial figures was grounded in their claim to knowledge—of legal texts as well as of the hermeneutical rules for the interpretation of these texts (Walzer et al. 2000: 248). Jewish judges did not possess the coercive means of state officials. Rather, their judicial decisions were enforced by virtue of the belief of those appearing before them in the validity of Jewish law and in the competence of their judgement. Whereas judgement was the prerogative of laymen as well as scholars, a penalty could be meted out only by an expert (*mumḥe*). Nevertheless, the effectiveness of a punitive ruling was dependent on the willingness of the general public to endorse it, as judges had little if any real means of coercion. The collective will of the community was therefore crucial for the execution of a judicial decision, imbuing the judicial procedure with a distinct social dimension, of which the most explicit expressions were ostracism (*shamta*) and excommunication (*ḥerem*) (Elon 1994: 19, 23).

Ecclesiastical Justice

Although the ecclesiastical judiciary was consolidated following its formal endorsement during the reign of Emperor Constantine (r. 306–37), pre-Constantinian episcopal courts are illuminating as early prototypes of this institution. The bishop's court was established as part of a broader endeavour to provide the individual believer with a communal framework founded upon Christian principles of normative behaviour. As such, the court was perceived as one of the principal aspects of the bishop's role as protector of his community (Brown 2001: 67; Harries 1999: 73). Christians were expected to settle their legal concerns in episcopal courts, which gradually assumed a position analogous to that of the Roman civil system (Humfress 2007: 154). By the fourth century, ecclesiastical courts were recognized as formal judicial institutions in the Roman Empire. In 318, the *episcopalis audientia*, the episcopal tribunals, received the state's formal recognition.[4] Despite common features between the *episcopalis audientia* and secular imperial institutions, the bishop's court, unlike its secular counterpart whose jurisdiction pertained only to civil matters, gradually came to possess jurisdiction over both civil and religious matters, and moreover, from a Roman legal point of view, was considered an institution of arbitration.

[4] On the *episcopalis audientia*, see Vismara 1937; *The Theodosian Code*, 1.27.1.; Selb 1967; Ziegler 1971: 167–74; Lamoreaux 1995; Harries 1999: 191–211; Rapp 2005: 242–52; Lenski 2001: 83–92.

Further east, under Sasanian rule, the East Syrian Church sought to create its own autonomous judicial institutions (Macomber 1968: 181; Krikorian 1981; McDonough 2005: 253–5; Erhart 2001: 127; Baum and Winkler 2003: 20; Payne 2010: 400). The reign of the Sasanian monarch Yazdegerd I (r. 399–420) marked the beginning of an era of tolerance toward non-Zoroastrian minorities in the Sasanian Empire. The synod of 410 announced Yazdegerd's 'Edict of Toleration' for the East Syrian Church, granting it autonomous standing within the Sasanian Empire and promising the state's enforcement of ecclesiastical judicial decisions. Just below the catholicos, East Syrian bishops functioned as judges and had their decisions enforced through the mechanisms of the Sasanian state. Whereas the catholicos stood at the top of this legal order, East Syrian bishoprics, scattered over a wide territorial jurisdiction, facilitated the judicial activities of local ecclesiastical judges.

Unlike rabbinic law, early ecclesiastical legal principles were restricted to matters of religion. Nonetheless, our evidence suggests that under both Roman and Sasanian rule ecclesiastical judges were expected to rule on worldly affairs as well, that is, to apply what is commonly termed as secular law, or civil law, pertaining to rules dictated by private and civil rights. Ecclesiastical judges under late Roman rule are known to have resorted to Roman imperial law, with the assistance of lay legal advisers (assessores) (Humfress 2007: 206), while fifth- and sixth-century East Syrian legal collections suggest the incorporation of civil legal principles into the ecclesiastical legal system itself and of rulings by clergymen in areas of civil law (Selb 1981–9: I. 42; Rose 1982: 160; Erhart 2001: 127; Mathisen 2001: 4).

Pre-Islamic and Early Islamic Justice

By 632, following Muhammad's death, the young Muslim community was still in the process of defining its legal doctrine and institutions. It is likely that Islamic principles of justice, as known from the Quran, had already been articulated at this stage, or else were formulated shortly thereafter. Yet the tribes about to emerge from Arabia did not yet have at their disposal anything that may be described as a coherent legal apparatus capable of adequately attending to the needs of the fledgling Muslim community. While Islamic law in general and its early judicial institutions in particular trace their origins to the time of Muhammad, their development should be considered in light of the non-Muslim legal traditions and practices that were prevalent in the areas that fell under Islamic rule and pre-Islamic Arabian practices. Modern scholars seem to agree about the emergence of Islamic law and judicial practices from older legal traditions and administrative arrangements, though they part ways on the question of the exact sources. The three main regions described in modern scholarship as providing inspiration for Islamic law are Arabia, the Fertile Crescent, and Iraq (Tyan 1938: I. 119, 131–2, 138; Schacht 1959; Schacht 1966: 26; Crone 1984: 167; Morony 1984: 37, 85; Crone 1987b: 8, 15, 107–8; Motzki 2002: xv; Hallaq 2005: 8, 19; Jany 2008: 149).

The question of origins aside, it is reasonable to assume that the first generations of Muslims to settle outside Arabia carried with them an Arabian legal heritage, better known as Arabian customary law (Khadduri 1955: 20; Hallaq 2005: 18). According to Wael Hallaq (2005: 8), Arabian societies and cultures 'provided the larger context in which Islam, as a legal phenomenon, was to grow'. This is why the rulings of the first generations of Muslim judges were most likely based on the only system with which they were familiar, namely that of customary Arabian practices.

It is in Arabia that the precedent of the prophet, an Arabian arbiter and the first Muslim arbiter, provided the immediate judicial model upon which future generations of Muslim jurists would seek to ground the principles of Islamic justice. In addition to the teachings of the Quran, the principal source on which the first generation of Muslim *qāḍīs* based their rulings was prophetic practice, the *sunna*.[5] With time, however, as Islamic societies expanded and new challenges required new solutions, the Quran and *sunna* were augmented by additional sources of judicial reasoning (Schacht 1966: 26; Goitein 1968: 162–3; Zaman 1997: 9; Hallaq 2005: 53; Masud, Peters, and Powers 2006: 6).

Justice in the Early Islamic Period

With the exclusion of criminal law, non-Muslim protected communities (*dhimmīs*) were granted legal autonomy by their Muslim overlords, giving their judicial institutions jurisdiction over a wide range of legal affairs in the realms of religious and civil laws (Fattal 1958: 344–65; Goitein 1967–93: II. 311; Libson 2003: 81). Accordingly, the vast majority of cases brought before non-Islamic courts involved family law, monetary affairs, and issues of morality and religious conduct (Goitein 1967–93: II. 2).

Rabbinic judicial arrangements and practices in the period under discussion are often portrayed in modern scholarship within the framework of broader historiographic accounts (for exceptions, see Assaf 1924; Hurvitz 1995). A crucial hindrance to studies dealing with rabbinic judicial practices in the early Islamic period is the scarcity of extant evidence. This methodological difficulty is particularly acute for the period between the Islamic conquest and the second half of the ninth century and is eased significantly from the tenth century and on—a time for which substantial data offered by documents from the Cairo geniza in general and gaonic responsa in particular. Thus, for the period leading up to the late ninth century, modern scholarship has been largely inclined to base its analysis on the premise of a general institutional continuity from the times of the Talmudic sages (Brody 1998: xix).

[5] Tyan 1938: I. 68; Schacht 1966: 10; Bravmann 1972: 175; Crone and Hinds 1986: 48; Hallaq 2005: 4–5, 46–51.

Far more evidence is available about the social history of the eastern churches after the Islamic conquest, yet here too, direct evidence about the exact nature of the ecclesiastical judicial organization is slim (Kaufhold 1984: 91). Consequently, as in the case of Jewish studies, modern scholarship has failed to produce comprehensive accounts that deal exclusively with the question of the ecclesiastical judicial administration. Instead, the topic has been addressed through two broader perspectives—the history of the eastern churches under early Islamic rule, and the history of eastern Christian ecclesiastical law. In this context, the individual histories of the various churches are of particular relevance. While these churches shared a common juridical background, their separate existence over time introduced a gradual codification of legal collections that were built upon or in dialogue with local legal traditions (Selb 1981–9: I. 39; II. 77; Hage 1999; Kaufhold 2005; Humfress 2007: 206; Pennington 2007: 387). Thus a substantial part of our knowledge regarding the state of the ecclesiastical judiciaries in the early Islamic period derives from the Christian legal literature composed around that time.

The most comprehensive study on the Islamic judiciary remains Émile Tyan's 1938 oeuvre *Histoire de l'organisation judiciaire en pays d'Islam*. In the decades since its publication, the topic has been addressed predominantly in numerous studies on the history of Islamic law and jurisprudence. Unlike the limited nature of the sources that shed light on Jewish and Christian judicial institutions, the Islamic source material is ample and highly diverse, including judicial manuals (*adab al- qāḍī* 'the etiquette of judging'), biographic dictionaries, historiographic narratives, *belles-lettres*, and formal judicial decrees (Masud, Peters, and Powers 2006: 2).

Judicial Centralization in the Context of Social Fragmentation

Their unique character and independent formation notwithstanding, the Jewish, Christian, and Islamic judicial organizations exhibit not a few striking similarities. Underlying these similarities is a crucial interplay between religion and society, between religious law and social life. Legal stipulations not only provided practical guidance to believers regarding their religious practices, their daily affairs, and their encounters with adherents of other religions, but also instilled in their minds a notion of membership in confessional units that transcended local affiliations. In this respect, a centralized judicial apparatus played a crucial role in sustaining communal membership and cohesion. Legal scholars and social historians acknowledge the role of law in general and of its judicial application in particular as a means of social control, particularly through the monopolizing of norms (Mann 1986: 7, 22; Satlow 1996: 274, 294; Rosen 2000: 35; Hurvitz 2003: 986). The attempts of the confessional leaders under discussion to achieve these goals should be considered in the context of a multiplicity of social and religious powers of some judicial capacity or another, a predicament that oftentimes forced central confessional leaderships to share their judicial authority with other social agents, such as prominent merchants, landowners, scholars, holy men, and courtiers (Mann 1986: I. 17–18; MacEvitt 2008: 12; Rustow 2008: 70; Rustow 2009: 133–59).

Gaonic Centres vis-à-vis Regional Communities

Rabbinic judicial institutions and practices should be considered against the background of a constant tension between the centralist positions of the gaonic academies in Palestine and Iraq, on the one hand, and regional conditions, on the other. A significant contributing factor to this tension seems to have been the simple fact of the physical distance between the academies and the various regional communities, which not only solidified the latter's subordination to the former but also served as a catalyst for the development of local customs (Libson 2003: 34). The geʾonim of Babylonia presented themselves and were perceived by their supporters throughout the Near East and the Mediterranean Basin as heirs to a long chain of authorities dating back to the times of the early Rabbanite sages in Palestine and Babylonia (Gil 2004: n. 87; Brody 1998: 56–8). Accordingly, they claimed legal supremacy and maintained the office of the *bet ha-din ha-gadol* (great court), over which would preside the second in rank to the gaʾon, the *av bet din* (head of the court). At the same time, the gaonic centre in Palestine presented itself as the legal court of the entire Jewish diaspora (Lifshitz 1982–3: 268). And while rabbinic communal institutions in gaonic times did gradually assume a more institutionalized character than that of the communal institutions of antiquity, still, the hierocratic principle was maintained (Brody 1998: 38), meaning that gaonic centres were acknowledged as a supreme court and the responsa issued there were considered binding rulings (Lifshitz 1982–3: 268, 276).

The tenth-century *Epistle of Rabbi Nathan the Babylonian* paints a portrait of a territorial division of administrative jurisdictions, *reshuyot*, allocated to the exilarch, the two geʾonim of Babylonia (of Sura and Pumbedita), and the gaʾon of Palestine (Neubauer 1887–95: II. 78, 85–7; Hurvitz 1995: 166–8). Within each jurisdiction, the exilarch or the gaʾon directly controlled the judicial appointments of regional communities. In exchange for regularly supplying judges (or affirming their appointment) and supervising their work, the head of the *rashut* received an annual income from each community. These centralist prerogatives are mentioned also in a letter from 1036 outlining the authority of the Palestinian gaʾon. The document is a draft of a letter to a Jewish notable in Egypt in which the Palestinian gaʾon requests a renewal of his appointment from the Fatimid caliph al-Mustanṣir (r. 1036–94). The document lists a series of prerogatives traditionally reserved for the gaʾon, including the exclusive right to appoint and dismiss communal officials and oversight of the judicial courts (Goitein 1980: 70–6; see also Rustow 2008: 294–6).

While the exact jurisdictions and complete application of the *reshuyot* is hard to establish, the extant evidence suggests that such arrangements were anything but theoretical; regional communities within the *reshuyot* did indeed submit to the authority of the four centres (Mann 1919–20: 336; Sklare 1996: 80–3, 97–8; Brody 1998: 125–6). But this historiographic view requires some qualification. Although Rabbanite regional leaders shared a common pattern of expressing loyalty to the gaonic centres, it would be wrong to treat in similar terms the Jewish communities outside the *reshuyot* and those within them. The Jewish communities that had begun by the late tenth century to consolidate their local institutions in North Africa, Sicily, and even before that in Spain, were beyond the direct authority of the central academies in Babylonia and Palestine, in both theory and practice (Ben-Sasson 1996; Ben-Sasson 2004; Cohen 1997: 73–86). Their relations with the gaonic centres appear to have been inconsistent, with some regional leaders maintaining close relations with more than one of the gaonic academies in Iraq and Palestine, and others manifesting relations that ranged from complete subordination to nominal salutation (Ben-Sasson 1996: 401; Bareket 1999: 111). Alongside to the numerous geniza letters and gaonic responsa that attest to the intimate relations between graduates of the gaonic academies and their former masters in important regional centres, such as Fusṭāṭ and Qairawān, there are also indications that certain regional Rabbanite leaders operated more independently (Goitein 1967–93: II. 4, 12; Gil 2004: 154–6, 167–82; Cohen 1997: 79). The latter, it has been argued, were not prepared to treat gaonic responsa as judicial verdicts, fearing these may undermine their own authority (Lifshitz 1982–3: 297). But despite their hegemonic aspirations, and particularly from the end of the tenth century and on, the geʾonim acknowledged their dependence on the recognition of their authority by regional leaders and no less on the donations sent to the academies by regional communities. Thus they ultimately legitimized the autonomous standing of regional judicial institutions and accommodated themselves to it (Ben-Sasson 1996: 298, 304).

The Ecclesiastical Leadership and the Challenges of Legal Diversity and Internal Divisions

As an institution, the office of the ecclesiastical judge continued to function after the Islamic conquest despite the change in political circumstances. Canon 6 of an East Syrian synod from 676 provides a vivid image of the manner in which justice was to be administered, at least from the standpoint of ecclesiastical officials. The canon stipulates that lawsuits among Christians are to be brought before the judgement of individuals who have been designated by the bishop. The principle of judicial hierarchy can be discerned through the canon's appeal to litigants to forward their petition to the bishop himself if they are dissatisfied with the verdict they received or harbour doubts about the integrity of the ecclesiastical officials who issued it (*Synodicon orientale*, 484–5). Thus, supreme judicial powers were held by the head of the church, who in turn delegated that power along a hierarchical chain of officials, starting with the metropolitans, continuing with the bishops, and reaching down to archdeacons and priests (Selb 1981–9: I. 129, 194, 201, 203; Kaufhold 1984: 92). Serving at the top of the judicial hierarchy, the ecclesiastical judge is not only the supreme judicial officeholder but also appoints and oversees the work of other judges within his jurisdiction. These judges were appointed from among the clergy, an arrangement that greatly contributed to the centralization of ecclesiastical power in general and of its judicial prerogatives in particular but also held significant risk for the church. Unlike its position under late Roman rule or even under Sasanian rule, the ecclesiastical court under Islam did not enjoy the formal sanction of the state. Moments of crisis, such as a temporary vacancy in the patriarchal office, served as ripe opportunities for various parties within the churches and outside them to undermine ecclesiastical authority, leading to a state of administrative havoc.[6] Thus, patriarchs took pains to assure the loyalty of their clergy, an endeavour that is highly attested in the numerous synodical recordings.[7]

Generally speaking, the eastern churches continued to run their affairs almost undisturbed under early Islamic rule,[8] while their social significance even increased. In addition to ecclesiastical and monastic affairs (ranging from property to disciplinary issues), the themes of eastern Christian synodical canons from the early Islamic period reflect a growing concern with administrating justice among the laity. The ecclesiastical jurisdiction was gradually extended to questions of marriage, inheritance, charity, usury, slavery, orphans and widows, property, and various disputes (Selb 1981–9: I. 149–50, 215). The process of incorporating civil regulations into ecclesiastical law, which had already been initiated by the East Syrian church under Sasanian rule, not only intensified under Islamic rule but also came to cut across denominational boundaries. The evidence suggests that, within a few centuries of the conquest, civil regulations became part and parcel of the ecclesiastical legal codifications of the different churches. The impetus for this development may be gleaned from a remark made by the East Syrian catholicos Timothy I (d. 823), linking the trend of Christian recourse to non-Christian (i.e. Islamic) tribunals to the church's failure to provide its believers with a civil legal code (Putman 1975: 61). The first significant attempt to create a comprehensive ecclesiastical legal code that would include civil regulations appears to have been that of the East Syrian cleric Išōʿbokt (eighth century; exact dates unknown) (Kaufhold 1971: 22). In the introduction to his law book, Išōʿbokt laments a reality in which

> the Christians are divided based on the laws stipulated in the land of the Romans and those in the land of the Persians. The latter are further distinguished from those in Babylonia, Khuzistān, and Mēšān. Similarly, there are differences in legal affairs in additional places, as even [between] districts and towns. Although the Christian belief is one, the law is not one and not the same. (Sachau 1907–14: III. 9)

6 Macomber 1968: 181; see for example in the introduction to the electing synod of the East Syrian patriarch Ḥnanišōʿ II (d. 780) in 775, in *Synodicon orientale*, 515.

7 Putman 1975: 31; Simonsohn 2011: 11 and the examples in ch. 5.

8 Rémondon 1972: 262; Wipszycka 1972: 52–4; Walmsley 1992: 254; Figueras 1994; Schick 1995: 85ff.; Foss 1997: 192, 198; Stroumsa 2008: 55–60, 76.

Išōʿbokt explains this state of legal disorder by the fact that Christian judges inconsistently rely on early and later legal sources, leaving much to personal discretion. Thus, while religious figures like Išō'bokt may have been reluctant to include temporal concerns within the ecclesiastical jurisdiction, they could no longer accommodate the absence of a unified ecclesiastical code that includes civil law regulations.

Parallel efforts seem to have been initiated by West Syrian ecclesiastical jurists as well. A collection of synodical acts and civil regulations found in a manuscript from 1204 displays an undisturbed legal link between the first ecumenical councils and the acts of a synod held in 1153. Though it is hard to determine when and how civil regulations came to be included in West Syrian legal collections, it is useful to note the compiler's introductory note to this West Syrian collection:

> We begin to write the book that contains all the new canons of the later patriarchs . . . and all the laws, judgments, sentences, and heritages and the rest [of the administrative affairs] of the Greek kings (i.e. Roman emperors), as well as of all the judgments, laws, sentences, heritages, [legislation regarding] liberation of slaves, and of all the properties and the rest [of the administrative affairs] of the Arab rulers under whose sentences the believers act and whose laws they accept. (Vööbus 1975–6: Vol. 368, 23)

We may assume that life under Islamic rule induced ecclesiastical authorities to incorporate civil regulations into their legal collections, thus allowing their courts to expand their jurisdiction over their dispersed congregations. Here it is noteworthy that, whereas the East Syrian church was already forced to adapt to non-Christian rule before the Islamic conquest, the churches of the West Syrians, at least those of the former Roman Empire, faced this challenge only after the Islamic consolidation of power (Crone 1980a: 71 n. 55). In both cases, the expansion of ecclesiastical law was designed, among other things, to address the risk of ecclesiastical leaders losing control over their communities.[9]

Caliphs and Scholars

The pre-Islamic institution of arbitration did not disappear following the rise of Islam. Early Islamic sources attest to the presence of arbiters centuries after the Islamic judicial apparatus had taken form, thus forcing the incorporation of this institution into Islamic law (Tillier 2009: 309, 313). This is reinforced by the fact that the first Muslims who settled outside Arabia chose to sustain their tribal organization.[10] S. D. Goitein (1968: 134) has noted that '*ḥukm al-Jāhiliyya*, judgement according to

[9] Kaufhold 1971: 24–2; Kaufhold 1984: 91, 94; Rose 1982: 160, 165; Crone 1987b: 12; Selb and Kaufhold 2005: 51–64. Similar efforts were made in the Armenian church in the second half of the seventh century; see Mardirossian 2004: 400.

[10] Van Ess 1991–7: II. 124; Crone 1980b: 25–33; Carver 1996: 208; Wheatley 2001: 10.

arbitrary opinion or established local practice, did not disappear immediately... but was replaced gradually... by a legal system worked out on religious lines'. In fact, the persistence of pre-Islamic Arabian customs was reflected not merely in the institution of the arbiter but also in the type of law to which early Muslim judges made reference in their judgement. In an eighth-century administrative treatise, the Abbasid secretary 'Abdallāh b. al-Muqaffa' (d. *c.*758) criticized Iraqi Muslim judges for rendering judgements based on a customary practice (*sunna*) that was not prescribed by the prophet or in the Quran (Hallaq 2005: 38). Ibn al-Muqaffa' called for a comprehensive legal reform that would bring Muslim judges under the direct authority of the caliph and restrict their legal points of reference to the quranic teachings and the prophetic example. Thus, the image that emerges of the judicial arrangements of the period shortly after the Islamic conquest echoes the fact that it took centuries—perhaps until the tenth century—for Muslim judicial practices to take on a more concrete and established shape (Coulson 1959: 20; Hallaq 2005: 2–3, 5). The process entailed not only the formation of fixed institutions and their legal references but also the arrangement of these institutions into a fixed hierarchical order.

Underlying and guiding the formation of Islamic judicial institutions was an eagerness to replace those institutions that were directly identified with the chaos of pre-Islamic times. Instead of the divisions and lack of leadership that typified the pre-Islamic era, Muslim jurists sought to bring about an order that would be founded on an Islamic outlook and characterized by such qualities as unity, administrative hierarchy, division of tasks, and centralization. At the core of this image we find the office of the *qāḍī*, a newly developed judicial institution that stood in opposition to that of its pre-Islamic antecedent, the *ḥakam*. Whereas the latter was the product of an era of ignorance and chaos, the office of the *qāḍī* was to serve as a manifestation of an ideal society.

It is commonly acknowledged that a central feature of the development of the Islamic judicial administration was the growing specialization, independence, and localization of *qāḍī*s around the eighth century (Schacht 1966: 26; Hallaq 2005: 97). As long as the Muslims remained within the boundaries of their garrison towns, the jurisdiction of the *qāḍī*s was restricted to them. Yet once Muslims began to expand their settlement beyond their military confinements, the needs associated with the regulation of life amidst a confessionally and socially mixed environment began to emerge, impacting dramatically on the growth and elaboration of the Islamic judicial office. Yet despite attempts by the state to control the territory notionally under its sovereignty, 'inadequate means of communication and inadequate public finances' prevented it from applying its authority in full.[11] It is in this context that the Umayyad and even more so the Abbasid governments (661–750, 750–1258 respectively) sought to bring Muslim judicial officers under greater control through an intimate involvement in their appointment and by laying down clearer definitions of their qualifications and

[11] Von Grunebaum 1946: 1; see also Coulson, 1956: 216; Schacht 1966: 49; Cahen 1970: 530.

prerogatives (Hallaq 2005: 57–8). A principal record of these definitions from as early as the second century of Abbasid rule is the vast literature of *adab al-qāḍī* (the etiquette of judging), where religious scholars compiled a long series of professional instructions, pertaining not only to judicial conduct but also to matters of appointment, jurisdiction, procedural law, and directives for the issuing of documents (see Schneider 1990). The creation of the office of the 'chief judge' (*qāḍī al-quḍāt*), early in Abbasid rule, should be understood in this context as well. The chief judge, who sat in the capital of the caliphate, acted as the supreme judicial authority in the empire (von Grunebaum 1946: 163; Jany 2008: 156–8). By establishing this office, the caliphate was able to place provincial *qāḍīs* under stricter surveillance and supervision (Schacht 1966: 50; Hallaq 2005: 80); by the time of the legal reforms of Abbasid caliph Hārūn al-Rashīd, the procedure had become fully formalized (r. 786–809) (Bligh-Abramski 1992: 41, 56).

But the caliphate was not alone in trying to dominate the judicial apparatus—other sectors within the empire possessed similar ambitions. Very shortly after Ibn al-Muqaffaʿ composed his memorandum, the *qāḍī* of Baṣra, ʿUbayd Allāh al-ʿAnbarī (d. 784–5), wrote an epistle to the ʿAbbāsid caliph al-Mahdī (r. 775–85), in which he sought to place the office of the *qāḍī* under the direct authority of the jurisconsults (*al-aʾimma al-fuqahāʾ*). The relative chronological proximity between al-ʿAnbarī's suggestions and those of Ibn al-Muqaffaʿ's suggests that the two men shared similar concerns. Yet while al-ʿAnbarī sought to subordinate the judge to the spiritual authority of the jurisconsults, Ibn al-Muqaffaʿ appears to have favoured a caliphal authority that embodied both secular and religious authorities (Zaman 1997: 5–6; Tillier 2006: 152–4). One implication of the growing presence of religious scholars in the caliphal court and outside was a growing attempt on the part of these circles to achieve influence over the *qāḍī*'s office at the expense of local government officials, specifically, the vizier and governors (Kennedy 1981: 29; Bligh-Abramski 1992: 42; Hallaq 2005: 62, 79). Here, joint membership in a legal school (*madhhab*) and kinship served to consolidate political factionalism.[12] It is under circumstances of mixed loyalties that *qāḍīs* found themselves at the centre of conflicting doctrinal affiliations, local rivalries between families, and court–periphery tensions. *Qāḍīs* were forced to choose between their allegiance to local urban elites and the caliphal court and its direct agents. By choosing to ally with the state, the *qāḍī* won its support and was officially able to secure his office. Yet such an allegiance came with a price, for not only the *qāḍī*'s independence but also his moral integrity were thereby compromised, at least in the eyes of certain scholarly circles (Rebstock 1999: 15; Jany 2008: 157; see also Wensinck 1922). While institutionally the *qāḍī*'s court may have been in allegiance with the caliphal centre or local forces, such independence should not be confused with that of the *qāḍī*'s legal profession. According to Hallaq, 'judicial independence became the

[12] Coulson 1956: 216; Coulson 1964: 87; Kennedy 1981: 29; Rebstock 1999: 14–15; Bulliet 1972: 62–3; Berkey 2003: 203, 206; Tillier 2011.

hallmark of Islamic legal tradition. As a rule, no authority could redirect cases or interfere in the process of adjudication.'[13]

Institutional Multiplicity

The geʾonim, patriarchs, and caliphs all shared a common concern to enforce their supreme judicial authority over their respective communities within a vast territorial stretch. Thus, the geʾonim insisted upon the subordination of regional rabbinic courts, the patriarchs acted in the same way towards their ecclesiastical judicial agents, and likewise the caliphal court vis-à-vis the *qāḍī* courts. These efforts, however, were not restricted to particular institutions but were aimed, rather, at what appear to have been highly diverse social settings. These settings offered an institutional diversity that owed its origins to a much older set of arrangements that pre-dated the Islamic period, in which the individual could choose to settle disputes or validate contracts before a variety of judicial authorities (Simonsohn 2011: ch. 1).

Ordained, Expert, and Lay Rabbanite Judges

The historical process that saw the expansion of Jewish communities in the western part of the Mediterranean entailed also the gradual formation of diverse judicial arrangements (Elon 1994: I. 48). Given the dispersion of Jewish communities under early Islamic rule, one cannot speak of rabbinic judicial institutions within a unified administrative framework of checks and balances. The documents found in the Cairo geniza describe regional communities of elaborate organizations, whose subordination to the gaonic centres was often voluntary.[14] Whether directly subordinate to the gaonic court or not, these regional communities hosted a variety of judicial institutions, a result not only of contemporaneous circumstances but also of the institutional diversity that was already prescribed in early rabbinic sources.

One of the main regional institutions mentioned in gaonic responsa is the 'court of high standing' (*bet din ḥashuv*), over which presided regional scholars (Hurvitz 1995: 169). In most cases, these judges were graduates of either the gaonic academies or a local institution of learning (*bet midrash*), and as such were considered ordained (sing. *samukh*) judges (sing. *dayyan*) (Ben-Sasson 1996: 272, 279; Rustow 2008: 267). In Egypt, the supreme head of the Jewish community, attested as early as the late tenth century, was known by the title 'head of the Jews' (*raʾīs al-Yahūd*). The Egyptian head of the Jews was also considered the highest judicial authority. As such, he would extend his judicial authority over judges in local communities outside the old part of the Egyptian

[13] Hallaq 2005: 83; on Islamic judicial review, see Powers 1992, esp. p. 338.

[14] Goitein 1967–93: II. 5ff.; Ben-Sasson 1996: 401ff.; Ben-Sasson 2004: 189.

capital. Goitein referred to the juridical authority of the head of the Jews in Egypt as 'the most conspicuous aspect of his office'. As the highest ranking judicial figure in his community, the *ra'īs* would not himself sit in judgement. At the beginning of the eleventh century, his judicial authority was still conditional on gaonic approval, though public consent was becoming increasingly important. There is some evidence that, in the capacity of his judicial office, the *ra'īs*, like the ga'on, also responded to queries from members of the Jewish community in Egypt.[15]

While geniza letters often speak of a single officially recognized judge, designated 'the court' (*bet din*) (Goitein 1967–93: II. 316), judicial proceedings in fact normally took place before a tribunal of three judges (Assaf 1924: 46–8; Goitein 1967–93: II. 312; Elon 1994: I. 27). At the same time, formal ordination through one of the academies or a local institution of learning was not exclusive for the legitimizing of a judicial office. Indeed, according to Goitein, rabbinic judicial institutions were comprised largely of laymen (Goitein 1967–93: II. 314; see also Mann 1919–20: 364); and especially where legal specialists were unavailable, judicial roles were assumed by individuals whose legitimacy derived from their standing within their community and their learned background (Hurvitz 1995: 170). These men were often designated as the local elders (*zeqenim*). They were either local communal leaders or men of limited legal training.[16] Though the elders were often prominent members of their congregations whose primary occupations were of a private nature, they are frequently referred to in the sources as a formal communal institution (Goitein 1967–93: II. 58–60). Unlike the communal head and expert judges, however, the elders assumed judicial responsibilities for ad hoc purposes (Ben-Sasson 1996: 329).

In addition to individuals, the collective authority of the congregation (*qahal*) appears to have possessed some judicial power as well (Nakhalon 2001: 4, 13, 15, 24–6, 83). This feature was characteristic of communities that followed the Palestinian tradition, though it may also have prevailed in other communities that simply lacked a formal judicial court. The duty of the congregation to decide on a legal question applied particularly to cases in which a member of the congregation felt that his rights had been violated in some manner. Under such circumstances, that member had the right to stop the public prayer and have his grievance redressed through a procedure called 'calling upon the Jews' (*istighātha ilā al-Yahūd* or 'calling Israel for help' (*mustaghith ilā Yisrā'el*) (Goitein 1967–93: II. 324; Ben-Sasson 2004: 182). Although the congregation did not assume a formal judicial role, its endorsement of the complaint would significantly increase its force, as the congregation would then press the local rabbinic court to follow up with a judicial resolution of the matter.[17]

15 On the office of head of the Jews in Egypt, see Goitein 1967–93: II. 23ff.; Cohen 1980; Sela 1994. In North Africa, see Ben-Sasson 1996: 347ff.; on the judicial prerogatives of this office, see Goitein 1967–93: II. 33–4; on the *ra'īs* as a halakhic authority responding to legal queries, see Bareket 1999: 124–5.

16 On this, see a responsum written by Rav Hayya (d. 1038) in Lewin 1941: 209–10 (response no. 490).

17 Assaf 1942 108; Ben-Sasson 1996: 332, n. 233; Gil 1992: doc. 217.

Another indication of the operation of judicial bodies not appointed by the academies or involving legal specialists can be found in a responsum addressed to scholars from an institution of learning in Qayrawān, in which the eleventh-century gaʾon Rav Hayya (d. 1038) drew a distinction between courts that were under the direct authority of the Babylonian academies and those that were not (Harkavy 1887: 80, no. 180). The latter he described as 'tribunals in Syria' (*'arka'ot she-be-Surya*), echoing the reference in the Babylonian Talmud to a judicial forum over which presided laymen (*hedyoṭot*).[18] Nonetheless, the geʾonim sought to retain a position of legal supremacy also in the case of these latter communities, despite their remoteness and lack of ordained judges (Libson 2003: 35). Well aware of the risk of forfeiting the relevance of their leadership, they attempted to avoid disputes with regional communities by exhibiting a lenient approach toward local custom.[19]

Ecclesiastical and Non-ecclesiastical Judicial Authorities

The Christian communities that came under Islamic rule in the second half of the seventh century were heirs to a judicial setting in which the ecclesiastical court was only one among a variety of judicial options. Modern scholars of late antiquity have convincingly demonstrated the rich and dynamic nature of judicial arrangements available to and sought by Christians under the late Roman and Sasanian Empires (Simonsohn 2011: ch. 1). Life under the two empires afforded the individual a great diversity of judicial institutions whose authority derived from a variety of sources, including imperial sanction, religious affiliation, social rank, and interpersonal relationships. Imperial magistrates, ecclesiastical officials, urban aristocrats, village headmen, local notables, and pious individuals on both sides of imperial boundaries were all in a position to oversee the implementation of legal commitments and the peaceful resolution of disputes.

This institutional diversity, though scarcely mentioned in the available sources from the early Islamic period, does not appear to have disappeared after the Islamic conquest and was evidently a source of great concern for the ecclesiastical leadership. While the above-mentioned canon of the East Syrian church from 676 exhorts Christians to settle their lawsuits only before those individuals designated by the church, it also betrays an ecclesiastical preoccupation with the judicial competition posed by unappointed individuals. The canon insists that 'lawsuits and quarrels between Christians should be judged in the church; and should not be taken outside [it], as [in the manner of] those who are without a law; but rather they should be judged before judges who are appointed by the bishop . . .'. Believers are warned 'not to take their affairs outside

[18] BT Sanhedrin 23a; on lay judges in geniza documents, see Goitein 1967–93: II. 322; see also Elon 1994: I. 27; Hurvitz 1995: 172.

[19] Nakhalon 2001: 13, 24–6; Libson 2003: 38.

the church' and reminded that 'no one from amongst the believers may usurp, on his own authority, the judicial decisions over the believers, without the permission of the bishop and the consent of the community' (*Synodicon orientale*, 484–5). The canon does not allow for more than speculation regarding the particular identity of those who 'usurp' these judicial prerogatives. In other instances, however, the church's objection gave way to collaboration, as can be inferred from a decree issued by the East Syrian patriarch Ḥnanišōʿ II (d. 780), who sought to exploit the executive powers of a Christian layman in a legal dispute involving the inheritance of a widow (Sachau 1907–14: II. 27).

Despite their remoteness from East Syrian and West Syrian spheres of influence, cases of non-ecclesiastical figures of judicial capacity from Egypt and Palestine can further illuminate the phenomenon. Seventh-century papyri from Nessana speak of a group of figures, independent of the ecclesiastical administration, who in the framework of their office as village headmen fulfilled arbitration roles within their community (Stroumsa 2008: 60, 76). For early Islamic Egypt we find evidence indicating tensions between ecclesiastical and lay judicial authorities (Riedel 1900: 232, 271). Here the figure of the *archon*, a lay member of the Coptic church, appears as someone who fulfilled judicial tasks in collaboration with the church.[20] In addition, Coptic papyri from the period shortly after the Muslim conquest attest to the endurance of pre-Islamic civil institutions, most notably that of the *pagarchos* (Schiller 1932: 9, 16–17; Steinwenter 1955: 53; Foss 1997: I. 2–12). The office of the latter was a secular judicial institution that was administered by a Christian official who was subject to the authority of the Muslim governor.

It appears, however, that for the most part the authority of Christian lay individuals who held judicial prerogatives was not welcomed by the churches. Canon 27 of a West Syrian synod of 794 rejects the intervention of non-ecclesiastical authorities: 'None of the worldly ones (i.e. secular) has authority to speak among priests regarding ecclesiastical affairs. Therefore, if one has a lawsuit or a say (i.e. complaint), he should be brought before the bishop of his city' (Vööbus (1975–6: vol. 376, 14, no. 27). Canon 4 of a West Syrian synod held in 817 supports the notion of Christian laymen serving in an extra-ecclesiastical judicial capacity. The canon attests to the presence of Christian dignitaries who would intervene on behalf of those condemned by the church. Such figures are mentioned in different West Syrian canons as 'those who are outside the fold of the church', 'the dignitaries of the Christians', or even 'the Christians whose force is hard' (Vööbus 1975–6: Vol. 376, 32–3).

It stands to reason that the Christians who lived under early Islamic rule were not very different from those depicted by Peter Brown in his famous essay on the holy man in the late Roman Empire.[21] Here, too, judicial services were offered by figures of spiritual reputation who were not part of the ecclesiastical apparatus. As in earlier times, church authorities were unhappy with such trends. This is attested in a position

[20] Evetts 1904–14: III. 9; 'Archon', *The Coptic Encyclopedia*.

[21] Brown 1971; Brown 1998.

attributed to the late seventh-century West Syrian bishop Jacob of Edessa, who refused to grant stylites judicial authority, claiming that 'they have ascended the pillar not in order to become judges of the people and to administer the laws . . . [T]hey have not been called or appointed for this by God or by the chiefs of the priests' (Vööbus 1975–6: Vol. 368, 228).

While Jacob's position refers to the judicial authority of stylites, it may be indicative of a general attitude toward the temporal prerogatives of men whose authority did not derive from ecclesiastical appointment but rather from their holy position. Within this category we may also include monks. There is some indication that, in the period under discussion, monks also assumed administrative positions of a temporal nature. Thus, a canon issued in a West Syrian synod in 896 prohibits monks from assuming communal leadership posts in what appears to be small Christian communities in the northern parts of the Fertile Crescent (Vööbus 1975–6: Vol. 376, 64–5). While the canon makes no reference to judicial responsibilities, these should not be ruled out. Given this various data, and even while a full understanding of the components of Christian non-ecclesiastical judicial authority in the early Islamic period remains to be gathered, it seems safe to argue that the judicial setting was by no means monolithic. Instead, it offered a diverse institutional setting in which bishops, priests, holy men, and lay figures simultaneously fulfilled certain judicial roles.

Islamic Judicial Diversity

As noted earlier, the formation of the Islamic judiciary and its various institutions was a gradual process driven by an amalgamation of political, intellectual, religious, social, and cultural factors. According to Joseph Schacht, the first caliphs neither applied nor indeed envisioned an 'Islamic system of administration of Justice'; such a system would eventually develop in response to later challenges (Schacht 1966: 16). It seems safe to assert that somewhere around the late ninth–early tenth century, Muslims were able to settle their legal concerns before a variety of judicial institutions such as that of the arbiter, the *qāḍī*'s court, the governor's office, the police (*shurṭā*), the board of grievances (*maẓālim*), and the office of the inspection of the markets (*ḥisba*), to list only the most notable offices. This institutional multiplicity should be considered alongside another important feature of the Islamic state, namely its inability to serve as the sole patron of judicial institutions. Both multiplicity and the lack of state hegemony were manifestations of a constant tension between an Islamic political ideology and traditional practices, and the attendant changes in the balance of power between Islamic central forces and local ones. While Islamic law was, formally, the sole point of reference in the administration of justice, in practice, the state had a limited ability to legislate or to insist upon the uniform implementation of its laws (von Grunebaum 1946: 1). Instead, it sponsored or acted alongside the legal enterprises of jurists and provided the infrastructure for the implementation of the law. Although the *sharīʿa* was the only formally recognized legal order, its exploitation by various social groups introduced a diverse legal setting, which in turn facilitated a notable institutional variety.

The Islamic judicial structure was organized around a number of well-defined offices. At the top of this structure stood the caliph, the formal successor of Muhammad, who according to certain caliphal circles in the eighth and ninth centuries embodied both temporal and spiritual powers. The judicial office of the 'commander of the faithful' stemmed from the concept that Islam is 'the community of Allah', the umma, whose first judicial authority was Muhammad.[22] Well into Umayyad rule (661–750), during which the ancient Arabian practice of arbitration continued to play a central role alongside the newly introduced office of the *qāḍī* (Schacht 1966: 24), the Muslims began to adopt one of the main principles of the judicial organizations of their Roman and Sasanian predecessors: a hierarchical organization in which the head of state acts as the highest judicial figure and delegates his authority to regional governors, who in turn extend their authority to local magistrates.[23]

Under the Abbasids, the judiciary was gradually broken down into separate jurisdictions, leaving the *qāḍī* court in charge only of questions of religious law (Bligh-Abramski 1992: 58). Administratively, local *qāḍī*s acted within a judicial hierarchy, passing on judicial prerogatives to a lower class of judges (*nuwwāb*) and entrusting them with full or partial jurisdiction over small towns (Johansen 1999: 86–7). Two (or more) *qāḍī*s could serve within the same geographical jurisdiction, with each addressing distinct legal matters, such as penal or family law (Hallaq 2005: 80). This specialization is thought to have reached its high point in the ninth century. Yet the *qāḍī* did not operate alone. Not only did the institution of the pre-Islamic *ḥakam* continue to constitute a judicial option, but evidence also indicates that other figures, like the head of the police (*shurṭā*) and tribal officials (at least during the first century after the conquest) continued to fulfil judicial roles as well (Goitein 1967–93: II. 371; Bligh-Abramski 1992: 46–9).

An important aspect of Abbasid policy was the creation of a board of grievances, or office for the investigation of complaints, known as the *maẓālim* court.[24] Initially headed by the chief administrator of the caliphal court, the vizier, this judicial institution was originally established to enable litigants to lodge complaints against the government, including miscarriage of justice claims, particularly against *qāḍī*s (Nielsen 1985: 4; Hallaq 2005: 99). With time, however, the *maẓālim* became another form of tribunal, administered by an official who bore the title 'the overseer of grievances' (*nāẓir al-maẓālim* or *ṣāḥib al-maẓālim*), and as such, it handled matters

[22] Von Grunebaum 1946: 142; Goitein 1968: 131; Crone and Hinds 1986: 44–5; Hallaq 2005: 43.

[23] Schacht 1966: 24–5, 50; Kennedy 1981: 35; Morony 1984: 37–41; Bligh-Abramski 1992: 43, 58; Jany 2008: 149; Foss 1997: Part I.2.

[24] Cf. Schacht 1966: 51; Morony 1984: 86; according to Schacht and Morony, the office was initiated already under the Marwanids 684–750.

of a secular nature, like property and commercial affairs.[25] Unlike the *qāḍī*, who had to rely on the cooperation of the police for the enforcement of his decisions, the court of the *maẓālim* acted on behalf of the ruler and thus had access to means of enforcement (Rebstock 1999: 14). Despite the nature of legal affairs under its jurisdiction, the *maẓālim*'s classification as a secular judicial institution has rightly been described as misleading, since not only was the caliph's justice considered religious, but 'the dialectical relationship between the regular judgeship and *maẓālim* reflects as much their complementarities as their interchangeability' (Tillier 2009: 59; see also Coulson 1964: 130; Schacht 1966: 51).

A third judicial office that was introduced by the Abbasids around the ninth century and held civil and criminal judicial prerogatives is the 'inspection of the markets' (*ḥisba*) (Schacht 1966: 25; Silverstein and Sadan 2004: 344). The establishment of this office was a further blow to the *qāḍī*'s jurisdiction. In the narrow sense, the role of the inspector (*muḥtasib*) was to oversee commercial activities and address disputes that arose in the market, but in practice, he was entrusted with the moral supervision of the community and hence claimed judicial powers that had previously been reserved for the *qāḍī* (von Grunebaum 1946: 165). It should be noted, however, that the Islamic office of the *muḥtasib* was likely introduced already prior to the ninth century under a slightly different heading (*ṣāḥib al-sūq* rather than the later attested *muḥtasib*), and should therefore be considered in relation to the pre-Islamic institution of the market overseer, attested in Roman and rabbinic legal traditions (Schacht 1966: 25; Crone 1987b: 107–8).

With the establishment of the *maẓālim* and the *ḥisba*, the *qāḍī*'s jurisdiction was gradually limited to matters pertaining to Islamic law, the *sharīʿa* (Schacht 1966: 64; Bligh-Abramski 1992: 58). As a result, modern scholars hold the view that *qāḍī*s were increasingly drawn from a background of religious learning with a specialization in religious law. While the *qāḍī* may have received his formal appointment from the caliphal court, in practice, his allegiance to local scholars grew stronger and the legitimacy of his office relied heavily on their support (Hallaq 2005: 79).

Conclusion: Justice and Community

The Jewish, Christian, and Muslim communities at the centre of this discussion operated simultaneously on religious and social levels, rendering their religious affiliations and social memberships inseparable, at least from the standpoint of religious elites.[26] Accordingly, social aggregations were carved along religious lines and

[25] Ziadeh 1960: 65; Coulson 1964: 128–9; Schacht 1966: 51; Nielsen 1985: 4–6; Powers 1992: 316; for a summary of the *maẓālim*'s jurisdiction and method of practice, see Nielsen 1985: 17–25.

[26] Von Grunebaum 1946: 2, 6, 145; Baer 1950: 14; Goitein 1967–93: I. 262, II. 397; Rose 1982: 159, 161; Elon 1994: I. 6.

organized in accordance with a set of rules whose primary source and point of reference was scripture. These rules provided the most basic principles of the law and the legal platform on which future elaborations would be made (von Grunebaum 1946: 143; Hallaq 2005: 31; Walzer et al. 2000: xiii, xxxix). With time, confessional laws expanded to such an extent that they encompassed every aspect of life within the community, thereby creating legally self-contained theocracies.[27] Consequently, the practical application of these legal orders by means of a judicial apparatus was crucial, not only as the most solemn expression of religious ideals but also as a conspicuous marker of uncompromising socio-religious sovereignty.

For the modern observer, the lack of practical means of enforcement of the sort possessed by modern-state judicial institutions may suggest the feeble state of the confessional administrations surveyed above. Yet public consent, on which was predicated the implementation of rabbinic, ecclesiastical, and *sharʿi* justice, functioned in their case as a significant source of power. In principle, those who chose to appear before a Jewish judge agreed in advance to accept his ruling and its application (Goitein 1967–93: II. 316). The most effective and often only sanction available to Jewish judicial institutions was the proclamation of ostracism and excommunication (Mann 1919–20: 335–6, 341; Assaf 1922: 89; Ben-Sasson 1996: 302–3; Frenkel 2006: 169–73). Given the social nature of this penalty, its effectiveness depended not only on the cooperation of the culprit himself but on the voluntary adherence of the community as a whole. Indeed, the records suggest that also in the case of corporal punishments, particularly imprisonment, flagellation, and the shaving of the culprit's head and beard for certain offences, the meting out of such measures depended largely on the cooperation of the public.[28] Public consent was also a prerequisite for the implementation of ecclesiastical sentences. Despite what appears to have been a highly institutionalized set of arrangements, ecclesiastical judges relied mostly on excommunicating measures to enforce their decisions. Accordingly, outside the formalities of the ecclesiastical hierarchy, these judges were almost entirely dependent on the goodwill of their community for the implementation of their verdicts (Selb 1981–9: 214; Villagomez and Morony 1999: 314–15; for Egypt, see Foss 1997: I. 267). Like his non-Muslim counterparts, if to a lesser extent, the *qāḍī*, too, despite his identification with the ruling majority and formal affiliation to the state, seems often to have lacked direct means of enforcement, relying instead on the collaboration of the local police (von Grunebaum 1946: 165).

Indeed, the reliance of judicial decisions on public consent suggests an important bond between justice and community, in which the latter was committed to a social

[27] Khadduri 1955: 25; von Grunebaum 1946: 144–5; Coulson 1959: 13; Schacht 1966: 1, 48; Goitein 1967–93: II. 311; Putman 1975: 61; Selb 1981–9: I. 43; Rose 1982: 163–5; Elon 1994: I. xlix; Mathisen 2001: 1; Nakhalon 2001: 13, 15.

[28] Mann 1919–20: 344–5; Assaf 1922: 16; Aptowitzer 1937. Flogging and disciplinary flogging: Goitein 1967–93: I. 259; Ben-Sasson 1996: 340.

contract that in turn stemmed from a principle commitment to God, his covenant, and his temporal agents. Thus, any breach of communal jurisdictions was perceived as a blunt transgression of communal boundaries and a betrayal of God (Simonsohn 2011, chs 4, 6). The position of the ninth-century East Syrian patriarch Timothy I toward those 'Christians, men or women, who appear before outside judges' was articulated in terms of no less than an act of idolatry, bearing harsh consequences: 'And if they go to judges outside, how can they be Christian? For Paul has said to them: *You cannot partake of the table of the Lord* (1 Cor. 10: 21) and in another table. And *you cannot drink the cup of the Lord and the cup of Beliʿal*' (Sachau 1907–14: II. 67). Likewise, geniza documents record the annual practice of excommunicating Jews who appeared before Muslim judges on the seventh day of the Festival of Tabernacles on the Mount of Olives (Gil 1992: 167). Such attitudes reflect the severity attributed to the phenomenon of extra-confessional litigation and, perhaps more importantly, the decisive role played by judicial institutions in sustaining the interplay between the religious and social aspects of communal membership.

It is against the backdrop of this social paradigm and in light of the social and institutional diversity discussed above that we should interpret the endeavours of confessional leaders of the three religions to centralize their judicial administrations. The formal position of the geʾonim, patriarchs, and caliphs as the supreme judicial authorities of their respective communities was of utmost importance for sustaining their de facto power. Judicial authority afforded these leaders crucial means with which to fulfil their supervisory and coordinating functions. Yet such prerogatives exceeded mere technicalities, as they also gave these leaders the capacity to implement their understanding of the law and to shape public opinion in a manner that legitimizes their leadership. The growing independence of local *qāḍīs*, along with the growing prominence of Islamic scholarly circles, posed a challenge to the caliphal office, rendering its weight in the provinces nominal in most cases (Coulson 1956: 216). Thus, calls for reform, like that of Ibn al-Muqaffaʿ, were designed specifically to counter these trends toward an increasingly decentralized judicial administration (Zaman 1997: 4–6). Similar concerns over decentralization are reflected in Īšōʿbokt's depiction of a reality in which Christians adhere to a diversity of legal traditions, and in the tenth-century *Epistle of Nathan the Babylonian* portraying gaonic jurisdictions in a historical moment of a growing independence on the part of regional Jewish communities. Here, judicial agents, namely ordained Rabbanite scholars, Christian clergymen, and Muslim judges (*qāḍī*, *nāẓir al-maẓālim*, *muḥtasib*), provided the infrastructure. Confessional judges acted as local representatives of central authorities and implementers of their laws, thereby granting the various centres the legitimacy and the social control they sought to attain.[29]

[29] Putman 1975: 32, 34; Nielsen 1985: 1; Sklare 1996: 81; Brody 1998: 59; Rebstock 1999: 14.

References

The Apostolic Constitutions, ed. J. Donaldson. 1870. Edinburgh: T. & T. Clark.

Aptowitzer, A. 1937. 'Flogging and Disciplinary Flogging in Geonic Responsa'. In Hamishpat ha-'Ivri, 33–104.

Assaf, S. 1922. *Punishment after the Close of the Talmud.* Jerusalem: H.mo.l.

Assaf, S. 1924. *Jewish Legal Courts and their Procedures in the Post-Talmudic Period.* Jerusalem: Defus ha-Po'alim.

Assaf, S., ed. 1942. *Teshuvot Ha-geonim Mi-kitve-yad She-bi-genizat Cambridge.* Jerusalem: Mekitse Nirdamim.

Baer, Y. 1950. 'The Origins of the Organization of the Jewish Community of the Middle Ages'. *Zion* 15: 1–41.

Bareket, E. 1999. *Fustat on the Nile: The Jewish Elite in Medieval Egypt.* Leiden: Brill.

Baum, W. and Winkler, D. W. 2003. *The Church of the East: A Concise History.* London: Routledge.

Ben-Sasson, M. 1996. *The Emergence of the Local Jewish Community in the Muslim World: Qayrawan, 800–1057.* Jerusalem: Magnes.

Ben-Sasson, M. 2004. 'Religious Leadership in Islamic Lands: Forms of Leadership and Sources of Authority'. In J. Wertheimer, ed., *Jewish Religious Leadership: Image and Reality.* New York: Jewish Theological Seminary, I. 177–209.

Berkey, J. 2003. *The Formation of Islam: Religion and Society in the Near East, 600–1800.* New York: Cambridge University Press.

Bligh-Abramski, I. 1992. 'The Judiciary (*qāḍīs*) as a Governmental-Administrative Tool in Early Islam'. *Journal of the Economic and Social History of the Orient* 35 (1): 40–71.

Bravmann, M. M. 1972. *The Spiritual Background of Early Islam: Studies in Ancient Arab Concepts.* Leiden: Brill.

Brody, R. 1998. *The Geonim of Babylonia and the Shaping of Medieval Jewish Culture.* New Haven: Yale University Press.

Brown, P. 1971. 'The Rise and Function of the Holy Man in Late Antiquity'. *Journal of Roman Studies* 61: 80–101.

Brown, P. 1998. 'The Rise and Function of the Holy Man in Late Antiquity, 1971–1997'. *Journal of Early Christian Studies* 6 (3): 353–76.

Brown, P. 2001. *Poverty and Leadership in the Later Roman Empire.* Wantage: University Presses Marketing.

Bulliet, R. 1972. *The Patricians of Nishapur: A Study in Medieval Islamic Social History.* Cambridge, MA: Harvard University Press.

Cahen, C. 1970. 'Economy, Society, Institutions'. In P. M. Holt et al., eds, *The Cambridge History of Islam.* London: Cambridge University Press, 511–38.

Carver, M. O. H. 1996. 'Transitions to Islam: Urban Roles in the East and South Mediterranean, Fifth to Tenth Centuries AD'. In N. Christie and S. T. Loseby, eds, *Towns in Transition: Urban Evolution in Late Antiquity and the Early Middle Ages.* Aldershot: Scolar, 184–212.

Cohen, M. 1980. *Jewish Self-Government in Medieval Egypt.* Princeton: Princeton University Press.

Cohen, M. 1997. 'Jewish Communal Organization in Medieval Egypt: Research, Results and Prospects'. In N. Golb, ed., *Judaeo-Arabic Studies.* Amsterdam: Harwood, 73–86.

The Coptic Encyclopedia, 1991. New York: Macmillan.

Coulson, N. J. 1956. 'Doctrine and Practice in Islamic Law: One Aspect of the Problem'. *Bulletin of the School of Oriental and African Studies* 18 (2): 211–26.
Coulson, N. J. 1959. 'Muslim Custom and Case Law'. *Die Welt des Islam* (n.s.) 6 (2): 13–24.
Coulson, N. J. 1964. *A History of Islamic Law.* Edinburgh: Edinburgh University Press.
Crone, P. 1980a. 'Islam, Judeo-Christianity and Byzantine Iconoclasm'. *Jerusalem Studies in Arabic and Islam* 2: 59–95.
Crone, P. 1980b. *Slaves on Horses: The Evolution of the Islamic Polity.* Cambridge: Cambridge University Press.
Crone, P. 1984. 'Jāhilī and Jewish Law: The *Qasāma*'. *Jerusalem Studies in Arabic and Islam* 4: 153–202.
Crone, P. 1987a. *Meccan Trade and the Rise of Islam.* Princeton: Princeton University Press.
Crone, P. 1987b. *Roman, Provincial and Islamic Law: The Origins of the Islamic Patronate.* Cambridge: Cambridge University Press.
Crone, P. and Hinds, M. 1986. *God's Caliph: Religious Authority in the First Centuries of Islam.* Cambridge: Cambridge University Press.
Dagron, G. et al., eds. 1993. *Evêques, moines et empereurs (610–1054) Histoire du Christianisme: des origines à nos jours*, Vol. IV. Paris: Desclée.
Ducellier, A. 1996. *Chrétiens d'Orient et Islam au Moyen Age: VIIe–XVe siècle.* Paris: A. Colin.
Eddé, A.-M. et al., eds. 1997. *Communautés chrétiennes en pays d'Islam, du début du VIIe siècle au milieu du XIe siècle.* Paris: SEDES.
Elon, M. 1994. *Jewish Law: History, Sources, Principles.* 4 vols. Philadelphia: Jewish Publication Society.
Erhart, V. 2001. 'The Development of Syriac Christian Canon Law in the Sasanian Empire'. In Mathisen 2001: 115–29.
Evetts, B., ed. and trans. 1904–14. *History of the Patriarchs of the Coptic Church of Alexandria* (*PO* 2–4). 4 vols. Paris: Firmin-Didot.
Fattal, A. 1958. *Le Statut légal des non-musulmans en pays d'Islam.* Beirut: l'Institut de Lettres Orientales.
Figueras, P. 1994. 'The Impact of the Islamic Conquest'. *ARAM* 6: 283–90.
Foss, C. 1997. 'Syria in Transition, AD 550–750'. *Dumbarton Oaks Papers* 51: 189–269.
Frenkel, M. 2006. *The Compassionate and the Benevolent: The Leading Elite in the Jewish Community of Alexandria in the Middle Ages.* Jerusalem: Ben-Zvi Institute.
Gil, M. 1992. *A History of Palestine, 634–1099.* Cambridge: Cambridge University Press (originally published in Hebrew in 1983, 3 vols).
Gil, M. 2004. *Jews in Islamic Countries in the Middle Ages.* Leiden: Brill (originally published in Hebrew in 1997, 4 vols).
Goitein, S. D. 1967–93. *A Mediterranean Society: The Jewish Communities of the Arab World as Portrayed in the Documents of the Cairo Geniza.* 6 vols. Berkeley: University of California Press.
Goitein, S. D. 1968. *Studies in Islamic History and Institutions.* Leiden: Brill.
Goitein, S. D. 1980. *Palestinian Jewry in Early Islamic and Crusader Times.* Jerusalem: Yad Itzhak ben Zvi.
Gould, G. 1993. *The Desert Fathers on Monastic Community.* Oxford: Clarendon Press.
Von Grunebaum, G. E. 1946. *Medieval Islam: A Study in Cultural Orientation.* Chicago: University of Chicago Press.
Hage, W. 1999. 'Die Kirche "des Ostens": Kirchliche Selbständigkeit und kirchliche Gemeinsamkeit im funften Jahrhundert'. In G. J. Reinink and A. C. Klugkist, eds, *After*

Bardaisan: Studies on Continuity and Change in Syriac Christianity in Honour of Professor Han J. W. Drijvers. Leuven: Peeters, 141–8.

Hallaq, W. 2005. *The Origins and Evolution of Islamic Law*. Cambridge: Cambridge University Press.

Harkavy, A. E., ed. 1887. *Zikhron la-rishonim ve-gam la-akhronim*. Berlin [no publisher].

Harries, J. 1999. *Law and Empire in Late Antiquity*. Cambridge: Cambridge University Press.

Hecht, N. S. et al., eds. 1996. *An Introduction to the History and Sources of Jewish Law*. Oxford: Clarendon Press.

Humfress, C. 2007. *Orthodoxy and the Courts in Late Antiquity*. Oxford: Oxford University Press.

Hurvitz, N. 2003. 'From Scholarly Circles to Mass Movements: The Formation of Legal Communities in Islamic Societies'. *American Historical Review* 108 (4): 985–1008.

Hurvitz, Y. 1995. 'Jewish Legal Courts in the Geonic Period'. *Mahanayim* 13: 166–77.

Jany, J. 2008. 'Persian Influence on the Islamic Office of *Qāḍī al-Quḍāt*: A Reconsideration'. *Jerusalem Studies in Arabic and Islam* 34: 149–68.

Johansen, B. 1999. 'The All-Embracing Town and its Mosques: *Al-Miṣr al-ǧāmiʿ*. In *Contingency in a Sacred Law: Legal and Ethical Norms in the Muslim Fiqh*. Leiden: Brill, 77–106 (originally in *La Revue de l'Occident Musulman et de la Méditerranée* 32 (1981): 139–61).

Kaufhold, H., ed. 1971. *Syrische Texte zum islamischen Recht: Das dem nestorianischen Katholikos Johannes V. bar Abgare zugeschreibene Rechtsbuch*. Munich: Verlag der Bayer. Akad d. Wissenschaft; Beck in Komm.

Kaufhold, H. 1984. 'Der Richter in den syrischen Rechtsquellen: Zum Einflus islamischen Rechts auf die christlich-orientalische Rechtsliteratur'. *Oriens Chistianus* 68: 91–113.

Kaufhold, H. 2005. 'La Littérature pseudo-canonique syriaque'. In M. Debié et al., eds, *Les Apocryphes syriaques*. Paris: Geuthner, 147–67.

Kennedy, H. 1981. 'Central Government and Provincial Elites in the Early Abbasid Caliphate'. *Bulletin of the School of Oriental and African Studies* 44: 26–38.

Khadduri, M. 1955. *War and Peace in the Law of Islam*. Baltimore: Johns Hopkins Press.

Krikorian, M. 1981. 'Autonomy and Autocephaly in the Theory and Practice of the Ancient Oriental Churches'. *Kanon* 5: 114–29.

Lamoreaux, J. 1995. 'Episcopal Courts in Late Antiquity'. *Journal of Early Christian Studies* 3 (2): 143–67.

Lenski, N. 2001. 'Evidence for the *Audientia Episcopalis* in the New Letters of St. Augustine'. In R. Mathisen, ed., *Law, Society and Authority in Late Antiquity*. Oxford: Oxford University Press, 83–97.

Lewin, B. M. 1941. *Otzar ha-ge'onim, vol. 10: Gittin* Jerusalem: Mosad ha-Rav Kuk.

Libson, G. 2003. *Jewish and Islamic Law: A Comparative Study of Custom during the Geonic Period*. Cambridge, MA: Harvard University Press.

Lifshitz, B. 1982–3. 'The Legal Status of the Responsa Literature'. *Shenaton ha-mishpat ha-ʿivri* 9–10: 265–300.

McDonough, S. 2005. *Power by Negotiation: Institutional Reform in the Fifth-Century Sasanian Empire*. Ph.D. thesis, University of California.

MacEvitt, C. 2008. *The Crusades and the Christian World of the East: Rough Tolerance*. Philadelphia: University of Pennsylvania Press.

Macomber, W. 1968. 'The Authority of the Catholicos Patriarch of Seleucia-Ctesiphon'. *Orientalia christiana analecta* 181: 179–200.

Mann, J. 1919–20. 'The Responsa of the Babylonian Geonim as a Source of Jewish History'. *The Jewish Quarterly Review* (n.s.) 10 (2/3): 309–65.
Mann, J. 1920–2. *The Jews in Egypt and in Palestine under the Fāṭimid Caliphs*. 2 vols. London: Oxford University Press.
Mann, M. 1986. *The Sources of Social Power*. 2 vols. Cambridge: Cambridge University Press.
Mardirossian, A. 2004. *Le Livre des canons arméniens de Yovhannes Awjnec'i: église, droit et société en Arménie du IVe au VIIIe siècle* (*CSCO* 606 *subsidia* 116). Leuven: Peeters.
Masud, M. K., Peters, R. and Powers, D. S. 2006. 'Qadis and their Courts: An Historical Survey'. In Masud, Peters, and Powers, eds, *Dispensing Justice in Islam: Qadis and their Judgments*. Leiden: Brill, 1–44.
Mathisen, R., ed. 2001. *Law, Society and Authority in Late Antiquity*. Oxford: Oxford University Press.
Morony, M. 1984. *Iraq after the Muslim Conquest*. Princeton: Princeton University Press.
Motzki, H. 2002. *The Origins of Islamic Jurisprudence: Meccan Fiqh before the Classical Schools*. Leiden: Brill.
Ibn al-Muqaffa', 'A. 1976. *Al-risāla fī al-ṣaḥāba*, ed. and trans. C. Pellat. Paris: G. P. Maisonneuve et Larose.
Nakhalon, A., 2001. *The* Kahal *and its Enactments in the Geonic Period*. Jerusalem: Institute for Research in Jewish Law, Hebrew University.
Neubauer, A., ed. 1887–95. *Mediaeval Jewish Chronicles and Chronological Notes*. 2 vols. Oxford: Clarendon Press.
Nielsen, J. S. 1985. *Secular Justice in an Islamic State: Maẓālim under the Baḥrī Mamlūks, 662/1264–789/1387*. Leiden: Nederlands Instituut voor het Nabije Oosten.
Payne, R. 2010. 'Persecuting Heresy in Early Islamic Iraq: The Catholicos Ishoyahb III and the Elites of Nisibis'. In A. Cain and N. Lenski, eds, *The Power of Religion in Late Antiquity*. Burlington, VT: Ashgate, 397–409.
Pennington, K. 2007. 'The Growth of Church Law'. In A. Casiday and F. W. Norris, eds, *The Cambridge History of Christianity*. Cambridge: Cambridge University Press, 386–402.
Powers, D. 1992. 'On Judicial Review in Islamic Law'. *Law and Society Review* 26 (2): 315–42.
Putman, H. 1975. *L'Église et l'islam sous Timothée I*. Beirut: Dar el-Machreq.
Rapp, C. 2005. *Holy Bishops in Late Antiquity: The Nature of Christian Leadership in an Age of Transition*. Berkeley: University of California Press.
Rebstock, U. 1999. 'A Qadi's Errors'. *Islamic Law and Society* 6 (1): 1–37.
Rémondon, R. 1972. 'L'Église dans la société égyptienne à l'époque Byzantine'. *Chronique d'Égypte* 47: 254–77.
Riedel, W., ed. and trans. 1900. *Die Kirchenrechtsquellen des Patriarchats Alexandrien*. Leipzig: Deichert.
Rose, R. 1982. 'Islam and the Development of Personal Status Laws among Christian Dhimmis: Motives, Sources, Consequences'. *The Muslim World* 72 (3–4): 159–79.
Rosen, L. 2000. *The Justice of Islam: Comparative Perspectives on Islamic Law and Society*. Oxford: Oxford University Press.
Rustow, M. 2008. *Heresy and the Politics of Community: The Jews of the Fatimid Caliphate*. Ithaca, NY: Cornell University Press.
Rustow, M. 2009. 'At the Limits of Communal Autonomy: Jewish Bids for Intervention from the Mamluk State'. *Mamlūk Studies Review* 13 (2): 133–59.
Sachau, E., ed. and trans. 1907–14. *Syrische Rechtsbücher*. 3 vols. Berlin: G. Reimer.

Satlow, M. 1996. 'Texts of Terror: Rabbinic Texts, Speech Acts, and the Control of Mores'. *Association of Jewish Studies Review* 21 (2): 273–97.

Schacht, J. 1959. 'Foreign Elements in Ancient Islamic Law'. *Journal of Comparative Legislation and International Law* 32: 9–17.

Schacht, J. 1966. *An Introduction to Islamic Law*. Oxford: Clarendon Press.

Schick, R. 1995. *The Christian Communities of Palestine from Byzantine to Islamic Rule*. Princeton: Darwin.

Schiller, A. A. 1932. *Ten Coptic Legal Texts*. New York: The Metropolitan Museum of Art.

Schneider, I. 1990. *Das Bild des Richters in der 'adab al-qaḍˇī'-Literatur*. Frankfurt: Peter Lang.

Sela, S. 1994. 'The Head of the Rabbanite, Karaite and Samaritan Jews: On the History of a Title'. *Bulletin of the School of Oriental and African Studies* 57: 255–67.

Selb, W. 1967. 'Episcopalis audientia von der Zeit Konstantins bis zur Novelle XXXV Valentinians III'. *Zeitschrift des Savigny-Stiftung für Rechtsgeschichte* 84: 162–217.

Selb, W. 1981–9. *Orientalisches Kirchenrecht*. 2 vols. Vienna: Osterreichischen Akademie der Wissenschaften.

Selb, W. and Kaufhold, H., eds. and trans. 2005. *Das syrich-römische Rechtsbuch*. Vienna: Osterreichischen Akademie der Wissenschaften.

Silverstein, A. and Sadan, J. 2004. 'Ornate Manuals or Practical *Adab*? Some Reflections on a Unique Work by an Anonymous Author of the 10th century CE'. *Al-qanṭara* 25 (2): 339–56.

Simonsohn, U. 2011. *A Common Justice: The Legal Allegiances of Christians and Jews under Early Islam*. Philadelphia: Pennsylvania University Press.

Sklare, D. 1996. *Samuel ben Hofni Gaon and his Cultural World*. Leiden: Brill.

Steinwenter, A. 1955. *Das Recht der koptischen Urkunden*. Munich: Beck.

Stroumsa, R. 2008. *People and Identities in Nessana*. Ph.D. thesis, Duke University.

Synodicon orientale ou recueil de synodes nestoriens, ed. and trans. J. B. Chabot. 1902. Paris: Imprimerie nationale.

The Theodosian Code, trans. C. Pharr. 1952. Princeton: Princeton University Press.

Tillier, M. 2006. 'Un traité politique du IIe/VIIIe siècle: l'epitre de 'Ubayd Allāh ibn al-Ḥˇasan al-'Anbarī au calife al-Mahdī'. *Annales Islamologiques* 40: 152–4.

Tillier, M. 2009. *Les Cadis d'Iraq et l'état abbasside (132/750–334/945)*. Damascus: Ifpo.

Tillier, M. 2011. 'The Qadis of Fustat-Misr under the Tulunids and the Ikhshidids: The Judiciary and Egyptian Autonomy'. *Journal of the American Oriental Society* 131 (2): 207–22.

Tyan, É. 1938. *Histoire de l'organisation judiciaire en pays d'Islam*. 2 vols, Paris: Librairie du Recueil Sirey.

Van Ess, J. 1991–7. *Theologie und Gesellschaft im 2. und 3. Jahrhundert Hidschra: Eine Geschichte des religiösen Denkens im frühen Islam*. 6 vols. Berlin: Walter de Gruyter.

Villagomez, C. and Morony, M. 1999. 'Ecclesiastical Wealth in the East Syrian Church from Late Antiquity to Early Islam'. In G. J. Reinink and A. C. Klugkist, eds, *After Bardaisan: Studies on Continuity and Change in Syriac Christianity in Honour of Professor Han J. W. Drijvers*. Leuven: Peeters, 303–15.

Vismara, G. 1937. *Episcopalis audientia*. Milano: Società editrice 'Vita e pensiero'.

Vööbus, A., ed. and trans. 1975–6. *The Synodicon in the West Syrian Tradition* (*CSCO* 367–8, 375–6 *Scr. Syri.* 161–4). Leuven: Secretariat du CSCO.

Walmsley, A. 1992. 'The Social and Economic Regime at Fihl (Pella) between the 7th and 9th Centuries'. In P. Canivet and J. P. Rey-Coquais, eds, *La Syrie de Byzance à l'Islam VIIe–VIIIe siècles: Actes du Colloque International, Lyon—Maison de l'Orient Méditerranéen,*

Paris—Institut du Monde Arabe, 11-15 Septembre 1990. Damascus: Institut Francais de Damas, 249–61.

Walzer, M. et al., eds. 2000. *The Jewish Political Tradition*, Vol. I: *Membership*. New Haven: Yale University Press.

Wensinck, A. J. 1922. 'The Refused Dignity'. In T. W. Arnold and R. A. Nicholson, eds, *A Volume of Oriental Studies Presented to Edward G. Browne*. Cambridge: Cambridge University Press, 491–99.

Wheatley, P. 2001. *The Places Where Men Pray Together: Cities in Islamic Lands, Seventh through the Tenth Centuries*. Chicago: University of Chicago Press.

Wipszycka, E. 1972. *Les Ressources et les activités économiques des églises en Égypte du IVe au VIIIe siècle*. Brussels: Fondation Égyptologique Reine Élisabeth.

Zaman, M. Q. 1997. 'The Caliphs, the "'Ulamā'", and the Law: Defining the Role and Function of the Caliph in the Early 'Abbāsid Period'. *Islamic Law and Society* 4 (1): 1–36.

Ziadeh, F. 1960. "*Urf* and Law in Islam'. In J. Kritzeck and R. B. Winder, eds, *The World of Islam: Studies in Honor of Phillip K. Hitti*. London: Macmillan, 60–7.

Ziegler, K.-H. 1971. *Das private Schiedsgericht im antiken römischen Recht*. Munich: C. H. Beck.

CHAPTER 10

JEWS AND MUSLIMS IN CHRISTIAN LAW AND HISTORY

JOHN TOLAN

How does Christianity explain the existence of the two rival Abrahamic faiths, Judaism and Islam? What place does it allow in Christian society for Jews and Muslims? The responses to these questions are many, and in this brief article it will only be possible to examine a few prominent examples. Rather than a survey of Christians' attitudes towards Jews (or Judaism) and Muslims (or Islam), we will examine how Christian law accommodated Jews and Muslims as residents of Christian societies and the roles that Christian thinkers assigned to Judaism and Islam in a Christian scheme of history. The emphasis will be on a few salient examples from the fourth century (when Christianity obtains social and intellectual predominance in the Roman Empire) to the nineteenth (when Christianity loses that predominance in Europe).

During the life of Jesus, various apocalyptic movements within Judaism anticipated the imminent arrival of the Messiah and the instauration of the new Jewish kingdom. Jesus himself seems to have taught that the end of history was near and certainly many of his followers, in the first generations following his death, taught that the end was near (Matt. 25: 31–46; Luke 24: 49); the extent and nature of Jesus' apocalypticism continues to provoke scholarly debate (Aune 2006: 7–8). The apocalyptic predictions of the prophets, in particular the Book of Daniel, revisited and revised in the New Testament (above all in the Book of Revelation) assured Jesus' followers that the persecutions they were experiencing would soon come to an end, the pagan Roman Empire (cast as the new Babylon) would be crushed, and a new era of justice and peace would dawn. Yet when Constantine proclaimed the edict of Milan in 313, the persecutions ceased and Rome turned from persecutor to ally of the church. Churchmen had to rethink apocalyptic schemes of history and Christian legislators had to define through law the confines of the church and its relationship to Roman society.

1. Jews and Christian Rome

A. Jews in Roman and Byzantine Law

In the fourth and fifth centuries, as Christianity became the dominant religion of the Roman Empire, imperial decrees outlawed pagan sacrifices and ordered the closing of pagan temples, yet at the same time offered guarantees to Jews: synagogues were protected; soldiers were not be billeted in synagogues; Jews were not to be summoned to court on the Sabbath; they were protected from insult and injury on the part of Christians. Yet at the same time that these laws protected Jews, other laws restricted them, prohibiting them from serving in certain positions of authority, from proselytizing among Christians (Linder 2006; Mathisen 2014). These laws were promulgated by emperors from Constantine onwards, often reacting to specific events and to requests from the people concerned: Jews worried by Christian violence, or Christian bishops concerned about Jewish proselytism. These laws reflect individual reactions to specific situations, rather than a concerted attempt to define relations between Christians and Jews (Nemo-Pekelman 2010). Yet when Theodosius II had many of these laws grouped together into one chapter of his *Theodosian Code* (438), it provided a clear place for Jews as a protected but inferior minority in a Christian Roman Empire.

Judaism became a tolerated but inferior religion. Indeed, one might say simply that it became a religion (Boyarin 2004). Earlier, pagan Roman emperors had granted privileges and protections to Jews, just as they had granted similar privileges to other subjected peoples. In legal terms, Jews represented one among many subjected peoples (*gentes*), and were not defined in terms of religion. The rise of Christianity, a breakoff Jewish sect, to dominance in the Roman Empire changed that. In the fourth and fifth centuries, Christian churchmen and Christian emperors struggled to organize and structure the institutional church and to define the contours of orthodox belief and practice: Christianity became a religion, and as such its constituent parts (hierarchy, rites, and doctrine) were set down. While the emperors who promulgated these laws at times lambasted Judaism as a 'superstition', some of the laws defined it as a 'religion' and indeed institutionalized it along the lines of that of the church. A hierarchy of Jewish officials was recognized and given, quite explicitly, the same privileges as the high officials of the Christian church, creating what Amnon Linder has called a 'Jewish Church' (Linder 2006: 157).

Among the prerogatives of this Jewish 'clerical' elite was to exercise justice in communal affairs. Several laws point to difficulties in establishing boundaries between Roman and Jewish jurisdiction: Jews were subjected to Roman laws, yet could submit their affairs to their own authorities to settle internal disputes. Several laws mention cases of Jews refusing to recognize the authority of judgements rendered by Jewish judges and appealing to Roman judges. This will remain an issue throughout the Middle Ages and the early modern period: Jews are recognized, and given privileges, as a community; the community regulates itself and disciplines its wayward members. Justinian ordered major new compilations of law during his reign; these texts, referred to collectively as the *Corpus iuris civilis*, reiterated a number of the laws from the *Theodosian Code* concerning Jews and included various new laws, in which one sees a similar mix of protection and restriction. Ralph Mathisen has plausibly suggested that the reiteration of a number of restrictive laws (on, for example, intermarriage between Christians and Jews) suggests that these laws were frequently ignored, and that 'it would appear that, after the spate of Jewish legislation in the early fifth century, Jews were largely left to themselves and the laws regulating their behavior were largely ignored' (Mathisen 2014). Justinian's *Corpus iuris civilis* became the foundation text for subsequent Byzantine law and had a profound influence on European law, particularly from the eleventh century. While several ninth-century emperors of Constantinople attempted to force Jews to convert, on the whole the status accorded by these laws was respected (Dagron 1993; Sharf 1995).

B. Jews in the Emerging Christian Conception of History

In the first centuries of Christianity, Christians of the Roman Empire endured sometimes intense, but in fact unequal and sporadic persecution; in the fourth century, Christianity became first an officially tolerated religion within the empire, then a more or less official state religion during the reign of Theodosius I (379–95). Many early Christians had a profoundly apocalyptic view of history, with Rome assigned the role of the 'whore of Babylon', persecutor whose demise would bring on the end of time. This changed in the fourth century, as the empire became Christian, and Christian writers assigned a salvific role to Rome, whose dominion came to be seen as a divinely ordained tool for the dissemination of Christianity. Subsequent Christian writers would have to explain the vicissitudes of the history of Rome and the church in the light of God's plan of history which began at the creation and would culminate in the Last Judgement. One important issue they had to grapple with—and the one that interests us here—is the role that non-Christians (past, present, and future) played in this divinely authored drama that is human history.

Eusebius of Caesarea is in many respects the father of Christian history. Eusebius' *Chronicle* is an ambitious and unparalleled effort to write universal history fusing the mythical and historical narratives of widely varying sources from different cultures: Egypt, Assyria, Persia, Greece, etc. Renouncing any effort to blend these sources into a seamless narrative, he rather laid them out in multiple parallel columns, thus emphasizing the synchronicity of people and events in different cultures. While the organization into parallel columns confers legitimacy on all these variant historiographical traditions, a closer look shows that two of the traditions predominate: the Hebrew and the Roman. The *Chronicle*'s tables commence with the life of Abraham: God's covenant with Abraham thus is the key foundational event in human history. Moreover, the multiple columns (eight at some places) of the *Chronicle* progressively dwindle in number, as conquest causes fusion of empires (and of their histories) (Williams and Grafton 2006: 141). Rome is represented first as one column among many, but it progressively comes to dominate the *Chronicle* as it conquers and absorbs nations. After Octavian's victory over Antony at Actium, only two columns remain: Rome and the Jews. The Jewish column abruptly closes with the sack of Jerusalem by Titus and Vespasian in 70: from that point on, Eusebius' *Chronicle* has one unrivalled column, that of Rome. Eusebius was a close adviser to Constantine, and this disposition of his *Chronicle* graphically displays the triumph of a Roman Empire chosen by God as his vehicle for the dissemination of Christianity. The Jews, through their double revolt represented by the rejection of Christ the Messiah and the revolt against Roman power, lose their place in history as they literally disappear from Eusebius' *Chronicle*. Eusebius' traditional Greek learning is subsumed into a system defined and dominated by the twin systems of Jewish and Roman history: while Hebrew tradition provides the key to structuring and understanding the past, the present and future belong to Rome. It would be hard to find a clearer image of the place assigned to Jews in the new Christian Rome; Jerome translated Eusebius' *Chronicle* into Latin and it thus became the foundational work of Christian historiography in both Greek and Latin. Whereas early Christians awaited the destruction of Rome which would herald the new millennium, for Eusebius Constantine's conversion changed everything. In his *Life of Constantine*, after describing how the emperor had new Christian sanctuaries built in Jerusalem, he writes, 'this being perhaps that fresh new Jerusalem proclaimed in the prophetic oracles' (Eusebius 1999: 135–6). In other words, the celestial Jerusalem had already descended to earth, thanks to the conversion of the emperor and his transformation of the Lord's city. The new kingdom that God's people had fervently awaited had arrived: it was Constantine's new Christian Empire.

Augustine, in his *City of God*, written a century after Eusebius' *Chronicle*, called into question the central role of Rome in Christian history. Writing in response to pagans who claimed that the sack of Rome by the Goths in 410 was caused by the abandonment of the gods of Rome and the adoption of Christianity, Augustine reduced Rome to one empire among many and denied it any superiority or special legitimacy. Roman power, like that of previous empires, was based on the brute force of conquest. Indeed, the peace imposed by Roman emperors was propitious to the spread of Christianity. The city of God is comprised of the elect, whose members lived as *peregrini*, foreigners, on this earth. Human society is a *civitas permixta*, a mixed community where the citizens of the earthly and worldly cities are inextricably intertwined. Over and against those who saw Rome's current tribulations as so many signs of the approaching end, Augustine affirmed that it was impossible to know when the end would come. Those Christians who hoped for the imminent millennium were misled, for the millennium had already been realized: the promised kingdom of God was to be understood spiritually as the reign of the church (Fredriksen 1999).

In various works, Augustine addresses the role of Jews in Christian society (Signer 1999). In the *City of God* (18.46) he explains that the Jews who put Jesus to death and failed to believe in him were in consequence crushed by the Romans and sent into exile among the nations. Since they are found everywhere, they serve as witnesses, 'living letters of the law': proof in the flesh both of the truth of the scriptures which they preserve in the original Hebrew and of the humiliation meted out by Christ to those of his people who refuse to recognize him as their Lord. While Christian heretics (such as the Donatists) should be compelled to conform with the Catholic faith, Jews should be allowed to live in peace among Christians. They preserve in error the ancient covenant and through their error, and their subservient place in Christian society, serve as unwitting witnesses to the superior truth of Christianity (Cohen 1999). Moreover, the Jews will, of their own will, massively convert to Christianity at the end of time: this, indeed, will be one of the signs that the end is near.

Christian historiography is subsequently marked by two contrasting tendencies: a Eusebian tradition sacralizing Rome (and subsequent Christian kingdoms), and an Augustinian tradition denying the sacral nature of rulership, conceding only that rule by force is a necessary evil. Many medieval authors display a mixture of Eusebian and Augustinian perspectives. Hugh of St Victor wrote and taught in the Augustinian convent of St Victor of Paris, one of the key seats of learning in twelfth-century Europe (Sicard 1991). In his *De sacramentis*, Hugh sets out his theology of history. God, architect of the world and planner of its history, communicates with us through events. 'In the divine utterance', explains Hugh, 'not only words but even things have a meaning' (Hugh of St Victor 1961: 121). Christian history is linear, and Hugh rejects the 'errors' of the ancient philosophers who saw time as cyclical (Sicard 1991: 135). Between the two cosmic dramas of creation and apocalypse, Hugh situates two major human dramas: the Fall, a unique event in which man lost his privileged place in the universe that God created, and the restoration or redemption, which is human race's slow progress towards that perfection which it had once lost. Hugh follows the traditional division of history into six periods which had been prefigured in the six days of the creation. But he also adds another traditional division into three ages. First 'before the law' (from Adam to Moses) is the age in which humanity is ruled by 'natural law', as dictated by human reason. Under natural law humanity progressed and became ready to receive God's law through Moses, marking the beginning of the second age (from Moses to Christ), 'under the law' (even though most of humanity, ignoring Mosaic Law, still followed natural law). Finally, humanity progresses to the point where it is ready to receive redemption through Christ's incarnation, which marks the beginning of the third and final age 'under grace'.

In this view of history, the present and the future belong to Christianity, while non-Christians follow legitimate but superseded laws. This distinction between three laws is taken up by jurists, in particular in the twelfth-century *Decretum* attributed to Gratian, which is the foundation text of medieval canon law in Latin Europe. While Hugh had emphasized the chronological progression between the three laws, Gratian insists on the fundamental identity and compatibility between them. God created us with reason, which enables all humans to understand the fundamental notions of justice that make up natural law: the *lex gentium* (law of nations), to the extent that it respects universal natural law, is thus completely compatible with Christian law which subsumes it. This is in part Gratian's response to the renewed study of Roman law, which he in this way both legitimizes and subordinates by incorporating it into Christian law. What the Law of Moses added to natural law was *mystica*, strictures unable to be perceived through reason alone, such as the prohibition of pork or the injunction of circumcision. The law of Christ affirms and transforms that of Moses, for Jesus himself had affirmed, 'Do not think that I have come to abolish the Law or the Prophets; I have not come to abolish them but to fulfil them' (Matt. 5: 17). Hence, for Gratian, when the church replaces circumcision with baptism, this is not an abrogation of the law; it is merely the fruit of understanding the law in its new, spiritual sense, rather than in the literal, carnal sense (Chodorow 1972; Southern 1995: 264–318).

The law of Moses is thus subsumed in and superseded by the law of Christ: this is a trope found in countless texts, by theologians, chroniclers, and others, throughout the Middle Ages. It finds vivid expression in iconographic representations of the synagogue and the church. Outside the south transept portal of the cathedral of Strasbourg, for example (*c.*1220), Synagogue is presented as a blindfolded young woman, her head hanging down, with a broken lance in her right hand (sign of her lost power) and the tablets of the law of Moses which seem to be slipping out of her left hand, sign that she still is clinging weakly to the old law. Over and against this figure of blindness is the Church triumphant, a proud crowned woman with a piercing gaze, holding the symbols of her covenant with Christ: the cross in her right hand and the chalice of the Eucharist in the left (Rowe 2011). This vision of Judaism bowed and subservient pervades theological and legal texts of the period (Sapir Abulafia 2011). Throughout Europe, communities of Jews lived in the cities (and in some areas in the countryside) and often played important roles in trade and, increasingly, in finance. Various European rulers issued laws guaranteeing safety and often some degree of legal autonomy to these Jewish communities. Pope Callixtus II (1119–24) issued a bull *Sicut Judaeis*, which offered specific protections to Jews living within Christian society. Callixtus' letter does not survive, nor does that of his successor Eugenius III (1145–53), but both are referred to by Pope Alexander III, who issues his own bull *Sicut Judaeis* sometime between 1159 and 1181, in which he prohibits Christians from forcing Jews to convert or imposing penalties on those Jews who do convert. He further bars Christians from injuring Jews or taking money from them, disrupting Jewish festivals, exacting additional services, or desecrating Jewish cemeteries to extort money.[1] Later popes were to reissue this bull, sometimes with minor variations.

Dozens of the legal texts compiled by Gratian in his *Decretum* provide concrete examples of the subordinate but protected role assigned to Jews in Christian society. While the church claimed no jurisdiction over Jews, it did attempt to regulate and limit Christian interaction with Jews, prohibiting Christians from sharing meals with Jews or

[1] Notice no. 103877, RELMIN project, 'The Legal Status of Religious Minorities in the Euro-Mediterranean World (5th–15th Centuries)'; Telma Web edition, IRHT, Institut de Recherche et d'Histoire des Textes—Orléans http://www.cn-telma.fr/relmin/extrait103877/.

having sexual intercourse with them—much less marrying them. Jews were not to own Christian slaves (a rule later interpreted as a ban on the employment of Christian servants); they were not to exercise authority over Christians.[2] In the judicial landscape of medieval Europe, multiple systems of justice overlapped (and sometimes were in outright rivalry with each other): seigniorial courts, royal courts, municipal courts, ecclesiastical courts, and rabbinical courts (which treated disputes within the Jewish communities). In theory, Jews were prohibited from bearing witness against Christians or exercising any jurisdiction or authority over them: this principle is found in Roman law, in canon law, and in many texts of civic law. Yet in fact, throughout Europe we find numerous laws that allow Jews to bear witness against Christians in disputes concerning them and that allow disputes between Jewish and Christian individuals to be judged by a mixed group of Christians and Jews. As in Rome and Byzantium, these restrictive laws are often reissued and reiterated, suggesting that they were enforced only sporadically.

2. The Middle Ages and Early Modernity

A. Irruption of the Saracens into the Christian Scheme of History, Seventh to Thirteenth Centuries

If Jews and Judaism play a large part in the Christian scheme of history, Muslims and Islam are, at least at first glance, completely absent. Indeed while Islam or the Quran was often referred to as *lex Sarracenorum* (the law of the Saracens) or *lex Mahumeti* (the law of Muhammad), there was never any question that it could represent a legitimate law: there was no room for a fourth phase of history after the triumph of Christianity. While, for many canon lawyers, the rule of Muslim princes could be legitimate to the extent that they respected natural law, the *lex Sarracenorum* itself was at best a hodgepodge of Jewish, pagan, and heretical elements mixed with Christian truths.

Medieval Christian writers did not speak of 'Islam' or 'Muslims', words unknown (with very few exceptions) in western languages before the sixteenth century (Tolan 2002: xv). Instead, Christian writers refer to Muslims by using ethnic terms: Arabs, Turks, Moors, Saracens. Often they call them 'Ishmaelites', descendants of the biblical Ishmael, or Hagarenes (from Hagar, Ishmael's mother). Ishmael, according to Genesis, was Abraham's eldest son, born of Hagar, handmaid of his wife, Sarai (subsequently Sarah). The angel of the Lord who announced to Hagar the birth of her child tells her

[2] For online editions of these texts, with commentary and translations, see Notice no. 1510, RELMIN project, 'The Legal Status of Religious Minorities in the Euro-Mediterranean World (5th–15th centuries)' Telma Web edition, IRHT, Institut de Recherche et d'Histoire des Textes—Orléans <http://www.cn-telma.fr/relmin/auteur1510/>.

'he will be a wild man; his hand will be against every man, and every man's hand will be against him; and he shall dwell in the presence of all his brethren' (Gen. 16: 12). Sarah later bears a child, Isaac. When Isaac is weaned his parents have a feast, and Sarah sees Ishmael mocking his younger brother; she tells Abraham, 'Cast out this bondwoman and her son: for the son of this bondwoman shall not be heir with my son' (21: 10). God tells Abraham to heed his wife, consoling him by announcing that 'of the son of the bondwoman will I make a nation'. This is the same message God sends to Hagar in despair in the desert. Indeed, Ishmael lived to father twelve sons, 'twelve princes according to their nations' who 'dwelt from Havilah unto Shur, that is before Egypt, as thou goest toward Assyria' (Gen. 25: 16–18). The scheme of twelve tribes of Ishmael is no doubt meant to correspond to the twelve tribes of Israel, and in the list of Ishmael's sons one finds names that correspond to tribes or peoples, but also to towns. It seems that the biblical term Ishmaelite was first used to refer to small groups in the Transjordan, and later expanded to designate a wide range of nomadic peoples living south and east of Palestine (Retsö 2003: 220–9). It is a band of Ishmaelite merchants who buy Joseph in the desert from his brothers and who resell him in Egypt (Gen. 37–9). The Christian allegorical interpretation of the story of Abraham and his two sons begins in the New Testament itself, in Paul's letter to the Galatians. The two sons signify the two covenants: the first, born of the flesh from Hagar (which Paul associates with 'mount Sinai in Arabia'), is the covenant of bondage; the second, born of the spirit from Sarah, associated with Jerusalem, is the covenant of freedom (Gal. 4: 22–31).

While learned treatises often refer to Ishmaelites, the far commoner term in the Middle Ages was Saracen (*Sarracenus* in Latin, *Sarrasin* in Old French). The term, of obscure origin, was used by Greek and Latin writers of late antiquity to refer to Arab-speaking tribes of the Arabian Peninsula (Tolan 2012a). Eusebius seems to be the first author to treat the terms Saracen and Ishmaelite as essentially synonymous: he mentions *Σαρακηνοί* in several of his works, presenting them as the descendants of Ishmael. But it is Jerome who develops a vivid and negative image of Ishmaelite/Saracen marauders. The angel's words to Hagar, that Ishmael would be a 'wild man' and that 'his hand will be against every man', are fulfilled, for Jerome, in the acts of his descendants: the Ishmaelite marauders who attack towns and monasteries. In his commentary on Ezekiel, Jerome mentions the Midianites, Ishmaelites, and Hagarenes, saying that the latter 'now call themselves Saracens, falsely usurping the name of Sarah, thus appearing to be born of a free lady'. The *Agareni* are the descendants of Hagar; they can also be called Ishmaelites, descendants of Ishmael. As for the term 'Saracens', Jerome gives it a polemical etymology: these descendants of the illegitimate child of a slave-girl want to usurp the rights of the free-born descendants of the patriarch Isaac. This etymology seems to be Jerome's own invention; it is destined to a long posterity. Two centuries before the birth of Muhammad, Jerome proffers a polemical image of Saracens as deserts marauders, enemies of civilization and Christendom, who seek to usurp the heritage of Isaac. He has little to say about their religion: he at one point mentions that they worship Venus, yet elsewhere describes how St Hilarion had converted some of them to Christianity (Tolan 2012a).

Christian chroniclers in Latin Europe, when contemplating the meteoric rise of the 'Saracens' in the seventh and eighth centuries of the Christian era, turned quite naturally to the authorities they held most reliable: the Bible and the writings of church fathers such as Jerome. Bede, a monk at the Northumbrian monastery of Jarrow in the early eighth century, had heard of the Saracens' conquests in the East, their subjection of Africa, and their raids into Spain and Gaul. He turned to Genesis and to Jerome's commentary on Genesis and concluded that 'Now, [Ishmael's] hand is against all men, and all men's hands are against him, to such an extent that the Saracens hold the whole breadth of Africa in their sway, and they also hold the greatest part of Asia and some part of Europe, hateful and hostile to all' (Bede 2008: 278–9). For Bede, as for Jerome, the words that the angel spoke to Hagar bear important meaning not only for comprehending biblical history, but for understanding eternal truths about the descendants of Ishmael, the Saracens, whose ferocity is clearly announced by the angel: it is an immutable characteristic of a clearly identifiable people. While for modern historians (not to mention medieval Muslim writers) the rise of Islam marks a clear break in the history of the 'Saracens', from the biblically informed vision of Christian history, that transformation is imperceptible: Bede's Saracens are essentially the same as Jerome's.

Hence it should come as no surprise that many European authors, knowing little or nothing about Islam, portrayed Saracens in the guise of pagan idolaters: the more colourful descriptions, in crusade chronicles and epic poems, show them worshipping a panoply of idols, chief among them 'Mahumet'. The epic poems describe fierce battles between Saracens and Christians and often culminate in the destruction of the Saracens' idols. In the *Chanson de Roland*, the Saracens themselves, in a fit of pique after losing to the Christian army, topple the idols of their gods; the Christian knights, as they invest the city of Saragossa, finish the job off by smashing with hammers the remaining idols they find in the 'sinagoges' and 'mahumeries'. This image of the pagan Saracen lives on in the *chansons de geste*, liturgical drama, saints' lives, and in various Latin chronicles, until the fifteenth or sixteenth centuries, assuring the Christian readers of the truth of their own religion (Tolan 2002: 105–34).

But most authors who wrote about the *lex Sarracenorum* portrayed it as a deviant, heretical form of Christianity. We find this already in John of Damascus, an eighth-century Christian who served in the administration of the Umayyad caliphate in Damascus and subsequently became a monk in the Palestinian monastery of Mar Saba, where he wrote an encyclopedic exposition and refutation of the 100 heresies that endangered Christendom: the 100th was the heresy 'of the Ishmaelites'. The proponents of this heretical doctrine, John explains, deny the divinity of Christ and the reality of his crucifixion. They accuse Christians of idolatry when they venerate the cross, but they themselves practise idolatry when they kiss the black stone of the Kaʿba (Tolan 2002: 50–9).

Theophanes composed his *Chronigraphica* in Constantinople around 815 (Tolan 2002: 64–6). Theophanes claims that the Jews had first flocked to Muhammad, thinking he was their long-awaited Messiah; when they saw him eating camel (a forbidden food), they realized their error, yet some of them stayed with him out of fear 'and taught him illicit things directed against us Christians'. Theophanes describes Muhammad's marriage to Khadīja and his travels in Palestine where he sought out the writings of Jews and Christians. Muhammad had an epileptic seizure, and at this Khadīja became distressed; he soothed her by telling her: 'I keep seeing a vision of a certain angel called Gabriel, and being unable to bear his sight, I faint and fall down.' Khadīja sought the advice of 'a certain monk living there, a friend of hers (who had been exiled for his depraved doctrine)'; this heretical monk seems to be based on the Christian figures Bahira and Wariqa of Muslim tradition. The monk told Khadīja that Muhammad was indeed a prophet to whom the angel Gabriel came in visions. Theophanes recounts that Muhammad promised to all who fell fighting the enemy a paradise full of sensual delights: eating, drinking, and sex. He said 'many other things full of profligacy and stupidity'.

A far more learned and elaborate polemic (and one which was to have a far greater impact in Latin Europe), was the *Risālat al-Kindī*, written by a ninth- or tenth-century Baghdad Christian (Tartar 1985; Tolan 2002: 60–6) The *Risālat al-Kindī* is both polemical and apologetical: it attacks Muslim doctrine and provides a defence of key Christian doctrines that would be distasteful to Muslims. Its author defends the Trinity while affirming God's unity; far be it from a true Christian to say that 'God is the third of three'. Does not God, in the Bible, refer to himself in the plural? God has many attributes, he asserts, two of which are eternal: life and knowledge. Life corresponds to Christ the Word (λογός, *kalima*), knowledge to the Holy Spirit (πνευμα, *rūh*); thus the Trinity can be proven from a reflection on God's nature. The Christian author makes a concerted attack against Muhammad, in order to prove that he was no prophet. He recounts Muhammad's biography in as acerbic and derogatory fashion as possible, showing all the while a good knowledge of the Quran and early Muslim historiography. He notes that Muhammad had first been an idolater and had enriched himself through trade and through his marriage with Khadīja. Wishing to rule over his tribe, he decided to pretend to be a prophet; his companions, gullible nomads who knew nothing of the signs of prophecy, believed him. He and his followers enriched themselves through war and pillaging. These acts, for the Christian writer, are enough to prove that Muhammad was not a prophet; the failures of some of the expeditions (especially the battle of Uhud) even more so: a true prophet would have foreseen (and avoided) defeat. This Christian monk is particularly shocked by Muhammad's sexual life, which he attacks with gusto. Muhammad himself, he says, claimed to have the sexual powers of forty men. He presents a catalogue of Muhammad's fifteen wives, dwelling on the scandals surrounding Zaynab and 'Â'isha. He criticizes the practice of ablutions, Ramadan fasts, the pilgrimage rites at Mecca. This work circulated among Arabic-speaking Christians in Spain. Twelfth-century Latin polemicist Petrus Alfonsi used it in his *Dialogues against the Jews*, which for good measure contains a chapter attacking Islam, largely derived from the *Risālat al-Kindī*. Peter, abbot of Cluny, commissioned a translation of the work, along with the Quran and other works, in 1142; this Latin translation accompanied the Quran translation in manuscripts and early printed editions.

We find a similar portrayal of Islam as a heretical deviant of Christianity in the works of various Latin authors of the twelfth century. Anastasius the Librarian translated Theophanes' *Chronographica* into Latin in the 870s; this translation was one of the few widely available sources about Muhammad in Western Europe before the twelfth century: supplying information, for example, in the monastic chronicles of Sigebert de Gembloux and Hugh of Fleury (Kedar 1984: 33–5, 86–9).

Several twelfth-century Latin authors created more elaborate and more colourful portraits of Muhammad as a wily pseudo-prophet, founder of a heretical sect: Adelphus, Embrico of Mainz, Gautier de Compiègne, Guibert of Nogent. (Tolan 2002: ch. 6). While the details of these polemical biographies of Muhammad differ from author to author, the portrait they sketch is essentially the same. A heretical Christian monk takes the young camel-driver Muhammad under his wing, corrupts his spirit, and plots to make him leader of the Arabs by having him pretend to be a prophet. In order to convince the people of his divine mission, Muhammad performs a number of bogus miracles: he hides pots of milk and honey in the desert, then claims that God had placed them there. He trains a dove to eat grains from his ear and affirms that it is the angel Gabriel come to speak with him. He writes a book of law which he places on the horns of a bull; when the bull erupts in the midst of the assembled people, they acclaim him as a divine messenger. The revealed law encourages its adepts to indulge in polygamy and incest: the amassed people accept these injunctions with great enthusiasm. When at last the false prophet dies, he is laid in an iron coffin, which is placed in a temple with magnets in the ceiling: the coffin floats in mid-air, which the Arabs take as a sure sign of his divine election. These authors make the prophet of Islam into a colourful trickster, who through clever ruses manages to trick a multitude into following his law. The goal is not only to denigrate Islam and its prophet, but also to explain its successes, which would be the result of its debauched morals and of the false miracles.

B. Jews and Muslims in Christendom: Thirteenth to Fifteenth Centuries

In 1215, Pope Innocent III presided over the fourth Lateran Council, which sought to promote an ambitious agenda of church reform, launch a new crusade to recover Jerusalem, and affirm the spiritual and temporal authority of the pope. The council reaffirmed a number of principles meant to govern the relations between Christians and non-Christians, here specifically noting that these laws applied both to Jews and to 'pagans' (i.e. Muslims) who lived in Christian territories. First, they should be able to exercise no authority over Christians. They are prohibited from publicly mocking Christians during Holy Week. Those who convert to Christianity are not to be allowed to return to their original religion. One of the canons requires Jews and Saracens to wear distinctive dress, in order that they may be easily recognized so that Christians may avoid illicit sexual relations with them. While the canon does not state what their specific dress should be, three years later, King Henry III requires English Jews to wear, on their outer garments, a white badge in the shape of the tablets of the law that Moses had received on Mt Sinai.[3]

Innocent III showed particular zeal in policing the boundaries between religious communities and in prohibiting what he saw as illicit relations between Christians and Jews. In a series of letters to King Philip II of France and to various French prelates, the pope complains that the king and his officials not only permit Jews to practice usury, they use coercion to help Jews collect their debts. Moreover, Jews in France employ Christian servants, including wet nurses, in their homes; Jews sell to Christians meat or wine which they do not deem fit for their own consumption. Worse, some of them openly mock Christian practice (veneration for the cross, Easter festivities) and even kill unsuspecting Christians. Innocent indeed reaffirmed the papal protection of Jewish communities when he reissued the *Sicut iudeis:* yet he ominously added that that protection would be offered only to those Jews 'who have not presumed to plot against the Christian Faith' (Grayzel 1966: 95). Innocent's successors continued to reissue the bull into the fifteenth century.

Yet by the thirteenth century, the place of Jews was more and more endangered in many parts of Europe. It is beyond the scope of this essay to relate the increasing incidents of anti-Jewish violence beginning in the late eleventh century (when crusaders attacked Jewish communities in the Rhineland), or the accusations that Jews desecrated the host or ritually murdered Christians. These stories have been told many times, and there is considerable scholarly debate about the causes and dynamics of these developments. Suffice it to say that a combination of crusading rhetoric, deep resentment concerning Jewish moneylending, and missionary efforts of the new mendicant orders created volatile situations. One of the consequences was a string of expulsions from different European polities: Bologna in 1178, the French royal domain in 1182, Britanny in 1240, Perugia in 1279, Gascony in 1288, Anjou in 1290, France in 1306 and again in 1394, and so on into the following centuries. There were also expulsions of Muslims from Sicily (1220), from Lucera (1300), and from various areas of Christian Spain. Some of these expulsions were only temporary, some remained limited and local. In 1492, Isabel of Castile and Ferdinand of Aragon expelled the Jews from Spain; the expulsion of the Muslims was to follow several years later. Jews were subsequently expelled from Portugal, Provence, and various Italian cities. The result was a massive migration of Jews towards the Maghrib, the Ottoman Empire, the Netherlands, and Central and Eastern Europe. There was no longer an Augustinian consensus that Jews

[3] Lateran IV: Notice n° 30326, RELMIN project, 'The Legal Status of Religious Minorities in the Euro-Mediterranean World (5th–15th centuries)'; Telma Web edition, IRHT, Institut de Recherche et d'Histoire des Textes—Orléans <http://www.cn-telma.fr/relmin/extrait30326/>. Henry III: Notice n° 252108, RELMIN project, 'The Legal Status of Religious Minorities in the Euro-Mediterranean World (5th–15th centuries) Telma Web edition, IRHT, Institut de Recherche et d'Histoire des Textes—Orléans <http://www.cn-telma.fr/relmin/extrait252108/>.

should be allowed to live subordinate in Christendom: where Jewish communities exist, they do so at the prerogative, if not the whim, of Christian rulers. The debate over whether these rulers should allow Jews to reside in their realms was complicated by the eruption of the war of religions.

C. Christian History as Seen in the Sixteenth Century: Martin Luther

In the writings of Martin Luther, we find both a profound continuity with medieval writings on Judaism and on Islam and a major reorientation, as Luther tries to understand them in relation both to 'true' (reformed) Christianity and to the errors of the papists. Luther is one of the sixteenth-century Christian authors who thought and wrote most extensively on Judaism and Islam, and his work was of course to have a profound impact on subsequent Protestant thought and was in the twentieth century cited with approbation by Nazi ideologues (Probst 2012). While Luther wrote extensively on both rival faiths, his concerns were rarely those of a missionary attempting to convert Jews or Muslims. He sought rather to explain God's scheme of history to his readers and to protect them from the dangers and temptations offered by the devil, in the form of Jewish, Muslim, and papist doctrines and practices.

While Luther's view of the place of Jews in the Christian scheme of history is in many respects the same as that established over a thousand years earlier by church fathers from Eusebius to Augustine, it is distinguished by two essential elements: first a keen apocalyptic sense that the end of history is near, and second a conviction, in his early works, that if the Jews have yet to see the light of Christian truth, the fault lies not so much with the Jews themselves but with the papacy and clergy who have failed both to preach the Gospel to the Jews and to show through their life and works a true example of Christian piety (Kaufmann 2006). In his *That Jesus Christ was Born a Jew* (LW 45: 199–229; *Daß Jesus Christus ein geborner Jude sei*, WA 11: 314–36), Luther presents rather standard Christological exegetical interpretations of key Old Testament passages: Isaiah 7: 14 (on the Virgin birth), Genesis 49: 10–12 ('The sceptre shall not depart from Judah . . . until the *shiloh* comes', which proves for Luther that the *Shiloh*, or Messiah has already come), and the seventy weeks prophesied by Daniel 9: 24–7, which, according to Luther's complex calculations, show that the Messiah was born 1,500 years previously. None of these arguments are new, yet Luther thinks that good (Protestant) Christians can convince Jews where 'monks and papists' have failed miserably. If Jews have not wanted to convert, it is largely because they have been so persecuted by Christians: if the apostles had treated the Gentiles so poorly, none of them would have converted either. We treat them like dogs, refuse their commerce, force them into the base profession of usury, make absurd accusations against them. 'If I had been a Jew and had seen such dolts and blockheads govern and teach the Christian faith, I would sooner have become a hog than a Christian' (p. 200).

Yet in later works, Luther's attitude towards Jews hardened, perhaps because he realized that they were no likelier to be convinced by Protestant arguments than they had been by those of Catholics. He also came to see Jews as the devil's agents who sought to weaken the faith of Christians. Around 1538, Luther composed his *Against the Sabbatarians, letter to a good friend* (LW 47: 65–98; *Wider die Sabbather an einen guten Freund*, WA 50: 312–37). Who these Sabbatarians actually were, what they believed and practised, and even whether they existed have been the objects of scholarly debate. For Luther, Jews, 'making inroads ... with their venom and their doctrine' (p. 65), have induced Christians to undergo circumcision, have taught them that the Messiah has not yet appeared, and have led them to believe that the Jewish law is eternal and that it should be adopted by Gentiles. Gone is the optimism he showed in *That Jesus Christ was born a Jew;* if even good Christians can make few inroads with the stubborn Jews, that should come as no surprise: they refused to listen to their own prophets. The chief culprits are the rabbis, who for centuries have taught erroneous and absurd interpretations of the Law of Moses, given as they are to 'babbling and lying' (p. 78) such that 'If I were Moses, I would give my pupils, the Jews, a good box on the ears' (pp. 81–2). Luther aims to establish two key truths in this tract: that God inflicted on the Jews the current 'Roman' exile, which began with the destruction of the Temple in 70 CE, as punishment for horrible sins, as the rabbis themselves acknowledge: what they do not acknowledge was that this sin was the refusal to recognize Jesus Christ as their long-awaited Messiah. Luther then seeks to show that the Jews no longer are Jews: since the destruction of the Temple and the beginning of their current exile, they are no longer able to perform key stipulations of the law, involving the Temple and the priesthood. Sure, they point to rules they *do* still follow, for example those concerning dietary restrictions. But it is as if someone whose house had burned down proffered scattered bricks and charred timbers as proof that his house was still standing. No longer optimistic that Jews can be convinced of Christian truth, Luther provided his Christian readers with proofs of their error. For Luther, Jews sought to draw Christians into their corrupt faith, either fully or partially, and in some cases succeeded: this was a clear sign that their presence in Protestant Europe, even as a numerically insignificant minority, was dangerous to the faith.

Hence in his later works Luther comes to the conclusion that Jews should be expelled by Christian princes in order to protect the true church. The tone is particularly virulent in *On the Jews and their Lies* (LW 47: 137–306; *Von den Juden und ihren Lügen*, WA 53: 417–552), a long and rambling diatribe written in response to a Jewish anti-Christian tract which Luther had read. Luther lambastes the Jews for their triple arrogance: they show undue pride in their birth, in their circumcision, and in the fact that they received the Law from God on Mount Sinai. This pride leads them to despise the *Goyim*, whom they believe it is legal to rob, cheat, and kill. Whereas in earlier works Luther had dismissed the hostile stories of how Jews poisoned wells and killed Christian children, he now asserts that these stories and worse are probably true. They curse us Christians in their synagogues every Saturday, Luther asserts, and affirm that our Lord is the son of a whore. 'Learn from this, dear Christian, what you are doing if you permit the blind Jews to mislead you,' he warns his reader: 'Be on your guard against the Jews' (p. 172).

Beyond warning his reader, Luther has seven quite concrete proposals. 'First, to set fire to their synagogues or schools' (p. 268). Second, to raze and destroy their houses. Third, to take away prayer books and Talmuds. Fourth, to forbid their rabbis to teach, under pain of death. Fifth, to abolish safe conduct: since they have no honest business to conduct, let them stay at home (Luther seems to have forgotten that their homes were to be razed). Six, prohibit usury. And seventh, 'I recommend putting a flail, an ax, a hoe, a spade, a distaff, or a spindle into the hands of young, strong Jews and Jewesses and letting them earn their bread in the sweat of their brow, as was imposed on the children of Adam' (p. 272). In an age of vehement anti-Jewish polemics, Luther's stand out as particularly violent.

Luther's assessment of Muslims (or 'the Turks', as he invariably calls them) is in a similar way based on his apocalyptical sense of history with the pope as the principal ally of Antichrist (Francisco 2007). In 1518, in defence of his ninety-five theses, Luther affirmed that the Turk served as 'the lash and rod of God'; those who seek to fight the Turk rather than combating their own iniquities oppose God's will (*Explanations of the Ninety-Five Theses*, LW 31: 83–252 (citation p. 92); WA 1: 525–628). God is punishing Christians for their sins, notably those of the corrupt church: the way to stop the Turkish threat is not to muster armies, but to make penance. Luther develops this theme in greater detail in 1528, when, in the aftermath of Sulayman the Magnificent's annexation of much of Hungary, there was a real risk of large swaths of the German lands falling under Ottoman dominion. While Luther acknowledges that the emperor has the right and duty to defend his empire against the Turk, he affirms in his *On War against the Turk* (1529) that the most effective means of protection remain repentance and prayer in order to 'take the rod out of God's hand' (LW 46: 161–205 (citation p. 170); *Vom Kriege wider den Türcken* WA 30 III: 107–48). Luther's message is the same in his *Appeal for Prayer against the Turk* of 1541: 'The Turk, you see, is our "schoolmaster". He has to discipline and teach us to fear God and to pray. Otherwise we will do what we have been doing—rot in sin and complacency' (LW 43: 219–41 (citation p. 224); *Vermahnung zum Gebet wider den Türkcen* WA 51: 585–625). Just as the Israelites refused to listen to their prophets and needed to be whipped by the king of Babylon, so do Christians need the chastisement of the Turk.

Beyond assigning to the 'Turk' the role of scourge or schoolmaster, Luther struggled to understand the place of Islam in God's plan: he sought out material on the rites and beliefs of the Muslims and on their attitudes towards Christians. One of his principal sources was a veritable best-seller in the fifteenth and sixteenth centuries: George of Hungary's *Book on the Rites and Customs of the Turks.* George had been taken captive in 1438, at the age of 16, and taken to Istanbul, from which he managed to escape twenty years later. His treatise provides a vivid description of the social and religious life of the Ottoman capital. Luther himself wrote a Latin preface to the 1530 re-edition of George's treatise, in which he pays particular attention to the meticulousness with which Muslims practise their rites:

> The religion of the Turks or Muhammad is far more splendid in ceremonies... than ours, even including that of the religious or all the clerics. The modesty and simplicity of their food, clothing, dwellings, and everything else, as well as the fasts, prayers, and common gatherings of the people... are nowhere seen among us—or rather it is impossible for our people to be persuaded to them. Furthermore, which of our monks, be it a Carthusian... or a Benedictine, is not put to shame by the miraculous and wondrous abstinence and discipline among their religious? Our religious are mere shadows when compared to them, and our people clearly profane when compared to theirs. Not even true Christians, not Christ himself, not the apostles or prophets ever exhibited so great a display. This is the reason why many persons so easily depart from faith in Christ for Muhammadanism and adhere to it so tenaciously. I sincerely believe that no papist, monk, cleric, or their equal in faith would be able to remain in their faith if they should spend three days among the Turks. (Henrich and Boyce 1996: 259)

In other words, the Turks are better Catholics than the papists themselves: convinced that their merit is reflected in their works, they excel in charity, fasting, devotion, and prayer. If one is measured by works, the Turks outshine the papists. Proof, for Luther, that Catholics are doomed, more even than the Turks, for placing their hope in ceremonies, indulgences, fasting, and the like, rather than in faith. Or, as he will put it in his *Appeal for Prayer against the Turks*: 'the Pope's devil... is bigger than the Turk's devil' (LW 43: 227). Luther uses the pious Turk to bash (literally and figuratively) the dissolute papist.

Luther also sought to counter those Germans who admired Muslims for their piety and justice and who would prefer the Sultan's dominion to the oppression at the hands of their compatriots. 'Some praise the Turk's government because he allows everyone to believe what he will so long as *he* [the Sultan] remains the temporal lord' (*On War against the Turk*, LW 43: 175). 'Since now', he writes in 1530, 'we have the Turk and his religion at our very doorstep, our people must be warned lest, either moved by the splendour of the Turkish religion and the external appearance of their customs, or offended by the meagre display of our own faith or the deformity of our customs, they deny their Christ and follow Muhammad' (Henrich and Boyce 1996: 260). This fear pervades Luther's writings on Islam: fear not merely of conquest of the German lands by the Ottoman armies, but—what was of course much worse for Luther—of the attraction that Turkish culture and Muslim religion would exercise on the Sultan's German subjects, leading them to convert to Islam, or rather, as Luther puts it, to apostatize, to 'become Turks'.

For these two reasons, then—as a stick to bash papists and as a means to discourage apostasy—Luther sought, starting in the 1520s, to learn more about Islam. He turned, quite naturally, to the works of medieval scholars and polemicists who had confronted Islam from the twelfth to the early fourteenth centuries. In the 1520s, he came across a Latin manuscript of the *Contra legem Saracenorum*, an early fourteenth-century tract by Dominican missionary Riccoldo da Montecroce. In 1542, the Basel city council jailed two publishers who wanted to print, in Latin, a collection of texts about Islam including

Robert of Ketton's twelfth-century Latin translation of the Quran and Riccoldo's *Contra legem*. The city fathers proclaimed that it was dangerous to publish the 'fables and heresies' of the Quran. Luther intervened to convince the council that the Quran should be printed since there was no better way to combat the Turks than to permit everyone to see for themselves Muhammad's 'lies and fables'. The Quran was published the following year, with a preface by Luther. 1542 was also the year in which Luther published his own German translation of Riccoldo's *Contra legem Saracenorum*. It is striking that when it comes to understanding the role of Islam in history, Luther and his contemporaries can do no better than to study, publish, and translate the work of Catholic medieval authors who confronted the same problems before them.

3. Secularization of European Society and Changing Notions Of Judaism and Islam

A. Towards Religious Relativism?

The cornerstone of the medieval Roman church's vision of history was the church's own key role in God's plan: only through and by the church could humanity, collectively and individually, obtain salvation. 'Extra ecclesiam nulla salus', 'there is no salvation outside the church', is a doctrine reiterated by a number of medieval popes, notably Innocent III in 1215 and Boniface VIII in 1302. Thirteenth-century Parisian theologian William of Auvergne devoted a full chapter of his *De fide et legibus* to the refutation of the idea, which he attributes to Muhammad, that 'everyone is to be saved in his faith or law or sect, as long as he believes it to be good and from God and does it to please him'. Clearly contact with Jews and Muslims created doubts among some Christians as to the universal nature of the Catholic church, doubts which ecclesiastics sought to combat (Tolan 2012b).

In the sixteenth century, reports arrived in Europe of the peoples of the Americas and of their religious practices. Were these the lost tribes of Israel, whose primitive Judaism had degenerated? Or 'pagans' untouched by biblical religion? If these people had never been evangelized, how could a just God justify *extra ecclesiam nulla salus*? This, combined with the wars of religion that split Europe, raised serious doubts about the universality of the church and its mission. Inquisitorial records from Spain, from Portugal, and from the two countries' American empires record many cases of people, at all levels of wealth and education, expressing such doubts or affirming that good Muslims, Jews, Lutherans, or Indians could achieve salvation (Schwartz 2008).

Among European intellectuals, these issues provoked the emergence of new approaches to the study of religion (Stroumsa 2010). While the proponents of these methods were often deeply committed religious, some of them showed a keen desire to understand the rival religions per se and not simply through polemical lenses. Foremost in this effort were Jesuit missionaries such as José de Acosta, whose *Historia naturál y morál de las Indias* (1590) offered a rich description of religious practices of various groups of native Americans, practices which he indeed saw as snares of the devil, yet tried to understand in part by comparing them to those of ancient Israel, Christianity, and pagan Greece and Rome (Stroumsa 2010: 16–18). Or Matteo Ricci and his fellow Jesuit missionaries to China in the late sixteenth and early seventeenth centuries, who adapted to the norms of the Confucian elite in order to gain acceptance from them. These Jesuits sought, like their Dominican and Franciscan rivals, to evangelize non-Christians. Yet they sought to do so through a deep and to a large extent sympathetic understanding of the language, culture, beliefs, and practices of those they sought to convert. But their experience posed serious questions about the very nature of religion: was there a universal 'natural' religion, of which Judaism, Christianity, and Islam were simply historically specific manifestations? What was the purpose of religion in a well-functioning society?

These developments coincided with the emergence of modern philology, which scholars now turned on the Bible itself and, subsequently, on other foundational texts of the world's principal religions. What are the consequences of this for the place of Judaism and Islam in Christian law and history? There were, of course, continuities with medieval polemical strategies, as we have seen in the case of Luther; yet there were also efforts to understand contemporary, post-biblical Judaism on its own terms, if only the better to missionize Jews. Such is the case of Protestant scholar Johannes Buxtorf, who published his *Judenschul* in German in 1603 and then in Latin as *Synagoga judaica* in 1604. Buxtorf provoked a response by Venetian Rabbi Leone da Modena, whose *I riti degli Ebrei* (1637) was the first presentation of Jewish practice by a Jew for a non-Jewish audience (Stroumsa 2010: 41).

Judaism plays a key and ambivalent role in the emergence of European atheist and anti-religious discourse in the Enlightenment. Dutch Jews of the seventeenth century wrote polemics against Christianity; since these Jewish communities were dominated by Portuguese *conversos*, nominal Christians who returned to Judaism (and who were unschooled in the Talmud), their arguments focused on undermining the Christian reading of the Old Testament, in particular by pointing out that Jesus did not at all correspond to the Messiah that the Jews awaited. While these texts were written for a Jewish audience, they found eager readers among disaffected Christians (Popkin 1992). The caricature of Jesus found in the medieval *Toledot Yeshu*, a mocking, hostile biography of Jesus known to various Enlightenment authors (including Voltaire), is similar to the disparaging image of Muhammad in Christian polemics. The anonymous author of the *Traité des trois imposteurs* (1719) uses these polemical legends to present religion as essentially a means for a priestly elite to deceive and control the masses (Anderson 1997; Berti et al. 1996). But the biggest charlatans were the three great impostors Moses, Jesus, and Muhammad. Moses, a magician trained in Egypt, was a despot and impostor. Jesus was no better: he managed to convince a bunch of imbeciles that his mother was a virgin and his father the Holy Spirit. Muhammad is presented as a false prophet according to the traditions of medieval Christian polemics. What is new is that the author presents Moses and Jesus as impostors alongside Muhammad.

Indeed, polemical attacks on Judaism and on the Catholic church sometimes took the form of learned treatises on comparative religion. Henry de Boulainvillier, in his *Abrégé de l'histoire universelle jusqu'à l'Exode,* compares early Judaism to contemporary religions of Egypt and China, and concludes that the early Jews showed more superstition and ignorance (Sutcliffe 2003: 110–11). In his *Life of Mohamed* (1730), he presents the prophet as a divinely inspired reformer who spread knowledge of the One God as far as the Oxus. Muhammad preserved all that was best in Christianity and abolished its vices: the cult of relics and icons, and the grasping greed and inordinate power of superstitious monks and clergy (Tolan 2010). Boulainvillier's works were influential: among his readers were Gibbon and Voltaire.

Gibbon devotes a long chapter of his *Decline and Fall of the Roman Empire* to the life of the prophet and the Islamic conquests. The impostor figure, indeed, has not disappeared: Muhammad 'consulted the spirit of fraud or enthusiasm, whose abode is not in the heavens, but in the mind of the prophet' (Gibbon 1932: 80). Yet he affirms that 'the creed of Mohammed is free from suspicion or ambiguity; and the Quran is a glorious testimony to the unity of God' (Gibbon 1932: 82). He echoes Boulainvillier (whom he cites frequently) in praising Muhammad for instituting tithes for the benefit of the poor. Even in his death, the prophet showed himself worthy of emulation, a model of humility and penance. The violence of the Quran, often the object of Christian polemicists, pales in comparison with that of the Torah. Gibbon's portrayal of Muhammad is on the whole sympathetic, though tinged with condescension. Muhammad is a pious man and a brilliant leader, who gave his people a unity and purpose that allowed them to subject half the world to their rule. Yet his Arabs and Muhammad are proud and simple people: fierce warriors, emotional, impulsive, lustful, not prone to reflection. Gibbon explains this character as the result of the influence of climate and environment.

B. The Emancipation of the Jews

While Jewish communities continued to live, and in some cases to thrive, in Central and Eastern Europe, they did so as communities. In the multi-religious, multi-ethnic empires of the Ottomans and Habsburgs, Jews were among the many semi-autonomous communities. The same is true of France (where they are marginally present beginning in the sixteenth century) and in England (where Cromwell had permitted the admission of Jews in 1656), and elsewhere in Europe. As long as the state retained a strong identification with Christianity (Catholic or Protestant), adherents of other religions, in particular Jews, had a distinct and subservient legal status. As long as states recognized groups with specific rights and privileges, Jews were simply one group among many; but as soon as states accord equal rights to all citizens, corporate or communal identities become problematic.

Increasingly, Enlightenment thinkers argued that the state should no longer be associated with one religion and that adherents of all faiths should enjoy the same legal freedoms and be subject to the same obligations. John Toland published in 1714 a pamphlet addressed to the British Parliament entitled *Reasons for naturalizing the Jews in Great Britain and Ireland: on the same foot with all other nations: containing also a defence of the Jews against all vulgar prejudices in all countries*. Other Enlightenment thinkers similarly argued that Jews should be full citizens with equal rights. Various European rulers abolished key aspects of traditional European Jewry law: in 1781, Holy Roman Emperor Joseph II abolished the Jewish badge and taxes on Jewish travellers; he subsequently abolished other regulations concerning Jews, in particular on where they could live. The American and French revolutions were to bring these ideals into practice: Jews were granted equal rights by the US constitution in 1789, and the new French republic proclaimed the emancipation of French Jews in 1791. In the parliamentary debate leading to the emancipation decree, Stanislas de Clermont-Tonnerre proclaimed, 'we must grant everything to the Jews as individuals and nothing to them as a nation' (Hermon-Belot 1999: 59). In other words, a French Jew was a Frenchman with equal rights to any other Frenchman, to whom the same laws applied; there was to be no recognition of group rights of Jews, or of the authority of rabbis in any area other than those defined as strictly religious. Napoleon's armies brought the principles of emancipation to much of Europe. While these laws were in many cases reversed after Napoleon's defeat, the principle of emancipation was subsequently adopted in many parts of Europe, including in the German Reich by 1871 (Birnbaum and Katznelson 1995). Yet putting these principles into practice was often another matter, as there was considerable resistance from both Jews and non-Jews. Napoleon's solution to the problem was to create a new national Jewish representative organization, the 'Grand Sanhédrin', a new post-revolutionary version of a Jewish body of governance that had disappeared some seventeen centuries earlier (Hermon-Belot 1999: 78–81).

The Enlightenment and the liberal regimes of the nineteenth century brought legal emancipation to European Jewry, putting an end to discriminatory legal status and in theory making them fully equal citizens and eradicating the bases of any anti-Semitic prejudice. That this optimistic Enlightenment-Liberal ideal failed to work as its proponents hoped is of course one of the great historical tragedies of nineteenth- and twentieth-century Europe, but it is well beyond the scope of this chapter. Suffice it to say that not only did old forms of religious prejudice against Jews survive, and indeed thrive, but new virulent strains of secular anti-Semitism, based on race rather than religion, came to the fore. The same can be said of attitudes towards Islam: while it now was possible, in the wake of Boulainvillier and Gibbon, to admire Muhammad and his reforms, the figure of the prophet was in many respects secularized, presented as a great statesman and lawgiver more than as a prophet. His law was often portrayed as appropriate to a rough and uncultured desert people: climate and race now predominate as factors that justify and explain the inferiority of the Arabs, displacing (but not eradicating) religious explanations.

Abbreviations Used

LW: *Luther's Works* (55 volumes; Philadelphia: Fortress Press 1955–75).
WA: Martin Luther, *D. Martin Luther's Werke: Kritische Gesamtausgabe (Weimarer Ausgabe)*. 121 vols; Weimar: H. Böhlaus Nachfolger 1883–2009.

References

Anderson, A. 1997. *The Treatise of the Three Imposters and the Problem of the Enlightenment.* Lanham: Rowman & Littlefield.

Aune, D. 2006. *Apocalypticism, Prophecy and Magic in Early Christianity*. Tübingen: Mohr Siebeck.

Bede. 2008. *On Genesis*. Liverpool: Liverpool University Press.

Berti, S., Charles-Daubert, F., and Popkin, R., eds. 1996. *Heterodoxy, Spinozism, and Free Thought in Early-Eighteenth-Century Europe: Studies on the 'Traité des trois imposteurs'.* Dordrecht: Kluwer Academic.

Birnbaum, P. and Katznelson, I., eds. 1995. *Paths of Emancipation: Jews, States and Citizenship*. Princeton: Princeton University Press.

Boyarin, D. 2004. 'The Christian Invention of Judaism: The Theodosian Empire and the Rabbinic Refusal of Religion'. *Representations* 85: 21–57.

Chodorow, S. 1972. *Christian Political Theory and Church Politics in the Mid Twelfth Century: The Ecclesiology of Gratian's Decretum*. Berkeley: University of California Press.

Cohen, J. 1999. *Living Letters of the Law: Ideas of the Jew in Medieval Christianity*. Berkeley: University of California Press.

Dagron, G. 1993. 'Le Traité de Grégoire de Nicée sur le baptême des juifs'. *Travaux et mémoires* 11: 313–57.

Eusebius. 1999. *Life of Constantine*. Oxford: Clarendon Press.

Francisco, A. 2007. *Martin Luther and Islam: A Study in Sixteenth-Century Polemics and Apologetics*. Leiden: Brill.

Fredriksen, A. D. 1999. 'Apocalypticism'. In A. Fitzgerald, ed., *Augustine through the Ages: An Encyclopedia.* Grand Rapids, MI: Eerdmans, 49–53.

Gibbon, E. 1932. *Decline and Fall of the Roman Empire*. New York: Modern Library.

Grayzel, S. 1966. *The Church and the Jews in the XIIIth Century: A Study of their Relations during the Years 1198–1254, Based on the Papal Letters and the Conciliar Decrees of the Period.* New York: Hermon Press.

Henrich, S. and Boyce, J. 1996. 'Martin Luther—Translations of Two Prefaces on Islam: Preface to the Libellus de ritu et moribus Turcorum (1530) and Preface to Bibliander's Edition of the Qur'ân (1543)'. *Word & World* 16: 250–66.

Hermon-Belot, R. 1999. *L'Emancipation des juifs en France*. Paris: Presses Universitaires de France.

Hugh of St Victor. 1961. *The Didascalicon of Hugh of St. Victor: A Medieval Guide to the Arts.* New York: Columbia University Press.

Kaufmann, T. 2006. 'Luther and the Jews'. In P. Bell and S. Burnett, eds, *Jews, Judaism and the Reformation in Sixteenth-century Germany*. Leiden: Brill, 69–104.

Kedar, B. 1984. *Crusade and Mission, European Approaches toward the Muslims.* Princeton: Princeton University Press.

Linder, A. 2006. 'The Legal Status of the Jews in the Roman Empire'. In S. Katz, ed., *The Cambridge History of Judaism*, Vol. IV: *The Late Roman-Rabbinic Period.* Cambridge: Cambridge University Press, 128–73.

Mathisen, R. 2014. 'The Citizenship and Legal Status of Jews in Roman Law during Late Antiquity (ca. 300–540 CE)'. In J. Tolan, N. De Lange, and L. F. Capucine Nemo-Pekelman, eds, *Jews in Early Christian Law: Byzantium and the Latin West, 6th–11th c.* Turnhoult: Brepols.

Nemo-Pekelman, C. 2010. *Les Juifs et le droit à Rome (IVe–Ve siècles).* Paris: Honoré Champion.

Popkin, R. 1992. 'Jewish Anti-Christian Arguments as a Source of Irreligion from the Seventeenth to the Early Nineteenth Century'. In M. Hunter and D. Wooton, eds, *Atheism from the Reformation to the Enlightenment.* Oxford: Clarendon Press, 159–81.

Probst, C. 2012. *Demonizing the Jews: Luther and the Protestant Church in Nazi Germany.* Bloomington: University of Indiana Press.

Retsö, J. 2003. *The Arabs in Antiquity: Their History from the Assyrians to the Umayyads.* London: Routledge.

Rowe, N. 2011. *The Jew, the Cathedral, and the Medieval City: Synagoga and Ecclesia in the Thirteenth Century.* Cambridge: Cambridge University Press.

Sapir Abulafia, A. 2011. *Christian-Jewish Relations 1000–1300: Jews in the Service of Medieval Christendom.* London: Longman.

Schwartz, S. 2008. *All Can be Saved: Religious Tolerance and Salvation in the Iberian Atlantic World.* New Haven: Yale University Press.

Sharf, A. 1995. *Jews and Other Minorities in Byzantium.* Jerusalem: Bar-Ilan University Press.

Sicard, P. 1991. *Hugues de Saint-Victor et son école.* Turnhout: Brepols.

Signer, M. 1999. 'Jews and Judaism'. In A. Fitzgerald, ed., *Augustine through the Ages: An Encyclopedia.* Grand Rapids, MI: Eerdmans, 470–4.

Southern, R. 1995. *Scholastic Humanism and the Unification of Europe.* Oxford: Blackwell.

Stroumsa, G. 2010. *A New Science: The Discovery of Religion in the Age of Reason.* Cambridge, MA: Harvard University Press.

Sutcliffe, A. 2003. 'Judaism in the Anti-Religious Thought of the Clandestine French Early Enlightenment'. *Journal of the History of Ideas* 64: 97–117.

Tartar, G. 1985. *Dialogue islamo-chrétien sous le Calife al-Ma'mûn (813–834): les épîtres d'al-Hashimî et d'al-Kindî.* Paris: Nouvelles Éditions Latines.

Tolan, J. 2002. *Saracens: Islam in the Medieval European Imagination.* New York: Columbia University Press.

Tolan, J. 2010. 'European Accounts of Muhammad's Life'. In J. Brockopp, ed., *Cambridge Companion to Muhammad.* Cambridge: Cambridge University Press, 226–50.

Tolan, J. 2012a. 'A Wild Man, Whose Hand will be against All: Saracens and Ishmaelites in Latin Ethnographical Traditions, from Jerome to Bede'. In W. Pohl et al., eds, *Visions of Community: Ethnicity, Religion and Power in the Early Medieval West, Byzantium and the Islamic World.* Farnham; Burlington, VT: Ashgate, 513–30.

Tolan, J. 2012b. '"Tra il diavolo di Rustico e il ninferno d'Alibech": Muslims and Jews in Boccaccio's Decameron'. In A. Eisenbeiß and L. Saurma-Jeltsch, eds, *Images of Otherness in Medieval and Early Modern Times: Exclusion, Inclusion and Assimilation*. Berlin, Munich: Deutscher Kunstverlag, 133–41.

Williams, M. and Grafton, A. 2006. *Christianity and the Transformation of the Book: Origen, Eusebius, and the Library of Caesarea*. Cambridge, MA: Harvard University Press.

CHAPTER 11

BEYOND EXCLUSIVISM IN THE MIDDLE AGES

On the Three Rings, the Three Impostors, and the Discourse of Multiplicity

DOROTHEA WELTECKE

Introduction

Giovanni Boccaccio (1313–75) in his collection of stories, *The Decameron*, told the tale of the loving father who owns one precious ring and fabricates another two to bequeath these seemingly equal rings to his three sons he holds equally dear. The sons, however, quarrel on after his death as to who has received the genuine ring. A solution to their contention does not seem possible. This famous story has been welcomed as the beginning of religious scepticism, tolerance, and even religious comparative thought. The same holds true for the enigmatic aphorism that Moses, Jesus, and Muhammad are three impostors who seduced the world. To many modern authors these two perspectives on the three Abrahamic religions even seemed to be interchangeable (Niewöhner 1988). In the modern interpretation Boccaccio's tale represented the discovery of the similarity or, rather, equality of the three Abrahamic religions, the impossibility to decide on their truth claims, and, consequently, the imperative to respect and tolerate the religious other. The tale of the three impostors seems to push the same argument further by insisting that not only the truth claims were similar, but that they were also evenly false.

Scholars in early modern Europe were the first to identify their own claims for religious tolerance and secularism with these propositions. The tale of the three impostors first appeared in the late seventeenth century as an anonymous atheist pamphlet. The ring parable was most prominently constructed by the poet Gotthold Ephraim Lessing in his play 'Nathan the Sage' from 1779. Since then the two tales have become very prominent in western debates; they are codes for critical and liberal attitudes towards religion.

The narration and the proverb thus appear to represent very rare medieval voices that go against the tide in a world which, on the face of it, was self-referred and largely either ignorant or hostile towards other faiths. In the present chapter these two intertwined topics, first the tales of the rings and the three impostors and secondly the medieval conceptions of religious respect beyond or in spite of absolute truth claims, will be sketched. The aim is to categorize and contextualize first the source material and secondly some of the conceptions that can be found in the medieval discourse. Due to the current state of research, an equal treatment of all the religions or comprehensiveness cannot be attempted.

I The Tales of The Three and The One and The Discourse of Multiplicity

The Tales of the Three and the One

For centuries, scholars were fascinated by the tale of the three rings and the epigram of the three impostors. The exact number of versions is difficult to estimate as more texts have continually come to light, stemming from all the different cultures of the Abrahamic religions between the Iberian Peninsula and Central Asia (for collections see Niewöhner 1988; Shagrir 1997). In recent years the search for a primordial version has been given up (Poorthuis 2005). Instead, the different tendencies of the narrations were studied more closely. For the present, this set of texts may be called the 'tales of the three and the one'. They may be grouped into two main types. The first is the type of the treasure stories. Here, rings, pearls, or one precious stone represent the religions. These treasures are much desired, a loving father may bequeath them, they are characterized either as true or false, falsified or confused, retained by only one or nobody.

The oldest version was told by Patriarch Timotheus of the Church of the East (780–832) in his famous dialogue between the patriarch himself and the Calif al-Mahdi. Here, a pearl everybody desires to own is thrown into a dark house. While most people seize a worthless stone, one person might have found the real pearl. It is only when the house is illuminated that it will be known who was lucky. It is clear that the concept of a single absolute truth is not questioned, either by the characters in this story or by Timotheus. The narrator may be said to have opened up a space for mutual respect between the religions. His main intention was, however, to circumvent a comment on the internal disunity of Christianity, when challenged on this point by the caliph.

A second type of the 'tales of the three and the one' is stories about humans. Here, among other characters, three comrades, pilgrims, sages, daughters, or impostors represent the religions. The stories of the treasures and of humans are often combined as in the parable by Boccaccio, where three sons are correlated with three rings. The three humans are sometimes explicitly characterized as a Jew, a Christian, and a Muslim. As representatives of their religions the three humans interact. They meet on a road or in a forest. The heroes of the story engage in a trialogue or in a dialogue with a king. They may also fight or compete for a cake or a heritage and outwit one another. The figures are sometimes constructed on the same hierarchical level or classified as one prince and two disloyal servants, for example. These domestics mislead and harm the son of the king by various means, especially by falsifying a vital message they had been entrusted with by the king.

In the most radical version, Moses, Jesus, and Muhammad themselves are the protagonists. These narrations do not qualify as atheistic statements, as they do in the early modern era, but functioned as vilifications of religious enemies in the Middle Ages (Weltecke 2010). These polemical versions of the story of the three and the one are very rare. During the tenth century they first were hurled against the esoteric movements of an uprising group called the Qarmatians in Bahrain and against the Isma'ili movement in Egypt (Madelung 1959; Massignon 1920). The Qarmatians had established a Persian Mahdī against the rule of the Arabic Muslims and saw themselves as superseding the existing religions. In a very gross manner, later writers sought to expose them by demonstrating their derision of the established religion, law, and rule. The leader of the Qarmatians, for example, is said to have relieved himself on top of the Kaʿba he had stolen and broken into two pieces. Since the thirteenth century the sentence of the three impostors has also been ascribed to western figures, again for polemical purposes.

The stories of the three and the one could be adapted to any of the three religions. In all of them are elements of deceit, practical joke, and error. In many versions love and fidelity are featured as well. Most stories display a clear victory of one of the competing parties. Some seem to be undecided, especially in the confrontation with a mighty lord as in the case of Timotheus. Thus, they have no uniform tendency, apart from indeed stressing the existence of the one and only truth. The truth, however, may not be open to the protagonists of the narration. In one of the versions, thus, the Sultan Saladin is said (by a Latin Christian) to have destroyed a precious table and divided it into three. He did not know which of the three gods (!) was the most powerful and accordingly donated a part to each of them. The historical Sultan Saladin (1137/8–1193) was a figure mystifying the Latin world for his military power and his apparent magnanimity (Möhring 1993). Our narrator deflates the hero as he presents him as a simpleton who, by not deciding, rendered his treasure worthless (Jansen Enikel 1972).

The narrations obviously play with the tension between knowledge and deception, between one truth and conflicting claims, between authenticity and forgery, between force and the cleverness of the powerless. Very important are also motifs like similarity versus equality, unity versus disunity, or competition versus cooperation. Some stories are multi-layered and complicated. This is certainly true for Boccaccio's parable (Ó'Cuilleanáin 1984). His version is framed by an encounter between a mighty Muslim lord, Saladin, who wants to exact money for his wars, and a rich Jewish subject, Melchizedek, who does not want to risk his wealth. By asking Melchizedek about the true religion and threatening him with either a punishment for blasphemy or apostasy, Saladin intends to coerce Melchizedek into paying. The ring parable is Melchizedek's cunning answer, which Saladin accepts in good humour. After Saladin has demonstrated his power and is outwitted by Melchizedek, the Muslim lord and the Jewish moneylender become friends for life. They both change from being tyrannic and avaricious towards each other to being reliable and open-handed. Their relationship now functions to both their satisfaction. A Christian female narrator again frames the story on yet another level. Thus the set of threes is completed a second time. The Christian lady stands above the quarrels between Jew and Muslim and, as we might infer from the bias of the rest of the story, knows better. The detached Christian lady explains that she is not concerned with the truth of religion, but with acts of humans.

Obviously many problems of the complicated relations between people of different interests, levels of power, and religions are interwoven in the 'stories of the three and the one'. Yet although they have been seen as rare examples of a debate and relativism not expected in the Middle Ages, they are on the contrary not the only texts which touch these topics. In fact, there was a constant stream of narrations, historiography, and theological writings. In comparison with these complex works the short and often amusing narrations of the three and the one reduce the complex issues to a few emblematic elements. They represent the popular strand of writings on religious diversity.

Secular Literature

The wealth of writings which comment on religious multiplicity may be roughly grouped as follows: many histories and even some astrological works enlighten the cause and function of religious multiplicity. Bickering religious representatives and the problem of truth claims were already treated extensively in the preface to the world famous collection of parables known as the 'Kalila wa Dimna'. The prelude was written in Sassanian Iran of the sixth century (de Blois 1990) and, together with the collection of parables, disseminated to all the four corners of the Eurasian world. The novels of thirteenth-century Europe extensively treat the relation between the world of the Christian knights and a mighty other. These historical and poetical works of many genres communicate with the theological strands of their region and period. To analyse secular literature in view of its perception of the other has been a vivid field of research for many decennia.

Theological Genres

Polemical and apologetical literature almost always not only defined one's own propositions but also explained origins and causes of religious multiplicity in general. As an outcome, Muslim experts drove encyclopedic descriptions of theological traditions and sects already in the ninth and tenth centuries CE to a height unreached by western Christianity until the modern era (Gilliot 2002; van Ess 2011). Even in terms of their internal denominational multiplicity they often strove to surpass Judaism and Christianity. Following a narrative tradition, the number of the internal Jewish sects was given as 71, the Christians as 72 and the Muslims as 73. Writers of heresiographical treatises like Mohammed al-Shahrastānī (1076–1153 CE) took great pains to lay out different theological teachings and name the leaders of movements. Poems and tracts on the hereafter construct hell and heaven and populate these areas also with members of religions outside one's own religion.

Conflicting truth claims but also plurality as a problem in itself that needed explanation were most systematically treated in religious dialogues and comparative examinations. These tracts were designed as disputations in front of a king, as colloquia, or as a collection of letters and may be seen as elaborated versions of the 'tales of the three and the one'. Authors explained different theological propositions to their own flock. They acknowledge the fact that individuals are born into one religion and accept its truth claims as matter of fact. Yet, they encourage individuals to reach a higher level of religious understanding, so that their affiliation becomes a matter of choice as well as of rational thought and enquiry.

As far as the Abrahamic religions are concerned, religious plurality was most extreme in Central and Western Asian as well as in North African cities under Muslim rule. Still, diversity was also experienced and analysed within the frame of the Latin church.

Legal Literature and Juridical Acts

Legal texts and their comments, be it commentaries to the Talmud or responsa by Ashkenazi rabbis, tracts by Muslim jurists, or law-books by eastern Christian clerics classify religious affiliations and regulate relations. By way of commentary and debate they also constantly reflect these categories. Especially valuable are the inquisitorial records of the medieval religious inquisitions in the Latin West, produced from the mid-thirteenth century to the fifteenth century. As only few people wrote down their personal outlooks on life and religion, these protocols open up the rare opportunity to learn about the propositions of lay people (Edwards 1985).

The Discourse of Multiplicity

The tales as well as the manifold other texts indicated here are sources for what may be termed the medieval discourse of multiplicity. Within this discourse the roles of the participants differed according to power relations within their communities and their surrounding society at large. The wealth and the complexity of this discourse should not come as a surprise, nor should its aspects of religious doubt, comparison, and reasoning. The Middle Ages are the decisive period for the formation of the Abrahamic religions in terms of the development of their institutions, their teachings, and their mutual polemics and relationships. The religions themselves are, in fact, also a product of the various inter- and inner-religious relations and contacts (Wasserstrom 1995). Their sacred books in parts already reflect interreligious contacts (see for example Quran 5: 48) and so do later commentaries on them.

Most societies had to find means of organizing multiplicity by way of law, privileges, or informal practices. Religious equality was not aimed at. The laws ensured discrimination between a leading religion and those religions tolerated in its realm. The historical practices beyond these laws, however, display every shade between religious violence and peaceful cohabitation. The writings sketched above faced the reality of multiplicity, shaped practices, and were in turn shaped by them. At the same time, the multi-voiced discourse upheld the ideal of religious unity. In what follows some aspects of this discourse will be presented. Following the line of the material just sketched we will concentrate on strands which go beyond sheer exclusivism and reveal respect for the other.

II On Human and Religious Respect In Medieval Discourse

Analytical Models

Binary categories are usually implied in historical and philosophical research on interreligious interaction. Religions are characterized as 'tolerant' versus 'intolerant' or 'violent' versus 'peaceful'. The religious cultures in general are said to distinguish mainly between the binary opposition of 'believer' or 'non-believer'. Jan Assmann (2003) introduced a binary distinction between 'true' and 'false' in religion or between the true and false God as the fundamental monotheistic category. Assmann named this category the 'Mosaic distinction', a term which has engendered many scholarly debates.

For the medieval situation, however, these categories are in need of revision. While binary categories clearly existed in order to simplify affiliations and social positions for certain purposes, religious categories of the Middle Ages on the whole were more complex. Legal and theological teachings classified many more groups than merely believers versus unbelievers. Medieval Islam, for example, distinguished between believers, people of the book (mainly Jews, Christians), and idolaters. The scholastic theologian Thomas Aquinas (*c.*1225–74) also stressed that 'unbeliever' was a collective noun designating in fact different phenomena. This notion had practical consequences. The Latin inquisition as a rule had no power to question Jews and Muslims well into the Late Middle Ages (Yerushalmi 1970).

Therefore, other than binary oppositions are welcome as analytical tools. Ecumenical theological studies of the last century developed a model based on three categories. These studies distinguish between (a) exclusivist religions (adherents of other religions are in error), (b) inclusivist religions (adherents of other religions may know parts of the truth), and (c) pluralistic or universalistic religions (every religion is equally close to the truth). A slightly different picture emerges when the three categories are correlated not with the question of dogmatic truth but with God's assumed reaction to the different religions. Accordingly, exclusivists expect all others to go to hell, inclusivists expect some may be saved after all, and pluralists expect all religious paths to be equally salvific as long as the believer strives to please God (Khalil 2013). Prospects for a life after death when God rewards or punishes the deeds of humans on earth are very prominent in all the Abrahamic religions during the Middle Ages.

As a fourth category religious scepticism will be named. While present-day theological models often expressly exclude religious scepticism from the debate (Mensching 1955), secular historians and philosophers are very interested in these strands. A fifth category is not concerned with religious truth but with the value of human life as such, regardless of religious affiliation. In what follows these five categories will be applied in order to distinguish different strands of thought which open ways for mutual understanding and respect.

Anthropological Universalism

In Boccaccio's ring parable the loving father, who is equally fond of his three sons, is an important motive. Whatever the differences between the sons, they are all embraced by the same affection. This idea is the basis for one important strand of thought, which may be termed anthropological universalism. Anthropological universalism may not limit dogmatic or soteriological exclusivism in any way. It turned towards the common humanity, regardless of the religious differences.

This universalism is displayed in works of secular literature mentioned above, for example in some of the German epics of the High Middle Ages (Stein 1933). Especially the epics *Parzival* and *Willehalm* by Wolfram of Eschenbach (d. *c.*1220) must be named in this respect. Wolfram was not interested in depicting other religions realistically; he instead constructed unspecified 'pagans'. Wolfram, however, made sure that these foreign opponents of the Christians were just as brave, chivalric, and faithful and thus had to be treated with knightly respect. A central point in the novel *Willehalm* is the great address by Lady Gyburc to the council of war. Gyburc urges the Christians to spare the pagans, because every human being, the Christian before baptism included, is a pagan by birth. As she herself had been a pagan before she converted, the anthropological similarity and indeed identity of Christian and pagan is demonstrated in her person.

With their treatment of the encounter of religious enemies, Wolfram and Boccaccio were not reflecting fierce crusade propaganda, yet their propositions were well in line with official doctrine. Legal and theological teachings of Latin Christianity held that the pagan possesses his land and life by natural right. Christians may only fight in self-defence and in defence against sins violating natural law (Muldoon 1979). While these theories did not prevent religious violence, a basic legal protection of life and property of non-adherents of the dominant religion was established within all monotheistic cultures of the Middle Ages. Only heretics or apostates in Christian or in Muslim dominated societies could expressly forfeit these elementary securities (Griffel 2000; Lourdaux and Verhelst 1976). In Jewish societies and in Christian communities under Muslim rule no physical violence was legitimate or executed.

Anthropological universalism is often confused with religious relativism or pluralism because medieval thinkers are not expected to respect the well-being of representatives of—in their view—untrue religions.

Inclusivism

The 'tales of the three and the one' often contain the motive of a single father or king, representing God. The idea of one common God is in fact a very important inclusivistic proposition, contradicting the idea of a stable 'Mosaic distinction' mentioned above.

a. Dogmatic inclusivism

Dogmatic inclusivism was a very widely spread attitude. Even if numerous Jewish and Muslim thinkers denounced Christians as idolaters or many Christian theologians censured Jews and Muslims as traitors and heretics, a lot of thinkers of the three religions stressed the common traditions. Other religions—like Buddhism or more local beliefs in Eurasia, for example—were expressly excluded from this understanding. Especially in the Middle East the shared theological and philosophical backgrounds served in fact as the basis for both religious demarcation and inclusivism. The other two religions could either be negatively framed as deviations or positively as steps towards the absolute truth.

In this context the many religious tracts and dialogues written by Jews, Christians, and Muslims respectively, in Asia or in Europe, should be mentioned. They are often characterized by a reverential tone towards adherents of other religions. They stress the common grounds of their teachings. Especially writings for missions and interreligious diplomacy stressed inclusive propositions and could point out emphatically how near the religious enemy in fact already approached the truth. Many religious dialogues and examinations demonstrate great anthropological and even religious esteem. Yet none of the authors of these tracts and dialogues, be it the Jew Ibn Kammūna (*c.*1215–1284 CE) in Baghdad or the Latin Christian Ramon Llull (1232–1316) in Mallorca, would cede the superiority of their own religion (Lewis and Niewöhner 1992).

Very far-reaching dogmatic inclusivism may be found as the medieval cultures embraced the ancient philosophical traditions and adapted them to their theology. The translation and adaptation of traditions helped to spread not only philosophical writings but also religious teachings across religious borders. Within its own chain of logic arguments the scholars could accept a philosophical and even a theological teaching as correct, even if it originated from a religious doctrine they did not share. Within certain contexts, they chose not to debate the religious bearings of a specific teaching.

This is true for the famous *Letters of the Brethren of Purity* from around the tenth century CE, which cite a broad variety of spiritual and philosophical sources from India to Greece. The letters originated in Muslim circles but have also been widely read by Jewish scholars. The authors often found very affirming words for non-Muslim teachings; their dogmatic inclusivism is very liberal indeed. Often no comparative evaluation is given at all. Yet the superiority of Islam remains (Alí de Unzaga 2010). During the twelfth and thirteenth centuries Latin scholastic thinkers, too, made ample use of ancient philosophy as well as of Jewish and Muslim sources. It is of no consequence for the present argument whether their approach to non-Christian philosophy led to a genuine conception of a double truth (philosophical and theological) or not. One could also mention the scientific and spiritual works by the Syriac Orthodox scholar Gregorius Bar ʿEbroyo (1226–86), who appreciated the Muslim theologian al-Ghazālī, without ever wavering in his conviction of the superiority of Christianity as a doctrine (Teule 1992).

Dogmatic inclusivism has often been interpreted as religiously relativistic. Consequently inclusivist works have been misunderstood as pluralistic. This is also the case for an apologetic tract, the *Bustān al-Uqūl* written by a Yemenite Jewish scholar in a period of crisis and persecution. Nathanael al-Fayyūmī (*c.*1090–*c.*1165) intended to keep the wavering members of his community with his flock and to prevent conversion. He provided the Jews of Yemen with both strong and inoffensive arguments against polemical assaults and aggressive mission. Nathanael's advice to Jews under threat was to accept Muhammad's prophethood to the Muslims as genuine and to remain with Judaism as the true and superior religion revealed to the Jewish people.

In modern scholarship inclusivism has occasionally been connected with heterodoxy. On the contrary, however, inclusivism has always been one possible strand of orthodoxy. It is true that several unorthodox figures like the enigmatic mystic Ibn Hallāj (d. 922 CE) voiced a liberal inclusivist attitude. Yet his sympathy for non-Muslims was not the reason for his persecution (Massignon and Mason 1982: I. 191ff.).

Dogmatic inclusivism was not always welcome to the other parties concerned. Inclusivist supersessionism could be engrossing and posed a potential threat to the religious inferior. Writers like Judah Halevi (1075–1141) realized this constellation as dangerous for his communities. In the *Book of Kuzar (Kuzari)* he therefore argued for strict soteriological exclusivism, excluding even converts from God's presence in the world to come. Still his rabbi hoped that at the end of all days all the people who had derided the Jews before, would then embrace their faith. The prospect of an eschatological conversion of all the peoples is often expressed throughout the spiritual literature.

b. Soteriological inclusivism

Soteriological inclusivism was not necessarily combined with dogmatic inclusivism. Soteriological inclusivism also appears in the religious cultures of Latin Christians and

Muslims alike. In his great poem on the hereafter, the *Commedia*, Dante Alighieri (1265–1321), for example, grouped virtuous Muslims and innocent un-baptized into limbo, not into hell. Here, we encounter the Sultan Saladin (1137–93), the Andalusian philosopher Averroes (1126–98), or the Persian physician Avicenna (*c.*980–1037). Their names were mentioned with great admiration by the Latin scholars of the time. With this grouping, Dante was not breaking ground for a liberal avant-garde but remained fully in line with scholastic theology.

For centuries, theologians had defined certain conditions under which the non-Christians could even be received in heaven. They wanted to reconcile the theology of the all-merciful God with absolute truth claims (Capéran 1934). Thomas Aquinas made it clear that, in contrast to the heretic, the unbeliever was damned for his sins, not for his false religion. Those unbelievers who had never had the chance to listen to the gospel and who had taken great care to lead a virtuous life, he said, had implicitly wished for baptism without knowing it. Those individuals could be included in salvation. Saladin could certainly have heard the gospel, thus he only qualified for the limbo. But others, living before Christ or in the remote distance, could not. Accordingly, we meet some of these unbelievers in Dante's Paradise.

Islam, too, developed a limited inclusivism to allay the teaching that the non-Muslim invariably would go to hell. In the eyes of well-respected Muslim scholars the impossibility to have heard about God's revelation to Muhammad could indeed, together with virtuousness, qualify a non-Muslim for reception into heaven. Controversies arose as to what exactly 'no possibility to hear' would imply. Thus, inclusivist propositions of different grades were formulated. The theologian al-Ghazālī (1058–1111) designed a very limited option. The Sufi mystic Ibn al-ʿArabī (1165–1240), who was also a pronounced dogmatic inclusivist, opened the window somewhat further. He accepted that mankind followed different paths to God, which were, apparently, all created by him. The political, dogmatic, and soteriological superiority of Islam, however, was not suspended by Ibn al-ʿArabī (Legenhausen 1999; Khalil 2013). This is also true for the well-known mystic called Mevlana or al-Rūmī (1207–73). Mevlana's modest, respectful and inclusivist poems have been very popular in the western liberal thought of the last 200 years and have regularly been misunderstood as pluralistic (Lewis 2001).

For some medieval Jewish thinkers, like Moses Maimonides (1135/8–1204), it was understood that the righteous among the nations would be included in God's salvation. While the fate of the unbeliever was fiercely disputed among Christian and Muslim theologians, this was much less a theological problem for Jewish theologians.

Religious Scepticism and Individualistic Faith

Another motive common to many of the 'tales of the three and the one' is doubt about the truth and the possible deception by fraud. When criteria are lacking, a rejection of all the religious truth claims may be a logical consequence. Orthodox religious leaders considered this thought a constant danger. Even the existence of the ever-disputing theologians themselves could become the ultimate argument in this line of thought. The outspoken medieval Muslim polemicist Ibn Ḥazm stressed this point (Turki 1979). There were indeed individuals who did not believe in the existence of God (Weltecke 2010). Yet, no satisfying proof has been found that the pluralist proposition could switch into an atheist one.

A strand that can well be accounted for as a reaction to the different truth claims may be termed individualistic faith. Where a decision was impossible, simple adherence to a personal faith and ethical rules seemed to be the solution. Such was the reaction of the above-mentioned figure of Burzōē the physician. In the introduction to the *Kalila wa-Dimna* he asserts that he turned his back on all the belief systems and pursued his own path of salvation instead. He stressed, however, his intention to please God and to save his soul. Clearly Burzōē's account was widely known, for example to the physician Samau'al al-Maghribī, who converted to Islam in the year 1163 (Samau'al al-Maghribī 1964). In the lively debates of the first centuries of Muslim rule a number of thinkers expressed strong criticism of the truth claims of Judaism, Christianity, and Islam, their sacred scriptures, their cosmological myths, but would not abandon some individual religious ideas of God. These 'freethinkers' have been of great interest for research (Stroumsa 1999).

Combined with a hearty contempt for ecclesiastical authorities, this line of reasoning may also be found in the Latin West, voiced by uneducated laymen and women. Central Asia and northern India as a scene of a remarkable religious productivity by individual ascetics should be mentioned here, too. Ultimately the quest for a personal relation to God and a rejection of the teachings and claims by religious authorities was one of the most vigorous driving forces, which constantly caused new religious movements and teachings to emerge.

Pluralism: Dogmatic or Soteriological

a. Denominational pluralism

For a long time scholars have been studying internal struggles and denominational differences in the religions. Especially well known are the two main branches of Islam, Shi'a and Sunna, the different medieval churches (Latin church, Orthodox churches, eastern churches) and the two branches of Judaism, the Rabbanites and the Karaites. Yet, there were many more smaller or larger groups. The truth claims of these denominations could be just as absolute vis-à-vis their internal enemies as they were towards other religions. A long tradition of polemics accompanies their relations. Scholars even argued that the exclusivism of the monotheistic religions was more pronounced towards internal factions than towards other religions. This thesis, however, cannot be confirmed.

In medieval Judaism, separations and ferocious polemics remained (Lasker 1981), but traditions were very rarely ousted as non-Jewish. Thus, their mutual contentions demonstrate that cohabitation, exchange, fierce polemics, and topographical separation could in fact take place at the same time (Rustow 2008). Muslim and Christian attitudes differ in theory. From their point of view internal deviance was no protected form of religious life. As is well known, episodes of violent persecution arose in some areas of medieval Islam and of Latin Christianity. At the same time cohabitation could be a normal experience of everyday life.

Certain periods witnessed the development of genuine pluralistic strands of theological thought that sought to bridge the gaps. On the whole these pluralistic movements were not ousted as heretical. The first strong pluralistic movement within Christianity occurred during the twelfth and the thirteenth centuries, about 800 years after the first establishment of parallel churches. Authors like the Armenian theologian Nerses of Lampron (1153–98) and the Syriac Orthodox scholar Bar ʿEbroyo were leading the field. They declared dogmatic and ritual differences, which had been considered to be absolutely vital in the past, to be mere varieties of the same theology and practice (Pinggéra 2000; 2006). They considered the diverse branches of Christianity as equally true and salvific without arguing for dogmatic and ritual uniformity. By this method the diversities, which had long been part of the respective religious identities, remained unoffended. The same method of decreasing the importance of differences was used in inter-Muslim exchange. Thus, declaring teachings as equal but not insisting on their actual sameness was one established inter-denominational theory of pluralism in the Middle Ages.

In his *Book of the Dove*, Bar ʿEbroyo used a second method to open up a pluralistic perspective. He declared that while he had been very interested in scholastic disputation in the past, he now considered dogmatic discourse as futile and altogether abstained from it. Instead of quarrelling he 'wholly eradicated the root of hatred from the depth of [his] heart' (trans. Wensinck 1919: 60). Bar ʿEbroyo devalued cognitive and speculative theology in favour of spiritual contemplation. In fact, he also bridged a religious border in this work by quoting extensively from al-Ghazālī's 'Deliverance from error' (without naming his source), who in this work also argued for the path of the mystics. Al-Ghazālī for his part likewise stressed the deficiencies of scholastic disputations in favour of the religious practice by the mystic, to whom dogmatic differences were less important. As may be expected, inter-denominational pluralism has often been confused with interreligious pluralism in modern scholarship.

b. *Interreligious pluralism*

In the 'tales of the three and the one' there is much debate on the similarity and the value of the three religions; yet a genuine pluralist version, where all the three religions are equally *true* in the narrator's mind, is not known. This is in accordance with the status of pluralism in the Middle Ages. Interreligious pluralism used much the same theory as inter-denominational pluralism to overcome exclusivist positions. Different practices were declared as equally valid and various theological teachings as mere variances of the same true message. However, genuine pluralism violated the limits religious authorities were ready to tolerate and also the common opinions of the population.

Recent movements like the 'theology of religions' and other endeavours for peace between different belief-systems have caused a search for past vestiges of the pluralistic position. Thus, in the quest for medieval roots of contemporary intentions many inclusivists or anthropological universalists were read as pluralists. This led to misreadings of scholars like Meister Eckhart (*c.*1260–before 1328), Peter Abelard, Boccaccio, Marsilio Ficino (1433–99), Nicolas of Cusa (1401–64), Nathanael al-Fayyūmī, Mevlana/al-Rūmī, Ibn al-ʿArabī, and others, some of which have been mentioned above. These writers were inclusivists at most. Sources for the pluralist proposition cannot easily be found as the voices had little chance to be recorded or were not able to express themselves in writing.

Concerning the question whether other religions are salvific, the following positive responses could be given: in order to reconcile the theology of the all-compassionate God with his justice, the punishment in hell and its eternity were widely discussed mainly within Christian and Muslim societies. Both Christianity and Islam largely opted for the eternity of hell and punishment. However, already in early Christianity the idea was brought up that God could not wish for a perpetual suffering of sinners. Around the year 500, the theology of all-redemption was again expressed, this time by a Syriac writer, mystic, and ascetic, Stephen bar Sudhailē (*fl. c.*500 CE). In the *Book of Hierotheos*, Stephen envisaged how in the end all created beings, humans, angels, demons, and devils, would dissolve in God. While Syriac Orthodox authorities sympathized with Stephen's theology, they considered the doctrine of a finite hell heretical. Apart from the very limited opportunity described above, the salvation of the unbeliever was not possible within the accepted theology of medieval Christianity in general. At the same time, there were mystical strands in Greek as well as in Syriac theology that kept the idea of all-redemption alive during the centuries. Books were copied and the teaching debated. Until at least the thirteenth century Syriac copies of the *Book of Hierotheos* were produced and much sought after (Pinggéra 2002).

A comparable debate took place within medieval Islam. Heresiographers like Shahrastani mentioned authors who proposed universalistic salvation at the end of all days or a finite punishment of the souls in hell (Shahrastani 1986: 75). Ibn al-ʿArabī hoped that the sinners in hell would not experience their abode as an eternal suffering (Khalil 2013: 69). Surprisingly enough, a tract by the radical polemicist for Muslim orthodoxy, Ibn Taymiyya (1263–1328 CE), is known for explicitly suggesting a finite hell and an all-redemption (the tract is not translated, see Khalil 2013: 80ff.). Up to the present, the debate on the authenticity and the content of Ibn Taymiyya's treatise have been very controversial. In this piece written at the end of his life, Ibn Taymiyya stated, against the weight of tradition, that there was in fact no consensus on the eternity of hell and gathered quotations both from the Quran as well as from comments and traditional sayings of the prophet Muhammad (*ḥadīth*). In fact, in order to support his argument he gathered valuable vestiges of an ongoing debate otherwise lost. Here, too, the idea remained alive even if the leading majority of theologians never accepted it.

In Jewish soteriology, again, the eternity of punishment was no line of demarcation between orthodoxy and deviancy. Eschatological all-redemption was neither considered impossible nor outright deviant. After all it was not considered a burning issue. In Kabbalist circles in Spain an ethical-juridical principle (*tikkun olam*, repairing the world) received strong eschatological meanings as the mystics now thought that law-abiding Jews could in fact move cosmic forces and help to bring about the salvation of the entire world (Rosenthal 2005).

Even more radical was a second strand which took immediate redemption of all people, regardless of their religion, for granted. Since the early thirteenth century several established Latin theologians realized that this pluralist proposition existed among their flock. One of them was the scholar Guillaume Peyrault (*c.*1190–1271). Guillaume wrote a chapter on 'the error of the one who says that everybody can be saved in his respective faith and religion' (Guillelmus Peraldus 1629: 106–10). Guillaume also documented the argument in favour of this proposition. God the all-merciful could not have created so many pagans (here: Muslims) and Jews with the intention to damn them all to hell. Therefore it was necessary to assume that other faiths were equally dear to him. This assertion kept emerging in Latin theological works, protocols, and also in historical works right up to the end of the Middle Ages. All recorded pluralists lacked a sophisticated education. No scholar is known to have supported the proposition that all religions are equally true, valid, or salvific.

Muslim authors such as al-Nawawi (1234–78 CE) were arguing just in the same way as Guillaume Peyrault that those who doubted that only Islam was true and considered other religions just as valid, were to be considered unbelievers (Khalil 2013: 8). In Islam and Judaism also unorthodox individuals are described as pluralists in historiographical or polemical works. These assertions are difficult to verify (van Ess 1991–7: IV; van Ess 2011; Wasserstrom 1995). Mention should also be made of the religious teachings and practices that, among other features, bridged the antagonism between Islam and Hinduism in northern India. As yet they have not been taken into account sufficiently in this debate. The propositions found in the Persian realm of writing between Central and South Asia need to be taken more into consideration in future studies on pluralism (Roychoudhury 1941; Grobbel 2007).

In conclusion, on the basis of the current state of research it is certain that pluralistic propositions had always been alive during the entire Middle Ages in the different sections of the Abrahamic religions. Yet they were marginalized. Therefore, to identify individuals proves to be much more difficult than for the other, more accepted strands sketched above.

Conclusion

The narrations of the rings and of the three impostors are the tip of the iceberg of the discourse of multiplicity. All levels of society were involved in this discourse, and thus its topics found their way into the popular culture to which the 'tales of the three and the one' belong. The discourse of multiplicity then and now was and is shaped by power interests, hierarchies, and unequal opportunities of participation. During the Middle Ages, those voices that sought to demarcate the borders between the religions and maintain the superiority of their own truth claims were dominant. The aim to keep the communities in line, however, did not impede the development of respectful theories; on the contrary. Medieval worlds went far beyond simple distinctions between 'us' and 'they' or 'believer' and 'non-believer'. It is true, religious differences could be understood as exclusive alternatives and legitimate violence. But at other times many more distinctions and shades could be distinguished.

Several different strands of thought were isolated here, which show different levels of ethical and religious respect towards the other. The majority of these lines of thought were quite accepted by the religious authorities. Only pluralism, while existing, remained on the margins. Dogmatic inclusivism accepted different religions as partly true. As was seen, this inclusivism in itself was not necessarily combined with positive salvific expectations for adherents of other religions; neither did dogmatic exclusivism exclude them. One could defend the idea that God would save some of the unbelievers, in spite of their entirely false beliefs. Dogmatic exclusivity could even be combined with soteriological universalism. This teaching would sustain that all the unbelievers would eventually be saved, in spite of their false beliefs.

Some of the strands of respectful thought invented in the Middle Ages are rather prominent today: to respect the common humanity regardless of religious differences, to embrace the idea of a common God or to declare theological teachings, rituals, and practices as equally true or salvific but not insisting on their sameness.

References

Alí-de-Unzaga, O. 2010. 'Ikhwan al-Safa', in D. Thomas et al., eds., *Christian-Muslim Relations. A Bibliographical History. Volume 2 (900–1050)* Leiden: Brill, 306–11.

Assmann, J. 2003. *Die Mosaische Unterscheidung oder Der Preis des Monotheismus.* Munich, Vienna: Hanser.

Bar 'Ebroyo, Gregorius. 1919. *Bar Hebraeus' Book of the Dove*, trans. A. J. Wensinck. Leiden: Brill.

de Blois, F. 1990. *Burzoy's Voyage to India and the Origin of the Book of Kalilah wa Dimna.* London: Royal Asiatic Society of Great Britain & Ireland.

Boccaccio, Giovanni. 1976. *Decameron.* Vittore Branca, ed. Mailand: Pr. L'Accademia della Crusca.

Capéran, L. 1934. *Le Problème du salut des infidèles.* Toulouse: Grand Séminaire.

Edwards, J. 1985. 'Religious Faith and Doubt in Late Medieval Spain'. *Past and Present* 120: 3–25.

al-Ġazzālī, Abū-Ḥāmid Muḥammad Ibn-Muḥammad. 2001. *Deliverance from Error and Mystical Union with the Almighty. Al-Munqidh min al-ḍalāl*, ed. G. F. McLean, trans.

M. N. Abdul-Rahim Rifat. Washington, DC: Council for Research in Values and Philosophy.

Gilliot, C. 2002. 'Islam, "sectes" et groupes d'opposition politico-religieux (VIIe–XIIe siècles)'. *Rives Nord-Méditerranéennes* 10: 35–52.

Griffel, F. 2000. *Apostasie und Toleranz im Islam: Die Entwicklung zu al-Ġazālīs Urteil gegen die Philosophie und die Reaktionen der Philosophen*. Leiden, Boston: Brill.

Grobbel, G. 2007. 'Das Dabistan-i madahib und seine Darstellung der Religionsgespräche an Akbars Hof'. In B. Reinert and J. Thomann, eds, *Islamische Grenzen und Grenzübergänge*. Bern: Lang, 85–130.

Jansen Enikel. 1972. *Jansen Enikels Werke*, ed. P. Strauch. MGH. Dt. Chroniken 3, Dublin and Zürich: Weidmann.

Khalil, M. H., ed. 2013. *Between Heaven and Hell: Islam, Salvation, and the Fate of Others*. Oxford, New York: Oxford University Press.

Lasker, D. J. 1981. 'Rabbinism and Karaism: The Contest for Supremacy'. In R. Jospe, ed., *Great Schisms in Jewish History*. New York: Center for Judaic Studies and University of Denver, 47–72.

Legenhausen, M. G. 1999. *Islam and Religious Pluralism*. London: al-Hoda.

Lessing, G. E. 1966. *Nathan der Weise*. Peter Demetz, ed. Frankfurt a.M.: Ullstein.

Lewis, B. and Niewöhner, F., eds. 1992. *Religionsgespräche im Mittelalter*. Wiesbaden: Harrassowitz.

Lewis, F. D. 2001. *Rumi: Past and Present, East and West. The Life, Teachings and Poetry of Jalāl al-Dīn Rumi*. Oxford: Oneworld.

Lourdaux, W. and Verhelst, D., eds. 1976. *The Concept of Heresy in the Middle Ages (11th–13th C.): Proceedings of the International Conference Louvain May 13–16*. Leuven: The Hague University Press.

Madelung, W. 1959. 'Fatimiden und Bahrainqarmaten'. *Der Islam* 34: 34–88.

al-Maghribī, Samau'al. 1964. *Ifḥām al-Yahūd: Silencing the Jews*, ed. and trans. M. Perlmann. New York: American Academy for Jewish Research.

Massignon, L. 1920. 'La Légende "De tribus impostoribus" et ses origines islamiques'. *Revue de l'histoire des religions* 82: 74–8.

Massignon, L. and Mason, H. 1982. *The Passion of Al-Hallaj: Mystic and Martyr of Islam*. Princeton: Princeton University Press.

Mensching, G. 1955. *Toleranz und Wahrheit in der Religion*. Heidelberg: Quelle & Meyer.

Möhring, H. 1993. 'Der andere Islam: Zum Bild vom toleranten Sultan Saladin und neuen Propheten Schah Ismail'. In O. Engels and P. Schreiner, eds, *Die Begegnung des Westens mit dem Osten. Kongressakten des 4. Symposions des Mediävistenverbandes in Köln aus Anlass des 1000. Todesjahres der Kaiserin Theophanu*. Sigmaringen: Thorbecke, 131–55.

Muldoon, J. 1979. *Popes, Lawyers, and Infidels: The Church and the Non-Christian World 1250–1550*. Liverpool: Liverpool University Press.

Niewöhner, F. 1988. *Veritas sive Varietas: Lessings Toleranzparabel und das Buch von den drei Betrügern*. Heidelberg: Schneider.

Ó'Cuilleanáin, C. 1984. *Religion and the Clergy in Boccaccio's 'Decameron'*. Rome: Ed. di Storia e Letteratura.

Peraldus, Guillelmus. 1629. *Summa virtutum ac vitiorum*. 2 vols., ed. R. Clutius. Cologne: Boetzer (various editions).

Pinggéra, K. 2000. 'Christologischer Konsens und kirchliche Identität: Beobachtungen zum Werk des Gregor Bar Hebraeus'. *Ostkirchliche Studien* 49: 3–30.

Pinggéra, K. 2002. *All-Erlösung und All-Einheit: Studien zum "Buch des heiligen Hierotheos" und seiner Rezeption in der syrisch-orthodoxen Theologie.* Wiesbaden: Reichert Verlag.

Pinggéra, K. 2006. 'Nerses von Lambron und die armenische Kirche des 12. Jahrhunderts: Erneuerung und Identität in Konflikt'. In M. Tamcke, ed., *'Dich, Ararat, vergesse ich nie!' Neue Beiträge zum Schicksal Armeniens und der Armenier.* Münster: Lit, 25–46.

Poorthuis, M. 2005. 'The Three Rings: Between Exlusivity and Tolerance'. In B. Roggema, M. Poorthuis, and P. Valkenberg, eds, *The Three Rings: Textual Studies in the Historical Trialogue of Judaism, Christianity and Islam.* Leuven, Dudley, MA: Peeters, 257–85.

Rosenthal, G. S. 2005. 'Tikkun haOlam: The Metamorphosis of a Concept'. *The Journal of Religion* 85 (2): 214–40.

Roychoudhury, M. 1941. *The Din-i-Ilahi or the Religion of Akbar.* Calcutta: Calcutta University Press.

Rustow, M. 2008. *Heresy and the Politics of Community: The Jews of the Fatimid Caliphate.* Ithaca, NY: Cornell University Press.

Shagrir, I. 1997. 'The Parable of the Three Rings: A Revision of its History'. *Journal of Medieval History* 23 (2): 163–77.

al-Shahrastānī, Abu al-Fath b. 'Abd al-Karim. 1986. *Livre des religions et des sectes (Al-Milal wa-l-niḥal). Traduction avec introduction et notes.* 2 vols, ed. and trans. D. Gimaret and G. Monnot. Leuven: Peeters.

Stein, S. 1933. *Die Ungläubigen in der mittelhochdeutschen Literatur von 1050 bis 1250.* Berlin: Eisner.

Stroumsa, S. 1999. *Freethinkers in Medieval Islam: Ibn al-Râwandî, Abû Bakr al-Râzî, and their Impact on Islamic Thought.* Leiden: Brill.

Teule, H. G. B. 1992. 'Barhebraeus' Ethicon, al-Ghazâlî and Ibn Sina'. *Islamochristiana* 18: 73–86.

Timotheus I, Patriarch der Kirche des Ostens. 2011. *Timotheos I., Ostsyrischer Patriarch: Disputation mit dem Kalifen al-Mahdī*, ed. and trans. M. Heimgartner. Leuven: Peeters.

Turki, A. M. 1979. 'La Refutation du scepticisme et la théorie de la connaissance dans les Fiṣal d'Ibn Ḥazm'. *Studia Islamica* 50: 37–56.

van Ess, J. 1991–7. *Theologie und Gesellschaft im 2. und 3. Jahrhundert Hidschra: Eine Geschichte des religiösen Denkens im frühen Islam.* 6 vols. Berlin and New York: De Gruyter.

van Ess, J. 2011. *Der Eine und das Andere: Beobachtungen an islamischen häresiographischen Texten.* 2 vols. Berlin and New York: De Gruyter.

Wasserstrom, S. M. 1995. *Between Muslim and Jew: The Problem of Symbiosis under Early Islam.* Princeton: Princeton University Press.

Weltecke, D. 2010. *'Der Narr spricht: Es ist kein Gott': Atheismus, Unglauben und Glaubenszweifel vom 12. Jahrhundert bis zur Neuzeit.* Campus Historische Studien; Frankfurt.

Yerushalmi, Y. H. 1970. 'The Inquisition and the Jews of France in the Time of Bernard Gui'. *Harvard Theological Review* 63 (3): 317–76.

PART III

SCRIPTURE AND HERMENEUTICS

CHAPTER 12

HISTORICAL-CRITICAL READINGS OF THE ABRAHAMIC SCRIPTURES

NICOLAI SINAI

THERE can be little doubt that the modern scholarly engagement with the Bible and the Quran in the western world has been dominated by what is customarily called 'historical criticism' or 'the historical-critical method' (Soulen and Soulen 2001: 78–80). The compound adjective 'historical-critical' only seems to have gained programmatic currency in biblical studies around 1800 (Kraus 1982: 176), but the second component of the term is already employed in Ludwig Cappellus' *Critica sacra* (1650), a manual of biblical exegesis which, among other topics, treats the transmission of the biblical text and establishes methodological principles for the assessment of textual variants (Kraus 1982: 49–50, 83–4; Burnett 2008: 789–92). Cappellus is perhaps best known for an earlier work (published anonymously in 1624) which demonstrates, against the orthodox Protestant dogma of the divine origin of all aspects of the Hebrew text of scripture, that the biblical vowel signs were only introduced in the fifth or sixth century CE (Kraus 1982: 31–5, 48). An even more sustained application of the 'critical' mindset is Richard Simon's *Histoire critique du Vieux Testament* (1678), which ventures far beyond issues of textual criticism and argues, as Thomas Hobbes and Isaak de la Peyrère had already done in the 1650s (Hobbes 1996: 252–3 (ch. 33); Nellen 2008: 817–23), that the Pentateuch cannot have been composed by Moses alone (Kraus 1982: 65–70; Rogerson 2008: 838–43). By way of a preliminary definition, we may thus say that to study the Bible, or any other text, *critically* is to set aside traditional presuppositions about its origin, transmission, and meaning, and instead to follow, as Hobbes put it, the 'light . . . which is held out to us from the books themselves' (Hobbes 1996: 252); and to pursue such a critical enquiry from a *historical* perspective is to take an overriding interest in what the text in question might have meant to its original addressees or human author(s), and how these and later redactors and transmitters contributed to its present shape.

Due to the paradigmatic status which the historical-critical approach has enjoyed in modern scholarship, any student of the historical interactions and structural homologies within the Abrahamic family of religions would do well to give some thought to the methodological underpinnings of historical-critical readings of religious writings, which were to a significant extent developed and honed by scholars grappling with the Bible. The present chapter is meant to assist in such a self-reflective endeavour. I shall begin by attempting to transcend the more or less lexical definition of historical criticism given above and to further carve out its hermeneutical peculiarities.

The Hermeneutics of Traditional Scriptural Exegesis

Although describing Judaism, Christianity, and Islam as 'scriptural religions' may be a simplification, it is certainly a defensible one: the notion of a revealed or inspired corpus of literature seems to be inscribed into the very genome of all historical descendants of the biblical tradition. Normally, recognition of a particular text as constituting 'scripture' is expressed in terms of genealogical statements about how the text's proximate human author or transmitter—for example, Moses, the apostolic authors of the Gospels, or Muhammad—came to function as a conduit for divine communications, or to receive divine inspiration. Nevertheless, endowing a text with scriptural authority is not simply a matter of such explicit affirmations of revelatory status: it also requires a special kind of hermeneutics, which Moshe Halbertal has characterized as applying an extreme version of what modern philosophers call the 'principle of charity' (Halbertal 1997: 27ff.). In order to throw into relief some of the defining features of historical-critical interpretation, it will be useful to briefly survey the most important principles of traditional scriptural exegesis.

As John Barton has observed, treating a certain text, or a collection of texts, as constituting scripture (at least in the common sense of the term) generally entails the 'hermeneutical imperative' that it ought to be read as containing teachings which are both individually true and collectively consistent (Barton 1996: 73). This imperative may manifest itself, for example, in attempts to resolve apparent contradictions between different scriptural passages, or to defuse tensions between scripture and the worldview espoused by its interpreters.[1] To be sure, the twin postulate of scripture's truth and coherence is not always applied to the entire corpus: traditional Islamic

[1] This can be achieved either by insisting that the reader adapt his worldview to the literal sense of scripture (for example, by denying evolutionism in favour of creationism), or by reading contemporary beliefs into scripture (for example, by arguing that the Bible or the Quran allude to modern science).

exegetes often consider certain earlier quranic commandments to have been 'abrogated' by later ones; and Mark's Jesus insists that the establishment of marriage as an indissoluble bond in Gen. 2: 24 overrides the Mosaic permission of divorce (Deut. 24: 1), said to have been decreed merely 'for the hardness of your hearts' (Mark 10: 5). Nevertheless, it seems correct to insist that hermeneutical practices which we would recognize as endowing a text with properly scriptural status must uphold the truth and coherence at least of a significant chunk of it.

In addition to being true and consistent, scriptural texts are also generally assumed to be transhistorically *significant*—i.e. they are credited with an abiding formative and normative relevance for contemporary believers (Barton 1996: 73–6; Halbertal 1997: 3). Many scriptural interpreters will thus display a concern with maintaining and extending the respective text's foundational role for the way in which a community (or a scholarly elite within it) understands God, the world, and itself; with the scriptural derivation of moral or legal norms; and with unlocking scripture's potential for individual ethical or spiritual progress (Sinai 2009: 16–21). Finally, it should be noted that canonical practices of reading also engender an intense concentration of intellectual energy on details which in a profane text would be viewed as negligible or even 'subsemantic' (Barton 1996: 77): a text credited with canonical authority is presumed to repay any amount of exegetical pondering that its human interpreters are capable of. One may call this the assumption of scripture's exegetical inexhaustibility (Sinai 2009: 10–16).

Going beyond the preliminary clarification of 'historical criticism' given above, we may thus say that to interpret the Bible (or the Quran) from a historical-critical perspective is not only to be prepared to question established opinions about its origin, transmission, and meaning, but to systematically suspend the traditional postulates of consistency, abiding truth, and contemporary significance that endow these texts with scriptural authority in the first place. The earliest explicit articulation of this second and stronger understanding of historical criticism is found in Benedict Spinoza's (d. 1677) landmark *Tractatus theologico-politicus* (1670). The next section therefore proposes to take a closer look at this foundational manifesto of modern biblical hermeneutics.[2]

Spinoza's Understanding of Historical-Critical Hermeneutics

Spinoza explicitly rejects the postulate that scripture is 'everywhere true and divine', laid down as an a priori foundation for discovering its 'true sense' (Spinoza 1925: 9; English translation in Elwes 1883–4: 8 [henceforth cited in brackets]), and complains

[2] My discussion of Spinoza draws on and partly reproduces Sinai 2010. For a recent study of the *Tractatus*, see Nadler 2011.

that this assumption has all too often led interpreters to 'wring their own figments and opinions out of the sacred text' (Spinoza 1925: 97 [98]). Spinoza, by contrast, would have the exegete bracket the question whether the biblical text has anything to say which contemporary readers will be able to accept as true and relevant: 'we are at work not on the truth of what is said, but solely on its sense' (Spinoza 1925: 100 [101]). In interpreting the Bible, then, we are to engage in an extensive exercise in double-entry bookkeeping: whatever we contemporary interpreters may believe to be true about God, man, and the world is not allowed to directly determine the beliefs about God, man, and the world that we ascribe to, say, the ancient Israelites.[3] Linguistic and historical data come to replace the interpreter's theological, scientific, and other beliefs as the background against which the plausibility of a given interpretation is to be gauged: safeguarding or maximizing the truth and significance of a text—which constitute primary concerns of traditional scriptural exegesis—cease to be legitimate grounds for discarding a literal and commonsensical understanding of a particular passage in favour of an allegorical one or a complex harmonization with another passage. The interpreter of scripture must resolutely resist the temptation of reading it too charitably, of mistaking 'the mind of the Prophets and the Historians [who composed the biblical writings] with the mind of the Holy Spirit and the true nature of the matter' (Spinoza 1925: 105 [106]).

Spinoza himself provides an example for the exegetical procedure he has in mind. When it is stated in Deut. 4: 24 that God is a 'consuming fire', are we to understand that Moses believed God materially to be a fire, or are we to construe the statement as a metaphor? According to Spinoza, the relevant consideration must not be which one of the various possible interpretations conforms to what we take to be a reasonable view of the nature of God: there is nothing to guarantee that the Pentateuch might not contain unreasonable theology. Instead, we are to base our interpretation of the verse on an understanding of the text's historical background, which to Spinoza means that we must interpret it in the light of the other theological views expressed in the Pentateuch and according to the semantics of ancient Hebrew. Hence, if we are unable to provide evidence that in ancient Hebrew calling someone a 'fire' could carry a metaphorical meaning, we will be forced to take the text literally, 'however repugnant it may be to reason' (Spinoza 1925: 100–1 [102]). Although Spinoza maintains that a metaphorical reading of the above statement in fact turns out to be correct, his hermeneutics thus opens up the very real possibility that the Bible may turn out to be grossly *mistaken*—or, as scholars would start to put it towards the end of the eighteenth century, to contain 'myths' (Kraus 1982: 147–51 and Kümmel 1973: 101–4, 111–12)—and to be *inconsistent* (given that, as Spinoza registers, other biblical verses teach that God has no likeness

[3] However, at a very basic level any such exercise in double-entry bookkeeping must involve some measure of hermeneutic charity: for while we may attribute to a past culture views that directly contradict our own, it is certainly part of the interpreter's task to explain how holding such beliefs is a rationally intelligible thing to do, given certain historical circumstances.

to any visible thing, see Spinoza 1925: 101 [102]). As the important Enlightenment theologian Johann Salomo Semler (d. 1791), who fully subscribed to the basic principles of Spinoza's hermeneutics,[4] was to observe a century later, scripture may even turn out to be theologically and ethically *irrelevant*: 'it is therefore false to assume that Holy Scripture always, and in the first instance, brings about men's edification and must also be directly employed to that end' (Kümmel 1973: 66). When Johannes Weiß argued in his 1892 work *Die Predigt Jesu vom Reiche Gottes* that the historical Jesus was not a forerunner of nineteenth-century liberal theology but an apocalyptic prophet announcing the imminent end of the world (Schweitzer 1911), he provided a striking illustration for the radical otherness that might accrue to scripture on the basis of Spinoza's hermeneutics.

Although historical-critical scholarship has undergone significant refinement since Spinoza, I would submit that its basic approach—which is well summarized by the frequently reiterated maxim that the Bible must be interpreted in the same way as any other text[5]—has remained recognizably similar to the methodology set out in Spinoza's *Tractatus*. By virtue of suspending the a priori assumptions discussed above, historical-critical interpreters are bound to be highly sensitive to tensions, inconsistencies, and redundancies within scripture, as well as to divergences between scripture and later tradition, and to be disinclined to resort to non-literal strategies of reading or complex harmonizations in order to resolve such anomalies. Instead, they will typically seek to understand the text at hand in the light of views, concepts, and modes of expression current in the historical situation from which it originated, and of events and developments contemporaneous with it. This implies both that a text's historical context will play a fundamental role in determining what it is that the text is saying; and that traditional assumptions about its dating and ascription become falsifiable if there is reason to doubt that its style and content are historically plausible under the historical circumstances to which it has so far been assigned. A celebrated early instance of this sort of reasoning is Lorenzo Valla's demonstration in 1440 that the so-called 'Donation of Constantine', supposedly an official decree by which the Emperor Constantine had given over the western part of the Roman Empire to Pope Sylvester, could not have been composed in the fourth century CE. It is a consequence of Spinoza's hermeneutics that the traditional ascription, or even the explicit self-ascription, of biblical works can be prosecuted on the same grounds: de Wette's claim that the Book of Deuteronomy was a product of the seventh century BCE rather than having been authored by Moses, or Wellhausen's late dating of the priestly law (see below), are epistemological siblings of Valla's argument.

[4] 'An interpreter ought not to interject anything of his own ideas into the writing he wishes to interpret, but to make all he gets from it part of his current thinking and make himself sufficiently certain concerning it solely on the basis of its content and meaning' (quoted in Kümmel 1973: 66).

[5] See the citations from various seventeenth- and eighteenth-century authors in Reventlow 2008: 860–1 and Kümmel 1973: 50, 58, 61, 87, as well as Stroumsa 2010: 49–61.

Against a simplistic view of historical criticism as simply more 'neutral' than traditional scriptural exegesis, it bears pointing out that it is likewise based on assumptions which it does not, and indeed cannot, itself justify:

(i) A text can only be legitimately taken to signify something that was historically 'thinkable' and 'sayable' for ordinary (albeit highly educated and intelligent) humans at the time of its composition. As a result, crediting a text with a genuine foretelling of future events becomes hermeneutically inadmissible. The fact that chapter 11 of the Book of Daniel, supposedly set in the sixth century BCE, appears to foretell events occurring during the second century BCE thus supplies an argument to the effect that the Book of Daniel can only have been composed in the second century.

(ii) The historical events and developments against which a text is situated 'must be understood in terms of historical analogy; what was possible to occur in biblical times must be possible in the present and vice versa' (Hayes 2008: 998). Therefore, in reconstructing the historical reality behind the text, miraculous divine interventions are to be eschewed in favour of psychological, political, economic, or social categories of explanation.

These postulates are obviously rooted in a distinctively modern understanding of the material world as a self-contained field of causally interconnected occurrences, in which every event is caused by other events from within the system: divine or other supernatural interventions thus cease to be part of the explanatory toolkit.[6]

The Origins of the Historical-Critical Approach

The remainder of this chapter will attempt to convey a sense of the rich diversity of modern biblical and quranic scholarship that has developed around the core hermeneutical commitments sketched above on the basis of Spinoza's *Tractatus*. Before turning to the subsequent history of the discipline, however, it is important to briefly look back and examine how the new exegetical approach pioneered by Spinoza and Simon crystallized. A good point of departure for such retrospection is the question of the genesis of the Pentateuch. As intimated above, Hobbes, Spinoza, and Simon all contest the traditional belief that the Pentateuch was composed by Moses and instead argue that it can only have reached its final shape at a much later time; Spinoza, for example, singles out Ezra as the most probable editor of the sequence of historical

[6] Human agents, of course, are often seen as requiring an exception to this general view of the world as a causally self-contained system—see, for example, Descartes's understanding of humans as immaterial minds interacting with the material world.

books reaching from Genesis to Kings. In support of this position, Hobbes and Spinoza invoke various passages whose literal sense suggests the perspective of post-Mosaic writers, such as the description of Moses' death and burial in Deut. 34: 5–6, or Gen. 12: 6 ('At that time the Canaanites were in the land'), which presupposes the later Israelite takeover of Canaan (Hobbes 1996: 253; Spinoza 1925: 119 [121–2]; Nadler 2011: 108–10). Simon adds further references to various repetitions and inconsistencies that likewise cast doubt on the Pentateuch's unitary authorship (Simon 1685: 31–40 [book 1, ch. 5]).

Such textual observations have a centuries-long prehistory. This is signalled by Spinoza himself, who opens chapter 8 of the *Tractatus* with a citation from the Jewish exegete Abraham ibn Ezra's (d. 1164) commentary on Deut. 1: 1. The quotation enumerates various verses from the Pentateuch—such as Gen. 12: 6—that are prima facie incompatible with Mosaic authorship.[7] Havah Lazarus-Yafeh has suggested that Ibn Ezra could have been influenced by Islamic polemicists like Ibn Ḥazm (d. 1064), whose 'Book of Opinions on Religions, Sects, and Heresies' presents a long list of the Bible's geographical and chronological inconsistencies, theological impossibilities, and moral abominations in order to prove the quranically inspired charge that the Jews have 'falsified' the text of the Torah (Lazarus-Yafeh 1992: 26–35).[8] Lazarus-Yafeh's conjecture that elements of medieval Islamic polemics against Judaism, transmitted through Jewish scholars like Abraham ibn Ezra, resurface in Spinoza's *Tractatus* is furthermore supported by the fact that Ezra the scribe, whom Spinoza took to be the final editor of the historical writings of the Hebrew Bible, is cast in a similar role by Ibn Ḥazm.[9] It should also be noted that the statement describing God as a 'consuming fire' from Deut. 4: 24, employed by Spinoza in order to demonstrate proper exegetical procedure, is already cited by Ibn Ḥazm as an illustration of the shocking anthropomorphism of the Bible.[10] As Lazarus-Yafeh emphasizes, such a polemically motivated close reading of the Bible pre-dates the Islamic Middle Ages (Lazarus-Yafeh 1992: 28, 130–3), and Ibn Ḥazm's sources may ultimately reach back to ancient authors like the second-century pagan philosopher Celsus[11] or Marcion.[12]

[7] Spinoza 1925: 118–20 (120–3). For a more detailed exposition of the passage see Nadler 2011: 108–9, who points out that Spinoza gravely overstates Ibn Ezra's position.

[8] On Ibn Ḥazm and his *Kitāb al-fiṣal* see Adang 1996: 59–69.

[9] On Ezra in Islamic polemics see Lazarus-Yafeh 1992: 50–74. Already the sixteenth-century scholar Andreas Masius had suggested that the books of Joshua, Judges, and Kings were only compiled by Ezra and that the Pentateuch continued to be edited 'long after the time of Moses' (Rogerson 2008: 839).

[10] See Lazarus-Yafeh 1992: 17–18, with n. 29 (who does not note the overlap with Spinoza).

[11] According to Celsus, as cited by Origen, the books of the Hebrew Bible 'do not admit allegories, but are utterly ridiculous myths' (Schott 2008: 46–7). The parallel to Ibn Ḥazm's assertion that the contradictions to be found in the Torah and the Gospels 'do not admit allegorical interpretation' (Lazarus-Yafeh 1992: 26) is suggestive. Like Ibn Ḥazm, Celsus was also scandalized by the moral improprieties that the Bible attributes to the patriarchs, such as Lot's incest with his daughters (cf. Schott 2008: 47 and Lazarus-Yafeh 1992: 33–4).

[12] Marcion argued that the Mosaic God of justice, commanding to take 'an eye for an eye', could not be identical with the God of love proclaimed by Jesus, and also identified various contradictions within the Hebrew Bible (Metzger 1988: 90–4).

Nevertheless, it is not obvious that textual discoveries of the sort adduced by Abraham ibn Ezra must necessarily be viewed as affording a sort of Archimedean point from which to lift traditional Jewish and Christian beliefs about the origin of the Bible off their foundation. The passage about Moses' death and burial, for example, is already highlighted, and conveniently domesticated, in the Talmud: 'Is it possible that Moses whilst still alive would have written "So Moses . . . died there" (Deut. 34: 5)? The truth is, however, that up to this point Moses wrote, from this point Joshua, son of Nun, wrote.'[13] And a Christian allegorist like Origen (d. *c.*254) could freely admit Celsus' point that the Bible contained 'impossibilities and contradictions', in order to then go on to maintain that such impossibilities constitute 'stumbling blocks' inserted by the Holy Spirit in order to direct the reader of scripture to a spiritual layer of meaning hidden beneath its literal surface sense (Turner 2010: 76). The prominence which early modern writers like Spinoza give to such long-recognized anomalies therefore requires a separate explanation. The most pertinent one is surely the emphasis on the literal sense of the Bible that can already be found in late medieval exegesis (Grant and Tracy 1984: 87–91; Smith 2008: 55–60) and then received a powerful boost by the Reformation.[14] If scripture was to function as the exclusive arbiter of theological truth over and against ecclesiastic tradition, it had to possess one 'simple' and 'literal' sense, as Luther insisted (Raeder 2008: 375). Despite the fact that Luther was still committed to a Christological interpretation of the Old Testament (Raeder 2008: 377–8), historical and philological considerations thus came to be recognized as important ways of access to the sense of scripture. Luther himself raised the possibility that the final editing of the Book of Isaiah might have been undertaken by someone other than the prophet (Raeder 2008: 389; Kraus 1982: 16), and Andreas Bodenstein von Karlstadt cited Deut. 34: 5, among other verses, as prima facie speaking against the view that Moses was the author of the Pentateuch (Kraus 1982: 28–31). Thus, textual observations of the sort put forward by Abraham ibn Ezra were only able to display their full force as a result of the unprecedented theological weight that Protestant hermeneutics imposed on the literal sense of the Bible. From this perspective, Spinoza's tongue-in-cheek presentation of his exegetical approach as a consistent application of the Reformationist principle of *sola scriptura*, while certainly a rhetorical artifice, does not appear to be so far off the mark after all (Spinoza 1925: 99 [100]).

Another important precondition for the work of Spinoza and Simon was of course the significant increase of philological expertise in Greek and Hebrew that owed as much to Renaissance humanism as to the Reformationist emphasis on the primacy of scripture. A crucial first step consisted in printings of the Hebrew and Greek text of the Bible becoming available at the beginning of the sixteenth century (Schenker 2008). The foundations for a proper command of Hebrew grammar and lexicography by Christian interpreters were established by Johannes Reuchlin (d. 1522) and Conrad

[13] Babylonian Talmud, *Menaḥot* 30a, quoted after Lazarus-Yafeh 1992: 10.

[14] Kraus 1982: 6–16; Grant and Tracy 1984: 92–9. See also the chapters on individual Reformers in Sæbø 2008.

Pellican (d. 1556), who paved the way for the impressive philological erudition displayed in Hugo Grotius' *Annotata ad Vetus Testamentum* (1644) (Kessler-Mesguich 2008; Kraus 1982: 26–7, 50–3). During the same period, and in partial imitation of the established procedures of classical scholarship, the methodology of textual criticism was honed, reaching a first apogee in Cappellus' *Critica sacra* (1650).[15] Thus, over the course of the 150–200 years preceding Spinoza and Simon, Christian interpreters of the Bible had systematically acquired a previously non-existent set of textual and linguistic skills without which the novel hermeneutical approach outlined in the previous section would not have been feasible. Incidentally, it may be remarked that in doing so, they attained for the first time a level of philological competence comparable to that routinely expected of Islamic interpreters of the Quran, who from the ninth century on had taken a close interest in grammatical and lexicographical issues and quranic reading variants.

Biblical Criticism after 1700

Utilizing analytical categories coined by the historian of science Thomas Kuhn, one might characterize the works of Spinoza and Simon as marking an exegetical shift of 'paradigm' followed by a period of 'normal science', in which ever more data is accumulated and the theoretical models used to explain this data become ever more refined (Kuhn 1962). In spite of the important differences between canonical and historical-critical hermeneutics highlighted above, it must be emphasized that there is at least one significant commitment that historical-critical 'normal science' has inherited from traditional biblical exegesis: its commitment to a close reading of the biblical text which, while adhering to the same general principles that govern the interpretation of ordinary historical documents, nevertheless deems the Bible to merit an amount of philological attention that one would not normally accord to 'profane' writings—a sort of latter-day equivalent of what was called the 'assumption of scripture's inexhaustibility' above. In this respect, the consolidation of historical-critical practices of close reading after Spinoza and Simon, in spite of contributing to a partial subversion of the Bible's religious authority, was nevertheless squarely predicated on the latter. This was certainly a result of the fact that in eighteenth- and nineteenth-century Germany, the historical-critical study of the Bible increasingly came to be practised within Protestant theological faculties.

While the present chapter obviously cannot hope to do justice to such a centuries-long collaborative scholarly enterprise, it will be useful to provide at least one illustration for the further development of historical-critical Bible scholarship since the early eighteenth century. In order to link this to the preceding sections, I shall again

[15] As pointed out by Kraus 1982, 582 (n. 3 on § 14), Cappellus explicitly acknowledges the paradigmatic role of a work by Heinrich Stephanus on Cicero (1557).

concentrate on the genesis of the Pentateuch. A decisive advance over the works of Spinoza and Simon occurred when Jean Astruc (d. 1766), the personal physician of Louis XIV of France, realized that the two creation accounts at the beginning of the Book of Genesis are marked by a systematic preference for different divine names, namely, the term 'Elohim' (Gen. 1: 1–2: 3) and the tetragrammaton YHWH (Gen. 2: 4–3: 24). In a book published in 1753, Astruc proposed that this state of affairs could be explained by assuming that the two narratives stemmed from two different sources on which Moses had drawn in composing the Book of Genesis. Remarkably, the same discovery had already been made about four decades earlier by Henning Bernhard Witter, but had subsequently fallen into oblivion (Lods 1925). Witter and Astruc mark the birth of the Documentary Hypothesis, i.e. the theory that repetitions, incongruities, and anomalies of the sort catalogued by Simon could be accounted for by postulating that the Pentateuch in its present form had been compiled from a number of originally independent works with significantly different terminological and theological characteristics. Astruc's approach was taken up by Johann Gottfried Eichhorn (d. 1827), who in his German introduction to the Old Testament (1780–3) conducted his own source-critical analysis of Genesis based on Astruc's general principle (Rogerson 1984: 19–20). In 1798, Karl David Ilgen proposed an important refinement of the Documentary Hypothesis by distinguishing two different sources using the divine name 'Elohim'. Various alternative models to the Documentary Hypothesis that were proposed during the first decades of the nineteenth century were ultimately abandoned (Whybray 1995: 12–28).

While Astruc and Eichhorn had still considered Moses to have been responsible for the compilation of the Pentateuch, subsequent Old Testament criticism was marked by increasing doubts about the biblical account of ancient Israelite history. Already Johann Severin Vater (d. 1826) and Wilhelm Martin Leberecht de Wette (d. 1849) saw the Pentateuch as a comparatively late work dating from the seventh or sixth century BCE (Rogerson 1984: 34–5), thus broadly agreeing with Spinoza's dating. De Wette was also responsible for a hypothesis that was to become a veritable cornerstone of Pentateuchal scholarship: in his 1805 dissertation, he argued that the Book of Deuteronomy was not composed by the same author as the other books of the Pentateuch and that it was in part identical with the 'book of the law' which according to 2 Kings 22–3 was discovered in the Jerusalem Temple in the eighteenth year of King Josiah of Judah (622 BCE). Rather than being a work of Moses, de Wette maintained that Deuteronomy had only been composed under Josiah in order to support the latter's centralization of the sacrificial cult in Jerusalem (Rogerson 1992: 39–43). For the first time, it seemed, part of the Pentateuch had been securely placed in a specific historical situation—although it should be noted that contemporary scholarship has found reason to question the historicity of the report from 2 Kings, thus undermining de Wette's chronological anchor point (Würthwein 1994).

Drawing on the work of Ilgen and de Wette, Hermann Hupfeld and Eduard Riehm in 1853 and 1854 formulated the classic version of the Documentary Hypothesis which postulated four Pentateuchal source layers: one using the tetragrammaton (the

'Yahwist'), two using the divine name 'Elohim' (the 'Elohist' and the Priestly Source), and the Book of Deuteronomy (Kraus 1982: 247–8). The Documentary Hypothesis reached its consummation with Julius Wellhausen's (d. 1918) *Prolegomena to the History of Israel*, first published in 1878, which demonstrated, on the basis of earlier work by Karl Heinrich Graf and Abraham Kuenen, that the Priestly Source with its extensive legal portions (now found in Leviticus and Numbers) was in fact younger than Deuteronomy and postdated the classical literary prophets such as Amos and Hosea.[16] The 'Mosaic' law accordingly emerged as the youngest element of the Pentateuch—a groundbreaking inversion of the biblical view of Israelite religious history, which, unlike Hobbes' or Spinoza's somewhat casual denial of the Pentateuch's Mosaic authorship, was based on a painstaking, multi-generational sifting of texts. Although Pentateuchal scholarship continued to evolve in the first half of the twentieth century, cultivating a new interest in questions of literary genre and in the oral traditions underlying the literary sources of the Pentateuch, Wellhausen's formulation of the four-source theory of the Pentateuch survived virtually unchallenged until the 1970s. Since then, scholars have developed various alternative models, although these generally retain important elements of nineteenth-century Pentateuchal source criticism.[17] Partly in recognition of the fact that theories about the literary and redactional prehistory of the Pentateuch and other biblical books are, at least to some degree, inevitably hypothetical, recent decades have also seen a growing emphasis on the end product that has emerged from these processes, i.e. on the final shape of individual biblical writings, or even the Hebrew Bible as a whole (Sheppard 1992).

Before moving on to the Quran, one seminal development in the history of the discipline must be briefly touched upon: the discovery of the Hebrew Bible's ancient Near Eastern context. By the 1850s, Grotefend, Rawlinson, Champollion, and Hincks had made groundbreaking contributions to the decipherment of Old Persian and Akkadian cuneiform and Egyptian hieroglyphs (Wiesehöfer 2001: 231–42; Allen 2010: 8–9; Cathcart 2011). Their work made it possible to read the numerous ancient Near Eastern documents that were being discovered over the course of the nineteenth century, such as the thousands of clay tablets excavated at Nineveh. An early product of this new type of scholarship was George Smith's *The Chaldean Account of Genesis* (1876), offering translations of Babylonian texts which showed close parallels with the biblical accounts of the creation and the deluge. Spinoza had assumed that the historical background of the biblical writings would have to be reconstructed on the basis of the Bible itself, and this had essentially remained the approach even of Wellhausen (although the latter had supplemented the biblical data by parallels from pre-Islamic Arabic religion, assumed to preserve vestiges of the primitive stage of Semitic religion). For the first time, the new material that was now becoming available offered direct glimpses into the Bible's wider cultural context.

16 On the 'path to Wellhausen' see Rogerson 1984: 257–72.

17 A detailed overview of some recent approaches is given in Zenger et al. 2004: 92–122.

It is perhaps understandable that the striking parallels between the primeval history in Genesis 1–11 and ancient Near Eastern texts such as the Enuma Elish or the Atrahasis story led some scholars to conclude that much of the Bible was little more than a distant echo of Mesopotamian civilization, a position forcefully expressed in Friedrich Delitzsch's (d. 1922) lectures on 'Babel und Bibel', delivered in 1902, which triggered a famous controversy (Johanning 1988; Lehmann 1994). Contemporary scholarship has reached a much more nuanced perspective than Delitzsch and has transcended the heady triumph of discovery by rightly emphasizing the Bible's deliberate recasting of, and implicit polemics against, ancient Near Eastern notions.[18] The availability of the new ancient Near Eastern material has therefore required biblical studies to undergo a crucial learning process that can perhaps be summed up by saying that intertextual comparison does not imply reductionism—a truth to which we will have occasion to return in the next section, dealing with the emergence of modern quranic scholarship.

The Historical-Critical Study of the Quran

For more than a millennium, Christians had been accustomed to reviling the Quran as a rehash of Christian heresies, and its presumed author Muhammad as an 'impostor' and a 'false prophet' (Bobzin 2004). Any first-hand discussion of the Quran was thus closely bound up with anti-Islamic polemics.[19] A precondition for the modern western study of the Quran was therefore the gradual dissipation of such a primarily polemical stance (Stroumsa 2010: 124–44). This change in attitude is well illustrated by the Catholic theologian Johann Adam Möhler (d. 1838), who, in spite of ascribing the Quran's rejection of the divinity of Jesus to Muhammad's 'ignorance' and 'misapprehensions', criticized the traditional view that the Islamic prophet was a religious impostor as rendering inexplicable the genesis of the Quran, and speaks with respect of the latter's 'highly original piety, its touching devotion and [its] peculiar religious poetry' (Möhler 1839: 357, 370).[20] The Quran, then, was not a deliberate fabrication aimed at furthering Muhammad's craving for power, but a genuine expression of human religiosity, and as such could be seen to deserve dispassionate study. While the historical-critical study of the Bible emerged when European scholars started to read the Bible with significantly *less* charity than before, that of the Quran was born when western scholars began to read it *more* charitably (although in no way going so far as to assume its truth or coherence). Like the Bible, the Quran thus ceased to be

[18] For a comparative overview see Clifford 1994.

[19] As emphasized in Burman 2007, the polemical function of medieval Latin translations of the Quran should not lead one to overlook that, despite their philological limitations, they constituted bona fide attempts at rendering the Arabic original.

[20] I owe my awareness of Möhler's article to Bobzin 1999: 16–17.

evaluated primarily in terms of whether or not it corresponded to what was taken to be theologically (or morally, or cosmologically) true.

The view that Muhammad had practised conscious deception was also rejected in Abraham Geiger's (d. 1874) *Was hat Mohammed aus dem Judentume aufgenommen* ('What did Muhammad Borrow from Judaism?', 1833) (Geiger 1898: 25; cf. Sinai 2008), the earliest scholarly treatment of the Quran that still figures in contemporary western publications. Geiger's impressive catalogue of quranic 'borrowings' from biblical and rabbinical literature was superseded in the 1930s by Heinrich Speyer's even more comprehensive *Die biblischen Erzählungen im Qoran*, but even today a full picture of the complicated ways in which the Quran is intertwined with the religious landscape of late antiquity—for example, with Syriac Christianity—has yet to emerge. In marked contrast to the Hebrew Bible, for which comparative work of the sort carried out by Geiger only began to be feasible with the rediscovery of the ancient Near East in the last decades of the nineteenth century, after more than a century of intense source-critical analysis, the modern western study of the Quran was from its inception intensely focused on intertextual comparison with biblical and post-biblical Jewish and Christian literature. As a result, the temptation of intertextual reductionism was even more acute in quranic studies than in biblical scholarship: for all their erudition, Geiger, Speyer and others often tended to assume that the Quran simply replicates a given Jewish or Christian narrative or concept.[21] As in the case of the Bible, however, many scholars would now readily admit that the Quran does not simply and invariably 'borrow' from earlier traditions, but frequently appropriates and inflects them in line with its own theological agenda and purposes, often in highly sophisticated and creative ways (Griffith 2008: 115–16).

Geiger's treatise was followed, in 1843 and 1844, by two works by Gustav Weil (d. 1889), a study of the life of Muhammad and a brief 'historical-critical introduction to the Quran'. Weil's most lasting contribution consisted in his attempt to reconstruct the chronological order in which the texts now collected in the Quran had originally been promulgated by Muhammad. Weil's division of the quranic material into four periods (three Meccan, one Medinan) (Weil 1844: 54–80) was further refined in Theodor Nöldeke's (d. 1930) *Geschichte des Qorâns* (1860), which in a thoroughly revised and enlarged edition prepared between 1909 and 1938 has remained an important reference work until today (Nöldeke 1909–38).[22] The notion that the quranic material can be reorganized into a linear series of texts datable to different stages of Muhammad's prophetic career, as well as the distinction between suras and verses reportedly revealed at Mecca and at Medina, is already prominent in traditional Islamic exegesis, where Weil's and Nöldeke's four-period chronology clearly has its point of departure (Weil 1843: 363ff.). Nonetheless, the Weil–Nöldeke chronology is meant to be

21 For a case study, see Nicolai Sinai, 'Pharaoh's Submission to God in the Qur'an and in Rabbinic Literature: A Case Study in Qur'anic Intertextuality', forthcoming in a volume edited by Holger Zellentin.

22 The question of chronology is treated in vol. I, 58–234.

based primarily on stylistic and terminological criteria immanent in the Quran itself, such as the extreme divergences in verse length exhibited by different suras, rather than on extra-quranic reports of frequently dubious authenticity. The four-period chronology may thus be seen as a methodological and functional analogue to the Documentary Hypothesis. The question to what extent Weil's and Nöldeke's chronological reordering stands in need of revision or should even be replaced by an entirely different approach will certainly remain on the agenda of quranic scholars for some time to come. The problem is closely bound up with that of determining the scope of the textual units that are to be dated: do these consist in brief passages encompassing merely a few verses, or can we assume that at least the short and mid-sized suras, and perhaps even the longest ones, are unified literary wholes?[23]

Weil's work was also paradigmatic insofar as it closely linked the study of the Quran to that of the life of Muhammad, an approach inherited from medieval Islamic scholarship. The Quran itself offers little more than indirect and frequently opaque allusions to its historical context, yet post-quranic Islamic literature contains an extensive corpus of traditions dealing with the biography of Muhammad (*sīra*) and the revelation of specific quranic verses. Writing in 1851, Ernest Renan was therefore able to famously declare Islam to have been 'born in the full light of history' and the life of Muhammad to be 'as well known to us as that of any reformer of the 16th century' (Renan 1851: 3 [my translation]). Subsequent scholarship has been forced to take note of the strong likelihood that this highly detailed body of material may only have emerged over the course of the first two Islamic centuries and consequently does not afford us direct access to the Quran's historical milieu of origin—an insight which, incidentally, is not confined to western scholarship and has recently been underscored by the Tunisian historian Hisham Djait (Sinai 2011). It was mainly due to two famous books published in 1977—John Wansbrough's *Quranic Studies*, and *Hagarism* by Patricia Crone and Michael Cook—that the historical reliability even of the basic chronological and geographical framework of the *sīra* tradition has also become subject to sustained doubt, including the Quran's provenance from the western Arabian towns Mecca and Medina, and its traditional dating to the first decades of the seventh century. As a result, the almost instinctive projection of later Islamic historiography and exegesis on the text of the Quran that characterizes the work of earlier western scholars has now deservedly fallen into discredit. Even if, as I believe, cogent reasons can be adduced in favour of a suitably revised version (rather than dismissal) of the traditional narrative of Islamic origins, such scepticism should in no way be seen as excessive or superfluous: as demonstrated by de Wette's and Wellhausen's redatings of Deuteronomy and the Priestly Source, and F. C. Baur's view that the Gospel of John was not composed before the second half of the second century CE (now generally rejected), the construction,

[23] The first position, associated with the name of Richard Bell, has been criticized—persuasively, in my view—in Neuwirth 1981. For a holistic reading of a long (Medinan) sura see Cuypers 2009.

evaluation, and, if needs be, dismissal of historical counter-narratives is an integral part of the historical-critical commitment to bracketing commonly received beliefs and opinions.

Concluding Remarks

As I have argued above, to read scripture historically-critically is to systematically suspend the question of its truth, coherence, and contemporary relevance; to be attentive to inconsistencies and redundancies within scripture, as well as between scripture and later beliefs; and to account for the textual phenomena thus observed by means of historical models, which often include complicated redactional processes. It must be emphasized, though, that nothing about this approach prevents the historical critic from discovering the Bible or the Quran to exhibit considerable literary artistry (instead of mechanically, and often quite arbitrarily, dissecting them into earlier and later textual layers); or from finding them to be engaged in a highly sophisticated debate with previous traditions (instead of reducing them to mere reverberations of things said before). Although it would be easy to compile a martyr's memorial of the historical-critical study of scripture, the proposition that a religious commitment to the Bible or the Quran is compatible with the historical-critical approach, and may even have important things to learn from it—a conviction expressed not only by Christian theologians, but also, for instance, by the Egyptian scholar Naṣr Ḥāmid Abū Zayd (d. 2010)[24]—should therefore not be lightly dismissed.

References

Adang, C. 1996. *Muslim Writers on Judaism and the Hebrew Bible: From Ibn Rabban to Ibn Hazm*. Leiden: Brill.

Allen, J. 2010. *Middle Egyptian: An Introduction to the Language and Culture of Hieroglyphs*. 2nd edn. Cambridge: Cambridge University Press.

Barton, J. 1996. 'The Significance of a Fixed Canon of the Hebrew Bible'. In M. Sæbø, ed., *Hebrew Bible/Old Testament: The History of Its Interpretation*. Vol. I: *From the Beginnings to the Middle Ages (Until 1300)*. Göttingen: Vandenhoeck & Ruprecht, 67–83.

Bobzin, H. 1999. *Der Koran: Eine Einführung*. München: Beck.

Bobzin, H. 2004. 'Pre-1800 Preoccupations of Qur'ānic Studies'. In J. D. McAuliffe, ed., *Encyclopaedia of the Qur'ān*. Vol. IV. Leiden: Brill, 235–53.

Burman, T. E. 2007. *Reading the Qur'ān in Latin Christendom, 1140–1560*. Philadelphia: University of Pennsylania Press.

Burnett, S. G. 2008. 'Later Christian Hebraists'. In Sæbø 2008: 785–801.

[24] On Abū Zayd and his predecessors see Wielandt 2002: 131–7.

Cathcart, K. J. 2011. 'The Earliest Contributions to the Decipherment of Sumerian and Akkadian'. *Cuneiform Digital Library Journal.* <http://www.cdli.ucla.edu/pubs/cdlj/2011/cdlj2011_001.pdf> (accessed 7 February 2013).

Clifford, R. J. 1994. *Creation Accounts in the Ancient Near East and in the Bible.* Washington, DC: Catholic Biblical Association.

Cuypers, M. 2009. *The Banquet: A Reading of the Fifth Sura of the* Quran, trans. Patricia Kelley. Miami: Convivium.

Elwes, R. H. M., trans. 1883–4. *The Chief Works of Benedict de Spinoza.* Vol. I. London: G. Bell & Sons.

Geiger, A. 1898. *Judaism and Islam*, trans. F. M. Young. Madras: M.D.C.S.P.C.K. Press.

Grant, R., with Tracy, D. 1984. *A Short History of the Interpretation of the Bible.* 2nd edn. Philadelphia: Fortress.

Griffith, S. 2008. 'Christian Lore and the Arabic Qur'ān: The "Companions of the Cave" in *Sūrat al-Kahf* and in Syriac Christian Tradition'. In G. S. Reynolds, ed., *The Qur'ān in its Historical Context.* Abingdon: Routledge, 109–37.

Halbertal, M. 1997. *People of the Book: Canon, Meaning, and Authority.* Cambridge, MA: Harvard University Press.

Hayes, J. H. 2008. 'Historical Criticism of the Old Testament Canon'. In Sæbø 2008: 985–1005.

Hobbes, T. 1996. *Leviathan*, ed. J. C. A. Gaskin. Oxford: Oxford University Press.

Johanning, K. 1988. *Der Bibel-Babel-Streit: Eine forschungsgeschichtliche Studie.* Frankfurt am Main: Peter Lang.

Kessler-Mesguich, S. 2008. 'Early Christian Hebraists'. In Sæbø 2008: 254–75.

Kraus, H.-J. 1982. *Geschichte der historisch-kritischen Erforschung des Alten Testaments.* 3rd edn. Neukirchen-Vluyn: Neukirchener Verlag.

Kuhn, T. 1962. *The Structure of Scientific Revolutions.* Chicago: University of Chicago Press.

Kümmel, W. G. 1973. *The New Testament: The History of the Investigation of its Problems*, trans. S. McLean Gilmour and H. C. Kee. London: SCM.

Lazarus-Yafeh, H. 1992. *Intertwined Worlds: Medieval Islam and Bible Criticism.* Princeton: Princeton University Press.

Lehmann, R. G. 1994. *Friedrich Delitzsch und der Babel-Bibel-Streit.* Freiburg: Universitätsverlag; Göttingen: Vandenhoeck & Ruprecht.

Lods, A. 1925. 'Un précurseur allemand d'Astruc, Henning Bernhard Witter'. *Zeitschrift für die Alttestamentliche Wissenschaft* 43: 134–5.

Metzger, B. 1988. *The Canon of the New Testament: Its Origin, Development, and Significance.* Oxford: Oxford University Press.

Möhler, J. A. 1839. 'Ueber das Verhältniß des Islams zum Evangelium'. In Möhler, *Gesammelte Schriften und Aufsätze*, ed. J. J. I. Döllinger. Vol. I. Regensburg: G. J. Manz, 348–402.

Nadler, S. 2011. *A Book Forged in Hell: Spinoza's Scandalous Treatise and the Birth of the Secular Age.* Princeton: Princeton University Press.

Nellen, H. J. M. 2008. 'Growing Tension between Church Doctrines and Critical Exegesis of the Old Testament'. In Sæbø 2008: 802–26.

Neuwirth, A. 1981. *Studien zur Komposition der mekkanischen Suren.* Berlin: De Gruyter.

Nöldeke, T. 1909–38. *Geschichte des Qorāns.* Revised by F. Schwally, G. Bergsträsser, and O. Pretzl. 3 vols. Leipzig.

Raeder, S. 2008. 'The Exegetical and Hermeneutical Work of Martin Luther'. In Sæbø 2008: 363–406.

Renan, E. 1851. 'Mahomet et les origines de l'islamisme'. *Extrait de la Revue des deux mondes*, livraison du 15 déc. 1851.

Reventlow, H. G. 2008. 'English Deism and Anti-Deist Apologetic'. In Sæbø 2008: 851–74.
Rogerson, J. W. 1984. *Old Testament Criticism in the Nineteenth Century: England and Germany*. London: SPCK.
Rogerson, J. W. 1992. *W. M. L. de Wette: Founder of Modern Biblical Criticism. An Intellectual Biography*. Sheffield: Sheffield Academic.
Rogerson, J. W. 2008. 'Early Old Testament Critics in the Roman Catholic Church—Focusing on the Pentateuch'. In Sæbø 2008: 837–50.
Sæbø, M., ed. 2008. *Hebrew Bible/Old Testament: The History of Its Interpretation*. Vol. II: *From the Renaissance to the Enlightenment*. Göttingen: Vandenhoeck & Ruprecht.
Schenker, A. 2008. 'From the First Printed Hebrew, Greek and Latin Bibles to the First Polyglot Bible, the Complutensian Polyglot: 1477–1577'. In Sæbø 2008: 276–91.
Schott, J. M. 2008. *Christianity, Empire, and the Making of Religion in Late Antiquity*. Philadelphia: University of Pennsylvania Press.
Schweitzer, A. 1911. *The Quest of the Historical Jesus*, trans. W. Montgomery. London: Adam and Charles Black.
Sheppard, G. T. 1992. 'Canonical Criticism'. In *Anchor Bible Dictionary*. Vol. I. New York: Doubleday, 861–6.
Simon, R. 1685. *Histoire critique du Vieux Testament*. 2nd edn. Rotterdam: Reinier Leers.
Sinai, N. 2008. 'Orientalism, Authorship, and the Onset of Revelation'. In D. Hartwig et al., eds, *'Im vollen Licht der Geschichte': Die Wissenschaft des Judentums und die Anfänge der kritischen Koranforschung*. Würzburg: Ergon, 145–55.
Sinai, N. 2009. *Fortschreibung und Auslegung: Studien zur frühen Koraninterpretation*. Wiesbaden: Harrassowitz.
Sinai, N. 2010. 'Spinoza and Beyond: Some Reflections on Historical-Critical Methodology'. In W. Schmidt-Biggemann and G. Tamer, eds, *Kritische Religionsphilosophie: Eine Gedenkschrift für Friedrich Niewöhner*. Berlin, New York: De Gruyter, 193–214.
Sinai, N. 2011. 'Hisham Djait über die "Geschichtlichkeit der Verkündigung Muḥammads"'. *Der Islam* 86: 30–43.
Smith, L. 2008. 'Nicholas of Lyra and Old Testament Interpretation'. In Sæbø 2008: 49–63.
Soulen, R. N. and Soulen, R. K. 2001. *Handbook of Biblical Criticism*. Louisville, KY: Westminster John Knox Press.
Spinoza. 1925. *Opera*. Vol. III, ed. C. Gebhardt. Heidelberg: Carl Winters Universitaetsbuchhandlung.
Stroumsa, G. G. 2010. *A New Science: The Discovery of Religion in the Age of Reason*. Cambridge, MA: Harvard University Press.
Turner, D. 2010. 'Allegory in Christian Late Antiquity'. In R. Copeland and P. T. Struck, eds, *The Cambridge Companion to Allegory*. Cambridge: Cambridge University Press, 71–100.
Weil, G. 1843. *Mohammed der Prophet, sein Leben und seine Lehre*. Stuttgart: Metzler.
Weil, G. 1844. *Historisch-kritische Einleitung in den Koran*. Bielefeld: Velhagen & Klasing.
Whybray, R. N. 1995. *Introduction to the Pentateuch*. Grand Rapids, MI: Eerdmans.
Wielandt, R. 2002. 'Exegesis of the Qur'ān: Early Modern and Contemporary'. In J. D. McAuliffe, ed., *Encyclopaedia of the Qur'ān*. Vol. II. Leiden: Brill, 124–42.
Wiesehöfer, J. 2001. *Ancient Persia from 550 BC to 650 AD*, trans. A. Azodi. London: Tauris.
Würthwein, E. 1994. 'Die Josianische Reform und das Deuteronomium'. In *Studien zum Deuteronomistischen Geschichtswerk*. Berlin, New York: De Gruyter, 188–216.
Zenger, E. et al. 2004. *Einleitung in das Alte Testament*. 5th edn. Stuttgart: Kohlhammer.

CHAPTER 13

INTERPRETERS OF SCRIPTURE

CAROL BAKHOS

> 'And if all the trees of the earth were pens and the oceans ink, with many more oceans for replenishing them, the word of God would never come to an end.' Quran 31: 27
>
> 'Turn it over again and again, for everything is in it.' *Pirke Avot* 5: 22
>
> '*Commentary* questions discourse as to what it says and intended to say; it tries to uncover that deeper meaning of speech that enables it to achieve an identity with itself, supposedly nearer to its essential truth; in other words, in stating what has been said, one has to re-state what has never been said. In this activity known as commentary which tries to transmit an old, unyielding discourse seemingly silent to itself, into another, more prolix discourse that is both more archaic and more contemporary—is concealed a strange attitude towards language: to comment is to admit by definition an excess of the signified over the signifier.' Foucault 1975: xvi–xvii.

Readers of the Bible and Quran continue to unpack and tease out new meaning of a biblical narrative or quranic verse that resonates for the reader personally or throws light on a current social or political matter. The canon of scripture is fixed, but political, social, and religious exigencies give rise to different interpretations of it. Particular contexts give shape to the ways in which exegetes revitalize the word of God. This is as true of the church fathers, the rabbis, and the muffasirūn as it is of interpreters of sacred texts today.[1]

[1] This is a somewhat expanded version of chapter one of my monograph, *The Family of Abraham* (Cambridge, MA: Harvard University Press, 2014).

Ancient and modern Jewish, Christian, and Islamic scriptural interpretation share many fundamental assumptions inherent to the hermeneutical process. They approach scripture as a seamless whole, perfect in its message to humanity. The word of God is neither self-contradicting, nor subject to mutability. Its interpretation on the other hand is far from monolithic, and betrays differing perspectives. Interpretation must be understood as a contextualized activity. The very questions addressed, the manner in which they are addressed and answered—who is addressing and answering and to what audience—all factor into understanding scriptural interpretation. In other words, awareness of the historical situatedness of the interpreter and of that which is interpreted provides a portal into exegetical texts and the practices that inform specific readings of scripture.

'An interpretation', writes Heidegger (1962: 192–3), 'is never a presuppositionless apprehending of something presented to us. If, when one is engaged in a particular kind of interpretation, in the sense of exact textual interpretation, one likes to appeal [*beruft*] to what "stands there", [but] then one finds that what "stands there" in the first instance is nothing other than the obvious undiscussed assumption [*Vormeignung*] of the person who does the interpreting.' What 'stands there' is twofold: one must attempt to grasp what 'stands there' for the rabbis who interpreted scripture, for the muffasirūn, interpreters of the Quran, and for the Christian church writers, and also to recognize what 'stands there' for us as interpreters of the received tradition. The process of interpretation is never purely philological, even when it is explicitly stated as such. In attending to our own presuppositions—from which we are never free, but an awareness of which and through which we better understand and elucidate the past and present—we are better attuned to the very movement between the text and interpreter, and between the interpretation and ourselves. This recognition of our own situatedness allows us to appreciate the ways in which the literature we will examine is itself the very expression of the experience of the historically situated interpreter and text.

What follows is an overview of Jewish, Christian, and Muslim interpretative traditions of the late antique, early medieval periods that played a role in later exegetical developments. Far from exhaustive, this general discussion seeks to familiarize the reader with underlying exegetical concepts, some common to all three Abrahamic religions, some unique to each, as well as with several important works and interpreters whose impact is detectable in contemporary exegesis.

The stories in the Hebrew Bible and Quran are characteristically terse, and in the case of the Quran elliptical, and thus readers are left with many unanswered questions about the details of any given narrative. Exegetes creatively expand stories as well as bridge gaps therein. At the same time, troubling passages are explained away in order to whitewash the patriarchs who are depicted as embodying religious teachings and behaving in exemplary ways. Clothed in layers of tradition scriptural characters take on a life of their own, and events are imbued with meaning exceeding the literal reading of the text. The accretion of traditions and confessional assumptions shape preconceived images and scriptural personages.

Ancient Jewish Biblical Interpretation

In *Biblical Interpretation in Ancient Israel* (1985), Michael Fishbane draws attention to how the Bible, the very source for exegesis, includes numerous examples of interpretation. That is, many biblical passages re-tailor earlier material to construct new meaning. The inner-biblical exegetical phenomenon takes on many forms and functions and is consonant with later interpretative literature. Our enquiry into Jewish biblical interpretation is, however, limited to a period spanning the ancient and early medieval eras, and will focus on midrash—rabbinic biblical interpretation.

The Septuagint, a Greek translation of the Pentateuch, and the Aramaic translations, the targumim, are biblical translations. Although their intent is not to explicate the Bible, to the extent that translation per force is a form of interpretation, they possess some of the qualities of interpretation. Translations of specific words or phrases considered problematic in Hebrew often, although not necessarily, convey theological or philosophical concerns. For example, 'the image of God' is rendered 'the glory of God', and the 'mouth of God' is 'the voice of God'.

Forms of scriptural amplification include *Jubilees*, an elaborate narrative covering events that take place from Genesis to Exodus 12, the *Genesis Apocryphon*, one of the Dead Sea Scrolls extant in fragmentary form, and the *Biblical Antiquities* of Pseudo-Philo that ends with the death of Saul. These works embellish biblical stories but the question remains whether they take the stories of the Bible as their starting point, or whether they are renditions of biblical stories. In other words, one should not readily assume the canonical status of the Bible at this stage, and therefore while they exhibit embellishments and amplifications of biblical stories, it is debatable whether or not they should be considered forms of biblical interpretation.

One of its earliest interpreters was Philo of Alexandria (20 BCE–50 CE), who commonly attributes Greek philosophical views to biblical characters. He was a Jewish Hellenistic philosopher and interpreter of scriptures whose approach to the Bible made less of an impact on Palestinian rabbinic interpretation than it did on patristic exegesis. His interest in the etymologies of Hebrew names, a form of allegorical interpretation, was for example adopted and popularized by early church exegetes.[2] Philo was more concerned with philosophical matters and understanding biblical personages in light of Hellenistic philosophical values. His approach to reading scriptures was shaped by a commitment to Judaism and Stoic philosophy.

Another early interpreter of the Bible is the ancient Jewish historian Josephus (37–*c.*100 CE). His account of the history of the Jewish people from the biblical period must be considered part of the long trajectory of Jewish scriptural interpretation. Josephus promises to cover the entire biblical history systematically, and by and large

[2] For an overview of Philo's life and work, see Kamesar 2009a, especially the two articles in the volume: Kamesar 2009b and Runia 2009.

delivers on that promise. His retelling of biblical events and character embellishments contributed to the reception of the Bible in antiquity. His depiction of the Jewish forefathers resonates with Greek thought and culture. For example, Josephus' Abraham is a Greek philosopher who combats Chaldean views that maintain the power of heavenly bodies. Abraham's discovery of God comes about through celestial contemplation, recognition of the irregularity of the stars, which effect changes in the land and sea: 'For he said that if they had the power they would have provided their own orderliness; but since they lack this, it is evident that as many things as they contribute to our increased usefulness they perform not by their own authority but in accordance with the power of their commander, on whom alone it is proper to confer honor and gratitude' (*AJ* 1.156; trans. Feldman 2000: 57).[3] This portrayal of Abraham as one who refutes the divine power of heavenly orbs is also found in Philo, who commonly attributes Greek philosophical views to biblical characters.

Previous scholarship drew a connection between the pesharim of Qumran and rabbinic midrash. The pesher ('interpretation') of prophetic works of the Bible found at Qumran exhibit similar traits with those of rabbinic midrash, namely the atomistic approach to scriptural verses, the employment of double entendre, anagram, and paronomasia. It, however, is a distinct form of interpretation and should not be conflated with rabbinic forms of interpretation. Although there are no traces of the pesher proper in the New Testament, it also shares affinities with New Testament uses of prophetic literature. The Qumran pesher, however, is future oriented and prophetic literature functions in the New Testament as a key to unlocking the meaning of past events.[4]

In common parlance, midrash (Hebrew root *drš*, 'to investigate, seek, search out, examine') refers generally to interpretation of any text, sacred or secular, ancient or contemporary. In its strictest sense, however, it is a process of scriptural exegesis that characterizes classical rabbinic interpretation. It also refers to the vast and varied rabbinic compilations of the late antique and medieval periods that preserve oral traditions prior to their redaction (*c.* fifth to the thirteenth centuries). Midrash, both the process and the very fruit of that process, grew out of an attempt to understand laconic or obscure biblical verses in order to make meaning out of scripture. Midrash is the means by which the rabbis made biblical ordinances relevant, taught moral lessons, told stories, and maintained the Jewish meta-narrative that shaped and continues to sustain the Jewish people. The Bible was a means to look both backward and forward. They probed it for responses to the burning theological issues of the day, for answers to a changing reality.

Not all rabbinic interpretation, however, should be understood as a response to contemporary religious or social concerns. Gaps in the biblical text, superfluous

[3] With respect to Josephus' argument, namely that if the celestial spheres had their own independent power, then they would have arranged for their own uniformity, Feldman observes: 'it is the celestial phenomena that are the originating cause of all that happens and that they alone determine the future'.

[4] For a general introduction to the Dead Sea Scrolls, see VanderKam 2010.

wording, and seeming contradictions occupied the rabbis' attention. Midrash's verso-centric, intertextual orientation is its fundamental feature, but not all midrashim can be understood in these hermeneutic terms. Social, theological, and political issues precipitated by historical events such as the rise of both Christianity and Islam played a role in the development of rabbinic interpretation.

Compilations of Midrash

There are generally two kinds of rabbinic compilations of this period: aggadic exegetical and homiletic compilations. The former are ordered according to biblical verses, and the latter are a series of sermons based on a specific verse under discussion. The premier examples of aggadic exegetical compilations are *Genesis Rabbah and Lamentations Rabbah*, two of the Midrash Rabbah collections of the books of Torah and the five *megillot* (scrolls)—Lamentations, Esther, Ruth, Song of Songs, and Ecclesiastes.[5]

In addition to *Leviticus Rabbah*, *Deuteronomy Rabbah*, and *Numbers Rabbah*, other compilations such as *Peskita de Rab Kahana* on selected passages or sections read on special Sabbaths or festal days are arranged homiletically. In these works, chapters comprise homilies that cohere around a particular topic. The collections of homilies moreover share a structural arrangement: a series of proems (*petiḥtot*), the body (*gufa*) of the homily, and an eschatological ending or peroration. The *petiḥta* (proem), a verse usually from the Writings, especially from Psalms or the Wisdom Literature, although also sometimes from the prophets, is also an earmark of the aggadic compilations, whether exegetical or homiletical. Through a chain of interpretations, the seemingly extraneous verse is connected to the verse under discussion. This structure exemplifies a fundamental aspect of midrash, namely the desire to unite the diverse parts of the tripartite canon—Torah, Prophets, and Writings—into a harmonious, seamless whole that reflects the oneness of God's Word.

Halakhic midrashim, the earliest midrashic collections, deal primarily with issues of halakha, rabbinic law. They are also exegetical by nature and thus often provide word-by-word explications on verses in Exodus, Leviticus, Numbers, and Deuteronomy. Later compilations, which are more difficult to date, include *Midrash Psalms (Tehilim)*, *Exodus Rabbah*, *Tanna de-be Eliyahu*, also known as *Seder Eliyahu*, and the Tanhuma-Yelamdenu literature, which consists of a group of homiletic midrashim on the Torah.

The broad designation of compilations as either halakhic or aggadic belies the fact that halakhic midrashim contain aggadic material and vice versa. Whether halakhic or aggadic, late antique or early medieval, the midrashic locus of exegesis is a biblical word or phrase. Punsters par excellence, the rabbis were keen on making philological

[5] For an introduction to rabbinic texts, see Strack and Stemberger 1992 and Millar et al. 2013.

associations. They culled *TaNaKh* for verbal affinities; they spun stories and drew connections in order to elucidate a given verse. Every letter of a word, every phrase, was open to interpretation, for the Word of God is expressed in a specific way in order to teach or explain something. Nothing in scripture is superfluous and every word has meaning, in fact many meanings, some more apparent than others. One will often find contradictory statements from various rabbis made about the meaning of a word, and one interpretation is not more acceptable than another. The multiplicity of meaning does not challenge scriptural authority, but rather attests to its infinitude.

Midrashic Methods

Rabbinic exegetical methods employed in halakhic and aggadic midrashim vary. The *qal vaḥomer* (literally 'light and heavy') establishes an argument based on the inference that if something applies in a minor case, it will also apply in the major. This form of reasoning is found in both halakhic and aggadic midrashim, and was common in Graeco-Roman argumentation (*a minore ad maius*). The *gezera shavah*, however, is more common to halakhic midrashim. By means of verbal analogy, a particular detail of a biblical law in one verse is derived from the meaning of the word or phrase in the other. Other rules that characterize halakhic midrashim include the *binyan av* (a specific law in one verse may be applied to all other similar cases), *klal uprat*, *prat uklal* (rules of inference between general and specific statements and vice versa), and *hekkesh* (inference by analogy, whether explicit or implicit between two subjects—not words—within the same or similar context).

These aforementioned rules are employed in halakhic exegesis, but biblical non-legal passages are often explained by paronomasia (wordplay). Philology provides a linchpin for rabbis to draw analogies between verses. It also can take the form of *gematria*, whereby the arithmetical value of Hebrew letters is used to interpret a word or verse, and *notarikon*, shorthand writing whereby individual letters are used to signify words. In other words, Hebrew words are understood as acronyms so that each letter stands for another word, which in turn forms a phrase or sentence.

An important feature of rabbinic compilations is the inclusion of competing opinions on how to interpret a verse. Consider, for instance, this midrash from Genesis Rabbah:

> 'So it came about that the Lord scattered them (*vayafeẓ*) from there over the face of the entire world and they stopped building the city.' (Gen. 11: 8) R. Yudan said: The people of Tyre went to Sidon and the Sidonites to Tyre, while *Miẓraim* [Egypt] retains his land. R. Nehemiah said: Everyone held onto their own land for their original settlement was there, and to that they returned. So what is meant by '. . . the Lord scattered them . . .'? All the peoples entered the mountain peaks and absorbed their own inhabitants. The Rabbis said: *vayafeẓ* is to be read *vayaẓef* (swept away): the sea came up and swept away thirty families. R. Pinchas said in

> R. Levi's name: No misfortune comes to a man which does not profit somebody. Whence were those thirty families replaced? From Abraham, sixteen from the sons of Keturah and twelve from Ishmael, and as for the remaining two—And the Lord said unto her, 'Two nations are in your womb' (Gen. 25: 23). (*Gen. Rab.* 38: 10)

The midrash concerns God's response to humanity's building of a tower after the great flood (Gen. 11: 8): 'The Lord came down to look at the city and tower [called Babel in verse 9] that man had built, and the Lord said, "If, as one people with one language for all, this is how they have begun to act, then nothing they propose to do will be out of their reach. Let us, then, go down and confound their speech there, so that they shall not understand one another's speech." Thus the Lord scattered them from there over the face of the whole earth.' What does it mean that God scattered the people from there over the whole earth? Didn't the people already 'branch out over the earth' after the Flood? Rabbi Yudan understands the scattering to mean that people exchanged places, but Rabbi Nehemiah interprets it as meaning that people went back to where they belonged before the Flood. In the third explanation, the rabbis, true to form, transpose letters, turning *vayafeẓ*, 'scattered', into *vayaẓef*, 'swept away', and explain that the verse means that thirty families were swept away and replaced by the progeny of Abraham. Where did the rabbis come up with thirty? From the nations or families of Abraham: twelve from Ishmael, two from Isaac, and sixteen from the children Abraham has with Keturah. The image is that of sweeping away and scattering—sweeping away nations that engage in building a tower to reach the heavens, and scattering Abraham's family throughout the world.

The example illustrates recurring aspects of rabbinic interpretation. First, it asks what is meant by the scattering of people from over the face of the whole earth, in light of Gen. 10: 32: 'the nations branched out over the earth after the Flood'. It tackles the question by offering different explanations, including one based on wordplay, and it exemplifies the intertextuality of rabbinic biblical interpretation.

In addition to wordplay, we find scores of stories, maxims, and parables, *meshalim* (sg. *mashal*). The Hebrew parables about kings are the signal form of narrative in rabbinic exegetical literature. Nearly all rabbinic *meshalim* consist of a bipartite structure—the fictional narrative, which is the *mashal* proper, and its application, the *nimshal*, which usually concludes with a biblical verse serving as the *mashal*'s prooftext. Formulaic phrases mark the two parts: *mashal le*, 'it is like' (also, *mashal lema hadavar dome le*, or simply *le*), and *kakh*, 'so, too, similarly' (Stern 1991).

Thesaurus-like anthologies characterize the post-classical, mid-late medieval period of rabbinic literature. Noteworthy are the *Yalkut Shim'oni* (known simply as the *Yalkut*), *Yalkut ha-Makhiri*, and the *Midrash Ha-Gadol*. The *Yalkut*, compiled from more than fifty works and covering the entire span of the Jewish Bible (TaNaKh), is one of the most well-known and comprehensive anthologies. There are several other collections of midrashic works of this period, collections that blend collation and commentary. A noteworthy work of the eighth/early ninth century that falls into the category of neither midrash nor anthology is *Pirke de Rabbi Eliezer* (*PRE*).[6] It transmits both classical rabbinic and non-rabbinic material and utilizes earlier motifs and narratives from the Second Temple period.[7] The status of *PRE* in the rabbinic corpus is problematic. Its narrative structure as biblical expansion is similar to that of the book of *Jubilees* (second century BCE), and its style is significantly different from that of earlier midrashim. Even though several sources were used, its structure indicates that it is ostensibly the work of one author, probably a Palestinian. It seems to represent a transition between the mythical perspective of rabbinic literature and that of Kabbalah.[8] Given its dating and the inclusion of material that betrays familiarity with Islam, the composition sits at literary as well as cultural crossroads.

This later period saw a rise in commentaries on the Bible, but the interest in midrash continued nevertheless. Midrashim of the ancient and early medieval periods were often mentioned or alluded to in Bible commentaries. Even today they find their way into contemporary sermons, for they are part of the very bedrock of the Jewish tradition that exhorts readers of the Bible to 'turn it over again and again, for everything is in it' (*Pirke Avot* 5: 22).

The later rabbinic compilations include stories found in Islamic sources. While previous scholarship generally assumed that the Islamic texts adapted Jewish material, recent scholars have compellingly argued for a more fluid circulation of stories and motifs that may indeed have originated in Islamic circles.[9]

Christian Biblical Interpretation

Many literary genres shaped early Christian biblical interpretation. Through the use of homilies, letter writing, and commentary, the church fathers engaged the meaning of individual verses as well as entire passages and entire books of the Bible. The role scriptural interpretation played in the formation of doctrine and indeed in all areas of the life of the church contributed to Christianity's vitality and development over the centuries. It both influenced and was influenced by doctrinal discussions. How the early Christian exegetes understood biblical passages throws light on the manner in which Christian communities conceived of themselves.

[6] For a general introduction to *PRE*, see Zunz 1954: 134–40, 417–24; Friedlander 1981: xiii–lvii; Strack and Stemberger 1992: 332–3. On the use of narrative in PRE, see Meir 1980; Elbaum 1986b: 57–62; Elbaum 1991–2: 99–126; Elbaum 1986a: 97–117. On the folkloristic aspects of *Pirke de Rabbi Eliezer*, see Stein 2005; Adelman 2009; Sacks 2009; Treitl 2010.

[7] Adelman 2009 contends that *PRE* preserves mythic narratives of the Pseudepigrapha of the Second Temple period.

[8] Rubenstein 1996: 158. Cf. Dan 1974, esp. 21, 135–6; Urowitz-Freudenstein 1994. And see especially Shinan 1979: 162–5, Elbaum 1996: 245–66.

[9] For discussions and illustrations of this phenomenon, see Firestone (1990), Lassner (1993), Lowin (2006), and Bernstein (2006).

Like their Jewish counterparts, Christian interpreters made sacred texts relevant to Christian audiences. Lessons from the lives of biblical characters became accessible and practical. This is especially true given that most Christians could not read the Bible. Thus, what they understood to be God's word was mediated by the church fathers. In retelling the biblical story for edifying purposes, early church writers in a sense 'rewrote' the narrative. They also engaged in internecine debates on theological matters and drew on scripture to bolster their beliefs.

The fathers of the church unequivocally accepted the inspired nature of Christian scriptures. They differed with respect to determining the meaning of the divine word, when to take it figuratively, and when to read it literally. The term literal refers to the sense of scripture intended by the writer. That is to say, the literal sense may be metaphorical. Christian exegetes acknowledged that the explicit literal meaning may also include an implicit sense. Early Christian scriptural interpretation took into account the need to consider a variety of approaches to scripture; otherwise how was one to understand Exod. 21: 24, 'eye for eye, tooth for tooth', when, for example, a toothless baby is murdered? Or, how does one read anthropomorphic statements about God in Genesis (e.g. Gen. 3: 8)? As Chrysostom (347–407) would explain (*Hom. in Ps.* 9.4), 'We interpret some passages by the letter, others with a meaning different from the literal and figurative' (Kannengiesser 2006: 171). In his analysis of early Christian exegesis, the scholar Charles Kannengiesser notes that even the most literal-minded exegetes who rigorously 'applied the rules and principles of a philological analysis to the sacred text' instinctively approached 'the literality of the biblical text as gifted in itself with supernatural power. "The meaning deserves to be explored because divine scripture says nothing that would be useless or out of consideration ..." (Ambrosiaster, *Quaestiones* 10,1)' (Kannengiesser 2006: 175). The meaning of the literal sense was not always apparent, and often proved problematic. Cultural chasms resulted in unfamiliar phrases and foreign geography. The 'ordinary' sense of a word or phrase was not always readily available, so Christian writers consulted lists, among them those of Philo, whose interpretation of proper names often opened up the meaning of obscure terms. The interest in etymology harks back to Homer and Hesiod and generally speaking played a role in the development of allegorism. In Christian circles, Origen (*c.*185–*c.*253 CE) believed in the significance of the original meaning of Hebrew names, but unlike Jerome he did not compose an *Onomastikon* ('Book of Names').

Interpreters were primarily concerned with maintaining the continuity between the Old and New Testament. The notion that Christians are the spiritual inheritors of the Old Testament with respect to its sacred teachings and divine revelation is paramount to understanding early church interpretation. Through allegory and typology, Christian exegetes fostered the unity of the testaments. 'The New is in the Old concealed, the Old is in the New revealed', ran a popular medieval Latin saying (quoted by Pelikan 2005: 95). The notion that the Old and New Testaments are intrinsically connected, not as two separate parts of a whole, but as one in which each testament is part and parcel of the other, is fundamental to understanding Christian approaches to scripture.

One sign of that intrinsic connection is the Christological reading of prophetic literature. Beginning with Paul, the events of the OT prefigured Jesus and the church. They, in turn, unfasten the deeper meaning of events recorded in the OT. Examples of prefiguration include Adam as a topos of Jesus in Paul's writing. The fulfilment statements in Matthew exemplify how the New Testament reads the prophetic writings of the Old Testament. Other examples include Matthew 21: 42–3 and Acts 8: 26ff., in which Isaiah 53: 7–8 is explicitly read as a reference to Jesus:

> Now the passage of the scripture that he [Ethiopian eunuch] was reading was this: 'Like a sheep he was led to the slaughter, and like a lamb silent before its shearer, so he does not open his mouth. In his humiliation justice was denied him. Who can describe his generation? For his life is taken away from the earth' [Isa. 53: 7–8]. The eunuch asked Philip, 'About whom, may I ask you, does the prophet say this, about himself or about someone else?' Then Philip began to speak, and starting with this scripture, he proclaimed to him the good news about Jesus. (Acts 8: 32–5)

The second century CE controversy with Marcion and the ongoing debates with Gnostic thinkers contributed to this very linkage between the Old and New Testaments as many writers went to great lengths to respond to theological challenges that compromised the relationship between both Testaments. Gnostic dualism and disregard for the material world led some to reject the Old Testament entirely, for it was deemed a product of a foolish Demiurge in contrast to the supreme, good God of the New Testament.[10] Marcion also dismissed the Old Testament *in toto*. The testaments, even his New Testament, which differed from what eventually became canonized, to his mind, were irreconcilable. Marcion believed that the God of the Old Testament was vengeful yet righteous, but for many Gnostics the creator God of the Old Testament was inherently evil, proof of which could be found in the world he created. Early church exegetes employed a variety of strategies in order to secure the relationship between the Old and New Testaments, throwing light on the meaning of individual words, phrases and verses, and entire stories. A brief review of terms commonly used in discussions of patristic methods of interpretation—such as 'literal sense' and 'plain sense', allegory, typology, and *theoria*—may be helpful (see Kannengiesser 2006 and Simonetti 1994).

The relationship between the literal and spiritual 'sense' of scripture was often referred to in terms of 'lower' or 'closer' and 'higher' and 'deeper'. The relationship between the literal and spiritual 'senses' of scripture informs the use of allegory in Christian exegesis. Allegory is a Hellenistic term derived from the Greek, 'to say something else in public speech'. It is a form of interpretation, as I. Christiansen explains, 'thanks to which a core idea ("Ideeneinheit") implicitly included in the letter is explicated, a notion equivalent to the written expression but of a broader significance being joined to it' (as translated in Kannengiesser 2006: 250). In Greek antiquity, commentators produced allegorical interpretations of Homer and Hesiod. The Latin

[10] Not all Gnostics took this approach. Others, such as the Valentinian, Ptolemy, displayed a more nuanced position. See Simonetti 1994: 16 for a brief discussion of Ptolemy's *Letter to Flora*.

tradition, too, utilized allegory for exegetical purposes; there is no shortage of it in Philo.[11] In every instance, allegory is a means by which pagan, Christian, as well as, to some degree, Jewish interpreters situated themselves vis-à-vis society and culture.[12]

Typology is a form of allegorical interpretation. According to the writings of the church fathers, a biblical place, person, event, or institution can function as a type, or *typos*, insofar as the place, person, event, or institution signifies someone or something that will be fulfilled or manifested in the future through God. What sets typology apart from allegory is connection to historical reality: typology attaches itself to history, whereas allegory need not have any connection to an original event in order to derive meaning. Isaac, Joseph, Joshua, and David are regarded as *typoi* of Jesus. Typological readings are widespread among the church fathers.

Events such as the crossing of the sea are read typologically. Thus, in *Ps. Barnabas* (12: 2–3), the prayer of Moses as he extends his hands during the battle between the Israelites and the Amalekites is understood as a *typos* of the cross and crucifixion. In Dialogue with Trypho, the law as discussed in the OT is a *typos* of Christ and the church. Gregory of Nyssa explains the Red Sea as a *typos* of baptism. Theodore of Mopsuestia provides numerous examples of how the events in the Old Testament are understood as *typoi* of events in the New Testament. Thus the liberation of the Israelites from Egypt is read as a prefiguration of the death of Jesus and freedom from sin.

Not all early Christian interpretation is by nature non-literal. Clement, for example, draws on Old Testament characters to exhort believers to behave morally. He employs exempla throughout his writings. Cain, Esau, and Aaron illustrate the effects of jealousy, and Abraham, Job, and David display the virtue of humility. And, while early Christian exegetes interpreted the couple in the Song of Songs as Christ and the church, Theodore read it as a love song, and hence did not accept its canonicity.

When discussing early Christian interpretation, scholars of patristics[13] often refer to two general schools of interpretation, the Alexandrian and the Antiochene, even though the later was not a formal school (*didaskaleion*). Although scholarship in the field has adhered to this rigid dichotomy, customary distinctions such as 'Alexandria vs. Antioch' have recently been modified in order to underscore the importance of figural representation to all forms of early Christianity (Young 1989; Nassif 1996; Trakatellis 1996; Kannengiesser 2002). Not only are there instances when an Antiochene scholar allegorizes a verse that an Alexandrian takes literally, but these categories homogenize the exegetical process such that differences among interpreters

[11] As Kannengiesser (2006: 249) mentions, traces of allegorism in Hellenistic Judaism are found in Aristobulos (mid-second century BCE). Fragments of his *Commentary on Pentateuch* are found in Eusebius of Caesarea's *Praeparatio evangelica* 8.10, 12.2.

[12] For a discussion of the use of allegory in ancient Alexandria, see Dawson 1992. For an excellent discussion of allegory in midrash, see Kister 2013.

[13] For an excellent overview of patristic studies, see Clark 2008.

within a school are obfuscated.[14] Antiochene exegetes, for example, may in fact use the same method but come to different interpretations.

One of the leading figures of the Alexandrian school is Clement of Alexandria (*c.*150–*c.*215 CE), for whom the gospel is the fulfilment and realization of the law. Scripture is written with intention, but that intention is not necessarily immediately perceptible. Scripture operates on two levels according to Clement. One level is intended for immediate consumption, but the other level requires deeper enquiry and exegetical ability. The Word of God was revealed mysteriously, and every word, jot, or tittle was written with intention even if it is not readily known (*Strom.* 1.9.45, 4.25.160). It is therefore of no surprise that allegory was favoured, for if scripture is expressed on the first level, it would still require assistance.

Philo's influence is palpable in Clement's work. Like Philo, Clement (*Strom.* 1.3.30–1) illustrates how Abraham represents faith, Sarah wisdom, and Hagar pagan culture. But even while Clement continues his traditions, there is a major difference—Clement's traditions are Christocentrically oriented.

The characteristics that mark the work of Origen (*c.*185–*c.*253 CE), among them allegory, etymology, and the symbolism of numbers, may be found in the work of his predecessors, such as Clement, but it was under Origen (*c.*185–*c.*253 CE) that the school of Alexandria reached its apex. Known for his encyclopedic learning and productivity, and for his staggering facility with the biblical text, Origen stands out as one of the greatest scholars of the early church. His interpretation took the form of commentaries on entire books, homilies preached in Caesarea, and scholia—that is, collections of explanations for select passages in Exodus, Leviticus, Isaiah, and Psalms 1–15. Other exegetes tended to concentrate on a few books of the Old Testament; the more expansive Origen included Ecclesiastes and Job. In fact, he wrote on all the books of the Old and New Testaments. As one scholar observes, 'Origen made biblical hermeneutics into a real science, and, in that sense, he conditioned decisively all subsequent patristic exegesis' (Simonetti 1994: 39). What he received from his predecessors he widened and deepened, and at the same time he produced what is perhaps the first attempt at a critical edition of the Old Testament, his sixfold Bible, commonly known as the *Hexapla*. Although he knew no Hebrew and thus relied on rabbis for the significance of Hebrew names, he set himself the task of producing the most reliable biblical text by placing six translations side by side.

Origen's approach to scripture was philological and marked by the recognition of the inexhaustibility of the word of God. His *De principiis* outlines a theory of exegesis that informed his interpretative work and espouses notions generally accepted by Christian exegetes—that scriptures convey knowledge about God and Jesus, the world, and evil, and demonstrate divine salvific actions. In *De principiis* 4.3.5, Origen notes that while all of scripture has a spiritual significance, that is not the case with respect to the literal, since one can identify several instances where the literal sense is impossible.

14 See the discussion of Frances M. Young (1983) of how Origen and Eusthatius of Antioch treat Saul's meeting with the witch of Endor in 1 Samuel 28, as well as Hay 1964.

For Origen, every word of the Bible had a possible spiritual message; Theodore (see below), in contrast, renounced his allegorical readings and emphasized the historical dimension of scripture which in his view undermined allegory. But even Theodore, who took an extreme position, understood the non-literal dimensions of scripture, and those who took their cue from Philo and Origen did not diminish the intrinsic value accorded the letter. Literal and allegorical readings are intertwined.

The Alexandrian exegete Didymus the Blind (*c.*313–398) was heavily influenced by Origen and admired by Jerome. Like his Alexandrian predecessors, Didymus read scripture in order to unveil the supernatural mysteries therein. Thus, etymologies of Jewish names are pregnant with meaning, as are animals and numbers. While he read beyond the literal, unlike Origen he was far less concerned with textual criticism.

We see Origen's influence in Didymus' *Commentary on Genesis*, putatively the oldest commentary by a Greek Christian author on the first book of the Bible. Didymus makes the same distinction between the lighter, spiritual bodies of the prelapsarian period and the weighty body after the Fall. Furthermore, he draws on Philo's interpretation of Sarah and Hagar. Whereas Sarah is emblematic of perfect virtue, Hagar symbolizes a preliminary stage leading up to virtue. After Didymus who lived to the end of the fourth century, the Alexandrian school's importance diminished.

Unlike Alexandria, where an actual school was established under the aegis of a local bishop, in Antioch we find a group of exegetes and theologians who came together for a common purpose, although some such as the founder of the school, Diodorus (late fourth century), took on private teaching roles (Simonetti 1994: 67). The Antiochene school, which flourished in the fourth and fifth centuries, is often described as anti-allegorical, but such a portrayal is inaccurate.

Theodore of Mopsuestia (*c.*350–428), one of the leading figures of the school of Antioch, would in 553 be renounced as a heretic at the Second Council of Constantinople for his Christological views, but at the time of his death he was regarded as one of the outstanding biblical exegetes and theologians of his time. Known today as the Father of Nestorianism, Theodore was a towering critic of Origen's allegorical interpretation. He maintained a literatist orientation as well as one directed toward eschatological readings of scripture.

Gregory of Nyssa (*c.*335–*c.*395) came from an illustrious family in Cappadocia. Along with his brother Basil, who was Bishop of Caesarea, and Gregory of Nazianzus, he is recognized as one of the three great Cappadocians whose sundry writings left an enduring impact on the teachings of the church. His exegetical work reveals a deep admiration for Origen to the extent that his hermeneutical principles by and large played a role in Gregory's writing. Gregory uses the term *historia* as designating the literal wording or actual event and *theoria*, like the Alexandrians, to mean *allegoria* or *dianoi* (the 'deeper meaning'). Cyril of Alexandria, for example, used the word for the allegorical sense. For Antiochian exegetes, *theoria* was prophetic vision. One of Gregory's major works, *The Life of Moses*, is divided into two parts—the first summarizes Moses' life (*historia*), and in the second he draws moral and spiritual lessons from it (*theoria*).

John Chrysostom (347–407), 'the golden-mouthed', was a close friend and classmate of Theodore's and a fellow monk. Renowned for his oratory excellence that earned him his name, Chrysostom was an interpreter of scriptures whose literary legacy was unsurpassed among the Greek church fathers. In addition to the exegetical homilies that make up the largest part of his writings, he wrote sermons, treatises, and letters. He adhered to the Antiochene exegetical precepts, yet, as he explains, 'We interpret some passages by the letter, others with a meaning different from the literal, others again as literal and figurative' (*Hom. in Ps.* 9.4, quoted in Kannengiesser 2006: 171).

Ephrem (*c.*306–373) is considered one of the best-known writers of the golden age of Syriac literature, which spanned the fourth and eighth centuries. He is best remembered for his teaching and scriptural interpretation. His extensive oeuvre may be divided between prose, including expository as well as rhetorical works, and poetry. He was most famous for his poems: dialogue poems and metrical homilies (*mêmrê*) and 'teaching songs' (*madrashê*), often referred to as hymns (Palmer 1993).[15] According to Jerome, these compositions were recited publicly after the reading of scriptures (Griffith 2006: 1407). As many have noted, their closest analogues might be 'the Hebrew *Piyyutim*, synagogue songs which enjoyed great popularity in Palestine from the eighth century on, and which feature biblical themes and literary devices very similar to those regularly used by Ephraem' (Griffith 2006: 1400). The purpose of *madrashâ* (singular), however, is akin to its Hebrew cognate, *midrash*, to instruct.

The Syriac and Greek traditions refer to him as having commented on all the books of the Bible, however, his *Commentary on Genesis* is the only extant work in Syriac. Many of his commentaries are preserved in Armenian and some are preserved in Syriac fragments. Rather than giving a verse-by-verse exposition, Ephrem focused on passages that he considered significant, such as the first three chapters of Genesis on creation and the Adam and Eve narrative.

Ephrem's exegetical works point to a familiarity with Jewish interpretation and reflect the influence of his Mesopotamian milieu. They are also shot through with Christian faith. But one can say that of all his work:

> The scriptures are set up
> like a mirror;
> one whose eye is clear
> sees there
> the image of the truth.
> Set up there
> is the image of the Father;
> depicted there
> is the image of the Son,
> and of the Holy Spirit. (Griffith 2006: 1416)

[15] For a general introduction, see Matthews and Amar (1994: 3–56) and Griffith (2006).

Whether in his refutations against those who hold opposing theological views, in his commentaries, or in his *mêmrê* and *madrashê*, his concern was to draw the reader or listener closer to truth which for him is the life, death, and resurrection of Christ:

> See, the Law carries
> all the likenesses of him.
> See, the Prophets, like deacons,
> carry
> the icons of the Messiah.
> Nature and the scriptures
> together carry
> The symbols of his humanity
> and of his divinity. (Griffith 2006: 1417)

Indeed, as highly regarded as his prose was, it was his poetical works that brought him wide acclaim, for it was through them that he conveyed his theological teachings, displayed his mastery of Semitic poetic devices, and exhibited his artistic genius.

Most scholars of patristic literature prominently place Cyril of Alexandria (*c.*375–444 CE) among writers who helped shape Christian thought. There is no question that he was a key figure in theological controversies of the fifth century but he was also a prolific biblical commentator. As Robert Wilken suggests, Cyril's exegetical work is best understood by turning to Cyril's own words: 'In Christ we bloom again to newness for life.' 'For Cyril', writes Wilken, 'the renewal of all things in Christ is the central skopos of the Bible.' He continues: 'Christ is Cyril's true subject matter. Yet without the Bible there is no talk of Christ. Cyril knew no way to speak of Christ than in the words of the Bible, and no way to interpret the words of the Bible than through Christ' (Wilken 2006: 864–5). This is amply illustrated in his *Glaphyra*, an exegetical treatise on the Pentateuch. Cyril's commentary on select passages such as the story of Cain and Abel, the flood narrative, Abraham, the institution of Passover, the theophany on Mount Sinai, the cleansing of lepers, and the reconnaissance into the Promised Land is Christologically oriented. Abel and Joshua are figures of Christ.

Cyril is a good example of how an Alexandrian exegete can engage in literal interpretation. He shows restraint in the spiritual interpretation of Old Testament figures. The literal interpretation of biblical verses is more developed than in other writers of the Alexandrian school. Moreover, his literal reading of passages in the Pentateuch is extensive. Thus, for example, while Jonah is a figure of Jesus with respect to the three days which he spent in the belly of the fish, he is not a figure of Jesus when he tried to escape God's command to speak to the Ninevites. Cyril rejects Origen's figurative reading of the story. Cyril's exegesis is characterized by a moderate position vis-à-vis the Alexandrian and Antiochene approaches.

Jerome and Augustine are two of the greatest interpreters of scripture in the West. Each produced systematic commentaries. With Jerome as the primary exception, generally speaking, western authors rarely engaged in philological examinations of scripture. Origen's influence permeated the exegesis of western authors. The prominent tendency was to interpret allegorically, yet they displayed a wide variety of attitudes. Ambrosiaster (later half of the fourth century), the name given to an anonymous exegete who wrote a Latin commentary on Paul's thirteen epistles (Hebrews was not included), for example, is an exception to the tendency to engage in allegory. And yet, scriptural verses are understood spiritually or figuratively (Kannengiesser 2006: 1083).

Jerome (*c.*347–419/420) may be charged with lacking originality or methodological coherence; however, there is no shortage of philological rigour to his commentaries. Even during his lifetime he gained authority in the realm of sacred scripture. Augustine's correspondence with him attests to his widespread reputation. His translation of the Old Testament, the Vulgate, directly from the Hebrew contributed to his renown as one knowledgeable in scriptural matters, and more importantly became the bases 'on which would rest from now on any edifice of the explication of the Scriptures in the Christian West' (Jay 2006: 1114).

Origen's profound influence on him is clear in Jerome's *Hebraic Questions on Genesis*, but his approach, unlike Origen's, is twofold, taking into account the literal and spiritual senses of scripture (Jay 2006: 1104). Moreover, he engaged with rabbinic sources to an unprecedented degree. Jerome's personal trajectory equipped him with the proper exposure to the cultural and philological tools necessary to produce commentaries that enriched Christian exegesis. As Pierre Jay (2006: 1114) writes:

> Positioned by his personal itinerary at the crossroads of a classical Latin training, a biblical culture very largely Greek, and of a serious Hebrew initiation, the *uir trilinguis* that Jerome knew himself to be thus appears at this winding down at the end of the fourth century as an exceptional mediator in the service of scripture: between the heritage of ancient culture and the newness of Christian experience, between Jewish traditions and the Church's tradition, between the Greek East and the Latin West.

Even the briefest overview of Christian interpreters must include Augustine (345–430 CE) whose interpretative work took on many forms—homily, commentary, and *quaestio*. His *De doctrina Christiana* (*On Christian Teaching*) is largely a treatise on biblical interpretation. In it he espouses the notion that there is a multiplicity of interpretations one may offer for a scriptural passage. 'Sometimes not just one meaning but two or more meanings are perceived in the same words of scripture,' writes Augustine. He continues: 'Even if the writer's meaning is obscure, there is no danger here, provided that it can be shown from other passages of the holy scriptures that each of these interpretations is consistent with the truth.'[16] Augustine also appreciated the rhetorical devices used in scripture: 'The literary-minded should be aware that our Christian authors used all the figures of speech which teachers of grammar call by their Greek name of tropes, and that they did so more diversely and profusely than can be judged or imagined by those who are unfamiliar with scripture or who gained their knowledge of figures from other literature.'[17]

[16] Augustine, *On Christian Teaching* 3.27.38 (1997: 86–7). [17] Ibid.

In addition to *De doctrina christiana* (*On Christian Teaching*), two other works mark an important phase in Augustine's career as biblical commentator: *De genesi ad litteram* (*The Literal Meaning of Genesis*), a unique attempt to produce a proper commentary of scripture; and *Confessions*. Especially in the *Confessions* we encounter the inextricable links between the human condition and scriptural interpretation and are exposed to the ways in which theology, philosophy, and one's personal spiritual journey commingle with exegetical endeavours. In these works Augustine affirms both the diversity and oneness of scripture, and in theory celebrates the diversity of opinions as long as an interpretation draws us toward love of God and of neighbour.[18]

Early Christian interpreters exhibited two tendencies. On the one hand, their wish to read the Old Testament Christocentrically, against Jews and Gnostics, pushed them toward allegory; on the other, the dangers of the Gnostics' exaggerated allegorism fostered a more literal interpretation of scriptural sources. Despite the prominence of symbolic interpretation among Christian exegetes, then, the early church writers cannot be characterized as mere allegorists. Loosely speaking, the Alexandrian and Antiochene schools represented these two trends—the Alexandrians on the allegorical side, the Antiochenes on the literal side—but recent scholarship has benefited from moving beyond the oversimplification of earlier decades.

Quranic Exegesis

'Tafsīr' is derived from the root *fassara*, to explain, to expound, and refers both to the act of interpreting, exegesis, and explanation and to actual corpora of interpretation.[19] The chronological span of tafsīr literature is expansive; its scope is vast and its physical size voluminous. It exhibits the cumulative and innovative nature of the exegetical enterprise par excellence. Extant commentaries on the Quran represent a sustained engagement that continues to the present.

Traditional tafsīr commentaries hew to a fairly standard format. As their starting point they take the quranic chapters from first to last, and they include a range of interpretations attributed to earlier authorities. While the individual commentator (*muffasir*) preserves exegetical traditions, at the same time, through his selection process, he transforms the tradition. As McAuliffe (2003: 312) observes, 'The authorities that he cites define and demarcate the exegetical lineage within which he writes. Further, it is in the very process of selection, organization, presentation, and assessment of this material from one's exegetical predecessors that the individuality and originality of the particular commentator demonstrates itself.'

[18] *On Christian Teaching* 1.35.39; *Confessions* 12.30.41–31.42.

[19] Another related term is *ta'wīl*, exegesis, interpretation, from the verb *ta'awwala*, which originally meant, 'to apply a verse to a given situation'. See Gilliot 2001–6.

The *isnād* (chain of transmission, plural *asānīd*) goes all the way back to the Companions and successors of the prophet. These reports provide the basis of the extensive tafsīr compilations.[20] Traditional commentaries include an isnād and the very interpretation, the *matn*. Given the breadth of the tafsīr corpus, generalizations are untenable. We can safely assert, however, that Muslim exegetes repeatedly addressed questions and concerns having to do with when and why a verse was revealed (*asbāb al-nuzūl*), the meaning of an uncommon word or phrase, syntactic matters, and morphological irregularities. Quranic exegesis of the classical period—roughly from al-Ṭabarī (d. 923 CE)[21] to the twelfth century—is intertextual to the extent that parallel words and phrases occurring in other verses are brought to bear on the meaning of the verse at hand. Furthermore, *ḥadīth* traditions are also included in the commentaries.

Often, tafsīr literature is divided into two broad categories: *al-tafsīr bi'l-ma'thūr* (also known as *tafsīr bi'l-riwāya*) and *tafsīr bi'l-ra'y*. The first refers to inherited tradition and is more conservative and constrained, whereas the second is based on personal opinion. About *al-tafsīr bi'l-ra'y*, it is reported that Muhammad categorically stated: 'Whoever talks about the Quran on the basis of his personal opinion (*ra'y*) or from a position of ignorance will surely occupy his seat in the Fire!'[22] As other *ḥadīths* indicate, during the classical period exegesis itself was less of a concern than the issue of whether or not someone unqualified would venture into such matters (McAuliffe 1991: 20–1). The prevalence of *tafsīr bi'l-ma'thūr* may be attributed to Ibn Taymiyya (1263–1328) whose exegetical paradigm categorically rejected as valid sources other than those inherited (Saleh 2010; Saleh 2011). While scholars today continue to use these categories to categorize tafsīr, one must question their analytical utility. The very act of selecting and organizing 'received tradition' reveals that which is unique to the muffasir.[23]

Saleh offers an alternative tripartite categorization: the encyclopedic, or as Goldfeld (1988: 6) labelled them, 'collective commentaries', which include the major, massive works of tafsīr that, while disseminating a sea of sources, in turn become foundational sources for later interpreters. Included among this type of tafsīr are the works of al-Ṭabarī, al-Thaʿlabī, al-Wāḥidī, and al-Rāzī, to name a few. The second type of tafsīr is the '*madrasa*-style work'. Appreciably shorter and oriented toward topics, these commentaries served a pedagogic or ideological purpose. 'They summarized the issues

[20] For some literature on the debate as to the reliability of the chains of transmission, see Juynboll 1983; Motzki 1991; Sezgin 1992; Leemhuis 1988; Cook 1981: 107–16; Berg 2003: Berg 2000; McAuliffe 1991: 23–6. See Gilliot 1990a, who examines the mythic dimensions of the Companion Ibn 'Abbās, considered by some the father of *tafsīr bi'l-ma'thūr*.

[21] For a superb biography of al-Ṭabarī, see Robinson 2005. See also Rosenthal 1989: 5–134; Kennedy 2008; Gilliot 1988; Gilliot 1994; Gilliot 1989.

[22] Ibn Kathīr, *Ṭafsīr al-Qur'ān al-ʿaẓim*, 1.5, quoted from McAuliffe 1991: 20. McAuliffe notes that in the introduction to his commentary, *Jāmiʿ al-bayān* 1.77–9, al-Ṭabari enumerates variants on the prophet's denunciation of *al-tafsīr bi'l-ra'y*.

[23] It is important to note that the use of the terms was ideologically driven, as a Sunnī (of the Salafī type) endeavour to suppress 'heretical' interpretations. For a discussion of the genealogy of the term, see Saleh 2010.

in tafsīr', writes Saleh, 'and usually avoided the larger context of a given hermeneutical problem' (Saleh 2010: 21). Examples include al-Wāḥidī,[24] al-Zamakhsharī, and al-Bayḍāwī. The third type is a supercommentary, or textual gloss (*ḥāshiya*),[25] on several *madrasa*-style commentaries such as al-Zamakhsharī's *al-Kashshāf* and al-Bayḍāwī's *Anwār al-tanzīl*. These *ḥāshiya*-style commentaries were used in the *madrasa* curriculum.[26]

Muqātil Ibn Sulaymān al-Balkhī (d. 150/767) was born in Balkh, in modern day Afghanistan, and lived in Iraq, but his scholarly pursuits sent him on peregrinations as far as Beirut and Mecca (Muqātil b. Sulaymān 1979–89; Gilliot 1990b). The scholarly consensus maintains that his tafsīr is most likely the earliest extant quranic commentary. Muqātil ibn Sulaymān was one of the earliest mufassirūn to show less of an interest in grammar and more on narrative expansion. Although he was roundly considered a great quranic commentator, later generations denigrated his contribution. This sea change, according to Claude Gilliot, 'betrays a discernible historical trend of backward projection, whereby ancient scholars come to be judged according to standards which only find widespread acceptance long after the scholar in question has died' (Gilliot 2001–6).

Because Muqātil drew heavily on isrā'īliyyāt literature, he was accused of having borrowed his narratives from the Jews. He was also reproached for anthropomorphisms, and was heavily criticized for not providing chains of transmission for his exegesis. Viewing him as unreliable and a liar, later Sunni traditionalists (*aṣḥāb al ḥadīth*) did not mention his corpus of interpretation. It is important to note that Muqātil engaged with the Quran at a time when *asānīd* were not considered the fixed pathways of transmission. Moreover, his work was composed before the mu'tazilite attack on anthropomorphism developed. In any event, there is no question that his work left an indelible mark on these later exegetes.

The incorporation of *ḥadīths*, around 38,000, and 13,000 different isnāds in al-Ṭabarī's al-Tafsīr alone, is staggering (Robinson 2005: 337). In attempting to be as comprehensive as possible, al-Ṭabarī includes interpretations that he himself did not favour. Sometimes his preferences are made explicit; at other times they are subtly revealed by the way in which the *ḥadīths* are arranged. In either case, he constantly

24 al-Wāḥidī is listed under the first category for one of his works, *al-Basīṭ*, and here for his other work, *al-Wasīṭ*.

25 The ḥāshiya has three meanings: the margin of pages, in which notes were written, the note itself, and gloss, which is a comparatively later usage developing over time. See Rosenthal 2012. To date, very little is written about the subject, yet it is of central importance in the development of the Islamic scholarly tradition.

26 Rippin 1994: 70 suggests that in addition to locating texts of tafsīr, as either 'in an academic setting devoted to the study of Qur'ān in its many aspects' or as popular, 'where a preacher uses the Qur'ān for the edification of his audience', we consider a third situation that is 'less scholarly but yet semi-learned, one that would work on a fairly local level to produce people sufficiently familiar with the Qur'ān so that they might become respected persons within their own groupings'.

displayed independent judgement (*ijtihād*),[27] favouring reasoned, commonsensical interpretations over those marked by flights of fancy.

Unlike Muqātil, whose reception by his contemporaries was less than favourable, al-Ṭabarī was regarded by his peers as a foremost authority. A scholar's scholar and consummate compiler, he laboriously gathered and systematically organized the exegetical, linguistic, and historical opinions of previous generations on the verses of the Quran, which resulted in his al-Tafsīr, the most celebrated example of the *tafsīr bi'l-ma'thūr* (based on reports) approach. His other crowning achievement, which he wrote before his commentary, is his *Ta'rīkh al-rusul wa-al-mulūk* (*The History of the Prophets and Kings*, also known as the Annals, Ta'rīkh al-Ṭabarī), a universal history of the world.[28]

Al-Ṭabarī's general theory of exegesis has been described as resembling a family tree: 'There are several main stems from which descend the various branches' (Khalidi 2008: 4). The three main stems are God, Muhammad, and the scholarly community, and from these stems we derive the fundamental exegetical principles of quranic interpretation, which include the following (Khalidi 2008: 4–5):

1. The moral and legal implications of a verse must be applied generally unless it is restricted in a prophetic *ḥadīth*.[29] While most *āyāt* (verses) of the Quran deal with a particular situation, the moral or legal implication is valid for all similar occasions. This principle is already witnessed in early exegetical writings.
2. Verses have both exoteric (*ẓāhir*) and esoteric (*bāṭin*) meaning. An interpreter cannot jettison the exoteric meaning in favour of the esoteric unless the esoteric meaning or a prophetic *ḥadīth* furnishes reason to do so.[30]
3. Ambiguity in a verse cannot be resolved by bringing another verse, even if that verse is unambiguous. Such analogies are not acceptable.[31] Rather, each verse must be interpreted on its own, and done so exoterically, that is, according to the literal or apparent meaning.
4. The Quran possesses no ambiguities. It is manifestly clear (*bayān*). No word, not even a letter, of the Quran can be rendered meaningless or incorrect.
5. Mastery of the Arabic language is a prerequisite. The meaning of an *āya* (verse) is determined according to proper Arabic usage.

[27] According to Rosenthal 1989: 56, 'His own views leaned toward moderation and compromise.'

[28] For a complete, annotated English translation with useful historical and philological notes, see the thirty-eight-volume *History of al-Tabari*, Yar-Shater (1985–99). Volumes of special interest are Vol. I, *The History of al- Ṭabarī*, trans. Franz Rosenthal (1985); Vol. II, *Prophets and Patriarchs*, trans. William M. Brinner (1987); and Vol. III, *The Children of Israel*, trans. William M. Brinner (1991).

[29] It would be worthwhile to compare the rabbinic rule of *kelal uperat, perat ukelal* (rules of inference between general and specific statements and vice versa) to al-Ṭabarī's principle.

[30] As Khalidi 2008: 6, notes, when it comes to questions of human freedom, and anthropomorphic verse, al-Ṭabarī is willing to 'entertain a less than fully exoteric interpretation'.

[31] Compare *gzera shavah*, the rabbinic hermeneutical rule of analogy: a particular detail of a biblical law in one verse is derived from the meaning of the word or phrase in the other.

6. What precedes or follows a specific pericope is important in determining meaning. Passages must be understood in context (*siyāq*).
7. Whenever there is a case of conflict regarding variant readings or questions of pronunciation, the orthography of the Qurans in common use (*rasm al-maṣāḥif*) serve as arbiters.
8. The authority of experts in specialized fields of learning such as grammar and history is highly regarded when several variant readings are acceptable.
9. With respect to generic nouns (*ism li-kull*), all meanings are equally possible.
10. That which is unspecified should not be rendered specific. Arbitrarily specifying details or presuming knowledge (*takalluf*) in order to fill in gaps in a verse such as providing the answers to 'who', 'when', or 'how much', assumes a false kind of authority.[32]

Aḥmad b. Muḥammad al-Thaʿlabī (d. 427/1035), a native of Nīshāpūr, was a prominent mufassir, considered by some 'the most important Quran exegete of the medieval Islamic world' (Saleh 2009: 323).[33] His major exegetical work, *al-Kashf wa'l-bayān 'an tafsīr al-Qur'ān* (*The Unveiling and Elucidation in Quran Exegesis*), commonly known as *al-Kashf*, is a massive interpretation of the Quran. Characteristics that set al-Thaʿlabī's work apart from other medieval commentaries include the self-conscious manner in which he embarked on the task before him. The introduction evaluates the status of the field, enumerates all utilized sources, discusses earlier exegetes, and explains why the Muʿtazilite tafsīr tradition, for example, was not included. Al-Thaʿlabī drew on personal notes from well over three hundred scholars and, meticulous in amassing material, availed himself of all recensions (Goldfeld 1984). Because it also included most of al-Ṭabarī's material, it became the treasured resource for later exegetes. Al-Thaʿlabī is also known for his *Qiṣaṣ al-Anbiyā'*, a recounting of the prophets preceding the birth of Muhammad.

Fakhr al-dīn al-Rāzī (d. 606/1209) is one of the most important commentators and theologians of the medieval period, perhaps only second to al-Ṭabarī. In addition to his extensive quranic commentary, *Mafātīḥ al-ghayb* (*Keys to the Unseen*), which is also referred to as *Tafsīr al-Kabīr* (*The Great Commentary*), he wrote other major works that display his philosophical and theological proclivities. Written in scholastic fashion, his exegetical commentary exemplifies the method of *tafsīr bi'l-ra'y*. Theological and philosophical issues raised in quranic verses are addressed dialectically. Arguments and opinions reign supreme, and less consideration is given to the authority of the prophet and his Companions (*al-ṣaḥābah*).

Born in Bosra in 1300, Ibn Kathīr was a historian and traditionalist of Mamlūk, Syria. Most famous for his *al-Biddāya wa-l-nihāya*, a major historical work that became the basis of later works, Ibn Kathīr also produced a Quran exegesis, *Tafsīr al-Qur'ān al-ʿaẓīm*, and a popular *qiṣaṣ* work.

[32] This is antithetical to the rabbinic penchant to fill in the lacunae of biblical verses.

[33] Saleh describes *al-Kashf* as an 'epoch-making work' (Saleh 2009: 324). See Saleh (2004).

Interpretation of the Quran takes on other forms, among them histories and stories of the prophets. The *Qiṣaṣ al-Anbiyā'* (The Stories of the Prophets), which share details found in Jewish and Christian sources, fill in the gaps of the quranic narrative, and flesh out characters with homiletic and historical flourishes.[34] These stories are also known as the *isrā'īliyyāt*,[35] a term applied to narratives about the 'children of Israel' (Banū Isrā'īl),[36] that is, the ancient children of Israel. A precise definition of the term has eluded scholars; perhaps it is best defined as Muslim renditions of narratives also found in the Jewish tradition.

Qiṣaṣ al-anbiyā', unlike the Quran itself, are ordered for the most part chronologically. In fact, linear chronology may be considered the most significant aspect of this literature. As Roberto Tottoli notes, 'If, in historiography, the succession of prophets constitutes the initial stage of a history based on three periods—prophets, Muḥammad, and Islamic history—the *Qiṣaṣ al-anbiyā'* represent a type of genre limited to the description of the first among these. Here, in a temporal and literary space that goes from creation to the advent of Muhammad, medieval Islamic authors gather stories and traditions of different kinds to alternate with and link to Quran verses and passages' (Tottoli 2009: 469).

During the early Islamic period, those gathering traditions looked favourably on these stories, considered early testimonies of the true religion, Islam. In fact, in the Quran God instructs Muhammad to consult those who have read the Book if he doubts what God reveals to him (10: 94). Consulting these traditions for legal advice, however, was prohibited, and by the fourteenth century the term *isrā'īliyyāt* had come to designate dubious traditions with objectionable content (Tottoli 1999; Calder 1993). Ibn Kathīr (d. 1373) was in all likelihood the first to use the term systematically to designate unreliable traditions of direct Jewish origin (Tottoli 1999: 206). In any event, the normative attitude toward the *isrā'īliyyāt*[37] did not prevent their wide readership

[34] For an introduction, see Brinner 2002 and Tottoli 2002. For a flawed but useful compendium of legends associated with biblical and quranic personages, see Schwartzbaum 1982.

[35] While I refer to the terms interchangeably, some scholars argue that the generic term *qiṣaṣ al-anbiyā'* covers three different categories: legends about creation, legends about prophets, and stories dealing specifically with the Israelites (*isrā'īliyyāt*) and their rulers, beginning with the death of Moses and their entry into the promised land. Others, however, are of the opinion that the *qiṣaṣ al-anbiyā'* are a subdivision of the *isrā'īliyyāt*. See discussion in Adang 1996. For an introduction to the stories of the prophets, see Klar 2009.

[36] On isrā'īliyyāt, see Tottoli 1999; Schöck 1993: 39–54; Adang 1996: 8–10; and McAuliffe 1998: 345–69. McAuliffe comments that 'perhaps the most felicitous translation is that provided by Jacob Lassner, who dubs the whole genre "Jewish memorabilia,"' but the term, as she herself observes, is sometimes attributed to 'the earlier *ahl al-kitāb*', even though 'the association with Jews predominates' (346). Awn 1983: 9, like some other scholars, points out: 'The qiṣaṣ literature should not be viewed as wholly derivative from Jewish and Christian sources, for it underwent substantial Islamization at the hands of Muslim preachers and commentators. Cross-fertilization occurred, with details, nuances and embellishments traded back and forth among the various religious communities. Finally, the influence of these tales on indigenous non-Christian or Jewish pre-Islamic beliefs should not be discounted.'

[37] Wahb ibn Munnabih (654/55 to 728 or 732), of Persian or Yemeni descent, is inextricably associated with isrā'īliyyāt. Because his writings appear to have drawn heavily from Jewish and Christian sources,

and preservation in various literary corpora throughout the centuries. The terms *Qiṣaṣ al-anbiyā'* and *isrā'īliyyāt* should not be conflated, for the latter is a pejorative term that develops much later than the former.[38] After all, Ibn Kathīr produced his own collection of *Qiṣaṣ al-anbiyā'*. *Isrā'īliyyāt* implies judgement on the reliability of a tradition in contrast to *Qiṣaṣ al-anbiyā'*, which are perfectly acceptable.

In the introduction to his *Tales of the Prophets* (*'Arā'is al-Majālis fī Qiṣaṣ al-Anbiyā'*), the eleventh-century Quran commentator al-Tha'labī, whose collection of tales is one of the most widely known, enumerates five reasons for transmitting stories about the prophets: 1. It was a 'manifestation of his prophethood and a sign of his mission.' 2. 'God told him about the noble characters of the preceding messengers and prophets, the saints and pious men, and praised them, so that these men would serve him as a model and example, so that his people might avoid the transgression of those commandments for which the nations of the prophets were punished and for which they deserved punishments and chastisements.' 3. In order to confirm him and make his nobility as well as his people's known. 4. To serve as instruction and guidance. 5. To keep the memory and legacy of preceding prophets and saints alive (Brinner 2002: 3–5). They affirm Muhammad as prophet, and offer moral instruction. Through the preceding prophets' exemplary behaviour, they guide all who are subject to transgressions. Accounts of the moral depravity of previous generations and the fate they faced as a consequence of their wretchedness assure Muhammad and his followers of God's favour bestowed on those who live righteously. They also secure the prophetic legacy for posterity. Far from being dry didactic disquisitions, these fanciful, colourful tales entertain and edify. They convey Muslim beliefs and mores in the same way that Jewish aggadah, non-legal narrative, not only fills in scriptural and theological lacunae, but also transmits rabbinic teachings and religious, social, and cultural values.

In addition to collections of tales of the prophets, there exist copious compilations of extra-quranic traditions dealing with quranic narratives and personae. The historical works of the late ninth and early tenth centuries synthesize earlier traditions and in turn become foundational for later writings.[39] The massive classical history of al-Ṭabarī, *Ta'rīkh al-rusul wa'l-mulūk*, for example, was copied or abridged to suit the purposes of later chroniclers. His monumental account spans the period from the

later Muslim sources look down upon his writings. See Adang 1996: 10–12 for a brief discussion of his role in disseminating Jewish and Christian traditions. On Wahb b. Munabbih, see Khoury 1972; Kister 1974; Abbott 1977.

[38] Compare Vajda 2012, who subsumes *Qiṣaṣ* under the broader Isrā'īliyyāt category. Adang (1996: 9) adopts the term 'to indicate the whole genre of Islamicized biblical legends'.

[39] A great deal has been written on Islamic historiography. See Rosenthal 1968; Khalidi 1994; Robinson 2003; Humphreys 1991; 1989: 271–90. For a focused discussion of two of the major histories and the use of sources, see Athamina 2008. This triumph of collection over composition that prevailed during the emergence of Islamic historiography in the ninth century may be an oversimplification. Robinson 2003 describes three phases of the development of the genre of historiography and it is in the second phase, from *c.*730 to *c.*830, that we can speak of Islamic historiography: 'By 830, biography, prosopography and chronology had all emerged in forms that would remain recognizable throughout the classical period' (Robinson 2003: 24).

creation of the world to 914–15, the last years before his death. Indeed, the synthetic corpus of this indefatigable collector of traditions, considered an author by some (Hodgson 1968),[40] is hardly a mere collection of random reports.

Robinson writes: 'Certainly anyone who has written history can only marvel at the variety and number of al-Ṭabarī's sources: by any reasonable standard, he was an extraordinarily resourceful scholar. It is not only the scale of his work that is marvelous, however. Just as impressive is its overall coherence. It is a hugely ambitious narrative that begins with creation and ends with the year 915, and which pivots around the birth of Islam: the career of the prophet, the conquests and early caliphs—the culmination of God's will for human history. It is precisely this coherence that gives rise to the suspicion that al-Ṭabarī was doing more than merely collecting and arranging' (Robinson 2003: 35).[41] His *Taʾrīkh*, 'emphatically traditionalist, moderate and catholic' (ibid.) became the standard of the period.

Volumes of quranic exegesis play an important role in the Islamic tradition and the production of different collections over the centuries reflects heterogeneity often overlooked when discussing 'the' Islamic tradition.

As in the Jewish and Christian traditions, pre-modern readers of scripture assumed its immutability, explained seeming contradictions, and demonstrated its timeless efficacy. They made the Word of God relevant to their contemporary concerns, and smoothed out seemingly irreconcilable verses in accordance with deeply held theological notions.

References

Abbott, N. 1977. 'Wahb b. Munabbih: A Review Article'. *Journal of Near Eastern Studies* 36: 103–12.

Adang, C. 1996. *Muslim Writers on Judaism and the Hebrew Bible: From Ibn Rabban to Ibn Hazm*. Leiden: Brill.

Adelman, R. 2009. *The Return of the Repressed: Pirqe de-Rabbi Eliezer and the Pseudepigrapha*. Leiden: Brill.

Athamina, K. 2008. 'The Historical Work of al-Balādhurī and al-Ṭabarī: The Author's Attitude towards the Sources'. In H. Kennedy, ed., *Al-Tabari: A Muslim Historian and his Work*. Princeton: Darwin Press, 141–55.

Augustine. 1997. *On Christian Teaching*, trans. R. P. H. Green. Oxford: Oxford University Press.

Awn, P. 1983. *Satan's Tragedy and Redemption: Iblīs in Sufi Psychology*. Leiden: Brill.

[40] Hodgson briefly discusses al-Ṭabarī's method of selecting *hadīth* reports and illustrates how the process of selecting anecdotes is quite deliberate.

[41] He continues: 'In fact, it is now becoming clear that he and his contemporaries *were* [emphasis his] doing much more than that. Late ninth- and tenth-century compilers impressed their vision upon the material not merely by selecting and arranging pre-existing *akhbār*, but by breaking them up, by rephrasing, supplementing and composing anew' (35–6).

Berg, H. 2000. *The Development of Exegesis in Early Islam: The Authenticity of Muslim Literature from the Formative Period.* Richmond: Curzon.

Berg, H. 2003. 'Weaknesses in the Arguments for the Early Dating of Qur'ānic Commentary'. In J. D. McAuliffe, B. D. Walfish, and J. W. Goering, eds, *With Reverence for the Word: Medieval Scriptural Exegesis in Judaism, Christianity, and Islam.* Oxford, New York: Oxford University Press, 329–45.

Bernstein, M. S. 2006. *Stories of Joseph: Narrative Migrations between Judaism and Islam.* Detroit: Wayne State University Press.

Brinner, W. M., trans. 2002. *Lives of the Prophets: As Recounted by Abū Isḥāq Aḥmad Ibn Muḥammad Ibn Ibrāhīm al-Thaʿlabī.* Leiden: Brill.

Calder, N. 1993. 'Tafsīr from Ṭabarī to Ibn Kathīr: Problems in the Description of a Genre, Illustrated with Reference to the Story of Abraham'. In G. R. Hawting and A.-K. A. Shareef, eds, *Approaches to the Qur'an.* New York: Routledge, 101–40.

Clark, E. 2008. 'From Patristics to Early Christian Studies'. In D. Hunter and S. A. Harvey, eds, *The Oxford Handbook of Christian Studies.* Oxford, New York: Oxford University Press, 7–42.

Cook, M. 1981. *Early Muslim Dogma: A Source-Critical Study.* Cambridge: Cambridge University Press.

Dan, J. 1974. *Hasipur Haʿivri Bimei Habeinayim.* Jerusalem: Keter.

Dawson, D. 1992. *Allegorical Readers and Cultural Revision in Ancient Alexandria.* Berkeley: University of California Press.

Elbaum, Y. 1986a. 'From Sermon to Story: The Transformation of the Aqedah'. *Prooftexts* 6: 97–117.

Elbaum, Y. 1986b. 'On the Character of the Late Midrashic Literature'. *Proceedings of the Ninth World Congress of Jewish Studies.* 4 vols. Jerusalem: World Congress of Jewish Studies, III. 57–62.

Elbaum, Y. 1991–2. 'Rhetoric Motif and Subject-Matter: Toward an Analysis of Narrative Technique in Pirke de-Rabbi Eliezer'. *Jerusalem Studies in Jewish Folklore* 13 (14): 99–126.

Elbaum, Y. 1996. 'Messianism in Pirke de-Rabbi Eliezer: Apocalypse and Midrash'. *Teudah* 11: 245–66.

Feldman, L., trans. 2000. *Judean Antiquities 1–4.* Vol. III of *Flavius Josephus: Translation and Commentary,* ed. S. Mason. Leiden: Brill.

Firestone, R. 1990. *Journeys in Holy Lands: The Evolution of the Abraham–Ishmael Legends in Islamic Exegesis.* Albany, NY: State University of New York Press.

Foucault, M. 1975. *Birth of a Clinic: An Archaeology of Medical Perception,* trans. A. M. Sheridan Smith. New York: Vintage.

Friedlander, G., trans. 1916. *Midrash Pirke de Rabbi Eliezer.* London; repr. New York: Sepher-Hermon Press, 1981.

Gilliot, C. 1988. 'La Formation intellectuelle de Tabari (224/5–310/ 839–923)'. *Journal asiatique* 276: 201–44.

Gilliot, C. 1989. 'Les Oeuvres de Tabari (mort en 310/923)'. *Mélanges de l'Institut Dominicain d'Études Orientales du Caire* 19: 49–90.

Gilliot, C. 1990a. 'Les Débuts de l'exégèse coranique'. *Revue du monde musulman et de la Méditerranée* 58: 83–100.

Gilliot, C. 1990b. *Exégèse, langue, et théologie en Islam: l'exégèse coranique de Tabari (m. 311/ 923).* Paris: Libr. J. Vrin.

Gilliot, C. 1994. 'Mythe, récit, histoire du salut dans le commentaire coranique de Tabari'. *Journal asiatique* 282: 237–70.

Gilliot, C. 2001–6. 'Exegesis of the Qur'ān: Classical and Medieval'. In J. D. McAuliffe, ed., *Encyclopaedia of the Qur'ān*. Leiden: Brill.

Goldfeld, I. 1984. *Qur'ānic Commentary in the Eastern Islamic Tradition of the First Four Centuries of the Hijra: An Annotated Edition of the Preface of al-Tha'labī's 'al-Kashf wa'l-bayān 'an tafsīr al-Qur'ān'*. Acre: Srugy.

Goldfeld, I. 1988. 'The Development of Theory on Qur'ānic Exegesis in Islamic Scholarship'. *Studia Islamica* 67: 5–27.

Griffith, S. H. 2006. 'Ephraem the Exegete (306–373): Biblical Commentary in the Works of Ephraem the Syrian'. In Kannengiesser 2006: 1395–428.

Hay, C. 1964. 'Antiochene Exegesis and Christology'. *Australian Biblical Review* 12.

Heidegger, M. 1962. *Being and Time*, trans. J. Macquarrie and E. Robbinson. New York: Harper & Row.

Hodgson, M. G. S. 1968. 'Two Pre-modern Muslim Historians: Pitfalls and Opportunities in Presenting Them to Moderns'. In J. U. Nef, ed., *Towards World Community*. The Hague: W. Junk, 53–68.

Humphreys, R. S. 1989. 'Qur'anic Myth and Narrative Structure in Early Islamic Historiography'. In F. M. Clover and R. S. Humphreys, eds, *Tradition and Innovation in Late Antiquity*. Madison: University of Wisconsin Press, 271–90.

Humphreys, R. S. 1991. *Islamic History: A Framework for Inquiry*. Princeton: Princeton University Press.

Jay, P. 2006. 'Jerome'. In Kannengiesser 2006: 1094–133.

Juynboll, G. H. A. 1983. *Muslim Tradition: Studies in Chronology, Provenance and Authorship of Early Ḥadīth*. Cambridge: Cambridge University Press.

Kamesar, A., ed. 2009a. *The Cambridge Companion to Philo*. Cambridge: Cambridge University Press, 2009.

Kamesar, A. 2009b. 'Biblical Interpretation in Philo'. In Kamesar 2009a: 65–94.

Kannengiesser, C. 2002. 'A Key for the Future of Patristics: The "Senses" of Scripture'. In P. M. Blowers et al., eds, *In Dominico Eloquio—In Lordly Eloquence: Essays on Patristic Exegesis in Honor of Robert Louis Wilken*. Grand Rapids, MI: Eerdmans.

Kannengiesser, C. 2006. *Handbook of Patristic Exegesis: The Bible in Ancient Christianity*. Leiden: Brill.

Kennedy, H., ed. 2008. *al-Ṭabari: A Muslim Historian and His Work*. Princeton: Darwin Press.

Khalidi, T. 1994. *Arabic Historical Thought in the Classical Period*. New York: Cambridge University Press.

Khalidi, T. 2008. 'Al-Ṭabarī: An Introduction'. In H. Kennedy, ed., *al-Tabari: A Muslim Historian and His Work*. Princeton: Darwin Press, 1–11.

Khoury, R. G. 1972. *Wahb b. Munabbih*. Wiesbaden: Harrassowitz.

Kister, M. 1974. 'On the Papyrus of Whab b. Munabbih'. *Bulletin of the School of Oriental and African Studies* 37: 547–71.

Kister, M. 2013. 'Allegorical Interpretations of Biblical Narratives in Rabbinic Literature, Philo, and Origen: Some Case Studies'. In G. A. Anderson, R. A. Clements, and D. Satran, eds, *New Approaches to the Study of Biblical Interpretation in Judaism of the Second Temple Period and in Early Christianity*. Leiden: Brill, 133–84.

Klar, M. 2009. 'Stories of the Prophets'. In Rippin 2009: 339–49.

Lassner, J. 1993. *Demonizing the Queen of Sheba: Boundaries of Gender and Culture in Postbiblical Judaism and Medieval Islam*. Chicago: University of Chicago Press.

Leemhuis, F. 1988. 'Origins and Early Development of the tafsīr Tradition'. In Rippin 1988: 13–30.
Lowin, S. 2006. *The Making of a Forefather: Abraham in Islamic and Jewish Exegetical Narratives*. Leiden: Brill.
McAuliffe, J. D. 1998. 'Assessing the Isrā'īliyyāt: An Exegetical Conundrum'. In S. Leder, ed., *Story-telling in the Framework of Non-Fictional Arabic Literature*. Wiesbaden: Harrassowitz, 345–69.
McAuliffe, J. D. 1991. *Qur'ānic Christians: An Analysis of Classical and Modern Exegesis*. Cambridge: Cambridge University Press.
McAuliffe, J. D. 2003. 'An Introduction to Medieval Interpretation of the Qur'ān'. In J. D. McAuliffe, B. D. Walfish, and J. W. Goering, eds, *With Reverence for the Word: Medieval Scriptural Exegesis in Judaism, Christianity, and Islam*. Oxford, New York: Oxford University Press, 311–19.
Matthews, E. G., Jr and Amar, J. P., eds. 1994. *St. Ephrem the Syrian: Selected Prose Works*. Washington, DC: Catholic University Press.
Meir, O. 1980. 'Hasipur Hadarshani Bemidrash Qadum Ume'uchar'. *Sinai* 86: 246–66.
Millar, F., Cohn, Y., and Ben-Eliyahu, E., eds. 2013. *Handbook of Jewish Literature from Late Antiquity, 135–700 CE*. New York: Oxford University Press.
Motzki, H. 1991. 'The Muṣannaf of 'Abd al-Razzāq al-Ṣanʿānī as a Source of Authentic Aḥadīth of the First Century A.H.'. *Journal of Near Eastern Studies* 50: 1–21.
Muqātil b. Sulaymān. 1979–89. *Tafsīr Muqātil ibn Sulaymān*, ed. 'Abdallāh Maḥmud Shihāta. 5 vols. Cairo: al-Hay'a al-Miṣriyya al-ʿĀmma lil-Kitāb.
Nassif, B. 1996. '"Spiritual Exegesis" in the School of Antioch'. In B. Nassif, ed., *New Perspectives on Historical Theology: Essays in Memory of John Meyendorff*. Grand Rapids, MI: Eerdmans, 343–77.
Palmer, A. 1993. 'A Lyre without a Voice: The Poetics and the Politics of Ephrem the Syrian'. *ARAM* 5: 371–99.
Pelikan, J. 2005. *Whose Bible Is It? A History of Scriptures through the Ages*. New York: Viking.
Rippin, A. 1994. 'Tafsīr Ibn 'Abbās'. *Jerusalem Studies in Arabic and Islam* 18: 38–83.
Rippin, A., ed. 2009. *Blackwell Companion to the Qur'ān*. Malden, MA: Wiley-Blackwell.
Robinson, C. 2003. *Islamic Historiography*. Cambridge: Cambridge University Press.
Robinson, C. 2005. 'al-Ṭabari'. In *Dictionary of Literary Biography*. Vol. 311: *Arabic Literary Culture, 500–925*, M. Cooperson and S. Toorawa, eds, Farmington Hills: Thomson Gale, 332–43.
Rosenthal, F. 1968. *A History of Muslim Historiography*. 2nd rev. edn. Leiden: Brill.
Rosenthal, F., trans. 1989. *The History of al- Ṭabarī*. Vol. I: *General Introduction and From the Creation to the Flood*. Albany: SUNY Press.
Rosenthal, F. 2012. 'Ḥāshiya'. In P. Bearman et al., eds, *Encyclopaedia of Islam*. 2nd edn. Brill Online.
Rubenstein, J. 1996. 'From Mythic Motifs to Sustained Myth: The Revision of Rabbinic Traditions in Medieval Midrashim'. *Harvard Theological Review* 89 (2): 131–59.
Runia, D. T. 2009. 'Philo's Influence on the Church Fathers'. In Kamesar 2009a: 210–30.
Sacks, S. 2009. *Midrash and Multiplicity: Pirke de-Rabbi Eliezer and the Renewal of Rabbinic Interpretive Culture*. Berlin: De Gruyter.
Saleh, W. 2004. *Formation of the Classical Tafsīr Tradition: The Qur'ān Commentary of Al-Thalabi (D. 427/1035)*. Leiden: Brill.
Saleh, W. 2009. 'Hermeneutics: al-Thaʿlabī'. In Rippin 2009: 323–37.

Saleh, W. 2010. 'Preliminary Remarks on the Historiography of tafsīr in Arabic: A History of the Book Approach'. *Journal of Qur'anic Studies* 12: 6–40.

Saleh, W. 2011. 'Marginalia and Peripheries: A Tunisian Historian and the History of Qur'anic Exegesis'. *Numen* 58: 284–313.

Schöck, C. 1993. *Adam im Islam: Ein Beitrag zur Ideengeschichte der Sunna*. Berlin: K. Schwartz.

Schwartzbaum, H. 1982. *Biblical and Extra-Biblical Legends in Islamic Folk-Literature*. Beiträge zur Sprach- und Kulturgeschichte des Orients. Walldorf-Hessen: Verlag für Orientkunde Dr. H. Vorndran.

Sezgin, F. 1992. *Studies in Early Hadith Literature: With a Critical Edition of Some Early Texts*. 3rd edn. Indianapolis: American Trust Publications.

Shinan, A. 1979. *Aggadatam Shel Meturgamnim*. Jerusalem: Makor.

Simonetti, M. 1994. *Biblical Interpretation in the Early Church: An Historical Introduction to Patristic Exegesis*, trans. J. A. Hughes. Edinburgh: T&T Clark.

Stein, D. 2005. *Maxims, Magic, Myth: A Folkloristic Perspective of Pirkei de Rabbi Eliezer*. Jerusalem: Magnes Press.

Stern, D. 1991. *Parables in Midrash*. Cambridge, MA: Harvard University Press.

Strack, H. L. and Stemberger, G. 1992. *Introduction to the Talmud and Midrash*, trans. and ed. M. Bockmuehl. Minneapolis: Augsburg Fortress, repr. 2009.

Tottoli, R. 1999. 'Origin and Use of the Term Isrā'īlīyyāt in Muslim Literature'. *Arabica* 46: 193–210.

Tottoli, R. 2002. *Biblical Prophets in the Qur'ān and Muslim Literature*. Richmond, VA: Curzon.

Tottoli, R. 2009. 'Narrative Literature'. In Rippin 2009: 467–81.

Trakatellis, D. 1996. 'Theodoret's Commentary on Isaiah: A Synthesis of Exegetical Traditions'. In B. Nassif, ed., *New Perspectives on Historical Theology: Essays in Memory of John Meyendorff*. Grand Rapids, MI: Eerdmans, 313–42.

Treitl, E. 2010. *Pirke de-Rabbi Eliezer: Text, Redaction and a Sample Synopsis*. Ph.D. dissertation. Hebrew University of Jerusalem.

Urowitz-Freudenstein, A. 1994. 'Pseudepigraphical Support of Pseudepigraphal Sources: The Case of PRE'. In J. C. Reeves, ed., *Tracing the Threads: Studies in the Vitality of Jewish Pseudepigrapha*. Atlanta: Scholars Press, 35–54.

Vajda, G. 2012. 'Isrā'īlīyyāt'. In P. Bearman et al., eds., *Encyclopedia of Islam*. 2nd edn. Brill Online.

VanderKam, J. C. 2010. *The Dead Sea Scrolls Today*. 2nd edn. Grand Rapids, MI: Eerdmans.

Wilken, R. 2006. 'Cyril of Alexandria (ca. 375–444)'. In Kannengiesser 2006: 840–69.

Yar-Shater, E., ed. 1985–99. *History of al-Tabari*. Albany: SUNY Press.

Young, F. M. 1983. *From Nicaea to Chalcedon: A Guide to the Literature and its Background*. Philadelphia: Fortress.

Young, F. M. 1989. 'The Rhetorical Schools and their Influence on Patristic Exegesis'. In R. Williams, ed., *Making of Orthodoxy: Essays in Honour of Henry Chadwick*. Cambridge: Cambridge University Press.

Zunz, L. 1954. *Hadrashot beYisrael*, ed. and suppl. H. Albeck. Jerusalem: Mossad Bialik.

CHAPTER 14

THE FINALITY OF PROPHECY

DAVID S. POWERS

The verb *to prophesy*, from the Greek *prophemi* (*pro* = 'for' or 'forth' + *phemi* = 'to speak', i.e. 'to say beforehand' or 'to foretell'), refers to a wide range of activities that defy any single categorization but which include divination, visions, auditions, and oracles.[1] These activities are associated with men and women who possess distinctive personal characteristics, speak or write in a special idiom, and act in a specific social setting. The prophet straddles the boundary between humanity and the divine. Through inspiration or ecstasy, she or he experiences a call from beyond and, as a result, feels compelled to proclaim an instruction, exhortation, warning, or prediction to members of her or his community. Thus understood, prophecy may be said to include four components: a transcendental source, a message, a human transmitter, and an audience.

Evidence of prophecy in the Near East can be traced back to the beginnings of recorded history. An early reference to a prophet occurs in a ration list drawn up in Lagash in the twenty-first century BCE. Over the course of the next 2,500 years, prophecy flourished throughout the region. In Arabia a man named Muhammad who was born *c.*570 CE is said to have received a series of communications from God over a period of twenty-three years between 610 and 632 CE. These communications were subsequently recorded in writing, collected, and redacted in the text known as the Quran. On one occasion, the Quran refers to Muhammad as 'the seal of the Prophets', a phrase that is understood by most Muslims and many non-Muslims as signifying that prophecy came to an end upon the death of Muhammad in 632 CE. In this chapter, I shall attempt to situate this claim in the context of the understanding of biblical and post-biblical prophecy in the Near East in antiquity and late antiquity.

[1] I wish to thank Jon Levenson and colleagues and students in the Near Eastern Studies Department at Cornell for comments on an earlier draft of this chapter. Any remaining errors are mine alone.

Prophets in the Hebrew Bible and in Post-biblical Texts

The Hebrew Bible suggests that the activity of prophets is similar to that of seers and soothsayers: 'Formerly, in Israel, when a man went to inquire of God, he would say, "Come, let us go to the seer", for the prophet of today was formerly called a seer' (1 Sam. 9: 9). A seer is an individual endowed with special knowledge who is subject to the influence of a supernatural entity. Through that entity, the seer receives a communication that is inaccessible to others and gives voice to that communication in a verbal utterance that is distinguished by its extraordinary content, complex style, rhyme, and/or cadence. The seer was sought out and received compensation for his or her oracles, which typically dealt with mundane issues such as the meaning of a dream, paternity of a child, or location of a lost animal.

The *navî* or prophet of the Hebrew Bible is a person who receives a call from God to transmit a divine message and who responds to that call by attempting to establish 'the ways of God'. A prophet serves as a source of guidance, receives visions, has dreams, preaches a word from God, and is often scorned or rejected by his or her immediate audience. The biblical prophet par excellence was Moses, who spoke with God face to face (Deut. 34: 10). Other biblical figures identified as prophets include Abraham (Gen. 20: 7), Miriam (Exod. 15: 20), Nathan (2 Sam. 7: 2), and Deborah (Judg. 4: 4). Indeed, one verse in Psalms may suggest that *all* of the patriarchs were prophets. Shortly after mentioning the 'offspring of Abraham' and 'descendants of Jacob' (Ps. 105: 11), the psalmist quotes the divinity as commanding: 'Do not touch my anointed ones, do not harm My prophets' (Ps. 105: 15). Subsequently, rabbis and church fathers expanded the ranks of prophets to include men (Adam, Noah, Jacob, and David) and women (Sarah, Miriam, Deborah, Hannah, Abigail, Hulda, and Esther) who are not identified as prophets in the Hebrew Bible. Although earlier prophets did not leave a record of their prophecies, later prophets are said to have received a divine instruction to record their respective messages (Jer. 30: 2, 36: 2, Hab. 2: 2; cf. Dan. 12: 4). The Hebrew Bible includes seven books attributed to Major Prophets (1 and 2 Joshua, 1 and 2 Samuel, Isaiah, Jeremiah, and Ezekiel), two books thought to have been written by figures acting under prophetic inspiration (Judges and Kings), and twelve books attributed to Minor Prophets (Hosea, Joel, Amos, Obadiah, Jonah, Micah, Nahum, Habakkuk, Zephaniah, Haggai, Zechariah, and Malachi). The Book of Malachi ends with a prognostication of the future appearance of the prophet Elijah (Mal. 3: 23).

The closure and canonization of the Hebrew Bible raised questions about the subsequent status of prophecy. Several biblical verses suggest that at a certain point in time God ceased to communicate with humanity, whereupon prophets disappeared: 'No signs appear for us; there is no longer any prophet; no one among us knows for how long' (Ps. 74: 9; cf. Amos 8: 11, Mic. 3: 6–7, Isa. 63: 11, Lam. 2: 9, and Zech. 13: 2–4). This break in communication between God and humanity was expected to last until the

End Time, when 'your sons and your daughters shall prophesy, your old men shall dream dreams, and your young men shall see visions' (Joel 3: 1). One encounters a similar idea in post-biblical texts. According to 1 Macc. 9: 27, following the death of Judas Maccabee, 'there was great distress in Israel, such as had not been seen since the time that prophets ceased to appear among them' (cf. 1 Macc. 4: 46, 14: 21). Similarly, the Qumran community believed that prophecy had ceased but would return at the end of time. A passage in the Community Rule scroll exhorts the sons of Aaron to follow the directives of the first men of the Community 'until the prophet comes, and the Messiahs of Aaron and Israel' (*Community Rule* 9.9–11).

The status of prophecy was disputed in post-biblical times. Some rabbis held that prophecy continued to function, albeit without rabbinic authority. Other rabbis held that prophecy ended with Jeremiah, who was 'the last of the prophets' (*Pesiqta de-Rab Kahana* 13.14; cf. *Abot de-Rabbi Nathan A* 1; *Qohelet Rabbah* 12.7), or that 'the Holy Spirit came to an end in Israel' following the deaths of the last three Minor Prophets, Haggai, Zechariah, and Malachi (*b. Sot.* 48b; cf. *y. Sot.* 9.13, 24b). According to *Seder Olam Rabbah* 30, 'there were prophets prophesying by the Holy Spirit' until the time of Alexander the Macedonian. The assertion that prophecy had ceased—whenever that event may have occurred—bolstered the authority of the rabbis as interpreters of the now closed and canonical text of the Hebrew Bible.

In fact, prophet-like activity continued to manifest itself among Jews in late antiquity, now in the form of dreams and the so-called *bat qol* (lit. 'a small voice'), that is to say, a disembodied heavenly voice—identified with the Holy Spirit—that provides for ongoing revelation in the absence of true prophecy: '[Y]et they were still able to avail themselves of the *bat qol*' (*b. Sanh.* 11a; cf. *b. Sot.* 48b; *y. Yoma* 9b; *Canticles Rabbah* 8.9, no. 3). One also finds evidence of prophet-like activity at Qumran, where, as noted, members of the community were waiting for the return of prophecy at the eschaton. At the same time, however, they attached great importance to the so-called Teacher of Righteousness, an inspired figure who was empowered to interpret the words of the ancient prophets for the benefit of his community and to reveal 'the hidden things in which Israel had gone astray' (*Damascus Document* 3.12–15). In function—if not in form—the Teacher of Righteousness appears to have performed the task of prophecy. In addition, the fact that the Qumran community rejected the reputed prophets of their adversaries suggests that the followers of those 'prophets' regarded them as true prophets. Be that as it may, prophet-like activity continued in late Second Temple Judaism.

Prophecy in the New Testament

Christians interpret numerous passages in the Hebrew Bible as presaging the life and career of Jesus, e.g. Deut. 18: 15, in which Moses is reported to have said: 'The Lord your God will raise up for you a prophet from among your own people, like myself; him you shall heed.' This prophecy is said to have been fulfilled by Jesus. In Acts 3: 18, Peter asserts: 'In this way God fulfilled what he had foretold through all the prophets that his Messiah would suffer.' Similarly, Christians interpret the closing reference in Mal. 3: 23 to the future appearance of the prophet Elijah as an allusion to John the Baptist who, in turn, will foretell the coming of Jesus.

The church fathers taught that the gift of prophecy was withdrawn from the Jews and conferred upon the Christians: '[T]he gifts that had previously resided among your people have now been transferred to us' (Justin Martyr, *Dialogue with Trypho* 82.1; cf. ibid. 53.3–4; Origen, *Contra Celsum* 7.8; Athanasius, *On the Incarnation* 39–40). The transference of prophecy to the Christians was regarded as a punishment of the Jews for their rejection of Christ.

Just as the rabbis taught that prophecy ended with either Jeremiah, Malachi, or Alexander the Great, some Christian scholars taught that prophecy ended with Jesus. One biblical witness for this teaching is found in Dan. 9: 24, where Daniel uses the verb *laḥtom* ('to seal' or 'to confirm') in connection with a 'prophetic vision' (*ḥazôn ve-nabî*). In context, *laḥtôm* refers to the 'confirmation' of a prophetic vision after a period of 'seventy weeks'. Subsequently, however, the church fathers reinterpreted this verse in such a manner as to suggest that it signifies the end of prophecy. Tertullian (d. 220 CE) glosses the verse as follows: 'In fact, when Christ was baptized . . . all the abundance of past spiritual gifts ended in Christ, who has sealed all visions and prophecies, which he has fulfilled by his coming.' Similarly, the Syriac-Christian author Aphrahat (d. *c.*345 CE) writes, '. . . the Messiah came and was killed in fulfillment of the vision and the prophets . . . Understand, my beloved, and perceive, that the [seventy] weeks were fulfilled; the visions and the prophets have ceased . . .'. In the eyes of Tertullian and Aphrahat, the fulfilment of the biblical prediction by Jesus signalled the end or cessation of all further prophetic activity.

Other church fathers taught that prophecy would resume at some point in the future in the form of the Holy Spirit. The return of the Holy Spirit was linked in turn to the appearance of a figure identified as the *paráklētos* (Gr. 'advocate' or 'comforter'). In John 14: 26, for example, Jesus is quoted as saying, 'But the *paráklētos*, the Holy Spirit, whom the Father will send in my name, will teach you everything, and remind you of all that I have said to you' (cf. John 15: 26, 16: 7, 16: 16, 26).

Thus, many Jews and Christians appear to have shared the view that true prophecy had been suspended but would resume at some point in the future—albeit at a different time, in a different form, and for a different reason.

Prophetic Movements in Late Antiquity

In the second and third centuries CE, several religious movements took the name of a founder who claimed to be a true prophet. The Elkasaites were a Judaeo-Christian movement composed of the disciples and followers of Elkasai who lived in Parthia. *Circa* 100 CE, Elkasai claimed to have received new revelations delivered to him by a giant angel. These revelations were recorded in a book that subsequently was brought to Rome by Alcibiades of Apamea, a member of the movement. The Elkasaites were rejected by church theologians as heretics.

Another prophetic movement emerged around the figure of Montanus who, in the second half of the second century CE, claimed to be a prophet of God through whom the Paraclete had spoken. Montanus was joined by two young women who left their husbands and also began to prophesy. Montanism was a Christian movement that originated in Asia Minor and later spread throughout much of the Roman Empire. Originally known as the New Prophecy, Montanism advocated reliance on the spontaneity of the Holy Spirit. The movement lasted until the sixth century CE.

A third prophetic movement emerged around the figure of Mani, whose father is said to have been an Elkasaite. Mani was born *c.*216 CE near Ctesiphon in southern Iraq. At the ages of 12 and 24 he had visionary experiences in which a heavenly twin instructed him to leave his father's religion and teach the true message of Christ. Like Montanus, Mani claimed to be the Paraclete promised in the New Testament; he also claimed to be an Apostle of Christ. He taught that Divine Wisdom is common to all of the great religions, but that this wisdom had been corrupted by the followers of earlier prophets—Adam, Zoroaster, Buddha, and Jesus. Mani claimed to possess a complete and truthful understanding of this wisdom. Later Muslim authors refer to him as 'the Seal of Prophets', possibly under the influence of Q. 33: 40 (see below). Following Mani's death in 276 CE, Manichaeism spread rapidly, reaching Rome and Egypt by the end of the third century and China by the end of the sixth.

A New Arabian Prophet

From the twenty-first century BCE down to the first quarter of the seventh century CE, prophecy flourished in various forms throughout the Near East, in Anatolia, Syria-Palestine, Iraq, and Iran. Although the rabbis and church fathers taught that true prophecy had either ceased or been suspended, many Jews, Christians, and other monotheists were living in anticipation of the return of prophecy. It is against the background of this anticipation that the rise of a new prophetic movement in Arabia is best understood.

In 610 CE, God resumed contact with humanity by sending a series of messages to an Arab tribesman who had been chosen as a new prophet. These messages were delivered and received over a period of twenty-three years, first in Mecca between 610 and 622 and then in Medina between 622 and 632.

The earliest revelations were short narrative units in rhymed prose. A typical example is sura 108 ('The Abundance'), which contains three verses, each ending in *-ar*:

1. *Innā aʿtaynāka al-kawthar*	We have indeed given you abundance.
2. *Fa-ṣalli li-rabbika wa'nḥar*	So pray to your Lord and sacrifice.
3. *Inna shāniʾaka al-abtar.*	The one who hates is the one cut off.

Like the Hebrew Bible, the new revelation posits a connection between prophecy and soothsaying. The form, content, and style of the early revelations reminded the prophet's immediate audience of the oracular utterances of a soothsayer (*kāhin*)—or the verses of a poet (*shāʿir*). In response to an implied accusation that the new prophet was nothing more than a soothsayer and/or poet, the Quran retorts: 'It is not the speech of a poet—little you believe. Nor is it the speech of a soothsayer—little you are reminded' (Q. 69: 41–2; cf. 52: 29, 81: 22). Rather, the communications received by the prophet had been conveyed to him by 'a noble messenger' (Q. 69: 40, 81: 19) or angel (2: 97–8). The source of these communications was not daemonic but divine.

The Quran identifies the human recipient of these divine messages as either a *rasūl* (pl. *rusul)*, literally 'one sent with a message', or a *nabī* (pl. *nabiyyūn*, *anbiyāʾ*), literally 'prophet' (cf. Hebrew *navî*). The word *rasūl* or messenger occurs 236 times in the Quran in the singular and ninety-five times in the plural. In both forms, it signifies a human agent sent by God to deliver a message to his people—usually in the form of a book—in a language that they understand. The word *nabī* or prophet occurs seventy-five times in the Quran, generally referring to a man who continues an earlier religious law, albeit without bringing a new book. On occasion, the terms overlap and are applied to one and the same person. Thus Ishmael (Q. 19: 54–5), Moses (19: 51), Jesus (19: 30, 61: 6), and Muhammad (33: 40, 7: 157) are identified as both messengers and prophets.

The Quran may be said to contain a theory of prophecy: at more or less regular intervals in time, God intervenes in history by delivering a message to a prophet. Prophets emerge in succession in accordance with *sunnat allāh* or divine providence (see e.g. Q. 33: 38). The quranic understanding of prophecy is typological, that is to say, all of the prophets, including the new Arabian messenger-prophet, possess characteristics and undergo experiences that are uniform, coherent, and consistent. Like his predecessors, the Arabian prophet offers guidance, experiences unusual physical and psychological states, is the recipient of visions and dreams, preaches reward and punishment, is rejected by unbelievers, and, in his capacity as a messenger, brings a new revelation in the form of a book. The typological identity between the new Arabian prophet and his biblical predecessors confirms the authenticity of his mission and the truth of his message; conversely, the success of the new prophet's mission validated the missions of his predecessors.

The men who are identified as prophets in the Quran are not identical to those identified as prophets in the Hebrew Bible. On the one hand, the prophets in the Quran are all biblical figures—with the exception of the otherwise unattested Arabian prophets Hūd, Ṣāliḥ, and Shuʿayb. On the other hand, none of the Major or Minor Prophets—with the exception of Jonah—is identified as a prophet in the Quran.

Some rabbis, it will be recalled, taught that prophecy had been suspended following either the destruction of the First Temple, the closure of the Hebrew Bible, or the career of Alexander the Great, and that it would not resume until the arrival of the Messiah. Similarly, some church fathers taught that prophecy had been suspended following the death of Jesus and would not resume until the appearance of the Paraclete. At the turn of the seventh century CE, Jews had been waiting for the arrival of the Messiah for approximately 1,000 years, while Christians had been waiting for the Paraclete for over 500 years. The Quran understood that a significant period of time had passed since the death of the last biblical prophet and/or the death of Jesus, and that both Jews and Christians were waiting for a resumption of some form of prophetic activity. This temporary gap in divine communication with mankind is identified in the Quran as a *fatra* or 'interval of time between two events'. This interval ended when God chose Muhammad as his next messenger. The new message was addressed *inter alia* to Jews and Christians, as stated in Q. 5: 19: 'O People of the Book (*ahl al-kitāb*), Our messenger has come to you, making things clear to you after an interval (*fatra*) between messengers, so that you cannot say, "No bearer of good tidings or warner has come to us." A bearer of good tidings and warner has come to you. God has power over everything.' The appearance of the new Arabian prophet ('a Messenger from among yourselves', Q. 9: 128) was understood as a fulfilment of Deut. 18: 15 and John 14: 26: The suspension of revelation had been lifted, true prophecy had returned, God had resumed communication with humanity, and another messenger had arrived.

As the most recent link in the succession of prophets, the new Arabian prophet brought a message to his community that was essentially identical to that of the earlier biblical prophets. The Quran insists that its message is the same as that of the Hebrew Bible and New Testament. The relationship between these three texts is embodied in the terms *confirmation*, *correction*, and *completion*.

The Quran repeatedly asserts that it *confirms* the message of the earlier scriptures, using the verbal noun *taṣdīq* ('confirmation') and the active participle *muṣaddiq* ('one who confirms'). In Q. 61: 6, the Divinity instructs his prophet to recall the following statement attributed to Jesus: 'O Children of Israel, I am God's messenger to you, confirming (*muṣaddiq^{an}*) the Torah that was before me, and giving you good tidings of a messenger who will come after me, whose name will be *aḥmad* (literally, "more worthy of praise").' Here Jesus not only confirms the message of the Torah, but also anticipates the future appearance of a more praiseworthy (*aḥmad*) messenger—universally understood by Muslims as a reference to Muhammad. Just as Jesus previously confirmed the Torah, Muhammad now confirms both the Torah and the New Testament. Several verses announce that the new Arabic revelation confirms 'what was before it' (e.g. Q. 2: 97, 6: 92, 10: 37, 12: 111, and 35: 31), 'the Book of Moses' (Q. 46: 12) or 'all the Scriptures before it' (Q. 5: 48). Other verses specify that the new revelation confirms the scriptures sent previously to the Jews and the Christians: 'He has sent down to you the Scripture in truth, confirming what came before it. And He sent down the Torah and the Gospel' (Q. 3: 3). Jews and Christians are commanded to believe in the new revelation because it confirms their respective scriptures: 'O you who have been given the Scripture, believe in what We have sent down, confirming what is with you...' (Q. 4: 47; cf. 2: 41, 3: 81). Conversely, members of the new community of believers are instructed to believe in the new revelation because it confirms the revelations sent previously to the Jews and Christians: '[I]t is the truth, confirming what is with them [namely the People of the Book]...' (Q. 2: 91). The Hebrew Bible, New Testament, and Quran are thus successive links in a chain of divine revelations that all bear the same message.

The essential identity of these three scriptures is qualified, however, by the contention that the Hebrew Bible and New Testament were subjected to 'tampering' (*taḥrīf*) or 'alteration' (*tabdīl*). The Quran charges Jews and Christians with failing to understand the original meaning of their scriptures, forgetting what was revealed, and altering the text of their scriptures. Q. 2: 79 warns: 'Woe to those who write the Scripture with their own hands and then say, "This is from God", so that they may sell it for a paltry price...' (cf. 3: 75). According to Q. 5: 13, the Israelites '...change words from their places and they have forgotten a part of that by which they were reminded...' (cf. 4: 46; 5: 41). These misunderstandings or manipulations of the Hebrew Bible and New Testament by Jews and Christians are *corrected* by the Quran, which thereby restores the original form and/or meaning of the earlier scriptures. And by restoring the original meaning of the earlier revelations, the Quran *completes* the cycle of divine communication to humanity.

Thus, the Quran *confirms* the truth of the earlier scriptures while at the same time *correcting* certain misunderstandings of their contents, thereby *completing* the cycle of divine communication with mankind that began with the first biblical prophet.

Islamic sources teach that the divine communications received by Muhammad were recorded in writing during his lifetime and subsequently compiled, redacted, and edited on two occasions, first during the caliphate of Abū Bakr (r. 632–4 CE) and again during that of ʿUthmān (r. 644–56). These two projects are said to have resulted in the production of a uniform consonantal skeleton that accurately represented the content of the revelations received by Muhammad. Once this standard canonical text had been established, all non-conforming codices are said to have been burned, shredded, or immersed in water. It now became the responsibility of the Muslim community to ensure that the Quran would not be forgotten, manipulated, or misunderstood, as happened earlier with the Hebrew Bible and New Testament. If the Muslims succeeded in this task, there would be no need for God to send another prophet to mankind.

In theory, of course, prophecy might continue. What was to prevent God from intervening in history at some point in the future by choosing yet another prophet and sending him to a community that had not yet been exposed to the Quran? It was to block this possibility, in my view, that the doctrine of the finality of prophecy was introduced.

The Finality of Prophecy

The Quran contains a single reference to Muhammad's status as 'the seal of Prophets'. In this revelation, Muhammad is mentioned by name and characterized as 'the messenger of God and the seal of Prophets (*khātam al-nabiyyīn*)'. The expression 'the seal of Prophets' is widely understood by Muslims as signifying that Muhammad was the last prophet. The historical circumstances in which this verse is said to have been revealed are documented in Islamic sources with remarkable precision and in vivid detail.

The revelation in which Muhammad is identified as 'the seal of Prophets' would become verse 40 of *Sūrat al-Aḥzāb* ('The Confederates'), which is composed of seventy-three verses. This sura is said to have been revealed to the prophet in 5/626–7, the year in which a coalition of pagan and Jewish 'confederates' attacked Medina but were repelled—with divine assistance—at the Battle of the Trench. For the next six years, Muhammad continued to receive communications from God. Upon his death in 11/632, however, prophecy is said to have come to an end.

Q. 33: 40 is the fifth verse in a five-verse pericope located in the middle of *Sūrat al-Aḥzāb*. These five verses read as follows:

> 36 When God and His messenger have decided a matter, it is not for any believing man or woman to have any choice in the affair. Whoever disobeys God and His Messenger has gone astray in manifest error.
>
> 37 [Recall] when you said to the one on whom God and you yourself have bestowed favor, 'Keep your wife to yourself and fear God', and you hid within yourself what God would reveal, and you feared the people when God had better right to be feared by you. When Zayd had finished with her, We gave her to you in marriage, so that there should be no difficulty (*ḥaraj*) for the believers concerning the wives of their adopted sons, when they have finished with them. God's command was fulfilled.
>
> 38 There is no difficulty for the prophet in that which God has ordained for him: God's practice (*sunnat allāh*) concerning those who passed away previously—God's command is a fixed decree.
>
> 39 Who conveyed God's messages and feared Him and no one else apart from God. God is sufficient as a reckoner.
>
> 40 Muhammad is not the father of any of your men, but the messenger of God and the seal of the Prophets. God is aware of everything.

The termination of the office of prophecy was surely a matter of great historical import—indeed, one might say that it was a matter of cosmic significance. It is therefore curious that v. 40 is said to have been revealed in connection with—in fact, as a direct consequence of—an amorous episode involving the prophet Muhammad, his adopted son, and the latter's wife. Let us attend to the relationship between v. 40 and the other four verses in the pericope and to the 'logic of revelation'. For the moment, we ignore v. 36 and proceed directly to v. 37.

In v. 37, the authorial voice ('We')—presumably God—orders a male addressee ('you')—presumably Muhammad—to recall a conversation between Muhammad and a third party ('the one on whom . . .'). This verbal exchange took place at an unspecified time in the recent past between Muhammad and the third party, who is characterized as 'the one on whom God and you yourself have bestowed favor'. In the continuation of the verse, this doubly favoured man is identified as 'Zayd'. The mere mention of Zayd's name is noteworthy: apart from Muhammad, Zayd is the only Muslim who is identified by name in the Quran. The continuation of the verse suggests that Zayd was Muhammad's adopted son, as confirmed by Islamic tradition. At the time of the verbal exchange, Zayd wanted to divorce his unnamed wife and Muhammad wanted to marry the woman. God reminds Muhammad that he had been hiding something within himself and—remarkably—rebukes the prophet for putting his fear of men above his fear of him. God then grants his prophet permission to marry the woman ('We gave her to you in marriage'), but only on the condition that Zayd no longer had any sexual desire for his wife (he was 'finished with her'). Previously, one surmises, a sexual union with the former wife of one's adopted son was regarded as a sin or act of disobedience. Verse 37 modifies the sexual taboo by introducing a distinction between the wife of an adopted son and that of a natural son: henceforth, no sin would be associated with a marriage between a man and the former wife of his adopted son. Verses 38–9 then compare Muhammad's experience to that of earlier prophets. Finally, v. 40 announces that Muhammad is sonless—or, to be precise, that he has no adult sons—after which it characterizes him as 'the messenger of God and the seal of Prophets'.

Islamic tradition teaches that v. 40 was revealed about a man named Zayd. Who was this man who is said to have been the *sabab* or cause of the revelation of this unique quranic witness to the finality of prophecy? According to Islamic sources, Zayd's birth name was Zayd b. Ḥāritha b. Sharāḥīl al-Kalbī. As a youth he was captured and, *c.*605 CE, acquired as a slave by Muhammad. Zayd's family tracked him down in Mecca, where his father Ḥāritha attempted to ransom his son. Of his own free will, Zayd chose continued slavery with Muhammad over freedom and reunification with his birth family. Following this demonstration of absolute loyalty, Muhammad adopted Zayd as his son in a formal ceremony attested by witnesses in the sacred precinct in Mecca. The adoption entailed two important legal consequences: Zayd b. Ḥāritha al-Kalbī became Zayd b. Muhammad al-Hāshimī; and mutual rights of inheritance were created between father and son. At the time of the adoption Zayd would have been between 25 and 30 years old, that is to say, he was a man. He was now Muhammad's son and heir—indeed, his sole heir.

When Muhammad received his first revelation in 610 CE, Zayd was either the first person or the first adult male to join the community of believers. He was known as the Beloved of the Messenger of God. In Mecca, Zayd married Umm Ayman, an Abyssinian woman who bore him a son, Usāma b. Zayd b. Muhammad, known as the Beloved Son of the Beloved of the Messenger of God.

Shortly after the hijra to Medina in 1/622, Zayd asked his father for permission to take as his second wife Zaynab bt. Jaḥsh, the beautiful granddaughter of ʿAbd al-Muṭṭalib and the prophet's paternal cross-cousin. Initially Muhammad was opposed to the marriage but Zayd stubbornly pressed his case. Eventually, Muhammad agreed and sent an agent to convey the marriage proposal to Zaynab. Upon hearing the proposal, Zaynab protested that she did not want to marry Zayd for she was, by her own estimation, 'the most perfect woman of Quraysh'. God now intervened in history to settle the matter by revealing the first verse of the pericope that ends with verse 40: 'When God and His messenger have decided a matter, it is not for any believing man or woman to have any choice in the affair. Whoever disobeys God and His Messenger has gone astray in manifest error' (Q. 33: 36). Zayd did marry Zaynab, although it was not long before he began to complain to his father about his wife's behaviour and to ask him for permission to divorce the woman. Muhammad had a better idea. One day, the prophet went to the couple's residence with the intention of admonishing his daughter-in-law. Upon his arrival, only Zaynab was at home, wearing a light dress. As she was in the act of rising to her feet, Muhammad caught a glimpse of Zaynab's body and was sexually attracted to her. When Zayd returned home later that day, Zaynab regaled him with the story of the strange encounter with her father-in-law. Zayd was now more determined than ever to divorce his wife. He reportedly ceased having sexual relations with her, thereby satisfying the quranic stipulation that he must be 'finished' with his wife before she might remarry. Curiously, Muhammad instructed his son *not* to divorce Zaynab ('Keep your wife to yourself and fear God'), despite the fact that he was in love with the woman. The prophet understood that his attraction to his daughter-in-law had brought him to the brink of committing a sin. Fearing public outcry, Muhammad kept his desire for Zaynab a secret.

God now made a second intervention in this episode by sending down the revelation that would become v. 37 of *Sūrat al-Aḥzāb*. As noted, this revelation legitimized the union between Muhammad and Zaynab by drawing a distinction between marriage with the former wife of a natural son (which continued to be forbidden—see Q. 4: 23), and marriage with the former wife of an adopted son (which was henceforth legitimate). Following the revelation of v. 37, Zayd divorced Zaynab, who then observed the *ʿidda* or waiting-period; when it was determined that she was not pregnant, Muhammad married her. It must have been in the interval between the divorce and the marriage that Muhammad informed Zayd that he was no longer his father (*'lastu bi-abīka'*), whereupon Zayd b. Muhammad, the Beloved of the Messenger of God, the first adult male to become a Muslim, the one upon whom both God and his prophet had bestowed favour, and the only Muslim apart from Muhammad to be identified by name in the Quran, lost his status as the prophet's son and heir.

Lest there be any question about Zayd's status, God now made a third intervention in this episode by sending down the revelation that would become v. 40 of *Sūrat al-Aḥzāb*: 'Muhammad is not the father of any of your men, but the messenger of God and the seal of Prophets. God is aware of everything.' The opening clause of this verse establishes that neither Zayd nor any other adult male within the community of believers could claim to be Muhammad's son. In this manner, God ensured that when the prophet died five years later, in 11/632, he would not have a son who might succeed him as either a prophet or as the leader of the community. (Zayd's status as a potential successor was mooted by his untimely death as a martyr at Muʾtah in southern Jordan in 8/629.)

The prophet's repudiation of Zayd raises several questions: Was it in fact necessary for Muhammad to disown Zayd as his son? Is it not the case that v. 37 legitimized the prophet's marriage to Zaynab by introducing a distinction between the former wife of a biological son and that of an adopted son? Suppose for the sake of argument that Zayd had continued to be Muhammad's adopted son. Would Muhammad have committed a sin or act of disobedience by marrying Zaynab after Zayd had divorced her? In fact, there is nothing in the language of v. 37 to suggest that there would have been any problem with the prophet's marriage to Zaynab. If so, then why did Muhammad repudiate Zayd? It was this question, in my view, that necessitated God's fourth and final intervention in this episode. Shortly after the divinity had introduced the distinction between biological and adopted sons in v. 37, he abolished the institution of adoption—thereby transforming the distinction into the proverbial distinction without a difference. The abolition of adoption is found in what would become vv. 4–5 of *Sūrat al-Aḥzāb*:

> 4 God has not put two hearts inside any man . . . nor has He made your adopted sons your [real] sons. That is what you say with your mouths, but God speaks the truth and guides to the [right] way.
>
> 5 Call them after their fathers. That is fairer with God . . .

Lest there be any doubt about the status of the institution, the prophet himself is reported to have said: 'There is no adoption in Islam; the custom of the Age of Ignorance (*jāhiliyya*) has been abolished.'

The Quran indicates that the designation of Muhammad as 'the seal of Prophets' was a direct consequence of an amorous episode involving the prophet and the wife of his adopted son Zayd. This episode produced not only a reform of marriage law and the abolition of adoption but also the theological doctrine of the finality of prophecy. One wonders about the direction of historical causation. Is there any other way to explain the emergence of the key theological doctrine? And what is the connection between this doctrine and Muhammad's sonlessness? In an attempt to answer these questions, let us take a closer look at the quranic understanding of prophecy.

Prophetology in the Quran

The Quran teaches that the biblical prophets were chosen by God from a single, divinely privileged lineage. The first two prophets were Adam and Noah. Subsequently the pool from which prophets were chosen was narrowed to Abraham and his descendants ('the seed of Abraham'). Beginning with Abraham, all of the biblical prophets identified in the Quran are members of this family. Remarkably, the Quran suggests—without explicitly saying so—that prophecy is the exclusive possession of a single, divinely privileged lineage. Thus, Q. 57: 26 states that God assigned prophecy and the Book to the progeny (*dhurriyya*) of Noah and Abraham. Q. 4: 163 identifies successive generations of prophets within a single family: 'We have made revelations to you, as We made them to Noah and the prophets after him, and as We made them to Abraham and Ishmael and Isaac and Jacob and the tribes . . .' According to Q. 29: 27, the office of prophecy is limited exclusively to Abraham and his lineal descendants. In fact, all of the biblical prophets mentioned in the Quran are members of this family: Adam, Noah, Abraham, Lot, Ishmael, Isaac, Jacob, Joseph, Moses, Aaron, David, Solomon, Job, Jonah, Elijah, Elisha, Zechariah, John the Baptist, and Jesus.

In the quranic worldview, true prophecy is the exclusive possession of a single family and the office of prophecy is transmitted from father to son. One might say that the office of prophecy is hereditary (although the 'gene' for prophecy may remain dormant for one or more generations). In order to qualify as a prophet, one must be a member of this family. Nowhere in the Quran, however, is Muhammad identified as a lineal descendant of Abraham (or Noah or Adam). It is therefore no coincidence that the *Sīra* of Ibn Isḥāq (d. 150/767), as redacted by Ibn Hishām (d. 218/833), opens with a section entitled 'Muhammad's Pure Descent from Adam' in which Muhammad's genealogy is traced back to Abraham through twenty-nine intervening links, then from Abraham to Noah through ten links, and finally from Noah to Adam through eight links (cf. Gen. 5: 1–31, 10: 21, and 11: 10ff.; and Matt. 1: 1–17). The list is as follows:

> **Muḥammad**—'Abdallāh—'Abd al-Muṭṭalib (whose name was Shayba)—Hāshim (whose name was 'Amr)—'Abd Manāf (whose name was al-Mughīra)—Quṣayy (whose name was Zayd)—Kilāb—Murra—Kaʿb—Luʾayy—Ghālib—Fihr—Mālik—al-Naḍr—Kināna—Khuzayma—Mudrika (whose name was 'Āmir)—Ilyās—Muḍar—Nizār—Maʿadd—'Adnān—Udd (or Udad)—Muqawwam—Nāḥūr—Tayraḥ—Yaʿrub—Yashjub—Nābit- Ismāʿīl—**Ibrāhīm, the friend of the Compassionate**—Tāriḥ (who is Āzar)—Nāḥūr—Sārūgh—Rāʿū—Fālikh—'Aybar—Shālikh—Arfakhshadh—Sām—**Nūḥ**—Lamk—Mattūshalakh—Akhnūkh, who is the prophet Idrīs according to what they allege, but God knows best (he was the first of the sons of Adam to whom prophecy and writing with a pen were given)—Yard—Mahlīl—Qaynan—Yānish—Shīth—**Adam.** (*Source*: Ibn Hisham, *Sīra*, trans. Guillaume, p. 3)

By creating a genealogical connection between Muhammad, on the one hand, and Abraham, Noah, and Adam, on the other, Islamic tradition established that Muhammad was in fact a member of the family that holds exclusive rights to the office of prophecy. He was thus qualified to be a prophet.

Depending on one's vantage point, genealogy may be used to establish a connection not only with the past but also with the future: Looking backwards in time, it was important for the early community of believers to establish a direct genealogical connection between Muhammad and Abraham; looking forwards in time, it was essential for that community to establish that Muhammad had no adult sons. These Muslims understood that if Muhammad did have a son who not only attained physical maturity but also outlived his father, then the office of prophecy would have passed to that son and/or to his descendants. In that case, however, Muhammad would not have been the last prophet. Conversely, if Muhammad was to be the last prophet, he could not be remembered as having a son—biological or adopted—who attained physical maturity and outlived him. The theological doctrine of the finality of prophecy demanded that the man who brought the office of prophecy to an end must be sonless. One might say that Muhammad's sonlessness was a theological imperative.

The reciprocal relationship between the finality of prophecy and Muhammad's sonlessness brings us back to the question of historical cause-and-effect: Was the theological doctrine a seemingly unintended consequence of a love affair involving Muhammad, Zayd, and Zaynab, as Islamic tradition teaches? Or was this narrative formulated after the fact in order to establish that Muhammad was sonless and was therefore the last prophet? As noted, Islamic tradition teaches that *Sūrat al-Aḥzāb* was revealed in 5/626–7. Let us bracket the traditional chronology and posit, for the sake of argument, that the doctrine of the finality of prophecy was post-Muhammadan. As the doctrine developed, there would have been a need to formulate a 'revelation' in which the divinity predicted that Muhammad would be sonless when he died. Where, when, and by whom might such a 'revelation' have been formulated?

The Chronology of Revelation

Islamic tradition's identification of 5/626–7 as the year in which vv. 36–40 of *Sūrat al-Aḥzāb* were revealed to Muhammad may be questioned on several grounds.

First, the traditional chronology makes it appear as if the divine pronouncement of Muhammad's sonlessness was made six years before the prophet's death in 11/632. This is curious, as Muhammad reportedly had numerous wives and concubines, was sexually active, and was fertile.

Second, the designation of Muhammad as the last prophet is a hegemonic and supersessionist claim that would best have been made from a position of supreme power. Such a claim makes no sense in a Meccan context and little sense in a Medinan context. In Mecca, Muhammad was charged with persuading pagans and polytheists that there was only one God, that this God communicated with mankind through prophets, and that he was one of those prophets. In Medina, the audience for Muhammad's message expanded to include Jews who may have been waiting for the return of true prophecy but who—with only a few exceptions—rejected his claim to be a prophet. In this Hijazi context, there would have been little or no force to the claim that Muhammad was the *last* prophet.

Third, between the years 632 and 700 CE, Arab-Muslim armies defeated the Byzantines and Persians and conquered much of the Near East. In 661 the Umayyads took control of the rapidly expanding Islamic empire and moved its capital to Damascus, where 'God's Caliphs' ruled over a polity composed largely of Jews and Christians who were waiting for the return of true prophecy. The hegemonic claim to be the custodians of God's final message to mankind makes better sense in Umayyad Damascus between the years 661 and 700 than it does in Mecca or Medina between the years 610 and 632.

The Redaction of the Quran

Recent scholarship has suggested that the consonantal skeleton of the Quran remained open and fluid for three-quarters of a century between the death of the prophet in 11/632 and that of the caliph ʿAbd al-Malik in 86/705 (see Déroche 2009). As the text was being compiled, edited, and redacted, problems were identified and solved and mistakes were made and corrected. There is good reason to believe that verses were added, revised, and/or removed from the text. The five-verse pericope that stretches from v. 36 to v. 40 of *Sūrat al-Aḥzāb* may have been one such addition to the text of the Quran (Powers 2009: 71).

The early community of believers is reported to have experimented with the formulation and placement of the quranic reference to the finality of prophecy. In the standard version of Q. 61: 6, it will be recalled, Jesus confirms the message of the Torah and anticipates the appearance of a more praiseworthy messenger—understood by Muslim exegetes as a reference to Muhammad: 'I am God's messenger to you, confirming the Torah that was before me, and giving you good tidings of a messenger who will come after me, whose name will be more praiseworthy (*aḥmad*).' A substantially different version of this verse is said to have been preserved in the codex of the Companion Ubayy b. Kaʿb (d. between 19/640 and 35/656): 'I am God's messenger to you, bringing you an announcement of a prophet whose community will be the last one among the communities (*ākhir al-umam*), and by means of whom God seals the messages and prophets (*yakhtum allāh bihi al-anbiyāʾ wa'l-rusul*)' (Jeffery 1937: 170). Here God seals or confirms the messages of earlier prophets by sending a new prophet whose community will be the last community to receive a divine revelation. One wonders about the relationship between Ubayy's version of Q. 61: 6—which is not found in the standard version of the Quran—and Q. 33: 40.

In addition to the first and second redaction projects sponsored by Abū Bakr and ʿUthmān, respectively, the Quran is said to have been redacted for a third time during the caliphate of ʿAbd al-Malik b. Marwān (r. 65–86/685–705), who reportedly took a personal interest in the text of the Quran and instructed his adviser al-Ḥajjāj b. Yūsuf (d. 95/714) to revise it. Al-Ḥajjāj is said to have changed the consonantal skeleton of eleven words, established the canonical order of verses and chapters, and introduced for the first time vowels and diacritical marks. He is also reported to have resolved certain unidentified disagreements over the consonantal skeleton of the Quran by removing several verses. Copies of the newly revised text were sent to Egypt, Syria, Medina, Mecca, Kufa, and Basra. As happened following the redaction sponsored by ʿUthmān, all non-conforming codices are said to have been recalled and destroyed.

The redactional project undertaken by al-Ḥajjāj at the request of ʿAbd al-Malik provides a reasonable historical context in which a five-verse pericope that provides a divine witness for the doctrine of the finality of prophecy might have been formulated. ʿAbd al-Malik certainly had the motive and opportunity to insert five carefully formulated verses into *Sūrat al-Aḥzāb*. Indeed, Islamic tradition remembers that massive editorial changes were made to this sura—albeit without providing any details about those changes. What is known—or reported—is that the chapter originally had 200 verses. One hundred and twenty-seven of these verses are said to have been removed, leaving seventy-three. One suspects that if 127 verses could be removed from the sura, five verses could have been added.

Two Options—In Lieu of a Conclusion

I have presented two different approaches to the religio-historical context in which the Islamic theological doctrine of the finality of prophecy was introduced.

The first approach is that of Islamic tradition, which teaches that the theological doctrine was introduced in 5/626–7 in connection with an episode involving the prophet Muhammad, his adopted son Zayd, and the latter's wife Zaynab bt. Jaḥsh. During the course of this episode, God is said to have intervened in history on four separate occasions: after Zaynab rejected a marriage proposal from Muhammad on behalf of his adopted son Zayd, God conveyed a revelation to his prophet in which he declared that Zaynab had no choice in the matter 'after it had been decided by God and His messenger'. This revelation would become v. 36 of *Sūrat al-Aḥzāb*. Not long thereafter, Muhammad himself fell in love with his daughter-in-law, whereupon God sent down a revelation in which he introduced a distinction between the former wife of a natural son and that of an adopted son. The purpose of this revelation was to facilitate Muhammad's marriage to Zaynab. This revelation would become v. 37 of *Sūrat al-Aḥzāb*. Shortly thereafter, God sent down a revelation in which he presumptively declared that Muhammad would die sonless and identified him as 'the seal of Prophets'. This revelation would become v. 40 of *Sūrat al-Aḥzāb*—and the sole Quran witness to the doctrine of the finality of prophecy. Finally, God sent down instructions that effectively abolished the institution of adoption. These instructions would become vv. 4–5 of *Sūrat al-Aḥzāb*.

Alternatively, we may view the doctrine of the finality of prophecy in the context of historical developments in the Near East in the second half of the first century AH: the Quran asserts that it confirms, corrects, and completes the divine revelations sent previously to the Jews and Christians. Following the death of the prophet and the conquest of the mountain arena, the new community of believers began to collect, edit, and compile the text that would become the Quran. This project was not finally completed until the reign of the fifth Umayyad caliph ʿAbd al-Malik, who ruled over a rapidly expanding empire composed largely of Jews and Christians, many of whom were waiting for the return of true prophecy. In an effort to quash this expectation, the caliph instructed al-Ḥajjāj to formulate the 'revelations' that would become vv. 36–40 of *Sūrat al-Aḥzāb* and to insert these new 'revelations' into the middle of the sura. By linking the doctrine of the finality of prophecy with Muhammad's sonlessness, the Muslim community transformed the earlier Jewish and Christian doctrine of the suspension of prophecy into the distinctive Islamic doctrine of the finality of prophecy.

Bibliography

Primary Sources

The Life of Muhammad: A Translation of Ibn Isḥāq's Sīrat Rasūl Allāh, trans. A. Guillaume. 1955. Oxford: Oxford University Press.

Mujāhid b. Jabr. 1410/1989. *Tafsīr*, ed. Muḥammad ʿAbd al-Salām Abū al-Nīl. Cairo: Dār al-Fikr al-Islāmī al-Ḥadītha.

Muqātil b. Sulaymān. 1424/2003. *Tafsīr*. ed. A. Farīd. 3 vols. Beirut: Dār al-Kutub al-ʿIlmiyya.

The Qurʾān, trans. A. Jones. 2007. Exeter. E. J. Gibb Memorial Trust.

al-Qurṭubī. 1387/1967. *al-Jāmiʿ li-aḥkām al-Qurʾān*, ed. ʿAbd al-Munʿim ʿAbd al-Maqṣūd. 20 vols. Cairo: Dār al-Kutub al-Miṣriyya.

al-Ṭabarī, Muḥammad b. Jarīr. 1954–68. *Jāmiʿ al-bayān ʿan taʾwīl āy al-Qurʾān*. 30 vols. in 12. 3rd edn. Cairo: Muṣṭafā al-Bābī al-Ḥalabī.

Secondary Sources

Alexander, P. S. 1995. '"A Sixtieth part of Prophecy": The Problem of Continuing Revelation in Judaism'. In J. Davies et al., eds, *Words Remembered, Texts Renewed: Essays in Honour of John F. A. Sawyer*. Sheffield: Sheffield Academic Press, 414–33.

Bijlefeld, W. A. 1969. 'A Prophet and More than a Prophet? Some Observations on the Qurʾanic Use of the Terms "Prophet" and "Apostle"'. *Muslim World* 59: 1–28.

Colpe, C. 1989. *Das Siegel der Propheten: Historische Beziehungen zwischen Judentum, Judenchristentum, Heidentum und frühem Islam*. Berlin: Institut Kirche und Judentum.

Cook, L. S. 2011. *On the Question of the 'Cessation of Prophecy' in Ancient Judaism*. Tübingen: Mohr Siebeck.

Déroche, F. 2009. *La Transmission écrite du Coran dans les débuts de l'islam: le codex Parisino-petropolitanus*. Leiden: Brill.

Evstatatiev, S. 2002. 'On the Perception of the *Khātam al-Nabiyyīn* Doctrine in Arabic Historical Thought: Confirmation or Finality'. In *Studies in Arabic and Islam: Proceedings of the 19th Congress: Halle, 1998*. Leuven: Peeters, 455–67.

Friedmann, Y. 1986. 'Finality of Prophethood in Sunnī Islam'. *Jerusalem Studies in Arabic and Islam* 7: 177–215.

Friedmann, Y. 1989. *Prophecy Continuous: Aspects of Aḥmadī Religious Thought and Its Medieval Background*. Berkeley: University of California Press.

Heschel, A. J. 1996. 'Prophetic Inspiration in the Middle Ages (Until the Time of Maimonides)'. In Heschel, *Prophetic Inspiration after the Prophets: Maimonides and Other Medieval Authorities*, ed. M. M. Faierstein. Hoboken, NJ: Ktav.

Jassen, A. P. 2007. *Mediating the Divine: Prophecy and Revelation in the Dead Sea Scrolls and Second Temple Judaism*. Leiden: Brill.

Jeffery, A. 1937. *Materials for the History of the Qurʾān*. Leiden: Brill.

Jeffery, A. 1952. *The Qurʾān as Scripture*. New York: Russell F. Moore.

Petersen, D. L. 2000. 'Defining Prophecy and Prophetic Literature.' In M. Nissinen, ed. *Prophecy in Its Ancient Near Eastern Context: Mesopotamian, Biblical, and Arabian Perspectives*. Atlanta: Society of Biblical Literature, 33–44.

Powers, D. S. 2009. *Muḥammad is Not the Father of Any of Your Men: The Making of the Last Prophet*. Philadelphia: University of Pennsylvania Press.

Powers, D. S. 2014. *Zayd*. Philadelphia: University of Pennsylvania Press.

Pregill, M. E. 2011. 'Ahab, Bar Kokhba, Muḥammad, and the Lying Spirit: Prophetic Discourse before and after the Rise of Islam'. In P. Townsend and M. Vidas, eds, *Revelation, Literature, and Community in Late Antiquity*. Tübingen: Mohr Siebeck.

Reeves, J. C. 2011. *Prolegomena to a History of Islamicate Manichaeism*. Sheffield: Equinox.

Simon, R. 1997. 'Mānī and Muḥammad'. *Jerusalem Studies in Arabic and Islam* 21: 118–41.

Stroumsa, G. 1986. '"Seal of the Prophets": The Nature of a Manichaean Metaphor'. *Jerusalem Studies in Arabic and Islam* 7: 61–74.

Waldman, M. R. 2012. *Prophecy and Power: Muhammad and the Qur'an in the Light of Comparison*. Sheffield: Equinox.

Watt, W. M. 1955. 'His name is Aḥmad'. *Muslim World* 43: 110–17.

Zwettler, M. 2010. 'A Mantic Manifesto: The Sūra of "The Poets" and the Qurʾānic Foundations of Prophetic Authority'. In J. L. Kugel, ed., *Poetry and Prophecy: The Beginnings of a Literary Tradition*. Ithaca, NY: Cornell University Press, 75–119.

CHAPTER 15

APOCALYPTICISM, MILLENARIANISM, AND MESSIANISM

LUTZ GREISIGER

Introduction: Endings and Beginnings

Apocalypticism is a deeply paradoxical phenomenon. What instantly comes to mind when hearing or reading of 'the apocalypse' is an imagery of the world ending in unprecedented disasters and destruction: the pre-eminent expression of collective angst. The fears aroused by these scenarios of doom notwithstanding, they are also an object of fascination and frequently even yearned for, promising a solution to inherent, seemingly irremediable problems of 'the world as we know it'. As Gershom Scholem made clear, apocalypticism is driven by a devastating critique of history and the present reality: 'If there is anything which, in the view of these seers, history deserves, it can only be to perish'—indeed a profoundly 'pessimistic' outlook (Scholem 1971: 10). Yet this characterization is just as correct as it is misleading.

To begin with there is plenty of evidence for another, pronouncedly 'optimistic' strand within the spectrum of the notoriously 'defeatist' millenarianisms that is closely related to—and, in fact, has partly inspired—the modern secular idea of progress (Amanat 2000: 248–55; Moorhead 2000; Williamson 2008; Ashcraft 2011). Indeed the hope for a *millennium*, an age of peace and bliss, as such does by no means refer to a state *beyond* history but to a pending, *intra*mundane and *intra*historical reality preceding 'the end'. Even the (non-millenarianist) apocalypticists' worldview, though it might be pessimistic towards history, is markedly confident in regard to the fate of humanity, or its chosen part, when this history will come to its well-deserved end: for them that will be the day of reward for their devotion and righteousness, under a *new heaven* and on a *new earth* (Isa. 65: 17; Rev. 21: 1; Q. 14: 48), in God's company. Apocalypticism does not simply announce 'the end' but the *completion* of history, the conciliation of contradictions, and an essentially better world to come.

The overall theme of the phenomena to be dealt with on the following pages is not pessimism, therefore, but rather hope, a *radical optimism*, the direct product of a profound discontent with the respective present conditions. It is this radical optimism that has acted, and continues to act, as the most efficacious ferment of the major and minor transitions in the course of the intertwined histories of the Abrahamic Religions. Albeit by no means an exclusive feature of these traditions (Landes 2011; Wessinger 2011) it is here that we find perhaps the most elaborate and ubiquitous manifestations of apocalyptic thought and the apocalyptic impulse.

Research

The modern academic study of apocalypticism has, for the largest part of its history, almost exclusively been the domain of Christian scholars. It had long led the humble existence of a rather outlandish, even suspicious, sub-discipline of biblical studies, before it finally began to attract considerable and growing attention during the second half of the last century (not least inspired by the findings of ancient manuscripts in Qumran and Nag Hammadi in the 1940s that contained hitherto unknown apocalyptic materials). As late as the beginning of the 1970s, Klaus Koch still felt compelled to call upon his colleagues to finally start paying due attention to this 'neglected area of biblical studies' (Koch 1972). But this reluctance continues making itself felt in other disciplines as well. A textbook example for the persistent aversion of many historians to acknowledge and examine apocalypticism as a major factor in social, political, and cultural developments is the tenacious conviction, repeated in countless publications, that the year 1000 CE had *not* caused any significant endtime expectations among Christians. It took more than a century until this misjudgement was corrected, and the unsurprising observation irrefutably substantiated, that the first turn of the millennium after Christ was indeed rife with apocalyptic, millenarian tension (Landes et al. 2003).

One of the milestones in the above-mentioned growth of apocalyptic studies was the great multi-disciplinary colloquium held in 1979 in Uppsala, on 'Apocalypticism in the Mediterranean and the Near East' (Hellholm 1983). Although its title determined no temporal restrictions to the subject area, it is significant that all the published papers were concerned with the 'classical' period of apocalyptic(ism) (*c.*200 BCE–200 CE), a state of affairs maintained at the follow-up convention in Anaheim, California, in 1989 (Collins and Charlesworth 1991). Despite the thematic breadth of both conferences—the ancient Greek, Mesopotamian, and Persian worlds were well covered—it is the Israelite, early Jewish, and early Christian developments that were at the focus of their interest. Medieval, modern, and Islamic themes remain out of view, and, still more serious, attempts at systematic comparative and/or transcultural studies are virtually absent (cf. McGinn 1998: 9–10). What motivates this scholarship, then, is rather evident: it is the recognition of the significance of apocalyptic(ism) for the complex historical shift that led from the Jewish tradition through the Jesus movement to early Christianity. This preoccupation finds perhaps its most radical expression in the famous provocative dictum of Ernst Käsemann (1969) that 'apocalyptic... was the mother of all Christian theology'.

For many of the scholars active in the field, furthermore, the problem of apocalyptic has been primarily one of literary genre and literary compositions, an approach, to be sure, that has not failed to evoke criticism. In studying these textual sources, it has frequently been demanded, one should make a clear distinction between form and content, between (textual) 'apocalypses' and 'apocalypticism' or 'apocalyptic eschatology', as well as apocalyptic movements (Koch 1972; Collins 1979: 3–4; Collins 1998: 2–14; McGinn 1998: 4–5, 10; cf. below). Political, sociological, psychological aspects of apocalypticism have, nonetheless, remained widely underappreciated.

While a wealth of scholarly literature concerned with early Jewish and early Christian apocalypticism(s) has been produced the number of publications devoted to the Islamic part of the field is—given the enormous significance of apocalyptic discourses and movements for its history—lamentably small. Even worse is the situation regarding the 'minor' Abrahamic traditions, as e.g. the Samaritan (Dexinger 1989) and Karaite (Walfish and Kizilov 2011: 491–3) ones; the numerous late antique Christian and para-Christian groups such as the Elchasaite (Jones 2004), Montanist (Daley 1991: 18–19, 34–7; Rankin 1995; Trevett 1996; Butler 2006), Donatist (Frend 1982) movements; the various Islamic currents or offshoots of mainstream Islamic traditions as the Ismāʿīliyya (Daftary 2007), Druze, Nuṣairiyya-ʿAlawiyya (Friedman 2010: 8–16, 235–8), the Bābi movement and the Bahāʾī religion (MacEoin 2009) or the Aḥmadiyya; and the modern Christian movements or traditions emerging from Christianity as the Latter Day Saints, or Mormons (Eliason 2001), the Adventist (Morgan 2001) and Rastafarian (Edmonds 2003) traditions—to name but a few. Just as none of the 'major' Abrahamic traditions is fully comprehensible, neither is any of these 'minor' ones, if the initial and often persisting apocalyptic impulses that shape them are not or not sufficiently regarded.

While, furthermore, discussions about 'apocalyptic origins' have broadly considered possible impacts of cultural traditions from the environments of early Judaism and Christianity on the emergence of apocalyptic(ism) (Hellholm 1983; Collins and Charlesworth 1991; Cohn 2001), questions of *mutual* influences of apocalyptic discourses in the history of different (either Abrahamic or non-Abrahamic) traditions, apart from a limited number of studies (e.g. Cook 2002; Cook 2005a; Cook 2005b; Voß 2011; Greisiger 2014), remain largely unaddressed.

Notably since the 1990s scholars, in particular from the United States, have engaged in a large-scale paradigm-shift by creating the interdiscipline of (the as yet uninstitutionalized[1]) *millennial studies*. Besides trying to make up for the above-mentioned

[1] An exception was the *Center for Millennial Studies* at Boston University, founded by Richard Landes in 1996 and defunct since 2003 (Landes 2011: xviii–xix; <http://www.mille.org>).

shortcomings of 'classical' apocalyptic studies, this endeavour aims at broadening the scope of research to an all-encompassing one, integrating phenomena from all kinds of religious traditions, geographical spaces, and historical periods as well as including modern secular currents, into one single approach to *millennialism* as a universal phenomenon. A major focus has been the sociological aspects of millennial movements, largely underexamined by previous scholarship (Robbins and Palmer 1997; Landes 2000; Landes 2011; Wessinger 2011).

Around the year 2000 the number of publications on apocalypticism and millennialism/millenarianism substantially increased, obviously an effect of the rising public interest in 'the millennium' and a corresponding demand for studies of the topic on the side of academic publishers. Apocalyptic and millennial studies owe a number of fundamental works to that boom, among them the *Encyclopedia of Millennialism and Millennial Movements*, edited by Richard Landes (2000), and the three-volume *Encyclopedia of Apocalypticism*, actually a handbook covering the whole field in more than forty articles, edited by John J. Collins, Bernard McGinn, and Stephen J. Stein (2000). In recent years this solid foundation for future research has been further expanded by two *Oxford Handbooks*, one on *Eschatology* (Walls 2007) and another on *Millennialism* (Wessinger 2011), evidence of the sustained academic interest in and growing awareness of the significance of apocalyptic and related studies.

The study of apocalypticism/millenarianism has had an impact on disciplines far beyond their own traditional boundaries. Field research among a millennial sect, conducted by a research group around social psychologist Leon Festinger in the 1950s, led to a full-fledged new theory when seeking to explain the surprising reaction of the sect's members to the failure to materialize of the prophecy around which their worldview was constructed. Instead of turning their back on their leader and her predictions in disillusionment, they began a large-scale proselytizing campaign in order to convince as many others of the truth of that prophecy, thus evading the obvious refutation of their belief by reality. Since Festinger's and his colleagues' work the theory of *cognitive dissonance* that resulted from their analysis has become a much-used tool in psychological and sociological studies (Stone 2000).

The generalized approach of millennial studies has advanced the field of research considerably, while its tendency to conceive millennialism as an anthropological constant might involve the danger of levelling out parts of the field's phenomenal diversity. In doing so it tends to blur or ignore the analytical achievements of classical apocalyptic studies. When dealing with Abrahamic apocalypticism, scholars of millennial studies at times indeed slot these all too casually into their own new analytical grid—by, for instance, declaring 'apocalypticism' as simply 'synonymous with "catastrophic millennialism"' (Wessinger 2011: 717; cf. Stein 2002: 211). Abrahamic apocalyptic scenarios, however, do not inevitably involve an imminent catastrophic disruption but frequently conceive of redemption as a process—which in this framework is categorized as 'progressive millennialism' regardless of the notion of millennium involved, if any (Wessinger 2011: 721). In any case, the structural, comparative approach of millennial studies, illuminating though its result may be, will certainly not render the study of *historically* related traditions as the Abrahamic ones, and their common features grown out of these historic relations, irrelevant.

Recent research on Abrahamic apocalypticism has been increasingly focused on its counter-propagandistic role in political opposition to the powers that be (Horsley 2004; Bockmuehl and Paget 2009; Greisiger 2014). At the same time the long disregarded role apocalypticism has played from Muhammad on and continues to play in the Islamic world has started to attract due attention to, though it remains largely underrepresented within, the field. It is here, furthermore, that the close interplay of apocalyptic and political discourses and movements—including their frequent violent excesses—in the Abrahamic traditions become most apparent (Amanat 2000; Arjomand 2002; Cook 2005c; Amanat 2009; D. Cook 2011; Filiu 2011; Landes 2011: 421–66; Shoemaker 2012: 118–96). A more comparative-systematic research on the varieties of Abrahamic apocalypticism will doubtlessly shed new light also on the proneness to political radicalism and violence so often associated with them generally and with their Islamic manifestations in particular. It may not be too audacious to predict that such a research will lead to the realization that all Abrahamic apocalypticisms have much in common in terms of their inner structures and dynamics as well as in their effects on the surrounding societies.

All in all the study of Abrahamic apocalypticism presents itself as a remarkably imbalanced field of research, and any attempt to substantially amend this state of affairs within the limits of the present essay would be condemned to failure. It may, however, give a tentative outline of a field of study yet to be established, defined, and developed.

Terms, Types, and Features

Apocalypticism is commonly seen as a specific variety of eschatology. The generic term *eschatology*, derived from the Greek *eschata* (sg. *eschaton*), 'last things' and *logia*, 'talk', 'order', is used to refer to (1) 'last things' at and beyond the end of the individual's life—death, resurrection and the verdict over one's soul at the final judgement, and to (2) collective, universal 'last things', catastrophes at the final stage of history, one or a sequence of decisive battles between the forces of good and evil, the resurrection of the dead, judgement, the destruction of this imperfect and its replacement by a perfect world under God's rule. For the sake of a maximum of clarity the present chapter will make use of the differentiation between *eschatological*, as signifying the talk, perceptions, and doctrines about 'last things', and *eschatic*, when referring to those 'last things' proper.[2]

[2] The term seems to have come into use only recently, particularly in the works of German theologians; see e.g. Herms 2003: 147; Härle 1995: 605 n. 8; Wolter 2009: 12 n. 8 (relating these terms to similar ones, such as *pneumatic/pneumatological* and *ontic/ontological*).

The closely interrelated phenomena labelled as *apocalypticism*, *messianism*, and *millenarianism/millennialism* in their essence all fall under the category of collective or universal eschatology. All three terms bear the unmistakable mark of one and a half centuries of western, predominantly Christian scholarship. *Apocalyptic* and *apocalypticism* are derived from the last book of the New Testament, the Revelation (*apokalypsis*) of St John which originally served as the prototype and 'reference work' for a great number of—mostly extra-canonical—Jewish and Christian writings.[3] *Messianism* is a term derived from *messias*, the Graecicized form of the Aramaic *meshīḥā* (*mashiaḥ* in Hebrew), 'anointed one', 'messiah', whose Greek translation, *christos*, furthermore is the origin of the English *Christ*. Finally *millenarianism* and *millennialism* (with all their spelling variants), from the Latin *mille anni*, 'a thousand years', and the synonymous *chiliasm*, from the Greek *chilia [chronia]*, 'a thousand [years]', all refer, again, to the Book of Revelation where there is revealed to the seer the coming of a thousand years, a *millennium*, of the binding of Satan and of peace and prosperity for the chosen part of humankind (Rev. 20: 1–3). Despite this Christian bias and in the (current) absence of an alternative applicable to the Abrahamic traditions as a whole and exclusively, it is reasonable to stick to the terms' accepted usage, while defining them as precisely as possible.

First, it is advisable to distinguish between *apocalyptic* and *apocalypticism*, understanding by the latter term discourses around a set of basic assumptions about the universe and its history and future as well as social movements engaged in such discourses and (betimes) acting upon them, while using the former term when referring to literary expressions of these ideas composed and/or utilized by their proponents. *Apocalyptic*, as a noun, in this sense is not congruent with the (however defined) literary genre of *apocalypse(s)*—countless textual sources that address apocalyptic themes have little or nothing in common with 'classical' apocalypses (cf. e.g. Collins 1998: 264–8). The adjective *apocalyptic* may refer to all these aspects and therefore ought to be disambiguated in the respective context of usage. Finally, authors of apocalyptic texts (including orally transmitted ones), apocalypt*ists*, ought to be distinguished from apocalypt*icists*, actors in apocalyptic discourses and movements.

The systematic/comparative study of the field in the Abrahamic religions will do well to start the investigation from the analytical category of *apocalypticism*, in order not to mask out any manifestation in whatever sources (including non-literary ones), as well as covering all other aspects, cultural, social, psychological, etc. The very word points at a central feature all manifestations of apocalypticism share: they revolve around truths that God has *revealed*, often through some angelic intermediary, to an elect human

Bernard McGinn has proposed an equivalent distinction of *eschatology* and *apocalypticism* as the one 'between viewing the events of one's own time in the light of the End of history and seeing them as the last events themselves' (McGinn 1998: 4). To solely term presentist eschatology as *apocalypticism*, however, would inappropriately exclude countless cases of futurist views of the eschatic events from the field of apocalyptic thought.

[3] The term was first introduced by Lücke 1832.

recipient who, in turn, reveals these truths to an audience of believers. Hence the apocalyptist's message claims a validity close to that of the holy scriptures held by the tradition he or she stands in. Typically apocalyptic texts are ascribed to some dignitary of the past (*pseudepigraphy*, 'false ascription'), frequently the very founder of that tradition, the claim of whose authorship serves the actual apocalyptist as a pseudonymous guise and the source of authority and trustworthiness of his visions.

The content of this two-way revelation usually consists of eschatological and cosmological knowledge (in varying proportions) otherwise inaccessible to ordinary mortals (Rowland 1982; Collins 1996; Collins 1998). The two aspects are closely interconnected. While the eschatological dimension is obviously part of the spatiotemporal structure of the universe, the fact of the revelation of the world's setup is itself conceived of as a sign of the approaching eschatic events, indeed as already a part of these events (e.g. Dan. 12: 4; 1 Cor. 13–14; Rev. 22: 10). This revealed nature of the universe, often provided to the apocalyptist in the course of a visionary journey through the heavenly spheres (Himmelfarb 1993; Collins 1996; Shoemaker 2012: 239–40, 256–7), is marked by sharp—spatial, temporal, and ethical—dualisms: it consists of two distinguished yet closely interrelated realms, the heavenly one of the divine and angelic beings and, its mirror image as it were, the mundane world inhabited by us humans. In the present aeon this universe is also the arena of a continuous struggle between the forces of good and evil, in which every human, as well as every supernatural being, is partisan of either side. In the aeon to come the good forces will prevail; it is envisioned as reserved for the chosen part of humankind, usually including the righteous individuals from earlier generations who will have been raised from the dead, whereas all others, just like their metaphysical 'allies', Satan and his hosts, will be subject to perdition.

Frequently apocalypticists expect that future aeon of cosmic purity and perfection to come about only after a millennium-like interim period in which earthly conditions will already reach a near-to-ideal state. The terms *millenarianism* and *millennialism*, both derived from *millennium*, are commonly used synonymously (Landes 2000; Wessinger 2011: 4, 22, 720). Two different available words however allow for a terminological differentiation by connecting each with a distinct notion. *Millennialism* may be used in the universalized sense current within millennial studies, as referring to beliefs in a breakthrough to a time profoundly better than the present. In contrast, *millenarianism* and *millenarian* may be reserved for discourses involving a millennium in the narrower sense, a penultimate period of near perfection preceding the actual end of history, as it is so particularly widespread and specified in Abrahamic traditions. This usage would then render *millenarianism* a sub-category of *millennialism*. Finally, the adjective *millennial*, contextual clarification provided, may be employed in connection with both categories as referring to the respective eschatic period or new age.

The proponents of millenarianism may expect the catastrophic and/or revolutionary upheaval commonly associated with 'the apocalypse' to initiate either the millennial interim period or, otherwise, only the new aeon at the end of days. The two types resulting from this alternative have, in Christian Protestant apocalyptic discourses since the nineteenth century, been termed *premillenarianism* (Second Coming,

Resurrection, Final Judgement, etc. *preceding* the Millennium) and *postmillenarianism* (those events *following* the Millennium) (Landes 2000: 578–89; Moorhead 2000; Stein 2000; Hill 2001). Similar diverging ideas have been observed in Jewish contexts (Ravitzky 1996: 79–144; Morgenstern 2006) and may most likely be found in other Abrahamic traditions as well.

Yet apocalypticism does not necessarily involve a millennium or similar interim period. In many, perhaps even most cases apocalyptic scenarios envisage the final disruption to occur without delay: history will reach its end, the world will be consumed, the dead will be raised and brought before their judge to be cast into hell or enter the post-historic Paradise or Heaven (Moorhead 2000; Shoemaker 2012). This sub-type of apocalypticism may be termed *amillenarian(ist)* or go without any particular qualification. The term *amillenarianism* (or *amillennialism*) has sometimes been used in a rather narrow sense, as referring to the view held by certain Christians that the millennium had already commenced with the foundation of the church in a spiritual manner and is not to be expected as a material, future reality (Wessinger 2011: 716). The *a-* in *amillenarianism*, however, does not do more than express the absence of a millennium, and does not imply a particular line of reasoning to reach this view. The term therefore should be kept open for all apocalyptic scenarios that do not involve an intermediary period. Regarding the above-mentioned application it stands to reason to consider equating the millennium with the age of the church as a proper form of millenarianism without an *a-*. To differentiate this subcategory from the 'conventional' *futurist* millenarianism one may use the terms *praeterist* or *realized* millenarianism.

History, as envisioned by the apocalypticist, is marked by determinism and periodization: since eternity each and every event has been predestined in God's master plan and the unfolding of this plan discloses its pattern, bit by bit. Jewish and Christian traditions know of four successive empires that, over the course of history, rule the world—and prevent its redemption—a figure based on certain vision narratives in the biblical Book of Daniel (Dan. 2 and 7). The author of these narratives wished to see the fourth and last empire identified with the Seleucid kingdom of Hellenistic Syria, then, *c.*165 BCE, dominating his native Judaea, and sought to convince his audience of its imminent downfall which would make way for the messianic kingdom of the endtime. This apocalyptic pattern of 'reading history', however, survived the end of the Seleucids and the role of the fourth and last kingdom was inherited by the successor world power, the Roman Empire. This reinterpretation in turn was adopted by early Christians and, in the fourth century, survived another turn of the tide when that last empire became Christian. That its end would mark the end of history as a whole has remained a fundamental conviction of many Jews and Christians (as well as, occasionally, Muslims). In the absence of a 'real' Roman Empire different powers, as e.g. the Vatican or the European Union, have been 'appointed' to be its present manifestation. Besides this four-empires scheme, the course of history has frequently been divided into periods of seven (days, weeks, years, etc.), on the analogy of the creation week, most notably as comprising a succession of a total of seven millennia. The significance popularly ascribed to calendrical turns of millennia (and *centennia*, centuries) as in

1999/2000, and the 'apocalyptic angst' they arouse, has its roots in this historico-apocalyptic reckoning (Landes 1988; Irshai 2000; Cook 2002: 344–50; Landes et al. 2003; Cook 2005a: 41–6, 84–97).

Many apocalyptic scenarios involve the expectation of the appearance (or reappearance) of a human, or semi-human redeemer, a messiah who will lead the good forces in their final battle with the forces of evil, as a military commander or spiritual saviour, or both (Neusner et al. 1987; Daley 1991, s.v. *Christ, second coming of*; Frankel 1991; Saperstein 1992; Collins 1995; Horbury 1998; Goldish 2004; García-Arenal 2005; Tucker 2008; MacEoin 2009; Searcy 2011). *Messianism*, like millenarianism, is a special case of apocalypticism. The expectation of a millennium-like period and that of the coming of a messianic redeemer frequently (although not inevitably) occur together; according to the two types of millenarianism the messiah may be conceived as reigning over his eschatic empire or kingdom either in a quasi-political, or in spiritual fashion, seizing actual power at the beginning of the millennium or at its end, respectively (Ravitzky 1996; Landes 2000: 578–89; Morgenstern 2006). In any case the messiah acts as God's direct envoy on earth which lends his reign a theocratic legitimacy unattainable by any human rule.

Established religious communities generally adopt a conservative attitude towards reality. They are looking for the source of their adherents' spiritual welfare back in time, towards one or a chain of founding figures (Abraham/Ibrāhīm, Moses/Mūsā, Jesus/ʿĪsā, Muhammad, etc.), who are believed to have been in closer contact to the divine sphere than anyone now living would be ever worthy of being granted. Under these conditions, new revelations, the prerequisite of apocalyptic and millenarian impulses, are frequently presented as renewed deeper insights into long established truths (Matt. 5–7; Q. 2: 129–40), just as the eschatological future they project appears as the mirror image of a past Golden Age (Paradise, the reign of the kings David and Solomon, the Apostolic Age, the Rāshidūn caliphate or the caliphate as such, the moral order of the 'Righteous Ancestors [*al-Salaf al-Ṣāliḥ*]', etc.). Adherents of apocalyptic movements, despite the frequently revolutionary effects they spark off, conceive of God's agenda for their presence as directed not simply at a global renewal but equally at a restitution of that bygone Golden Age (Sharon 1983: 19–24; Cook 2005a: 126–30, 226–9). This 'reactionary utopianism' has in some contexts been termed *restorationism* (Brooke 1994; Casey and Foster 2011) or *primitivism* (Bozeman 1988) and is part of the inherent dialectic of apocalypticism (Landes 2011: 26–9, s.v. *Millennialism, restorative*).

Dynamics

Perhaps the most fundamental appeal that apocalypticism exerts on humans is that it presents them with a solution to the perpetual dilemma of theodicy, the question of how there can be one god, being both essentially benevolent and omnipotent, and still allowing for misery, repression, terror—in short: evil—to prevail in his creation. The apocalypticist has an impressively simple answer to this agonizing question: the seeming contradiction is not to be solved under present conditions, in a synchronical manner, but only in a diachronical perspective, where there will come a time when God will act (anew) as the almighty *and* gracious lord of the universe, when he will extirpate the forces of evil from the world and grant those chosen by virtue of their faith and righteousness a life of peace and abundance (Cohn 2001; Amanat and Bernhardsson 2002: 2; Landes 2011: 8, 12).

There is plenty of evidence from throughout the Abrahamic traditions for the decisive role apocalyptic expectations have played in movements, upheavals, and revolutions most historians are used to analysing in political terms. From the Bar-Kokhba Revolt (Schäfer 2003) through the ʿAbbāsid, Fāṭimid and Almohad Revolutions (Sharon 1983; Halm 1996; Arjomand 2002; García-Arenal 2005) to Savonarola (Weinstein 2011) and the Münster Rebellion (Williams 2000: 553–88): hopes for imminent salvation and revolutionary programmes frequently appear in indissoluble amalgams (Cohn 1970).

This political dimension, it has been argued, does not come by mere coincidence. Apocalypticism was long, largely under a Marxist paradigm, discussed as the expression of an awakening political consciousness, a proto-revolutionary reaction to real political and economic contradictions (Hobsbawm 1959; Hill 1972). More recently the model of *relative deprivation* has been applied to explain the socio-political and psychological dynamic of apocalypticism, arguing that actors in such movements feel that their access to economic and/or symbolic capital falls short of what they justifiably expect, and they therefore are inclined to resort to millennial hopes (Cook 1995: 35–46). On closer inspection, however, apocalyptic movements, while frequently finding adherents predominantly among the lower social strata, seem just as often to appeal to middle and upper class groups, indeed may be triggered by an experience of success and triumph, rather than decline and deprivation (Cook 1995; Ravitzky 1996; 2000; Horsley 2010).

Another factor in the dynamic of apocalyptic movements that has only recently found scholarly attention is the functioning of communicational processes, in particular of the rhetoric of apocalyptic argument and persuasion (O'Leary 1994). *Belief* in revelations about the true nature and imminent overturn of reality thus fades into the background and apocalyptic rhetoric turns out to be a means to communicate radical criticism of the present reality, a criticism that nevertheless tends to turn into the readiness to perceive one's present as the time of denouement, the separation of good and evil, when it is going to become clear, once and for all, who stands on the 'right side' of the divinely wrought great correction.

The dynamic of any apocalyptic discourse or movement is further informed by the interaction of the eager, dissident, revolutionary agitators or activists with their antagonists, the vindicators of the present order and opponents of any premature imminent expectation or attempts at (radical) reviews of the accepted tradition and authorities, let alone revolutionary actions—in the metaphorical typology of Richard Landes the conflict between apocalyptic 'roosters' and 'owls' (Landes 2011: 40–52). In fact apocalyptic traditions themselves often carry with them strong rejections of any attempt to know the date and time of the eschatic events' commencement (Matt. 24: 36; *b. Sanh* 97b; Q. 7: 187). Not only are ordinary humans prohibited from such prescience, they are also warned against all too readily putting their faith in self-proclaimed heralds of the imminent redemption (Matt. 7: 15–16, *y. Ta'an* 4: 5, 68d).

Many Abrahamic apocalyptic traditions, especially those involving the expectation of a messiah, envision the forces of evil in the eschatic struggle to be led by a counter-messianic figure, known, among other manifestations, as the *Antichrist* to Christians, as *Armilos* (*Armilus*) to Jews (from the early Middle Ages on), and as the *Dajjāl* to Muslims. Virtually all narratives about this anti-messiah depict him as a great seducer who, underhandedly enabled by Satan himself, makes the masses believe him to be the actual redeemer, thus rising to world leadership, whereupon he shows his true demonic face, starts a massive persecution of the resisting faithful, and finally is being confronted, vanquished, and killed by the true messiah. Defaming one's enemy as the anti-messiah or his henchmen has been a powerful propaganda weapon in countless religious conflicts to this day. In the context of apocalyptic movements it has been readily utilized by both 'roosters' and 'owls' (McGinn 2000; Brandes and Schmieder 2010; Delgado and Leppin 2011).

In fact, like any other discourses, apocalyptic ones are in their whole readily utilizable by quite different, even opposing factions: those dissatisfied with the socio-economic or political conditions they live in, or experiencing an incomplete process of emancipation or takeover, may draw on apocalyptic rhetoric or action in order to claim and achieve advancement of their cause through critique or overthrow of the prevailing order, the demise of which they see as God's firm resolution. Those on the other hand who are in control of this order frequently refer to apocalyptic arguments, warning their subjects or 'flock' of the menace of heresy, their possible loss of divine favour, the seizure of power by a satanic pseudo-messiah, and the horrors of the eschatic cataclysms. Conservatives at times even draw on apocalyptic scenarios projecting the imminent victory of their own cause, as the only one in accordance with God's will.

Once the apocalypticists enter *apocalyptic time*, a phenomenon occurring in great variety (Baumgarten 2000; Landes 2011, esp. 29–36), they experience reality in a radically different way: accepted interpretations of the world are no longer valid; established religious and secular authorities have become irrelevant; persisting, even aggravating evils are seen as but the 'birth pangs of redemption'; violence, including that committed by the awakened themselves, as part of the great concluding battle of the forces of good and evil, in which the former will soon prevail. A frequent consequence of this (anticipatory) experience of a radically different reality is a revolutionary attitude towards traditional conceptions and practices of holy or ceremonial law like the Torah or the *Sharī'a*. This *antinomianism* or *hypernomianism* may assume different shapes, from moderate reforms to radical, anarchic overthrow of any legal limitation to the free development of the divinely inspired members of the eschatic community (Scholem 1971: 78–141; Scholem 1973; Dunn 1990; Landes 2000, s.v.; Amanat and Bernhardsson 2002: 4–10; Wright 2005; Daftary 2007, s.v. *ibāḥa*; MacEoin 2009: 214–18, 645–57; Wolfson 2009: 161–99).

Themes like the problem of theodicy and its apocalyptic solution, the unfolding of God's plan in history and its anticipated completion, may frequently be approached as mere areas of scribal erudition and 'theoretical' contemplation. Above all, however, it is the sense of urgency that triggers the original impulse of any apocalyptic discourse or movement, the imminent expectation of a shift from the corrupt present aeon to a perfect future one. The readiness to accept and welcome all kinds of radical changes (considered a restoration of original purity or not) that arises from this expectancy acts as a catalyst of actual changes in religious, sociocultural, and political history. All apocalyptic literature, however much revision and redaction it might have undergone, originates in this impulse and, as a by-product as it were, is only later given its textual form: 'Writing is generally an owl's medium, a retrospective act, almost inherently hostile to apocalyptic discourse' (Landes 2011: 47).

Once a group of believers has entered apocalyptic time, even a 'failed prophecy' of the impending eschatic consummation, however obvious its non-materialization, may not dissuade them from their faith. In many cases it is for them more feasible to resort to adaptive strategies that allow for maintaining this state of consciousness than to return to 'normal time' (Stone 2000). The believers may thus establish an ideology of (partly) realized redemption and institutionalize a charismatic leadership and/or hierocracy to govern the community of the chosen and administer the salvific divine gifts among them. Since, however, this realized redemption, the source of authority and communal order, retains a provisional state and its full realization remains yet to be accomplished, institutions and authority, however developed and refined in the course of time, never reach a state of indisputability but may be, and frequently are, subject to opposition in the name of another, new, apocalyptic impulse, arising from the conviction that the anticipated concluding phase of the redemptive process is to begin *now*, at last. At this point the dynamic cycle of Apocalyptic movements and religious traditions rooted in them may start anew. Through this process many, if not all, Abrahamic religions, as well as the bulk of their subdenominations, have emerged, been formed, and evolved.

Endings and Beginnings in History

The prehistory of Abrahamic apocalypticism lies in a religious current of ancient Israel and early Judaism known as prophecy. Divination techniques were a widespread feature of the ancient Near Eastern cultures and the practitioners of these techniques, employed by either a temple or the royal court, soon formed a class of religious professionals. These prophets were acting as mouthpieces of the respective god or goddess, uttering the divine messages in human language. The more firmly this practice was established and institutionalized the stronger grew the actual power of prophets within the society: speaking in the name of a deity—usually in favour of the king and ruling class—they reached a position that also enabled them to justifiably criticize existing political and social conditions (Nissinen et al. 2003). In the ancient Israelite society this common phenomenon assumed a peculiar shape when, through the crucial period of the Judaean upper class's Babylonian exile (587–538/16 BCE) and subsequent re-establishment and reorganization in *Eretz Israel*, the Jewish religion evolved. In this process the prophets (Hebr. *nevi'im*) played a decisive role: they called upon their audience to act in accordance with (what they perceived as) the will of God in order to maintain the covenant between him and his chosen people, and warned of the impending withdrawal of the divine favour in times of human misconduct. After the catastrophe of 587 BCE, they announced the 'Day of the Lord', the recovery of God's grace, the renewal of the covenant, to become manifest in the return from exile, the reconstruction of the Temple, the destruction of Israel's enemies, and the formation of a society in harmony with the Torah of God, shaped by righteousness, social justice, and graciousness. It is with this propaganda that the prophets at one and the same stroke reinforced strict monotheism, 'solved' the problem of theodicy emerging with it, and set the tone for apocalyptic eschatology: wickedness is to be eradicated soon and the chosen ones are to experience unhindered outpouring of the divine grace in the near future (Koch 1983; Cook 1995; Collins 2000; Cohn 2001: 141–62; Gnuse 2011: 244–6).

During the Second Temple period (516 BCE–70 CE) the conviction gained prevalence among the Jews that prophecy had been the privilege of a bygone age and God would not speak to his people through select individuals anymore. Now the reappearance of prophets was to be expected only on the eve of and during the messianic age (S. L. Cook 2011). New prophecies thus would meet with public approval only if they either were credibly presented as rediscovered ones from earlier ages (pseudepigraphy) or if the audience was or could be convinced that the last days had actually arrived. It was exactly this latter idea that took root with those who joined the movement centred around the messiah Jesus of Nazareth (Rowland 2010), one of the most momentous apocalyptic movements in the history of the Abrahamic religions.

Throughout this history the potentially destabilizing eschatological claim implied in any proclamation of a renewed prophecy met suspicion and resistance on the side of the conservative elites, frequently leading to suppression, persecution, and hush-up, as in the second century Phrygian Christian-millenarianist movement known as Montanism (Rankin 1995; Trevett 1996; Butler 2006), in the Shabbatean, Jewish messianic movement of the seventeenth and eighteenth centuries (Scholem 1973; Liebes 1993: 92–113; Idel 1998: 183–211; Goldish 2004), or the successive Sheykhī, Bābī, and Bahā'ī movements of mid-nineteenth-century Persia (Sharon 2004; MacEoin 2009), to randomly pick but these three examples.

As is well known, the concept of prophethood is of central significance for Islam: Already the early followers of Muhammad put their faith in him as the (last) prophet (*nabī*) and messenger, or apostle (*rasūl*), of God. These concepts are part of the movement's inheritance from the religious environment, dominated as it was by Jewish, Christian, and closely related traditions (Donner 2010: 27–34, *passim*), against which it asserted itself by the very claim of renewed prophecy. The widespread apocalyptic expectancy and fluid religious situation among the inhabitants of the

Arabian peninsula at the time is further indicated by the number of contenders for the dignity of prophethood and political opponents of Muhammad his followers had to cope with—essentially a struggle for divinely appointed leadership of the eschatic congregation of the awakened (Donner 2010: 97–106; Shoemaker 2012).

Prophecy, historically preceding the emergence of apocalypticism, thus became—whether in the form of applying scriptural predictions to the respective present, circulating new pseudepigraphal prophecies, or of active public prophesying—an essential element and distinctive mark of apocalyptic discourses and movements.

Abrahamic apocalypticism in its earliest forms developed, as we have seen, during the exilic and early post-exilic periods within a multi-religious environment of Mesopotamian and, after the collapse of the Babylonian empire (539 BC), Persian (Zoroastrian) traditions. The question as to how much influence on the development of early Abrahamic apocalypticism may be attributed to these traditions (or, it should be added, the other way round) might never satisfactorily be answered, beyond generalizations such as: it is highly unlikely that neighbouring religious communities would not have shared a good deal of their respective concepts about the world and its future prospects. At any rate it is important to note that Abrahamic apocalypticism was not created *ex nihilo* but originated in a religiously diverse and sophisticated cultural environment (Clifford 2000; Hultgård 2000; Cohn 2001; Foster 2002; Kreyenbroek 2002; Gnuse 2011).

The political realization of the redemptive scenario the prophets had pictured, the return from exile to the Promised Land and the rebuilding of the Temple, failed to engender the utopian society of righteousness, justice, and the renewed covenant with God. In the eyes of many living in Second Temple Judaea their age was not only lacking the spirit of prophecy, the divine presence itself was absent from the newly erected Temple, along with the Ark of the Covenant and other essentials from King Solomon's shrine of old. As this perception of absence led to a localization of his abode in heaven, God's eschatic return, suspended to the (near) future, became a scenario of dramatic change, an irruption of the transcendent into this world. Furthermore, in the political realm the perceived deficiency of the present became manifest in another absence: that of the kings from the Davidic dynasty (Barker 1991: 133–77).

Thus, the return of the Glory of God to his earthly sanctuary to reside among his chosen people again and the coming of an anointed ruler from the descendants of King David became closely related eschatological motifs expressing the Jewish hopes for a restoration of their onetime statehood in covenant and communion with God, yet a restoration that would transcend any previous historical reality in material splendour and spiritual majesty. The Second Temple period evolved into a heyday of apocalypticism: pious Jewish sectarians communicated this message in vision narratives and prophecies, allegedly of heroes from Israel's glorious past, like the Babylonian Jewish courtier Daniel (Dan. 7–12), the primeval progenitor Enoch (Charlesworth 1983: 5–90), the prophets Ezekiel and Zephaniah (ibid.: 487–95, 497–516), Ezra the scribe (ibid.: 517–59), etc.

The expectation of the messiah (or, at times, of two or more messiahs) to establish his eschatic kingdom went rampant among lower and upper strata of the post-exilic

Jewish society (Neusner et al. 1987; VanderKam 2000), from the Qumran sect (Collins 1995; Martínez 2000) to the followers of Jesus of Nazareth. Announcing the 'kingdom of God'—as approaching and as in some sense having already arrived, predicting the destruction of the Herodian temple and its replacement by a new and perfect one (Matt. 24: 1–2, 26: 61; Mark 13: 1–2, 14: 58; Luke 21: 5–6; John 2: 19–20), and at his entry into Jerusalem being welcomed by the crowd as the 'Son of David . . . who comes in the name of the Lord' (Matt. 21: 9; Mark 11: 9; Luke 19: 38; John 12: 13), Jesus clearly was seen by his adherents as the awaited messiah who would reign in the eschatic age of divine grace, universal peace, and bliss. With his death on the cross (which caused a grave *cognitive dissonance* among them) they began preaching with renewed fervour that he had undoubtedly been the redeemer and had been taken up into heaven only to return at any moment in glory to complete the divine revolution. The more the Second Coming was delayed the further their speculations about Jesus's messianic ministry in past, present, and future, their ideas about the conditions of God's grace and the nature of his covenant, diverged from the traditional Jewish mindset. With Paul of Tarsus' mission among the Gentiles, although clearly meant to accomplish the old prophetic promise of a conversion of all mankind to faith in the God of Israel, mediated through his *christos*, the movement eventually turned into an entirely new religion (Dunn 1999; Allison 2000; de Boer 2000; Horbury 1998; Horsley 2000; Dunn 2006; Fredriksen 2010).

Jewish apocalyptic traditions were absorbed into the religious worlds of ancient Christian groups and much of the respective literature has survived only thanks to their being translated or adapted into and transmitted through eastern Christian languages and literatures (Charlesworth 1983; VanderKam and Adler 1996). Rabbinic Judaism largely ignored or depreciated apocalyptic traditions which had caused such a grave break-away and moreover, in the course of the two great uprisings against Roman domination, had proven to be a potentially deadly peril to the sheer survival of the Jewish community: the famous Jewish War (66–73 CE), that culminated in the destruction of the Jerusalem Temple and the revolt led by the aspirant for the messianic office, Shimʿon bar Kokhba (132–5 CE), in the wake of which Jews were banned from Jerusalem and the city destroyed and replaced by a pagan Roman garrison town. But also the Christian doctrines, in particular Roman-Byzantine orthodoxy, when it acquired, in the fourth century, the status of the official imperial religion, demanded an adjustment to the political realities irreconcilable with the apocalypticists' notorious recalcitrance. Had many early Christian millenarianists combined Jewish apocalyptic hopes for a restoration of the people, statehood, and cultic centre of Israel with Christian expectations of Christ's return and rise to world power (Heid 1993), the church fathers now tended to downplay the material, political, and collective dimension of the inherited apocalyptic outlook in favour of the spiritual, transcendental, and individual (Daley 1991).

The above-noted tendency within Second Temple Judaism towards radically transcendentalizing the conceptions of God and his abode, together with the traditional apocalyptists' cosmological speculations, gave rise to a mystical movement whose adherents strove to approach the godhead on its heavenly chariot-throne (*Merkava*) by ascending through its outer halls (*Hekhalot*), the spheres in between earth and heaven (Mach 2000). Thus these adepts abandoned the apocalyptic timeline and realized, as it were, the eschatic bliss of God's presence in the here and now through meditation and visions. Similarly close connections between mystic practices and apocalyptic discourses occur time and again in the history of the Abrahamic religions, from the 'ecstatic (or prophetic) Kabbalah' of Abraham Abulafia (1240–after 1291) and the Kabbalistic school of Isaac Luria (1534–72) and Hayim Vital (1543–1620) (Idel 1998; Dan 2002: 121–7, 203–12) through Joachim of Fiore (1135–1202) and the Joachite movement (Reeves 1993), to the recurrent impacts Sufi traditions and orders had on mahdist, messianic movements (García-Arenal 2005; Searcy 2011). If apocalypticism is 'a social mysticism' (Landes 2011: 13), mysticism may well be described as an individualist, ahistorical, presentist apocalypticism.

A widespread apocalyptic expectancy, similar to the one during the late Second Temple and early post-Temple periods, took hold of large parts of the population in the Near Eastern provinces of the Byzantine Empire and their surroundings during the first decades of the seventh century. Under the onslaught of the Sasanid-Persian armies (602–28) the fourth empire had begun to totter, which could not but raise messianic expectations among Jews and Christians. Some Jews even took messianic action, fought alongside the Persians against the Byzantines, and subsequently instituted a short-lived semi-autonomous regime in Jerusalem and attempted to re-establish the cultic centre on the Temple Mount (Donner 2010: 15–16; Greisiger 2014).

It was in the same period of renewed apocalyptic agitation that a new religious movement emerged among the inhabitants of the Arabian peninsula, initiated and led by the prophet Muhammad (*c.*570–632), which was to evolve into Islam and was—like any novel impulse in the history of the Abrahamic religions—pronouncedly apocalyptic: the Quran abounds in warnings of the approaching eschatic events, referred to as 'The Hour (*al-sāʿa*)', that would be accompanied by cosmic disasters and lead to the day when the earth would be profoundly transformed into or replaced by a new and refined one, all living creatures and angels would be destroyed, and instantly the dead would be resurrected—narratives enriched by numerous motifs from Jewish and Christian apocalyptic traditions, most notably the return of Jesus as a redeemer (Arjomand 2002: 112). With 'The Hour' at hand Muhammad's ministry was, in his and his followers' view, not to create a new religion but to restore the pure original faith of Abraham/Ibrāhīm to save as many people from damnation at the Final Judgement as possible. Initially not demanding that Jews and Christians abandon their respective faiths but striving to integrate them into an eschatic community of believers in the renewed truth underlying all three traditions (Cook 2005b; Donner 2010: 68–74; Shoemaker 2012: 118–218), the movement adopted an inclusivist attitude familiar to Jewish and Christian apocalyptic discourses and movements as well (cf. the above remarks on Paul).

The three successive civil wars (*fitan*, sg. *Fitna*; 656–61, 680–92, 744–50), themselves seen by many contemporaries as symptoms of the approaching end, 'signs of The Hour', are the context of the earliest appearances of the (primarily Shīʿite) concept of the Mahdī, the 'rightly guided' redeemer and restorer of the pure religion and just societal order, as well as similar, less commonly accepted redeemer figures (the Qaḥṭānī and Sufyānī), and gave birth to the two major Islamic traditions known as the Sunni and Shīʿī as well as to the first, Umayyad, dynasty of caliphs (661–750) (Arjomand 2002; D. Cook 2011). The interplay of apocalypticism and political developments is rarely as discernible in earlier periods but a comparison with more recent cases may demonstrate that this connection certainly is the rule, rather than the exception (Collins, McGinn, and Stein 2000: Vols. II and III; Wessinger 2011). *Ex eventu* prophecies, created *after the event* they purported to predict, during the early Islamic period frequently served as a media of political propaganda, providing a precedent for the analytical approach of apocalypticism as rhetoric (O'Leary 1994).

Conclusion

The apocalyptic outlooks of numerous contemporary religious currents throughout the Abrahamic worlds mostly escape the general and even the greater part of the academic public in 'the west'. In fact most of the groups and movements usually labelled religiously radical or fundamentalist, like the spectrum of jihadist groups (from the relatively moderate Muslim Brotherhood to al-Qaeda to the Islamic State/IS(IS)) (Cook 2005c; Landes 2011: 421–66), the Christian Evangelical and Charismatic movements (Boyer 1992; Kaplan 1997; Newport and Gribben 2006; Gribben 2011), or the Israeli Jewish settler movement (Ravitzky 1996: 79–144; Ravitzky 2000), see themselves as actors in an apocalyptic drama, either unfolding in our present or to be unleashed in the near future.

Besides the currently ever growing influence of these radical 'fringe' groups and their gradually blending into the respective sociocultural and religious 'mainstreams', what lends significance to the study of apocalypticism is its deep roots in the Abrahamic traditions at large, deep enough that they reach the very origins of these traditions and run along their entire history.

Writing the history of apocalypticism in the Abrahamic Religions would be tantamount to giving an account of their origins, inherent dynamics, their divergent and convergent developments, interrelations and conflicts, spanning a period of several millennia. The historical, integral, and systematic study of this vast field, just as much as it is a promising undertaking, remains largely a desideratum of the comparative study of religions.

References

Allison, D. 2000. 'The Eschatology of Jesus'. In Collins, McGinn, and Stein 2000, I. 267–302.

Amanat, A. 2000. 'The Resurgence of Apocalyptic in Modern Islam'. In Collins, McGinn and Stein 2000, III. 230–64.

Amanat, A. 2009. *Apocalyptic Islam and Iranian Shiʿism*. London: Tauris.
Amanat, A. and Bernhardsson, M., eds. 2002. *Imagining the End: Visions of Apocalypse from the Ancient Middle East to Modern America*. London: Tauris.
Arjomand, S. A. 2002. 'Millennialism and Revolution in Early Islamic History'. In Amanat and Bernhardsson 2002: 106–25.
Ashcraft, W. M. 2011. 'Progressive Millennialism'. In Wessinger 2011: 44–65.
Barker, M. 1991. *The Gate of Heaven: The History and Symbolism of the Temple in Jerusalem*. London: SPCK.
Baumgarten, A. I., ed. 2000. *Apocalyptic Time*. Leiden, Boston: Brill.
Bockmuehl, M. and Carleton Paget, J., eds. 2009. *Redemption and Resistance: The Messianic Hopes of Jews and Christians in Antiquity*. London: T&T Clark.
de Boer, M. C. 2000. 'Paul and Apocalyptic Eschatology'. In Collins, McGinn, and Stein 2000: 345–83.
Boyer, P. S. 1992. *When Time Shall Be No More: Prophecy Belief in Modern American Culture*. Cambridge, MA: Harvard University Press.
Bozeman, T. D. 1988. *To Live Ancient Lives: The Primitivist Dimension in Puritanism*. Chapel Hill, NC: University of North Carolina Press.
Brandes, W. P. and Schmieder, F., eds. 2010. *Antichrist: Konstruktionen von Feindbildern*. Berlin: Akademie.
Brooke, J. L. 1994. *The Refiner's Fire: The Making of Mormon Cosmology, 1644–1844*. Cambridge: Cambridge University Press.
Butler, R. D. 2006. *The New Prophecy and 'New Visions': Evidence of Montanism in the Passion of Perpetua and Felicitas*. Washington, DC: Catholic University of America Press.
Casey, M. W. and Foster, D. A., eds. 2011. *The Stone-Campbell Movement: An International Religious Tradition*. Knoxville, TN: University of Tennessee Press.
Charlesworth, J. H., ed. 1983. *Old Testament Pseudepigrapha*. Vol. I: *Apocalyptic Literature and Testaments*. New York.
Clifford, R. J. 2000. 'The Roots of Apocalypticism in Near Eastern Myth'. In Collins, McGinn, and Stein 2000, I. 3–38.
Cohn, N. R. C. 1970. *The Pursuit of the Millennium: Revolutionary Millenarians and Mystical Anarchists of the Middle Ages*. London, New York: Oxford University Press.
Cohn, N. R. C. 2001. *Cosmos, Chaos, and the World to Come: The Ancient Roots of Apocalyptic Faith*. 2nd edn. New Haven, London: Yale University Press.
Collins, A. Y. 1996. *Cosmology and Eschatology in Jewish and Christian Apocalypticism*. Leiden, Boston: Brill.
Collins, J. J. 1979. *Apocalypse: The Morphology of a Genre*. Semeia 14. Missoula, MT: Scholars Press.
Collins, J. J. 1995. *The Scepter and the Star: Messianism in Light of the Dead Sea Scrolls*. Grand Rapids, MI: Eerdmans.
Collins, J. J. 1998. *The Apocalyptic Imagination: An Introduction to Jewish Apocalyptic Literature*. 2nd edn. Grand Rapids, MI: Eerdmans.
Collins, J. J. 2000. 'From Prophecy to Apocalypticism: The Expectation of the End'. In Collins, McGinn, and Stein 2000, I. 129–61.
Collins, J. J. and Charlesworth, J. H., eds. 1991. *Mysteries and Revelations: Apocalyptic Studies since the Uppsala Colloquium*. Sheffield: JSOT.
Collins, J. J., McGinn, B., and Stein, S. J., eds. 2000. *The Encyclopedia of Apocalypticism*, 3 vols. New York, London: Continuum.

Cook, D. 2002. *Studies in Muslim Apocalyptic*. Princeton: Darwin Press.
Cook, D. 2005a. *Contemporary Muslim Apocalyptic Literature*. Syracuse, NY: Syracuse University Press.
Cook, D. 2005b. 'The Beginnings of Islam as an Apocalyptic Movement'. In S. O'Leary and G. S. McGhee, eds, *War in Heaven, Heaven on Earth: Theories of the Apocalyptic*. London: Equinox, 79–94.
Cook, D. 2005c. *Understanding Jihad*. Berkeley, London: University of California Press.
Cook, D. 2011. 'Early Islamic and Classical Sunni and Shi'ite Apocalyptic Movements'. In Wessinger 2011: 267–83.
Cook, S. L. 1995. *Prophecy & Apocalypticism: The Postexilic Social Setting*. Minneapolis, MN: Fortress Press.
Cook, S. L. 2011. *On the Question of the 'Cessation of Prophecy' in Ancient Judaism*. Tübingen: Mohr Siebeck.
Daftary, F. 2007. *The Ismāʿīlīs: Their History and Doctrines*. 2nd edn. Cambridge: Cambridge University Press.
Daley, B. E. 1991. *The Hope of the Early Church: A Handbook of Patristic Eschatology*. Cambridge: Cambridge University Press.
Dan, J. 2002. *The Heart and the Fountain: An Anthology of Jewish Mystical Experiences*. Oxford, New York: Oxford University Press.
Day, J., ed. 2010. *Prophecy and the Prophets in Ancient Israel: Proceedings of the Oxford Old Testament Seminar*. New York: T&T Clark.
Delgado, M. and Leppin, V., eds. 2011. *Der Antichrist: Historische und Systematische Zugänge*. Fribourg, Stuttgart: Academic.
Dexinger, F. 1989. 'Samaritan Eschatology'. In A. D. Crown, ed., *The Samaritans*. Tübingen: Mohr Siebeck, 266–92.
Donner, F. M. 2010. *Muhammad and the Believers: At the Origins of Islam*. Cambridge, MA: Harvard University Press.
Dunn, J. D. G. 1990. *Jesus, Paul, and the Law: Studies in Mark and Galatians*. London: SPCK.
Dunn, J. D. G. 2006. *The Partings of the Ways between Christianity and Judaism and their Significance for the Character of Christianity*. London: SCM.
Dunn, J. D. G., ed. 1999. *Jews and Christians: The Parting of the Ways AD 70 to 135*. 2nd edn. Grand Rapids, MI, and Cambridge: Eerdmans.
Edmonds, E. B. 2003. *Rastafari: From Outcasts to Culture Bearers*. Oxford, New York: Oxford University Press.
Eliason, E. A, ed. 2001. *Mormons & Mormonism: An Introduction to an American World Religion*. Urbana, IL: University of Illinois Press.
Filiu, J.-P. 2011. *Apocalypse in Islam*. Berkeley: University of California Press.
Foster, B. R. 2002. 'Mesopotamia and the End of Time'. In Amanat and Bernhardsson 2002: 23–32.
Frankel, J., ed. 1991. *Jews and Messianism in the Modern Era: Metaphor and Meaning*. New York. Oxford: Oxford University Press.
Fredriksen, P. 2010. 'Judaizing the Nations: The Ritual Demands of Paul's Gospel'. *New Testament Studies* 56: 232–52.
Frend, W. H. C. 1982. 'The North African Cult of Martyrs: From Apocalyptic to Hero-Worship'. In T. Klauser and E. Dassmann, eds, *Jenseitsvorstellungen in Antike und Christentum: Gedenkschrift für Alfred Stuiber*. Münster: Aschendorff, 154–67.

Friedman, Y. 2010. *The Nuṣayrī-ʿAlawīs: An Introduction to the Religion, History and Identity of the Leading Minority in Syria*. Leiden, Boston: Brill.

García-Arenal, M. 2005. *Messianism and Puritanical Reform: Mahdīs of the Muslim West*. Leiden, Boston: Brill.

Gnuse, R. 2011. 'Ancient Near Eastern Millennialism'. In Wessinger 2011: 235–51.

Goldish, M. 2004. *The Sabbatean Prophets*. Cambridge, MA; London: Harvard University Press.

Greisiger, L. 2014. *Messias · Endkaiser · Antichrist: Politische Apokalyptik unter Juden und Christen des Nahen Ostens am Vorabend der arabischen Eroberung*. Wiesbaden: Harrassowitz.

Gribben, C. 2011. *Evangelical Millennialism in the Trans-Atlantic World, 1500–2000*. Basingstoke: Palgrave Macmillan.

Halm, H. 1996. *The Empire of the Mahdi: The Rise of the Fatimids*. Handbook of Oriental Studies, sect. 1: The Near and Middle East 26. Leiden: Brill.

Härle, W. 1995. *Dogmatik*. Berlin, New York: De Gruyter.

Heid, S. 1993. *Chiliasmus und Antichrist-Mythos: Eine frühchristliche Kontroverse um das Heilige Land*. Bonn: Borengässer.

Hellholm, D., ed. 1983. *Apocalypticism in the Mediterranean World and the Near East: Proceedings of the International Colloquium on Apocalypticism, Uppsala, August 12–17, 1979*. Tübingen: Mohr Siebeck.

Herms, E. 2003. 'Schleiermachers Eschatologie nach der zweiten Auflage der "Glaubenslehre"'. In *Menschsein im Werden: Studien zu Schleiermacher*. Tübingen: Mohr Siebeck.

Hill, C. 1972. *The World Turned Upside Down: Radical Ideas during the English Revolution*. London: Temple Smith.

Hill, C. E. 2001. *Regnum Caelorum: Patterns of Millennial Thought in Early Christianity*. 2nd edn. Grand Rapids, MI, and Cambridge: Eerdmans.

Himmelfarb, M. 1993. *Ascent to Heaven in Jewish and Christian Apocalypses*. New York, Oxford: Oxford University Press.

Hobsbawm, E. J. 1959. *Primitive Rebels: Studies in Archaic Forms of Social Movement in the 19th and 20th Centuries*. Manchester: Manchester University Press.

Horbury, W. 1998. *Jewish Messianism and the Cult of Christ*. London: SCM.

Horsley, R. A. 2000. 'The Kingdom of God and the Renewal of Israel: Synoptic Gospels, Jesus Movements, and Apocalypticism'. In Collins, McGinn, and Stein 2000: I. 303–44.

Horsley, R. A. 2004. *Hidden Transcripts and the Arts of Resistance: Applying the Work of James C. Scott to Jesus and Paul*. Leiden, Boston: Brill.

Horsley, R. A. 2010. *Revolt of the Scribes: Resistance and Apocalyptic Origins*. Minneapolis, MN: Fortress.

Hultgård, A. 2000. 'Persian Apocalypticism'. In Collins, McGinn, and Stein 2000; I. 39–83.

Idel, M. 1998. *Messianic Mystics*. New Haven, London: Yale University Press.

Irshai, O. 2000. 'Dating the Eschaton: Jewish and Christian Apocalyptic Calculations in Late Antiquity'. In Baumgarten 2000: 113–53.

Jones, F. S. 2004. 'The *Book of Elchasai* in its Relevance for Manichaean Institutions, with a Supplement: The *Book of Elchasai* Reconstructed and Translated'. *Aram* 16: 179–215.

Kaplan, J. 1997. *Radical Religion in America: Millenarian Movements from the Far Right to the Children of Noah*. Syracuse, NY: Syracuse University Press.

Käsemann, E. 1969. 'The Beginnings of Christian Theology'. *Journal for Theology and the Church* 6: *Apocalypticism*: 17–46.

Koch, K. 1972. *The Rediscovery of Apocalyptic: A Polemical Work on a Neglected Area of Biblical Studies and its Damaging Effects on Theology and Philosophy*. London: SCM.

Koch, K. 1983. *The Prophets: The Assyrian Period*. Philadelphia: Fortress.

Kreyenbroek, P. G. 2002. 'Millennialism and Eschatology in the Zoroastrian Tradition'. In Amanat and Bernhardsson 2002: 33–55.

Landes, R. A. 1988. 'Lest the Millennium be Fulfilled: Apocalyptic Expectations and the Pattern of Western Chronography 100–800'. In W. Verbeke et al., eds, *The Use and Abuse of Eschatology in the Middle Ages*. Leuven: Peeters, 137–211.

Landes, R. A. 2000. *Encyclopedia of Millennialism and Millennial Movements*. New York, London: Routledge.

Landes, R. A. 2011. *Heaven on Earth: The Varieties of the Millennial Experience*. Oxford: Oxford University Press.

Landes, R. A. et al., eds. 2003. *The Apocalyptic Year 1000: Religious Expectation and Social Change, 950–1050*. Oxford, New York: Oxford University Press.

Liebes, Y. 1993. *Studies in Jewish Myth and Jewish Messianism*. New York: State University of New York Press.

Lücke, F. 1832. *Commentar über die Schriften des Evangelisten Johannes*, pt. 4, Vol. I: *Versuch einer vollständigen Einleitung in die Offenbarung Johannis und die gesammte apokalyptische Litteratur*. Bonn: Eduard Weber.

MacEoin, D. M. 2009. *The Messiah of Shiraz: Studies in Early and Middle Babism*. Leiden: Brill.

McGinn, B. 1998. *Visions of the End: Apocalyptic Traditions in the Middle Ages*. 2nd edn. New York: Columbia University Press.

McGinn, B. 2000. *Antichrist: Two Thousand Years of the Human Fascination with Evil*. San Francisco: Harper.

Mach, M. 2000. 'From Apocalypticism to Early Jewish Mysticism?' In Collins, McGinn, and Stein 2000: I. 229–64.

Martínez, F. G. 2000. 'Apocalypticism in the Dead Sea Scrolls'. In Collins, McGinn, and Stein 2000: I. 162–92.

Moorhead, J. H. 2000. 'Apocalypticism in Mainstream Protestantism 1800 to the Present'. In Collins, McGinn, and Stein 2000: III. 72–107.

Morgan, D. 2001. *Adventism and the American Republic: The Public Involvement of a Major Apocalyptic Movement*. Knoxville, TN: University of Tennessee Press.

Morgenstern, A. 2006. *Hastening Redemption: Messianism and the Resettlement of the Land of Israel*. Oxford: Oxford University Press.

Neusner et al., eds. 1987. *Judaisms and their Messiahs at the Turn of the Christian Era*. Cambridge: Cambridge University Press.

Newport, K. G. C. and Gribben, C., eds. 2006. *Expecting the End: Millennialism in Social and Historical Context*. Waco, TX: Baylor University Press.

Nissinen, M. et al., eds. 2003. *Prophets and Prophecy in the Ancient Near East*. Atlanta: Society of Biblical Literature.

O'Leary, S. D. 1994. *Arguing the Apocalypse: A Theory of Millennial Rhetoric*. New York: Oxford University Press.

Rankin, D. 1995. *Tertullian and the Church*. Cambridge: Cambridge University Press.

Ravitzky, A. 1996. *Messianism, Zionism, and Jewish Religious Radicalism*. Chicago, London: University of Chicago Press.

Ravitzky, A. 2000. 'The Messianism of Success in Contemporary Judaism'. In Collins, McGinn, and Stein 2000: III. 204–29.

Reeves, M. 1993. *The Influence of Prophecy in the Later Middle Ages: A Study in Joachimism.* Notre Dame, IN: University of Notre Dame Press.
Robbins, T. and Palmer, S., eds. 1997. *Millennium, Messiahs, and Mayhem: Contemporary Apocalyptic Movements.* New York, London: Routledge.
Rowland, C. 1982. *The Open Heaven: A Study of Apocalyptic in Judaism and Early Christianity.* London: SPCK.
Rowland, C. 2010. 'Prophecy in the New Testament'. In Day 2010: 410–30.
Saperstein, M., ed. 1992. *Essential Papers on Messianic Movements and Personalities in Jewish History.* New York: New York University Press.
Schäfer, P., ed. 2003. *The Bar Kokhba War Reconsidered: New Perspectives on the Second Jewish Revolt against Rome.* Tübingen: Mohr Siebeck.
Scholem, G. 1971. *The Messianic Idea in Judaism and Other Essays on Jewish Spirituality.* New York: Schocken.
Scholem, G. 1973. *Sabbatai Ṣevi, the Mystical Messiah, 1626–1676.* Princeton, London: Princeton University Press.
Searcy, K. 2011. *The Formation of the Sudanese Mahdist State: Ceremony and Symbols of Authority, 1882–1898.* Leiden, Boston: Brill.
Sharon, M. 1983. *Black Banners from the East.* Vol. I: *The Establishment of the ʿAbbāsid State: Incubation of a Revolt.* Jerusalem: Magnes.
Sharon, M. 2004. *Studies in Modern Religions and Religious Movements and the Babi-Bahaʾi Faiths.* Leiden, Boston: Brill.
Shoemaker, S. J. 2012. *The Death of a Prophet: The End of Muhammad's Life and the Beginnings of Islam.* Philadelphia: University of Pennsylvania Press.
Stein, S. J. 2000. 'Apocalypticism Outside the Mainstream in the United States'. In Collins, McGinn, and Stein 2000: III. 108–39.
Stein, S. J. 2002. 'American Millennial Visions: Towards Construction of a New Architectonic of American Apocalypticism'. In Amanat and Bernhardsson 2002: 187–211.
Stone, J. R., ed. 2000. *Expecting Armageddon: Essential Readings in Failed Prophecy.* New York, London: Routledge.
Trevett, C. 1996. *Montanism: Gender, Authority and the New Prophecy.* Cambridge: Cambridge University Press.
Tucker, W. F. 2008. *Mahdis and Millenarians: Shīʿite Extremists in Early Muslim Iraq.* Cambridge: Cambridge University Press.
VanderKam, J. C. 2000. 'Messianism and Apocalypticism'. In Collins, McGinn, and Stein 2000: I. 193–228.
VanderKam, J. C. and Adler, W., eds. 1996. *The Jewish Apocalyptic Heritage in Early Christianity.* Assen: Van Gorcum.
Voß, R. 2011. *Umstrittene Erlöser: Politik, Ideologie und jüdisch-christlicher Messianismus in Deutschland, 1500–1600.* Göttingen: Vandenhoeck & Ruprecht.
Walfish, B. D. and Kizilov, M., eds. 2011. *Bibliographia Karaitica.* Leiden, Boston: Brill.
Walls, J. L., ed. 2007. *The Oxford Handbook of Eschatology.* Oxford, New York: Oxford University Press.
Weinstein, D. 2011. *Savonarola: The Rise and Fall of a Renaissance Prophet.* New Haven, London: Yale University Press.
Wessinger, C., ed. 2011. *The Oxford Handbook of Millennialism.* Oxford: Oxford University Press.
Williams, G. H. 2000. *The Radical Reformation.* 3rd edn. Kirksville, MO: Truman State University Press.

Williamson, A. H. 2008. *Apocalypse Then: Prophecy and the Making of the Modern World.* Westport, CT, London: Praeger.
Wolfson, E. R. 2009. *Open Secret: Postmessianic Messianism and the Mystical Revision of Menaḥem Mendel Schneerson.* New York: Columbia University Press.
Wolter, M. 2009. *Theologie und Ethos im frühen Christentum: Studien zu Jesus, Paulus und Lukas.* Tübingen: Mohr Siebeck.
Wright, N. T. 2005. *Paul in Fresh Perspective.* Minneapolis, MN: Fortress Press.

PART IV

RELIGIOUS THOUGHT

CHAPTER 16

THE ABRAHAMIC RELIGIONS AND THE CLASSICAL TRADITION

PETER E. PORMANN

WRITING about the classical tradition in the three Abrahamic religions of Judaism, Christianity, and Islam resembles writing about these religions themselves. All three have, at different times, come into close contact with the Graeco-Roman heritage. All three originate in the Fertile Crescent, a region of the world that became thoroughly Hellenized after the conquests of Alexander the Great in the late fourth century BCE. All three religions also endeavoured to find an accommodation with the surrounding Greek culture at different times. This is true for Judaism and Christianity in the first centuries CE, but it also applies to Islam, which actively engaged with the classical tradition during its formative period. Nor was the contact between the Abrahamic religions and Graeco-Roman thought limited to some initial period. Rather, theologians and thinkers belonging to the three confessions drew on Greek ideas again and again.

It is also important to stress from the outset that this fruitful encounter between Graeco-Roman and Abrahamic civilizations did not occur in isolation. The Septuagint, the Greek translation of the Hebrew Bible, for instance, was first produced for the Jewish community: it became a Jewish classic (de Lange 2013). Later, however, Christians so much appropriated it that many Jews grew less and less comfortable with using it and referring to it. Great Jewish thinkers of Greek expression such as Philo of Alexandria or Flavius Josephus also had a profound influence on Christian writers. Likewise, the Graeco-Arabic translation movement during the heyday of the Abbasid dynasty not only influenced Christians and Muslims, but also many Jewish thinkers, not least the great Maimonides (Mūsā ibn ʿUbayd Allāh, known in Hebrew as Rabbi Moshe ben Maimon, or Rambam; d. 1204). And Arabic-writing philosophers and physicians such as Avicenna and Averroes—both profoundly influenced by Greek thought—became core curriculum in the nascent European universities.

One of the defining features of the Abrahamic religions that ties them closely together is undoubtedly their constant recourse to the classical tradition. It is, therefore, difficult to do justice to this topic, as it is so vast. To tackle it here, I have decided to offer no more than a number of vignettes: I shall briefly discuss some salient examples that can illustrate the close links that the Abrahamic religions have both with each other and with the classical tradition. I shall first look at the strong relationship between early Christian theology, as expressed in the so-called apologetic literature, and Greek thought; here, the scholarship of Franz Overbeck will provide a guiding line. Then I shall turn to the concept of 'wisdom of Greek' or 'Greek wisdom' that we find mentioned in the Talmud and in later Jewish exegetical texts. Moreover, the seminal Graeco-Arabic translation movement of the ninth century will come under scrutiny. The figure of 'the philosopher of the Arabs', al-Kindī, in particular will illustrate how Muslims sought an accommodation between religion as revealed through the prophets and philosophical truths that can be attained through human intelligence. Next, the example (that we have already mentioned) of Maimonides will illustrate how much influence the translation movement exerted on later thinkers. But it will also show how the same philosophical and theological problems that were debated in late antiquity by Christians and Jews continued to interest thinkers from all three confessions in the Arabic and the Latin traditions of the Middle Ages. Finally, the examples of the Ottoman court and of the modern Arab world will illustrate that the engagement with the classical tradition continues until today.

Christian Apologetic Literature

> *οὐκ ἔνι Ἰουδαῖος οὐδὲ Ἕλλην, οὐκ ἔνι δοῦλος οὐδὲ ἐλεύθερος, οὐκ ἔνι ἄρσεν καὶ θῆλυ. πάντες γὰρ ὑμεῖς εἷς ἐστε ἐν Χριστῷ Ἰησοῦ.*
>
> There is neither Jew nor Greek, neither slave nor free, neither man nor woman. For you are all one in Jesus Christ.
>
> St Paul, Letter to the Galatians (3: 28)

The connection of Christianity to Greek culture is a particularly intimate one, as its foundation text, the New Testament, was written in Greek, namely in a variety of Greek known as *koinē* or 'common' Greek. This said, there have been some scholarly speculations whether certain parts of the New Testament such as St Matthew's Gospel were originally drafted in Aramaic. St Paul, whose theology as expressed in his letters had a crucial influence on the early community, mastered Greek to perfection; and he was himself a Roman citizen. One could approach the question of Christianity's relationship with the classical tradition from a thousand vantage points. In the following, I shall discuss the interpretation of one historian of the early church whose analysis is both astute and compelling. He is Franz Overbeck (1837–1905), who spent most of his career in Basel, where he befriended Friedrich Nietzsche. Within Overbeck's massive oeuvre, I shall focus on his works on patristic literature, written late in his life (Overbeck 1994–2010: Vol. III).

Overbeck saw the development of liberal theology during the nineteenth century with a very critical eye (Law 2012). Liberal theologians such as Adolf von Harnack (1851–1930) sought an accommodation between the modern society of their time and the Christian message. Overbeck thought that they fundamentally misunderstood the core Christian belief. According to him, the earliest Christians believed in the imminent second coming of Christ: the world was about to end, and they lived in the expectation of this event. With the world, history would come to an end as well. As St Paul stated in the opening quotation above, societal, ethnic, and gender differences became irrelevant in the face of Christ's message to repent and believe in the gospel. Yet, the world did not end, nor did Christ return. Rather, the fledgling community had to organize itself differently. Jesus had announced the immediate coming of the kingdom of Heaven, but, instead, the church arrived.

Christianity had to endeavour to find an accommodation in these circumstances and with the surrounding society. One might say that the doctrine of the coming of the Messiah was a core Jewish and Christian belief, only that the two differed in who the Messiah was. The early Christian community perpetuated the life of total abandonment in the expectation of doomsday through monasticism. For Overbeck, this was one strategy through which the church could survive in the new circumstances. The other main strategy was to defend Christian ideas by adapting them to a culturally Greek audience. This is the main feature of the so-called apologetic literature, of the writings of the early church fathers from the second century onwards. It is here that the influence of Greek thought on Christianity was felt particularly strongly.

In two works in particular, Overbeck argued that the writings of the early Christian community differ radically in form from the later apologetic literature; these works are the *About the Beginnings of Patristic Literature* (*Über die Anfänge der patristischen Literatur*), first published in 1882 (Overbeck 1994–2010: III. 33–90); and the *About the Beginnings of Church Historiography* (*Über die Anfänge der Kirchengeschichtsschreibung*), first published in 1892 (Overbeck 1994–2010: III. 113–202). Overbeck notes first of all that the different books and letters that make up the *New Testament* are not literary works, but rather historical documents. In other words, he uses the term 'literature (Literatur)' in a narrower sense than one would expect. The letters by St Paul, for instance, arise from concrete historical situations that often elude us today: they are letters, not literature. Likewise, the four Gospels are *sui generis*: they recount the life, death, and resurrection of Jesus, but not in a historiographical way. Finally, the Book of Revelation records John of Patmos' vision of the apocalypse. Even the Acts of the Apostles (Apostel*geschichte* in German) is a unique document rather than a literary or historiographical creation. For nobody writes gospels, revelations, or acts of the apostles in the later period under his own name. Later histories often begin with repeating or retelling events contained in Eusebius' *Ecclesiastical History*, but never with retelling the Acts of the Apostles. For

Overbeck, the pseudepigraphic literature has no relevance here, for the very reason that it contains later fabrications.

Therefore, the New Testament should not be regarded as literature; its form—a key term for Overbeck—is radically different from the early patristic literature that begins in the second century AD, with Irenaeus (d. *c.*200) being one of its earliest extant exponents. Overbeck defines this literature as 'Graeco-Roman literature which is confessionally Christian and pursues Christian interests (*griechisch römische Literatur christlichen Bekenntnisses und christlichen Interesses*)'. When Clement of Alexandria (d. *c.*215) or Eusebius of Caesarea (d. *c.*340) write their works defending Christianity, they write in Greek for a Greek-speaking and Greek-thinking audience. But more importantly, their works belong in their form (or genre, one might nowadays say) to Greek literature. Just as the early Christians differed radically in their beliefs from their later co-religionists, so the writings of the New Testament do not resemble in their form the writings of later apologetic authors.

Overbeck's analysis of how Christianity developed as a result of its engagement with Greek ideas emphasizes the differences between early Christian belief on the one hand, and Christian theology as it evolved from the second century onwards. In this, he differed radically from other Enlightenment and post-Enlightenment thinkers who were keen to point out the differences between the sacred tradition as represented by the Abrahamic traditions and secular science which they associated with Greek thought (I shall return to this point in the conclusions). Some of the same Enlightenment thinkers also wanted to construe an essential difference between Judaism and the classical tradition, but this endeavour, too, is fraught with problems, as we shall see.

Wisdom of Greek (*Ḥokhmat Yevanit*)

ואל תשיאך חכמת יונית אשר
אין לה פרי כי אם פרחים [. . .]
שמע דברי נבוניה נבוכים בנויים
על יסוד תהו וטיחים
ותשוב לך בלב ריקם ונעור
ופה מלא ברב שיגים ושיחים.

Let not wisdom of Greek (*ḥokhmat yevānīt*) carry you away
which produces no fruits but flowers
[. . .]
Listen to the confused words of those who understand it,
[words] built on a foundation of chaos and plaster;
it returns to you with a void and empty heart
and with a mouth full of abundant prater and babble.

Abū l-Ḥasan al-Lāwī (Judah Halevi, d. 1141)

The question of how religion and society should relate to Greek culture and thought did not only arise in Christianity, but also in Judaism. From the Middle Ages onwards, Jewish thinkers have often discussed this problem with reference to the concept of '*ḥokhmat yevanit* (wisdom of Greek)' or *ḥokhmah yevanit* (Greek wisdom). The exact meaning of this phrase was already disputed in the Talmud, where we find it in a number of places (see Jospe 2009, whose argument I largely follow here). There is, for instance, an account of the sack of Jerusalem under Pompey that was made possible by the treachery of 'an old man who knew the wisdom of Greek (זקן מכיר בחכמת יונית)', because he could communicate in this language. The passage ends with a malediction: 'Cursed be the person who raises pigs, and cursed be the man who teaches his son the wisdom of Greek (וארור האדם שילמד את בנו חכמת יונית).' In another passage, Rabbi Yishmaʿel is said to have responded to an eager student who had learnt the whole Torah by heart that he should only study the 'wisdom of Greek' 'at a time that belongs neither to the day nor to the night (בשעה שאינה לא מן היום ולא מן הלילה)'. This is an allusion to Jos. 1:8, 'but thou shalt meditate therein [sc. in the book of the law] day and night (והגית בו [ספר התורה] יומם ולילה)'.

These accounts raise two exegetical questions: what does 'wisdom of Greek' mean here; and was its study forbidden in the Talmud. Both these questions are actually addressed in the explanation of the first account about the sack of Jerusalem; there we find that one rabbi distinguished between Greek language (*lashon yevanit*) and 'wisdom of Greek'. The implication appears to be that Greek language is not forbidden; rather its use is rather necessary 'in the land of Israel'. And even learning wisdom of Greek and Greek hairstyles are acceptable in the case of someone who is 'close to the government (מפני שהוא קרוב למלכות)'. Moreover, the first story may only suggest that communication with the enemy in Greek is bad. Some exegetes such as Rashi and Maimonides therefore explained the expression 'wisdom of Greek' here as knowledge of a secret Greek cipher.

In the second passage, rabbi Yishmaʿel's injunction to study the wisdom of the Greek neither during the day nor during the night appears to be a simple *schêma katà merismón*: time is divided into day and night, and if you forbid to do something both during the day and during the night, you simply prohibit this activity at all times. But Rabbi Yishmaʿel clearly wants to put an over-ambitious student in his place. Therefore, his remark may well contain an amount of irony. In any case, the issue at hand here is the neglect of studying the Torah (*biṭul Torah*), not the study of Greek thought in general. Therefore Jospe (2009) follows Saul Lieberman in his conclusion that 'the study of Greek Wisdom is not forbidden *per se*' and that 'none of the early Rabbinic sources mentions the direct prohibition of the study of either the Greek language or Greek Wisdom' (Lieberman 1962: 100, 102).

Even in later times 'wisdom of Greek' can clearly be used in a pejorative way, as the opening quotation from the poem *Your words are fragrant like myrrh* by Judah Halevi shows. Judah (d. 1141) was an important intellectual and poet who lived in

Muslim Spain. In the quotation, he states that the wisdom of Greek bears no fruit, but resembles idle talk that only dazzles and confuses. Did he, however, reject Greek learning in general? Nothing could be further from the truth, as his Neoplatonic outlook shows. Rather, his criticism is aimed at certain Aristotelian philosophers who held the world to be eternal, and not created by God. In other words, 'wisdom of Greek' as a concept has a negative ring, but Judah uses it selectively: specific aspects of Greek doctrine are idle chatter, not all of Greek thought. Likewise, when one looks at the ample literature of so-called responsa (or Jewish legal opinions), one sees a nuanced picture. Even rabbis who have a rather sceptical attitude towards Greek philosophy do not quote the examples from the Talmud discussed above in support of an outright ban.

Some stories in the Jewish past such as the revolt of the Maccabees or that of Bar Kochba at Massada seem to tell a story of Jewish resistance against an occupying power and its culture. But obviously the relationship between Judaism and Greek thought is far more complex. We should not forget, for instance, that the Septuagint, the Greek translation of the Hebrew Bible, was first a Jewish classic (de Lange 2013), and many Jews thought and wrote in Greek first, the most prominent example being Philo of Alexandria. But even the uprising against the Romans in CE 66 is chronicled in Greek by Flavius Josephus (d. *c.*100 CE), and he is also one of our main sources for Jewish life in Palestine at that time. Therefore, it comes as no surprise that even the language of the Talmud is replete with words and expressions derived from Greek, including for some of its religious institutions. And the rejection of 'wisdom of Greek' in the Talmud cannot be interpreted as a Jewish orthodoxy pitched against Greek culture.

Here, a comparison with Islam and its alleged relationship to Greek culture is useful. The founder of Islamic Studies, Ignaz Goldziher (1850–1921), wrote a seminal article about 'the attitude of the old Islamic orthodoxy towards the ancient sciences (*Stellung der alten islamischen Orthdoxie zu den antiken Wissenschaften*)' (Goldziher 1916). In it, he argued that an 'old orthodoxy', represented by thinkers such as Ibn Ṭaymīya (d. 1328), was opposed to Greek learning; the 'new orthodoxy' of Goldziher's day, represented by the Ottoman religious establishment, had no such opposition. Sabra (1987), Gutas (1998: 166–75), and others rightly refuted Goldziher's idea. They basically argue that Goldziher quoted a few disparate opinions without putting them in their right context. Goldziher then extrapolated from these few quotations what the core belief—the essence—of the 'old orthodoxy' was, namely to reject Greek learning. In other words, he essentialized Islam, with little regard to the overwhelming amount of conflicting evidence. The discussion of 'wisdom of Greek (*ḥokhmat yevanit*)' teaches a similar lesson: statements against Greek learning should not be taken out of context in order to pitch religious orthodoxy against Greek philosophy. Both rabbinic Judaism and Islam emerged in a heavily Hellenized world, and both were profoundly marked by the Graeco-Arabic translation movement, as we shall see next.

Graeco-Arabic Translation Movement

وينبغي لنا أن لا نستحي من استحسان الحق واقتناء الحق من أين أتى، وإن أتى من الأجناس القاصية عنا والأمم المباينة، فإنه لا شيء أولى بطالب الحق من الحق.

We must not be ashamed to admire the truth or to acquire it, from wherever it comes. Even if it should come from far-flung nations and foreign peoples, there is for the student of truth nothing more important than the truth.

Ya'qūb al-Kindī (d. *c.*873; trans. Adamson and Pormann 2012: 12)

The age of the Graeco-Arabic Abbasid translation movement has rightly been compared by Dimitri Gutas (1998: 8) to Pericles' Athens and Renaissance Italy. This translation movement took place from the second half of the eighth to the first half of the tenth century CE. In its wake, most philosophical, medical, scientific, and mathematical texts available in late antique Alexandria were rendered from Greek into Arabic. But the translated texts also included some verse such as the so-called *Menander Sentences* (pithy sayings in iambic trimetres attributed to the New Comedy playwright Menander, such as 'whom the Gods love dies young') (Pormann 2014), as well as the Alexander Romance, a somewhat mythical account of Alexander the Great's exploits (Doufikar-Aerts 2010). This translation movement had a tremendous impact on the three Abrahamic religions, as it shaped not only the philosophical, but also the theological thinking of prominent Jews, Christians, and Muslims.

We can distinguish three main phases in this translation movement. During an earlier first phase in the late eighth and early ninth century, individual texts such as Galen's *On Simple Drugs* and Euclid's *Elements* were rendered into Arabic by Christian translators such as al-Biṭrīq (Ullmann 2002, Pormann 2011) and Ḥajjāj ibn Yūnus ibn Maṭar. Then the mid-ninth century (from the 820s to 870s) marks the heyday of the Graeco-Arabic translation movement, where two distinct groups of translators had the greatest impact, namely Ḥunayn ibn Isḥāq's workshop and al-Kindī's circle. Finally, some Aristotelian texts such as the *Poetics* were rendered into Arabic in the first half of the tenth century in the context of the Peripatetic school of Baghdad, where Christians such as Abū Bišr Mattā were active.

Both the circle of the Muslim al-Kindī and the workshop of the Christian Ḥunayn deserve further scrutiny, as they illustrate the importance of inter-confessional collaboration. Little is known about al-Kindī's life for certain, apart from the fact that he could trace his ancestry to good Arab stock, that he hailed from Baṣra, that he was affluent, and that he rose to prominence in the courts of the Abbasid caliphs (Adamson and Pormann 2012). He came into contact with Greek mathematical texts translated during the first phase, such as Euclid's *Elements*, and took a great interest in the geometrical method of proof (Endress 2003; Gutas 2003). This led him to employ his wealth to sponsor Christians to translate key philosophical texts into Arabic, the two most prominent being the so-called *Theology of Aristotle* and the *Book on the Pure Good*, the latter being known in the Latin West as the *Book on Causes* (*Liber de causis*) (Endress 1973; Zimmermann 1987, 1994). We do not know exactly how this process of translation came about, but the following scenario appears likely. The *Theology of Aristotle* is actually a paraphrastic rendering of Plotinus' *Enneads*, end of book four to beginning of book six. 'Paraphrastic' here means that the resulting text often deviates from the original not only in its language, but also its philosophical content (Adamson 2002). For instance, Aristotelian concepts absent from the original are introduced into the translation. Moreover, on the level of style, we find some decidedly quranic overtones (Adamson and Pormann 2012: xxiv–xxvii). It seems likely that the translator of the *Theology* was the Christian Ibn al-Nāʿima al-Ḥimṣī, and we know from one manuscript that al-Kindī 'improved (*iṣlāḥ*)' it. One can therefore only speculate whether it was al-Kindī who revised the style of the translation in such a way that it would appeal to his fellow Muslims.

To make Greek philosophy acceptable and appealing to his co-religionists was part of al-Kindī's intellectual programme, as we can also see from his philosophical writings. Two examples can illustrate this. In *On First Philosophy*, dealing mainly with metaphysics, al-Kindī insisted that truth is always the same, irrespective of who discovered it, and that one therefore should seek it out from wherever one can find it (see the opening quotation at the start of this section). And in his *Epistle on the Quantity of Aristotle's Books*, al-Kindī distinguishes between two types of knowledge: prophetic knowledge and what one might call human knowledge. Prophets such as Moses or Muhammad were divinely inspired and had direct access to the truth. Normal human beings, however, need to work a lot harder to discover it, and philosophy offers the prime means to do so. Importantly, however, the truth of revealed religion and of philosophy is the same; only the modes of accessing it are different.

We also have one philosophical treatise by al-Kindī in which he explains a passage from the Quran, and notably from the sūra *The Merciful* (*al-Raḥmān*), verse six, which runs: 'and the stars and the trees bow themselves' (trans. Arberry 2008: 557). But what does it mean for the stars and trees to bow (or prostrate) themselves before God? Citing classical poetry as witness (*shāhid*, pl. *shawāhid*), al-Kindī argues that prostration here means obedience. It makes no sense to interpret this verse literally, as the stars have no limbs which to bend. They obey God, the Almighty, in their souls, and serve as the proximate agent cause for generation and corruption in the sublunar world. To put this differently, anything that happens here on earth is caused by the movement of the stars. But they do not move in a whimsical fashion or according to their own will, but according to the decree of the Creator; he is the ultimate cause for everything. This example illustrates how al-Kindī reconciled the cosmology developed by Aristotle and Claudius Ptolemy with the holy writ. As al-Kindī stated at the beginning of his *Epistle on the Prostration of the Outermost Body* (§ I.2; Adamson and Pormann 2012: 175): 'Upon my life, what Muhammad the truthful (may the blessings of God be upon him) has said and transmitted from God (the exalted and mighty) may indeed be understood wholly through reasonable deductions...' Therefore, there is no contradiction between reason and revealed religion.

Al-Kindī's circle provides one instance in which a Muslim patron, in this case al-Kindī himself, commissioned Christians to translate Greek texts. Ḥunayn ibn Isḥāq's workshop represents another such instance. In Ḥunayn's case, we are particularly well informed about how he went about translating from Greek into Arabic as he gave a detailed account of these translations of Galen (Käs 2010 with further references). We know that high-ranking members of the Abbasid elite—such as the Banū Mūsā, three sons of a famous highwayman turned plutocrat—often commissioned the Arabic translations, and paid handsomely for them. Not infrequently, this process of translation went via a Syriac intermediary: for example, Ḥunayn may translate from Greek into Syriac and then hand the task to produce an Arabic version to one of his collaborators (Bhayro et al. 2012, Pormann 2012, Vagelpohl 2011, all with further references). When translating medical texts, Ḥunayn and his collaborators would also take the religious sensitivities of their audience into consideration. When confronted with various deities of the Greek pantheon, they sometimes replaced them with 'God (*Allāh*)' or similar expressions (Strohmaier 2012).

It is hard to overestimate the impact of the translation movement on the development of Judaism, Christianity, and Islam. For many of their chief theologians and thinkers were profoundly indebted to Greek thought in Arabic translation, as the example of Mūsā ibn ʿUbayd Allāh ibn Maymūn, better known as Maimonides (d. 1204) demonstrates.

Maimonides between Medicine and Speculative Theology

Maimonides illustrates like few others the importance of Greek thought for Arabic culture. He is equally famous for achievements in three areas: codifying Jewish law in his massive work *The Repetition of the Law* (*Mishneh Torah*), as well as dealing with other questions of practical theology, for instance, in so-called responsa (or legal opinions); contributing to theological and philosophical debates, notably in his *Guide for the Perplexed* (*Dalālat al-ḥāʾirīn*, known in Hebrew as *Moreh Nevochim*); and writing a large number of influential medical monographs and treatises. We have already seen that Maimonides solved the problem of 'knowledge of Greek wisdom' by interpreting this expression as referring to a Greek cipher which enabled treason during the siege (and ultimate sack) of Jerusalem. I shall not deal here with other aspects of his works of practical theology. But his medical works demonstrate that Maimonides could not have had any compunction about studying Greek texts in Arabic translation, as he frequently refers to previous Greek authorities such as Hippocrates and Galen. For instance, he wrote a commentary on the Hippocratic

Aphorisms (Joosse and Pormann 2012); and he wrote his own books of *Aphorisms*, in which he often quotes previous Greek medical authorities; in the last chapter, he lists his doubts about Galen explicitly, thus displaying the same critical attitude as many Arabic-speaking physicians such as Abū Bakr Muḥammad ibn Zakarīyā᾽ al-Rāzī (d. *c*.925). He also practised medicine, notably serving as court physician to the Ayyūbid rulers; his medical 'swan song', for instance, offers advice to Saladin's son al-Afḍal about melancholy and heavily draws on the Greek physician Rufus of Ephesus (Pormann 2008: 185–8).

His views about philosophy and speculative theology owe an equally great debt to the Greek tradition. We can illustrate this with the topic of anthropomorphism: God is described in the Bible and the Quran as having a number of attributes such as 'wrathful'; but we also find references to his extremities. In Genesis, man is even said to be created in God's image. This then begs the question of whether God looks like man, whether he has human traits, be they physical (hands, arms, etc.) or mental (wrathful, etc.). The question of God's attributes already occupied Greek thinkers, and it continues to be debated by the proponents, of Islamic speculative theology (*kalām*) and philosophy, as well as Maimonides (Belo 2007). The opening chapter of Maimonides' *Guide for the Perplexed* offers an interesting example. His starting point there is the Bible verse where God says: 'Let us make man in our image (*beẓalmenu*) after our likeness (*kidmutenu*) (נעשה אדם בצלמנו כדמותנו; Gen. 1: 26)'. Does this mean that God has hands and feet, is made of flesh and blood? Maimonides denies this by deploying a twofold argument. First, he talks about semantics. He specifies that the word for physical shape in the Bible is *to᾽ar*; therefore, when *ẓelem* (image) and *demut* (likeness) are used in this verse, it must mean something else: the comparison is figurative. Put in Aristotelian terms, they are homonyms (*ism muštarak*; ὁμώνυμον). For this usage, too, he adduces a number of examples, such as 'I am like (*damiti*) a pelican in the wilderness (דמיתי לקאת מדבר) (Ps. 102: 7).' The speaker does not compare his physical appearance to that of a pelican; rather what the two have in common is to be forlorn and sad.

Maimonides thus rejected the anthropomorphic interpretation of this verse in Genesis, chapter 1, and he then offers his own: man is created in God's image in the sense that he possesses 'intellectual understanding (*idrāk ʿaqlī*)', or, to put it differently, because the divine intellect is connected to man (*min ağli l-ʿaqli al-ilāhīyi l-muttaṣili bihī*). To be sure, Maimonides developed a much more sophisticated philosophical theology in his *Guide for the Perplexed*. In this, he partly drew on al-Fārābī's notion of the negative attributes, which itself has its origin in late antiquity (Belo 2007). But this initial example can show that Maimonides continues debates that originate in antiquity. To give just two examples: both the Jewish thinker Philo of Alexandria (*fl.* 1st century CE) and the Christian philosopher John Philoponus (*fl. c.*500 CE) already adhered to a similar interpretation to that put forward by Maimonides. In his *On the Creation of the World* (§ 69), Philo states that

> nobody should apply the likeness [between man and God] to the outline of the body. For God is not anthropomorphous, nor is the human body god-like. The

word likeness is used to apply to the intellect that rules the souls. (τὴν δ' ἐμφέρειαν μηδεὶς εἰκαζέτω σώματος χαρακτῆρι· οὔτε γὰρ ἀνθρωπόμορφος ὁ θεὸς οὔτε θεοειδὲς τὸ ἀνθρώπειον σῶμα. ἡ δὲ εἰκὼν λέλεκται κατὰ τὸν τῆς ψυχῆς ἡγεμόνα νοῦν·)

Likewise, in his *On the Creation of the World* (6.6; ed. Reichardt 1897: 239) Philoponus says that it would be laughable and ultimately impious to think that the words 'image' and 'likeness' used in this verse apply to the body.

In this way, the first chapter of the *Guide for the Perplexed* illustrates how debates begun in antiquity continued in the medieval Islamic and Jewish writings; and they were to have a lasting effect on medieval Christian theology as well. This engagement with Greek thought was only made possible through the Graeco-Arabic translation movement of the eighth to the tenth centuries. But translations from Greek into Arabic continued to be produced even in the early modern period.

Interest in Greek and Latin at the Ottoman Court

Mehmet the Conqueror (r. 1444–6, 1451–81) not only took the city of Constantinople, but also took an active interest in Greek history and literature (Raby 1983). For instance, when campaigning near Troy, he asked about the tomb of great heroes such as Achilles and Ajax, at least according to a contemporaneous Greek source. He also studied some Greek, as his schoolbook exercises show, although he did not become totally proficient in this language. But he did commission a number of Greek manuscripts which were produced in his scriptorium; among them we find Arrian's *Anabasis*, an account of Alexander the Great's exploits; and a copy of the *Iliad*, now in the National Library in Paris. That his interest in these matters was not superficial is shown by the fact that he had a number of texts translated from Greek into Arabic. His main focus here was theology, notably texts explaining the doctrine of the Trinity. Yet, he also commissioned translations of the Neoplatonic philosopher Pletho.

George Gemistus Pletho (*c.*1355–1452) formed part of the Byzantine intellectual elite that went to Italy in the build-up to the Ottoman conquest; another prominent example includes his student Basil Bessarion (1402–70), who was later to become cardinal. He took a strong interest in Platonic and Neoplatonic writings; Pletho and his pupil Bessarion inspired Marsilio Ficino (1433–99) to establish the Platonic academy in Renaissance Florence. Unlike Bessarion, Pletho appears to have adhered to certain polytheism; he wrote, for instance, a hymn to Zeus, perhaps inspired by the example of the Stoic philosopher Cleanthes. He also penned *The Laws* (*Nomoi*), as did Plato before him. He was particularly known for his criticism of the Aristotelianism that dominated much of philosophical discourse, especially in the wake of Averroes being translated into Latin. Mehmet had these works translated into Arabic, so that he could peruse them (Akasoy 2002). The references to the Greek pantheon are largely retained in these translations, and the resulting Arabic text must have felt at least somewhat odd to read for any monotheist. For instance, there are direct addresses to Zeus, who is called God (*ilāh*).

The interest in Greek extended beyond Mehmet the Conqueror (Gutas 1998: 173–5). But we also find Latin medical texts being translated on quite a significant scale at the Ottoman court in the seventeenth century. The chief physician Ibn Sallūm commissioned a number of Latin medical works to be translated into Arabic and Ottoman Turkish (Pormann 2013b: 65–71). In the wake of these translations, even key elements of Paracelsus' new chemical medicine became available in Arabic. As Paracelsus himself drew on Greek sources, especially in the alchemical tradition, we have here an instance of the classical tradition indirectly influencing Ottoman medicine.

The important point, however, remains that the interest in Greek (and to a lesser extant Latin) continued well into the Ottoman period. This is yet another proof, if additional evidence be needed, that the so-called Islamic religious orthodoxy did not oppose the interest in Greek learning. And this interest continued even in the modern period.

Classical Studies and Islam's Modernity

The Greek and Roman classics remained an important point of reference for Arabic and Islamic culture also in the modern period beginning with the so-called *nahḍa*, the cultural 'awakening' that took place from roughly the 1870s to the 1950s (Pormann 2006). In the following, I shall highlight some salient examples that illustrate the various ways in which Arabs engaged with the classical tradition in modern times, taking Egypt as the prime example, because of both its cultural and economic importance during this period.

The first major event that marks the beginning of an active engagement with Greek literature in Egypt was the publication of an Arabic verse translation of the *Iliad* by Sulaymān al-Bustānī (1856–1925) in 1904 (Pormann 2007). The translator wrote a long preface to his work, in which he compared ancient Greek with classical Arabic poetry. He emphasized the many parallels between the former and the latter poetic traditions, both characterized by a strong oral element. Al-Bustānī was particularly interested in the so-called Homeric question, which asked whether both the *Iliad* and the *Odyssey* were written by one author called Homer, or whether they are in fact compilations resulting from long processes of oral composition. Al-Bustānī's translation was celebrated lavishly, and his ideas influenced subsequent generations of Egyptian intellectuals.

The greatest Arab playwright, Tawfīq al-Ḥakīm (1898–1987), argued fervently for a renewal of Arabic literature through contact with the Graeco-Roman classics. In the preface to his *Oedipus, the King* (*Ūdīb al-Malik*, published in 1949), he noted that during the medieval Graeco-Arabic translation movement, mostly non-literary texts were rendered from Greek into Arabic. For Arabic literature to experience its own renaissance, it would be necessary to take Greek poetry, drama, and literature more generally as a source of inspiration, just as various European literatures did during their Renaissance. It is, however, important to adapt the classical subjects to the religious and cultural sensitivities of the audience. He did this in a number of plays, such as *Pygmalion* (based on Ovid's *Metamorphoses*), and *Praxa or the Problem of Government* (drawing on Aristophanes' *Assemblywomen* with its female protagonist Praxagora). In both the areas of drama and epic, later authors continue to engage with the Graeco-Roman heritage. This can be illustrated by two examples: two full Arabic prose translations of the *Iliad* appeared over the course of two years (namely in 2002 and 2004); and an adaptation of Aristophanes' *Lysistrata*, called *Women's Peace* (*Salām al-Nisā'*), by the Egyptian playwright Lenin al-Ramlī, was produced on the Cairene stage in protest against the US invasion of Iraq in 2003 (Pormann 2014b).

The study of Greek and Latin had no greater champion in Egypt than Ṭāhā Ḥusayn, perhaps the most famous Arab intellectual of the twentieth century and a highly influential thinker. Ḥusayn learned Greek and Latin in Paris, and became convinced that Egyptians would only be able to write their own history once they had mastered the two classical languages, because many of the sources for this history were written in them. In his seminal work *The Future of Culture in Egypt* (*Mustaqbal al-thaqāfa fī Miṣr*), he argued fervently that specialist state schools teaching Greek and Latin ought to be set up; and that Classics must become part and parcel of the university curriculum. He failed in the former endeavour, but succeeded in the latter: Classics is now a well-established discipline in most Egyptian universities, including al-Azhar, the oldest Muslim university.

But classical studies also led to religious controversies, as two famous examples can illustrate. In the academic year of 1925–6, Ṭāhā Ḥusayn lectured on the origins of pre-Islamic Arabic poetry. He applied the methods that he had studied in Paris, and notably the historical criticism famously associated with Theodor Mommsen. Using the concept of radical doubt inherited from René Descartes, Ḥusayn claimed that the pre-Islamic poetry was essentially a fabrication of later times. For the most part, the earliest sources for this poetry date from the eighth century, and Ḥusayn argued that the authors of the collections in which they are preserved invented the odes of pre-Islamic Arabia. This poetry is extremely famous, and schoolchildren still study it and learn parts of it by heart. For this reason, Ḥusayn's suggestion that it was a fake provoked scandal in cultural, but also in theological terms. For the Islamic exegetical tradition relied heavily on pre-Islamic poetry to interpret the meaning of the Quran. When a word or phrase is obscure or in need of explanation, the commentator would quote so-called 'witnesses (*shawāhid*)' to elucidate its meaning; the rationale underlying this technique is that the language of the Quran and that of pre-Islamic poetry are similar to each other; if, however, these quotations are made up, then a large part of traditional Quran exegesis becomes unreliable. Therefore, the religious establishment took a dim view of Ḥusayn's ideas and endeavoured to have him convicted as an apostate.

Ḥusayn also influenced the next generation of Arab intellectuals, among them Louis ʿAwaḍ (1915–90). The latter provoked similar outrage when he argued in the 1960s that much of the *Epistle of Forgiveness* (*Risālat al-Ghufrān*) by the celebrated littérateur al-Maʿarrī drew on Greek sources.

In both these controversies, Egyptian scholars applied to their own tradition academic techniques that they mostly learned in the West: Ḥusayn used the tools of historical criticism and ʿAwaḍ those of comparative literature and literary criticism. But classical scholarship had a far more profound influence on key beliefs about the Quran itself (Pormann 2013a). In the nineteenth century, the idea crystallized that one could reconstruct the exact words of classical authors such as Sophocles, Euripides, or Plato through textual criticism—what was sometimes called 'Lachmann's method' after the German classicist Karl Lachmann (1793–1851). This is a method that strives for univocity: the classical author wrote one authoritative text that the modern scholar endeavours to reconstruct by drawing on the extant manuscripts (Timpanaro 2005). Now, both Ṭāhā Ḥusayn, a champion of modernization and engagement with the Graeco-Roman past, and Ibn ʿUthaymīn (1929–2001), a traditionalist and Salafist cleric from Saudi Arabia, adhered to the same notion that the text of the Quran is univocal, and that it can be reconstructed in the same form in which it was revealed to the prophet Muhammad. In their own way, both Ḥusayn and Ibn ʿUthaymīn are modernist: they reject the notion of ambiguity, whether textual or in meaning. In this, they go against centuries of traditional quranic exegesis which celebrated the complex character of the Muslim holy writ (Bauer 2011). Ḥusayn is conscious of his debt to classical scholarship, whereas Ibn ʿUthaymīn never studied it directly. And yet, both their views about the status of the quranic text ultimately derive from modernity's preoccupation with univocity that was so important in nineteenth-century classical scholarship.

Conclusions

וַֽ֭יַּדְרִיכֵם בְּדֶ֣רֶךְ יְשָׁרָ֑ה

And he led them forth by the right way
Psalm 107: 7

καὶ ὅπου ἐγὼ ὑπάγω οἴδατε τὴν ὁδόν. Λέγει αὐτῷ Θωμᾶς· κύριε, οὐκ οἴδαμεν ποῦ ὑπάγεις· πῶς οἴδαμεν τὴν ὁδόν; λέγει αὐτῷ Ἰησοῦς· ἐγώ εἰμι ἡ ὁδὸς καὶ ἡ ἀλήθεια καὶ ἡ ζωή· οὐδεὶς ἔρχεται πρὸς τὸν πατέρα εἰ μὴ δι' ἐμοῦ.

And whither I go ye know, and the way ye know. Thomas saith unto him, Lord, we know not whither thou goest; and how can we know the way? Jesus saith unto him, I am the way, the truth, and the life: no man cometh unto the Father, but by me.
John 14: 4–6

اهدنا الصراط المستقيم
صراط الذين أنعمت عليهم
غير المغضب عليهم
ولا الضالين

Guide us on the straight path,
the path of those on whom you bestowed favours
not those against whom one is angry
nor those who go astray

This short series of vignettes on the links between the Abrahamic religions and the classical tradition could do little more than highlight a few examples illustrating the close ties between the two. All three religions are closely connected to each other and had constant recourse to the classical past, which served as a source of inspiration for countless generations of theologians, philosophers, and thinkers. Already in the three languages mostly associated with the three monotheistic religions, namely Hebrew, Latin, and Arabic, we can see the great influence of Greek. Hebrew is replete with words of Greek origin, and they include, as we have mentioned, major institutions of rabbinical Judaism. Latin, of course, is the language most closely related to Greek, and here, too, we find countless loan words. But even in Arabic, and notably in the language of the Quran, we find quite a number of words that have Greek (and even Latin) origins. The only noun that is mentioned twice in the opening sura of the Quran (al-Fātiḥa), apart from God (*Allāh*), is 'path', or *sirāṭ* in Arabic. But *sirāṭ* comes from Latin *strata*, in the sense of *uia strata* or 'paved way', whence English 'street' and German 'Straße'. This highlights that the contacts between the various cultures run much deeper than just the contacts that I have detailed above.

The same could also be said for a number of key concepts that the Greek tradition shares with the Abrahamic religions, such as that of the 'straight path', or the 'right way'. The opening quotations to this section show that it represents an idea that was expressed in the Hebrew Bible, the Greek New Testament, and the Arabic Quran. For instance, when 'doubting' Thomas is asked to follow Jesus in St John's Gospel, he is at a loss as to where to go (Most 2005: 64): he does not know 'the way', to which Jesus replies that he is the way. Furthermore, the Christian religion is often referred to in the New Testament simply as 'the Way (*hē hodós*)' (Strohmaier 2012: 184). Likewise there are more than two dozen places in the Hebrew Bible where the expression 'straight path (דרך ישר/ה)' or 'good path (דרך טוב/ה)' occur. And we have already mentioned that the word 'path' is the only noun mentioned twice in the opening sura (*Sūrat al-Fātiḥa*). And the notion of the right or straight path can already be found in antiquity, as the example Callimachus (*Aitia* 1 fr. 1, 25–9 ed. Pfeiffer) shows: he urges the reader to take the narrow, untrodden path.

Especially during the Enlightenment, there were a number of thinkers who denied the close ties between the classical tradition and the Abrahamic religions (see e.g. Leonard 2012). A famous example is Ernest Renan (1823–92), who emphasized the Semitic character of the Judaism, Christianity, and Islam, and saw them incapable of scientific thinking, anchored in the Greek tradition. But our discussion here demonstrates that Renan and his fellow Enlightenment thinkers were clearly wrong in emphasizing the divide between Greek thought and the three monotheistic religions. In fact Judaism, Christianity, and Islam owe their very character to an active engagement with the classical tradition, which constitutes an important part of their shared heritage.

Further Reading

The subject is vast, so I am just going to mention some recent books and articles that will allow the reader to delve deeper into this topic. Goodman (2007) and Leonard (2012) look at the relationship between Jews and the Graeco-Roman world at different ends of the chronological spectrum, and are quite different in their focus, but well worth reading for the breadth of the learning and the depth of their analysis. For an impression how the Greek tradition fundamentally shaped Arabic philosophical thought, see Adamson and Pormann (2012); the classical study remains Gutas 1998, and Pormann 2011 contains a lot of relevant material. Law (2012) offers a good way into Overbeck's perception of Christianity with further references to English literature. Finally, Pormann (2013a and 2013b) offers examples of the classical tradition continuing to exert its influence on the modern Arab world.

References

Adamson, P. 2002. *The Arabic Plotinus: A Philosophical Study of the 'Theology of Aristotle'* London: Duckworth.

Adamson, A. and Pormann, P. E. 2012. 'More than Heat and Light: Miskawayh's Epistle on Soul and Intellect'. In A. Shihadeh, ed., *On the Ontology of the Soul in Medieval Arabic Thought*, special issue of *The Muslim World* 102 (3–4): 478–524.

Akasoy, A. A. 2002. 'Plethons (1360–1452) *Nomoi*: Ein Beitrag zum Polytheismus in spätbyzantinischer Zeit und seiner Rezeption in der islamischen Welt'. *Mirabilia* 2002, available at <http://www.revistamirabilia.com/nova/images/numeros/02_2002/15.pdf> (accessed 26 March 2013).

Arberry, A. J. 2008. *The Koran Interpreted*. Oxford World's Classics. Oxford: Oxford University Press.

Bauer, T. 2011. *Die Kultur der Ambiguität: Eine andere Geschichte des Islam*. Berlin: Verlag Der Weltreligionen.

Belo, C. 2007. 'Muʿtazilites, al-Ashʿarī and Maimonides on Divine Attributes'. *Veritas* 52: 117–31.

Bhayro, S. et al. 2012. 'The Syriac Galen Palimpsest: Progress, Prospects and Problems'. *Journal of Semitic Studies* 58: 131–48.

de Lange, N. 2013. 'The Septuagint as a Jewish Classic'. In S. Humphreys and R. G. Wagner, eds, *Modernity's Classics*. Heidelberg: Springer, 143–63.

Doufikar-Aerts, F. 2010. *Alexander Magnus Arabicus: A Survey of the Alexander Tradition through Seven Centuries. From Pseudo-Callisthenes to Suri*. Leuven: Peeters.

Endress, G. 1973. *Proclus Arabus: Zwanzig Abschnitte aus der Institutio theologica in arabischer Übersetzung.* Beirut: Orient-Institut der Deutschen Morgenländischen Gesellschaft; In Kommission bei F. Steiner, Wiesbaden.

Endress, G. 2003. 'Mathematics and Philosophy in Medieval Islam'. In J. P. Hogendijk and A. I. Sabra, eds, *The Enterprise of Science in Islam.* Cambridge, MA: MIT Press, 121–76.

Goldziher, I. 1916. 'Stellung der alten islamischen Orthdoxie zu den antiken Wissenschaften'. *Abhandlungen der königlich-preussischen Akademie der Wissenschaften,* Jahrgang 1915, philosophisch-historische Klasse, no. 8. Berlin: Verlag der Akademie; English translation by M. L. Swartz, 'The Attitude of Orthodox Islam toward the "Ancient Sciences"'. In M. L. Swartz, *Studies on Islam.* Oxford: Oxford University Press, 185–215.

Goodman, M. 2007. *Rome and Jerusalem: The Clash of Ancient Civilizations.* London: Allen Lane.

Gutas, D. 1998. *Greek Thought, Arabic Culture: The Graeco-Arabic Translation Movement in Baghdad and Early 'Abbāsid Society (2nd–4th/8th–10th Centuries).* London: Routledge.

Gutas, D. 2003, 'Medical Theory and Scientific Method in the Age of Avicenna'. In D. C. Reisman, ed., *Before and After Avicenna: Proceedings of the First Conference of the Avicenna Study Group.* Leiden: Brill, 145–62.

Jospe, R. 2009. 'Jafet in Sems Zelten: Oder was die Talmudweisen und jüdischen Philosophen unter "Weisheit des Griechischen" (חכמת יונית) verstanden'. *Judaica* 65: 281–322.

Käs, F. 2010–11. 'Eine neue Handschrift von Hunain ibn Ishâqs Galenbibliographie'. *Zeitschrift für Geschichte der arabisch-islamischen Wissenschaften* 19: 135–93.

Law, D. R. 2012. 'Franz Overbeck: Kierkegaard and the Decay of Christianity'. In J. Stewart, ed., *Volume 10, Tome I: Kierkegaard's Influence on Theology—German Protestant Theology.* Farnham: Ashgate, 223–38.

Leonard, M. 2012. *Socrates and the Jews: Hellenism and Hebraism from Moses Mendelssohn to Sigmund Freud.* Chicago: Chicago University Press.

Lieberman, S. 1962. *Hellenism in Jewish Palestine; Studies in the Literary Transmission, Beliefs and Manners of Palestine in the I century B.C.E.-IV century C.E.* 2nd edn. New York: Jewish Theological Seminary of America.

Most, G. W. 2005. *Doubting Thomas.* Cambridge, MA: Harvard University Press.

Overbeck, F. 1994–2010. *Werke und Nachlaß.* 9 vols. Stuttgart: Metzler.

Pormann, P. E. 2006. 'The Arab "Cultural Awakening (*Nahḍa*)", 1870–1950, and the Classical Tradition'. *International Journal of the Classical Tradition* 13: 3–20.

Pormann, P. E. 2007. 'The Arabic Homer: An Untold Story'. *Classical and Modern Literature,* 27–44; reprinted in *Muqāranāt (Comparisons)* 3 (2010): 24–43.

Pormann, P. E. 2008. 'Melancholy in the Medieval World: The Christian, Jewish, and Muslim Traditions'. In P. E. Pormann, *Rufus of Ephesus: 'On Melancholy'.* Tübingen: Mohr Siebeck, 179–97.

Pormann, P. E. 2012. 'The Development of Translation Techniques from Greek into Syriac and Arabic: The Case of Galen's On the Faculties and Powers of Simple Drugs, Book Six'. In R. Hansberger, M. Afifi al-Akiti, and C. Burnett, eds, *Medieval Arabic Thought: Essays in Honour of Fritz Zimmermann.* London: Warburg Institute; Turin: Nino Aragno Editore, 143–62.

Pormann, P. E. 2013a. 'Classical Scholarship and Arab Modernity'. In S. Humphreys and R. Wagner, eds, *Modernity's Classics: Ruptures and Reconfigurations.* Springer: Heidelberg, 123–41.

Pormann, P. E. 2013b. *Mirror of Health: Medical Science during the Golden Age of Islam.* London: Royal College of Physicians.

Pormann, P. E. 2014. 'Arabs and Aristophanes, Menander among the Muslims: Greek Humour in the Medieval and Modern Middle East'. *International Journal of the Classical Tradition* 21: 1–29.

Pormann, P. E., ed. 2011. *Islamic Medical and Scientific Tradition.* 4 vols. Routledge: London.

Pormann, P. E. and Joosse, N. P. 2012. 'Commentaries on the Hippocratic Aphorisms in the Arabic Tradition'. In P. E. Pormann, ed., *Epidemics in Context.* Berlin: De Gruyter, 211–49.

Raby, J. 1983. 'Mehmed the Conqueror's Greek Scriptorium'. *Dumbarton Oaks Papers* 37: 15–34.

Reichardt, W., ed. 1897. Philoponus, *On the Creation of the World* (*De opificio mundi*). Leipzig: Teubner.

Sabra, A. I. 1987. 'The Appropriation and Subsequent Naturalization of Greek Science in Medieval Islam: A Preliminary Statement'. *History of Science* 25: 223–43.

Strohmaier, G. 2012. 'Galen the Pagan and Ḥunayn the Christian: Specific Transformations in the Commentaries on *Airs, Waters, Places* and the *Epidemics*'. In P. E. Pormann, ed., *Epidemics in Context: Greek Commentaries on Hippocrates in the Arabic Tradition.* Berlin: De Gruyter, 171–84.

Timpanaro, S. 2005. *The Genesis of Lachmann's Method*, trans. Glenn Most. Chicago: University of Chicago Press.

Ullmann, M. 2002. *Wörterbuch zu den griechisch-arabischen Übersetzungen des 9. Jahrhunderts.* Wiesbaden: Harrassowitz.

Vagelpohl, U. 2011. 'In the Translator's Workshop'. *Arabic Sciences and Philosophy* 21: 249–88.

Zimmermann, F. W. 1987. 'The Origins of the So-called Theology of Aristotle'. In J. Kraye, W. F. Ryan, and C. B. Schmitt, eds, *Pseudo-Aristotle in the Middle Ages: The Theology and other Texts.* London: Warburg Institute, 110–240.

Zimmermann, F. W. 1994. 'Proclus Arabus Rides Again'. *Arabic Sciences and Philosophy* 4: 9–51.

CHAPTER 17

CONFESSING MONOTHEISM IN ARABIC (*AT-TAWḤĪD*)

The One God of Abraham and his Apologists

SIDNEY H. GRIFFITH

I The 'Oneness' of The One God

Jews, Christians, and Muslims together make up the Abrahamic faith communities who have sought, each in their own distinctive ways, to claim the heritage of the biblical patriarch for themselves. While each community of believers has painted its own portrait of Abraham, usually in counterpoint to the other communities' visions of 'God's Friend', as each one is pleased to call him (Isa. 41: 8; Jas. 2: 13; Q. 4: 125; see Levenson 2012), they all agree that scripturally speaking the patriarch Abraham was the first monotheist. What is more, each community explicitly identifies the one God it worships in reference to the one God of Abraham, Isaac (and/or Ishmael), and Jacob (Exod. 3: 6; Matt. 22: 32; Q. 2: 133). But the confessional profile of the 'oneness' of the one God that Jews, Christians, and Muslims alike confess has some remarkably different features in each community's articulation of the reasonableness of their own confessional formulas. It is no wonder then that in the wake of the Quran's critique of the adequacy of the Jewish and Christian professions of monotheism (*at-tawḥīd*), that by the ninth century CE in the Islamicate world, when scholarship in all three communities was being conducted in Arabic, the topic of God's 'oneness' and its meaning came up for discussion. The learned men (*al-ʿulamāʾ*), philosophers (*al-falāsifah*), and religious apologists (*al-mutakallimūn*) of each community undertook the systematic defence in the Quran's own Arabic language of the scriptural warrants of their own community's distinctive creedal expressions of monotheism. And nowhere did this conversation reach the level of sophistication that it achieved in the scholarly milieu of Baghdad and environs in the time of such philosophically inclined intellectuals as Abū Yūsuf Yaʿqūb ibn Isḥāq al-Kindī (d. 870), Abū Naṣr Muḥammad al-Fārābī (870–950), Abū ZakariyyahYaḥyā ibn ʿAdī (893–974), and Saʿadia ha-Gaʾon ibn Yūsuf al-Fayyumī (882–942), to name only the most prominent of them. In their hands the theoretical discussion quickly turned to the question of what it means to affirm that anything at all can be said to be one, a topic to which the Muslim philosopher al-Fārābī devoted a separate treatise, as did his Christian student and successor as the head of the Baghdadī school of Aristotelians, Yaḥyā ibn ʿAdī.[1]

Following a brief recollection of the interreligious, intellectual milieu of Abbasid Baghdad and her environs in the ninth and tenth centuries CE, the present study looks first into the broad range of the conversations about God's 'oneness' in Islamicate religious discourse before turning more particularly to a brief discussion of the circumstances of the treatises by al-Fārābī and Yaḥyā ibn ʿAdī just mentioned, along with reflections on the topic in the works of several Jewish writers in the milieu, such as al-Muqammiṣ, Qirqisānī, and Saʿadia. The purpose is to show how it was that these several writers, Muslim, Christian, and Jewish, focused their considerable intellectual acumen on a problem that defined one of the major differences between their respective confessional communities, namely how logically to speak of the concept of the 'oneness' of the one God in such a way that the different nuances in the expression of the monotheism of the Jews, Christians, and Muslims might emerge clearly in the Arabic-speaking idiom of the interreligious colloquy initiated by the challenge of the Quran.

II Interreligious Philosophy in Tenth-Century Baghdad

By the early years of the ninth century, many of the intellectual leaders, the *ʿulamāʾ* of the Jews, Christians, and Muslims, had already gravitated to Baghdad and her environs making the Abbasid city the major hub of intellectual life and interreligious colloquy within the World of Islam. Once the geʾonim of the Jewish academies of Sura and Pumbedita and the patriarchs of the Christian church of the East had relocated to the city early in the century, it was not long before Muslim thinkers there and nearby, such as Abū Yūsuf Yaʿqūb ibn Isḥāq al-Kindī and Abū Bakr Muḥammad ibn Zakariyā ar-Rāzī (85–925) were doing philosophy in Arabic in dialogue with the translated texts of Aristotle, Plato, Galen, and their classical interpreters, and the Muslim theologians (*al-mutakallimūn*) were exploring discursive modes of speech in which they might systematically articulate Islamic belief and practice. The latter in particular were faced

[1] Abū Naṣr al-Fārābī, *Kitāb al-wāḥid wa l-waḥdah*, ed. Mahdi (1989); Yaḥyā ibn ʿAdī, *Maqālah fī t-tawḥīd*, edited in Samir (1980) and in Khalifat (1988: 375–406).

with discerning and marking out the critical differences between Islamic beliefs on the one hand, and the doctrines of the older monotheists on the other hand, to whose teachings they were often reacting in criticism of their adequacy. The way forward had been prepared for these intellectual undertakings by the Graeco-Arabic translation movement, under way in largely Christian hands, with the support of the caliphal establishment, since the second half of the eighth century (Gutas 1998). By the tenth century masters such as the Christian logician Abū Bishr Mattā ibn Yūnus (d. 940), the Jewish thinker Sa'adia ha-Ga'ōn ibn Yūsuf al-Fayyūmī (882–942), and the Muslim Abū Naṣr al-Fārābī (d. 950) 'the second master' after Aristotle had joined the conversations, to be followed in the next generation by the Christian Yaḥyā ibn 'Adī (893–974), al-Fārābī's student, who in due course became the leader of the Aristotelians in Baghdad in the third quarter of the tenth century, a group that was largely made up of Yaḥyā's circle of students and disciples, both Christian and Muslim (Kraemer 1986a; 1986b).

On the philosophical front, in addition to medicine, logic and other topics, and along with the defence of the religious claims of their own religious communities, all the Baghdad thinkers of the period, Jews, Christians, and Muslims alike, were interested in ethical, moral, and political issues, both private and public. These included concerns about how best to dispel sorrows and achieve happiness, how to instil virtues and extirpate vices, how to envision 'the perfect man' (*al-insān al-kāmil*) and lead the philosophical life, and, not least, how best society should be structured and under which legal system (*sharī'a*) it should be governed. Interestingly, it is in this latter context that one often finds references to interreligious concerns and to the imperative for the cultivation of 'humane values' (*al-insāniyyah*) in the relationships between communities, almost as if for these thinkers philosophy itself and the philosophical way of life could provide the only reasonable approach to inter-communal dialogue and social harmony.[2] Finally, there was also the question of right religion. The scholars of the period, Jews, Christians, and Muslims, were eager to make use of their late antique philosophical heritage to commend the veracity of their own religious traditions. The Christian translator and philosopher Ḥunayn ibn Isḥāq seems to have envisioned this inter-communal role for philosophy already in the ninth century, according to a passage in the *Kitāb ādāb al-falāsifah*, a text often attributed to him. The bulk of the work is a collection of sayings of Greek and Persian sages and ancient philosophers, transmitted from both ancient and seemingly contemporary, gnomological sources (Gutas 1975; Zakeri 2004). But the opening narrative is an interesting, if idiosyncratic, discursive sketch of the history of philosophy, in which Ḥunayn assimilates even religious thinking and ritual behaviour into the realm of the philosophical way of life, portraying synagogues, churches, and mosques as virtual schools of philosophy (see the fuller discussion in Griffith 2008b).

[2] In this connection, see Watt (2005; 2007). See also the earlier essays Allard (1962); Vajda (1962); Wasserstrom (1995).

III God-Talk in Arabic

The earliest Arabic-speaking Muslim philosophers were concerned, like their Jewish and Christian counterparts, to explore the philosophical dimensions of *at-tawḥīd*, confessing that God is one. It is significant in this connection that the discussion of 'oneness' (*al-waḥdāniyyah* or *al-waḥdah*) and its philosophical implications, in the light of Greek logic and metaphysics, was high on the list of the concerns of the first two Muslim philosophers whose names are still widely known, Abū Yūsuf Yaʿqūb ibn Isḥāq al-Kindī and Abū Naṣr al-Fārābī. Al-Kindī, for whom, in the words of Gerhard Endress, the cultivation of 'philosophy was to vindicate the pursuit of rational activity as an activity in the service of Islam' (Endress 1997: 50), spoke at some length in his treatise *On First Philosophy* about divine existence and 'oneness' (Marmura 2005: 337–53; Adamson 2003). And he also wrote a treatise specifically dedicated to laying out his logical objections to the Christian doctrine of the Trinity, precisely in terms of what he took to be its incompatibility with confessing the 'oneness' of God. His text now survives only in the quotations from it included by Yaḥyā ibn ʿAdī in his refutation of al-Kindī's objections (Périer 1920–1: 3–21).[3]

The philosopher al-Fārābī, Yaḥyā ibn ʿAdī's Muslim teacher, was also much interested in the philosophical implications of 'one' and 'oneness', as we mentioned above, and in fact it was in drawing on his deep knowledge of the Alexandrian philosophical and logical tradition that al-Fārābī wrote the book entitled *Kitāb al-wāḥid wa l-waḥdah*, a book on 'the one and one-ness' (Mahdi 1989). In it he discusses in some detail what one means when one says that something is 'one', very much, it would seem, with the Muslim doctrine of *at-tawḥīd* in mind. Then, in due course, with al-Fārābī's ideas very much in the background of his own thinking, Yaḥyā ibn ʿAdī wrote his own aforementioned, philosophically and logically attuned monograph, *Maqālah fī t-tawḥīd*,[4] in order systematically and positively to set out his reasoning in defence of the Christian doctrine of the Trinity, or the 'trebling of the "oneness" of God' (*tathlīth waḥdāniyyat Allāh*), as Yaḥyā put it.

The ground was prepared for these logical and philosophical discussions of the implications of the doctrine of *at-tawḥīd* by controversies that had arisen in the late eighth and early ninth centuries among Arabic-speaking Muslim theologians (*al-mutakallimūn*) on the one hand, and between Jewish, Christian, and Muslim theologians on the other hand, about the divine attributes (*ṣifāt Allāh*), the Quran's 'beautiful names' (*al-asmāʾ al-ḥusnah*) of God. For Muslims, the controversies had largely to do

[3] Al-Kindī's text, extracted from Yaḥyā's treatise, is published independently, with discussion and a new French translation in Rashed and Jolivet (1998).

[4] Samir (1980: 375–406). See the English translation of the first third of Yaḥyā's essay, based on Khalifat's edition, in Uluç and Argon (2008). The translation extends from p. 375 to the middle of p. 384 of Khalifat's edition, omitting the final twenty-two pages, and two-thirds of the full text, albeit that n. 65 on p. 148 of the article would lead the unwary reader to think the entire text had been translated.

with how properly to understand the divine attributes recorded in the Quran in such a way that they neither implied anthropomorphism in God, nor compromised God's 'oneness', even by implication (Gimaret 1988). For Arabic-speaking Christians, the controversies among Muslims about the divine attributes provided the Christian apologists both with an opportunity to develop a new theological approach with which to defend the credibility of their traditional doctrine of the Trinity, and with a new idiom in which to express the doctrine in Arabic (Griffith 2012). Their purpose was to argue in favour of the logical and religious credibility of trebling the 'oneness' of God (*at-tathlīth*), without in any way compromising the affirmation that God is truly one (*at-tawḥīd*) (see the studies included in Griffith 2000). As we shall see, not only did the Muslim *mutakallimūn* find this line of argument flawed and unconvincing, but from early in the ninth century onward Jewish scholars too argued that positing independently subsisting, essential attributes in the divine being compromised monotheism.

It is generally agreed among scholars that the distinctive mode of Islamic theology, the *'ilm al-kalām* (Frank 1992; see also Frank 1968; van Ess 1982), soon to be adapted to their own needs by Jews and Christians, grew up initially with the Mu'tazilite school of thought, responding to developments in the study of theoretical Arabic grammar and including elements of formal, largely Aristotelian logic provided by the contemporary translation movement (Frank 1978; Gimaret 1988). The Mu'tazilites flourished from the eighth century to the mid-ninth century, after which their school was eclipsed in official, Islamic circles by the so-called Asharite, Maturidite, and Ḥanbalite movements, most of whose *'ulamā* nevertheless carried on in their works with the traditional methods of the *'ilm al-kalām* (van Ess 1991–7; Caspar 1987: 145–257. See also Watt 1998). The first generation of Christian *mutakallimūn* were contemporaries of the early Mu'tazilite *mutakallimūn* and the Christians composed their own *kalām* treatises much on the model of and often in the idiom of their Muslim counterparts, in an effort the more convincingly in their Islamic milieu to purchase a modicum of credibility for their own doctrines and to suggest the inadequacy, from the Christian point of view, of the current Islamic systems of thought (Griffith 2008a). There were similar developments *mutatis mutandis* in apologetic discourse among Arabic-speaking Jewish scholars in the same Baghdadī milieu, most notably in the work of Dāwūd ibn Marwān al-Muqammiṣ, who had at one time been an associate of a Christian *mutakallim*, Nonnus of Nisibis (Teule 2009). Al-Muqammiṣ' major work, the *'Ishrūn Maqālah*, was largely an exercise in *kalām* against Christian teachings, including Christian ideas about the 'oneness' of God, as we shall see (Stroumsa 1989; Sklare 1999).

The Christian philosopher Yaḥyā ibn 'Adī was heir to the earlier apologetic efforts of his own community's *mutakallimūn* and he even wrote a number of apologetic texts of his own in the *kalām* style, in defence of the doctrine of the Trinity (Haddad 1985; Swanson 2005). He defended the doctrine against the strenuous objections of the early Muslim critic of religious doctrines, Abū 'Īsā al-Warrāq (d. *c.*862; see Thomas 1996), whose text survives only in Yaḥyā's transcription of it in the course of his refutation of its arguments (Thomas 1992; see also Platti 1991). Like the earlier apologists, Yaḥyā approached the subject within the framework of the ongoing discussion of the divine attributes. But in his response to the objections of al-Kindī, and in his discussion of the precise sense of the terms 'the one' and 'oneness', in dialogue with the thinking of his teacher al-Fārābī, Yaḥyā left the methods of the *mutakallimūn* behind, and he engaged in the discussion in terms of what he took to be the common idiom of Aristotelian logic.

The philosopher al-Kindī had said that he would challenge the Christians for the unreasonableness of their 'trebling' (*at-tathlīth*) the oneness of God on the basis of 'logic and philosophy', and more specifically, on the grounds that their Trinitarian confession necessarily involved the repulsive idea of introducing 'composition' (*at-tarkīb*) into the godhead. He said the following about the *aqānīm/hypostases* of the Christian Trinity, by which, he specified, 'they mean "individual persons" (*ashkhāṣ*)':

> It is necessarily the case that each one of them is a composite of the substance which comprises them and of the particular property that particularizes it. Every composite is caused and nothing caused is eternal. Therefore, the Father is not eternal, nor is the Son eternal, nor is the Holy Spirit eternal. They are both eternal and not eternal; this is the ugliest absurdity. (Périer 1920–1: 4; Rashed and Jolivet 1998: II. 123)

In his response to al-Kindī, Yaḥyā argues that given the Muslim philosopher's own description of God as simultaneously 'God' (*ilāh*), as 'one' (*wāḥid*), and as 'substance' (*jawhar*), al-Kindī too faced a logical conundrum involving the notions of 'one' and 'three'. And Yaḥyā proceeds to find fault with al-Kindī's use of the categories defined in Porphyry's *Eisagôgê* to discredit the Christian doctrine, arguing that the Muslim philosopher had misunderstood and misused the technical terms involved when it came to his discussion of the Christian doctrinal formulas, but he overlooked the same difficulties involved in his own affirmations regarding the one God. In the end, according to Yaḥyā, the matter came down to the proper understanding of what one means when he predicates 'one' or 'many' of a subject. And he explains that God is said to be 'one' in number in reference to his 'substance'/'being' (*jawhar*), while in reference to his 'quiddity' or 'whatness' (*māhiyyah*), which, according to Yaḥyā, is essentially described as being 'generous/good' (*jawād*), 'wise' (*ḥakīm*), and 'powerful' (*qādir*), he is 'three'.[5] This triad of predicates, Yaḥyā argues, bespeaks actual 'meanings' or essential 'referents' in God, each one of which differs from the other two (Périer 1920–1: 12–13; Wolfson 1976).

Yaḥyā follows much the same line of reasoning in his treatise on *at-tawḥīd*, in which he goes to considerable lengths to dispose of what he considers to be logically faulty definitions of 'the one' (*al-wāḥid*), such as those usually employed by Muslim thinkers, and then he explains what he regards as the proper understanding of the predicate 'one' in reference to God: the Creator is one by definition, in reference to his being the

[5] Yaḥyā seems to have been the first of the Arabic-speaking apologists for the doctrine of the Trinity to use this triad, with its roots in the Alexandrian philosophical tradition, in the Trinitarian context. See Haddad (1985: 218–22).

subject of the predications of the divine attributes; he is three in reference to the three essential attributes (*ṣifāt*) of his being, 'goodness/generosity' (*jūd*), 'wisdom' (*ḥikma*), and 'power' (*qudra*), the existence of which are, according to Yaḥyā, logically and ontologically prior to the predication of all other divine attributes (Samir 1980: 242–64).

In his response to Abū ʿĪsā al-Warrāq's criticism of the doctrine of the Trinity, and in another important essay in defence of the doctrine, Yaḥyā spoke of the three hypostases of the one divine being/substance in comparison with yet another exemplary triad that some in the Aristotelian tradition had also described as 'one', the intellect (*al-ʿaql*), 'the subject of the act of intellection' (*al-ʿāqil*), and 'the object of the act of intellection' (*al-maʿqūl*), a threesome that bespeaks yet another instance of Yaḥyā's familiarity with earlier discussions of the 'one'; his teacher al-Fārābī, as we shall see, critiqued this very idea in his *On One and Unity* (Platti 1991: 20–1; Périer 1920, esp. 11–27; Mahdi 1989: 55). In both of these instances, one sees Yaḥyā ibn ʿAdī's turn away from the apologetic methodologies of the Muslim and Christian *mutakallimūn* of the preceding generations, while at the same time retaining their positioning of the problem of the Christian Trinity in terms of the current discussions about the ontological status of the divine attributes. The Christian *mutakallimūn* who preceded Yaḥyā had spoken of several different triads of divine attributes as composing what they proposed as the triad of essential divine attributes, bespeaking the corresponding essential referents in God, the existence of which, they had argued, is presumed for the predication of all other attributes.[6] In his treatises, Yaḥyā consistently uses the two sets of triads just mentioned, preferring later in his career the triad: *al-ʿaql*, *al-ʿāqil*, and *al-maʿqūl*. The distinguishing feature of Yaḥyā's triads is that unlike those that appear in the apologies of the *mutakallimūn*, both of his had their roots in the Aristotelian discussions of the First Cause and of the one and the many.

Thinking of himself as a logician who would go beyond the range of thought of the *mutakallimūn*, Yaḥyā ibn ʿAdī was determined to defend the credibility of the Christian doctrine of the Trinity in logical and philosophical terms, in the very idiom of the current philosophical discussion in the confraternity of the philosophers of tenth-century Baghdad about the meaning of predicating 'one' and 'oneness' of a subject. In this light one must turn then to a closer look at his *Maqālah fī t-tawḥīd*.

IV The Logic of Monotheism

According to the scribal note at the head of the copy of Yaḥyā ibn ʿAdī's *Maqālah fī t-tawḥīd* that is preserved in a seventeenth-century manuscript, he finished the work in the month of April, 940 CE (Samir 1980: 159), just ten years before the death of his teacher al-Fārābī (d. 950), during which time he, Yaḥyā, was presumably still very

[6] See the schematic presentation in Haddad (1985: 218–33).

much under the influence of 'the second master' after Aristotle. But Sahban Khalifat has suggested that Yaḥyā may have composed this work in the light of his reading of the Aristotelian commentator Ammonius' (*c.*435/445–517/526) *Kitāb ḥujjat Arisṭāṭālīs fī t-tawḥīd* (Khalifat 1988: 100). This first essay on *at-tawḥīd* is the earliest of a number of treatises in which over the following thirty years and more Yaḥyā would continue to develop his thought on the topic. It is instructive too to note at the outset that in the essay, unlike al-Fārābī who on the surface at least confined himself to the specifically philosophical and logical problems of 'the one' (*al-wāḥid*) and 'oneness' (*al-waḥda*), Yaḥyā immediately addressed himself to the topic in overt religious terms. He speaks up-front of how people differ about the meaning of what they affirm when they speak of the 'oneness' (*waḥdāniyyah*) of the Creator; Yaḥyā lists five examples, all of which he disowns as inadequate understandings when the subject is God.[7] They include those who say that 'oneness' means to deny multiplicity of the Creator, or that he has no likeness (*lā naẓīr lahu*). Yaḥyā mentions one unnamed contemporary *mutakallim*, who is alleged to have said of the Creator's 'oneness' that 'its meaning, and that of the existence He has, is that He is one in the sense of being the starting point for numbering'.[8] Then Yaḥyā mentions those who say that the meaning of 'the one' (*al-wāḥid*), when said of the Creator, is one (*aḥad*) of its meanings by which entities other than he are described. Finally there are those who say that the Creator is 'one' in every way, not multiple in any way, while others maintain that he is one in a certain way and multiple in another. As we shall see, Yaḥyā will later concede the validity of this position in the distinctive way in which he understands it. For now, he finds all of these understandings to be wanting in one way or another as their defenders uphold them, and he goes on to state his own purpose in writing his essay.

> Our purpose in this essay is to examine these beliefs one by one, and by means of sound proofs and clear arguments to expose the falsity of the false and to elucidate the truth of the truthful, in the briefest and clearest way we can. (Samir 1980: 163–4; Khalifat 1988: 375–6)

True to his word, Yaḥyā ibn ʿAdī then sets about the relentlessly logical task of demonstrating to his own satisfaction that the foregoing five understandings of 'oneness' as predicated of the Creator that he had just described are all in some way inadequate and even invalid as their upholders explain them when it comes to speaking of the one God. To follow the long and often convoluted paths of his reasoning and argumentation would take us too far afield to rehearse them here. He says at the conclusion of the exercise that having shown the error of the adversaries' definitions he must now set down what the real meaning of 'the One' is. He puts it this way: 'We say

[7] Al-Fārābī too begins his *On One and Unity* with a discussion of the ways in which something is said to be 'one' and he goes on at considerable length to discuss the one and the many and the ways in which something may be said to be simultaneously one and many. See Mahdi (1989: 36–57, 75–97), concluding with an epitome of the ways in which something may rightly be said to be 'one', pp. 97–102.

[8] Uluç and Argon render this difficult phrase as follows: 'The meaning of the One and His existence is that He is One in the sense of being the beginning of numbers' (Uluç and Argon 2008: 149).

"the One" is an existent being in which no otherness (*ghayriyya*) is to be found, whence it is one' (Samir 1980: 196; Khalifat 1988: 384; Uluç and Argon 2008: 156). Yaḥyā goes on to detail the divisions of 'one' as so defined and then to describe the ways or modes (*jihāt*) of 'one' in the several divisions of its predication of a subject and to relate them to the corresponding divisions and modes of speaking of 'the multiple'. This leads to his defence of the proposition that the Creator is rightly said to be 'one' (*wāḥid*) in one way of speaking and 'multiple' (*kathīr*) in another. While the Creator, or the 'First Cause', is 'one' in the sense that he is 'an existent being in which no otherness is to be found', according to Yaḥyā, he may also be said from another perspective to be 'multiple'. And Yaḥyā goes on to argue that the one God may reasonably be said to be 'multiple' due to the fact that creatures, the caused effects of the Creator's creation, are seen to bespeak the real presence of several states of being of the First Cause that Yaḥyā calls 'meanings' or 'objective referents' (*maʿānī*) of the 'one' Creator, or 'descriptions' (*awṣāf, ṣifāt*) of his 'whatness/quiddity' (*māhiyya)* that are more than 'one' and that are necessarily to be predicated of him as Creator. Yaḥyā reasons that these 'meanings', bespeaking objective referents in the divine essence, must logically be affirmed of the Creator's very being as true in 'act' (*fiʿl*) as opposed to mere 'potency' or 'power' (*quwwa*); each must be affirmed as proper to God's 'essence' (*dhāt*), as opposed to being predicated as an 'accident' (*ʿarad*); and each is affirmed in terms of its strict 'definition' (*ḥadd*), as opposed to being posited as a mere, non-essential 'attribution' (*mawzūʿ*). According to Yaḥyā, these essential 'meanings', 'objective referents', or 'descriptive predicates' bespeak 'bountifulness' (*al-jūd*), 'active power' (*al-qudra*), and 'wisdom' (*al-ḥikma*), as essential states of the divine being, 'which are more than "one", by means of which the First Cause and its "what-ness", "quiddity" are to be described' (Samir 1980: 242; Khalifat 1988: 398).

It is immediately evident that along with this line of reasoning, brought in toward the end of his essay, Yaḥyā has imported the technical terminology and the underlying grammatical premises of the discussions among the contemporary Muslim and Christian *mutakallimūn* about the ontological significance of the scriptural 'divine attributes' (*ṣifāt Allāh*), albeit that he presents his argument as a whole as a relentlessly logical and philosophical discussion about 'the One'. In fact, the three essential states of God's being that Yaḥyā argues must characterize the essence of the one God are the correlative states of being, bespoken by the 'attributes': *jawād* (*jūd*), *qādir* (*qudrah*), and *ḥākim* (*ḥikma*), the same triad of essential attributes he affirmed in his reply to al-Kindī mentioned above and in several others of his apologetic works. It is noteworthy that in the choice of these particular essential attributes, Yaḥyā is at odds with the varying triads of essential attributes normally proposed by earlier and contemporary Christian *mutakallimūn*, such as 'existing' (*mawjūd*), 'living' (*ḥayy*), and 'rational' (*nāṭiq*), without which they argued no others could reasonably be attributed (Haddad 1985: 218–22). Yaḥyā's choice of these three notably Aristotelian attributes of the First Cause is seemingly dictated by his determination to appear relentlessly philosophical in his argument and to avoid any suspicion of being under the influence of the *ʿilm al-kalām*, albeit that he has nevertheless, perhaps unwittingly, brought in that discipline's technical terms and grammatical assumptions about the necessary implications of predicating essential, descriptive attributes of God. After all, for Yaḥyā, as for the Christian *mutakallimūn*, the defence of the logical credibility of the Christian project of 'trebling the oneness of God' (*tathlīth waḥdāniyyat Allāh*) was the underlying reason for his logical defence of describing the Creator as simultaneously both 'one' and 'multiple', and for his argument that according to his definition of 'one', 'the one' comprises 'the multiple'.

As for Yaḥyā's rather negative definition of 'the one' as 'an existent being in which no otherness is to be found, whence it is one', it is clear that he was desperately trying to find a way to escape from the objection that even the positing of essential attributes of the one divine essence, one in being, entails notions of composition and quantity in some measure. As we shall see, the Jewish *mutakallim* al-Muqammiṣ had in the previous century already argued this very point in response to the allegations of the Christian *mutakallimūn* of his time that the essential attributes they predicated of God as indicative of the divine hypostases did not compromise God's 'oneness' in being. And Yaḥyā clearly also wanted to find a way around al-Fārābī's rejection of just such a line of reasoning as both the earlier Christian *mutakallimūn* and he, Yaḥyā, regularly employed in defence of the reasonableness of the doctrine of the Trinity. In the course of his descriptions of the ways in which the adjective 'one' might accurately be predicated of a subject, al-Fārābī had written as follows:

> 'One' may be predicated of anything, the quiddity of which is not divided by reason of a plurality of names and terms that are predicated of it, and the many terms concerning it do not refer to many 'meanings'/referents (*maʿānin*), nor do the inflections of a single phoneme predicated of it refer to many transformations, on the pattern of what some people say, e.g., among many such, *al-ʿaql*, and *al-ʿāqil*, and *al-maʿqūl*, [saying that] the multiple inflections do not refer to multiple transformations within it. (Mahdi 1989: 54–5)

While al-Fārābī doubtless had other logicians in the Aristotelian tradition in mind with this observation, who would have been familiar with the traditional triad he cites, and not just the contemporary Christian *mutakallimūn*, his reasoning does nevertheless counter the very arguments these *mutakallimūn* customarily employed, including Yaḥyā, who, as we have mentioned above, had adopted this very triad as illustrative of the ontological status of the hypostases of the one God in his own treatises precisely because of its Aristotelian pedigree.

It is remarkable that Yaḥyā ibn ʿAdī concludes his *Maqālah fī t-tawḥīd* without ever explicitly mentioning the Christian doctrine of the Trinity, and without ever arguing, as he did in other texts, that the three essential attributes of the First Cause, i.e. the Creator, namely 'bountifulness/goodness', 'power', and 'wisdom', are indicative of the three 'hypostases' (*aqānīm*) of the one God according to Christian belief. But it is nevertheless crystal clear that a compulsion to explore the logical requirements for the reasonable affirmation of this very doctrine is what pressed Yaḥyā to propose his rather eccentric definition of 'oneness', and motivated his efforts to show how what is essentially 'one' on that definition, i.e. the First Cause, might also be seen logically to be 'multiple' by reason of the necessary ontological features that in his judgement must logically be predicated of the one essence of the one Creator or the First Cause, by reason of the very quiddity or 'what-ness' of the Creator, determined by the close observation of the Creator's creatures, the products or effects of his creative actions and accomplishments.

It is clear that contemporary as well as latter-day readers of Yaḥyā's essay had many difficulties with his reasoning. At some point after the completion of the text, he added an appendix in which he speaks of its reception among those who were studying it (Samir 1980: 266–72; Khalifat 1988: 404–6). He complains of people ignorant of logic and the rules of reasoning who, unable to discern the true meaning of words, mock and laugh at his work. He mentions those solicitous for the best science, equipped with the virtues of understanding, who nevertheless demean and disdain the positions he takes. He also mentions people who accept his reasoning who have no doubt or misgiving about it and deem it to be right. But given the length of the text, he worries about these readers' grasp of the finer points. In the end, Yaḥyā says he wrote the appendix to caution readers not to be in too much of a hurry to make a decision about his reasoning, and not to make judgements on the basis of passing thoughts but to ponder and to think carefully about what he had written lest they too quickly neglect careful consideration and even-handedness in approaching his essay. The addition of the appendix therefore suggests that Yaḥyā's *Maqālah fī t-tawḥīd* had already gained a wide circulation and that it had been subjected to criticism by his fellow logicians in the school of al-Fārābī and beyond.[9]

V Contesting The Trebling of God's 'Oneness'

One can easily imagine how readily Yaḥyā's non-Christian readers would recognize the special pleading he engaged in as he strove to define 'one' and 'oneness' in a philosophical way that would allow him without contradiction to affirm both 'oneness' and 'three-ness' of the one God. Indeed the Christian *mutakallimūn* before him and after

[9] An additional note is sometimes appended to Yaḥyā's text in its Coptic transmission in which he offers a solution to the doubt that some readers of his essay had raised about his position that nothing exists without being qualified by some description or other that is a true description, thereby providing grounds for affirming that what is 'one' from one perspective may be seen as 'multiple' from another. The doubt was that this position ruled out the possibility of there being anything at all that could be said to be simply 'one' (*wāḥid mufarrad*). Yaḥyā's solution was to point out that such a doubt arises only in the imagination of someone who thinks that what exists along with something else does not then exist itself. See Samir (1980: 273–7). This additional note is not published in Khalifat, *The Philosophical Treatises* (1988).

him pursued the same elusive goal, usually working more in the vein of the *ʿilm al-kalām*. But after Yaḥyā they more and more thought of themselves as purveyors of a philosophical theology. As for Yaḥyā himself, it is not unlikely that he thought he was taking al-Fārābī's thinking about the ways in which something that is 'one' may also be said to be 'many' a step further than the master would have thought it could go. And Muslim apologists and polemicists, following in the wake of al-Kindī, continued to point out the errors in logic that they perceived in Christian reasoning such as Yaḥyā's, beginning with those to whom he replied in the appendices to his *Maqālah fī t-tawḥīd*. Jewish scholars in the same milieu, from the ninth century onward had also been quick to take issue with such Christian efforts to treble the oneness of the one God, leading them as well to explore more fully the notion of oneness.

Writing probably already in the first half of the ninth century, the Jewish *mutakallim* Dāwūd ibn Marwān al-Muqammiṣ, who had for some time been under the tutelage of the Syriac-speaking Christian scholar Nonnus of Nisibis (d. after 862), had already taken up the question of what it means to say that God is one. In chapter 8 of his *ʿIshrūn Maqālah*, al-Muqammiṣ provides what in the wider Baghdadī milieu may well be the earliest detailed discussion of what the word 'one' means for a monotheist (Stroumsa 1989: 164–72; Vajda 1967). Having reviewed six possible ways in which the term 'one' can be used; he concludes, recalling in the process the views of some other 'monotheist scholars (*al-ʿulamāʾ al-muwaḥḥida*)' as he calls them, that God is one in simplicity and one in both essence and act, and he says:

> God is one in that there is no diversity in His essence, and one in that there is none equivalent to Him in His essence, and one in that there is none who is His peer or similar to Him in His act. (Stroumsa 1989: 172)

The 'monotheist scholars' whom al-Muqammiṣ mentioned in the lines just preceding this definition were in all probability Christians (Stroumsa 1989: 172 n. 60), a feature of the text that clearly bespeaks the inter-communal character of the discussion about God's oneness already in early Abbasid times. Al-Muqammiṣ then turns to a somewhat detailed refutation of the trebling of the oneness of God as the Christian *mutakallimūn* in his milieu defended it (Stroumsa 1989: 172–83). He mentions their explanations of how the one God in one substance may be said to be simultaneously three *hypostases/aqānīm* without contradiction by offering analogies with created substances that can be said to be both three and one, such as three gold dinars with different inscriptions. He also mentions the *kalāmic* argument the Christian *mutakallimūn* employed, according to which the one divine substance may be said to be characterized by three essential 'characteristic traits' or 'properties' that are indicative of the three *hypostases* of the one God, thereby indicating his familiarity with the contemporary Christian defence of the reasonableness of the doctrine of the Trinity on the basis of their interpretation of the ontological significance of the divine attributes (*ṣifāt Allāh*), as was mentioned above. According to al-Muqammiṣ, neither the analogies nor the interpretation of the *hypostases* as three essential divine attributes can be logically defended because they inevitably involve additions of some sort to the one divine being of the one God, thereby compromising the notion of oneness.

Just about a century after al-Muqammiṣ' time in Baghdad, Abū Yūsuf Yaʿqūb al-Qirqisānī (*fl. c.*940) also found it necessary in his discussion of the phrase in Deuteronomy 6: 4, 'the Lord is one', to expatiate on the meaning of the oneness thus affirmed of the one God. And in the process, with some adjustments, he appropriated al-Muqammiṣ' earlier disquisition on the subject, listing six opinions of scholars on God's oneness, highlighting in particular God's simplicity, 'He is one, not of a composite essence', and the fact that there is none like him, 'He is not an effect, but rather He is the cause of every effect' (Ben-Shammai 1982). On this basis, elsewhere in his *Kitāb al-anwār wal-marāqib* Qirqisānī explicitly points out the logical inadequacies of the Christians' explanations of the verisimilitude of their affirmation of the three *hypostases/aqānīm* of the one divine 'being'/'substance' (*jawhar*), which they posit in view of their affirmation of God's essential attributes, the absence of which they claim to be inconceivable. Qirqisānī argues very adroitly that the Christians base their arguments on logical principles, but he says that their definitions of such technical terms as *jawhar*, for example, are at variance with the definitions given by the 'master of logic' (*ṣāḥib al-mantiq*), who said that while it is true that a *jawhar* is a substance that exists on its own, as the Christians say, it is also by definition susceptible to supporting various, even contrary accidents in existence. If one then claims that God is a substance/*jawhar*, as the Christians do, this would logically lead to unacceptable conclusions such as introducing numbering into the divine essence, which in turn bespeaks composition, which then inevitably compromises 'oneness'.[10]

Saʿadia ha-Gaʾōn (882–942) had likewise attacked the logic of Christian thinking in the matter of their defence of the doctrine of the Trinity on the basis of their positing the ontological priority and distinct individuality of select essential divine attributes that the Christian *mutakallimūn* argued must be subsistent in the one God's very being, attributes (*ṣifāt*) such as 'life' ('living') and 'knowledge' ('knowing'). Saʿadia argues that although elite Christians 'maintain that they adopted their belief in the trinity as a result of rational speculation and subtle understanding',[11] their reasoning nevertheless logically and inevitably leads to the unacceptable supposition that God is a composite, physical being. It was undoubtedly pressure from well-reasoned critiques of Christian apologies for the doctrine of the Trinity such as Saʿadia's that prompted Yaḥyā ibn ʿAdī to attempt to make a case for the reasonableness of the doctrine on the basis of a philosophical exploration of the meaning of 'one' and 'oneness', as he did in his *Kitāb at-tawḥīd*. But Moses Maimonides (1135–1204), looking back some 200 years later at the use Yaḥyā and other Christian thinkers made of Greek philosophy and logic to support the reasonableness of their religious convictions, found not philosophy in it but the beginnings of the *ʿilm al-kalām*. One can only imagine the chagrin that Yaḥyā would have felt at being classed by name among the *mutakallimūn*. As for Maimonides' opinion of the efforts

[10] See in this connection, Yaʿqūb al-Qirqisānī, *Kitāb al-anwār wal-marāqib; Code of Karaite Law*, ed. Nemoy (1939), vol. I, III.2, 2–7, pp. 186–90.

[11] Saʿadja b. Jûsuf al-Fajjûmî, *Kitâb al-Amânât wa'l-Iʿtiqâdât*, ed. Landauer (1880: 86), quoted in the English translation of Rosenblatt (1948: 103).

of the Arabic-speaking Christian apologists to defend the reasonableness of trebling the oneness of the one God on the basis of positing three essential attributes of God's being, the author of *The Guide of the Perplexed* had the following to say.

> If, however, you belong to those whose aspirations are directed to that high rank which is the rank of speculation, and to gaining certain knowledge with regard to God's being One by virtue of a true Oneness, so that no composition whatever is to be found in Him and no possibility of division in any way whatever then you must know that He, may He be Exalted, has in no way and in no mode any essential attribute, and that just as it is impossible that He should be a body, it is also impossible that He should possess an essential attribute. If, however, someone believes that He is one, but possesses a certain number of essential attributes, he says in his words that He is one, but believes Him in his thought to be many. This resembles what the Christians say: namely, that He is one but also three, and that the three are one.[12]

Clearly in this retrospective view, albeit it was not his immediate purpose, Maimonides put his finger on the heart of the matter of the issue of 'one' and 'oneness', and confessing the 'oneness' of God as the issue was discussed in the milieu of Baghdad and its environs in the heyday of Abbasid intellectual culture. The topic engaged the attention of the intellectuals of all three monotheist communities at the very moment in early Islamic history when the stimulus of translated Greek philosophical and logical texts came to the fore in the Arabic-speaking scholarly milieu in which the implications of the newly explicated, theoretical Arabic grammar were already engaging the attention of religious thinkers anxious to explore the full meaning of the Arabic Quran.

VI Intellectual Encounters in Islamicate Society

This quick review of the discussions about the meaning of 'one' and 'oneness', especially as affirmed of the one God by Jews, Christians, and Muslims in Baghdad and its environs in Abbasid times, highlights the inter-communal character of intellectual life there at a crucial period in the development of Islamicate society. Philosophers and *mutakallimūn* of the several Abrahamic families of believers clearly developed their distinctive discourses in Arabic in tandem with and in reaction to one another, albeit that they seldom mentioned one another by name.[13] Accordingly, it

[12] Moses Maimonides, *The Guide of the Perplexed*, trans. Pines (1963: I. 111).

[13] An exception to prove the rule is Yaḥyā ibn ʿAdī's reply to philosophical questions proposed to him by the Jewish scholar of Mosul in Iraq, Ibn Abī Saʿīd ʿUthmān al-Yahūdī, who sent his questions by the hand of one Bishr ibn Simsān ibn ʿUrs ibn ʿUthmān al-Yahūdī. See Pines (1955). The text is published in Khalifat (1988: 314–36). Yaḥyā also named the authors of works from which he quoted extensively for the purpose of refuting them, e.g. al-Kindī and Abū ʿĪsā al-Warrāq, as mentioned above.

is crucial for an adequate study of the works of any one or several of them that the enquiry be made within the purview of the others, whose often contrary views and characteristic formulations would have been very much on the mind of any writer within a particular tradition who strove to present his own community's views in counterpoint to those of his contemporaries who thought differently. Therefore any present-day study of the theological works of an Arabic-speaking, Jewish, Christian, or Muslim author of Abbasid times must for accuracy's sake proceed with the awareness of the broader, even interreligious dimension of the author's thought world. This was the case even in the most basic matter of confessing monotheism, the bottom line in Abrahamic faith. Arguably it was in the interreligious colloquies between Jews, Christians, and Muslims in Arabic-speaking Baghdad and environs in Abbasid times that the concept of monotheism received its most intense scrutiny prior to modern times.

References

Adamson, P. 2003. 'Al-Kindī and the Muʿtazila: Divine Attributes, Creation and Freedom'. *Arabic Sciences and Philosophy* 13: 45–77.

Allard, M. 1962. 'Les Chrétiens à Baġdād'. *Arabica* 9: 375–88.

Ben-Shammai, H. 1982. 'Qirqisānī on the Oneness of God'. *The Jewish Quarterly Review* 73: 105–11.

Caspar, R. 1987. *Traité de théologie musulmane* (vol. I: Histoire de la pensée religieuse musulmane, Collection 'Studi arabo-islamici del PISAI', no. 1; Rome: Pontificio Istituto di Studi Arabi e d'Islamistica, 145–257.

Endress, G. 1997. 'The Circle of al-Kindī: Early Arabic Translations from the Greek and the Rise of Islamic Philosophy'. In G. Endress and R. Kruk, eds, *The Ancient Tradition in Christian and Islamic Hellenism: Studies on the Transmission of Greek Philosophy and Sciences*. Leiden: Research School CNWS, School of Asian, African, and Amerindian Studies, 43–76.

Frank, R. M. 1968. 'The Kalâm, an Art of Contradiction-Making or Theological Science? Some Remarks on the Question'. *Journal of the American Oriental Society* 88: 295–309.

Frank, R. M. 1978. *Beings and their Attributes: The Teaching of the Basrian School of the Muʿtazila in the Classical Period*. Albany, NY: State University of New York Press.

Frank, R. M. 1992. 'The Science of Kalām'. *Arabic Science and Philosophy* 2: 9–37.

Gimaret, D. 1988. *Les Noms divins en Islam: exégèse lexicographique et théologique*. Paris: Cerf.

Griffith, S. H. 2000. *The Beginnings of Christian Theology in Arabic: Muslim-Christian Encounters in the Early Islamic Period*. Aldershot: Ashgate.

Griffith, S. H. 2008a. *The Church in the Shadow of the Mosque: Christians and Muslims in the World of Islam*. Princeton: Princeton University Press.

Griffith, S. H. 2008b. 'Hunayn ibn Isḥāq and the *Kitāb ādāb al-falāsifah*: The Pursuit of Wisdom and a Humane Polity in Early Abbasid Baghdad'. In G. A. Kiraz, ed., *Malphono w-Rabo-Malphone: Studies in Honor of Sebastian P. Brock*. Piscataway, NJ: Gorgias, 135–60.

Griffith, S. H. 2012. 'Doing Christian Theology in Islamic Terms: Unity and Trinity of God in Early Christian-Muslim Dialogue'. In N. Hintersteiner, ed., *Thinking the Divine in Interreligious Encounter*. Amsterdam, New York: Rodopi, 147–74.

Gutas, D. 1975. *Greek Wisdom Literature in Arabic Translation: A Study of the Graeco-Arabic Gnomologia*. New Haven: American Oriental Society.

Gutas, D. 1998. *Greek Thought, Arabic Culture: The Graeco-Arabic Translation Movement in Baghdad and Early 'Abbāsid Society (2nd-4th/8th-10th Centuries)*. London, New York: Routledge.

Haddad, R. 1985. *La Trinité divine chez les théologiens arabes (750–1050)*. Paris: Beauchesne.

Khalifat, S., ed. 1988. *Yahyā Ibn 'Adī: The Philosophical Treatises*. Publications of the University of Jordan; Amman: Department of Philosophy, Faculty of Arts, University of Jordan, 375–406.

Kraemer, J. L. 1986a. *Humanism in the Renaissance of Islam: The Cultural Revival during the Buyid Age*. Leiden: Brill.

Kraemer, J. L. 1986b. *Philosophy in the Renaissance of Islam: Abū Sulaymān al-Sijistānī and his Circle*. Leiden: Brill.

Landauer, S. 1880. Al-Fajjûmî, Sa'adja b. Jûsuf, *Kitâb al-Amânât wa'l-I'tiqâdât*. Leiden: Brill.

Levenson, J. D. 2012. *Inheriting Abraham: The Legacy of the Patriarch in Judaism, Christianity and Islam*. Princeton: Princeton University Press.

Mahdi, M., ed. 1989. al-Fārābī, Abū Naṣr, *Kitāb al-wāḥid wa l-waḥdah*. Casablanca: Toubkal.

Maimonides. 1963. *The Guide of the Perplexed*, trans. S. Pines. 2 vols. Chicago: The University of Chicago Press.

Marmura, M. E. 2005. *Probing in Islamic Philosophy: Studies in the Philosophies of Ibn Sina, al-Ghazali and Other Major Muslim Thinkers*. Binghamton, NY: Global Academic Publishing, 337–53.

Nemoy, L., ed. 1939. Al-Qirqisānī, Ya'qūb, *Kitāb al-anwār wal-marāqib; Code of Karaite Law*. 2 vols. New York: The Alexander Kohut Memorial Foundation.

Périer, A. 1920. *Petits traits apologétiques de Yahyâ ben 'Adî: texte arabe édité pour la première fois d'après les manuscrits de Paris, de Rome et de Munich, et traduit en français*. Paris: Gabalda & Geuthner.

Périer, A. 1920–1. 'Un traité de Yahyâ ben 'Adî: défense du dogme de la trinité contre les objections d'al-Kindî; texte arabe publié pour la première fois et traduit'. *Revue de l'Orient Chrétien*, 3rd series, 2 (22): 3–21.

Pines, S. 1955. 'A Tenth Century Philosophical Correspondence'. *Proceedings of the American Academy for Jewish Research* 24: 103–36.

Platti, E. 1991. 'La Doctrine des chrétiens d'après Abū 'Īsā al-Warrāq dans son traité sur la trinité'. *Mélanges de l'Institut Dominicain d'Études Orientales du Caire*, Vol. 20. Leuven, Paris: Peeters, 7–30.

Rashed, R. and Jolivet, J., eds. 1998. *Oeuvres philosophiques et scientifiques d'al-Kindī*. Vol. II, *Métaphysique et Cosmologie; Islamic Philosophy, Theology and Science*. Leiden: Brill.

Rosenblatt, S., trans. 1948. *Saadia Gaon, The Book of Beliefs and Opinions*. New Haven, London: Yale University Press.

Samir, K., ed. 1980. *Le Traité de l'unité de Yaḥyā ibn 'Adī (893–974): étude et édition critique*. Patrimoine Arabe Chrétien, 2; Jounieh, Lebanon: Librairie Saint-Paul; Rome: Pontificio Istituto Orientale.

Sklare, D. 1999. 'Responses to Islamic Polemics by Jewish Mutakallimūn in the Tenth Century'. In H. Lazarus-Yafeh et al., eds, *The Majlis: Interreligious Encounters in Medieval Islam*. Wiesbaden: Harrassowitz, 135–61.

Stroumsa, S., ed. and trans. 1989. *Dawūd ibn Marwān al-Muqammiṣ' Twenty Chapters (Ishrūn Maqālāt)*. Leiden: Brill.

Swanson, M. N. 2005. 'The Trinity in Christian-Muslim Conversation'. *Dialog: A Journal of Theology* 44: 256–63.

Teule, H. G. B. 2009. 'Nonnus of Nisibis'. In D. Thomas and B. Roggema, eds, *Christian-Muslim Relations: A Bibliographical History*. Vol. I: *600–900*. Leiden: Brill, 743–5.

Thomas, D. 1992. *Anti-Christian Polemic in Early Islam: Abū 'Īsā al-Warrāq's 'Against the Trinity'*. Cambridge: Cambridge University Press.

Thomas, D. 1996. 'Abū 'Īsā al-Warrāq and the History of Religions'. *Journal of Semitic Studies* 41: 275–90.

Uluç, T. and Argon, K. 2008. 'Reflections on the Unity/Trinity Polemics in Islamic Philosophy: Yaḥyā bin 'Adī and His *Maqālah fī al-Tawḥīd* (Treatise on Unity)'. *Journal of Middle Eastern and North African Intellectual and Cultural Studies* 4 (2): 148–56 (133–61).

Vajda, G. 1962. 'Le Milieu juif à Baġdād'. *Arabica* 9: 389–93.

Vajda, G. 1967. 'Le Problème de l'unité de Dieu d'après Dāwūd ibn Marwān al-Muqammiṣ'. In A. Altmann, ed., *Jewish Medieval and Renaissance Studies*. Cambridge, MA: Harvard University Press, 49–73.

van Ess, J. 1982. 'Early Development of *Kalām*'. In G. H. A. Juynboll, ed., *Studies on the First Century of Islamic Society*. Carbondale and Edwardsville, IL: Southern Illinois University Press, 109–23 and 230–41.

van Ess, J. 1991–7. *Theologie und Gesellschaft im 2. und 3. Jahrhundert Hidschra*. 6 vols. Berlin: DeGruyter.

Wasserstrom, S. M. 1995. *Between Muslim and Jew: The Problem of Symbiosis under Early Islam*. Princeton: Princeton University Press.

Watt, W. M. 1998. *The Formative Period of Islamic Thought*. 1st edn. Edinburgh: Edinburgh University Press, 1973; repr. Oxford: One World.

Watt, J. W. 2005.'The Strategy of the Baghdad Philosophers: The Aristotelian Tradition as a Common Motif in Christian and Islamic Thought'. In J. J. van Ginkel et al., eds, *Redefining Christian Identity: Cultural Interaction in the Middle East since the Rise of Islam*. Leuven: Peeters, 151–65.

Watt, J. W. 2007. 'Christianity in the Renaissance of Islam: Abû Bishr Mattâ, al-Fârâbî and Yaḥyâ ib 'Adī'. In M. Tamcke, ed., *Christians and Muslims in Dialogue in the Islamic Orient of the Middle Ages: Christlich-muslimische Gespräche im Mittelalter*. Beirut: Orient Institut and Würzburg: Ergon Verlag in Komission, 99–112.

Wolfson, H. A. 1976. 'The Philosopher Kindī and Yaḥyā b. 'Adī on the Trinity'. In *The Philosophy of the Kalām*. Cambridge, MA: Harvard University Press, 318–36.

Zakeri, M. 2004. 'Ādāb al-falāsifa: The Persian Content of an Arabic Collection of Aphorisms'. In E. Gannagé et al., eds, *The Greek Strand in Islamic Political Thought*. Beirut: Université Saint-Joseph, 173–90.

CHAPTER 18

PHILOSOPHY AND THEOLOGY

CARLOS FRAENKEL

1. Introduction: Abraham the Philosopher?

Unlike Pascal, who famously opposed the God of the philosophers to the God of Abraham, Isaac, and Jacob, Muslim, Jewish, and Christian philosophers in the medieval Islamic world claim that the God of the patriarchs and the God of the philosophers is one and the same. Let me illustrate their approach through the Muslim philosopher Averroes (d. 1198) and his Jewish colleague Maimonides (d. 1204), who were the two last important representatives of *falsafa*—the main medieval school of Arabic philosophy—in Muslim Spain. For them the main demonstration for God's existence is the physical proof that Aristotle worked out at the end of the *Physics* and in *Metaphysics*, book 12. In a nutshell Aristotle argues that motion is eternal and that the instantiation of eternal motion in the universe is the celestial spheres which eternally move stars and planets around the earth. Since the celestial spheres are finite bodies, they cannot contain the infinite force required to eternally keep moving. And since an infinite body is impossible, the spheres must be moved by an incorporeal mover—that is, God. Apprehending God in this way, Averroes and Maimonides argue, is the highest good for human beings, for the main component of the human good is intellectual perfection which is acquired through knowledge of the natural order, culminating in knowledge of God. Leaving aside the technical details of Aristotle's proof, the important point for my purpose is that both Averroes and Maimonides claim that the first to establish God's existence in this way was not Aristotle, but Abraham![1] This is precisely the point on which Abraham broke with

[1] See Averroes, *Long Commentary on the* Metaphysics, p. 1634 [Bouyges] and *Decisive Treatise*, p. 2 [Hourani]; Maimonides, *Book of Knowledge*, Laws Concerning Idolatry 1.3 and *Guide of the Perplexed* 3.29, p. 376 [Munk-Yoel]; p. 514 [Pines].

the star worshipping idolaters of his time: they did not understand that the celestial spheres require an incorporeal mover and thus took them to be the deity itself. Abraham is, of course, the founding father of Judaism, Christianity, and Islam. What Averroes and Maimonides are trying to do, therefore, is to embed the beliefs about the world and the good that, upon careful reflection, they came to see as true at the very foundation of their religious tradition by portraying Abraham as an accomplished philosopher. It is easy to see why they do this: they are philosophers, but Averroes is also a Muslim and Maimonides a Jew. Hence they interpret their religious tradition in light of their considered beliefs about the world and the good. This form of philosophical reinterpretation is typical for Muslim, Jewish, and Christian philosophers in the Islamic world: it is their way of doing justice to the truth they take to be embodied in their religious tradition.

The label 'philosophers' (*falāsifa*) became a kind of intellectual trademark that identified its bearers as the heirs of the philosophy of Plato and Aristotle and set them apart from other intellectual currents in the Muslim world, most importantly 'theology' (*kalām*). It is important to stress that the opposition of *falsafa* and *kalām* which represents a key intellectual axis in the medieval Islamic world does not imply that proponents of *falsafa* give priority to reason and proponents of *kalām* to revelation. Of the two main schools of medieval *kalām*, the Muʿtazila and the Ashʿariyya, the former is in a sense as fond of reason (*ʿaql*) as the *falāsifa*. Since reason proves, for example, that God is not only numerically one, but also incorporeal and without composition, the Muʿtazila are not shy to interpret figuratively all passages of their religious texts that entail any form of multiplicity in God (besides corporeal features, this also includes attributes like wisdom, power, life, compassion, and so forth if these are taken to refer to different aspects of God's nature). And yet for the *mutakallimūn* the role of philosophy remains instrumental: its twofold purpose is to clarify the prophetic religion, whose truth has been established independently through miracles, and to refute every opinion that contradicts it. For the *falāsifa*, by contrast, the prophet is first of all an accomplished philosopher who conceived God philosophically, while the representation of God in the religious sources is an 'imitation' of the philosophical conception that by means of parables and metaphors aims at conveying an approximate idea of God to non-philosophers. Although the philosophical conception of God thus coincides with the allegorical content of the parables and metaphors representing God in the religious sources, only philosophy can conceive God as he truly is and as he was conceived by the prophets. True philosophy thus constitutes the core of religion rather than being an instrument to confirm and defend independently existing religious doctrines.

2. The Intellectual Setting: Al-Ghazālī's *Deliverance from Error*

Philosophers and theologians were not the only ones who claimed to represent the truth of their religious tradition. A good introduction to the competing currents of thought in the medieval Islamic world is the *Deliverance from Error*, the intellectual autobiography of the great Muslim theologian al-Ghazālī (d. 1111). Al-Ghazālī's quest begins after he experiences the breaking of '*taqlīd*'—the loss of trust in the beliefs and values of his religious tradition that he had accepted on the authority of 'parents and teachers'. The bonds of *taqlīd* broke, al-Ghazālī writes, when he realized that he would have been just as fervent a Jew or Christian as he was a Muslim, had he been brought up in a Jewish or Christian community:

> As I drew near the age of adolescence the bonds of mere authority [*taqlīd*] ceased to hold me and inherited beliefs lost their grip on me, for I saw that Christian children always grew up to be Christians, Jewish children to be Jews, and Muslim children to be Muslims.[2]

If al-Ghazālī cannot rely on the authority of his religious tradition, can he rely on his own cognitive faculties—the senses and the intellect? He finds reasons to cast doubts on both. The senses tell us, for example, that the sun is the size of a *dinar* coin. Here the intellect can identify and correct the mistake. But can we trust the intellect? We can conceive of a higher cognitive faculty, al-Ghazālī argues, that would identify the mistakes of the intellect in the same way as the intellect identifies the mistakes of the senses. The fact that we do not have such a faculty or know about such mistakes does not mean that we do not make them, since we also would not know about the mistakes of the senses without the intellect. Al-Ghazālī's sceptical crisis only ends when God casts light into his heart, restoring trust in his cognition. The quest for knowledge thus cannot begin without God's help. Then al-Ghazālī describes how he 'scrutinized the creed of every sect' and 'tried to lay bare the inmost doctrines of every community' in order to 'distinguish between true and false, between sound tradition and heretical innovation'.[3] He examines the four main interpretations of Islam in his time, proposed by theologians, philosophers, Sufis, and Ismāʾīlis, which all claim to represent true Islam.

Theology or *kalām* (literally 'speech' or 'debate') for al-Ghazālī is, above all, an apologetic discipline. The aim of the *mutakallimūn* is to defend the orthodox faith through rational argument against heretics and rival religions. While he does not deny that this defence is important, it does not offer a secure path to knowledge because the truth of the orthodox faith is taken for granted.

By contrast, Muslim philosophers (*falāsifa*) such as al-Fārābī and Avicenna, whom al-Ghazālī describes as the heirs of Socrates, Plato, and Aristotle, claim to accept only that which has been strictly demonstrated according to Aristotle's logic. While al-Ghazālī agrees that a demonstrated claim—that is, the conclusion of a scientific syllogism as set forth in the *Posterior Analytics* ('*burhān*' in Arabic, translating the Greek *apodeixis*)—must be true, he denies that the *falāsifa* have, in fact, made good on their promise. The disciplines that al-Ghazālī recognizes as apodictic are logic and

[2] *Deliverance*, 69–70 [Saliba-Ayyad]; 21 [Watt].
[3] Ibid. 67–8 [Saliba-Ayyad]; 20 [Watt].

mathematics. Aristotle's physics and ethics also contain much that is true, although in ethics Aristotle took over much from ancient Sufis without crediting them. (Like the *falāsifa*, who claim that in following Aristotle they are actually following Abraham, al-Ghazālī here claims to be following old Sufi traditions.) In metaphysics, by contrast, the *falāsifa* simply kowtow to the authority of their Greek teachers and defend doctrines that are often at odds with Islam. In three cases he goes so far as to declare the *falāsifa* unbelievers (*kuffār*), a charge that carried no less than the death sentence with it: for denying the creation of the world, God's knowledge of particulars, and the resurrection of the dead. Hence *falsafa* not only fails to deliver certain knowledge, but also leads its adherents astray. Note that al-Ghazālī does not claim to be able to prove that the claims of the *falāsifa* in metaphysics are wrong. He only disputes that they can offer a demonstration. In a scientific syllogism, the logical inference must be valid and the premises *necessarily* true—that is either self-evident or deduced from self-evident propositions. According to al-Ghazālī, however, many of the premises used by the philosophers can be disputed. Consider the proof for God's existence that, as we saw above, relies on the premise that the world is eternal. The first and longest discussion of the *Incoherence of the Philosophers*—the work in which al-Ghazālī spells out the critique of *falsafa* sketched in the *Deliverance*—is devoted to showing that the *falāsifa* were unable to prove the eternity claim. But if from the standpoint of reason the world can be both eternal (Aristotle's position) and created (Islam's position), who decides that Aristotle is wrong and Islam is right? If reason cannot settle questions about God's existence, nature, and relation to the world, the authority of revelation must be based on something else.

The third school that al-Ghazālī examines is the *ahl al-taʿlīm*, the adherents of authoritative instruction. By this he means the branches of Shiʿite Islam who claim that knowledge can only be attained through unconditional submission to the infallible imam. The imam is the successor of the prophet and must be of his family which ensures his unique connection with God. He is the only person able to grasp the true hidden meaning (*bāṭin*) of the Quran and provide guidance to the religious community. Can the imam, then, unlike the philosopher, decide whether the world is eternal or created and other disputed questions? Al-Ghazālī's main problem with the *ahl al-taʿlīm* is that they cannot defend the supposedly infallible teachings of the imam against the slightest objection. When put to the test they turn out not to have real knowledge at all.

Finally al-Ghazālī turns to Sufism which offers both a theory and a practical path. The two main steps consist in liberating oneself from the attachments to this world (the 'mansion of deception') and then turning to God (the 'mansion of eternity'), culminating in the immediate experience or 'taste' (*dhawq*) of God. Not only does al-Ghazālī credit Sufism with a viable path to God, but he describes it as superior to knowledge, just as being drunk allows us to grasp drunkenness in a way that is superior to understanding its definition. According to al-Ghazālī, this is the foundation of prophetic revelation and the state that Muhammad attained when he is described as 'passionately loving [*ʿashiqa*] God'. The authority of Islam, then, is based on the Sufi path to God. On account of this authority Islam trumps Aristotle when the two are at odds as in the question of the world's eternity or creation.

3. Methodological Considerations

The medieval Muslim world stretched geographically from India in the east to Spain in the west and was characterized by the political and religious hegemony of Islam and by Arabic as the shared language of its inhabitants. At the same time, it was a multi-ethnic and multi-religious world that included significant Jewish and Christian minorities. On the one hand, Jews and Christians were not on equal footing with Muslims. They were subject to a number of restrictions such as the *jizya*, a special tax that non-Muslims had to pay to their Muslim rulers. But they were also recognized as *ahl al-kitāb*—people of a divinely revealed (albeit superseded) book—and benefited from extensive rights and protections that were only rarely abrogated (as during the Almohad rule in twelfth-century Muslim Spain). As a consequence, Jews and Christians not only enjoyed communal autonomy, but also participated in all walks of social, economic, and cultural life: from fashion, cuisine, and commerce to science, poetry, and theology. This social fabric has been described as 'creative symbiosis' by S. D. Goitein.[4] With respect to intellectual life, the case of the Jews is somewhat different from that of the Christians. The expansion of Christianity into the Graeco-Roman world led to the appropriation of Greek intellectual tools which in turn gave rise to a long tradition of systematic theological and philosophical reflection. This tradition has no parallel in rabbinic Judaism. Under Islam, by contrast, Jews were keen to take up and contribute to the emerging new intellectual discourses. As Shlomo Pines argued, up to the early modern period it is not possible to draw a meaningful intellectual boundary between Jews and Muslims: 'in its decisive period mediaeval Jewish thought was an offshoot of Arabic thought: the debates of Jewish philosophers can only be understood if one refers to the doctrinal differences obtaining among Arabic philosophers.'[5] Thus we find Jewish *mutakallimūn* like Saʿadia Gaon, Jewish *falāsifa* like Abraham ibn Daud and Maimonides, Jewish Sufis like Baḥya ibn Paquda and Abraham ben Maimonides, and Jewish appropriations of Shiʿite concepts—for example in Judah Halevi. While Christians, too, participated, they did so to a lesser degree than Jews, and in some disciplines—most importantly *kalām* and *falsafa*—more than others. As mentioned, Christians had a rich intellectual tradition of their own that not only long preceded the developments in the Muslim world, but also significantly helped to shape them.

The study of Muslim, Jewish, and Christian thought in the Middle Ages thus faces a number of challenges. For one thing neither of these traditions was monolithic. As al-Ghazālī's *Deliverance* illustrates, they included very different schools each of which

[4] See Goitein 1955. [5] Pines 1959: 61–2.

claimed to represent the truth (not to mention that the four schools described by al-Ghazālī were also internally diverse). In fact, the medieval attempts to define the boundaries of a religion—for example in al-Ghazālī's *Decisive Criterion for Distinguishing Islam from Unbelief* or in Maimonides' *Thirteen Principles*—are surely in part a response to the deep disagreements that al-Ghazālī documents. It is clear, moreover, that the different schools competed with each other, criticized each other, borrowed from each other, and so forth. Not being *mutakallimūn*, for example, is constitutive for the identity of the *falāsifa*. At times they appropriate and reinterpret concepts from rival schools. Thus al-Fārābī claims that the true imam is the philosopher-ruler in a work completed in Aleppo at the court of the Hamdanid ruler Sayf al-Dawla, a supporter of Shīʿite Islam centred on the authority of the imam.[6] Or Maimonides uses the term '*ʿishq*' that in Sufism refers to the passionate love of God to describe the intellectual love uniting the philosopher with Divine Reason.[7] This may well be an implicit response to the increasing popularity of Sufism in Egypt's Jewish community which Maimonides led. Hence studying each school in isolation—by writing, for example, a history of *kalām* or of *falsafa* or of Sufism—fails to capture the dynamic interaction between them. As Pines made clear, dividing the period up according to religious, rather than intellectual, affiliations is just as artificial. The characterization of Jewish philosophy as an 'offshoot' of Arabic thought, however, introduces another unhelpful division: that between original and derivation. Jewish thinkers in the Islamic world—Saʿadia Gaon, Judah Halevi, Baḥya ibn Paquda, Maimonides, and others—often stand out through the originality of their responses to the great philosophical, theological, and scientific questions of the time—regardless of the fact that they were Jews who wrestled with these questions within a Jewish framework. And the same can be said for Christian thinkers. Yet while it is true that a Jewish philosopher like Maimonides felt much greater intellectual affinity to a Muslim philosopher like al-Fārābī than to a Jewish *mutakallim* like Saʿadia Gaon, one cannot properly understand Maimonides without taking the distinctly Jewish character of his work into account. In fact, Maimonides did not write a single philosophical work strictly speaking. In a sense, all of his works are commentaries on the Law of Moses. His first important work is the *Commentary on the Mishna*, his last the *Guide of the Perplexed*, which is presented as a book of biblical interpretation. According to the introduction, Maimonides' goal is to explain 'the meanings of certain terms', as well as 'very obscure parables occurring in the books of the prophets' in order to show perplexed Jewish intellectuals that no real conflict exists between the teachings of the prophets and the teachings of the philosophers.[8] In addition to explaining the Law of Moses as a commentator, Maimonides also puts order into it as a legal scholar, most importantly in the *Mishneh Torah*, his fourteen-volume code of Jewish law. Similarly, one cannot coherently separate the philosopher Yaḥyā ibn ʿAdī from the Christian Yaḥyā ibn ʿAdī who spares no effort to make

[6] See *Virtuous City*, ch. 15.11. [7] See *Guide* 3.51.
[8] *Guide* 1, introduction, p. 2 [Munk-Yoel]; 5–6 [Pines].

philosophical sense of key Christian doctrines such as the Trinity and the Incarnation. And since, as we will see, the distinctive feature of Christ for Yaḥyā is that his intellect is perfectly united with God's, any philosophical insight contributing to intellectual perfection brings a person closer to Christ. On the other hand, some of the actually meaningful boundaries run across shared religious and intellectual affiliations—for example the theological debates between the Muʿtazilite schools of Basra and Baghdad, the debate about the validity of the Talmud between Rabbanites and Karaites (who both adopted the conceptual tools of Muʿtazilite *kalām*), or the debate about the nature of Christ between Melkites, Monophysites, and Nestorians. As this short sketch illustrates, adequately capturing the complicated relations between philosophical and theological commitments, intellectual context and religious identity is not at all straightforward and much scholarship remains bound by divisions that are not justified by the material.

4. Theology (Kalām)

Al-Ghazālī's characterization of *kalām* as concerned primarily with apologetics fits well with how the *falāsifa* see *kalām*. According to al-Fārābī it is the science that seeks the 'victory of the doctrines and actions prescribed by the religious Lawgiver and the refutation of all opinions contradicting them'.[9] Maimonides goes even further: the *mutakallimūn* bend the facts to make them conform to their preconceived religious beliefs instead of grounding their beliefs on a scientific examination of the facts.[10] To be sure, this portrait of *kalām* is at least in part skewed, in particular with respect to the first school of *kalām*, the Muʿtazilites. 'The first duty prescribed to you by God', writes ʿAbd al-Jabbar, a tenth-century Muʿtazilite theologian, is 'rational inquiry' (*al-naẓar*) because without it knowledge of God cannot be attained.[11] The commitment to reason (*ʿaql*) is just as distinctive in Saʿadia Gaon, the most prominent Jewish intellectual in the tenth century, who uses the tools of Muʿtazilite *kalām* to provide a scientific foundation for the core doctrines of the Jewish tradition. And the Christian theologian Theodore Abū Qurra had already argued in the ninth century that Christianity is the true religion because it accords with reason.[12]

The Muʿtazilites were also known as the 'people of justice and unity' (*ahl al-ʿadl wa-al-tawḥīd*) because demonstrating God's justice and unity was one of their chief concerns. Both doctrines were clearly not derived from the Bible or the Quran. On the contrary, the Muʿtazilites went to a great deal of trouble to align the religious texts with their philosophical concept of God by reinterpreting everything that on a literal

[9] *Enumeration of the Sciences*, 107–8 [Amin]; 27 [Najjar].

[10] See *Guide* 1.71.

[11] *The Book of the Five Principles*, 79.

[12] See his *Treatise on the Existence of the Creator and the True Religion*, 200–58 [Dick]; 1–25 [Lamoreaux].

understanding contradicted it. But why did Muslim, Jewish, and Christian theologians value reason so highly and turn issues like God's justice and unity into objects of rational enquiry? Do the religious sources—the Bible, the Quran—not provide authoritative answers to such questions?

For one thing, they noticed that the religious sources often advocated inconsistent positions. On a question as crucial as assessing what it means to transgress a divine commandment, for example, different verses in the Quran as well as in the Bible appear to support mutually exclusive views. On the one hand God's will is said to determine human actions, on the other hand human actions are said to arise from free will.[13] Surely such a conflict can be solved exegetically. But in order to decide what to take literally and what to interpret, reason must serve as an arbiter. And once the debate started its far reaching implications for the conception of God become apparent. How can God be called 'just' if he rewards and punishes actions that he himself determined? And conversely, how can he be called 'omnipotent' if he has no power over what human beings do?

Turning from God's justice to God's unity, a second context must be mentioned: the theological debates between intellectuals of different religious communities. Consider a debate between a Christian and a Muslim on the question of whether Christ is God and incarnated in a human body. The Gospel of John affirms it, the Quran denies it, but if the debate's participants do not recognize the authority of each other's religious texts, the appeal to reason as arbiter is again a way out of the impasse.[14] The same holds for the doctrine of the Trinity, another signature Christian doctrine that the Quran rejects. The historian al-Ḥumaydī (d. 1095) describes just such a debate:

> At the . . . meeting there were present not only people of various [Islamic] sects but also unbelievers, Magians, materialists, atheists, Jews and Christians, in short unbelievers [i.e. non-Muslims] of all kinds. Each group had its own leader, whose task it was to defend its views . . . One of the unbelievers rose and said to the assembly: we are meeting here for a debate [*munāthara*]; its conditions are known to all. You, Muslims, are not allowed to argue from your books and prophetic traditions since we deny both. Everybody, therefore, has to limit himself to rational arguments [*ḥujaj al-ʿaql*]. The whole assembly applauded these words.[15]

The principle at work is clear: the participants in the debate cannot rely on their religious texts because none of them is recognized as authoritative by everyone. The sense of a multitude of conflicting opinions conveyed by al-Ḥumaydi is corroborated elsewhere. The Christian theologian Theodore Abū Qurra, for example, sketches a thought-experiment in his *Treatise on the Existence of the Creator and the True*

[13] See Wolfson 1976: 601–2 and the biblical passages discussed in Saʿadya, *Beliefs and Opinions* 4.3 and 4.6.

[14] See, for example, the *Dispute between a Saracen and a Christian* attributed to the eighth-century theologian John of Damascus in Sahas 1972.

[15] al-Ḥumaydī 1983: 175–6.

Religion: a person raised in solitude without religion encounters proponents of the many competing religions in the Middle East. Since they all claim to represent the true religion, Theodore argues that we must 'lay the scriptures [*kutub*] to one side and ask the intellect [*ʿaql*]'.[16] For his part Saʿadia Gaon, after establishing that God created the world out of nothing, proceeds to refuting the views that disagree with what he determined to be the Jewish position. These are no less than twelve cosmological theories ranging from Plato and Aristotle to the Upanishads and the Manichaeans.[17] It is thus clear how theological debates within a religious community, as well as with representatives of other religious communities, were able to motivate the embrace of reason and the subordination of revelation to reason when the two were in conflict. This does not mean that the qualms of the *falāsifa* are entirely misplaced, even in the case of rationalist theologians. Thus Theodore, for example, spends much effort on rationally proving the Incarnation, but neither discusses God's existence nor numerical unity—two points that were not controversial in his intellectual context. Reason, then, does not seem to have the foundational role that the *falāsifa* claim it should have. It is used to resolve disputes, but not to systematically ground the religious project as a whole.

5. Philosophy (*Falsafa*)

From the eighth to the tenth century a large part of Greek philosophy and science was translated into Arabic. This was a highly impressive achievement: one civilization appropriated the system of knowledge of another and turned it into the basis of a vibrant and creative intellectual culture of its own. It was, moreover, not the project of some isolated intellectuals, but a large-scale enterprise carried out under the patronage of the political, social, and economic elite of the Abbasid caliphate (the second Sunni dynasty ruling the Muslim empire; it seized power from the Umayyads in 750). After the Greeks, the next significant period in the history of philosophy and science thus unfolded in the context of Islamic civilization. Its main intellectual centres were Baghdad, the residence of the Abbasid caliphs, and *al-Andalus* (Muslim Spain), the last stronghold of the Umayyads.[18] Christian translators played an important role in this process, translating either directly from the Greek or through the intermediary of Syriac translations. The motives behind the translation movement were complex: a science like medicine, for example, was of interest because of its practical usefulness. The *Topics*, the first Aristotelian work to be translated, offered the dialectical tools required for debating with intellectuals of other religious communities. Competition with Byzantium about which empire had achieved greater scientific sophistication also

[16] *Treatise on the Existence of the Creator*, 218 [Dick]; 9 [Lamoreaux]; cf. 255 [Dick]; 23 [Lamoreaux].

[17] See *Beliefs and Opinions* 1.3.

[18] For a good account of the translation movement, see Gutas 1998.

played a role. Among the justifications offered for the reception of the Greek texts was the claim that the Greeks themselves had derived their insights from ancient Persian wisdom and that the translation movement thus only restored this wisdom to its place of origin (note the similarity to the attempt of Averroes and Maimonides to trace their philosophical views back to Abraham).

Among the competing responses to the encounter with Greek philosophy, that proposed by al-Fārābī ultimately prevailed. Although, chronologically speaking, al-Fārābī is not the first Arabic philosopher, he shaped the identity of classical Arabic philosophy from the ninth century onwards.[19] To understand the place of philosophy in the medieval Islamic world, we must thus begin with an examination of al-Fārābī. In the *Book of Letters* al-Fārābī offers an account of the development of human knowledge of which the last two stages are associated with Plato and Aristotle. While at 'the time of Plato' knowledge reached the degree of certainty that can be achieved through dialectics, in Aristotle's time

> scientific speculation [*al-naẓar al-ʿilmī*] is completed and all its methods are distinguished, theoretical philosophy and universal practical philosophy are perfected, and no object in them remains to be investigated. [Philosophy] becomes an art that is only learned and taught.[20]

True philosophy, al-Fārābī claims, 'was handed down to us by the Greeks from Plato and Aristotle alone'.[21] Later Muslim, Jewish, and Christian *falāsifa* shared al-Fārābī's high regard for Plato and especially Aristotle. Averroes, for example, writes in his *Long Commentary on the* De anima that Aristotle 'was a model in nature and the instantiation that nature found for showing the highest human perfection'.[22] The great majority of Averroes' works are commentaries on Aristotle. They come in different formats and serve different purposes. Sometimes they take on the form of a systematic treatise on a philosophical topic, for example philosophical psychology or celestial physics. But all of them reflect what is undoubtedly Averroes' central intellectual concern: understanding Aristotle. Averroes thus bears eloquent witness to the *falāsifa*'s conviction that Aristotle was the best gateway to the truth.

This does not mean that true philosophy flourished only in Greece. Elsewhere al-Fārābī traces the origin of philosophy back to Mesopotamia where Abraham was born. From there it was transmitted to 'the people of Egypt', then 'to the Greeks where it remained until it was transmitted to the Syrians and then to the Arabs'.[23] Since al-Fārābī wrote most of his works in Baghdad, this suggests once more that he is merely returning philosophy to where it originally came from. Al-Fārābī's claim to inherit and continue Greek philosophy is made most clearly in *On the Appearance of Philosophy* where he describes the transmission of philosophy through a long chain of intermediaries from Aristotle to himself. While Christian authorities prohibited teaching parts of

[19] See Gutas 1998: 95–104 on the rise of the 'ideology of rationalism' in the ninth century.
[20] *Book of Letters*, sections 142–3. [21] *Attainment of Happiness*, 196 [Yasin]; 49 [Mahdi].
[22] p. 433 [Crawford]. [23] *Attainment*, 181 [Yasin]; 43 [Mahdi].

the philosophical curriculum because they perceived them as a threat to Christian doctrine, he is the first to restore philosophy to its full scope after the arrival of Islam.[24] As a historical document this text is of little interest, but it allows us to see how al-Fārābī situates himself in relation to ancient philosophy and how he conceives his own role in philosophy's transmission to the Muslim world. Al-Fārābī's portrait of his role in the transmission of philosophy was adopted by later *falāsifa* who take him to be the foremost philosophical authority after Aristotle.[25] Unlike seventeenth-century philosophers like Descartes who were keen to establish a 'new' philosophy after the Copernican revolution had blown the Aristotelian picture of the world into pieces, the *falāsifa* thus wanted to continue the true philosophy which they equated with the philosophy of Plato and Aristotle. While they did not pretend to originality, this does not imply that they were not original in many respects—in the way they interpreted and systematized their Greek sources, made them useful to their distinctive concerns, engaged in debates with *kalām* and other intellectual rivals, and so forth.

Since al-Fārābī did not encounter Greek philosophy as a living tradition, his first task was to bring the Greek texts that had been translated into Arabic back to life by explaining the importance of philosophy, introducing its methods and subjects, and commenting on its canonical works. Ensuring the continuity of philosophy is crucial, because, according to al-Fārābī, philosophy is the key to the best life. His second task is to clarify the relationship between philosophy and religion. Al-Fārābī rejects a number of views that had been proposed on this matter. On one end of the conceptual spectrum is a group of *mutakallimūn* that al-Fārābī describes in the *Enumeration of the Sciences*: because human reason is 'too weak' (*yaḍʿuf*) to guide us, they argue, we must rely on the supernatural revelation received by the prophets.[26] On the opposite side of the spectrum Muslim freethinkers like Abū Bakr al-Rāzī deny the need for prophetic guidance altogether, since God has bestowed reason on all human beings. The plurality of prophetic religions, moreover, and their claim to exclusive validity only give rise to religious strife in Rāzī's view.[27] The first Arabic philosopher, al-Kindī (d. *c.*870), occupies a middle ground. He modified philosophy to suit Islam in an unacceptable manner, according to al-Fārābī, which is why he omits al-Kindī in his account of the 'appearance of philosophy' in Islam.[28] Similarly Christian authorities prohibited

[24] On the anti-Byzantine stance reflected in the assessment of the Christians, see Gutas 1998: ch. 4.2. The issue seems to hinge on the teaching of the *Posterior Analytics* containing Aristotle's theory of the scientific syllogism. For al-Fārābī this is, of course, crucial given his concept of philosophy as a demonstrative science.

[25] Avicenna, for example, al-Fārābī's most important successor in the Muslim East, relates in his autobiography how he studied Aristotle's *Metaphysics* many times, but only succeeded in understanding it when he read it with al-Fārābī's commentary (*Sīra*, 32–4 [Arabic]; 33–5 [English]). For the Muslim West, see Maimonides' praise of al-Fārābī in his letter to Samuel ibn Tibbon: 'All that al-Fārābī wrote [...] is entirely without fault... for he excelled in wisdom [*haya muflag be-hokhmah*]' (*Letters*, 553). For the appreciation of al-Fārābī's works on logic by Averroes and his students, see Ibn Tumlūs, *Introduction to the Art of Logic*, 14–15.

[26] *Enumeration*, 108 [Amin]; 28 [Najjar].

[27] On Rāzī, see Stroumsa 1999: ch. 3.

[28] On al-Kindī, see Adamson 2006; on al-Kindī and al-Fārābī, see in particular 14–18.

teaching parts of the philosophical curriculum as we saw. Thus several questions arise: should prophetic guidance replace reason or, conversely, reason prophetic guidance? Must the teachings of reason at least be modified or partially prohibited to fit into a religious framework?[29]

Reviving the project of ancient philosophy requires, first of all, clarifying what this project is.[30] According to al-Fārābī's general outline in the *Attainment of Happiness*, its central concern is an enquiry into the constituents of human perfection or 'happiness' (*saʿāda*, translating Aristotle's *eudaimonia*), and into how to attain and disseminate it. In the *Philosophy of Plato* and the *Philosophy of Aristotle*, al-Fārābī explains how this project informs the writings of Plato and Aristotle. Of course the question arises whether Plato and Aristotle pursue the same project in the first place. Although Aristotle is superior to Plato, al-Fārābī stresses that the 'purpose' (*gharaḍ*) of their philosophy is the same.[31] To corroborate this he writes a treatise harmonizing their views on issues of apparent disagreement.[32] Then al-Fārābī establishes the order of the philosophical curriculum, most prominently in the *Enumeration of the Sciences*. A number of introductory works exhort to or prepare for the study of philosophy.[33] After all these preliminary steps, the strictly philosophical work can begin: explaining Aristotle. Since Aristotle agrees with Plato and at the same time is superior to him, no explanation of Plato is needed. The Greek philosophers left not only an outline of philosophy, but also of 'the methods [*ṭuruq*] to it and of the methods to re-establish it when it becomes confused or extinct'.[34] By 'the methods' al-Fārābī certainly means Aristotle's logic. Since his goal is to ensure the continuity of philosophy, providing the 'toolkit' for establishing and transmitting it is obviously a central concern to him. He thus commented on all parts of the *Organon* in the version inherited from the late ancient Alexandrian tradition—from Porphyry's *Eisagôgê* to the *Rhetoric* and the *Poetics*.[35] Much of al-Fārābī's authority for philosophers like Averroes and Maimonides rests, in fact, on his contribution to logic.[36] But he also commented on the philosophical

[29] Al-Fārābī's twofold task reflects challenges specific to introducing philosophy into the Muslim world. While historians of Islamic philosophy broadly agree that al-Fārābī's intellectual outlook was shaped by the late Alexandrian tradition of Neoplatonic commentators on Aristotle, the continuity between the philosophical curriculum in late ancient Alexandria and early medieval Baghdad accounts only partly for al-Fārābī's project.

[30] I do not claim that the following account corresponds to the chronological order in which al-Fārābī wrote his works, or that it reflects a preconceived plan which he systematically executed. What I propose is an interpretation of how several parts of al-Fārābī's corpus fit together.

[31] *Attainment*, 196 [Yasin]; 50 [Mahdi].

[32] See his *The Harmonization of the Opinions of the Two Sages, Plato the Divine and Aristotle*.

[33] See, for example, *Exhortation to the Path of Happiness*. For a comprehensive study of this genre's place in al-Fārābī's work, see Jaffray 2000.

[34] *Attainment*, 196 [Yasin]; 50 [Mahdi].

[35] On the inclusion of the *Rhetoric* and *Poetics* into the *Organon* and its philosophical implications, see Black 1990.

[36] For Averroes, see Ibn Tumlūs, *Introduction*, 14–15. For Maimonides, see *Letters*, 553.

sciences properly speaking, both theoretical (mathematics, physics, and metaphysics) and practical (ethics and politics).

To understand how al-Fārābī conceives the relationship between philosophy and religion we must look at his political philosophy which was mainly shaped by Plato. Scholars have long wondered why Aristotle's *Politics* was not translated into Arabic and why al-Fārābī—and the *falāsifa* in general—turned to Plato rather than Aristotle for their political philosophy despite considering Aristotle superior to Plato.[37] But recall that Aristotle's superiority, according to al-Fārābī, stems from the fact that his scientific method is superior to Plato's. Whereas in Plato's time knowledge was still pursued by means of dialectics, in Aristotle's time 'scientific speculation' was 'completed'—that is, reached the stage of '*burhān*' (demonstration), the method set forth in the *Posterior Analytics*. Aristotle himself, however, stresses that 'political philosophy' is not an exact science. Its premises and conclusions are only 'generally' (*epi to polu*) and not necessarily true.[38] For the *falāsifa* this means that political philosophy by its nature cannot generate more than dialectical propositions.[39] Hence even on al-Fārābī's conception of Greek intellectual history Plato would seem to be as good as Aristotle with regard to political philosophy. Arguably, Plato had given more thought to political issues than Aristotle. And the way he proposes to conceive the relationship between philosophy and political power in a virtuous *polis* and the role of philosophy in the pedagogical-political guidance of the citizens to virtue provided a much better conceptual framework for interpreting Islam and Judaism as philosophical religions than Aristotle's *Politics*. It is also not true that Aristotle plays no role in al-Fārābī's political thought. First and foremost the *Organon*, but also the *De anima* and the *Nicomachean Ethics*, provide crucial concepts that are integrated into the overall Platonic framework.

How, then, did Plato's political philosophy prove useful to al-Fārābī for determining the relationship between philosophy and religion? Throughout Plato's dialogues, the goal of his philosophical-political project remains the same: to make the citizens better by leading them to virtue.[40] In the Socratic dialogues the key to virtue is knowledge, which the Socrates of the Apology thinks is to some extent accessible to all citizens.[41] Knowing what is good for Socrates is a necessary and sufficient condition for doing what is good.[42] Political success thus consists in directing the citizens through philosophical enquiry to knowledge.[43] But from the middle dialogues onwards Plato no longer considered knowledge as sufficient for the task. When he came to see the human

[37] See, for example, Pines 1975. [38] *Nicomachean Ethics* 1.3, 1094b21–2.

[39] Al-Fārābī's commentary on the *Nicomachean Ethics* is not extant, but see the distinction between 'necessary' (*hekhraḥi*) and 'general' (*me'odi*) in the preserved Hebrew version of Averroes' *Middle Commentary on the* Nicomachean Ethics, 60–1.

[40] For a number of characteristic passages, see *Apology* 25a–c; *Protagoras* 318c–d, 319e–320b; *Gorgias* 464b–465a, 515b–521d; *Republic* 420b–421c; *Statesman* 296e–297b; *Laws* 630a–631d, 650b.

[41] See, for example, *Apology* 29d ff.; 30e; 33b.

[42] See, for example, *Charmides* 174b–c; *Laches* 199d–e; *Protagoras* 351b ff.

[43] Hence Plato praises Socrates as the only Athenian to practise 'the true craft of politics' (*Gorgias* 521d).

soul as having both rational and irrational parts, and most souls as dominated by one of the latter, the problem of non-philosophers—that is, of those who cannot be led to virtue through philosophy—became a central concern for him.[44] My understanding of Plato's solution is this: although philosophy remains a necessary condition for becoming perfectly virtuous, all human beings can be led to a lower level of virtue through a pedagogical-political programme designed by philosophers for non-philosophers. This explains the elaborate discussion that Plato devotes to non-philosophical devices—most strikingly in the *Laws*. The programme's main components are religious stories, laws, persuasive speeches, and religious practices. The crucial point for my purpose is that Plato abandons the Socratic attempt, portrayed in the *Apology*, to lead all citizens to virtue through philosophical enquiry. In the *Republic*, Plato, in fact, explicitly criticizes the use of the Socratic debate for testing the beliefs of non-philosophers, since it will cause them to lose the traditional beliefs in which they were brought up and they lack the ability to 'discover the true ones'. After having been 'law-abiding', therefore, they 'become lawless'.[45]

Al-Fārābī adopts Plato's fundamental premise that human beings are unequal by nature and divided into a minority of philosophers and a majority of non-philosophers.[46] In *Falsafat Aflāṭūn*, moreover, he clearly distinguishes between the Socratic method and the method advocated in Plato's later dialogues. 'Socrates', he claims, was only able 'to conduct a scientific investigation of justice and the virtues . . . but did not possess the ability to form the character of the youth and the multitude [*al-aḥdāth wa-al-jumhūr*].' The 'philosopher, the king and the lawgiver', by contrast, must be able to do both: to instruct 'the elect [*al-khawāṣṣ*]' by means of 'the Socratic method' and to form the character of 'the youth and the multitude' by means of a pedagogical-political programme.[47] From al-Fārābī's *Jawāmiʿ kitāb al-nawāmīs li-Aflāṭūn* [Epitome of Plato's *Laws*], we know that at a minimum, he was familiar with the main traits of the pedagogical-political programme that Plato had worked out in the *Laws*.

We saw that, in the *Ḥurūf*, al-Fārābī describes the process by which the theoretical and practical sciences reach perfection. This is followed by an outline of the two methods used for disseminating the results of this process to the political community. They correspond precisely to the two methods that we just saw: the 'instruction' of philosophers 'proceeds by demonstrative methods', whereas the instruction of non-philosophers, 'which is public, proceeds by dialectical, rhetorical or poetical methods'. This second kind of instruction in turn constitutes 'religion' (*milla*) which al-Fārābī takes to be an 'imitation of philosophy' (*muḥākīyya li-l-falsafa*).[48] Religion thus conceived fulfils precisely the role of Plato's pedagogical-political programme: 'through

[44] See, for example, *Republic* 581b–c. [45] See the entire passage 538c–539a.

[46] For the former, see *The Political Regime*, 89–91 [Najjar]; 44 [Najjar]. For the latter, see *Attainment*, 177–8 [Yasin]; 41 [Mahdi].

[47] *The Philosophy of Plato*, 21–2 [Rosenthal–Walzer]; 66–7 [Mahdi].

[48] *Attainment*, 185 [Yasin]; 44 [Mahdi]. Al-Fārābī's most elaborate discussion of religion is the *Book of Religion*.

religion, the multitude is taught, educated and given all that is needed to attain happiness.'[49] Its purpose is to convey 'theoretical and practical matters that have been inferred in philosophy, in such a way as to enable the multitude to understand them by persuasion or imaginative representation or both'.[50] Religion thus serves as the 'tool' of philosophy which makes philosophical contents accessible to non-philosophers.[51] God's description as a king in the religious texts, for example, is seen as a pedagogically useful metaphorical imitation of the philosophical doctrine of God occupying the first rank in the hierarchy of existents. The notion of the king conveys an approximate idea of God's rank to non-philosophers who cannot understand the ontological order, but who do understand the political order.[52]

For al-Fārābī, Plato's philosopher-king who has the task of guiding both philosophers and non-philosophers to the perfection and happiness possible to them, is replaced by the prophet.[53] The virtuous political community is, therefore, at the same time a virtuous religious community. The difference between the philosopher and the prophet is explained in terms of Aristotle's psychology: the prophet has not only perfected his intellect like the philosopher, but he also has a perfect imagination. And one of the imagination's functions, according to al-Fārābī, is precisely 'to imitate' things.[54] In other words: the prophet is not only a philosopher, but a poet and orator as well which allows him to guide both the philosophers and the non-philosophers in his community. It should be clear by now how the late ancient version of the *Organon* is integrated into this Platonic framework: the prophet instructs philosophers by presenting them with propositions about things as they truly are and then leads them to assent by providing a demonstration. To non-philosophers, on the other hand, he presents propositions that for the most part poetically imitate reality and then leads them to assent through rhetorical or dialectical arguments.[55] Thus religious texts for al-Fārābī consist mainly of metaphors, parables, and rhetorical and dialectical arguments.

One implication of conceiving religion as an 'imitation' of philosophy is that much of its content will be false if understood literally. God, for example, according to the philosopher, is not truly a king as he is poetically represented in the religious texts. But the representation is true if it is understood as a metaphor for God's ontological rank. A religious text is thus true when considered in terms of its allegorical content—that is, when the imitated doctrine is made visible behind the imitation. But if true religion coincides with true philosophy on the allegorical level, then the difference between the two—which seemed to be implied in the notion of 'imitation'—disappears. Only taken literally, religion is an imitation of philosophy. Taken allegorically religion and philosophy are the same.

[49] *Letters*, section 144. [50] Ibid., section 108. [51] Ibid., section 110.

[52] See, for example, *Attainment*, 185 [Yasin]; 45 [Mahdi], quoted by Averroes in his Commentary on Plato's *Republic*, 30. Cf. *Guide* 1.8–9.

[53] See in particular ch. 15 of the *Virtuous City*. See also Walzer 1957.

[54] See *Virtuous City* 14.2.

[55] See, for example, *Attainment*, 184 [Yasin]; 44 [Mahdi]. Cf. Black 1990.

Al-Fārābī can now address the concerns about reason and prophetic guidance of both the *mutakallimūn* and Abū Bakr al-Rāzī. Although reason is not too weak to guide us, this does not mean that the literal content of the prophetic teachings is redundant since God did not bestow reason *equally* on all human beings. As a consequence, reason on its own is not sufficient to lead humankind to perfection. And al-Fārābī can also respond to al-Kindī and Christian censors that there is no need to modify philosophy or prohibit parts of the philosophical curriculum, since a virtuous religion, correctly understood, is in complete agreement with philosophy.

Al-Fārābī uses traditional religious vocabulary to signal how religious doctrines can be philosophically reinterpreted. Thus 'divine revelation', for example, can be reinterpreted in terms of the human intellect's transition from potentiality to actuality.[56] Note, however, that al-Fārābī never explicitly identifies Islam with the philosophical religion resulting from this reinterpretation. He stresses, moreover, the possibility of multiple virtuous religions which share a true core embedded in different cultural materials. In the *Epitome of the* Laws, al-Fārābī traces this pluralism back to Plato: Plato mentions the *nomoi* of both Crete and Sparta 'in order to explain that there are many *nomoi* [*nawāmīs*] and that their multiplicity does not invalidate them [*kathrathuhā lā tubṭiluhā*]'.[57] This pluralism is also reflected in al-Fārābī's definition of religion:

> Religion consists of opinions and actions, determined and limited by conditions [*muqadarra muqayyada bi-sharāʾiṭ*], which are prescribed to the community by their first ruler who strives to attain a particular goal.[58]

The 'opinions and actions' constituting a religion are 'determined and limited' by the natural and cultural 'conditions' under which the religion was established. Hence a virtuous religion allows for multiple instantiations each of which is valid in its particular context. Their true core is

> reproduced by imitation for each nation and for the people of each city through those parables which are best known to them. But what is best known often varies among nations, either most of it or part of it. Hence these things are expressed for each nation in parables other than those used for another nation. Therefore it is possible that virtuous nations and virtuous cities exist whose religions [*milal*] differ, although they all have as their goal one and the same happiness.[59]

Al-Fārābī thus combines universalism with respect to the true content and goal of a virtuous religion with contextual pluralism concerning the laws, stories, exhortations, and practices of worship that 'imitate' the true content and serve as means for attaining the goal. This allows him to give an answer to Rāzī's charge that multiple prophetic religions give rise to religious strife. On al-Fārābī's view their claim to truth clearly must not entail a claim to exclusivity. Al-Fārābī thus provides a model for philosophically reinterpreting the religious traditions existing side by side in the Islamic world.

[56] See *Virtuous City* 15.10. [57] *Epitome* 1.2.
[58] *Religion* 1. [59] *Virtuous City* 17.2.

In a sense later *falāsifa* like Yaḥyā ibn ʿAdī, Averroes, and Maimonides do just that: they apply al-Fārābī's model to the interpretation of Christianity, Islam, and Judaism as philosophical religions. Al-Fārābī's universalism is expressed well in a passage of Yaḥyā's *Treatise on the Reformation of Morals*:

> One who loves perfection must also make it a habit to love people generally . . . and to be gentle and compassionate with them. Men are a single tribe [*qabīl*], related to one another; humanity [*insāniyya*] unites them. The adornment of the divine power is in all of them and in each one of them, and it is the rational soul. By means of this soul, man becomes man. It is the nobler of the two parts of man, which are the soul and the body. So man in his true being is the rational soul, and it is a single substance in all men. All men in their true being are a single thing, but they are many in persons. Since their souls are one, and love is only in the soul, all of them must then . . . love one another.[60]

In the entire treatise, Yaḥyā makes no explicit reference to Christianity. This does not mean that traditional religion can be neglected. But when he discusses the way of life of those who 'give people an interest in eternal life'—for example 'scholars' (*ahl al-ʿilm*) and 'monks' (*al-ruhbān*)—he says, ecumenically as it were, that among the things 'to be considered good for them' is 'attendance at churches and mosques and so forth'.[61] As we will see below, however, the passage just cited is not only compatible with Yaḥyā's Christian commitments, but can be read as the philosophical reinterpretation of a key Christian doctrine: the duty of loving one's neighbour.

A different example of the kind of universalism advocated by the *falāsifa* is the view that one should accept a true claim without regard to the religion of the person who makes it. In the words of al-Kindī:

> We ought not to be ashamed of appreciating the truth and of acquiring it wherever it comes from, even if it comes from races distant and nations different from us. For the seeker of truth nothing takes precedence over the truth, and there is no disparagement of the truth, nor belittling either of him who speaks it or of him who conveys it. No one is demeaned by the truth, rather all are ennobled by it.[62]

This attitude was, of course, crucial to justify the reception of pagan Greek philosophy in which al-Kindī and his intellectual circle were engaged. But it was also extended to philosophers of sibling religious communities as in the case of Maimonides who, like al-Kindī, instructs his readers 'to listen to the truth from whoever says it'.[63] In the instructions he left to a student about which philosophical works are worth studying, he does not recommend a single Jewish author. After the Greeks, in particular Aristotle and his commentators, the philosophers he praises are all Muslims: al-Fārābī who 'excelled in wisdom', for example, or Ibn Bājja whose 'treatises are all good for the person who understands'.[64] If someone proposes a definition of an animal species,

[60] *Reformation* 5.14. [61] Ibid. 3.43. [62] *On First Philosophy*, 103 [Abū Rīda]; 58 [Ivry].
[63] *Eight Chapters*, Preface. [64] *Letters*, 553.

explains the meaning of justice, or works out a proof for God's existence, what matters is not whether he is Greek, Jewish, Muslim, Christian, or anything else, but whether what he says is true.

Note, however, that the *falāsifa*'s universalism does not by itself commit them to recognizing multiple virtuous religions. After all, someone who belongs to a false religion may also hit on the truth occasionally. Even when they are willing to admit religious pluralism, they usually deny that different religions are *equally* virtuous. Averroes, for example, writes that a virtuous character can only be attained through

> the knowledge and exaltation of God by the forms of worship prescribed by the laws to [the members of the community] in each religion [*fī milla milla*], like sacrifices, prayers, supplications and similar utterances by which praise is rendered to God, exalted be he, the angels, and the prophets.[65]

While he thus allows that the practices and beliefs of different religions promote human perfection, he also argues that the practices and beliefs of Islam do so best. A 'wise man' (*ḥakīm*) must:

> choose the best religion of his time, even if they all are true for him, and believe that the better one will be abrogated [*yunsakh*] through one that is even better. For this reason the wise men who were teaching the people in Alexandria converted to Islam when the religion of Islam reached them, and the wise men who were in the Roman Empire converted to Christianity when the religion of Jesus, peace be upon him, reached them. And nobody doubts that among the Israelites were many wise men, as is clear from the books... attributed to Solomon.[66]

A little further Averroes claims that 'in our religion' practices like prayer and beliefs like the doctrine of the hereafter fulfil the purpose of a virtuous religion 'more perfectly' (*atamm*) than comparable practices and beliefs in other religions.[67] I thus take Averroes to be claiming that Islam is superior to Judaism and Christianity. Averroes does not say why Islam is superior in his view. Two explanations are possible. On the first, the degree of wisdom that a religion embodies depends on the moral and intellectual state of the community that the founder of the religion addresses. On the second, it depends on the degree of wisdom of the founder himself. Maimonides offers a good example of the first explanation. During their long sojourn in Egypt, he argues, the Israelites became habituated to the corrupt practices and beliefs of their pagan masters. Since human nature resists radical change, Moses could only reform, but not completely erase these practices and beliefs. Thus Moses retains the practice of sacrifices, but redirects it from idols to God. He also continues to speak of God as if he had human form. In these, as well as in many other cases, Moses, according to Maimonides, had to make concessions to the idol worship with which the Israelites

[65] *Incoherence of the Incoherence* 2.4, 581 [Bouyges]; 359 [Van den Bergh].

[66] Ibid. 583 [Bouyges]; 360–1 [Van den Bergh].

[67] Ibid. 584 [Bouyges]; 361 [Van den Bergh].

had been brought up.[68] Averroes could thus argue that Islam is superior to Judaism and Christianity, because it was established under more favourable religious-cultural circumstances. The second explanation can be illustrated through Yaḥyā's account of God's incarnation in Christ. Yaḥyā refers to Aristotle's claim that in the act of knowledge, the subject and object of knowledge become one. Thus the human intellect unites with the form of the thing that it apprehends. Since God is incorporeal and hence pure form, knowing God entails that the human being 'becomes united [*muttaḥad*] with his Creator mighty and magnificent through the intermediary of the intellect [*ʿaql*]'.[69] But if this is all that the Incarnation means, why should such a union be attributed to Christ alone and not to the prophets and the righteous who achieved knowledge of God as well? Yaḥyā's response to this objection is that nobody else 'reached Christ's degree' (*balagha mablaghuhū*) who alone attained 'perfect union' (*ittiḥād tāmm*) with God.[70] The difference between Christ and the prophets, therefore, is one of degree with respect to intellectual perfection.

Yaḥyā's philosophical Christology also allows us to discern the implicit Christian character of the universal humanism that he espouses in *The Reformation of Morals*. As we saw, all human beings partake in Divine Reason through their rational souls, which in turn is the defining feature of their humanity. In this sense 'men are a single tribe'. The more they perfect their rational souls, the more they unite with Divine Reason and hence with each other—that is, with the rational aspect of their selves. Since Christ is perfectly united with Divine Reason and thus identical with it, union with Divine Reason is at the same time union with Christ. In the end, then, Yaḥyā's commitment to universal rationalism is not distinct from his commitment to Christianity. And since Divine Reason unites all rational souls, the love of Divine Reason is at the same time the love of all human beings insofar as they are rational. It is thus as much a love of oneself as it is a love of others, which provides Yaḥyā with a philosophical interpretation of the Christian duty to love one's neighbour.

These examples should suffice to show that the relationship between the philosophical universalism of the *falāsifa* and their religious particularism is complicated. While they may all have agreed that Abraham was an outstanding philosopher, they usually also insisted on the superiority of their own Abrahamic religion.

6. Epilogue: Philosophy and Theology in the Latin West

When Christian philosophers in medieval Europe began to study Graeco-Arabic philosophy and science in Latin translation, they did not interpret Christianity as a philosophical religion. The fact that Christian philosophers in antiquity—for example

[68] See *Guide* 3.32. [69] *On the Necessity of the Incarnation*, 83. [70] Ibid. 85.

Clement and Origen of Alexandria—did propose such an interpretation, as did Yaḥya ibn ʿAdī, among others, in the Muslim world, implies that nothing in the nature of Christianity precludes it.[71] Yet while the relationship between philosophy and Christianity in the later Middle Ages took on different forms, the two always remained identifiable as two distinct traditions. Thomas Aquinas, for example, argues that central Christian doctrines such as the Trinity and Christ's Incarnation are beyond the reach of reason. Latin Averroists even allow for philosophy and Christian theology to contradict each other on core doctrines. This is the opposite of the position advocated by the *falāsifa*. For Yaḥya, for example, both the Trinity and the Incarnation can be explained within the framework of Aristotelian philosophy. They do not transcend reason's grasp, let alone contradict it. Thus Yaḥyā sees no tension between his philosophical and Christian commitments. The fact that in the medieval university philosophy and theology were taught in different faculties bears witness to their separation on the institutional level as well. The tensions between philosophy and Christianity culminated in the 1277 condemnation of 219 philosophical and theological theses by Bishop Tempier in Paris which further entrenched the division between Christianity and many of the teachings of the Graeco-Arabic philosophical corpus that had been translated into Latin. One could point to the fact that the Platonic framework underlying the interpretation of religious traditions as philosophical religions in the Muslim world did not play a significant role in the medieval Latin context. This, however, does not answer the question, but only moves it up one level: since Christian appropriations of this Platonic framework were available in patristic literature—for example in the works of Clement and Origen—it remains to be explained why it was not adopted for integrating Christianity with Graeco-Arabic philosophy in the Middle Ages. At any rate, medieval Latin Europe did not have a place for the philosopher Abraham who held the religious and philosophical identity of Muslim, Jewish, and Christian *falāsifa* together.

References

Abd al-Jabbār. 1979. *The Book of the Five Principles* (*Kitāb al-uṣūl al-khamsa*) in D. Gimaret, 'Les *Usul al-Hamsa* du Qadi Abd al-Jabbar et leurs commentaires'. *Annales Islamologiques* 15: 47–96.

Abū Qurra, Theodore. 1982. *Treatise on the Existence of the Creator and the True Religion* (*fî wujûd al khâliq wa-al-dîn al-qawîm*), Arabic in Ignace Dick, *Théodore Abuqurra: Traité de l'existence du Créateur et de la vraie religion*, Patrimoine arabe chrétien 3, Jounieh: Librairie Saint-Paul; Rome: Pontificio Istituto Orientale; Eng. trans. John C. Lamoreaux, Theodore Abū Qurra, Provo. Utah: Brigham Young University, 2005.

Adamson, P. 2006. *Al-Kindī*. Oxford: Oxford University Press.

Averroes. 1938–48. *Long Commentary on the* Metaphysics (*Tafsīr mā baʿd al-ṭabīʿāt*), ed. M. Bouyges. Beirut: Imprimerie Catholique.

[71] On Clement's and Origen's philosophical interpretation of Christianity, see Fraenkel 2012: ch. 2.

Averroes. 1953. *Long Commentary on Aristotle's* De Anima, ed. F. S. Crawford. Cambridge: The Medieval Academy of America.

Averroes. 1969. *Commentary on Plato's* Republic, Hebrew trans. S. b. Judah of Marseilles, ed. with Eng. trans. by E. I. J. Rosenthal. Cambridge: Cambridge University Press.

Averroes. 1992. *The Incoherence of the Incoherence* (*Tahāfut al-tahāfut*), ed. M. Bouyges. Beirut: Dār al-Mashriq, 3rd edn.; Eng. trans. S. Van den Bergh. 2 vols. E. J. W. Gibb Memorial Series, London: Luzac, 1954.

Averroes. 2000. *Middle Commentary on Aristotle's* Nicomachean Ethics, Hebrew trans. by S. b. Judah of Marseilles, ed. L. Berman. Jerusalem: The Israel Academy of the Sciences and Humanities.

Averroes. 2001. *Decisive Treatise* (*Faṣl al-maqāl*), Arabic ed. G. Hourani (corrections by M. Mahdi) with Eng. trans. C. Butterworth. Provo: Brigham Young University Press.

Avicenna. 1974. *Autobiography* (*Sīrat al-shaykh al-ra'īs*), ed. and Eng. trans. William Gohlmann. New York: SUNY Press.

Black, D. 1990. *Logic and Aristotle's 'Rhetoric' and 'Poetics' in Medieval Arabic Philosophy*. Leiden: Brill.

Butterworth, C., trans. 2001. *Alfarabi: The Political Writings: Selected Aphorisms and Other Texts*. Ithaca, NY: Cornell University Press.

al-Fārābī. 1884. *On the Appearance of Philosophy* (*Fī ẓuhūr al-falsafa*), in Ibn Abī Uṣaybiʿa 1884: II. 134–5.

al-Fārābī. 1943. *The Philosophy of Plato* (*Falsafat Aflāṭūn*), ed. F. Rosenthal and R. Walzer. London: Warburg Institute; Eng. trans. in Mahdi 1962.

al-Fārābī. 1961. *The Philosophy of Aristotle* (*Falsafat Arisṭūṭālīs*), ed. M. Mahdi. Beirut: Dār Majallat Shiʿr; Eng. trans. in Mahdi 1962.

al-Fārābī. 1964. *The Political Regime* (*Kitāb al-siyāsa al-madaniyya*), ed. F. Najjar. Beirut: al-Kāthūlīkīyah; partial Eng. trans. F. Najjar in Lerner and Mahdi 1972: 31–57.

al-Fārābī. 1968. *Book of Religion* (*Kitāb al-milla*), ed. M. Mahdi. Beirut: Dār al-Mashriq; Eng. trans. Butterworth 2001.

al-Fārābī. 1968. *Enumeration of the Sciences* (*Iḥṣā' al-ʿulūm*), ed. U. Amin. Cairo: Maktabat al-Anjlū al-Miṣrīyah; partial Eng. trans. F. Najjar in Lerner and Mahdi 1972.

al-Fārābī. 1969. *The Book of Letters* (*Kitāb al-ḥurūf*), ed. M. Mahdi, Beirut: Dār al-Mashriq; Eng. trans. of book 2 in *Medieval Islamic Philosophical Writings*, ed. Muhammad Khalidi. Cambridge: Cambridge University Press, 2005.

al-Fārābī. 1985. *Exhortation to the Path of Happiness* (*Kitāb al-tanbīh ʿalā sabīl al-saʿāda*), ed. J. al-Yasin. Beirut: Dār al-Manāhil; Eng. trans. Jaffray 2000: 401–30.

al-Fārābī. 1985. *The Principles of the Opinions of the Citizens of the Virtuous City* (*Mabādi' ārā' ahl al-madīna al-fāḍila*), ed. and Eng. trans. R. Walzer, *Al-Farabi on the Perfect State*. Oxford: Clarendon Press.

al-Fārābī. 1992. *The Attainment of Happiness* (*Taḥṣīl al-saʿāda*), in *al-Aʿmāl al-falsafiyya*, ed. J. al-Yasin, 119–225. Beirut: Dār al-Manāhil; Eng. trans. Mahdi 2001.

al-Fārābī. 1998. *Epitome of Plato's* Laws (*Jawāmiʿ kitāb al-nawāmīs li-Aflāṭūn*), ed. T.-A. Druart, *Bulletin d'Etudes Orientales* 50; partial Eng. trans. in Lerner and Mahdi 1972.

al-Fārābī. 1999. *The Harmonization of the Opinions of the Two Sages, Plato the Divine and Aristotle* (*Kitāb al-jamʿ bayna ra'yay al-ḥakīmayn Aflāṭūn al-ilāhī wa-Arisṭūṭālīs*), ed. and French trans. by F. Najjar and D. Mallet. Damascus: Institut Français de Damas; Eng. trans. Butterworth 2001.

Fraenkel, C. 2012. *Philosophical Religions from Plato to Spinoza: Reason, Religion, and Autonomy*. Cambridge: Cambridge University Press.

al-Ghazālī. 1953. *The Deliverance from Error* (*Munqidh min al-ḍalāl*), ed. Jamil Saliba and Kamil Ayyad. Damascus, 1939; Eng. trans. W. M. Watt in *The Faith and Practice of Al-Ghazālī*. London: George Allen and Unwin.

al-Ghazālī. 1997. *The Incoherence of the Philosophers* (*Tahāfut al-falāsifa*), Arabic with Eng. trans. M. E. Marmura. Provo: Brigham Young University Press.

al-Ghazālī. 2002. *Decisive Criterion for Distinguishing Islam from Unbelief* (*Fayṣal al-tafriqa bayna al-islām wa-al-zandaqa*), ed. M. Bījū. Damascus, 1993; Eng. trans. S. A. Jackson in *On the Boundaries of the Theological Tolerance in Islam: Abū Ḥāmid al-Ghazālī's 'Fayṣal al-Tafriqa'*. Oxford: Oxford University Press.

Goitein, S. D. 1955. *Jews and Arabs: Their Contact through the Ages*. New York: Schocken.

Gutas, D. 1998. *Greek Thought, Arabic Culture: The Graeco-Arabic Translation Movement in Baghdad and Early Abbasid Society*. London and New York: Routledge.

al-Ḥumaydī. 1983. *On the History of Scholars in Andalusia* (*Jadhwat al-muqtabis fī tārīkh 'ulamā' al-Andalus*), ed. I. al-Ibyārī. Beirut: Dār al-Kitāb al-Lubnānī.

Ibn Abī Uṣaybiʿa. 1884. *ʿUyūn al-anbāʾ fī ṭabaqāt al-aṭibbāʾ*, ed. August Müller. 2 vols. Königsberg: al-Wahbīyah.

Ibn Tumlūs. 1916. *Introduction to the Art of Logic* (*Madkhal li-ṣināʿat al-manṭiq*), ed. and Spanish trans. M. Asin. Madrid: Centro de Estudios Historicos.

Jaffray, A. 2000. *On the Threshold of Philosophy: A Study of Al-Fārābī's Introductory Works on Logic*, Ph.D. dissertation. Harvard.

al-Kindī. 1974. *On First Philosophy* (*Fī al-falsafa al-ūlā*), ed. M.ʿA. H. Abū Rīda in *Rasāʾil al-Kindī al-falsafīya*. 2 vols. Cairo, 1950–3, I. 97–162; Eng. trans. A. Ivry, in *Al-Kindī's Metaphysics*. Albany: SUNY Press, 1974.

Lerner, R. and Mahdi, M., eds. 1972. *Medieval Political Philosophy*. Ithaca, NY: Cornell University Press.

Mahdi, M., trans. 1962. *Al-Farabi's Philosophy of Plato and Aristotle*. Ithaca, NY: Cornell University Press.

Maimonides. 1931. *Guide of the Perplexed* (*Dalālat al-ḥāʾirīn*), ed. S. Munk and Y. Yoel. Jerusalem. Eng. trans. S. Pines. Chicago: University of Chicago Press, 1963.

Maimonides. 1963–8. *Commentary on the* Mishna, Arabic with Hebrew trans. J. Kafih in *Mishnah im perush rabbenu Mosheh ben Maimon*. Jerusalem: Mossad ha-Rav Kook.

Maimonides. 1963–8. *Thirteen Principles*, Arabic in *Commentary on the* Mishna.

Maimonides. 1975. *Eight Chapters*, Arabic in *Commentary on the* Mishna; Eng. trans. C. Butterworth and R. Weiss in *Ethical Writings of Maimonides*. New York: Dover.

Maimonides. 1988–9. *Letters of Maimonides* (*Iggerot ha-Rambam*), ed. Y. Sheilat. 2 vols. Ma'aleh Adumim: Ma'aliyot.

Maimonides. 1993. *Book of Knowledge* (*Sefer ha-maddaʿ*). Jerusalem: Mossad ha-Rav Kook.

Maimonides. 2000. *Mishneh Torah*, ed. S. Frankel. 12 vols. Jerusalem: Hosaat Shabtei Frankel.

Pines, S. 1959. 'A History of Arabic and Jewish Mediaeval Philosophy'. Project-Description from 1959, published by Carlos Fraenkel in 'Zur Integration von islamischem und jüdischem Denken: Eine unbekannte Projektbeschreibung von Shlomo Pines'. In *Münchener Beiträge zur Jüdischen Geschichte und Kultur* 2008: 61–2.

Pines, S. 1975. 'Aristotle's *Politics* in Arabic Philosophy'. *Israel Oriental Studies* 5: 150–60.

Saʿadya Gaon. 1960. *The Book of Beliefs and Opinions* (*Kitāb al-amanāt wa-al iʿtiqadāt*), ed. J. Kafih. Jerusalem: Sura; Eng. trans. Samuel Rosenblatt. New Haven: Yale University Press, 1948.

Sahas, D. 1972. *John of Damascus on Islam*. Leiden: Brill.

Stroumsa, S. 1999. *Freethinkers of Medieval Islam: Ibn al-Rawāndī, Abū Bakr al-Rāzī and their Impact on Islamic Thought*. Leiden: Brill.

Walzer, R. 1957. 'Al-Fārābī's Theory of Prophecy and Divination'. *The Journal of Hellenic Studies* 1: 142–8.

Wolfson, H. A. 1976. *The Philosophy of the Kalam*. Cambridge, MA: Harvard University Press.

Yaḥyā ibn ʿAdī. 1920. *On the Necessity of the Incarnation (Fī wujūb al-taʿannus)*, Arabic with French trans. Augustin Périer, *Petits traités apologétiques de Yaḥyā ben ʿAdī*. Paris: Gabalda & Geuthner, 69–86.

Yaḥyā ibn ʿAdī. 2002. *The Reformation of Morals* (*Kitāb tahdhīb al-akhlāq*), Arabic with Eng. trans. S. Griffith. Provo: Brigham Young University Press.

CHAPTER 19

SCIENCE AND CREATION

The Medieval Heritage

WILLIAM E. CARROLL

THERE are few periods in the history of the civilizations of the Mediterranean world more important for an understanding of the relationship between science and creation than that of the Middle Ages. What comes to be a traditional understanding of creation,[1] namely, that God's creative act involves nothing other than an exercise of divine power, raises questions for those who accept a first principle of the natural sciences that all coming into existence has its beginning in some previously existing thing. Thus, it is not possible—not even for an omnipotent God—to get something from absolutely nothing.

Most scholars deny that there is an explicit teaching of creation out of nothing in the Hebrew Bible, the Christian New Testament, or the Quran (May 1978). Indeed, unlike the Hebrew Bible, the Quran does not contain a full-blown creation story.[2] The idea of God's creating all that is 'out of nothing' has its source in scriptural texts, but it is ultimately a theological conclusion about what ought to be believed: a conclusion reached as believers came to terms with the content of their faith.

The development of the understandings of what it means for God to create is part of the wider story of the reception of Greek science and philosophy, and in particular of the texts of Neoplatonism and of Aristotle, in Muslim, Jewish, and Christian intellectual communities. In the Middle Ages, in each of these communities, there was a wide-ranging discussion of the relationship among theology, philosophy, and the natural sciences: between what reason and faith tell us about nature, human nature, and God.

[1] Of course, 'traditional' does not mean universally accepted. As we shall see, there are a variety of interpretations of what it means for God to create. Throughout the chapter I have used 'creation' to mean the act by which God creates, as distinct from the result of this act.

[2] There are passages which refer to God as the One 'who created the heavens and the earth, and what is between them, in six days', as well as references to the fact that 'God creates whatever He wills' (Q. 25: 59 and 24: 45). Also important is: 'When He wants anything He only has to say "Be" and it is' (Q. 36: 82).

The philosophical and scientific heritage of antiquity, especially as that heritage was mediated first through intellectual developments in the Hellenistic world (in particular in Alexandria) and eventually through the widespread translations of texts into Syriac, Arabic, and later into Latin, helped to create a kind of common intellectual space occupied by Jewish, Christian, and Muslim thinkers. Although scholars in these communities came to different judgements about that heritage and its relevance to what they believed about God and the world, they shared enough in common in order to influence one another in important ways.

A comprehensive survey of the discourse about creation and science is well beyond the scope of this chapter. In a way, I have offered a selected history of ideas, abstracted from social and political contexts. As the chapter proceeds, I draw comparisons among thinkers in the three traditions. There are several excellent histories of philosophical and theological developments in medieval Islam, Judaism, and Christianity which can be consulted for a fuller account than can be given here (Adamson and Taylor 2005; Arnaldez 1993; Burrell 1986; Burrell 1993b; Campanini 2004; D'Ancona 2005a; Davidson 1987; Gilson 1955; Leaman 1985; Rudavsky 2000).

Medieval Islam

The reception of Greek thought in the Islamic world is a complex story. Well before the rise of Islam, Nestorian Christians in Syria and Persia established centres of learning producing translations of Greek texts. The project of translation into Arabic, especially in Baghdad, from the ninth century on, included not only texts which might be described as strictly philosophical, but also medical (e.g. Galen), mathematical (e.g. Euclid), and astronomical (e.g. Ptolemy) texts. Among the more famous texts rendered into Arabic were Aristotle's *Metaphysics*, a paraphrase of Aristotle's *De anima*, the famous *Theology of Aristotle* (which is actually a rearranged Arabic version and paraphrase of the *Enneads* of Plotinus), and the *Book on the Pure Good* (what will come to be known in the Latin West as the *Liber de causis*) (D'Ancona 2005b) (see the chapter in this volume by Pormann).

Greek philosophy seemed particularly challenging to some Muslim theologians who came to view it with suspicion as an alien way of thinking. The intellectual heritage of the ancient world brought with it the view that the universe is eternal. An eternal world was generally thought to be the antithesis of a created world; it would not be dependent upon God as cause. Also, the world must be seen as created out of nothing, for if God were to fashion the world out of some pre-existent matter, there would be something—that very matter—which was not dependent upon God.

In order to defend a view of God as absolutely free and sovereign, it seemed that one must affirm that the world is temporally finite. If the universe has an absolute beginning, then its coming-into-existence would require a divine agent. Nevertheless, a crucial question which occupied the attention of Muslim, Jewish, and Christian scholars in the Middle Ages was: if the world is created by God, *must* it have a temporal beginning, i.e. must it be temporally finite? An eternal universe was, in the view of many, a necessary universe, either in the sense of not needing a cause, or in the sense of not being the result of God's free choice. Divine sovereignty and the radical contingency of the created order must be protected from the encroachments of Greek logic and an Aristotelian science which sought to discover the necessary nexus between cause and effect. For Aristotle, true knowledge meant the discovery of necessary truths—of what must be so and cannot be otherwise. But, any necessity posited in the created order seemed to threaten divine omnipotence—that somehow God was required or necessitated to act in a certain way—and, accordingly, some theologians embraced a radical occasionalism which saw events in the world as only the occasions for divine action. God alone is the true cause of all that happens.

One of the leading supporters of the translations of Greek texts was al-Kindī (*c.*801–866), who sometimes is known as the first philosopher in the medieval Islamic world (see the chapters in this volume by Pormann and Griffith). As Peter Adamson notes, al-Kindī oversaw the work of a group of translators in Baghdad and used the results in his own treatises (Adamson 2005: 33) He was keen to show how Greek philosophy could be useful in addressing questions raised in Islamic theology (*kalām*). In what survives of al-Kindī's *On First Philosophy*, he argues for the relevance of Greek metaphysics for Muslims. He brings together references from Aristotle and Neoplatonism, but he explicitly rejects the Aristotelian thesis that the world is eternal. It was clear for al-Kindī that creation had to mean that the world is temporally finite. This commitment to the necessity of creation's meaning that a created world cannot be an eternal world will be a topic which runs through discussions about creation in all three religious communities in the Middle Ages. In fact, al-Kindī, in the tradition of John Philoponus (*c.*490–570), thought that the world's having a beginning, and hence that it was created, could be demonstrated by reason (Adamson 2005: 38; D'Ancona 2005b: 17; Davidson 1987: 114). The argument is based on the impossibility of an actual infinity of the past, which would follow were the world to be eternal. Al-Kindī makes a crucial contribution to Arabic philosophy, because he sees the God of Aristotle as compatible with both Neoplatonic emanationism and the God of Islam (Adamson 2005: 38–9; D'Ancona 2005a: I. 282–351; D'Ancona 2005b; Lizzini 2009: 88–94).

The position which many Muslim theologians feared can be found in the works of al-Fārābī (870–950), who established a philosophical curriculum for the study of Plato and Aristotle, and of Avicenna (980–1037), whose writings in medicine, natural philosophy, and metaphysics proved to be extraordinarily influential. Their work offers an excellent example of the way in which Greek thought could be appropriated in the Islamic world. Al-Fārābi, in some respects like al-Kindī, combined features of Aristotelian and Neoplatonic thought: Aristotle's understanding of causation is extended to include the causing of being and intellection. What is of special interest is that al-Fārābi's reading of Aristotle includes the view that Aristotle understands that there is a Creator who is the One (important for Neoplatonists) and the efficient cause of all that is. He links this idea with the Demiurge in Plato's *Timaeus* (D'Ancona

2005a: I. 405). The details of this causation are set forth in terms of Neoplatonic emanationism (Reisman 2005: 57; D'Ancona 2005a: I. 400ff.; Lizzini 2009: 94–9).

Surely the most influential philosopher in the Islamic world, especially concerning discussions about creation, was Avicenna. For him, the view of God, as the absolutely necessary being, and the created order of things as only possible, is the key for an understanding of creation (Acar 2010; McGinnis 2010; Wisnovksy 2005; Druart 2005). Anything other than God is, in itself, only possible, and its existence, therefore, requires God's causing it to be.

> Things that are included in existence are subject to a rational division into two kinds. One of them is that which, when considered by itself, is not necessary in its existence. It is evident that its existence is also not impossible, otherwise it would not have been included in existence. This [kind of] thing is in the sphere of possibility. The other kind is that which, when it is considered by itself, necessarily exists. So we say: The necessary existent by itself has no cause, while the possible existent by itself has a cause. (Avicenna 2005: 1.6, 30)

In explaining the kind of agent causality which creation involves, Avicenna notes that there is an important difference between the ways in which metaphysicians and natural scientists discuss agent cause:

> ...the metaphysical philosophers do not mean by 'agent' only the principle of motion, as the naturalists [philosophers of nature] mean, but the principle and giver of existence, as in the case of God with respect to the world. (Avicenna 2005: 6.1, 195)

Thus, there is wider sense of cause than that which concerns the natural sciences. He observes that a reflection on what it means for something to be reveals that what something is, its essence, is different from whether a thing exists. On the basis of the ontological distinction between essence and existence, Avicenna argues that all beings other than God (in whom this distinction disappears) require a cause to exist. Since existence is not part of the essence of things, it needs to be explained by a cause extrinsic to the thing; and, ultimately, there must be an Un-caused Cause. Avicenna makes a point of noting that the created 'effect needs that which bestows existence on it always, permanently, as long as [the effect] exists' (Avicenna 2005: 6.1, 200).

One feature of Avicenna's explanation of all creatures' flowing from a primal source of being and intelligibility was that, since the source of all that is eternal, that which flows from this source must also be eternal. But, as we have seen, an eternal world was often seen as a necessary world, a world which had to come forth from God—a world, thus, which was not the result of the free creative act of God. Avicenna sought to be faithful to Greek metaphysics (especially in the Neoplatonic tradition) and also to affirm the contingency of the created order. Although the world proceeds from God by necessity and is eternal, it differs fundamentally from God in that *in itself* it is only possible and requires a cause to exist. God, on the other hand, is necessary in himself and thus requires no cause. Contingent existence, although not necessary in itself, is necessary through or by another. According to Avicenna, 'real existence' emerges as a new attribute for the contingent being of the created world (which was originally present as an essence or 'possibility' in the divine mind); it is 'a kind of added benefit bestowed by God upon possible being in the act of creation' (Kahn 1982: 8; Goodman 1992: 74). Creation, so understood, is 'out of nothing' in the sense of not out of anything actually existing. Creation causes what is possible in itself to be necessary, as a result of its being caused to exist (McGinnis 2010: 187).

A world without necessary relationships is an unintelligible world. Yet, at the same time, the fear was that a necessary world is a self-sufficient world, a world which cannot not be: the opposite, so it seemed, of a world created by God. At best a necessary world would only be a world which *must* surge forth from a primal source of being. Central to Islamic belief (and to Jewish and Christian belief, as well), however, is that God's creative act in causing the world to be is a free act. It is not clear that Avicenna's emanationist scheme is compatible with the idea of divine freedom. Avicenna thought of God, the Necessary Existent, as the ultimate agent cause of the world, yet he denied that God has the 'intention' to create the world. He does think that it is proper to say that God 'wills' the universe to be. Such willing is a necessary feature of divine intellection. God knows that the universe emanates from himself and, having such knowledge, God consents to what occurs (McGinnis 2010: 206–7). It is in giving consent to what God knows that God can be said to will what occurs.

Avicenna's project was to show how the multiplicity of things in the world has its source in the One in which there is no multiplicity whatsoever, how material things can have their source in an immaterial principle, and how the Necessary Existent can know the world of changeable things without itself being changed (Finianos 2007: 202).

The explanation Avicenna offered of the absolute origin of the world in terms of a necessary emanationist schema was attractive since it seemed to do justice to both necessity and dependence. *Necessity* is demanded by Greek science in order to protect the intelligibility of the world, since science discovers the necessary nexus between cause and effect. *Dependence* is demanded by theology to protect the 'originatedness' of the world. Creation for Avicenna is an ontological relationship—a relationship in the order of being—with no reference to temporality. In fact, Avicenna accepted the established Greek view that the universe is eternal. His view of the emanation of existing things from a primal source only made sense in an eternal universe. The question was—and is—whether an emanationist metaphysics can do justice to creation? Is it consistent with the God revealed in scripture? The eternity of the world and the paradoxical understanding of divine agency were sources of deep suspicion for opponents of Avicenna and others who accepted some version of emanationist metaphysics.

It was precisely such questions which led many in what came to be called *kalām* to react negatively to those, like Avicenna and al-Fārābī, who were in the tradition of *falsafa*. As Jon McGinnis puts it: 'The proponents of *falsafa* saw themselves as adopting, adapting, and generally extending the Graeco-Arabic philosophical and scientific tradition, while the advocates of *kalām* envisioned themselves as promoting a way of thought intimately linked with the Arabic language and the Islamic religion'

(McGinnis 2010: 14). There were at least two major schools within *kalām*, the Muʿtazilites and the Ashʿarites; the former favoured a reading of the Quran which relied on the demands of logic and reason, whereas the latter would argue that when it came to understanding God and the Quran one passed well beyond the domain of reason and logic and ought to rely simply on what the sacred text revealed—in a literal sense. One example, which highlights the difference between these two, concerns the question of whether the Quran itself, understood as the recitation of God, is created or is, in some sense, an integral feature of God and thus uncreated. The Muʿtazilites affirmed the former, the Ashʿarites the latter. Defending God's absolute freedom led many *kalām* thinkers to deny that natural entities possess any causal powers of their own. In natural philosophy, they preferred a version of atomism (associated with that of Epicurus) which left creatures to be more obviously susceptible to the actions of the Creator: a view which has come to be called 'occasionalism' (Dhanani 1994: 5; Burrell 1993a: 52–3).

A leading Ashʿarite thinker, al-Ghazālī (1058–1111), was the most famous opponent to what was considered to be threats to Islam in the thought of philosophers such as Avicenna. In *The Incoherence of the Philosophers* (*Tahāfut al-Falāsifah*) al-Ghazālī set forth a wide-ranging critique of Greek thought. Al-Ghazālī defended what he considered to be the orthodox Islamic doctrine of creation versus Avicenna's embrace of an eternal world. An eternal world, al-Ghazālī thought, was the very antithesis of a created one. For God to be an agent the effect of his act must have a beginning of its existence. An eternal world cannot be dependent upon an act of God, since an eternal world would be a completely self-sufficient world. In fact, al-Ghazālī claimed that, on philosophical grounds alone, all the arguments advanced for an eternal world fail. The incoherence which al-Ghazālī found in Avicenna's position was the affirmation of a world which is simultaneously eternal and created.

Although there is a dispute among scholars concerning al-Ghazālī's position on the existence of real causes in nature, other than God's causality, there are passages in his writings which support a denial of creaturely causality (Marmura 2005; Frank 1994). There could be no other real agent causes in the world, if one thought that God were all-powerful (Druart 2005: 342–5). In the *Incoherence*, he writes: 'The connection between what is habitually believed to be a cause and what is habitually believed to be an effect is not necessary according to us... Their connection is due to the prior decree of God, who creates them side by side, not in its being necessary in itself, incapable of separation' (al-Ghazālī, *Incoherence* 17.1 (1997: 170)). A famous example he gives is that when fire is burning a piece of cotton, fire is not the agent of the burning; rather it is God who is the cause of the burning and of what results. Nature does not possess its own intrinsic principles which serve as causes of the characteristic behaviour we observe. God is the only true agent cause.

Yet, Avicenna and other philosophers sought to understand the very causes in nature which al-Ghazālī denied existed. It would seem to many Muslim thinkers that one had to choose between Athens and Mecca, between Greek science and the revelation of the Quran. To seek to embrace both is, so they thought, to be incoherent. A fundamental error of the philosophers, according to al-Ghazālī, was their failure to achieve a correct understanding of causality. The relationship between God's continuing creative act, a manifestation of divine omnipotence, and whether as a result there is any metaphysical space, as it were, for other causes in nature, is a theme with which scholars in all three religious traditions had to wrestle. How ought one to understand the relationship between God as cause and creatures as causes? Indeed, as we have seen, can one speak of causality as predicated of both God and creatures?

Later in the twelfth century, Averroes (*c.*1126–98), in *The Incoherence of the Incoherence* (*Tahāfut al-Tahāfut*), defended the Greek philosophical tradition against al-Ghazālī. Averroes argued that eternal creation is not only intelligible, but is the most appropriate way to characterize the universe. Al-Ghazālī had thought that for God to be the cause of the world, that is, for God to be the agent who brings about the existence of the world, such causality required a temporal beginning. In other words, the world cannot be both eternal and the result of God's action, since whatever is the result of an action of another must come into existence after the initiation of the action of the other. Thus, what exists eternally cannot have another, not even a divine other, as its originating source. In reply, Averroes draws a distinction between two different senses of an eternal world: eternal in the sense of being unlimited in duration, and eternal in the sense of being eternally self-sufficient, without a cause. Thus, an eternal world, understood in terms of duration without beginning or end, does not conflict with God's eternity, understood in the sense of complete and total self-sufficiency.

Averroes notes that a world which is eternal, only in the sense of being unlimited in duration, would still require an external agent which makes it what it is. Thus, what makes the world eternal—in this sense of eternal—could be identified with that which causes it to be. On the other hand, a world which is eternal not only in the sense of unlimited duration but also in the sense of being completely self-sufficient would be entirely independent of any external cause. Its eternal existence would be rooted simply in what it is: it would exist necessarily, without cause. Averroes contends that philosophers, such as Aristotle, are committed to the eternity of the world only in the sense of unlimited duration and not in the sense of the world's being wholly self-sufficient. The distinction he draws, thus, is between a world which is eternally existent in itself and a world which is eternally existent by being made so (Kogan 1985).

Even though Averroes claimed that an eternal, created universe was indeed probable, he rejected the idea of creation out of nothing in its strict sense. He thought that creation consisted in God's eternally converting potentialities into actually existing things. For Averroes, the doctrine of creation out of nothing contradicted the existence of a true natural causality in the universe (Averroes, I. 133: 78). For if it were possible to produce something from absolutely nothing there would be no guarantee that particular effects required particular causes. In a universe without real natural causation, 'specific potentialities to act and to be acted upon are reduced to shambles' and causal relations 'to mere happen-stance' (Kogan 1985: 218). Thus, for Averroes, there could be no science of nature if the universe were created out of nothing (Ozcoidi 2001: 109–285). Averroes also defended the integrity of natural philosophy against what he considered an unwarranted emphasis on metaphysics in the thought, for example, of Avicenna.

For Avicenna, the changes which resulted in the coming into existence of new members of a species required the agency of a created intelligence, a Giver of Forms. Material beings themselves could produce only limited changes in the world—preparatory to the reception of a substantial form.[3]

The Jewish Tradition and Maimonides

In understanding what it means for God to create the world, Jewish thinkers began their reflection with an interpretation of the opening verse of Genesis. What did 'in the beginning' (*be-reshit*) and create (*bara*) mean? In the beginning, yes, but what sense of beginning? Some authors concluded that the beginning spoken of in Genesis was preceded by other beginnings: that God created other worlds before this one. Some were attracted to Plato's account in the *Timaeus*. Questions about the nature of time and whether there was time before the beginning of this world were common themes (Rudavsky 2000: 4–15). As with Muslim and Christian authors, Jewish commentators were influenced by philosophical traditions from antiquity; not only Plato and Plotinus, but also Aristotle. Although his work occurs in what is properly the ancient world (rather than the Middle Ages), Philo of Alexandria (d. 50) offers an extraordinary example of the ways in which philosophy can be used in the interpretation of the Bible.[4] Of special note is the role Plato's *Timaeus* plays for Philo, as well as Philo's claim that God is always active, never ceasing to create (Radici and Reale 1987: xxii and *Le allegori delle leggi* I. 5–6: 118).

It was the same translation movement which provided a spur for developments in philosophy in both Islam and Judaism (Harvey 2005: 350). Probably the first significant Jewish author in the Middle Ages to confront questions of creation in a significant way was Saʿadia (882–942) (see the chapter by Fraenkel in this volume). Saʿadia relied heavily on the work of Philoponus who argued against Aristotle's claim that the world is eternal and provided the philosophical arguments for a beginning of time which proved crucial for many later thinkers in all three religious traditions—but most notably among the *kalām*. In fact, Saʿadia's work played an important role in the transmission of Philoponus' arguments (Rudavsky 2000: 63; Davidson 1987: 86ff.). As we saw with some Islamic thinkers, Saʿadia thought that there was a strict distinction between a created universe and an eternal one. In his *Book of Beliefs and Opinions* (933), Saʿadia provides a systematic presentation of what he considered the fundamental

[3] '(N)atural efficient causes play the role of preparatory causes that dispose and prepare the matter by either moving it to some suitable place or altering certain qualitative features of the matter, rendering it receptive to the influence of a metaphysical efficient cause, which in its turn bestows the species form by which the substance is the kind that it is' (McGinnis 2010: 193).

[4] In one treatise, *On Providence*, Philo describes five different approaches to the question of the origin of the world. The one he embraces has creation understood in terms of God's first creating a kind of ideal model and then producing matter which he informs (Radici and Reale 1987: lix; *On Providence* I. 6).

tenets of Judaism. For him, the Bible tells us that the world is created out of nothing and this truth is confirmed by philosophical and scientific reasoning; here he has in mind the arguments of Philoponus.[5] Saʿadia observes that the 'first doctrine' of Judaism is: 'things are created; they are created by something external to them; and they are created out of nothing.' As Mauro Zonta (2009: 56–8) remarks, Saʿadia's is the first explicit affirmation in medieval Jewish thought of the doctrine of creation out of nothing.

Other Jewish authors following Saʿadia are not so explicit in affirming creation out of nothing. Ibn Gabirol (1021–58), who was influenced by a key figure in Jewish Neoplatonism, Isaac Israeli (*c.*855–*c.*955), seemed to think that creation means God's working with some pre-existent material (Rudavsky 2000: 65–6; Altmann 1979) The rejection of any biblical account of creation out of nothing is clear, however, in Abraham Ibn Ezra (1089–1164) and Abraham bar Ḥiyya (d. 1136). The latter thinks that the earth's being 'without form and void', as set forth in Genesis, suggests that there was a kind of potential existence prior to the beginning of the world, and creation means the bringing of things into existence from this potency. Ibn Ezra thought that 'to create' as set forth in Genesis meant to cut or to set a boundary, thus indicating that God was somehow forming things out of matter already in existence (Zonta 2009: 59–60; Rudavsky 2000: 5–6).

Surely the most significant Jewish thinker in the Middle Ages was Moses Maimonides (1135–1204), and his analysis of creation and science is an important part of the medieval heritage on this subject. The 'perplexed' in the title of his most famous work, *The Guide for the Perplexed*, are those who do not understand how it is possible for philosophical and scientific reflections to be compatible with both the revelation of the Hebrew Bible and the traditions of Jewish law. In the introduction to the *Guide*, Maimonides says that he seeks to explain the meaning of key terms in the Bible, especially those predicated of God, in order to help 'a religious man for whom the validity of the Law has been established in his soul' and made manifest in his life. Such a man may become perplexed as to whether he should follow his intellect because in so doing he may seem to have to renounce the foundations of the law. The righteous man may be perplexed as to whether philosophy and science are compatible with religious belief (Maimonides, *Guide* I, introduction (1963: 5)).

When discussing the doctrine of creation, Maimonides observes: 'There is no doubt that there are things that are common to all three of us, I mean the Jews, the Christians, and the Muslims: namely, the affirmation of the temporal creation of the world, the validity of which entails the validity of miracles and other things of that kind' (Maimonides, *Guide* I. 71 (1963: 178)). He thought that belief in the Trinity excluded Christianity from being a monotheistic religion. In the *Guide*, Maimonides offers a kind of dialectical discussion of creation in which he identifies three positions: (1) that of Moses and the Law, which affirms creation out of nothing and a temporal beginning;

[5] Although Saʿadia never explicitly mentions Philoponus, Davidson (1987: 95ff.) has shown that he did draw from at least two sets of proofs for creation which had been first set forth by Philoponus.

(2) that of Plato and others who reject as absurd the view that something can come from nothing; (3) the position of Aristotle and his followers who also reject the idea of something's coming from nothing and endorse an eternally existing world (Maimonides, *Guide* II. 13 (1963: 281ff.); Davies 2011: 28ff.). Maimonides does not think that Aristotle himself claimed to demonstrate the eternity of the world, despite what some of his followers maintain. Aristotle, according to Maimonides, thought that arguments for the eternity of the world were only probable (Maimonides *Guide* II. 15 (1963: 290); Seeskin 2005: 60–95).

It is clear that for Maimonides creation means something temporal, in the sense that existence comes after non-existence. '[T]he great controversy is over this point [question of the temporal creation or the eternity of the world], and this is the very point that Abraham our Father discerned.... It is the root of the Torah that the Deity alone is primordial and that He has created the whole out of nothing; whoever does not acknowledge this is guilty of radical unbelief and of heresy' (Maimonides 1972: 231).

Maimonides thought that whether the universe is eternal or 'temporally created' cannot, in principle, be known by reason with certainty. The most a believer can do is to refute the proofs of the philosophers bearing on the eternity of the world. He was critical of any claims to demonstrate that the world is not eternal and *therefore* created out of nothing.

In an interesting discussion of the reading of the opening of Genesis in the Jewish tradition, Maimonides notes that some Jewish sages thought that the Bible affirms the eternity of time, but he argues that such a view is inconsistent with the whole thrust of scripture which tells us that God acts through purpose. Purposeful action is the opposite of the kind of necessitarian view which follows from an eternal universe. To account for the great diversity of things, each existing in its own particular way, means that the Creator must freely choose to produce things in their very particularity. 'For us', he says, 'the matter is clear... namely, that all things exist in virtue of a purpose and not of necessity' (Maimonides II. 19 (1963: 303)). That God acts through purpose rather than necessity means, in turn, that the Bible does indeed teach a first moment in time, although it does not do so openly. This is so because for the Bible to be taken literally in its general teaching that God acts through purpose and freedom, the opening of Genesis needs to be interpreted in a way different from the literal sense, which appears to teach that 'there was a time before the existence of the sun'. A literal interpretation of Genesis (which Maimonides is arguing against) implies that God does not act through will and purpose because it seems that the text proclaims that there was a time before the creation described in Genesis (Maimonides, *Guide* II. 25 (1963: 327ff.); Davies 2011: 41).

Maimonides was particularly alert to what he considered to be the dangers of Neoplatonic emanationism in which the doctrine of creation and the eternity of the world are combined in a way that would deny the free activity of God. Maimonides distinguishes his position from that of Avicenna and Averroes, who concluded that the world is eternal, and from the position of al-Ghazālī and the *kalām*, who, although affirming a temporal beginning, also thought that reason could reach this conclusion.

Maimonides criticizes the methods of the *kalām* theologians, who, he says, claim first to demonstrate the temporal creation of the world out of nothing and then to argue from such a creation to the existence of God. In fact, he suggests that the better method is to prove that God exists, is One, and is incorporeal, on the assumption that the universe is eternal (Maimonides, *Guide* I. 71 (1963: 181–2)).

Along with Averroes, Maimonides was critical of those Muslim theologians who assigned all causal agency to God. Without the necessary nexus between cause and effect, discoverable in the natural order, the world would be unintelligible and a science of nature would be impossible. 'My purpose', he writes, 'is to explain to you, by means of arguments that come close to being a demonstration, that what exists indicates to us of necessity that it exists in virtue of the purpose of One who purposed; and to do this without having to take upon myself what the Mutakallimun have undertaken—to abolish the nature of that which exists and to adopt atomism, the opinion according to which accidents are perpetually being created [which they adopt in order to maintain their position of divine causation]' (Maimonides, *Guide* II. 19 (1963: 303); Fox 1990: 282).[6]

The Christian West and Thomas Aquinas

Early Christian thinkers, in the fourth, fifth, and sixth centuries, had already distinguished the Christian doctrine of creation from Hellenistic thought, by affirming that the world is not eternal and that it is created out of nothing (Baldner and Carroll 1997: ch. 1; Soskice 2010). By the thirteenth century, however, Christian theologians were working within a richer intellectual tradition, which included the thought of Muslim and Jewish thinkers as well as that of the Greeks, such as Aristotle, whose works had only recently been translated into Latin. In 1215 the Fourth Lateran Council officially declared the doctrine of creation out of nothing and the temporal beginning of the world to be dogmas of the Catholic church. It would be Thomas Aquinas (1224–74), later in the thirteenth century, who developed this doctrine more fully; and Thomas uses extensively the insights of Avicenna, Averroes, and Maimonides as he forges an account of creation which seeks to do justice to the demands of reason and Christian faith.

There were three general positions on creation and an eternal world which were defended by different Christian thinkers in the 1260s and 1270s. First, there is the claim of scholars such as Thomas Aquinas, Boethius of Dacia, and Siger of Brabant, all of whom followed the lead of Maimonides and argued that neither the eternity of the

[6] For a discussion of later Jewish thinkers—Gersonides (1288–1344), Hasdai Crescas (1340–1410), Joseph Albo (1380–1444), and others—see Davidson 1987 and Rudavsky 2000.

world nor its temporal finitude could be demonstrated by reason. All three believed, as a matter of faith, that the world did have a temporal beginning. Second, there is the claim of scholars such as Matthew of Acquasparta that, on the basis of the contradictions which would follow were one to posit that the world is eternal, we can know for sure, using reason alone, that the world had a temporal beginning.[7] There is a third general position, affirmed by Bonaventure, Henry of Ghent, and John Pecham. It is also a view which we find in the early works of Albert the Great. This is the view that creation out of nothing necessarily requires a temporal beginning to the world. This is not the same as the position which claims that the world cannot be eternal and therefore must be created because it had to have a beginning. The third position follows from what it means to be created, and the conclusion is that an eternal, created world is impossible. A created world, because it is created, must be a world which has a temporal beginning. Bonaventure, for example, thought that 'out of nothing' had to mean, in some sense 'after nothing', otherwise one would be arguing that 'nothing' was a constituent of things (in the manner, for example, of a table's being made 'out of wood'). Since such a construal of 'out of nothing' made no sense, out of nothing must mean 'after nothing' (Baldner and Carroll 1997; Clavier 2011). Bonaventure and Albert were following the analysis that came from Anselm's *Monologion* (c. 8). According to Anselm, if the expression *ex nihilo* is to have any positive meaning, if it is to mean anything more than a mere denial of material causality, then it must indicate a temporal beginning. It was the genius of Thomas, who acknowledged a considerable debt to Avicenna on this point, to see that the positive meaning of *ex nihilo* is that the creature is of itself really nothing—its non-being is naturally prior to its being—and that, therefore, the creature is completely dependent upon the Creator for its being.

There are important nuances in the arguments of those who fall into each of these broad categories, but with this general schema in mind, we can turn to the position of Thomas Aquinas. From his earliest to his last writings on the subject, Thomas maintains that it is possible for there to be an eternal, created universe.[8] On the basis of faith Thomas holds that the universe is not eternal. But he thinks that God could have created a universe which is eternal. Although reason affirms the intelligibility of an eternal, created universe, Thomas Aquinas thought that reason alone leaves unresolved the question of whether the universe is eternal. On this point, he follows Maimonides, and differs from Avicenna, since the latter thought that the universe must be eternal. Near the end of his career, in *De aeternitate mundi*, Thomas will take up, in his most sophisticated treatise on the subject, the intelligibility of an eternal, created universe.

[7] At times John Pecham appears to accept this argument, but it seems more likely that he did not think that it was strictly demonstrable that the world was temporally finite. Rather, his position is that it is true that the world is not eternal and 'a Christian who believes this can understand, with the help of reason, why it is true' (Dales 1990: 127).

[8] Thomas addresses the doctrine of creation in a magisterial way four times: *In II Sent.*, dist. 1, q. 1 (early to mid-1250s); *Summa contra Gentiles* II, cc. 6–38 (1259–64); *Questiones disputatae de potentia Dei* q. 3 (1265–6); and *Summa theologiae* I, qq. 44–6 (1266–8).

There he will write: 'to say that something has been made by God and that it has always existed, is not logically inconsistent' (Baldner and Carroll 1997: 119).

An eternal universe does not have to mean, as Maimonides, al-Ghazālī, and others argued, a necessary universe, a universe which is not the result of the free creative act of God. An eternal, created universe would have no first moment of its existence, but—as Avicenna had noted—it still would have a cause of its existence. Thomas did not think that there were compelling arguments for the eternity of the world. Contrary to the views of those who defended an eternal universe on the grounds that were the universe to have a temporal beginning there would have to be a change in God—God would have to change from not creating to creating—Thomas (following al-Ghazālī) argued that God eternally wills that the world (his effect) have a temporal beginning. Thus, there is no change in God.[9]

Indeed, Thomas thought that, leaving aside the question of whether the universe is eternal, reason alone can demonstrate that the universe is created. As he contends in his first magisterial treatment of creation in *Writings on the 'Sentences' of Peter Lombard*: 'not only does faith hold that there is creation, but reason also demonstrates it.'[10] Such a view sets Thomas apart from his teacher, Albert the Great, and his colleague at the University of Paris, Bonaventure. Albert, for example, as with many others, considered creation to be exclusively a theological notion: 'It ought to be said that creation is properly a divine work. To us, moreover, it seems astounding in that we cannot conclude to it because it is not subject to a demonstration of reason. And so not even the philosophers have known it, unless perchance some [should have known something] from the sayings of the Prophets. But no one ever investigated it through demonstration. Some, to be sure, have found certain probable reasons, but they do not prove [creation] sufficiently.'[11]

Thomas's metaphysical argument for God as cause of existence involves a combination of themes taken from an extension of Aristotle's claims for an unmoved mover to include divine efficient causality as a cause of being as such, and a recognition that there is a hierarchy of being in which each kind of being participates in an ultimate source of being: a source which is Being itself (*ipsum esse subsistens*).[12] Thomas employs in a novel way the distinction Avicenna drew between existence and essence in creatures to argue for God, the Creator, in whom this distinction disappears. Whereas for Avicenna, existence is something which comes to an essence, in a way analogous to an accident coming to a substance, Thomas thinks that existence is that which brings essence into actuality. Thomas's insight on this matter goes to the heart of

[9] Divine immutability was something which, for Avicenna, Maimonides, and Thomas Aquinas, was non-negotiable. Indeed, a commitment to it led Avicenna to argue that the universe must be eternal since he thought a temporal beginning would mean that God changed from not creating to creating.

[10] *In II Sent.*, dist. 1, q. 1, a. 2 (Baldner and Carroll 1997: 74).

[11] Albert the Great, *Super Sententiarum libros* 1.8 (Baldner and Carroll 1997: 27).

[12] The full argument can be found in Thomas Aquinas' *De potentia Dei*, q. 3, a. 5.

what he thinks it means for God to create (Burrell 2012: 67–8; Burrell 1993a: 32–3; Burrell 2010).

A key to Thomas Aquinas' analysis is the distinction he draws between creation and change, or as he often said: *creatio non est mutatio* (creation is not a change). The natural sciences have as their subject the world of changing things. Whenever there is a change there must be something which changes. It is true that from nothing, nothing comes; that is, if the verb 'to come' means a change. All change requires something which changes.

To create, on the other hand, is to be the radical cause of the whole reality of whatever exists. To cause completely something to exist is not to produce a change in something; to create, thus, is not to work on or with some already existing material. If there were a prior something which was used in the act of producing a new thing then the agent doing the producing would not be the *complete* cause of the new thing. But such a complete causing is precisely what the act of creation is. As Thomas writes in one of his later works, *On Separated Substances:* 'Over and above the mode of becoming by which something comes to be through change or motion, there must be a mode of becoming or origin of things without any mutation or motion through the influx of being [*per influentiam essendi*].'[13] To create is to give existence, and all things depend upon God for the fact that they are. God does not take nothing and make something out of 'it'. Rather, any thing left entirely to itself, separated from the cause of its existence, would be absolutely nothing. Creation is not exclusively some distant event; it is the continual, complete causing of the existence of whatever is. In a fundamental sense, creation is not really an event at all.

Contrary to the claims of Averroes, Aquinas thought that a world created *ex nihilo* (whether that world be eternal or temporally finite) was susceptible to scientific understanding. Creation so understood does not destroy the autonomy of that which is created. Created beings can and do function as real secondary causes, causes which can be discovered in the natural sciences. God as cause so transcends the created order that he can cause creatures to be causes. Thomas's understanding of analogical predication served him well in distinguishing between what it means for creatures to be causes and God to be a cause. A univocal sense of 'cause' results in a fundamental conflict between God's causing things to be and creatures as causes. God is not a competing cause in the world such that to attribute causal agency to him requires a diminution of causal agency to creatures, or vice versa. Creatures are what they are (including those which are free), precisely because God is present to them as cause. Were God to withdraw, all that exists would cease to be. Creaturely agency and the integrity of nature, in general, are guaranteed by God's creative causality.[14] Unlike

[13] Aquinas, *De substantiis separatis* c. 9, n. 49.

[14] Here is how Thomas Aquinas expresses this view in the *Summa theologiae* I, q. 105, a. 1: 'Some have understood God to work in every agent in such a way that no created power has any effect in things, but that God alone is the ultimate cause of everything wrought; for instance, that it is not fire that gives heat, but God in the fire, and so forth. But this is impossible. First, because the order of cause

Avicenna, who required an immaterial Giver of Forms to effect substantial change, Thomas thought that natural entities themselves were sufficient to account for these changes.

Thomas distinguishes between creation understood philosophically—as the complete dependence of all that is on God as cause—and creation understood theologically, which includes all that philosophy says and adds, among other things, that there is an absolute beginning to time. Thomas thinks, as does Avicenna, that metaphysics can prove that all things depend on God as cause of their existence. And with Avicenna, Thomas argues that there is no conflict between creation and any of the claims of the natural sciences, since the natural sciences have as their subject the world of changing things, and creation is not a change. Creation accounts for the existence of things, not for changes in things. Furthermore, Thomas thinks that God's absolute sovereignty, expressed, for example, in the doctrine of creation out-of-nothing, and so important to thinkers such as al-Ghazālī, does not require that one deny that there are real causes in nature. With Averroes, Thomas insists that the world is susceptible to scientific analysis in terms of causes in the world. But, as I have already noted, Thomas does not think, as Averroes does, that one must reject creation out of nothing in order to defend the possibility of a science of nature. Nor, according to Thomas, would an eternal universe have to mean a necessary universe, a universe which is not the result of God's free choice. With Maimonides, Thomas thinks that reason alone cannot know whether or not the universe is eternal. It is, he thinks, an error to try to reason to creation *ex nihilo* by attempting to show scientifically that the world has a temporal beginning. Nevertheless, for Thomas, reason can show, in the discipline of metaphysics, that the world has an *origin:* that it is created *ex nihilo*. The affirmation in faith that the universe has a temporal beginning perfects what reason knows about creation. Thomas's theological analysis of creation is much richer than just the recognition that the world has a beginning. He sees all things coming from and returning to God. Furthermore, the entire universe of creatures, spiritual and material, possesses a dynamic character, analogous to the internal dynamism of the Divine Persons of the Trinity. With the eyes of faith one sees the whole created order as 'footsteps' of the Trinity. Throughout, Thomas's theological understanding of creation is informed by his philosophical analysis; after all, Thomas is a philosopher because he is a theologian.

We find in Thomas's analysis of creation and its relation to the philosophical and scientific traditions which he inherits a confluence of the various questions and themes which informed (albeit in different ways) the thought of Muslim, Jewish, and Christian scholars. It is tempting to see a kind of progression over time which reaches its summit,

and effect would be taken away from created things, and this would imply lack of power in the Creator, for it is due to the power of the cause, that it bestows active power on its effect. Secondly, because the active powers which are seen to exist in things, would be bestowed on things to no purpose, if these wrought nothing through them. Indeed, all things created would seem, in a way, to be purposeless, if they lacked an operation proper to them, since the purpose of everything is its operation . . . We must therefore understand that God works in things in such a manner that things have their proper operation.'

as it were, in Thomas. We need to remember, however, that Thomas's position was not the only one in the Latin Middle Ages, nor, in important respects, was it the most widely accepted in Christian circles.

Conclusion

As we have seen, the idea of creation out of nothing was not the result of an obvious reading of Jewish, Christian, or Muslim scriptures. In all three religious communities the idea develops as philosophers and theologians consider what it means for God to create, in the context not only of scriptural revelation but also of various philosophical traditions (most notably Neoplatonism and Aristotelianism).

By the late thirteenth century there existed a profound series of reflections, in Islam, Judaism, and Christianity, concerning the relationship between creation and science. We have seen thinkers in all three traditions seeking to understand what it means for God to be the cause of all that is in the context of what science and philosophy tell us about the world. In wrestling with key topics concerning time and creation, divine freedom and emanation, and the like, these thinkers had to examine the relationship among the natural sciences, philosophy, and theology. The sophistication with which they engaged such topics is striking.

References

Acar, R. 2010. 'Creation: Avicenna's Metaphysical Account'. In Burrell et al. 2010: 77–90.

Adamson, P. 2005. 'Al-Kindi and the Reception of Greek Philosophy'. In Adamson and Taylor 2005: 32–51.

Adamson, P. and Taylor, R., eds. 2005. *The Cambridge Companion to Arabic Philosophy*. Cambridge: Cambridge University Press.

Altmann, A. 1979. 'Creation and Emanation in Isaac Israeli: A Reappraisal'. In I. Twersky, ed., *Studies in Medieval Jewish History and Literature*. Cambridge, MA: Harvard University Press, I. 1–15.

Aquinas, T. 2012. *Opera Omnia*. <http://www.corpusthomisticum.org/iopera.html>; accessed 30 May 2012.

Arnaldez, R. 1993. *À la croisée des trois monothéismes: une communauté de pensée au Moyen Âge*. Paris: Albin Michel.

Averroè. 1997. *L'incoerenza dell' incoerenza dei filosofi*, trans. M. Campanini. Torino: UTET.

Averroes. 1954. *Tahafut al-tahafut* (*The Incoherence of the Incoherence*), trans. S. van den Bergh. Cambridge: Gibb Memorial Trust.

Avicenna. 1978. *La Métaphysique du Shifa'*, trans. G. Anawati. 2 vols. Paris: J. Vrin.

Avicenna. 2002. *Metafisica*, trans. O. Lizzini and P. Porro. Milano: Bompiani.

Avicenna. 2005. *The Metaphysics of 'The Healing'*, trans. M. Marmura. Provo, UT: Brigham Young University Press.

Baldner, S. E. and Carroll, W. E. 1997. *Aquinas on Creation*. Toronto: Pontifical Institute of Mediaeval Studies.
Burrell, D. 1986. *Knowing the Unknowable God: Ibn-Sina, Maimonides, Aquinas*. Notre Dame, IN: University of Notre Dame Press.
Burrell, D. 1993a. *Freedom and Creation in Three Traditions*. Notre Dame, IN: University of Notre Dame Press.
Burrell, D. 1993b. 'Aquinas and Islamic and Jewish Thinkers'. In N. Kretzmann and E. Stump, eds, *The Cambridge Companion to Aquinas*. Cambridge: Cambridge University Press, 60–84.
Burrell, D. 2010. 'The Act of Creation with its Theological Consequences'. In Burrell et al. 2010: 40–52.
Burrell, D. 2012. 'Aquinas and Jewish and Islamic Authors'. In Davies and Stump 2012: 65–73.
Burrell, D. and McGinn, B., eds. 1990. *God and Creation*. Notre Dame, IN: University of Notre Dame Press.
Burrell, D. et al., eds. 2010. *Creation and the God of Abraham*. Cambridge: Cambridge University Press.
Campanini, M. 2004. *Introduzione alla filosofia islamica*. Rome: Editori Laterza.
Clavier. P. 2011. *Ex Nihilo*. 2 vols. Paris: Hermann.
Dales, R. 1990. *Medieval Discussions of the Eternity of the World*. Leiden: Brill.
D'Ancona, C., ed. 2005a. *Storia della filosofia nell'Islam medievale*. 2 vols. Torino: Einaudi.
D'Ancona, C. 2005b. 'Greek into Arabic: Neoplatonism in Translation'. In Adamson and Taylor 2005: 10–31.
Davidson, H. A. 1987. *Proofs for Eternity, Creation and the Existence of God in Medieval Islamic and Jewish Philosophy*. Oxford: Oxford University Press.
Davies, B. and Stump, E., eds. 2012. *The Oxford Handbook of Aquinas*. Oxford: Oxford University Press.
Davies, D. 2011. *Method and Metaphysics in Maimonides' 'Guide for the Perplexed'*. Oxford: Oxford University Press.
Dhanani, A. 1994. *The Physical Theory of the Kalām*. Leiden: Brill.
Druart, T. 2005. 'Metaphysics'. In Adamson and Taylor 2005: 327–48.
Finianos, G. 2007. *De l'existence à la nécessaire existence chez Avicenne*. Bordeaux: Presses Universitaires de Bordeaux.
Fox, M. 1990. *Interpreting Maimonides: Studies in Methodology, Metaphysics, and Moral Philosophy*. Chicago: University of Chicago Press.
Frank, R. 1994. *Al-Ghazali and the Ash'arite School*. Durham, NC: Duke University Press.
al-Ghazali. 1997. *The Incoherence of the Philosophers*, trans. M. Marmura. Provo, UT: Brigham Young University Press.
Gilson, E. 1955. *A History of Christian Philosophy in the Middle Ages*. London: Sheed & Ward.
Goodman, L. 1992. *Avicenna*. London: Routledge.
Harvey, S. 2005. 'Islamic Philosophy and Jewish Philosophy'. In Adamson and Taylor 2005: 349–69.
Kahn, C. 1982. 'Why Existence Does Not Emerge as a Distinct Concept in Greek Philosophy'. In P. Morewedge, ed., *Philosophies of Existence: Ancient and Medieval*. New York: Fordham University Press.
Kogan, B. 1985. *Averroes and the Metaphysics of Causation*. Albany, NY: The State University of New York Press.
Leaman, O. 1985. *An Introduction to Medieval Islamic Philosophy*. Cambridge: Cambridge University Press.

Lizzini, O. 2009. 'Il nulla, l'inesistente, la cosa: nota intorno all terminologia e alla dottrina del nulla e della creazione dal nulla nel pensiero islamico'. In M. Lenzi and A. Maierù, eds, *Discussioni sul nulla tra medioevo ed età moderna*. Firenze: Olschki Editore, 63–103.

McGinnis, J. 2010. *Avicenna*. Oxford: Oxford University Press.

Maimonides. 1963. *The Guide of the Perplexed*, trans. S. Pines. 2 vols. Chicago: The University of Chicago Press.

Maimonides. 1972. 'Letter on Astrology', trans. R. Lerner, in R. Lerner and M. Mahdi, eds, *Medieval Political Philosophy*. Ithaca, NY: Cornell University Press.

Marmura, M. 2005. 'Al-Ghazali'. In Adamson and Taylor 2005: 137–54.

May, G. 1978. *Schöpfung aus dem Nichts: Die Enstehung der Lehre von der creatio ex nihilo.* Berlin: Walter de Gruyter. (*'Creatio Ex Nihilo': The Doctrine of 'Creation out of Nothing in Early Christian Thought*, trans. A. S. Worrall. Edinburgh: T.&T. Clark, 1994.)

Ozcoidi, I. 2001. *La concepción de la filosofía en Averroes.* Madrid: Editorial Trotta.

Radici, R. and Reale, G., trans. and eds. 1987. *Filone di Alessamdria: la filosofia mosaica.* Milan: Rusconi.

Reisman, D. 2005. 'Al-Fārāībī and the Philosophical Curriculum'. In Adamson and Taylor 2005: 52–71.

Rudavsky, T. M. 2000. *Time Matters: Time, Creation, and Cosmology in Medieval Jewish Philosophy*. Albany, NY: The State University of New York Press.

Seeskin, K. 2005. *Maimonides on the Origin of the World.* Cambridge: Cambridge University Press.

Soskice, J. M. 2010. '*Creatio ex nihilo*: Its Jewish and Christian Foundations'. In Burrell 2010: 24–39.

Winter, T., ed. 2008. *The Cambridge Companion to Classical Islamic Theology*. Cambridge: Cambridge University Press.

Wisnovsky, R. 2005. 'Avicenna and the Avicennan Tradition'. In Adamson and Taylor 2005: 92–136.

Zonta, M. 2009. 'La "creazione dal nulla" nella filosofia ebraica medievale in terra d'Islam'. In M. Lenzi and A. Maierù, eds, *Discussioni sul nulla tra medioevo ed età moderna*. Florence: Olschki Editore, 53–62.

CHAPTER 20

MYSTICISM IN THE ABRAHAMIC RELIGIONS

MOSHE IDEL

1. Mysticism as Intensification of Performance, and Contact

Religious mysticism has two major components that are found, in various ways and degrees, in many of its manifestations. They are the intensification of religious life on the one hand, and eventually the feeling that a contact was established with a more sublime realm, widely understood as more spiritual than the 'normal' religious experience of a certain religion. Thus, we may speak about more general characteristics of mysticism, which differ from assumptions as to the existence of a special cognitive level that is specifically representative of the mystical experience. On the other hand, the type of intensification and the nature of the contact vary from one sort of mysticism to another, even within the same religion, and should be understood against the background of themes and ideals found in the specific religion within which the mystic operated. Most of the ideals shared by the specific mystics are also shared by the specific religious structures, which host the much more limited religious events described by scholars as mystical. Thus, a performative religion will intensify the religious acts, a religion based on faith will intensify the value of faith, and a more philosophically oriented religion will emphasize the importance of the intensified acts of cognition.

Mystics are, therefore, fundamentally more 'religious' than some of the other forms of religious elites, like for example the members of ordinary religious establishments, which are much more concerned with preserving the prevailing social-spiritual structures. In many cases, mystics sometimes claim to be more 'authentic' and in keeping with the 'original' or pristine ideals of a certain religion that have been allegedly 'betrayed' or at least neglected or forgotten by present religious elites. Thirteenth-century Christian forms of mysticism, especially in Italy, with their emphasis on the importance of poverty, are a major example of this claim for a renascence of a genuine betrayed spirituality with ancient roots. Contemporaneous Jewish mystics active in Western Europe, known as the Kabbalists, also claimed to restore an ancient Jewish spirituality, forgotten or neglected by some rabbinic authorities. This is the case of the authorship of the book of the *Zohar* attributed to a second-century rabbinic figure, of R. Baḥya ibn Paquda (eleventh-century Spain) who preached the allegedly 'lost' 'duties of the heart', and R. Abraham Abulafia (thirteenth century), who conceived himself to be a prophet. Revival is mentioned in the title of one of al-Ghazālī's most important books, *The Revival of Religious Sciences.* Or, to put it in more sociological terms, there are strong revivalist elements in mystical thinking, practice, and movements that isolate some ideals from the past. These are, to be sure, understood in new ways, but only in a few cases do they represent what a scholar—unlike a contemporary authority—would discern as heresy, from a theological or a phenomenological point of view.

The ways adopted by those spiritual figures in order to restore the ancient and allegedly betrayed values are somewhat different from the more common religious practices. Poverty, itinerant life, seclusion, intense dedication to contemplation or meditation, are sorts of activities that are supposed to facilitate the retrieval of a spiritual experience characteristic of a pristine, ancient spiritual past. Though rarely a case of strict innovation, mystical ideals and techniques are more often a restructuring of the old with new emphases and with the addition of elements taken from other cultures. From the literary point of view, many of the spiritual figures are also commentators, and the vast exegetical enterprises in mystical literatures are conspicuous.

However, the strong belief in spiritual values, and the deep emotional and intellectual investment in a type of behaviour intended to actualize them, constitute departures from the common way of religious life. They invite a more intense spiritual life by following a more specific religious path and then having some experience as the result of it. This intensification of religious life, more than the specifics of the techniques or the content of the experience, either restorative or new, seems to me to be a basic feature of many traditional forms of mysticism. In many cases, the intensification is described as culminating in reaching some contact with the divine realm. Therefore, the intensification of religious life, and the contact with what is conceived of as a spiritual sphere, are two main general features of mysticism that distinguish mystical literatures and experiences from other religious ones. This is the case also in the quietist forms of mysticism, where efforts are directed to a state of mind which strives not to exercise the will; these efforts are in themselves intense states of expectation. The new intensity of religious life creates what is perceived of as an alternative to what is envisioned—at least implicitly—as a more diluted form of religion, as fostered by present social structures, sometimes regarded as corrupted, and this is the reason why tensions often emerge between mystics and establishments. Thus, cases of sectarianism, polemics, and persecutions, which are conducive to extremism from the two sides, are often part of the emergence of the new spiritual ideals. In a way, mystical revivals are part of the phenomena of sociological and intellectual bifurcations. This departure of ways does not mean dramatic schisms, but even small divergences may attract sharp theological controversies. Not that the mystics attempted to present themselves as innovators, but any intensification also generates new emphases that are conceived of as alternatives, and thus as threats to the more common perceptions of a certain religion.

The intensification of activities changes the psychosomatic system and induces forms of experience which may have some characteristics in common with other mystical events. These intensifications may de-automatize ordinary behaviour and thus open the consciousness toward other forms of experiences. By paying special attention to carefully described patterns of behaviour and the ensuing experiences, a shift from a theological orientation takes place. To sum up my proposal: though traditional mystics belong to their respective religious traditions, and should be studied as such, they intensified their religious activity in order to reach stronger experiences than the regular religious ones in their tradition. This intensification is a more universal characteristic, which is nevertheless applied to different particularistic ways of religious behaviour. Some of these intensifications may take the form of acceleration of activities that will bring about the mystical experiences, which differ from each other from one religion to another, or even from one individual to another in the same religion.

The vast and diverse literatures commonly designated as religious mysticism can be approached from at least two main different perspectives. One is to see it as a universal phenomenon in many religions and to attempt to explore the common denominators of the different mystical literatures and experiences in order to discover and define the recurring universals. In many cases this approach is indebted to general psychological assumptions as to the nature of the soul and its special activities during what is described as a mystical experience as if present in all the forms of mystical experiences. This may be described as a synthetic approach, since it takes into consideration disparate literatures that are described as mystical, paying less attention to their cultural or religious contexts, and attempting to find the major characteristics that allegedly underlie them. The other major approach to religious mysticism is to consider it first and foremost against the specific background of the various religions from which it emerges. This is a more analytical approach, and it resorts to more philological, historical, sociological, and literary tools. Without using exactly the terms suggested above, the two approaches have been recently developed as competing alternatives in a series of collected articles initiated and edited by Steven T. Katz (1978, 1983) and Robert K. Forman (1990).

In line with an inclusive approach to the study of religion and mysticism, which strives to resort to many different methodologies, I suggest adopting elements from both approaches, without subscribing totally to the premises of either of the two. I believe that the approaches may at times function as correctives to each other, and complement each other much more than diverge. By assuming a very significant experiential component of the literatures to be surveyed below I do not claim that this element is identical in all of them but rather that there are significant differences between them.

2. Methodological Warnings

Assumptions as to the existence of distinct forms of mysticism that characterize each of the Abrahamic religions run against the plethora of mystical phenomena found in each of them. In other words, in each religion we may distinguish between many different approaches, a fact that problematizes the weight of phrases like Jewish, Christian, or Muslim mysticism as phenomenologically delineated from each other. This does not mean that we should not try to discern what is characteristic of each of the mystical phenomena in the three religions, by asking questions regarding the themes that are more or less important in each of them, or querying what is absent in one of them and prominent in the others. So, for example, the vision of Christian mysticism as focused on Christ, or of the Muslim and the Jewish ones as more focused on language, helps greatly in distinguishing between their general contours.

However, much more important is the distinction between different mystical trends found in each of the three religions. So, for example, there are dramatic differences between Christian orthodox mysticism, known as hesychasm, and Catholic mysticism, as demonstrated by the famous fourteenth-century polemic of Catholic thinkers against the main exponent of hesychastic thought, Gregory Palamas; in turn, both of them differ quite substantially from the Protestant forms of mysticism. In Judaism, distinctions between different schools of Kabbalah, and between it and other forms of philosophical mysticism on the one hand, and eighteenth-century Hasidism and other Kabbalists who opposed them fiercely on the other hand, is just one example of the diversity found in this religion. In Islam, the existence of many different orders, belonging to the two main versions of Islam, the Shiʿa and the Sunna, as well as the more heretical Ismāʿilis, and the fact that its mystical literatures have been written in various languages—for example Arabic, Persian, or Turkish—testify to its richness. The wide geographical range of the cultural centres of each of the three religious forms of mysticism, all found across more than one continent, warns against too simple a distinction even within one single religion. The three forms of mysticism display different attitudes toward the existence and role of mystical techniques that transcend the distinction between the three religions.

However, it is hard to distinguish between forms of mysticism found in the same geographical area but in different periods. So, for example, the first form of mysticism in Spain, Muslim Sufism of the eleventh–twelfth centuries, had a deep influence on Jewish mysticism, as seen for example in Rabbi Baḥya ibn Paquda's influential *The Duties of the Heart.* However, Sufism ended its career in the Iberian Peninsula when the most important Sufi master, Ibn al-ʿArabī, left al-Andalus for the Middle East; Kabbalah then started to flower there in the first decades of the thirteenth century, developing for almost three centuries until the expulsions from Spain (1492) and from Portugal (1496). In Spain some Sufi treatises were translated into Hebrew in the thirteenth century.

It is only after the expulsions of the Jews from the Iberian Peninsula, in the sixteenth century, that Spain produced its most important Christian mystics, Teresa d'Avila and

Juan de la Cruz. Whether these two towering mystics were influenced by Kabbalah is still an open question, though their belonging to *conversos*, namely to Jewish families who converted to Christianity, is more plausible. Despite this temporal stratification, it is plausible that some continuity may be discerned between the three forms of mysticism in the Iberian Peninsula.

Those are the reasons why many of the discussions below are general approximations, as they deal with the more widespread or well-known forms, ignoring less influential trends, especially provided the limited framework of the present exposition.

3. Mystical Techniques in Abrahamic Religions

Like many other forms of scholarship, the study of mysticism first began in West and Central Europe, and the intellectual propensities there coloured the manner in which mysticism has been depicted. This means that the more theological aspect of mysticism, namely the acquaintance with the nature of divinity, was conceived of as quintessential for understanding the nature of the mystical experience. A corollary to it was that the experiences were granted, freely, by the divinity to the aspirant. The role played by specific paths to reach divinity was neglected. Though certain rules that were part of the general ways of life in specific social-religious frameworks, monasteries, and orders—to say nothing of cells—have certainly been respected, they were conceived more as a form of preparation, and not as sufficiently effective in themselves to ensure the attainment of mystical experiences. Indeed, the forms of mystical experiences that may be correlated to a certain type of theology, even if a general one, are much more numerous than those that may be related to specific mystical techniques. The reason for this is simple: a scholar will be quite hesitant in reconstructing a mystical technique without solid evidence, but will more easily adventure in creating an affinity between a mystical experience and a theological stance, even if the latter is not mentioned explicitly by the mystic himself. Moreover, there are good reasons to assume that not all mystical experiences are related to mystical techniques. This relative absence of techniques is more evident in the Christian western forms of mysticism than in the Christian Orthodox ones, and more central in Hindu, Japanese, or Muslim forms of mysticism, than in the Christian ones. Phenomenologically speaking, Jewish mysticism is more similar to the Christian Orthodox forms, despite the fact that most of its main medieval developments took place in the Latin West. This is also the case with the Ashkenazi speculative schools that developed in Germany and France in the thirteenth century.

In lieu of a theological type of constructivism, which is problematic given the diversity of theologies active in the cases of some of the mystics (many of them elite figures and erudite scholars) there is also the danger of a constructivism of technique. Nevertheless, there is a certain substantial difference between the two forms of constructivism: while the theological one is prone to being exclusive, preventing, at least according to the methodology of Gershom Scholem and Robert Zaehner (Idel 2005: 4–16), extreme forms of mystical experience in Judaism, technical constructivism can be envisioned as inclusive: a variety of experiences can be induced by the same mystical technique—given the diversity of the spiritual physiognomies of the mystics—and in some cases a variety of techniques are available within the same mystical system. On the other side I am not aware of an explicit assumption that there are forms of experience that cannot be attained by the means of a certain technique. Though it is possible to postulate a certain affinity between the nature of the techniques and the content of the experience induced by these techniques, the nexus between them is not always organic, and unexpected experiences can be incited by these techniques. In other words, a certain theology is considered, by those scholars whom I propose to see as belonging to the 'Hegelian' approach, to be the representative of a certain religion, and at the same time, a closed system, and the nexus between it and the nature of the experience determined by a certain intrinsic logic. However, if we assume a significant affinity between the mystical experiences and the mystical techniques, we may speak about a form of relationship that is much more open-ended, and then attempt to offer forms of categorizations that will take into consideration the types of mystical techniques. Such a proposal has, perhaps, its strengths, but also its limitations, and the latter are worth emphasizing.

What impresses when reading the exercises of St Ignatius, Sufi mystical treatises, or some Kabbalistic writings is not just the existence of fascinating theologies that allow deep mystical transformations of the personality, but primarily the existence of detailed and sophisticated treatments of mystical techniques that are supposed to induce these mystical changes. Likewise, it seems that the specific *regula* of a certain order may bear evidence of its mystical character much more than the more general theology shared by all the Christian orders. It is in the *principium individuationis* of each of these religious structures, not only in their theologies, that clues for an understanding of the specifics of mystical experiences should be sought.

On the other hand, mystical experiences are not only a matter of recondite interpretation of sacred texts by resorting to a certain type of nomenclature, but may be conditioned by a sustained praxis of techniques and rituals. Strong affinities exist between the details of the rites and techniques used to trigger a certain experience, and the nature of that experience. Most of the details of those techniques stem from Jewish sources, some of them documented in late antiquity. Therefore, the description of those experiences in medieval Judaism should take into consideration both the speculative heritage stemming from the Greek and Hellenistic sources as mediated by Arabic sources, basically Neoplatonic and Hermetic, and sometimes also Sufi and Hindu elements, on the one hand, and the contribution of indigenous elements that pre-dated the nascent phases of Kabbalah, on the other.

Another aspect of the 'upward' approach that starts the study first with the more concrete aspects, puts in relief the importance of technique more than the nature of the divinity. The resort to the term 'ecstasy' is late in the history of mysticism, and it is related to the divestment from the body and implies much more of a human experience rather than a divine inspiration or a prophetic illumination. The main approach that describes the experience as a reflection of the supernal presence within man, in order to disclose some form of sublime information, theological in its nature, will be less concerned with ecstasy. However, focusing on this term does not reduce the religious experience to a psychosomatic event, but puts the emphasis upon those elements that are more available to the scholar, while keeping a more neutral position regarding the external elements—divine or others—that took part in the experience.

The main layers of Jewish literatures are concerned with detailed instructions dealing with the *minutiae* of religious performances, designated by the term *Halakhah*. The Halakhic mode of writing and behaving is a quintessential component of many forms of Judaism. The attention paid to the performance of commandments throughout the history of Jewish literature is paralleled by the special attention paid to those modes of action in the mystical literatures, and even to modes of action which are not nomian, but nevertheless enter into many details of precise performance. The 'technical' nature of Judaism in all its classical forms, which stresses the centrality of punctilious performance of commandments, invited a technical mode also in the mystical interpretations of these forms. In general, the techniques developed in medieval Kabbalah relied on the scale of value informing rabbinic Judaism: practices relating to the sanctity of the divine name, the study of the Torah, performance of commandments, and prayer. Those practices should be understood as forms of rituals, which may be defined by their 'apartness', namely, their distinctness from ordinary activities, and their 'scriptedness', namely, their ordered sequence of actions which makes them recognizable, to adopt a recent description of the nature of rituals. In the case of these four practices, both their distinctness and 'scriptedness' are conspicuous. When performed as linguistic rituals they were not only performed in Hebrew, a language that is not the vernacular of most of the authors to be discussed below, but were quite fixed and their activation broke the course of the ordinary life through the sanctity attributed to their performance. If this distinctness is obvious in most forms of Judaism, it is even more intensified in Jewish mystical literatures, which emphasized their efficacy and thus put a special emphasis on punctilious performance. A religion, or a certain type of mysticism, may include extreme experiences and expressions not only because some phrases are used—though the occurrence of such phrases is indubitably an important fact to be taken into account—but also if scholars are able to detect circumstantial factors that contrive to ensure the occurrence of the extreme experiences. Perhaps the recurrence of oblique indications, like the existence of techniques to return from an extreme mystical experience, or descriptions of bodily symptoms related to a certain experience, are as important as, or even more than, the theological criteria.

The difference between the theological and the technical approaches implies more than methods to deal with the role of an imponderable experience as part of the more general understanding of a certain form of mysticism. It assumes other dynamics that are formative of religious experience, especially in the case of mysticism: less dependent upon the nature of a reigning theology, on authority, or on abstract ideas, mysticism will be conceived as reaching its peak in extreme experiences if it will develop ways of reiterating these ideal experiences and transmitting them as ideals. I can imagine that a mystic who has undergone extreme mystical experiences will be more ready to write about techniques to retrieve these experiences, and as the esoteric nature of his lore becomes less important, he may attempt to impart his strong formative experience to others.

The different forms of mysticism should be examined not only with an eye to theological claims available and acceptable in a certain environment, but mainly by explicating their abstract tenets by resorting pre-eminently to semiotic, literary, anthropological, psychological, or neurological methods of investigation. This means also a certain restructuring of the corpora of mystical literature that will attract the attention of scholars: so, for example, in lieu of expatiating upon the nature of divine attributes or upon the emanative processes, the scholars of mysticism should inspect the large literature dealing with mystical rationales for the commandments or handbooks dealing with techniques to achieve mystical experiences, some of them still extant only in manuscript in Judaism, on hesychastic practices in Orthodox Christianity, and on the practice of *dhikr* and *Sama*ʿ in Islam. The Abrahamic mysticisms refer to special paths, designated as *via*, *tariqa*, or *derekh*, that are imagined to be conducive to extraordinary experiences. The affinity, or affinities, between the nature of mystical techniques and the ideal of mystical union will clarify the status of the ideal in a certain mystical network in a way that may be different from a network where the mystical techniques that show the way to reach such an experience are absent. Not less important are the detailed and complex speculations on the special nature of language and letters in Islamic mysticism, especially in the Shiʿah sect of Hurufiya and in Kabbalah, which hardly have parallels in Christian mysticism.

4. Mystical Theologies

It would be more reasonable to deduce the mystical nature of a system from its practices, and its general spiritual disciplines, rather than reduce mysticism to a spiritual potentiality related to a certain theological belief, or to abstract ideas like theism, pantheism, or panentheism. Instead of starting from above, namely with the theological stance, and deriving thus the kind of mysticism, I would prefer to start from below, namely with the details of the mystical practices, and advance then toward the experiences moulded by these practices. In my opinion, this approach is preferable also in the case of other areas of Jewish mysticism, like the emergence of Jewish myths from ritual, and not vice versa.

In lieu of an essentialist view that strives to decide, a priori, the nature of a mystical system from its theology, I would say that the nature of the concrete praxis, the spiritual disciplines as described by the mystics, may bear a crucial testimony for the mystical nature of a certain religion. Certainly, the notion that one basic theology informs a religion that developed over thousands of years is rather problematic, and if we assume that a mystic was exposed to more than one kind of theology at the same time, it is very difficult to decide which of these theologies were more influential for the mystical experience of a certain individual. This does not mean that theologies are not important for understanding mysticism in the three religions. However, their descriptions as simply monotheistic require much more elaborated analyses. Some forms of mysticism adopted more exclusive forms of theology, emphasizing the negative theology of Neoplatonic sources, while others assumed a more inclusive theology, which comprises a unity constituted of different divine powers or attributes, sometimes described as theosophy. Those divine structures or hierarchies mediate between the higher, sometimes unknown aspect of the deity and the created world, and may serve as a ladder of ascent for the soul or the mind of the mystic. This is the reason why sometimes the term mystical theology is used, following the title of a treatise by Pseudo-Dionysius. The complex *imaginaire* of the divine realm has trinitarian structures in Christianity, as is the case in Pseudo-Dionysius's treatises, sevenfold ones were important for some Ismāʿilis, and decadic ones are prevalent in Ismāʿīlīsm and in Kabbalah. In the two latter cases, those hierarchies involve also significant dynamic processes, like falls and ruptures within the pleromatic structures.

In this context the importance in the Abrahamic religions of the *scintilla animae*, or *apex animae*, namely the concept of the human soul as a divine spark, is related to theories of the immanence of the divinity within man, thus bridging the gap between God and man by means of following a mystical path.

5. Divine Names

Discussions of various divine names permeate most of the literature of Jewish mysticism, and they play a role of honour in both the Christian and Muslim ones. Speculations as to the existence of esoteric traditions among Jews are found in the works of early Christian writers such as Origen, Clement of Alexandria, and Irenaeus, and later in Talmudic literature. However, it seems that the first sustained discussion of the role of divine names can be found in the early sixth-century treatise on *Divine Names* by Pseudo-Dionysius, a text which had a deep impact on Christian mysticism, and even on Jewish mysticism. Devotion to the name of Jesus is known from the fifteenth-century Italian mystic Bernardino of Siena. In the three religions there are many discussions as to the numerous—seventy, seventy-two, or ninety-nine—or even infinite number of names of God, though sometimes God is conceived as unnamed. Those names were imagined as sharing something with the divine essence and thus a way to approach divinity.

The divine names were taken to constitute important components of techniques to achieve mystical experiences, as is the case in hesychasm and in Sufism throughout their history, among the late twelfth- and early thirteenth-century Hasidei Ashkenaz, in Abraham Abulafia's ecstatic Kabbalah and its various repercussions, until East

European Hasidism. This is a common denominator, though, to be sure, the names are different from one religion to another. In the main schools of Kabbalah divine names were taken to be an indispensable part of theurgical operations, especially those performed during prayer. By theurgical I mean recourse to performances, most of them nomian—namely the rabbinic precepts for regular prayers, which include divine names—in order to have an impact on the relations between the divine powers, the *sfirot.* This is just another form of contact with the divine realm. In many cases in Kabbalah, as well as in Christian mysticism, the divine names are conceived of as symbols for divine powers on the one hand, and for magical practices on the other.

6. Sacred Scriptures and The Graeco-Hellenistic Reservoir

Abrahamic religions are also religions of sacred scriptures. However, they alone cannot explain most of the elements found in the three mystical literatures. The interpretations offered for those texts and the manner in which mystical life has been envisioned by some of the religions' elites owe a lot to what I propose to call the Graeco-Hellenistic reservoir of speculative systems, mystery religions, mythology, magical and astrological traditions. The different interactions between the contents of this reservoir and themselves, and between their different combinations and the scriptural traditions, written and sometimes oral, may explain some of the main processes that produced the mystical traditions.

Mystical themes may be detected already in the sacred scriptures, though nowhere in them is there a more elaborated description of mystical experiences. In the Hebrew Bible we find verses like Psalm 16: 8, 'I set the Lord always before me', a verse that played an important role in the subsequent stages of Jewish mystical practices. The main impact of the sacred scriptures on mystics was the adoption of the lives of the holy men in the respective religions as paradigmatic figures, the details of whose behaviour, and sometimes even aspects of their death, should be imitated: Moses in Judaism, Jesus in Christianity, and Muhammad in Islam are not just founding figures of respective religions, but also transhistorical models to be imitated as much as it is possible.

However, the first significant encounter between the Jewish scriptural tradition and some parts of the reservoir is found in Philo of Alexandria's numerous writings, written in Greek. Here, the variety of speculative Greek thought has been employed in order to build up a philosophical-mystical understanding of the Hebrew Bible, conceived of as harbouring the most cherished Greek intellectual values. Philo's writings had a huge impact on early Christian mysticism and theology, though his direct impact on either Judaism or Islam is scant, if it exists at all. Extremely important is the possible impact of Philo, who may be described as a Middle Platonist, on Neoplatonism, especially on

Plotinus' view of mystical union, a view that left an indelible impact on many mystics from the Abrahamic traditions. This indirect impact changed the course of earlier mystical traditions toward a more spiritual-intellectual direction. By the dissemination of Plotinus' thought in their various Arabic versions, such as the *Theology of Aristotle*, the so-called *Sayings of the Greek Sage*, and in the shorter version of an influential book of a Neoplatonic philosopher, Proclus' *Elements of Theology*, known in the Middle Ages as *Liber de causis*, the three forms of Abrahamic mysticism had reached an important conceptual common denominator. Also the concept of emanation, which played an important role in the three forms of mysticism under scrutiny here, may have a common root in the Jewish Alexandrian book of the *Wisdom of Solomon*. Moreover, Neoplatonic traditions were combined since late antiquity with Stoic and Pythagorean elements, influencing first Christian mysticism, then Muslim mysticism, and only later the Jewish medieval forms of Kabbalah. So, for example, the Stoic, Cynical, and Epicurean ideal of *ataraxia* or *apatheia*, namely equanimity toward suffering, blame, or praise, or imperturbability, had a significant impact on the church fathers, and Meister Eckhart's *Gelicheit*, as well as on the Sufi concept of *istiwa*, which has been translated in Hebrew as *hishtavut*, being conceived of as a necessary condition for attaining a mystical experience.

However, other types of tradition found in the reservoir, such as Hermetic literature, astrology, and magic, also made their way into the three mystical literatures, sometimes together with the Neoplatonic trends, especially since the High Middle Ages. Some of those traditions reached Europe through medieval Arabic translations and sometimes also Hebrew ones, translated from Arabic, and in some fewer cases in Latin translations. Another wave of impact of these elements from the Greek and Latin originals made their ways into European culture and mysticism from the second half of the fifteenth century in the Italian Renaissance, especially in the influential translations of Marsilio Ficino, which entered the circuit of European elite culture at the same time and in the same circles as Jewish Kabbalah. Some of the amalgams of the Renaissance thought mentioned above had a lasting impact on western Esotericism, as in Rosicrucianism and Freemasonry.

7. Other Influences

In addition to the decisive influence of the Graeco-Hellenistic reservoir, it is possible to discern additional influences on the three forms of mysticism. According to Robert Zaehner (1960), a significant influence of Hindu mysticism is found in Muslim mysticism. In a more specific way in all the three mysticisms there are practices of breathing: this is the case of the Christian hesychasm, in some forms of Sufism, and in Abraham Abulafia's Kabbalah. It is plausible that, at least in the case of the Kabbalist, an impact of the Yogian distinction between three types of breathing is found: inspiration, respiration, and hold breathing. Patanjali Yoga was translated in the twelfth century into Arabic by al-Bīrūnī. In Kabbalah there are techniques of visualizing colours that correspond to divine powers during prayer, probably an impact of Tibetan practices related to mandala. The impact of Hindu and Buddhist collections of tales that were translated from Sanskrit via Pahlavi to Arabic and then to Hebrew and European languages served as a channel for transmitting certain concepts of eastern thought both in the Middle Ages and in pre-modern times. As pointed out by Henry Corbin (1982: 9–69; 1990), Zoroastrian influences are found in Iranian Sufism. It is plausible that Iranian theories on dualism, not necessarily via Manichaeism or Gnosis, but in their specific Zurvanic version had an impact on Kabbalistic thought, especially on theories of evil, though in the case of Christianity, the Cathar views have been regarded as heresy.

8. Mystical Union

The question of contact with the divinity or with median powers is part of many forms of mysticism, and in its most extreme forms it means a total fusion with the divinity described as *unio mystica*. Expressions of such experiences are found in the three forms of mysticism influenced by the terminology of Plotinus, especially the term *henosis*, which in many discussions has been used to interpret the Deuteronomic imperative to adhere to God (Deut. 10: 20). This contemplative-philosophical trend unifies many discussions in the Abrahamic forms of mysticism, and it overcame the more apophatic understandings of theology.

However, what is crucial for understanding the differences or the similarities between different forms of mysticism is not the very existence of mystical union experiences or their technical expressions, but the more comprehensive structures within which they eventually function. In matters of religion it is hard to assume that concepts function independently. The network of basic mystical notions defines the concept that enters it as much as the concept defines the dynamic network itself. Therefore, in lieu of resorting to detailed study of the theologies that were influential in a certain type of mysticism in order to discover whether these theologies allow extreme experiences and expressions, or would permit only moderate ones, it is also plausible to turn to an inspection of the mystical paths as a major avenue of describing the mystical nature of a certain religion. By investigating the various kinds of mystical paths and correlating them to the mystical ideals, it could be more reasonable to decide whether a certain ideal was cultivated in fact, rather than consisting in a theoretical goal. The detailed description and analysis of the mystical path, the question of occurrence of initiation rites, the intensity of the mystical techniques, altogether may testify as to the extreme nature of experiences more than the kind of theology that presides over a certain religion. Approached from this point of view, the place of mystical union in Jewish mysticism, as belonging to a performative religion, is quite substantial, despite the claims of Gershom Scholem to the contrary.

9. Mysticism and Extraordinary Powers

The direct contact with the divine is understood sometimes not only as a matter of a personal achievement that distinguishes the mystic from ordinary persons but also as the mystic's empowerment with special qualities, whether personal ones, namely clairvoyance, or transitive, such as thaumaturgic or magical powers. This concept of empowerment is shared by various religions and it is evident in the various perceptions of holy men in the Abrahamic religions: in the theories of western Christianity's view of saints and in the function of the *starets* in late Orthodox Christianity or the *ẓaddiq* in East European Hasidism. In the latter, a theory of conjugation between the extreme mystical union with God and the ability to perform miracles in this world has been explicated. In many cases founders of religions, and in some cases of mystical movements, have been conceived of as combining extreme mystical experiences with magical powers. In several cases in Christianity, the specific ascetic way of life could generate unusual corporeal effects, like special odours, a phenomenon known also in Judaism in the case of the messianic figure and Kabbalist Shabbtai Ẓvi.

10. Personal Redemption and Eschatology

The profound influence of Platonism and then of Neoplatonism, together with the centrality of the figure of Jesus Christ, contributed to a redemptive understanding of mystical experiences in Christianity. Basically a universalistic religion, Christian mysticism was concerned much more with individual redemption, namely a spiritual experience that can be accessed by the individual at any time, and much less with eschatology, which was part of the more apocalyptic genre. Though not pivoting around a redeemer who was already revealed, Muslim mysticism is similar to Christian mysticism as described above, and apocalyptic elements are even less central in Islam. This strong penchant toward individual redemption stems from common philosophical sources, which influenced both religions quite early by direct drawing from the Greek speculative sources, either by the intermediary of the impact of the Philonic synthesis, or by that of Pseudo-Dionysius. Aristotelian elements played a secondary role in those forms of mysticism, especially since they came later to the attention of Christian mystics, such as the early fourteenth-century Meister Eckhart. This is the reason why it is basically the soul, rather than the intellect, that is redeemed by its contact or union with the divine. The theme of the soul as a stranger in this world, and the body conceived of as tomb [*soma-sema*], played a significant role in those forms of mysticism, just as they did in Gnostic literatures.

To a great extent the earlier forms of Jewish mysticism, biblical, Qumran, rabbinic, and Heikhalot literature, are not concerned with Orphic-Platonic themes, as the soul–body dichotomy played a less significant role in them. However, in the Jewish mystical literatures of the Middle Ages, the role of this dichotomy increased dramatically as the result of the appropriation of Neoplatonism, first in Jewish philosophy and then in several forms of Kabbalah. From this point of view it is possible to discern a conspicuous common denominator in both the sources and the conceptual structures of these trends. Nevertheless, two major differences should be pointed out between the Jewish and the two other Abrahamic mysticisms: the much more pronounced role played by Aristotelian elements, especially the intellect as an organon of experience, as is evident in Abraham Abulafia's type of Kabbalah and its reverberations on the one hand, and the much more important role played by the nexus between the individual redemption and national eschatology on the other hand. Sometimes the redemptive experience has been interpreted by assuming the importance of preliminary experiences of personal redemption, which empowers a certain figure to play a public role as a national messiah. Or, to put it in other terms: spiritual forms of redemption connected to the individual have sometimes been combined with the national eschatology that was conceived in much more concrete, material terms of rebuilding a state and the Temple in Jerusalem, gathering the Jewish in exile, and restoring the ancient glory of the Israelites. Various attempts to balance an inner form of redemption as self-sufficient with the public role to be played by the mystic as a collective redeemer reverberate in the history of Jewish mysticism.

11. Social Frameworks for Mystics

Though a sociological approach to mysticism may appear to be a contradiction in terms, it is nevertheless interesting to compare the Abrahamic mystics from this point of view. Christianity and Islam harboured specific structures within which mysticism flowered. Monasteries and orders in Christianity, and orders in Islam, were frequently major frameworks which allowed the development of individuals that culminated in some mystical experiences. Encouraging special ways of life for their adherents through exceptional rules and practices, those frameworks were essential for the aspirations, attainments, and sometimes even the committing to writing of personal experiences. Moreover, by spending long periods of time in those fraternities, or sisterhoods, other types of ordinary life have been shaped, which combined from one side some forms of privation—asceticism in different forms—and some forms of enrichment by cultivating communities whose religious life was much more intense. To a great extent, these two forms of mysticism may be described following the Orphic-Platonic propensity, and as 'other-worldly oriented', to resort to Erich Neumann's distinction. This orientation occasionally came into conflict with the more institutional structures of the respective religions, and triggered tensions, critiques, and condemnations of the mystics by authorities—religious and secular—which caused their persecutions and sometimes even their eradication.

In Judaism, such social frameworks that separated the mystic from the community did not play a significant role. First and foremost because of family life: marriage and procreation were conceived of as quintessential requirements for a perfect Jewish life including that of the mystics, and the role of asceticism in the common use of the term was minimal, and its forms dissimilar to those of the two other Abrahamic religions. Though some forms of fraternities are known since the mid-eighteenth century in a Kabbalistic academy in Jerusalem, the famous Beit-El Yeshivah, family life continued nevertheless to be practised in accordance with rabbinic instructions. In many cases, Jewish mystics played central roles in the religious leadership of communities, which meant a direct or indirect involvement with the laymen. This leading role became more prominent in East European Hasidism from the end of the eighteenth century, where the person designated as the Righteous, or the *Ẓaddiq*, became the pivotal figure in the Hasidic groups, serving as an intermediary between the divinity and the community. To a great extent some popular Jewish forms of mysticism were intended to shape the behaviour of larger audiences more than was the case in the other two forms of Abrahamic mysticism. This is part of a this-worldly propensity more evident in Jewish mysticism.

In this context another basic difference is worth mentioning: the absence of writings stemming from feminine mystics, as authors. While in Christianity there are plenty of examples of women who experienced mystical experiences, and in Islam much less so but nevertheless there are, and some of their writings reached us, in Judaism the almost total absence of any role played by women in generating religious literature in general, and mystical literature in particular, is quite conspicuous. This phenomenon has to do with the absence of the special social frameworks mentioned above, the religious role played by the imperative to supply sexual fulfilment by the husband and especially by the imperative of procreation, and the prominent role played, de facto, by the mother in the education of the sons. The family and its obligations constitute the structural parallel of monasteries and orders, shifting the main activity of Jewish women from seeking spiritual experiences and writing confessional books as in Christianity, to procreating and sustaining the family. To a certain extent, the roles of the Jewish woman have been transferred to the feminine aspect of the divinity, the last of the ten *sfirot*, designated especially by the name *Shkhinah*—the divine presence, and then this theosophical stance also influenced the perception of the women.

12. Languages and their Implications

Christian and Muslim mysticism reflect the nature of their respective religions also by the languages in which the main literatures have been written. The two belonging to universal, non-national forms of religions, the diversity of languages represents both of the unifying factors: the main languages, like Greek, Latin, and Arabic, and the secondary languages, a long series of vernaculars, which constitute the specific backgrounds. In Judaism, a national religion, the central language was Hebrew (and to a certain extent also Aramaic, another cultic language that does not reflect a specific vernacular in the pertinent period), which is the language in which the vast majority of literatures conceived of as mystical have been composed. This is true not only of Kabbalah but also of East European Hasidism, which resorted very much to the vernacular Yiddish, including in the sermons delivered by the leaders on Sabbath afternoons; but when committed to writing they were printed in Hebrew. In Arabic and Spanish there are very few books of Kabbalah, much less than 1 per cent. These observations are important since they point to more centripetal tendencies in Jewish mysticism while in the two other religions the tendencies are more centrifugal. While constituting a smaller corpus of literature than the other two, Jewish mysticism includes a much more dialogical situation with the writing of previous mystics than in Christianity and Islam. The latter two were part of a more missionary type of attitude and the vernaculars were part of this approach, which is missing in Judaism, even more so when the basic assumption was that Kabbalah is an esoteric tradition, not to be revealed even to ordinary Jews, to say nothing of explicit rabbinic and Kabbalistic interdictions to disclose secrets to Gentiles.

This difference has to do also with another divergence: while in Judaism the confessional genre is much less developed (the autobiographical genre is scant) but the 'objective' aspects—exegetical, technical, and theological—which are more descriptive and esoteric, are more prominent, this is the inverse in the two other forms of mysticism, which are more subjective and exoteric, the different forms of Ismaili esotericism notwithstanding.

13. Mutual Influences

Similarities between forms of mysticism in the three Abrahamic religions are, however, not only a matter of common sources. There can be no doubt that there were also lateral influences of forms of mysticism in one religion on the other. Bernard McGinn (1991: 9–22), for example, speaks about the Jewish matrix of early Christian mysticism, especially Philo, and some Jewish elements are found in early Islamic mysticism, and in Ismāʿilism. It is undeniable that Muslim forms of mysticism influenced in quite a substantial manner Jewish medieval forms of mysticism, as is the case of R. Baḥya ibn Paquda, Abraham ben Maimon, and his entourage and descendants, and in the field of Kabbalah it is possible to discern influences of Ibn ʿArabi's school on some forms of ecstatic Kabbalah insofar as the concept of *ʿālam al-mithāl,* the world of the images, or the imaginal world as Henri Corbin translated it in his writings, is concerned. A few Ismāʿīlī treatises were translated into Hebrew, and their thought had an impact on Kabbalah. Moreover, some of the famous ecstatic exclamations of al-Ḥallāj are quoted in a Hebrew translation in a book of the fourteenth-century Provencal-Spanish author Moshe Narboni. John Scotus Eurigena's thought probably influenced theosophy in early Kabbalah. Early masters of Hasidism, flourishing in mid-eighteenth-century Eastern Europe, could be acquainted with Sufi material since this Hasidic movement was articulated in its inception in a region that was once part of the Ottoman Empire (or near it), and Turkish troops, the Janissaries, were permeated by Sufi propaganda, as well as with the eighteenth-century neo-hesychastic renascence that flowered in the northern Carpathian mountains. Evidently, Christian Kabbalah and its later offshoots owe much to the Jewish Kabbalah. In any case, it seems that the most formative influences on most of the stages of Jewish mysticism stem from the Muslim sources, while in the case of Christian mysticism, East and West, the sources are much more of Graeco-Latin extraction.

References

Corbin, H. 1982. *Temps cyclique et gnose ismaélienne*. Paris: Berg International Editeurs.

Corbin, H. 1990. *L'Iran et la philosophie*. Paris: Fayard.

Forman, R. K. C. 1990. *The Problem of Pure Consciousness*. New York, Oxford: Oxford University Press.

Idel, M. 2005. *Enchanted Chains, Techniques and Rituals in Jewish Mysticism*. Los Angeles: Cherub Press.

Katz, S. T. 1978. *Mysticism and Philosophical Analysis*. New York: Oxford University Press.

Katz, S. T. 1983. *Mysticism and Religious Traditions*. Oxford, New York: Oxford University Press.

McGinn, B. 1991. *The Foundations of Mysticism, Origins to the Fifth Century*. New York: Crossroad.

Zaehner, R. 1960. *Hindu and Muslim Mysticism*. New York: Schocken Books.

CHAPTER 21

POLITICAL THOUGHT

ANTONY BLACK

Introduction

The political thought of the three Abrahamic religions—Judaism, Christianity, Islam—contains an unexpected variety of ideas. All three claim descent from Abraham and his covenant with God. Christianity claims to be building on the foundations of the Old Testament, and Islam recognizes Moses and Jesus as prophets. But it is all too easy to exaggerate the extent to which they are in reality similar. The very notion of God underwent enormous changes, depending not least on what each proclaimed that the deity had done or was expected to do. When we speak of these as 'monotheistic religions', we should not imply identical or easily comparable notions of the deity. Their visions of the community of believers differed perhaps even more profoundly. These differences are perhaps most pronounced in the area of political thought. Some of these differences developed over time, but contrasting views of politics and the state often have—and still do—coexist at the same time within the same religion.

Religion and Politics

The three Abrahamic religions held widely differing views of the relationship between religion and politics, between the religious community and the state. Here too there were enormous differences within each. The Jewish people have undergone several political transformations. The ancient Hebrew tribes established a monarchy. The original Hebrew project was at heart political: Yahweh would make the Israelites a sovereign nation, in fact *the* sovereign nation with a position of (at least) moral supremacy over all the rest. This was extinguished by the Babylonians' conquest of Judah (587 BCE). This constituted an utter defeat for the political project of ancient Israel. During the Exile in Babylon (587–538 BCE), however, the Jews developed a new identity based on their religious law, on the Jewish people as a collective entity, and on their sacred history. These were now seen as the focal points of the covenant with Yahweh. Besides, a messiah would come, an ideal king who would restore the Jewish state. This would become a beacon for all peoples.

After the return to Jerusalem, Judaea became a province with religious and cultural autonomy within the Persian, and later the Seleucid, empires. From 167 BCE the monarchy of the Maccabees fought to regain political independence. Then in 63 BCE Judaea was conquered by Rome. There were two revolts aimed at re-establishing an independent Jewish state, in 66–73 and 132–5 CE. The failure of these induced the Jews to accept communal self-sufficiency within whatever heathen states there were, based on the observance of their religious law in their separate communities. This continued under Christian rule from the fourth century onwards, and under Islamic rule from the seventh century. Finally, in the late nineteenth century, there was a revival of the aspiration for an independent Jewish state. This drew inspiration both from the Hebrew Bible and from contemporary European nationalism. It led to the foundation of the state of Israel (1948); but 'Zionism' was not accepted by all Jews.

Christianity was, in theory at least, quite different. The application of the message of Jesus of Nazareth and his followers to politics and the state varied among Christians yet more dramatically. Christianity began as a religious movement with no interest in temporal power; the first Christians believed that Christ the Messiah would return very quickly and establish his new kind of kingdom, in which there would be no domination of humans by humans. So far as actual states were concerned, the first Christians became divided between some who saw the Roman Empire as intrinsically evil, and others who were willing to cooperate with the state authorities in the interests of public order and decency. When Christianity became the dominant religion in the Roman Empire, most Christians, especially the bishops, supported the Christian emperors as the representatives of God on earth. Such imperial Christianity continued in the eastern (Byzantine) empire until 1453, and then in Russia until 1917. In the West, where the Germanic kingdoms adopted Christianity, their kings also acquired a quasi-sacred status.

In one respect, nevertheless, Christianity remained different. Christians established a new kind of religious community, the church (*ekklesia*), different from most preceding religious organizations in that it saw itself as in principle separate from and independent of political power and the state. The church was to concern itself only with the spiritual affairs of its members and with preaching the gospel to non-believers. Under both Catholicism and Protestantism, this remained a permanent alternative to the state, whether as partner or antagonist.

In Western Europe, however, the papacy developed into what was in effect a spiritual monarchy for religious affairs and the church. There were repeated conflicts between the church, led by the papacy, and various kings. This led to the development of ideas about political society and the state as an autonomous domain separate from that of the church (Black 2008). In modern times, Christian doctrine has been used to support ideas across almost the entire political spectrum, from sacred monarchy to democracy, from liberalism to socialism, from non-violence to violent revolution.

Early Islam was at once a theological and a political project. It taught strict monotheism and the subjection of all peoples throughout the world to Muslim rule. The Muslim community itself was to be ruled by a caliph (deputy of the prophet Muhammad) or imam (leader).[1] After the death of Muhammad (632), the first controversies within Islam were not about theology but about politics. Who was entitled to lead the Muslim community? Some (proto-Sunnis, as it were) argued that the caliph must be elected from within Muhammad's tribe by tribal and religious leaders. Others, who may be seen as proto-Shiʿites, argued that Muhammad himself had designated his own successor, namely his son-in-law ʿAli, and that the true caliphs were those whom ʿAli and *his* successors designated.

After rebellions and civil wars, the Abbasids (750–1258) were accepted by the majority Sunnis as a de facto hereditary caliphal dynasty. To placate the Shiʿites, they also claimed kinship with the prophet. The Shiʿites, however, supported their own separate line of caliphs. The Twelver or Imami Shiʿites held that the Twelfth Imam had gone into hiding in the late ninth century but would one day return to restore a just Islamic state. Until then, one should refrain from political activity. This stance was reversed under the Twelver Safavid dynasty in Iran (1501–1722). A new school of Shiʿites now advocated active involvement in state affairs. Khomeini's revolution of 1979 took this a stage further by installing religious leaders as overseers of the state. By no means all Shiʿites, however, accept this approach.

The Ismāʿili (or Sevener) Shiʿites believed that the line had ended with the Seventh Imam in the late eighth century. They advocated the immediate, revolutionary implementation of an Islamic society. This was undertaken by a number of leaders claiming the status of Mahdī (expected one), alleged to be the precursor of the true leader. An Ismāʿili dynasty, the Fatimids, ruled Egypt from 969 till 1171. The later Ismāʿilis became non-violent, as they still are today. These disputes, reminiscent in their complexity of early Christian disputes about the Trinity, simply underscore the political underpinnings of Islam.

For the Sunni majority under the Abbasids, religious life and government became to a considerable extent separate. The one exception was Holy War (jihad): the drive towards extending the boundaries of Islam continued unabated. The *ʿulamā* (religious teachers, interpreters of the religious Law (*sharīʿa*)) functioned in alliance with, but structurally separate from, the political and military leadership of the various regional sultans. They endorsed the legitimacy of rulers and dynasties in exchange for patronage, such as the funding of religious colleges (*madrasas*). Sometimes they brought pressure on rulers to do more to enforce correct behaviour: this 'commanding the good and forbidding the bad' (Cook 2000) is the mantra of the Taliban (amongst others) today. When a dynasty's credibility declined, for example due to military failure (as in the case of the later Ottomans), Muslim rulers tended to fall back on their role as champions of orthodoxy, and here they needed the *ʿulamā*'s recognition. The

[1] Some late seventh- and early eighth-century caliphs tried to assume the title 'Deputy of God': Crone and Hinds 1986: 120.

enforcement of the *sharīʿah* in public life is the driving force behind Islamism today, and it is anything but new.

A new school of political thought developed in the nineteenth century in response to European conquests of countries previously under Muslim rule, such as Egypt and India. Some Muslim thinkers now advocated the acceptance of European ideas about constitutional democracy and the rule of law. These, it was argued, were actually based on the principles of original Islam. Political reform along these lines was seen as the only way to revive Islam as a world power.

In the twentieth and twenty-first centuries, Muslim political thought has become more diverse than ever. 'Modernists' accept much of liberal democracy as practised in the West, including a significant degree of separation of religious from political life. 'Islamists' or 'fundamentalists', on the other hand, have renewed the call for a return to original Islam, claiming that Islam contains within itself a complete political and economic programme, superior to anything the West has to offer. What is involved in such a programme varies considerably from one group to another. Shīʿism, meanwhile, which had long advocated political quietism in anticipation of the return of the Twelfth Imam, has produced its own version of Islamism in the Islamic Republic of Iran.

Land and Conquest

The basic idea behind all the Abrahamic religions is that certain people have entered into a special relationship with the deity which gives them special privileges. The prototype was God's covenant with Abraham, and subsequently Moses, that he would protect and favour the Israelites provided they recognized him as the only god, and kept his law (Torah). Islam, similarly, means submission to God and 'entry into a covenant of peace' (Crone and Cook 1977: 20).

This involved, first and foremost, land: Abraham was promised 'all the land that you can see' (Gen. 13: 15). God would enable them to acquire this land by ousting the existing inhabitants through conquest. This is a potent force behind Zionism today. Islam universalized the territorial claim: God decreed that the whole world was to be ruled by Muslims, and if people would not submit, they must be subdued by force. This was the basis for military jihad.

None of this appears in the 'new covenant' inaugurated by Jesus of Nazareth. Christians made no territorial claims. One of the most outstanding teachings of the New Testament was non-violence. The first Christians refused to serve in the Roman army. The Muslim martyr is someone who is killed while fighting for the true faith; the Christian martyr is someone who is prepared to die rather than to resist force with force. Leo Tolstoy (1828–1910) brought back non-violence to the forefront of Christian teaching. He corresponded with Mahatma Gandhi.

Early Christian non-violence may be seen in the context of the belief that Jesus the Messiah was about to return and establish his righteous kingdom by divine intervention: there was, therefore, no practical need for believers to fight. Some Twelver Shiʿites adopted a similar strategy in anticipation of the Return of the Twelfth Imam.

Christian views, however, underwent a metamorphosis as soon as Christianity became the official religion of the Roman Empire. Now it was seen as legitimate to defend the true faith against infidels and also heretics, by holy war if necessary. The Crusades were a mirror-image of Muslim jihad. In recent times, some Christians have used Old Testament texts to justify killing unbelievers occupying land which they believed God had promised to Christians just as he had promised Canaan to the Israelites, for example in North America and Australasia. The mainstream Christian view, however, has been that war is justified only in self-defence or for a just cause, such as the prevention of crimes against humanity (Russell 1975).

Lineage

Yahweh, having promised to make Abraham 'very fruitful', gave the land to Abraham and his descendants in perpetuity (Gen. 13: 16; 17: 2–9). The Hebrews occupied Canaan on the grounds of their Abrahamic lineage. There is a carry-over of this into Islam. Some Arabs claimed descent from Ishmail (either ʾIsmāʿīl' or 'Ishmael'), the son of Abraham by Hagar, the slave-girl of his wife Sarah; he is mentioned in the Quran after Abraham and before Isaac, as a prophet and recipient of revelation (Q. 2: 125, 133; 4: 163; 19: 54). Kinship of tribe and family have remained important in Muslim society and politics; lineage plays a significant role in establishing political legitimacy. Traditionally, a caliph had to be either from Muhammad's tribe (the Sunni view) or from his immediate family (the Shiʿite view), Kharijite meritocratic ideas notwithstanding. The Ottomans claimed descent from Uthman, the third rightly guided caliph. Even today, the kings of Morocco and Jordan claim descent from the prophet. Muslims, however, categorically reject any racial basis for membership of the community of believers. This was based solely on belief and behaviour.

Once again, the only trace of lineage in Christianity is the claim that Joseph, Jesus' nominal father, was descended from the house of David. Jesus had no actual father. He rejected any claim to privilege based on kinship to himself, and insisted that his followers be prepared to reject their own families. He ridiculed the Jews' claim to special status based on their descent from Abraham: 'God can make children to Abraham out of these stones here' (Matt. 3: 9).

Law

Yahweh dictated to Moses a law governing every detail of social and personal conduct, from morals to ritual to etiquette. Allah dictated a similarly all-embracing law to

Muhammad. The *sharīʿah* covered 'marriage, divorce, inheritance, slavery and manumission, commerce, torts, crimes, war, booty, taxation and more' (Crone 2004: 8–9). Once again, Christianity stands apart. The first Christians decided, after some debate, that observance of the Mosaic code was irrelevant to salvation. This eventually led to a distinction between the moral law, which was regarded as binding for Christians and indeed everybody, and other less important rules about social conduct and etiquette which were left for each society to interpret in its own way ('human' or 'positive' law).

The People

At the root of Judaism lies the idea that Yahweh chose the Jewish people in his covenant with Abraham. This was renewed with Moses but it stands as a covenant between God and his chosen people. Judaism emphasized the importance of each individual's commitment by decreeing that every seven years the Mosaic Law should be proclaimed to 'the people, men, women and dependants . . . aliens . . . (and) children too' (Deut. 31: 11–13; Neh. 8: 2–3).

Christianity was based on the individual's conversion, faith, and baptism. The result, nonetheless, was a community of believers, 'those called out', the church (*ekklesia*). In Islam, the community of believers (umma) was based, once again, on each individual's submission to God. Belief and prayer are individual acts but they find corporate expression in the Pilgrimage (ḥajj) and in Holy War (jihad).

In each case, the religious community was defined by its members' relationship with the deity. In relation to God everyone is equal. This had enormous consequences for the social thought of all three Abrahamic religions. The Mosaic code tried to eliminate social stratification by forbidding interest on loans and the sale of land outside the family. Islam, at least in theory, put all male Muslims on an equal footing; there was to be no priesthood.

Yet for long periods Christian and Muslim societies recognized class distinctions. In medieval Christendom they were justified by St Paul's comparison of the church to the human body: the performance of different functions by different individuals is essential to the well-being of the whole. Medieval Muslims adopted the four status groups of Indo-Iranian culture (commonly defined as men of religious learning, warriors, merchants, farmers). In theory these were equal but hardly in practice.

One momentous result of these faith-based associations was that, for Judaism, Christianity, and Islam, the most important social group is the people covenanted with God. Humanity at large hardly features in their social thought or moral teaching. Rather, they emphasize the exclusion of everyone else from the privilege of divine favour. In each religion, outsiders in principle have (with few exceptions) no status, no rights. The ancient Israelites were permitted to slaughter them as necessary. Islam decreed the same for those who refused to accept Islam, except for adherents of other monotheistic revelations.

Christianity was, once again, different but only to start with. For early Christians there was no question of using violence against those who refused to believe, however evil they might be. Yet there was a tension between believers' forbearance and the divine vengeance which would be visited upon unbelievers, and indeed heretics, at the Day of Judgement. In the light of this, Christians could perhaps afford to be tolerant. And this led Christians, once they were in control of society, to take all kinds of punitive measures against non-believers, including denial of property rights, expulsion, and, in the case of heretics (who should know better), execution. From the eleventh century onwards, Christian Europe became a persecuting society (Moore 1987). Islam was somewhat more tolerant. Adherents of other monotheistic faiths were allowed to practise their religion provided they paid a swingeing land-tax. They were strictly forbidden to proselytize.

Between 63 BCE and 1948, Jews, with very few exceptions, had no political power; non-Jews were just regarded as inferior (Shahak 1994). The more influence Orthodox Jews acquire in the state of Israel, the more this is reflected in state policy. While the chosen people of Judaism is a race, with the result that other ethnicities are regarded as of inferior status, Islam subsumed all differences of race and nation in the one umma, the only human organization that matters. The tribe still remained important in many Muslim societies, kinship in all of them. Christians, on the other hand, partly because the universal church is not a political unit, have often turned to membership of a territorial state, such as a medieval kingdom, or, in modern times, a nation, as the source of social identity and political legitimacy. Some Christians enthusiastically embraced an identity between state and nation, for example in Russia. Many Islamists, on the other hand, see the nation-state and national identity as expressions of paganism.

Government

Throughout their history, the Jews have believed that sovereignty belongs to Yahweh alone. The Torah is ambivalent about human kingship: it may be necessary but it is not altogether desirable, and wholly subordinate to the Torah (Melamed 7–9). It was with the people as a whole that Yahweh made the covenant. This set Hebrew political thought apart from that of all the other peoples of the ancient Near East, who regarded the monarch as the means by which divine beneficence was conveyed to humans, themselves in particular (Black 2009). Especially after the Exile, the Jewish monarch stood in the same utterly dependent relationship to God and the law as every other Jew. In Judaea after the Exile, certain political functions came to be ascribed to the people and the elders. The people—sometimes the elders and people—were seen as corporate political actors, either accepting or criticizing what kings were up to. They could play a role in deciding the succession. During the Middle Ages, Jewish thinkers continued to debate the desirability of kingship according to Jewish law, as well as emphasizing the subordination of any king to the law.

For early Christians, political authority of whatever kind was of secondary importance. Any ruler who upheld law and order and public decency was acceptable to God. After Roman emperors adopted Christianity, on the other hand, Christians endorsed the absolutism of the emperor as God's representative on earth. After about the eleventh century, Christian views about the status and duties of government came to differ sharply between East and West. In the East sacred absolutist monarchy became almost part of religious orthodoxy, in Russia down to the twentieth century.

In the West, by contrast, Christian leaders and theorists endorsed a wide variety of forms of government, ranging from feudal monarchy to republican city-states, and, later, representative democracy. It seems that the absence of any specific theory of government in the New Testament permitted a wide variety of alternatives. Feudal monarchy, in which power might be divided between king, nobles, and commoners, was seen as a manifestation of the organic complexity of the Body of Christ. Besides, Jesus had taught that a ruler should be a servant (*minister*). The notion that a king could be held to account if he blatantly broke the law may have derived from Germanic custom. This referred not only to divine law (moral or canon), but to the civil, man-made law of the state. A king who was flagrantly immoral or otherwise unsatisfactory could be brought to trial—either by the church (possibly the pope) or by his barons (here regarded as his equals: *pares*)—and even deposed. In modern times, it has been argued that constitutional democracy and the rule of law follow from principles of natural justice inherent in Christianity. But none of these developments took place in eastern Christendom.

The Jewish suspicion of any form of kingship was carried straight over into Islam.[2] Nonetheless, Muslims ascribed to the caliph—and other rulers (sultans), provided these could be shown to be, formally at least, the caliph's delegates—many of the absolutist features of Iranian monarchy. But all rulers were, in theory at least, obliged to adhere to the *sharīʿah*, and to fulfil specific religious functions not of their own devising. On the other hand, there was no formal process by which a ruler could be held to account for failing to do so.[3]

Political Philosophy

Muslims, western Christians, and Jews at various times adopted political ideas from non-Abrahamic sources. At the very beginning of the Abbasid caliphate, Ibn al-Muqaffaʿ (*c.*720–756?) tried to graft political ideas and customs from pre-Islamic Iran onto the caliphate. Caliphs adopted some of the ideas, language, and mannerisms of the

[2] One may compare this with ancient Rome.

[3] 'No medieval Muslim ruler . . . is on record as having gone to trial for having killed, tortured, jailed, or robbed innocent Muslims' (Crone 2004: 283).

Sasanian monarchy (*c.*224–651). A certain *Realpolitik*, partly associated with pre-Islamic autocracy, proved popular in bureaucratic and diplomatic circles: a ruler should be prepared to jettison the normal ethical rules when this is necessary to maintain his power and to promote Islam. *Advices to Kings* expressing these ideas became an accepted, widely disseminated, genre in the Muslim-ruled world right down to late Ottoman times.[4] When Machiavelli proposed a similar approach in the West, he was attacked for being immoral and irreligious.

The political ideas of ancient Greece and Rome entered the Abrahamic thought-world when, from the late eighth century, the works of Plato and Aristotle were examined and discussed by Muslim philosophers. No such discussion took place in the Christian East. This remained intellectually conservative until Peter the Great of Russia's opening to the West (*c.*1700). Al-Fārābī (*c.*870–950), Ibn Sīnā (980–1037), Ibn Rushd (1126–98), and others took up Plato's and Aristotle's doctrine that intellect and virtue are what matter in political life. They developed a strong affinity for Plato's idea of the philosopher-king, demonstrating that this was perfectly exemplified in the ideal of the caliphate. (The Jewish philosopher Philo of Alexandria (20/15 BCE–45/50 CE) had seen Moses as not only a prophet and lawgiver but also a Platonic philosopher-king (Melamed 2003: 23).) Plato's philosopher-ruler was none other than the genuine imam who lays down the laws by which people are to live ('the idea of Imam, Philosopher and Legislator is a single idea': al-Fārābī, *Happiness* in Lerner and Mahdi 1963: 78). His task is to educate people, whether by philosophy (for those capable of it), rhetoric (for everyone else), or force (jihad) (for those who refuse to accept the truth).

Al-Fārābī's originality, within the Muslim world, lay not so much in his idealism as in his conviction that all this could be discovered by means of the intellect alone. He insisted that what philosophy discovered by reason was nothing other than the order revealed by God to Muhammad. However, only a few unusually gifted individuals can arrive at this by reason alone; for everyone else, revelation remains necessary. He identified the characteristics of the various 'imperfect' states, such as tyranny and democracy, in terms of the beliefs held by their citizens. He derived most of this from Plato's *Republic*. Ibn Rushd cited the early caliphate and the rulers of Muslim Spain in his own day as examples of the transition from rule by the virtuous few to rule by the honour-seeking few, as envisaged by Plato. He described the contemporary city-states of Seville and Cordova as examples of self-seeking 'democracy'.

Jewish thinkers from the twelfth to the fifteenth centuries were also attracted by Platonic idealism. Moses was identified as 'the prototype of the Platonic philosopher-king' (Melamed 2003: 23), partly due to Muslim influence; for some, David and Solomon also made the grade. The future king-messiah would possess all the virtues of Plato's philosopher-king. Maimonides (1135–1204) supported the contentious view that monarchy is obligatory. Muslim and Jewish philosophers alike ignored the fact

[4] Some commentators refer to these as 'Mirrors for Princes', but this suggests a misleading comparison with medieval Europe.

that Plato, in the *Republic* at least, had in mind a committee or class of philosopher-rulers, rather than a monarch.

Ibn Khaldūn (1332–1406) held out the promise of a new development in social and political thought, by applying the method of analysis which Aristotle had used for the Greek city-state (*polis*) to the whole of 'human civilization'. He applied Aristotle's combination of empirical research and conceptual analysis to a wide sweep of historical phenomena, especially the Berber culture of his native North Africa (today's Tunisia). Historical events, such as the decline of the early caliphate, can only be understood by isolating the patterns which underlie all social change. Agricultural and pastoral societies (*badawa*) give rise to communities with a powerful collective identity (*'aṣabīya*), which, especially when combined with religious conviction as in the case of early Islam, enables them to conquer urban civilization (*hadara*). The new rulers establish a new regime; however, after some three generations, this in turn becomes softened and corrupted. People lose their sense of commitment to the community as a whole. They then fall prey to a new invasion from the 'wilderness'. One can see elements of this throughout Eurasia, for example in the rise of the Mongols.

But Muslim philosophy withered away. Ibn Khaldūn's innovative enterprise lay largely forgotten until European scholars unearthed it in the nineteenth century. Philosophy in the Muslim world had always been a minority movement. It was distrusted by the increasingly influential and powerful religious leaders (*'ulamā*), and driven underground. It left no lasting legacy in Muslim political thought. What shaped pre-modern Muslim political thought were legalistic interpretations of the Quran and *ḥadīth* (reports of what Muhammad had said or done). This trend had begun with Ibn Ḥanbal's attack on philosophy in its ninth-century heyday. Religious jurisprudence was deeply conservative and repetitious. Its practitioners made little attempt to render traditional ideas relevant to changed circumstances. It produced no new ideas.

Philosophers and theologians in the Christian West became acquainted with ancient Greek thought, in particular Aristotle, a good deal later, in the twelfth century. They adopted a different approach. They worked out a distinction between what could be known by reason alone, such as the existence of God and the basic moral code (which they called 'natural law'), and what could only be known by revelation, such as the Trinity, the Incarnation of God as man in the person of Jesus Christ, and self-sacrificing love as taught by Jesus. This difference between the Muslim and Christian approaches to revelation and reason may owe something to the more complex content of what Christians claimed to be revelation. The explanation of the Trinity and the Incarnation in the fourth century already required the use of Greek philosophical concepts. The subsequent revival of philosophical enquiry in the West was spurred on by disputes about the nature of the Eucharist (how could bread become Christ's flesh?) The attempt by some theologians to reject philosophy altogether, which had succeeded in Islamdom, failed in the western Christendom.

The use of political arguments based on reason alone was further facilitated by the ever present distinction between church and state. The church was clearly the product of revelation. On the other hand, the New Testament had little to say about the state. This, therefore, was an area which could be discussed by of means of philosophy.

Even before the twelfth century, ancient Roman ideas about power and justice, of which Muslims remained unaware, had become part of western political discourse. The notion of a republic in which citizens are free to make their own political decisions was embedded in the writings of Cicero; these had been in circulation since at least the ninth century. The rediscovery of the ancient Roman civil law in the eleventh century gave the West a wealth of legal and political ideas which formed the basis for due process and the rule of law.

Starting with Thomas Aquinas (*c.*1225–1274), western thinkers applied Aristotelian categories to contemporary institutions. And they used Aristotle to throw light on the outstanding contemporary problem in political theory, namely the relationship between church and state. It was an attempt to refute the papacy's claim to superiority over ordinary rulers which inspired the first comprehensive theory of the state in Marsilius of Padua (1275/80–1342/3).

One reason for this was surely that Christianity itself was, as we have observed, blessedly poor in political thought. The non-Abrahamic ancients were used to fill the gap; there was no contending revealed blueprint to compete with them. The fact that Italy and other parts of Europe were teeming with city-states—the subject matter of Aristotle's *Politics*—no doubt helped. Muslims, on the other hand, had no experience of the city-*state*; nor did they possess *Politics*.

Out of all this there developed in western Christendom an idea of human society and political authority as necessary for human life and well-being, simply because of the way we are. This was derived in part from non-Abrahamic antiquity, from the Roman idea of the public sphere (*res publica*), and from the Greek and especially Aristotelian idea of the *polis* (city-state/citizen-state) as the only community in which humans can learn to be good, and without which they cannot be good. European thinkers latched onto this partly because the medieval papacy claimed that only the (Abrahamic) community of the church, meaning in particular the clergy, could direct humans to virtue: therefore kings are obliged to do whatever is required of them by the clergy. To avoid the subordination implied in such 'papalism', rulers found refuge in a theory of the state. The distinction between 'ecclesiastical' and 'secular' power, between church and state, became more and more embedded in western culture. With it went the modern notion of the state. Muslims, on the other hand, could recognize only one community which leads to virtue, the umma presided over by the divinely established caliph or imam.

Modern Political Thought

Modern ('western') political theory, and liberal democracy itself, have become widely accepted in many parts of the world. But how much of this is actually of Abrahamic, that is to say (in this case) Christian, origin? From at least the eighteenth-century European Enlightenment onwards, political and social ideas inspired by Christianity have become inextricably intertwined with ideas of Roman and Greek origin and, furthermore, with innovative programmes and ideals devised by European thinkers and movements themselves. Some of these were Christian, many were not. It is important to note that all sorts of dissident, non-Christian, at times anti-Christian ideas could be expressed in Europe, for example by Machiavelli, Hobbes, Locke, and Rousseau, without their authors being murdered, judicially or otherwise, as tended to occur in the Muslim-ruled world.

The idea of human rights, of what we owe to other human beings simply in virtue of their humanity, had been put forward by Greek and Roman thinkers, notably the Stoics (Thorsteinsson 2010). Liberty, in the sense both of freedom of thought and expression, and political self-determination, derived from both Athens and Rome (not, however, from Plato). Democracy, broadly speaking, came from Athens.

But, despite these antecedents, there was something new about European thought. This was the insistence that such benefits ought to be extended to every human being, and that this is a matter of urgency. The idea of human rights as non-negotiable derives some of its force from the intransigency of New Testament teaching. Jesus insisted time and again that his 'new commandment' about how people should treat one another cannot be confined to members of any class or race, and that to act on it here and now is a precondition of salvation. Thus one may say that human rights were formulated by the Stoics but implemented by Christians, or under Christian influence: for example, the abolition of slavery. Justice, the rights of the deprived to sustenance and a minimum living standard, have often been articulated on philosophical grounds, but frequently derive their immediate urgency from a Christian emphasis (which may, of course, be adopted by non-Christians as well).

It was similar with democracy. In ancient Athens, 'the people (*demos*)' meant males whose parents were citizens—an elite, in other words. Republicanism—the doctrine that positions of power must be shared by many and must rotate by means of elections—was inspired in the first instance by Cicero and ancient Rome. It was also a natural development of the limits placed on royal authority by laws and parliaments, and of the constitutions of European cities and corporate bodies. It is possible, however, that the view that a republic is the *only* legitimate form of government, as opposed to one of several legitimate forms (including monarchy), was inspired by a rabbinic interpretation of an Old Testament criticism of the Israelite monarchy (1 Sam. 8; Nelson 2010). The Levellers deduced a right to universal suffrage from the intrinsic worth of every individual expressed in the New Testament.

Historical Islam had plenty to say about the rights of Muslims, but not about the rights of human beings as such. It advocated liberty, but only for right-thinking Muslims. Even today, only a tiny handful of Muslim thinkers are prepared to grant liberty and toleration to non-Muslims. Hardly any Muslim-majority state actually does so.

Muslims, with the exception of the most extreme Islamists, support democracy. But what they mean by this is universal suffrage for Muslims, including women maybe. It is difficult for devout Muslims to accept the election of a government intending to reduce the role of the *sharīʿah* in public life; none but the most moderate of Islamists would do so. Again, historical Islam knows nothing of the republican idea of rotation of those in power and constitutional limits on their powers. One reason why these were not conceived in traditional Muslim political thought was quite simply that there is no mention of them in the Quran or the *ḥadīth*. Some Islamists ridicule constitutional rules as 'mere technicalities' (Black 2011: 329).

Toleration of those who think differently from oneself is generally regarded as a core element of political morality. The Abrahamic religions have on the whole been less tolerant than other religious or philosophical systems. The Chinese empire and the ancient Roman Empire tolerated a wide variety of religious and philosophical opinions, though not political dissent. Jews have seldom been in a position to restrict others' beliefs. Having been subject to persecution, they have often been at the forefront of liberal reforms. Jews tend to tolerate non-Jews provided they do not hinder the Jewish project. This proviso is what makes the modern state of Israel increasingly intolerant of other faiths.

Muslims traditionally tolerated non-Muslim monotheists, though only as second-class citizens. Any Muslim who decided to change his or her religion incurred the death penalty. Today, many Islamists have become even less tolerant, persecuting anyone who is not a Muslim, or indeed the same kind of Muslim as themselves. Indeed, this idea of 'takfir' (namely considering even other Muslims to be non-Muslims and to target them) is almost as old as Islam itself; it began with the Kharijites in the mid-seventh century.

In pre-modern times, Christian states tolerated Jews but only on an ad hoc basis; they could be expelled at any time, and frequently were. Heretics and unbelievers were persecuted and could be executed. From the seventeenth century, however, some Christians argued in favour of toleration of different Christian sects and even of non-Christians. Milton and Locke were among the pioneers of the modern theory of toleration. But it was only with the American and French revolutions, both of them deeply influenced by the secularizing Enlightenment, that toleration of different beliefs or no beliefs became a norm.

Conclusion

All three Abrahamic faiths hold that divine revelation (to someone) is essential to our knowledge of truth and goodness. Within this paradigm, the 'Enlightenment' appeal to reason, science or (as in Rousseau) human feeling as a means to knowledge can only be taken so far. Some followers of each of the three religions in the twentieth and twenty-first centuries have reacted against Enlightenment approaches by arguing that *everything* that is worth knowing has been revealed by God (Euben 1997)—'fundamentalism' or, perhaps better, revelationism.

This has had an especially marked effect on Muslim political thought. Indeed it is a step that, as we have seen, had been taken once before in Muslim history. The result was that pre-modern Muslim political thought remained, like that of eastern Christendom, thoroughly conservative. Even Muslim modernists proceed on the assumption that a political programme or form of government can only acquire legitimacy if it can be deduced, by arguments, however contorted, from the Quran. Modern ideas have to be justified by reference to the revealed sources. But the Quran in itself does not point towards constitutionalism or liberty. It seems that modern Muslim political thought, when it has taken on board aspects of liberal democracy—or the whole of it—has invariably been reacting to outside developments.

On land, lineage, and law, Judaism and Islam have much more in common with each other than either has with Christianity. On membership of the community of believers, Christianity and Islam are more similar. Moreover, the differences between western and eastern Christianity seem, until very recently, at least as great as those between Christianity and reformed Judaism or liberal Islam.

Christianity stands out as the only Abrahamic religion which—at least in its western version—has endorsed non-Abrahamic political thought. Modern political philosophy developed within the context of western Christianity, and Christian thinkers have been at the forefront of its development. The category 'Abrahamic' sometimes obscures as much as it reveals.

References and Suggested Reading*

Black, A. 2008. *The West and Islam: Religion and Politics in World History.* Oxford: Oxford University Press.*

Black, A. 2009. *A World History of Ancient Political Thought.* Oxford: Oxford University Press.*

Black, A. 2011. *The History of Islamic Political Thought from the Prophet to the Present.* 2nd edn. Edinburgh: Edinburgh University Press.*

Burns, J. H., ed. 1988. *The Cambridge History of Medieval Political Thought c.350–c.1450.* Cambridge: Cambridge University Press.*

Cook, M. A. 2000. *Commanding Right and Forbidding Wrong in Islamic Thought.* Cambridge: Cambridge University Press.

Crone, P. 2004. *Medieval Islamic Political Thought.* Edinburgh: Edinburgh University Press.*

Crone, P. and Cook, M. 1977. *Hagarism: The Making of the Islamic World.* Cambridge: Cambridge University Press.

Crone, P. and Hinds, M. 1986. *God's Caliph: Religious Authority in the First Centuries of Islam.* Cambridge: Cambridge University Press.

Euben, R. L. 1997. 'Comparative Political Theory: An Islamic Fundamentalist Critique of Rationalism'. *The Journal of Politics* 59: 28–55.

Firestone, R. 2012. *Holy War in Judaism: The Fall and Rise of a Controversial Idea.* Oxford: Oxford University Press.*

Hampsher-Monk, I. 1992. *A History of Modern Political Thought: Major Political Thinkers from Hobbes to Marx.* Oxford: Blackwell.*

Lerner, R. and Mahdi, M., eds. 1963. *Medieval Political Philosophy: A Sourcebook.* Toronto, Free Press of Glencoe.
Melamed, A. 2003. *The Philosopher-King in Medieval and Renaissance Jewish Thought.* Albany, NY: State University of New York Press.
Moore, R. I. 1987. *The Formation of a Persecuting Society.* Oxford: Blackwell.
Nelson, E. 2010. *The Hebrew Republic: Jewish Sources and the Transformation of European Political Thought.* Cambridge, MA: Harvard University Press.
Russell, F. H. 1975. *The Just War in the Middle Ages.* Cambridge: Cambridge University Press.
Shahak, I. 1994. *Jewish History, Jewish Religion: The Weight of Three Thousand Years.* London: Pluto.
Thorsteinsson, R. M. 2010. *Roman Christianity and Roman Stoicism.* Oxford: Oxford University Press.

CHAPTER 22

RELIGIOUS DUALISM AND THE ABRAHAMIC RELIGIONS

YURI STOYANOV

The problem of the nature and dynamics of the interrelations between traditions of religious dualism and Judaism, Christianity, and Islam is of major importance for the exploration and understanding of some of the characteristic theological tensions and polemics within the Abrahamic religions. It also has significant implications for the investigation of and gaining new insight into the processes of the construction of their normative orthodoxies, especially in the spheres of devising strategies of defining and refuting doctrinal error, heterodoxy, and heresy. The non-confessional academic study of the interface between Abrahamic monotheisms and religious dualism, attempted dualist or near-dualist formulations of principal Abrahamic theological tenets and notions, as well as the provenance and re-emergence of dualist denominations and currents within the Abrahamic traditions, has progressed amid a series of long-standing and ongoing controversies and conflicting interpretations. Its progress has not been made any easier by the fact that research on the emergence and historical trajectories of religious dualist traditions (whether as or within 'high' religious systems or non-literate cultures) has continued to confront a series of serious religious and historical problems many of which still remain largely unresolved.

Since as a term in the study of religions 'dualism' has a relatively short but complex and controversial semantic history, it will be necessary to clarify first the history of its use in religio-historical, philosophical, and sociological contexts and discourses in order to avoid some of the characteristic terminological and semantic confusions that often accompany discussions of this problematic.

History of Research

As a term introduced by the English Orientalist Thomas Hyde (1636–1703) in 1700 (Hyde 1700: IX. 163–4), the term 'dualist' is, of course, an unattested socio-traditional self-designation among pre-modern religious communities and represents a typological construct to analyse and classify religious phenomena. Hyde used the term in relation to what he described as an ancient Persian belief in two principles, one eternal and one created (respectively labelled by Zoroaster the Light and the Dark) and in reference to the Persian Magi and the later Manichaeans who professed this teaching (analysis of Hyde's contribution to the study of Iranian religion, monotheism, and dualism in Stroumsa 2002). It was not long before the terms 'dualist' and 'duality' were employed in Iranian Zoroastrian frameworks by Hyde's influential scholarly contemporaries, Pierre Bayle (1647–1706) and Gotfried Leibnitz (1646–1716), while in 1734 the Protestant philosopher Christian Wolff in his *Psychologia rationalis* crucially employed the term 'dualism' to define philosophical systems like that of René Descartes (1596–1650), which postulate that mind and matter are two distinct substances, a terminological innovation which had a major impact on subsequent philosophical discourses regarding Cartesianism, transcendentalism, epiphenomenalism, predicate dualism, substance dualism, property dualism, etc. In the history of philosophy the term dualism came to be applied also in more general terms to philosophical systems that comprised significant and primary pairs of oppositions like Platonism (with its dualities between the mortal body and the immortal soul, the 'One' and the 'Many', the finite and the infinite, the world perceived by the senses and the world of eternal ideas comprehended by the mind) or the ontological distinction between the phenomenal and the noumenal world in Kantianism.

Notwithstanding its late, early eighteenth-century debut in philosophical discourse the term 'dualism' found thus wide currency in subsequent philosophical theories, controversies, and discussions. Characteristically, its use in the field of religious history and theology during the nineteenth century maintained its originally conceptualized association with the ancient Persian religion, the Magi, and Zoroaster. With the rapid progress of Oriental studies and disciplines such as the history of religions, historical theology, and ethnology in the latter half of the nineteenth century, the term came to be also applied in the expanding exploration of other ancient cultures and religions such as those of ancient Egypt and Mesopotamia. Simultaneously classical scholarship began to detect dualist currents in classical Greece and the Hellenistic world—especially within the pre-Socratic theorizing and systems, Orphism and Pythagoreanism, while ethnological research started uncovering dualist notions and scenarios in the preliterate cultures of northern America and Eurasia.

This widening of the thematic and geographical scope of the late nineteenth- and early twentieth-century study of religion and the fashionable quest to look for interconnections between often disparate religious traditions also led to the first more coherent and systematic efforts to determine the place of religious dualism in the history of religions on the whole. The nature of its relationship with monism, monotheism, and the Abrahamic religions continued to be a major research concern not only of theology but also of new and evolving disciplines of scholarly enquiry. For one of the founding fathers of sociology, Max Weber (1864–1920), along with the Indian doctrine of karma, the notions of original sin, predestination, and *deus absconditus*, Persian dualism derived from the experience of the irrationality of the world (Weber 1988: 554). According to other theories which found some currency during this period dualism represented an intermediate phase of passage between polytheism and monotheism (as a kind of necessary phase in the history of the religions) or emerged as a reaction or protest against monotheism (for instance, Henning 1951: 46). Other approaches, stipulating that monism/monotheism and dualism do not need to be categorically set against each other in the religio-historical and phenomenological sense, were also simultaneously articulated. Arguments were advanced, for example, that dualism can be defined as 'monotheism itself in two opposite and contrary aspects' (Pettazzoni 1920: 96, 112), that dualism and monism are intimately related not in terms of opposition but as a contrasted pair of notions (Stein 1909), or that 'in virtue of its precise definition of concepts' dualism acts as a corrective to monism's tendency to effect a premature synthesis (Eucken 1912: 101).

By that time the study of religion had been undergoing the manifold impact of the new historical-critical and comparative methods of investigation introduced and pioneered by the *Religionsgeschichtliche Schule*, which, with its prominent focus on what its representatives saw and reconstructed as a formative influence of ancient Iran and Mesopotamia on Judaism, Christianity, and Gnosticism, also affected the growing interest in and expanding exploration of the interrelations and borders between dualism and Abrahamic monotheisms. Some of the more far-fetched reconstructions of supposed archaic Iranian religious notions and mythic scenarios attempted within *Religionsgeschichtliche Schule*—such as the postulated Iranian myth of the 'redeemed redeemer', believed to have been adopted first in Gnosticism and then via Gnostic channels in Christianity (Reitzenstein 1921, 1929)—reinforced the inherited construct of Iran as the homeland of religious dualism and source for dualist trends in the Abrahamic religions.

Since the early twentieth century the growing evidence of the distinct patterns of dual organization developed in certain mostly preliterate societies has become the focus of intense and continuing theorizing in anthropological and sociological research exploring its provenance, evolution, social role, interaction with cultural factors, and ways of implementation and functioning. This progress of research on dual social organization systems inevitably went hand in hand with the study of the phenomenon of dual symbolic classification in such preliterate (as well as some later) societies, drawing on the polarity between primary and traditional pairs of opposites, accentuating variously the complementary or antagonistic nature of their relationship.

The accumulating evidence of these social and cultural classification systems and the new theories and methods applied to them had immediate and significant implications for the study of polarity, antagonism, complementarity, and contrariety in religious and cultural history and led to the formulation of some influential anthropological and sociological approaches to the problem of social bipartition and associated binary classificatory strategies. While some of these approaches chose a historicizing explanation of the phenomenon (seen as being thus the consequence of an earlier mixture of two different ethnic entities), for Émile Durkheim (Durkheim and Mauss 1903), his followers, and related theorists (Zolotarev 1964) the attested bipartite division of the social and natural spheres (and the related dualities of religious and mythological/cosmological notions) had its origins in binary models developed and functioning first in society itself. Despite making a number of major contributions to the study of binary schemes of structuring social/tribal relations and order as well as associated and consequent representations and categorizations through pairs of symbolic contraries, these historicizing and sociologizing approaches triggered sustained and wide-ranging criticism of reductionism.

Such criticism was especially evident in the influential works of structural anthropologists like Claude Lévi-Strauss and Rodney Needham (as well as related trends in social cultural anthropology) which instead proposed that dual social and cultural classification schemas derive from a 'deep structure' operating largely unconsciously in the human mind. Binary opposition was seen in this structuralist line of argument as the main mechanism of this 'deep structure', being thus intrinsic to the mind's perception of the world (Lévi-Strauss 1949, 1958; Blanché 1966: 15, *passim*) and as a primary factor and ultimate predicate of human consciousness, operating as an underlying ordering principle of social and cultural realities (Needham 1978, 1979, 1987).

Binary distinctions and classificatory mechanisms in the social and cosmological realms were thus a central research concern of structural anthropology which not only confirmed the significance of this problematic for anthropological and sociological theory (Needham 1973; Almagor and Maybury-Lewis 1989) but stimulated a number of studies and far-reaching debates across a range of fields, including the application of alternative methodologies of studying their function in literate and non-literate cultures, using, for instance, the hermeneutic approaches cultivated in the evolving discipline of the history of religions (Eliade 1969). Topics have ranged from the postulated correlations between binary differentiation and oppositions and the general formal characteristics of language (and even the bicamerality of the human mind), to the existence and manifestations of a 'polar mode of thought' in classical Greece (Lloyd 1966) and China (Granet 1973) and the transmutations of oppositional kinds of thinking and their religious and literary manifestations in medieval and early modern Europe (Clark 1997).

The consequent expanding (if somewhat unevenly) study of this problematic in such disparate fields resulted in a series of publications which have not always distinguished sufficiently the term dualism (including religious dualism) from duality, polarity, contrariety, and oppositional thought. This has led to some ambiguity and uncritical use in the application of the term dualism in scholarly and general literature as well as a frequent lack of terminological specificity, which has to be contrasted with the more terminologically well-defined and focused usage of the term in philosophical discourse once it was introduced in 1734. Symptomatically, the term dualism may have originally been employed in a religio-historical framework, but the parameters of its specific and valid usage were determined at first in philosophical discourse—such general and stricter parameters were not applied in earlier religious studies, especially in the field of monotheism and the Abrahamic religions. The process of more systematic phenomenological and comparative-historical exploration of religious dualism and its principal varieties commenced in earnest in the aftermath of the discovery of new sources for Manichaeism between the two world wars, the Nag Hammadi Gnostic corpus in 1945 and the Dead Sea Scrolls (between 1946 and 1952) and their ensuing publication. The resulting expansion of interest in as well as research and publications on the nature of religious dualism and its main forms has been of considerable relevance to the continuing study of the cosmologies, anthropologies, soteriologies, and eschatologies of the Abrahamic religions—as demonstrated by the intense debates surrounding the variously advanced prioritizations of the Jewish and Christian notions and layers in Manichaean syncretism, the posited existence of pre- and non-Christian Gnosticism or the provenance of what has been frequently seen and defined as dualistic themes, imagery, and language in the Dead Sea Scrolls.

Definitions of Religious Dualism and the Abrahamic Religions

Within the growing spectrum of approaches to and definitions of religious dualism there has been for some time a general agreement that a mere emphasis on the contrast between good and evil as fundamental moral dichotomies (so-called ethical dualism) and transcendence is not sufficient to qualify a religious tradition as dualist. Ideally, a similar criterion should be applied to the widely attested use of the traditional primary pairs of dual symbolic classification—light and darkness, life and death, etc. in world religions—the mere more extensive employment of this binary categorization in a given religious tradition should not be regarded as a defining symptom of religious dualism. Opinions and approaches have diverged, however, as to what type of relations between the different oppositional pairs are required at a systemic level to make such binary schemes dualistic, a divergence caused largely by the differing narrower/specific and broader/generalizing definitions of dualism as a religio-historic phenomenon.

The narrower definition has been largely conceptualized in the studies of Ugo Bianchi and other scholars working in the field of history and philosophy of religion (Bianchi 1961, 1983; Kippenberg 1999: 888; Casadio and Stroumsa 1999; Bianchi and Stoyanov 2004) which drew on the major advances in scholarship of religious dualism following the above-mentioned discoveries of Manichaean, Gnostic, and Qumran

Jewish sectarian texts as well as on the progress of research on the cosmogonies and cosmologies of non-literate societies and cultures. A version of this specific and narrowly confined definition was adopted in 1966 in the final document of the Messina Colloquium on the origins of Gnosticism (Bianchi 1967: xxviii) and while often qualified and challenged, Bianchi's definitions and methodology have found wide currency across the various disciplines of the study of religion as well as in strictly historical investigations of the ancient and medieval forms of religious dualism.

Defined in this particular and more specific sense, religious dualism views the existence of the cosmos and man as the outcome and interplay of two opposed supernatural agencies (co-eternal or not), which, in some of its principal versions, are also connected with the paradigmatic moral opposites of good and evil, and in contrast to the monotheistic theodicies and diabologies of the Abrahamic religions, represent two causal principles engaged in irreducible cosmic conflict (Bianchi 1961: 5–6; Casadio and Stroumsa 1999: 1004; Bianchi and Stoyanov 2004: 2504–5). The two opposite principles are seen thus as causes for the creation of the world and man which differentiates them also from binary and binitarian theologies which can use versions of dual symbolic classification to accentuate the notion of contrariety and conflict between the pairs of opposites and relate them respectively to two supernatural protagonists. Such theologies still cannot be defined as representative of religious dualism unless both these protagonists are also involved in the demiurgic acts of cosmogony and anthropogony. This definition seeks therefore to achieve terminological and methodological clarity by distinguishing the religious dualism of the two causal principles from religious systems which elaborate the notion of two supernatural principles associated with a binary system of opposites but without correlating both of them with the cosmogonic and anthropogonic processes.

This dichotomy applies not only to 'high' religious systems such as Zoroastrianism and currents within the Abrahamic religions, but also to the cosmogonies of preliterate cultures in Eurasia and North America in those cases where there emerges a second demiurgic figure, a demiurge-trickster, who moves from a position of collaboration with the first demiurge to a position of active opposition against him, expressed also in his own counter-creations (a notion developed in some versions of the regional 'earth diver' cosmogonies—Bianchi 1983: 57–194; Eliade 1970; Stoyanov 2000: 131–9). In this line of approach such a dichotomy seems particularly evident when some of these cosmogonies associate a divine pair of twins or brothers with the cosmogonic process. In certain cases they are perceived as acting in a complementary relationship but in others there is a definite transition to dualism, as the twins may be seen as involved in rivalry and opposition (often manifested in the respective creations), one of them being identified as a bad twin or a type of a demiurge-trickster. The non-biblical/non-Abrahamic earth-diver cosmogonies are especially relevant to the study of the interaction between Christian and Islamic heterodoxies and popular pre-Christian and pre-Islamic survivals of cosmogonic beliefs in Eastern Europe and Central Asia which has continued into modern times, displaying dualist elements in different stages of development and combination.

While this approach intends to narrow down the characteristics of the phenomenon of religious dualism vis-à-vis polytheism, monism, and monotheism, it has also to take into account the dynamics of interreligious and inter-denominational interplay in which religious borders are rarely solid and static but frequently porous and in flux. Studies of individual religious traditions and in the field of comparative religion have demonstrated on various occasions that tendencies and subcurrents approaching the above-defined religious dualism can exist in polytheistic, monistic, and monotheistic religious traditions (Bianchi and Stoyanov 2004: 2506–7). In the Abrahamic religions such undercurrents predominantly manifest as rudimentary or aberrant developments, being professed generally by sectarian and marginalized groups and figures who attract accusations of heresy and heterodoxy. However, in this approach tendencies towards developing religious dualism or the existence of short- or long-term dualist undercurrents in a religious tradition are not sufficient to characterize it overall as dualist, especially if it is cast in the Abrahamic mould.

Wider and generalizing definitions of religious dualism predictably have characterized as 'dualist' a larger number of religious traditions which in their view interpret the cosmos in terms of a pair of opposing antagonistic supernatural powers, controlling or struggling over the mastery of the world but without necessarily treating them as causal principles (for instance, Perkins 1997: 350; Meyers 2011: 94). Such definitions also can tend to equate dualism with the mechanism of dual symbolic classification, characterizing it as 'a tendency to classify phenomena into opposing groups' (Lange et al. 2011: 9). Applications of these broader definitions have been especially common in the field of early Judaism and Christianity studies since the 1960s, where more extensive recourses to binary categorizations and pronounced contrastive opposition of the primary polarities, usually on an asymmetrical and hierarchical basis, have been on various occasions described as representative of 'dualism' or 'dualistic thinking'.

Such applications have been often following and elaborating on James H. Charlesworth's influential broad definition of dualism in the context of the comparative exploration of the Dead Sea Scrolls and the Fourth Gospel, describing the phenomenon as 'a pattern of thought, an antithesis, which is bifurcated into two mutually exclusive categories (e.g. two spirits or two worlds), each of which is qualified by a set of properties and ethical characteristics which are contrary to those under the other antithetic category (e.g. light and good *versus* darkness and evil)' (Charlesworth 1968–9: 389). Even broader definitions of religious dualism have been ventured usually in the framework of interdisciplinary efforts to relate the phenomenon to a more generalized category of dualism as in an ongoing ambitious project for a 'cultural history of dualism' (Fontaine 1986–2011) in which dualism is defined as an unsolvable or unbridgeable opposition between two systems, concepts, principles, or groups of people (Fontaine 1986: I. 263, *passim*), a definition which is then applied to a variety of religious, cultural, political, and social phenomena in antiquity, the Middle Ages, the early modern and modern eras. *Longue durée* cultural-historical projects of the latter type are certainly commendable but given their interdisciplinary character they should be expected (at least to some extent) to draw on the various advances in the existing and growing anthropological and sociological work and theory on binary categorizations in the social and cultural spheres.

These recent applications of a broader notion of dualism to early Jewish and Christian concepts and views have not been matched as yet by similarly concerted attempts to introduce comparable generalizing approaches regarding dualism to the study of medieval, early modern and modern Judaism and Christianity, or Islam as a whole. Permeating a problematic which has been evolving as one of the most significant and topical in Abrahamic studies since the discovery of the Dead Sea Scrolls with such very wide concepts of 'dualism' has inevitably generated some intense debates about the feasibility and limits of looking for and discerning religious dualism as a defining core presence in early Jewish and Christian contexts or indeed whether 'dualist' is the appropriate term to characterize notions which have been synchronized within such ultimately monotheistic frameworks (among others, Shaked 1972; Stuckenbruck 2011). These debates have been also accompanied by the formulation of new dualist typologies which, while remaining generally confined to these specific sub-areas of Jewish and Christian studies, are at variance with the typologies already conceptualized to determine the place of dualism and its varieties in the overall history of religions.

Varieties/Typologies of Religious Dualism and the Abrahamic Religions

A commonly posited distinction between a radical variety of religious dualism (the belief in two coexisting opposed causal principles) and a mitigated version (in which the second principle 'descends' through a process of 'devolution' from a first and undivided source—as in Jonas 1958: 236–7) has been superseded by more elaborate typologies since the discovery of the Nag Hammadi and Qumran texts revolutionized the study of Gnosticism and early Judaism. The discovery of these texts led to increasing numbers of studies which, employing the newly redefined methods of form criticism, redaction history, and tradition history, broke into new territories, reassessing or refuting in the process the theories and arguments of the *Religionsgeschichtliche Schule* regarding, for example, the origins of Gnostic dualism which Hans Jonas also defined as anti-cosmic and eschatological (Jonas 1934: 5). The first more systematic attempt to formulate such a more elaborate typology of religious dualism was made in a series of studies by Ugo Bianchi (as an essential part of his long-term project to chart its *Weltgeschichte*) on the basis of the simultaneous and balanced use of comparative-historical and phenomenological approaches to the various historical and theological problems posed by dualist traditions and integrating material both from literate and non-literate religious cultures.

Bianchi's typology proposed three principal lines of distinction within the traditions representing (in accordance with his narrower definition) religious dualism (Bianchi 1973; Bianchi and Stoyanov 2004: 2507–9). The first line of distinction distinguishes radical or absolute dualism from moderate (or mitigated/monarchian/mild/softened) dualism. According to absolute dualism, as developed, in this line of argument, for example, by late Avestan and medieval Zoroastrianism, Manichaeism and some versions of medieval Christian (Paulician, Bogomil, and Cathar) dualist heresy, good and evil, light and darkness derive from two independent coeternal principles, irreducibly set against each other from eternity. In this approach radical dualist notions are also discernible in ancient Orphism, Empedocles' (490–430 BCE) cosmological teachings of the diametrically opposed cosmic principles of Love and Strife, some teachings of Platonism, and the Samkhya school of Hindu philosophy. In moderate or monarchian dualism, represented, for example, by some of the classical Gnostic systems and the anthropogonic doctrine of Plato's *Timaeus*, one of the two principles is seen as a secondary agency stemming from the other principle which is thus recognized as a sublime first cause.

The second line of distinction concerns the temporal framework within which the two principles function in opposition to each other. In dialectic dualism they are seen as acting eternally in what is often perceived as a cyclical and repetitive process of time—such motifs and elements are detectable in Orphism, in the teachings of Empedocles and Heraclitus (*c.*535–*c.*475 BCE), the atman-maya opposition in Hinduism, and the polarity and interplay of the universe's two basic principles of yin and yang in central trends of Chinese philosophy and Taoism. In eschatological dualism, with its focus on the eschatological events and ultimate purification of the world at the end of historical time, the evil or negative principle is destined to be vanquished in these last times and thus is not recognized as an eternal agency—notions shared in Zoroastrianism, Manichaeism, the principal Gnostic traditions, and medieval Christian dualist heresies of Bogomilism and Catharism.

The third line of distinction is related to the attitude to the physical world and matter. In cosmic or pro-cosmic dualism (as exemplified by Zoroastrianism), the physical world is treated essentially as a beneficent creation of the good principle, which is a 'Good Creation' and, although assaulted by evil, sin, and death, it is designed to bring about the ultimate destruction of the evil agency. Conversely, anti-cosmic dualism equates the physical world and matter with the principle of evil and darkness which are seen as totally opposed to the spiritual world and light. Anti-cosmic dualism is usually strongly anti-somatic, relegating the body to the evil world of matter and opposing it to the soul, with its origin in the realm of light and spiritual good. Anti-cosmic notions are traceable in some currents in Hinduism and Orphism to reach their dramatic and elaborate expressions in the cosmogonic, cosmological, and soteriological schemes of a variety of Gnostic systems and narratives, Manichaeism, and medieval Christian dualist Paulician, Bogomil, and Cathar movements.

On various occasions Bianchi and other religious historians have probed the important question of whether and in what manner this threefold typology and varieties of religious dualism his combined phenomenological and comparative-historical enquiry found differentiated within the 'high' religious systems could be applied to dualist tendencies, elements, and scenarios in non-literate religious cultures (Bianchi 1958/1983; Bianchi 1971). The final document of the Messina Colloquium on the origins of Gnosticism adopted a version of the above typology of religious dualism adding the category of metaphysical dualism as articulated in Plato and Platonism, viewing the world's constitution consisting of the 'dialectic of two irreducible and complementary principles' (Bianchi 1967: xxix). This document also recommended avoiding the term 'dualism' in reference to a 'purely dual principle' and psychological and ethical 'dualisms' when they do not exhibit real dualistic implications (Bianchi 1967: xxix). While widely accepted and employed in the field of history of religions, different aspects of Bianchi's typology have been subjected to discussion and reappraisal. Ioan Culiano, for instance, proposed that another dichotomy should be added to the 'three pairs' scheme: that of antihylic (against matter) versus prohylic dualism (Culiano 1992: 45), arguing at the same time that the mitigated dualist teachings of its first pair should not be regarded as belonging to religious dualism proper (Culiano 1992: 24).

Other typologies of religious dualism have been also advanced: Simone Pétrement, for example, shifts the main focus in her typology to the dichotomy of horizontal dualism (where the division is between beings on the same level as in Zoroastrian and Qumran dualism) and vertical dualism—where the division is between realities of different levels as in Platonic, Christian, and Gnostic dualism, as well as the Cartesian and Kantian philosophic systems (Pétrement 1946). In his analysis of Platonic, Gnostic, and Christian dualism, Arthur H. Armstrong proposes as a main line of division a distinction between cosmic dualism, defined as viewing the whole existence as constituted by the interaction of two opposite principles, and two-world dualism, which posits the division between two levels of reality, the normal and the higher one (Armstrong 1992). The cosmic dualism in this typology is further divided into four varieties: conflict-dualism of the Iranian pattern, in which the two principles are intrinsically opposed and in constant conflict; dualism in which the two principles are seen as independent but complementary or interacting in harmony—as frequently speculated in Chinese thought; and two types of dualism in which the second principle stems from the first, accordingly either in revolt or opposition against the first principle, or in harmony and collaboration with it.

Bianchi's influential typology and some slightly revised versions of its classifications (such as that of Culiano) were conceptualized and formulated from the broader perspective of the history of religions and thus one of their central concerns was the interface between world religions (as well as the religious cultures of non-literate societies) and the Abrahamic faiths in the frame of reference of a more restricted and clear delineation of religious dualism. Armstrong's and Pétrement's typologies were more concerned with defining dualism and the interactions of its versions in Platonic, Gnostic, and (non-Gnostic) Christian contexts. The progress of research on the Dead Sea Scrolls and the emergence of the first theories positing dualist tendencies or actual dualism in Qumran teachings and general worldview, as well as the growing interest in perceived parallels and even genetic links between Qumran and the New Testament (and early Christianity), led to the appearance of typologies intended to define and classify possible varieties of dualism predominantly in the contexts of a problematic which was attracting a great deal of attention in biblical, early Jewish, and Christian studies.

Such was the purpose of Charlesworth's typology of dualism (based on his above-mentioned wider definition of the phenomenon—Charlesworth 1968–9: 389), to provide a conceptual framework for the parallel study between the postulated dualistic pattern in the Dead Sea Scrolls (namely, the War Scroll) and the New Testament, specifically, the Fourth Gospel (a well-known treatment of what has been described on occasions as 'Johannine dualism' had been already put forward by Bultmann (Bultmann 1955: 15–32), who approached it as being of Gnostic extraction which itself was formulated under Babylonian and Iranian influences). Charlesworth theorized such a framework by proposing a sevenfold typology of dualism, defining its seven varieties as psychological dualism of two contrary inclinations found within man; physical dualism of the radical division between matter and spirit; metaphysical dualism—the opposition between God and Satan; cosmic dualism—signifying the concept of two opposing celestial spirits or two distinct divisions of the cosmos; ethical dualism—reflecting the bifurcation of mankind into two mutually exclusive groups in accordance with their virtues or vices; eschatological dualism—concerned with the rigid separation of time between the present age and the future one; and soteriological dualism—dividing mankind in accordance with faith or disbelief in a saviour. Meanwhile, research on the postulated dualist modes of thought in the Dead Sea Scrolls, predominantly in the *War Scroll* and the *Treatise of the Two Spirits* section in the *Community Rule* (but also in other documents), has attempted to define and even classify and establish the chronology of development of Qumran types of dualism(s), reaching some conflicting conclusions in the process. Such attempts have detected early 'ethical-cosmic' (Huppenbauer 1959) or stages of the development of eschatological, cosmic, and ethical varieties of dualism in the *War Scroll* and *Treatise of the Two Spirits*, while disagreeing, for example, whether ethical dualism was a primary or secondary conceptualization in the developmental scheme (von der Osten-Sacken 1969; Duhaime 1977, 1987).

There is an ongoing debate as to whether Qumran documents betray the presence or absence of dualist thought-patterns and whether the related notions and imagery display actual dualist tendencies or full-blown dualistic thinking. This debate has been complemented by further disputes, whether these patterns were a consequence of the external influence of Persian dualist traditions or internal development in Second Temple Judaism whose earlier stages can be detected in sapiential and apocalyptic literature (recent summaries of arguments and topics in Levison 2006 and the contributions to a special volume dedicated to dualism in Qumran, Xeravits 2010). Amid these debates Charlesworth's dualist typology, as applied to the study of early Judaism and Christianity, has on occasion been curtailed or augmented (Otzen 1975; Frey 1997). Frey, in particular, expands Charlesworth's definitions of metaphysical and cosmic dualism (and redefines their role in Qumran worldviews), and, drawing also on other approaches to dualist terminology and imagery in Qumran documents, adds four more types of dualism to his sevenfold scheme. These additional types are spatial dualism (denoting the division of the cosmos into two spatially separated parts like heaven and earth), theological dualism (in reference to the contrast between God and humanity), anthropological dualism of the opposition of the body and soul, and psychological dualism of the internalized contrast between good and evil, taking the form of contrary impulses engaged in a struggle within man (Frey 1997: 282–5). Elements of these typologies have been employed in the ongoing debates regarding the interrelations between what has been labelled (in accordance with the wider definition of the phenomenon) Qumran dualism and Johannine dualism in the Fourth Gospel (summary of recent research in Frey 2009; see also Bauckham 2000). When applied to Second Temple Jewish apocalyptic literature still other related typologies have been formulated, applied, for instance, to dualism in the Ethiopic Book of Enoch (1 Enoch) and defining its varieties as temporal, cosmic (understood as a sharp spatial division which has both vertical and horizontal aspects), and ontological—defined as an absolute distinction between divine and human (Nickelsburg 1991: 56–60). Still another approach, which otherwise asserts that 'Qumranic dualism' serves as a basic structural principle of the angelic, human, and material spheres of the universe and is manifested in physical light and darkness (Dimant 1998: 72–3), calls into question the very feasibility of the approach of identifying different dualist patterns (i.e. formulating dualist typologies) on the basis of the various 'dualistic formulations' in Qumran documents (Dimant 1998: 58–9).

Religious Dualism and the Study of Abrahamic Religions

It is self-evident that the application of the broader definitions of religious dualism in these currents of research on early Judaism and Christianity have extended significantly the criteria and presuppositions for categorizing a religious tradition or trend as dualist, generating rather expanded and expanding typologies of religious dualism. These typologies have tended to integrate some of the traditional components of what anthropological and sociological theory defines and analyses as dual symbol classification, as, for example, the division of a binary cosmos into two spatial parts, the notion of divine transcendence and other pairs of symbolic contraries which in the narrower definition of religious dualism would not qualify as dualist proper. As a consequence a number of religious currents, notions, and imagery in early Judaism and Christianity have been 'caught' in the enlarged conceptual net of such typologies and labelled as 'dualist'.

'Dualism' is, of course, a tool of interpretation, and as the debates over the interrelated use and meaning of other terms such as 'syncretism' in anthropology, sociology, and religious studies have shown, such terms can undergo re-semanticization in the respective discourses of these three disciplines. However, early Jewish and Christian studies are a sub-area of the study of the Abrahamic faiths and the history of religions in general and the redefinition and reapplication of a major typological construct like dualism as a rule should not take place in isolation from the existing and evolving patterns of its use in these broader fields (as well as ideally be informed by the corresponding typological and terminological developments in anthropological and sociological theories of dualism).

As with any other major general explanatory and descriptive category in the study of religion which may be subjected to recasting in novel scholarly discourses and contexts, some kind of consensus needs to be reached within religious studies scholarship on the whole as to the new revised meaning for the respective term (which needs to be as precise as possible) and its modified semantic delimitations. In the case of the recasting of 'dualism' as a semantically broadened typological construct in the above-discussed areas of early Jewish and Christian studies such consensus has not been reached and hardly sought. This significantly undermines the general usefulness of such broader definitions and typologies of religious dualism for the history of religions as a discipline and the possibility of them being successfully applied to other spheres of religious studies (including the study of the Abrahamic faiths as whole) beyond the confined field within which they have gained currency. The lack of such a needed terminological and typological consensus is highlighted, for example, by the fact that principal variants of religious dualism such as eschatological, cosmic (pro-cosmic), and metaphysical dualism in Bianchi-derived and -influenced classifications in the history of religion figure under the same label but denote completely different religious notions and attitudes in the classifications under the proposed broadened concept of dualism for early Judaism and Christianity (Charlesworth 1968/1969: 389; Frey 1997: 283–4). Needless to say, such a far-reaching re-semanticization of these principal types of religious dualism should have been preceded by a scholarly argumentation as to why their existing parameters of meaning in the history and philosophy of religion need to be radically redrawn in the case of early Jewish and Christian studies.

This broadened concept of dualism has thus a rather limited heuristic value outside the confined field of early Judaism and Christianity studies into which it was introduced. The concept has also some obvious inherent weaknesses which make it an inadequate tool, ill equipped for analysing and describing basic notions and views within the Abrahamic religions as well as for classifying phenomena and developments within their mainstream or marginalized and dissident trends. Generally, in this broadened version the concept has become too fluid and vague, capable of adopting as dualist any religious tradition and currents with a tendency towards developing bilateral symmetries or schemes of symbolic representations in terms of hierarchically and asymmetrically arranged pairs of opposites. Versions of such binary schemes (correlated with the cardinal religious and moral dichotomies) exist in varying degrees of rationalization and systematization in most religious traditions, including the normative theologies, cosmologies, soteriologies, and eschatologies historically conceptualized in the Abrahamic faiths. Hence the application of this broadened and to some extent indefinite notion of religious dualism, with its inbred predilection and potential to integrate in its typologies any religious trend or cluster of religious ideas and imagery employing the idiom of binary contrariety and oppositional values to the Abrahamic religions as whole, is bound to generate more confusion and misunderstanding rather than clarity. This concerns particularly such important areas in the study of the Abrahamic religions as their assimilation and recasting of Platonic and Neoplatonic traditions, the emergence of 'heterodox' and 'heretical' currents in their midst, developing tendencies towards or full-blown versions of the dualism of two causal principles, as well as their encounters and interchange with non-Abrahamic religions representing this type of dualism such as Zoroastrianism.

One of the main purposes of concepts such as religious dualism is to achieve clarity and mutual communicability in the scholarly dialogue and exchange across the disciplines of religious studies. In this context the study of the problematic arising from the interface between religious dualism and the Abrahamic faiths will be better served by the use of the concept in its more specific and confined meaning, as largely applied in the history of religions discipline to a range of fairly well-defined religious phenomena. Much specialized scholarly effort has already been focused on refining and clarifying the meaning and use of this more specific concept of religious dualism as a historico-genetic and phenomenological category in the disciplines of history and philosophy of religion and it certainly seems better equipped to anatomize and interpret the various aspects and stages of the interface between religious dualism and the Abrahamic faiths. In such a line of enquiry, for the sake of clarity and precision the concept of religious dualism should be restricted to belief systems which have developed binary schemes whose symbolic pairs of opposites are consistently correlated at the systemic level to two causal principles/supernatural entities. But particular attention should be paid also to religious tendencies, processes, and trends towards developing religious dualism (thus using it also as a dynamic, processual concept), whether remaining abortive and rudimentary or actually leading to near- or fully developed dualist formations and currents within the Abrahamic faiths. Such scholarly enquiry should consider both the phenomenological and historical (i.e. the models of interchange, interpenetration, contact diffusion, and acculturation) aspects of these Abrahamic-religious dualist interfaces.

There are several important areas of recent study and scholarly controversy which not only open promising venues for future research on these interfaces but raise some fundamental problems for the study of the Abrahamic religions. With the wide application of the broader concept of dualism in early Jewish and Christian studies, 'dualism' has become in a sense a kind of semantic trap, a catchword to brand and sketch otherwise complex and noticeable shifts in the conceptual world of early Judaism in the realms of theology, cosmology, and anthropology, new linguistic strategies to express these shifts, and a partial polarization of religious experience, at least in some quarters of Second Temple Judaism. These developments deserve a more nuanced analysis and new hermeneutical perspectives, including the controversy-ridden area of pro and contra arguments regarding possible external Iranian religious influences on the eschatology, angelology, demonology, novel satanology, and related new theodicy solutions in post-exilic Judaism (summary of earlier and recent debates in Winston 1966; Barr 1985; Stoyanov 2000: 54–60, 326–9). Arguments for such influences in biblical and early Judaism scholarship have not been sufficiently perceptive of ongoing debates (very relevant in this context) among Iranianists and religious historians on whether early Zoroastrianism represented radical dualism, 'dualist monotheism', or 'monotheistic dualism' as well as the related disputes on whether Zurvanism should be considered a 'heretical' monistic deviation from dualist Zoroastrianism or just its triadic version. These debates have been largely triggered by the notorious chronological problems posed by the nature of the primary sources for Zoroastrianism and the difficulties in separating the early stages of Zoroastrian thought from later sources. The opposing and contradictory views in this problematic area suggest that the existing arguments for a Zoroastrian or Zurvanite pedigree for the Qumran teachings of the 'Two Ways' and the 'Two Spirits', and the temporal and eschatological dimension of the postulated 'war dualism' in the War Scroll, etc. (summaries of recent debates in Stoyanov 2000: 61–5, 329–31; Levison 2006; Heger 2012: 227–311) need a cautious and balanced reassessment. New perspectives and opportunities for the exploration of this contested area of early Jewish studies have been offered, for instance, in studies of the language of dual opposition and contrastive and oppositional ideas in early Jewish sapiential and apocalyptic literature, leading to the blending of ethical, psychological, and cosmic dualities in the Qumran *Treatise of the Two Spirits* (Stuckenbruck 2011) and the dualist implications of the division of reality into two parallel worlds of heaven and earth (functioning according to different physical laws) in early Enochic and later Jewish revelatory and esoteric literature (Alexander 2011).

The strategies of rabbinic Judaism's elites to counter-balance these dualist tendencies in apocalyptic Judaism represents another important area of Abrahamic studies concerned with formulating, implementing, and standardizing responses to religious developments which could move towards and approach religious dualism. In the Talmudic period these strategies included polemics against the 'heresy' of the 'Two Heavenly Powers', apparently linked to speculations about the exalted status of an angel or vice-regent of the Lord (Segal 1977). Indeed such speculations may have been related to nascent Gnostic dualist cosmogonies, as in Jewish milieux preoccupied with theodicy, the exalted angel, having already assumed demiurgic functions, was subjected to satanization and the 'hierarchical duality' between him and God was radicalized and transformed into a 'conflicting dualism' (Stroumsa 1987: 172).

Rabbinic Judaism may have retained elements of the impact of the Platonic notion of soul–body duality on Jewish thought in the Hellenistic period (on figures such as Philo) but apocalyptic diabologies and the Enochic narratives of the fall of the Watchers lost their intensity during the Talmudic period, some related narratives being maintained, alluded to, or elaborated in aggadic literature. Some dualistic tendencies were also retained in the Jewish Merkabah (Divine Chariot) and later Hekhalot traditions, especially in the speculations surrounding the status and functions of the highest of the archangels and God's vice-regent, Metatron, as the 'Lesser Yahweh'.

Further study is needed to explore and contextualize the re-emergence and provenance of more explicit dualist tendencies in Judaism from the twelfth century onwards in early Kabbalistic traditions (along with some other parallels to Gnostic notions from late antiquity), particularly those concerned with the problem of evil and positing the existence of another, parallel world of a *sitra' aḥra*, waging a constant war with the 'side of holiness' (in contrast with the non- and anti-dualist theodicy in contemporary Jewish philosophy). In a development which also needs further close investigation, these dualist tendencies were magnified in the later Lurianic Kabbalah of Isaac Luria (1534–72), with the elaboration of its fundamental doctrines of the divine *ẓimẓum* (contraction), the break-up of the spiritual vessels and the discharge of the demonic *kelippot* (shells) in creation.

The process (and its socio-religious dimensions) through which early Christianity accepted some of the concepts of Satan and his opposition to God and man, as developed in post-exilic and particularly apocalyptic Judaism—with all their ambiguities and potential for radical new developments—has attracted some attention and debate (for instance, Pagels 1996). Early Christianity retained a tension between its monotheistic theology and the dualist implications of its evolving diabology and the evident spirit–flesh opposition in the New Testament. There are definite dualist tendencies in John and Paul; indeed although for some time the 'dualism' of the Fourth Gospel had been taken for granted, most recent studies have approached this problematic both from the perspectives of the broader and narrower concept of dualism (Barton 2007; Horton 2011) and referring to 'light–darkness imagery' rather than the commonly used until recently 'light–darkness dualism' in the Fourth Gospel (Bauckham 2000). The polemics through which the church fathers had to defend the evolving normative Christian tenets of evil as the privation of good and Godness against the more radical, dualist solutions of the origin of evil advanced in the contemporaneous Gnostic traditions of the second and third centuries has been also receiving some exhaustive attention in which the parameters of scholarly debate have been continuously expanding in challenging and stimulating directions. Some of the topics of this debate are central both to the understanding of religious dualism and the absorption and re-interpretation of Platonism in Abrahamic contexts. These include, for example, the continuities, inter-dependencies, and polemics among Platonist, Middle Platonist, Neoplatonist, Hermetic, Christian Gnostic, non-Gnostic Christian, and Origenist traditions regarding crucial notions such as the origin and nature of evil, matter, the figure of the Demiurge, and its relation to pro-cosmic and anti-cosmic religious attitudes.

The Christian churches' polemics against late antique and medieval Christian dualism were fundamental to the construction of Christian 'orthodoxy' and important and lasting heresiological constructs such as the heresiographic topoi regarding ever-resurgent and 'many-headed' 'Manichaeism', challenging Christendom with its successive reincarnations in various ages and sectarian milieux. Thus the study of the polemical struggle and legislation of the Christian clerical and political establishments against Christian dualist movements and groups in late antiquity and the Middle Ages is of considerable importance for the study of the formation and crystallization of anti-heretical strategies in Abrahamic contexts, including the construction of the fundamental heresiological constructs and formulas concerning religious deviance and dissent. In the case of the medieval Christian dualism of Bogomilism and the related Catharism, the predilection for using and elaborating earlier apocryphal and apocalyptic narratives in support of their dualist beliefs (Stoyanov 2000: 260–84) finds a telling parallel in late antique Gnosticism in which the creation of Gnostic secret dualist myths was a crucial part of the process of a 'self-conscious re-mythologization' by the Gnostic theorists (Stroumsa 1996: 54). In both cases this re-mythologization and creation of a dualist mythology was accomplished through an inverse exegesis of the normative scriptures to produce alternative accounts of cosmogony, fall, and salvation of the soul—which highlights the significance and continuity of radical scriptural hermeneutics as a primary factor of sectarian and dissident religious self-redefinition in Abrahamic contexts.

Although the diabology and cosmology of the Quran and early normative Islam was notably strictly monotheistic and anti-dualistic, veiled or explicit dualist tendencies eventually appeared in Islamic mystical and *ghulāt* (heterodox) traditions, as Islam expanded and encountered a multitude of other religious traditions. Still, one needs to distinguish the definite dualistic traits in such traditions from the heightened use of dualities and polarities, as in the system of ninth-century mystic al-Hakim al-Tirmidhi or the use of Zoroastrian themes and imagery in al-Sohrawardi's thought. The attacks of Sunni heresiologists against the Isma'ilis as followers of dualist Manichaeism clearly represent anti-dualist polemical clichés, whereas the actual history, disappearance, and survivals of Manichaeism in the medieval Islamic world still abound in major gaps (Reeves 2011). In this context the appearance of gnostic-like and dualist traits in the syncretistic and revelatory work *Umm al-kitāb* (Anthony 2011) and in the pre-Fatimid early Isma'ili cosmological tract of Abū 'Īsā al-Murshid (Halm 1996) deserve greater attention and study which could indicate whether their revival of dualist and gnostic tendencies is the outcome of an assimilation of Neoplatonic and related traditions from late antiquity or a novel religious synthesis in Islamic garb. Likewise, the dualist tendencies in the cosmology and diabology of Islamic heterodox communities such as the Alevi, the Yazīdīs, and the Ahl-i Haq need to be considered in the context of their conglomerate-like belief systems in which the later and locally adopted elements need to be differentiated from the more archaic components of their beliefs which include versions of the ancient and dualistically oriented earth-diver cosmogonic scenario (Stoyanov 2001).

Indeed the evidence of the coexistence and interpenetration between normative Abrahamic cosmogonies, on one hand, and Christian and Islamic heterodoxies and popular cosmogonic beliefs, on the other, has been substantially enriched by recent publications of more popular creation narratives from Eastern Europe and Central and

North-East Asia. A synthesis of the new evidence followed by reassessment of the theory of pre Christian/Islamic 'Eurasian dualism' and the dynamics of the interfaces of its cosmogonic lore with the standard Abrahamic cosmogonic narratives in a variety of Christian and Islamic contexts in Eastern Europe and Central Asia is certainly greatly overdue.

Finally, it seems significant that no influential religious dualist or near-dualist formulations (understood in the framework of the narrower definition of religious dualism) have been accomplished in Abrahamic contexts since the early modern period when the use of oppositional thought and polarities was still widespread, indeed flourishing, in West European religious, social, and cultural conceptual models before entering a decline in the eighteenth century (Clark 1997). Thus the waning of religious dualism in the Abrahamic traditions preceded the decrease of the popularity and application of polarity and binary thinking (especially in religious frameworks) in the modern era. The question how consequent and sporadic partial revivals of notions (but not systems) of religious dualism in modern and current syncretistic 'Neo-Gnostic' and New Religious Movements settings (with varied attitudes to the Abrahamic faiths) may relate to similar broader intellectual, cultural, and religious currents still remains to be explored as a whole.

References

Alexander, P. S. 2011. 'The Dualism of Heaven and Earth in Early Jewish Literature and its Implications'. In Lange et al. 2011: 169–86.

Almagor, U. and Maybury-Lewis, D., eds. 1989. *The Attraction of Opposites: Thought and Society in the Dualistic Mode.* Ann Arbor: Michigan University Press.

Anthony, S. 2011. 'The Legend of ʿAbdallāh ibn Sabaʾ and the Date of *Umm al-Kitāb*'. *Journal of the Royal Asiatic Society* 21 (1): 1–30.

Armstrong, A. H. 1992. 'Dualism: Platonic, Gnostic, and Christian'. In R. Wallis, ed., *Neoplatonism and Gnosticism.* Albany, NY: State University of New York Press, 33–55.

Barr, J. 1985. 'The Question of Religious Influence: The Case of Zoroastrianism, Judaism, and Christianity'. *The Journal of the American Academy of Religion* 53 (2): 201–35.

Barton, S. C. 2007. 'Johannine Dualism and Contemporary Pluralism'. In R. Bauckham and C. Mosser, eds, *The Gospel of John and Christian Theology.* Grand Rapids, MI: Eerdmans, 19–52.

Bauckham, R. 2000. 'The Qumran Community and the Gospel of John'. In L. H. Schiffman, E. Tov, and J. C. VanderKam, eds, *The Dead Sea Scrolls Fifty Years After Their Discovery.* Jerusalem: Israel Exploration Society, 105–15.

Bianchi, U. 1961. 'Le dualisme en histoire des religions'. *Revue d'Histoire des Religions* 159 (1): 1–46.

Bianchi, U. 1971. 'Dualistic Aspects of Thracian Religion'. *History of Religion* 10 (3): 228–33.

Bianchi, U. 1973. 'Il dualismo come categoria storico-religiosa'. *Rivista di storia e letteratura religiosa* 9 (1): 3–16.

Bianchi, U. 1983. *Il dualismo religioso: saggio storico ed ethnologico.* Roma: Edizioni dell'Ateneo.

Bianchi, U., ed. 1967. *Le origini dello gnosticismo/The Origins of Gnosticism: Colloquium of Messina, 13–18 April 1966—Texts and Discussions*. Leiden: Brill.

Bianchi, U. and Stoyanov, Y. 2004. 'Dualism'. In G. Casadio et al., eds, *Encyclopedia of Religion*. 2nd edn. New York: Macmillan, IV. 2506–14.

Blanché, R. 1966. *Structures intellectuelles, essai sur l'organisation systématique des concepts*. Paris: J. Vrin.

Bultmann, R. 1955. *Theology of the New Testament*. London: SCM.

Casadio, G. and Stroumsa, G. G. 1999. 'Dualismus'. In H. D. Betz et al., eds, *Religion in Geschichte und Gegenwart*. Tübingen: Mohr Siebeck, II. 1004–6.

Charlesworth, J. H. 1968–9. 'A Critical Comparison of the Dualism in 1QS 3:13–4:26 and the "Dualism" Contained in the Gospel of John'. *New Testament Studies* 15: 389–418.

Clark, S. 1997. *Thinking with Demons: The Idea of Witchcraft in Early Modern Europe*. Oxford: Oxford University Press.

Culiano, I. P. 1992. *The Tree of Gnosis: Gnostic Mythology from Early Christianity to Modern Nihilism*. San Francisco: Harper.

Dimant, D. 1998. 'Dualism at Qumran: New Perspectives'. In J. H. Charlesworth, ed., *Caves of Enlightenment: Proceedings of the American Schools of Oriental Research Dead Sea Scrolls Jubilee Symposium (1947–1997)*. North Richland Hills, TX: Bibal, 55–73.

Duhaime, J. 1977. 'L'Instruction sur les deux esprits et les interpolations dualistes à Qumrân (1QS III, 13–IV, 26)'. *Revue Biblique* 84: 566–94.

Duhaime, J. 1987. 'Dualistic Reworking in the Scrolls from Qumran'. *Catholic Biblical Quarterly* 49: 32–56.

Durkheim, E. and Mauss, M. 1903. 'De quelques formes primitives de classification'. *Année sociologique* 6: 1–72.

Eliade, M. 1969. 'Prolegomenon to Religious Dualism'. In *The Quest: History and Meaning in Religion*. Chicago: University of Chicago Press, 127–77.

Eliade, M. 1970. 'Le Diable et le bon Dieu, la prehistoire de la cosmogonie populaire roumaine'. In *De Zalmoxis a Gengis-Khan*. Paris: Payot, 81–130.

Eucken, R. 1912. 'Dualism'. In J. Hastings, ed., *Encyclopedia of Religion and Ethics*. Edinburgh, V. 99–101.

Fontaine, P. F. M. 1986. *The Light and the Dark: A Cultural History of Dualism*. Amsterdam: Gieben.

Frey, J. 1997. 'Different Patterns of Dualistic Thought in the Qumran Library: Reflections on their Background and History'. In M. Bernstein et al., eds, *Legal Texts and Legal Issues: Proceedings of the Second Meeting of the International Organization for Qumran Studies, Cambridge, 1995, Published in Honour of J. M. Baumgarten*. Leiden: Brill, 275–337.

Frey, J. 2009. 'Recent Perspectives on Johannine Dualism and its Background'. In R. Clements and D. R. Schwartz, eds, *Text, Thought, and Practice in Qumran and Early Christianity*. Leiden: Brill, 127–57.

Granet, M. 1973. 'Right and Left in China'. In Needham 1973: 43–58.

Halm, H. 1996. 'The Cosmology of the Pre-Fatimid Ismāʿīliyya'. In F. Daftary, ed., *Mediaeval Ismaʿili History and Thought*. Cambridge: Cambridge University Press, 75–83.

Heger, P. 2012. *Challenges to Conventional Opinions on Qumran and Enoch Issues*. Leiden: Brill.

Henning, W. 1951. *Zoroaster, Politician or Witch-Doctor*. London: Oxford University Press.

Horton, F. L. 2011. 'Dualism in the New Testament: A Surprising Rhetoric and a Rhetoric of Surprise'. In Lange et al. 2011: 186–209.

Huppenbauer, H. W. 1959. *Der Mensch zwischen zwei Welten: Der Dualismus der Texte von Qumran (Höhle I) und der Damaskusfragmente. Ein Beitrag zur Vorgeschichte des Evangeliums*, Zürich: Zwingli.

Hyde, T. 1700. *Historia religionis veterum Persarum eorumque Magorum*. Oxford.

Jonas, H. 1934. *Gnosis und spätantiker Geist*. Göttingen: Vandenhoeck & Ruprecht, vol. I.

Jonas, H. 1958. *The Gnostic Religion: The Message of the Alien God and the Beginnings of Christianity*. Boston: Beacon.

Kippenberg, H. G. 1999. 'Dualism'. In E. Fahlbusch and G. W. Bromiley, eds, *Encyclopedia of Christianity*. Grand Rapids, MI, and Leiden, I. 888–9.

Lange, A. et al., eds. 2011. *Light against Darkness: Dualism in Ancient Mediterranean Religion and the Contemporary World*. Göttingen: Vandenhoeck & Ruprecht.

Levison, J. R. 2006. 'The Two Spirits in Qumran Theology'. In J. H. Charlesworth, ed., *The Bible and the Dead Sea Scrolls*, Vol. II: *The Dead Sea Scrolls and the Qumran Community*. Waco, TX: Baylor University Press, 169–94.

Lévi-Strauss, C. 1949. *Le Structures élémentaires de la parenté*. Paris: Presses universitaires de France.

Lévi-Strauss, C. 1958. *Anthropologie structural*. Paris: Plon.

Lloyd, G. E. R. 1966. *Polarity and Analogy: Two Types of Argumentation in Early Greek Thought*. Cambridge: Cambridge University Press.

Meyers, E. M. 2011. 'From Myth to Apocalyptic: Dualism in the Hebrew Bible'. In Lange et al. 2011: 92–107.

Needham, R. 1978. *Primordial Characters*. Charlottesville, VA: University Press of Virginia.

Needham, R. 1979. *Symbolic Classification*. Santa Monica, CA: Goodyear.

Needham, R. 1987. *Counterpoints*. Berkeley: University of California Press.

Needham, R., ed. 1973. *Right and Left: Essays on Dual Symbolic Classification*. Chicago: University of Chicago Press.

Nickelsburg, G. W. E. 1991. 'The Apocalyptic Construction of Reality of 1 Enoch'. In J. J. Collins and J. H. Charlesworth, eds, *Mysteries and Revelations: Apocalyptic Studies since the Uppsala Colloquium*. Sheffield: JSOT, 51–64.

Otzen, B. 1975. 'Old Testament Wisdom Literature and Dualistic Thinking in Late Judaism'. In *Congress Volume: Edinburgh, 1974*. Leiden: Brill, 146–57.

Pagels, E. 1996. *The Origins of Satan*. Harmondsworth: Penguin.

Perkins, P. 1997. 'Dualism'. In E. Ferguson et al., eds, *Encyclopedia of Early Christianity*. 2nd edn. New York: Garland, 350–2.

Pétrement, S. 1946. *Le dualisme dans l'histoire de la philosophie et des religions*. Paris: Gallimard.

Pettazzoni, R. 1920. *La religione di Zarathustra nella storia religiosa dell'Iran*. Bologna: Nicola Zanichelli.

Reeves, J. 2011. *Prolegomena to a History of Islamicate Manichaeism*. London: Equinox.

Reitzenstein, R. 1921. *Das Iranische Erlosungsmysterium, religionsgeschichtliche Untersuchungen*. Bonn: Marcus & Weber.

Reitzenstein, R. 1929. *Die Vorgeschichte der christlichen Taufe*. Leipzig, Berlin: Teubner.

Segal, A. 1977. *Two Powers in Heaven: Early Rabbinic Reports about Christianity and Gnosticism*. Leiden: Brill.

Shaked, S. 1972. 'Qumran and Iran'. *Israel Oriental Studies* 2: 433–46.

Stein, L. 1909. *Dualismus oder Monismus: Eine Untersuchung über die doppelte Wahrheit*. Berlin: Reichl.

Stoyanov, Y. 2000. *The Other God: Dualist Religions from Antiquity to the Cathar Heresy.* London and New Haven: Yale University Press.
Stoyanov, Y. 2001. 'Islamic and Christian Heterodox Cosmogonies from the Ottoman Period—Parallels and Contrasts'. *Bulletin of the School of Oriental and African Studies* 64 (1): 19–34.
Stroumsa, G. G. 1987. *Another Seed: Studies in Gnostic Mythology.* Leiden: Brill.
Stroumsa, G. G. 1996. *Hidden Wisdom: Esoteric Traditions and the Roots of Christian Mysticism.* Leiden: Brill.
Stroumsa, G. G. 2002. 'Thomas Hyde and the Birth of Zoroastrian Studies'. *Jerusalem Studies in Arabic and Islam* 26: 216–30.
Stuckenbruck, L. T. 2011. 'The Interiorization of Dualism within the Human Being in Second Temple Judaism: The Treatise of the Two Spirits (1QS III: 13–IV: 26) in its Tradition-Historical Context'. In Lange et al. 2011: 145–69.
Von der Osten-Sacken, P. 1969. *Gott und Belial: Traditionsgeschichtliche Untersuchungen zum Dualismus in den Texten aus Qumran.* Göttingen.
Weber, M. 1988. 'Politik als Beruf'. In J. Winckelmann, ed., *Gesammelte politische Schriften.* 5th edn. Tübingen: Mohr (1st edn 1921), 505–61.
Winston, D. 1966. 'The Iranian Component in the Bible, Apocrypha, and Qumran: A Review of the Evidence'. *History of Religions* 5: 183–216.
Xeravits, G. G., ed. 2010. *Dualism in Qumran.* London and New York: T&T Clark.
Zolotarev, A. 1964. *Dual'naia organizatsiia pervobytnykh narodov i prozhozhdenie dualisticheskikh kosmogonii.* Moscow (written 1941).

PART V

RITUALS AND ETHICS

CHAPTER 23

PRAYER

CLEMENS LEONHARD AND
MARTIN LÜSTRAETEN

JEWS, Christians, and Muslims perform public liturgies. The study of Judaism, Christianity, and Islam must conceive liturgy and prayer in very broad terms in order not to exclude evidence that elucidates the subject. It is thus convenient to take general presuppositions about communal rituals and prayer among Muslims, Christians, and Jews as a point of departure and to organize the presentation of evidence along those lines.

1. Liturgy and Prayer as Performance: Typical Gestures and Postures

Prayers and liturgies are bodily performances: liturgies must be done, they cannot be only thought or imagined. They require a community of worshippers. While it is possible to assess some of their social functions and to map the changes they underwent throughout their history, their supernatural purposes and effects can only be analysed and presented as a description of the network of instructions, explanatory texts, and other evidence of the respective believers' opinions about them. Thus, they can be observed, documented, and interpreted but not understood. Although one can observe and describe some of their social functions and assess the participants' reaction to their experiences, the performance of liturgies cannot be fully grasped let alone replaced by textual information (Bell 1992).

The performance of Jewish statutory prayers is governed by an elaborate system of rules for the correct posture and gestures (Ehrlich 2004). Some of these continue or re-enact in a stylized way gestures and postures that were used in the Temple of Jerusalem, in other temples of the ancient world, and in contexts that highlighted social hierarchies. Some rather derive from behaviour at houses of study and schools or from general social customs. The most important part of the prayer, the *Amidah* (scientific translation and discussion: Langer 2003) indicates by its name—'standing (prayer)'—that one must stand during its performance. The worshippers bow at certain passages of this prayer (which is whispered in a low voice). During the rest of the service, the congregations mostly sit, rising just for certain moments, e.g. when the Torah scroll is lifted up in front of them. Some congregations practise a series of prostrations on the Day of Atonement. Some gestures in daily prayers require a certain status in the community. One of the most conspicuous of these may be performed only by members of the community who are of priestly descent (*kohanim*, Elbogen 1993: § 9b). The shape of the hands lifted up under the cover of the prayer shawl during this specific gesture was even adopted as an indication of the priestly status of certain persons on their tombstones. During the recitation of *Shma Israel* (comprising the biblical passages Deut. 6: 4–9; 11: 13–21; Num. 15: 37–41), worshippers cover their eyes with their hands and when saying *taḥanun*, a penitentiary prayer recited at the end of certain weekday prayers, each one covers his eyes leaning on one of his arms (Elbogen 1993: § 10). Any member of the congregation can theoretically lead the common prayer service. Dependent upon the Jewish movement and the style of the prayer as accepted by the congregation, a professional cantor (*ḥazan*) may assume that function.

As Christianity opposed the offering of animal sacrifices from its beginning, its earliest members avoided behaviours that were customary at temples or even the consumption of food that was regarded as typical for the cuisine of sacrifices (McGowan 1999). They preferred to adopt and adapt gestures and postures of its Graeco-Roman neighbours that were typical of club banquets, or symposia (Klinghardt 1996, Harland 2003). Furthermore, standing with uncovered head and outstretched arms was regarded as a typical posture for Christian prayer, as attested by the early third-century North African writer Tertullian (*Apology* 30.4), and was characterized in opposition to the respective pagan customs. In the course of the first centuries, the setting of the symposium was given up as focal point of inner congregational communication and worship. Thus, Christianity increasingly appropriated postures of devotion to worldly superiors such as the emperor or other forms of court behaviour (prostration, stylized prostration, and later kneeling; cf. for the historical context, Baldovin 2006). While Christian prayer or the participation in the Divine Liturgy of many Orthodox churches is typically performed in a standing posture, the introduction of pews in the churches of the Reformation and the Catholic church made sitting the most widespread posture for worshippers (for a concise survey, cf. Vereecke 1990). In eastern Christian churches, many gestures and movements of the clergy are concealed by a wall of icons. In reformed or Catholic services, the congregations tend to sit in front of the altar or pulpit in order to watch the precentor's actions and to listen to his or her words (Post 2003).

In Islam, the obligatory daily prayer (called *ṣalāt*) is described as a sequence of several *rakʿāt*, which originally meant 'bowings' but is used to designate prayer units which consist of a fixed set of movements. Each *rakʿa* starts with a Quran recitation which is performed standing, followed by a bow, a prostration, sitting on the knees, and a second prostration. At each prayer, this sequence is performed several times, framed by a standing opening and a final sitting. Kneelers or pews are not needed, only a clean space on the floor. Thus, mosques are usually furnished only with a carpeted floor. There is always one prayer leader (imam), but his liturgical role does not depend upon any kind of priestly status. He prays in the same direction and by the same set of movements as the other worshippers (*maʾmūmūn*). Friday prayers are exceptional as the preacher (*ḥāṭib*) stands on the pulpit for his sermons and sits down for the break between the two sermons (al-Muslim, Ǧumʿa, Bāb 156 (861–2)). All these movements are already described in the Quran as prayer gestures, enjoined by the prophet himself: standing (Q. 73: 2), bowing (Q. 77: 48), and prostration (Q. 53: 62). It is here where prayer became ritualized. The sequence of movements is supposed to be observed strictly, and exceptions are granted only to old or disabled people.

2. Texts

Jewish, Christian, and Muslim rituals use texts, which may be read, sung, murmured, or, in a few cases, only thought. As part of the performance of the ritual, texts function in a similar way to gestures. They may lose their semantic functions, or function as expressions of meaning which goes beyond what could be regarded as their plain sense (regarding the recitation of passages of the Book of Psalms for instance, Bradshaw 1995; Rappaport 1999: e.g. 151f.). Thus, the plain sense of their words need not reflect the interpretation of the ritual in the eyes of well-informed performers or ritual specialists. This can be exemplified from the rituals of the three traditions.

The widespread core unit of Jewish table prayers said before consumption of food is the *brakha* (blessing): 'Blessed are you, *Adonai* (a term that replaces the utterance of God's ineffable name), our God, king of the universe, who is bringing forth bread from the soil.' The blessing highlights bread as representing all food that is subsequently served during the meal. A similar blessing would be said over a cup of wine in formal meals. Ancient sources explain this *brakha* as allowing human use of what is actually God's property (*t. Brakhot* 4.1; Leonhard 2007). Neither the text of the *brakha* nor the gestures that accompany it allude to this special function. The form of the *brakha*—a standardized address of God followed by a relative clause—is ubiquitous in Jewish prayers (cf. Elbogen 1993: § 3 and Langer 1998a: 24–31 for its general structure). Unlike the frequently performed blessings over bread (and wine), the relative clause of many standard blessings indicates the praying persons' intention (especially in cases of prayers of intercession and requests addressed to God).

In the meditative Christian prayer of the rosary (two short prayer texts, repeated in a circular sequence and accompanied by the contemplation of biblical scenes; Duval 1988), in the rapid reading of sections of the Book of Psalms in Jewish and Christian daily prayers, and in the recitation of a sequence of epithets for God's name in the Muslim *ḏikr*, the words and sentences as well as narrative content recede into the background. These texts need not, moreover, fulfil a function in legal thinking about liturgies as in the case of the *brakha* mentioned above. Their performance attracts various explanations that may or may not refer to the reason why people started to recite them in the first place. Furthermore, certain texts may remain in use simply because nobody abolished them or because the shape of the liturgy is regarded as immutable. Thus, the Lord's Prayer was never abolished as part of the Eucharistic liturgies although it is not any more regarded as being necessary as a means of spiritual cleansing before the reception of the consecrated bread for which purpose it was inserted into the liturgy (Taft 1997).

All three traditions recite lines or pages from their canonical texts together with other, more recent compositions. Canonical texts are not always accentuated or treated with more reverence than others. An observer of the first liturgy of the Day of Atonement in Judaism might feel that the singing of a medieval poem, *Kol nidre* (Elbogen 1993: § 24.7), is performed with no less awe than the reading of the Torah on Sabbath mornings (Elbogen 1993: § 25–30). Traditional Catholic theology regards the recitation of the central prayer of the Eucharist as the only performance of the service that has an actual sacramental effect and this prayer remains the only piece of the liturgy of the Mass that requires a priest for its performance (see section 3 and cf. Power 1999 and Krosnicki 1998). The veneration of the faithful for it is much higher than for the reading of the Gospel. In Islam, the obligatory prayer texts and the positions for free private prayer (*du'ā'*) are strictly distinguished. The obligatory texts must be performed in properly pronounced Arabic (although the law schools differ with regard to the details of this rule). Furthermore, one has to make up for mistakes by extra prostrations at the end of the prayer. Free prayers, however, can be performed in the worshipper's native language. Over the centuries, the hierarchy of texts used in the rituals came to differ from the theoretical and extra-liturgical appreciation of canonical texts.

Nevertheless, the manifestation of the canonical status of a text can become one of the purposes of a ritual. In that case, the special text stands out from its context. It may be presented on a special carrier and performed in a unique way by an eminent person. Jews and Christians celebrate the solemn reading of biblical texts in their rituals. Due to the type of cantillation, the use of scrolls (vs. books), and the *brakhot* that encompass each reading of the weekly portion of the Torah in Jewish liturgies, it is perceived as more important than the ensuing reading of passages from the so-called 'Prophets' (*Neviim*), while the 'Writings' (*Ketuvim*) are not read at these occasions at all (Elbogen 1993: § 25–30). Since the Middle Ages, one of the five *Megillot* (Song of Songs, Ruth, Lamentations, Ecclesiastes, Esther) is read on each of the major festivals. The reading of the scroll of Esther should be accompanied by vivid reactions of the congregation in response to the course of the narrative. In many Christian traditions, the reading of a passage of the Gospel is performed in greater solemnity than the reading from other portions of the Bible during the celebration of a liturgy of the word (with or without Eucharist following), and the Gospel concludes the sequence of biblical readings (De Zan 1997; Jungmann 2003: 501–633). Jews were engaged in the public reading of biblical literature in their congregations from very early times. Outside the Land of Israel, this practice is known to pre-date the destruction of the Second Temple (70 CE). The ritualization of these reading services emerged, however, from customs encoded by the rabbis long after the destruction of the Second Temple (Langer 1998b). Thus, the typical shape of Christian and Jewish reading services developed independently of each other.

The readings are included in a normative network of gestures and postures. They must be read aloud and be heard by the members of the congregation, leading to the widespread use of electronic amplification devices in many Christian traditions. Conversely, the ubiquitous availability of microphones and loudspeakers considerably influenced the choice as well as the ways of production of liturgical texts, because the prayer leaders must now consider their congregations as an implicit audience to each word that they speak (taking the Catholic church in the Netherlands as an example: Post 2003).

In Islam, the recitation of the Quran is performed in cantillation and standardized pronunciation; the reciter must know when to pause and when to resume the recitation and at certain points of the text, the reciter is obliged to kneel (*sujūd at-tilāwa*). As texts of prayer, there are—besides the first sura—only a few verses to be recited, usually taken from the short suras 78 to 114 (*Juzʾ ʿamma*). The choice of the suras to be read is entirely at the cantor's discretion and there is no official cycle of readings or ordered lectionary. Besides prayer, Quran recitation plays an important role in everyday life, e.g. the complete Quran is read within the thirty days of the month of Ramadan. Some suras are recited on special occasions such as births, marriages, or funerals.

The course of study in Greek schools comprised the explanation and actualization of traditional texts. Similarly, Jews and Christians expounded biblical texts at the occasion of their groups' meetings. The scholarly methods for using and interpreting those traditional texts underwent considerable changes when they left the environment of the schools and were incorporated into more widespread rituals. Apart from the oral rhetoric performances that are obviously lost, large corpora of literary sermons were transmitted in both Judaism and Christianity (Heinemann and Jacobs 2007; Herr 2007; Dan and Carlebach 2007; Grégoire 1969; Moreno 1986), whereas in Islam sermons are only given at Friday prayers and on special occasions, e.g. eclipses and droughts, and are usually not written down and thus made part of the literary heritage of Islam. In Islam, sermons consist of prayer, exhortation, instruction, and at least one verse from the Quran. They are seen as religious duty because one should preach in Arabic even if the congregation is not capable of understanding it. Therefore in the Friday prayers of non-Arabic congregations, the same sermon is held once in Arabic and again in the respective language of the congregation.

Jewish, Christian, and Muslim theoreticians debate the role of the individual's *intention* during prayer. As soon as the recitation of texts becomes standardized and is performed unchanged over many generations, these texts become perceived as requiring bits of interpretation. Especially in cases where different interpretations of words, phrases, and ritual behaviour are possible or known, intention becomes perceived as an additional element of prayer besides words and actions. If intention and not just the visible, bodily performance of certain rites is regarded as crucial for the achievement of its effects, all three prayer traditions attempt to ensure the proper functioning of prayer by standardizing the thoughts of the prayer leader or the congregation (Langer 1998a: 23 for rabbinic sources on intentionality; Lacey 1940). In these cases, it is normative or at least recommended to think certain thoughts during the liturgies in order to abide by the ideal that outward performance should be consistent with intention. In many Christian churches, the individual participant is required to endorse certain theological tenets in order to be allowed to participate in certain liturgies. Thus, only a Catholic (*Codex Iuris Canonici* (*CIC*) can. 912 and 915; for exceptions see can. 844 § 4) is allowed to receive consecrated bread and wine. While this church would readily invite guests to other communal liturgies, in the case of the consumption of consecrated bread and wine, church membership, intention, and belief play a highly excluding role. In Islam, all Muslims who are capable of doing so in terms of age and mental ability are obliged to perform the prayer at least five times daily. Prayers of members of other religions or non-believers are considered to be invalid. Usually, non-Muslims are not allowed to enter a mosque at prayer time or to participate in Muslim worship.

3. Communal and Solitary Prayer

In spite of the highly privatized and mental acts mentioned above, communal liturgical activity is the primary way to perform prayers. Individuals learn how to pray by participating in the prayers of their communities, and they continue to use texts and motifs of communal prayers in their private ones (cf. Taft 1986: 367–73). Solitary prayer is therefore often interpreted as a substitute for—or at least as derived from—communal performances.

Thus, the Babylonian Talmud discusses the wording of solitary performances of the statutory prayers in dangerous situations or on journeys. The sages conclude with the abstract observation about prayer in these situations, stating that individuals should always associate themselves with the people of Israel (*b. Brakhot* 29b–30a; Langer 1998a: 20). In such special situations, one may dispense with the correct orientation of the body. Apart from emergency situations, some prayers may in general be carried out as private, mental acts of individuals that cannot be observed by others. Moreover, in Judaism and Christianity, silent prayer that is performed as continuously as possible is regarded as virtuous behaviour (cf. Leonhard 2014: 180–5). Such prayers need not be standardized. In Islam, one is only allowed to perform the daily prayer as a mental act (i.e. without the obligatory gestures and postures) in two types of special circumstances. First, ill and disabled persons who are not capable of performing the prescribed movements are allowed to combine prayers and to perform them standing with a sole movement of the head instead of bowings or prostrations or even in a sitting or lying position when they are not able to stand. Second, praying in the battlefield in times of war (Q. 4: 102) is discussed in the different Muslim schools. Some rule that warriors are allowed to shorten their prayer, to neglect the direction of prayer, and to reduce the movements to little hints, e.g. a movement of the eyes only.

The Christian churches did not develop models for minimal and irreducible forms of liturgies for emergency situations, in the case of the larger, communal celebrations, such as the Mass or the solemn performance of liturgies of the hours. Their performance was not regarded as necessary for the salvation of persons as individuals (Thomas Aquinas, *Summa theologica* 3.73.3 regarding the Eucharist). However, especially the Latin churches created systems of short forms for emergency situations with regard to baptism (Johnson 2007: ch. 6). Paradoxically, this led scholars to base their construction of the meaning of any sacramental performance on such reduced minimal forms which they came to regard as the essential core of the more elaborate performances. Thus, Thomas Aquinas regards the Institution Narrative (the priest's repetition of Jesus' words from the New Testament accounts of the Last Supper; 1 Cor, 11: 23–6; Mark 14: 22–5; Matt. 26: 26–9; Luke 22: 14–21) as the only effective piece of the whole Mass. Theoretically (because he would thus break the law of the church), the priest could omit the rest of the service that Thomas regards as mere 'decoration' (*Summa theologica* 3.78.1–4). Minimal forms of originally larger rituals and the claim that they are essentially the same as their much more elaborate cognates are important for ritual theory and practice, because Jews, Christians, and Muslims regard their performance—in an abbreviated way or in their full forms—as obligatory.

The obligation to pray is gendered in Judaism, Christianity, and Islam, while especially Christian churches (much less so Jews) added a complex web of status-related obligations, rights, and privileges with regard to communally performed rituals (Berger 2006, Synek 2006). In Islam, women at certain stages of the menstrual cycle and in the context of childbirth, children, and the elderly and frail are exempted from the obligation to perform the daily prayers. Women are also not obliged to take part in communal Friday worship in order to prevent the distraction of the male worshippers. As mosques may be equipped with balconies or separate rooms for women and men, both sexes may, however, participate in communal prayer. The rabbinic principle that time-bound commandments only concern people who dispose of the power to organize their time freely excludes women, slaves, and minors from the obligation to perform most liturgical duties (cf. *m. Qiddušin* 1.7). Nevertheless, women soon began to participate in communal worship in various degrees of architectural proximity to—and exclusion from—the men. Prayerbooks for women are among the early manuscripts of this genre. Today, such gender differences have been levelled out in some branches of Judaism (cf. Reif 1993: 223–5, 270, 313–14).

Christian churches differ in their degree of formulation of explicit laws obliging their members to participate in certain communal rituals. In the medieval Latin West the complexity of the performance of daily prayers increased to such an extent that only the more specialized clergy and the better-educated monks and nuns could fulfil this duty at all. Until today, lay members of the Catholic church are not obliged to perform the official ecclesiastical daily prayers. In the wake of this development, the churches created less demanding but also much less standardized and compulsory replacements for the canonical daily prayers (Taft 1986: 297–306). In contradistinction to Judaism and Islam, the Catholic and Orthodox churches emphasized the notion of vicarious prayer of religious specialists on behalf of laymen and developed strong status-related roles within the performance of certain rituals. While a Jewish or Muslim congregation may invite a prayer leader to organize and embellish the communal act of prayer, the members are themselves responsible for the fulfilment of their personal, obligatory prayer. In many Christian liturgies, the clergy play irreplaceable roles while the congregation functions much more as an audience, despite the individuals' duty to participate in the ritual.

Theoretically, the obligation to perform certain rituals could not only lead to the creation of abbreviated emergency forms but also to that of real substitutes. This phenomenon is hardly developed in Islam and Christianity. Yet, the rabbis solve the problem that the Torah commands them to perform rituals only at the Temple of Jerusalem, which was destroyed long ago. They suggest that the study of the Torah and/or prayer should be regarded as an effective replacement for the sacrificial liturgy at the Temple (cf. Langer 1998a: ch. 1). Thus they instruct their followers to pray the *Amidah* within the time-spans that were allotted to the performance of the twice daily sacrifice, including a third time on the Sabbath, because the priests had offered a third animal on that day. The Babylonian Talmud makes the implicit principle explicit: 'they arranged them (i.e. the daily prayers) according to the everlasting (i.e. the twice daily sacrifice)' (*b. Brakhot* 26b). Later texts expand and explain this principle (cf. *Pesiq. Rav Kah.* 6.3). The notion that prayer replaces the performance of sacrifices heavily influenced the creation of liturgical texts. Thus, many of the most common liturgical texts including elaborate liturgical poetry pertain to topics of the mandatory sacrifices of the Bible, the personnel at the Second Temple, or other aspects of rituals that cannot be performed any more after the destruction of the Temple, but that are commanded by the Torah. The reference to the Temple cult continues thus to function as a source of legitimization for—and interpretation of—many forms of later liturgical practice. Although rabbinic liturgies are designed to replace the Temple cult, their texts continue to deplore its loss and express hope for its future restoration. They are replacements of a cult that they emphasize to be irreplaceable drawing inspiration from this tension (cf. Stroumsa 2009: esp. ch. 3; Leonhard 2005).

The minimal requirements for the performance of communal rituals differ markedly between the three religions. In Islam, every obligatory prayer should be performed in a group—so at least two people are needed; solitary prayer is despised (al-Buḫārī, Ṣalāt, Bāb 87 (477)). One of them acts as prayer leader (imam). The Friday prayer and the two festive prayers are obligatory for all male believers who should gather at one place in order to symbolize the egalitarian fraternal community of believers. Unless there is not enough space available in the largest mosque of a town, several Friday prayers in different mosques of the same town are considered unrighteous and thus invalid. Validity of the Friday prayer requires—depending on the law school—a minimum of three to forty worshippers.

The more solemn parts of Jewish liturgies require the presence of ten adult Jewish men (called *minyan*) or ten men and women in certain denominations (recently even ten men and ten women in a few congregations). The *minyan* is regarded as a worthy representative of the people of Israel as a collective that can pray as such in God's presence.

While the large, solemn performances of grand public Christian rituals (like the consecration of a bishop or the dedication of a church building in the Catholic church; Calabuig 2000) typically require a considerable number of clergy and a large group of lay persons, the daily prayers and even the celebration of the Mass does not presuppose a quorum of participants. In the Catholic church, solitary performances of Masses by single priests continue to be debated since the late Middle Ages (cf. *CIC* can. 906). Jewish prayer may also be performed in large synagogues. Yet, Christian services and especially Catholic Masses may be performed together with hundreds of thousands of participants.

4. Space and Time

Prayer is oriented in space and organized in time. Due to its multifarious aspects, it oscillates between its functions of creating structures in space and time and of expressing structures that are claimed to be older than their manifestation by human beings or part of the basic organization of the cosmos.

4.1 Prayer and Space

All three religions celebrate and emphasize space and orientation. Yet, they also restrict the role of holy space in religious practice. Ever since Old Testament times, the canonical sources and many treatises of all three religions debate the tension between the claim of God's ubiquity or independence from spatial categories and the need of the congregation to dedicate rooms or buildings for their assemblies. Judaism (especially after the destruction of the Second Temple in Jerusalem), Graeco-Roman philosophers, Christianity, and Islam participated in the creation of a broad consensus that rejected the performance of sacrifices and thus the cult at the ancient temples. As all three religions started characteristically as movements in cities, they tended to build special structures for their meetings as soon as their social status allowed them to do so. Landscapes, whether untouched or changed by human beings in any way, do not play significant roles.

While Jewish prayer may be performed at any clean place (excluding, for example, latrines), it is typically and communally performed in synagogues, which are not regarded as sacred space. Yet, they are perceived as a special category of space which is derived from the presence of the Torah scrolls that are kept in a chest, typically on one of its walls that faces into the direction of Jerusalem (Fine 1998). Members of the congregation conduct themselves in this space with a heightened awareness of commandments and customs that should be kept also outside that building. Synagogue buildings are not consecrated.

In many Christian traditions, the dedication or consecration of church buildings occasion the lengthiest and most elaborate liturgies. They comprise above all acts that are interpreted as a cleansing of the building. Some are understood as expression of a transfer of possession to the church or as its inauguration by its first proper use. The Catholic church regards the placement of relics and the keeping of consecrated bread in a small container mostly in the east of the building as main factors (apart from the exclusion of demonic powers, especially in the Middle Ages) of the ongoing sacredness of the church building. The elaborate form of the central ritual of Orthodox and Catholic churches, the Divine Liturgy or the Mass, should be celebrated in a church building. Its performance outside of it is only envisaged for special occasions and in situations of need and distress. If a congregation disposes of a church building, it will perform most of its religious ritual acts within that building.

The obligatory daily prayer in Islam may be performed on any clean ground after defining a prayer space by spreading a prayer rug or a garment on the ground, which no one is allowed to cross (e.g. al-Buḥārī, Ṣalāt, Bāb 100 (509) or Aḥmad Ibn Ḥanbal, Musnād, iv, 2). The prayers of the festivals of the Breaking of the Fast (*ʿīd al-fiṭr*) and of the Sacrifice (*ʿīd al-aḍḥā*) are performed in a city square and not within a building. Only the Friday prayer is supposed to be performed in the mosque as the place of gathering. But even there, the individual prayer space (*as-sutra*) should be defined by means of special border-markers or a carpet. Throughout the ages, mosques were not regarded as space for sacrifices but as space for the gathering of the congregation and communal prayer. Originally non-Muslims were allowed to enter the building, but in the wake of the expansion of the cult of the saints and martyrs in Islam, many mosques came to be regarded as sacred space.

Thus, neither Judaism nor Islam perform prayers in order to consecrate a building; the Christian traditions mentioned are the only ones in which not only the performance of prayer as such but special liturgies create sacred space.

Despite modern Christian tendencies for the faithful to assemble in circular or elliptic form, in most church buildings, synagogues, and mosques the congregants face towards the east, towards Jerusalem, and towards Mecca respectively. In Judaism and Islam, this orientation remains the decisive spatial element that must be kept in the organization of prayer, even if no properly dedicated community building is available. The performance of the liturgy of hours by Catholic clergy does not require gestures, postures, or an orientation of the body whereas the orientation of the priest with regard to the congregation during the celebration of the Mass was and is debated until today.

4.2 Structures of Time

Individual prayer times and liturgies are framed by a perceptible beginning and a perceptible end. The elements of the frame and the very inception or ending of prayers can only vaguely be derived from the performance of the prayers themselves. Therefore, they continue to require social negotiation. Prayer times are expanded or reduced according to the needs of the respective communities. Therefore, different temporal boundaries may be applicable to different classes or participants' roles within the liturgies. In spite of negotiable or doubtful cases, participants in liturgies know when they are within the performance of the ritual and when they are not. The ritualization of certain acts of preparation for the liturgies is one of the means to extend the frames of prayer.

The standard Jewish prayerbooks invite their users into a multi-layered access to communal prayer on Sabbath mornings, beginning with solitary prayers upon waking up and performing basic acts of morning toilette, including the donning of *tfillin*, and later upon entering the synagogue. A further step of communality is achieved when the precentor summons the community to the recitation of Psalms. The service commences in its official form as soon as the first time *qaddish* is said, which requires a *minyan*. Similarly, many congregations mark the ending of the prayer with a song (like *Adon Olam*). Yet, even after this and while many of the members are leaving the room, further communal but less important prayers may be recited. Some communities reassemble inside or outside of the central room of the synagogue for the initial prayers of meals. In spite of the fact that the members of the congregation know quite well that the central service has ended, they will consider their participation in an ensuing meal as related to the communal meeting.

The structures of Christian meetings differ widely because of a great variety of customs and religious laws. More traditional churches tend to differentiate acts of preparation for the services between the laity and certain functionaries. The intensity of such preparatory acts shifts the perception of the beginning of the liturgies deeply into the time that precedes the actual inception of communal prayers. In some eastern churches, monks prepare the bread for the Divine Liturgy in an elaborate process—e.g. accompanied by the singing of Psalms. In many churches, clergy and laity observed strict fasting before their participation in the Mass. Today, such rules remain valid, although they may be alleviated in practice (as in the Catholic church; *CIC* can. 919). While churches mark the beginning of services by means of acoustic signals, the presiders already begin to say prayers while donning their ritual dress for the liturgies. Likewise, lavishly decorated combs made of precious materials remind the visitors to museums of the inception of the ritual long before the entry of the presiders into the main hall of the medieval church building. Similar to Jewish congregations, Christians may add meetings of less official status after the performance of what is regarded and framed as the core of the liturgy. The liturgical books and the general behaviour of the faithful indicate that they are aware of the beginning and end of this core service although its manifestation changed during the liturgical development of these rites.

While washing one's hands was part of the presiders' preparation for Mass as well as part of the ritual (as a preparation for the recitation of the central prayer of the Eucharist, *Apos. Con.* 8.11.2; [Pseudo-] Cyril of Jerusalem, *Mystagogical Catechesis* 5.2), it never attained to the same form as the ritual washing in Islam. However, in the Latin church of the Middle Ages, the cleansing of the community was performed in a stylized washing by means of sprinkling with consecrated water at the beginning of the service. Catholic churches still tend to set up small containers of consecrated water at the entrance of churches as a reduced and stylized lustration. The ritual washing in Islam instead is defined as a sequence of acts and texts to be uttered although there are different opinions about the necessity or composition of individual elements. Depending on the level of impurity, people are obliged to perform a partial ablution (*wuḍūʾ*)—i.e. a washing of the head, the arms, and the legs—or a full ablution (*ġusl*). Water is usually provided at the entry to a mosque. If no water is available, worshippers may perform a dry ablution by the use of sand or stones. Because of the phrases uttered, the ablution is not only an external but also an internal preparation for prayer. Although the washing is framed by the first and the second call for prayer, the effective prayer starts with the call '*Allāhu akbar*' (*takbīratu l-iḥrām*). After this, only words and acts of the prayer are permitted till the final call for peace (*taslīmatu l-iḥlāl*). Worshippers arriving too late for communal prayer are obliged first to say the *takbīratu l-iḥrām* before continuing prayer and are only allowed to say the *taslīmatu l-iḥlāl* after having prayed all the parts that they missed. Thus the elements marking the beginning and the end of prayer are clearly defined.

Prayer is organized in temporal circles, especially in Judaism and Christianity, less so in Islam. The texts used during its performance, its liturgical implements, as well as its special customs may explicitly or by way of establishing an otherwise meaningless difference refer to the time of the day, the lunar month (in Judaism), the lunar year (in Islam), or the solar year (in Judaism and Christianity). Larger divisions above the level of the year are much less important. Thus, the declaration of a holy year by the Catholic pope or the *Shmittah* (the seventh year in a cycle of seven years) are almost entirely irrelevant for daily prayer throughout the world.

After the destruction of the Second Temple, the rabbis re-established the most important festivals that had been celebrated there. Jewish congregations in the Diaspora may have marked some festivals by the performance of typical customs or rather by convening a congregational symposium. Apparently, most Diaspora communities kept the awareness that the celebration of the three major biblical pilgrim festivals was restricted to the Temple in Jerusalem. These are *Pesach* (commemorating the Exodus of the people of Israel from Egypt in spring), the festival of Weeks (*Shavuot*) fifty days after *Pesach*, and the festival of Tabernacles (*Sukkot*, in autumn; Elbogen 1993, § 23). In the perception of many Jews, the celebration of the Day of Atonement (*Yom Kippur*, four days before *Sukkot*) is the most solemn feast in the year, which is preceded by the celebration of New Year (*Rosh Hashana*). Both the Day of Atonement and the New Year festival are performed in a mood of awe, repentance, and fasting (Day of Atonement; Elbogen 1993: § 24). *Pesach* and *Sukkot* are accompanied by two festivals that elaborate aspects of these two; *Purim* (one month before *Pesach*) and *Chanukka* (about two months after *Sukkot*; Elbogen 1993: § 22). *Purim* is celebrated with customs of carnival centred on the narrative of the Book of Esther about the Jews' survival and victory in a dangerous court intrigue against them. Several narratives were created in order to weaken the association of *Chanukka* with the inauguration of the Temple and to create a loose connection with its season of the year, by means of symbolisms of light and darkness. Since the Middle Ages, the *Haggadah of Pesach*—a complex text consisting of biblical, rabbinic, medieval texts and poems, as well as additional material inspired by folk poetry in early modern Europe—is recited during the celebration of *Pesach* in families (or congregations; cf. for its origins Leonhard 2006: 73–118).

The first Christian congregations apparently rejected the customs of celebrating many of the appointed times that were regarded as essential markers of social and religious cohesion by other pagan or Jewish Greeks or Romans (cf. for Pesach, Leonhard 2006). They began to convene their groups at the first day of the week probably not before the early second century. In opposition to the restoration of Jewish celebrations of Pesach, Christians began to celebrate Easter which was, however, soon reformulated as the central commemoration of Christ's death and resurrection. Much of its initial meaning as an anti-Jewish festival was thus transformed and vanished from its explicit messages. Once established, Easter became the climax of an elaborate festival season. Its celebration transformed biblical narratives into liturgical performances along ritually structured time. In addition, a long period of preparation was added before the festival. Its former anti-Jewish thrust has been overcome today. Yet, Easter was a time of incentives to pogroms in medieval Europe. Towards the end of the second century, Christian communities began to regard the fifty days following Easter as a special season, calling it *Pentecost*, the Greek name for the biblical festival of the fiftieth day after the biblical *Pesach*. The historical relationship between the two festivals is unclear (Rouwhorst 2001a; Bradshaw and Johnson 2011: 69–74).

In the fourth century and most probably as a reconceptualization of the pagan interpretation of the season around the winter solstice, Christians created Christmas and Epiphany (Bradshaw and Johnson 2011: 123–68). Besides the Easter season, Christmas and Epiphany gave rise to a second cycle of festivals establishing a network of mimetic performances that restructured the whole year as a commemoration of the events told in the infancy narratives of Christ in the Gospels. Independent of the elaboration of Christian liturgies on the basis of biblical narratives, an ever increasing number of days of the year became marked as commemoration of saints in the Orthodox and Catholic churches.

Early Islam refused to adopt Jewish or Christian as well as pagan feasts. Besides the obligatory five prayers daily and the Friday prayer with preceding sermon there are only two annual feasts demanding special prayers: the Festival of the Breaking of the Fast (*ʿīd al-fiṭr*) at the end of the Ramadan fasting period and the Festival of the Sacrifice (*ʿīd al-aḍḥā*) on the tenth day of the month of pilgrimage. On both days, there is an additional special prayer time to be performed in the morning between sunrise and noon which is supposed to be celebrated in an assembly in the open space of a field (*muṣalla*) with a sermon following the prayer. It is considered a pious custom to stay awake the night before the festival day, praying, meditating, and reading the Quran. Before *ʿīd al-fiṭr*, it is customary to read the whole Quran within one month. Both feasts are celebrated in a festive ambience and it is common to exchange gifts and visit cemeteries. The original meaning of the pre-Islamic feast of *ʿĀšūrāʾ* was rejected in early Islam. Sunni Islam does not celebrate it to this day, whereas in Shiite Islam *ʿĀšūrāʾ* marks the end of a mourning period, and is celebrated as commemoration of the death of Ḥusayn by a procession with self-flagellation. There are also feasts carrying a certain religious character but not requiring special prayers: the feast of Muhammad's Night Journey (*Miʿrāj*) and Muhammad's birth (*Mawlīd an-Nabī*) emerged only after the initial formative period of Islam and have both been regarded as unlawful invention (*bidʿa*) by some legal authorities. Some Muslim denominations reject the feast of Muhammad's birth because they consider it as an imitation of the Christian feast of Christmas. They regard it as a counter-monotheistic adoration of Muhammad. The Muslim festivals depend on a strictly lunar calendar.

From the fourth century on, Judaism and Christianity began to assign certain biblical readings to each festival. Furthermore, Christian and Jewish clergy and poets began to align the topics of liturgical prayers and songs with the respective theme of the day (Rouwhorst 2002, cf. Rand 2014 regarding *piyyut*). This led to the creation of voluminous books that provided guidance and texts for the performance of an increasingly sophisticated system of public liturgies. Liturgical reforms sometimes reduced the complexity and abundance of rubrics and texts. Yet the space opened up by such movements was filled again in subsequent generations. In Islamic worship, there are no prescriptions regarding the selection of Quran readings.

5. Establishing and Crossing Borderlines

Individuals and groups use prayer as a token to express their belonging to communities and social strata. Thus, the public performance of rituals also legitimizes the division and internal organization of a society. Certain prayers are regarded as typical for the groups who perform them. Nevertheless, elements of ritual practice migrate between groups, changing their shapes or only the meanings that are attributed to them. These movements guarantee that even generally acknowledged borderlines between the groups include grey zones; it is the task of historical studies of liturgy and prayer to reconstruct the paths of these movements. Members of the three religions frequently shared geographical areas in the past, and their emergence and development can only be described as a cluster of closely related processes.

The contacts of Jews and Christians in medieval and modern Europe gave rise to customs that crossed the borders between the two religions. Yet, the meanings of *Chanukka* had already been shaped at the same time as—and possibly also in an implicit dialogue with—Christmas in late antique Christianity. The modern alignment of the two festival seasons even led to the expression of 'Chrismukka/Weihnukka' as a (partly humoristic) designation for this season (Kugelmann 2005). In spite of Jewish opposition, some Christian groups adopted the celebration of Pesach in the late twentieth century (Senn 1999). Conversely, denominations that regard themselves as crossing the borders between Christianity and Judaism combine elements of the Eucharistic prayer (especially its reformulation of the institution narratives) with the *Haggadah of Pesach*. Since the most recent Catholic revision of the instructions for the celebration of the Eucharist (1970), two short prayers based on the basic mealtime *brakhot* are recited by the priest in each celebration of the Catholic Mass (Lamberts 1997, Rouwhorst 2001b).

Elements of rituals and prayer can be interpreted as metaphors ('symbols'). They are said to refer to hidden meanings and imperceptible effects. For the learned insider, rites convey doctrinal meanings and have spiritual effects beyond what can be observed as their social functions. In fact, teaching the alleged meaning of rituals helps to uncover as well as to blur the visibility of their social effects.

As mentioned above, theories relate instances of prayer to sacrifice, claiming either to represent it or to replace it. Except for entirely marginal rituals, Jewish, Christian, and Muslim liturgies do not include the offering of sacrifices in the sense that animals or other goods at the disposal of humanity are dedicated to God, (partly) destroyed, or permanently withdrawn from human use. Nevertheless, liturgical texts and explanations are replete with sacrificial imagery.

Prayer is a means to create or invoke a special form of God's presence, beyond the general assumption of God's ubiquity, beginning with the Christian veneration of Christ's special presence in the bread and wine as consecrated during the Divine Liturgy, the Mass, or the Protestant *Abendmahl* and leading towards a heightened awareness of God's care for human beings during the public reading of the Bible or even simple communal prayer. Learned theories (like the theory of transsubstantiation in scholastic Catholic thinking) hold that this presence always remains a matter of belief and thus beyond experience and empirical proof. In Judaism, the cantillation of the Torah has been interpreted since late antiquity in similar terms as creating God's presence. Furthermore, the instructions for the gestures that should be performed during the prayer of the *Amidah* are also interpreted as a pious response to God's presence. Similarly, a special form of God's presence in *ṣalāt* is presupposed in Islam. Thus ritual purity is a basic requirement for the worshippers during the prayer towards Mecca, for the proper and exclusive enunciation of the Arabic wording of the prayer rite, as well as for the correct performance of the prescribed gestures and postures. Prayer is seen as the believer's submission to God's sovereignty and as the proper response to the revealed obligation to perform the different motions of the prayer rite as enjoined by the prophet.

6. Changes of Liturgies and Customs

Religious specialists as well as anthropologists may describe functions for groups and individuals that the liturgies fulfil. As long as these functions are mainly culled from the liturgies themselves, one could assume that the shape of liturgies should remain stable throughout the ages. However, it can be observed that especially Jewish and Christian (e.g. Yuval 2006), much less so Muslim, prayers, liturgies, and their interpretation changed significantly and frequently during the last two millennia of their coexistence. Even in cases of centuries of stability of one of their elements (as in the preservation of the ritual texts of the Catholic Mass between 1570 and 1970), other aspects of ritual performance and social functions may change drastically (e.g. Mitchell 2006 and Haquin 2006). As mentioned above, the mutual perception of the Abrahamic religions is one cause for such changes. In the nineteenth century, Reform Judaism rewrote several ancient prayers (for example *birkat haminim*, a prayer against heretics or evildoers which generations of Christian critics read as a curse against Christianity) that they regarded as potentially offensive towards their Christian neighbours (Langer 2012). More than a century later, the Catholic church reworded an intercession that used to ask for the conversion of all Jews to Christianity into a prayer for the Jews' steadfast adherence to the Torah: 'Let us pray also for the Jewish people, to whom the Lord our God spoke first, that he may grant them to advance in love of his name and in faithfulness to his covenant' (*The Roman Missal* 2011: 323).

The Muslim prayer rite is considered to have been fully developed within the first century after the prophet's emigration to Medina. The term 'the prayer' (*aṣ-ṣalāt*), in singular form and with definite article, is mentioned sixty-five times in the Quran, obviously in regard to a fixed prayer rite that seems to be quite stable from this time on because developments are normally rejected as unlawful inventions. Diverging opinions of the law schools on certain elements of the prayer rite and the oral tradition entail little differences in the shape of the prayer in different Muslim groups. In the formative period of early Islam, Christians and Jews were seen as belonging to the same community of faith and as being able to attain to salvation. Some parts of the newly introduced Muslim rites were obviously adopted from the Jewish and the Christian liturgies. The fact that Islamic liturgy and prayer remained more stable than Christian and Jewish liturgies does not imply that Muslim societies and groups changed less than Christian or Jewish ones.

7. Concluding Observations

Prayer and the performance of rituals help to establish and maintain borderlines between the Abrahamic religions as well as between groups within these religions.

Individual Jews, Christians, and Muslims may or may not regard one-time conversion ceremonies or rituals that are understood as carrying expressions of group adherence as a fundamental event in their lives. Yet, prayer offers to those who devote considerable periods of their time at tending to their religious affiliation a means to shape their identity in religious terms. Inclusion and exclusion are, therefore, important social functions of liturgy and prayer in these religions. The performance of liturgy and prayer rather divides than unites the Abrahamic religions.

As the Abrahamic religions emerged in roughly the same geographical area and expanded from there, not only religious ideas but also the practice and interpretation of rituals developed under mutual scrutiny. In many areas, this led to the migration of ritual elements between the Abrahamic religions, notably between Judaism and Christianity, much less so between these two and Islam. From a historical point of view, the three religions may have adopted and adapted features of the respective others among them. Yet, they are heavily indebted—directly as well as by way of opposition and supersession—to the religion(s) of ancient Greece and Rome regarding rituals and texts recited in prayers and liturgies.

References

Baldovin, J. F. 2006. 'The Empire Baptized'. In Wainwright and Westerfield Tucker 2006: 77–130.

Bell, C. 1992. *Ritual Theory, Ritual Practice*. New York, Oxford: Oxford University Press.

Berger, T. 2006. 'Women in Worship'. In Wainwright and Westerfield Tucker 2006: 755–68.

Bradshaw, P. F. 1995. 'From Word to Action: The Changing Role of Psalmody in Early Christianity'. In M. R. Dudley, ed., *Like a Two-Edged Sword: The Word of God in Liturgy and History. Essays in Honour of Canon Donald Gray*. Norwich: Canterbury Press, 21–37.

Bradshaw, P. F and Johnson, M. E. 2011. *The Origins of Feasts, Fasts and Seasons in Early Christianity*. Collegeville, Minnesota: Liturgical Press.

Calabuig, I. M. 2000. 'The Rite of the Dedication of a Church'. In Chupungco 1997–2000: V. 333–79.

Chupungco, A. J., ed. 1997–2000. *Handbook for Liturgical Studies*. 5 vols. Collegeville, MN: Liturgical Press.

Dan, J. and Carlebach, A. 2007. 'Homiletic Literature'. In *Encyclopaedia Judaica*. 2nd edn. IX. 507–16 [Gale Virtual Reference Library, accessed 7 March 2014].

De Zan, R. 1997. 'Bible and Liturgy'. In Chupungco 1997–2000: I. 33–51.

Duval, A. 1988. 'Rosaire'. In *Dictionnaire de Spiritualité*. Paris: Beauchesne, XIII. 937–80.

Ehrlich, U. 2004 [Hebrew 1999]. *The Nonverbal Language of Prayer: A New Approach to Jewish Liturgy*, trans. D. Ordan. Tübingen: Mohr Siebeck.

Elbogen, I. 1993 [1st edn 1913; updated Hebrew edn 1972]. *Jewish Liturgy: A Comprehensive History*, trans. R. P. Scheindlin. Philadelphia, New York, Jerusalem: Jewish Publication Society.

Fine, S. 1998. *This Holy Place: On the Sanctity of the Synagogue during the Greco-Roman Period*. Notre Dame, IN: University of Notre Dame Press.

Gerhards, A. and Leonhard, C. 2007. *Jewish and Christian Liturgy and Worship: New Insights into its History and Interaction*. Leiden, Boston: Brill.
Grégoire, R. 1969. 'Homéliaires'. In *Dictionnaire de Spiritualité*. Vol. X.1. Paris: Beauchesne, 597–617.
Haquin, A. 2006. 'The Liturgical Movement and Catholic Ritual Revision'. In Wainwright and Westerfield Tucker 2006: 696–720.
Harland, P. A. 2003. *Associations, Synagogues, and Congregations: Claiming a Place in Ancient Mediterranean Society*. Philadelphia: Fortress.
Heinemann, J. and Jacobs, L. 2007. 'Preaching'. In *Encyclopaedia Judaica*. 2nd edn, XVI. 467–75.
Herr, M. D. 2007. 'Midrash'. In *Encyclopaedia Judaica*. 2nd edn, XIV. 182–5.
Johnson, M. E. 2007. *The Rites of Christian Initiation: Their Evolution and Interpretation*, 2nd edn. Collegeville, MN: Liturgical Press.
Jungmann, J. A. 2003 [repr. Freiburg ^{5}1962]. *Missarum sollemnia: Eine genetische Erklärung der römischen Messe*. Bonn: Verlag Nova & Vetera.
Klinghardt, M. 1996. *Gemeinschaftsmahl und Mahlgemeinschaft: Soziologie und Liturgie frühchristlicher Mahlfeiern*. Tübingen, Basel: Francke.
Krosnicki, T. A. 1998. 'Liturgical Ministries'. In Chupungco 1997–2000: II. 161–71.
Kugelmann, C. 2005. *Weihnukka: Geschichten von Weihnachten und Chanukka* [= Chrismukkah: Stories of Christmas and Hanukkah]. Berlin: Nicolai.
Lacey, T. A. 1940. 'Intention (Theological)'. In *Encyclopedia of Religion and Ethics*. New York: Scribner's, VII. 380–2.
Lamberts, J. 1997. 'Preparation of the Gifts, Offertory or Celebrating Creation?' In *Questions liturgiques: Studies in Liturgy* 78: 16–33.
Langer, R. 1998a. *To Worship God Properly: Tensions between Liturgical Custom and Halakhah in Judaism*. Cincinnati: Hebrew Union College Press.
Langer, R. 1998b. 'From Study of Scripture to a Reenactment of Sinai: The Emergence of the Synagogue Torah Service'. *Worship* 72: 43–67.
Langer, R. 2003. 'The 'Amidah as Formative Rabbinic Prayer'. In A. Gerhards, A. Doeker, and P. Ebenbauer, eds, *Identität durch Gebet: Zur gemeinschaftsbildenden Funktion institutionalisierten Betens in Judentum und Christentum*. Paderborn: Schöningh, 127–56.
Langer, R. 2012. *Cursing the Christians? A History of the* Birkat HaMinim. Oxford: Oxford University Press.
Leonhard, C. 2005. '"Als ob sie vor mir ein Opfer dargebracht hätten": Erinnerungen an den Tempel in der Liturgie der Synagoge'. In A. Gerhards and S. Wahle, eds, *Kontinuität und Unterbrechung: Gottesdienst und Gebet in Judentum und Christentum*. Paderborn: Schöningh, 107–22.
Leonhard, C. 2006. *The Jewish Pesach and the Origins of the Christian Easter: Open Questions in Current Research*. Berlin: De Gruyter.
Leonhard, C. 2007. 'Blessings over Wine and Bread in Judaism and Christian Eucharistic Prayers: Two Independent Traditions'. In Gerhards and Leonhard 2007: 309–26.
Leonhard, C. 2014. 'Which Hymns were sung in Ancient Christian Liturgies?' In C. Leonhard and H. Löhr, eds, *Literature or Liturgy? Early Christian Hymns and Prayers in their Literary and Liturgical Context in Antiquity*. Tübingen: Mohr Siebeck, 175–94.
McGowan, A. 1999. *Ascetic Eucharists: Food and Drink in Early Christian Ritual Meals*. Oxford: Clarendon Press.
Mitchell, N. D. 2006. 'Reforms, Protestant and Catholic'. In Wainwright and Westerfield Tucker 2006: 307–50.

Moreno, M. A. 1986. 'Prédication'. In *Dictionnaire de Spiritualité*. Paris: Beauchesne, XII, 2.2052–64.
Post, P. 2003. *Space for Liturgy between Dynamic Ideal and Static Reality*. Groningen and Tilburg: Instituut voor Liturgiewetenschap.
Power, D. 1999. 'Theology of Eucharistic Celebration'. In Chupungco 1997–2000: III. 321–66.
Rand, M. 2014. 'Fundamentals of the Study of Piyyut'. In C. Leonhard and H. Löhr, eds, *Literature or Liturgy? Early Christian Hymns and Prayers in their Literary and Liturgical Context in Antiquity*. Tübingen: Mohr Siebeck, 107–25.
Rappaport, R. 1999. *Ritual and Religion in the Making of Humanity*. Cambridge: Cambridge University Press.
Reif, S. C. 1993. *Judaism and Hebrew Prayer: New Perspectives on Jewish Liturgical History*. Cambridge: Cambridge University Press.
Rouwhorst, G. A. M. 2001a. 'The Origins and Evolution of Early Christian Pentecost'. In M. F. Wiles and E. J. Yarnold, eds, *Papers Presented at the Thirteenth International Conference on Patristic Studies held in Oxford 1999. Ascetica, Gnostica, Liturgica, Orientalia*. Studia Patristica 35. Leuven: Peeters, 309–22.
Rouwhorst, G. A. M. 2001b. 'The Preparation of the Gifts in the Eucharistic Liturgy'. In *Jaarboek voor liturgie-onderzoek* 17: 213–35.
Rouwhorst, G. A. M. 2002. 'The Reading of Scripture in Early Christian Liturgy'. In L. V. Rutgers, ed., *What Athens Has to Do with Jerusalem: Essays on Classical, Jewish, and Early Christian Art and Archaeology in Honor of Gideon Foerster*. Leuven: Peeters, 305–31.
Senn, F. 1999. 'Should Christians Celebrate the Passover?' In P. F. Bradshaw and L. A. Hoffman, eds, *Passover and Easter: The Symbolic Structuring of Sacred Seasons*. Notre Dame, IN: University of Notre Dame Press, 183–205.
Stroumsa, G. G. 2009. *The End of Sacrifice: Religious Transformations in Late Antiquity*. Chicago, London: University of Chicago Press.
Synek, E. M. 2006. *'Wer aber nicht völlig rein ist an Seele und Leib . . .' Reinheitstabus im Orthodoxen Kirchenrecht*. Munich-Engling: Roman Kovar.
Taft, R. F. 1986. *The Liturgy of the Hours in East and West: The Origins of the Divine Office and its Meaning for Today*. Collegeville, MN: Liturgical Press.
Taft, R. F. 1997. 'The Lord's Prayer in the Eucharistic Liturgy: When and Why?' *Ecclesia Orans* 13: 137–55.
United States Conference of Catholic Bishops 2011. *The Roman Missal. [. . .] English Translation According to the Third Typical Edition. For Use in the Dioceses of the United States of America*. Washington, DC.
Vereecke, R. 1990. 'Gestures, Liturgical'. In P. Fink, ed., *The New Dictionary of Sacramental Worship*. Collegeville, MN: Liturgical Press, 503–13.
Wainwright, G. and Westerfield Tucker, K. B., ed. 2006. *The Oxford History of Christian Worship*. Oxford: Oxford University Press.
Yuval, Y. J. 2006. *Two Nations in Your Womb: Perceptions of Jews and Christians in Late Antiquity and the Middle Ages*. Berkeley, CA: University of California Press.

CHAPTER 24

PURITY AND DEFILEMENT

MOSHE BLIDSTEIN

Concepts and practices of purity and defilement are a central medium for articulating and embodying hierarchy, difference, and change in human culture and religions. The marking of members of the group as distinct from those outside it, the construction of the interior hierarchy of the group, and the specification of certain times, spaces, and actions as unique and differentiated from others, are all frequently achieved through language and practices of purity and defilement. *Religious* purity discourses and practises create such hierarchies primarily by constructing axes of purity and defilement in relation to different degrees of compatibility with the sacred or the divine. The Abrahamic religions made extensive use of this medium to structure their social, ritual, and moral worlds.

The force of these practices and discourses and their universality may be a result of their being an articulation of a universal human emotion, disgust, harnessed for the creation and expression of cultural structures and hierarchies (Haidt et al. 1997; Rozin et al. 2008). This basis lends purity discourse a number of its defining characteristics: both disgust, and impurity are commonly induced by substances crossing the body's borders, decaying substances, and things conceived as strange and irregular; both are created by physical substances as well as by moral affronts; and both can be allayed through rituals. Disgusting substances and actions are typically perceived as contagious, i.e. as producing negative results in their surrounding context (whether spatial, temporal, or social), going beyond their immediate vicinity. When disgust is co-opted for creating or supporting religious values, it may remain as a relatively unstructured emotion, unconstrained by clearly defined formulations or actions, or it may be expressed through ritual and formulas. In the former case, although the discourse of purity and defilement usually remains on the level of language without being structured into regular religious practice, it may have significant impact on the worldview and values of the adherents. In the latter case purification rituals are possible, whether for bodily or for moral defilements.

Purity and defilement are used in religious discourse and practice to evaluate and construct a highly varied range of phenomena; therefore, saying that something or someone is 'pure' or 'defiled' may have very different meanings in different contexts and domains. Rather than a unified or even diverse 'system' of purity and defilement, a better image is of purity and defilement as an idiom employed in religious discourse to construct order, institutions, and identity, and implemented in varying ways according to historical context and religious needs (Lemos 2013; Valeri 2000: 112–13).

The diverse usages of this purity and impurity idiom can be charted in several ways. A pervasive typology in recent scholarship is according to the origins or causes of impurity, which correlates to some extent to the type of rituals through which it is purified. In the study of Judaism and early Christianity, it is common to use the terms 'ritual impurity' and 'moral impurity' (Klawans 2000; for alternative terminologies, see Hayes 2007; Kazen 2002: 214–22; Freidenreich 2011). Ritual impurity results from bodily events, many of them non-intentional, such as birth, genital emissions, certain illnesses, and death. This impurity is temporary, creating some degree of disruption in social life; purification rituals return the default status of purity. As such, purification is a preparatory ritual, and its function is to allow a person to participate in social life, to enter sacred space, come in contact with a sacred object, or participate in a sacred ritual. The moral dimension of this type of impurity is significant, but indirect: it delineates the borders of society's structures and safeguards the sacred. Moral impurity results from particularly sinful behaviour. Its purification requires some moral change in the sinner, but also a social response and, in certain cases, elaborate rituals which assist in removing the impurity. Such impurity is seen as a force (demonic or otherwise) at battle with forces of holiness and purity, operating on both cosmic and personal levels. Purification (when possible) is therefore not a temporary measure to allow contact with the sacred, but a vanquishing of evil. Here, purity and defilement have a direct moral meaning; sin and impurity mingle and blur. To these two types David Freidenreich (2011: 27) adds *intrinsic impurity*, which is naturally inherent in a substance and therefore cannot be purified, only distanced from the person. Examples are the impurity of the pig in Islam and impure animals or the corpse in Judaism. This type is closely linked to the basic emotion of disgust discussed above.

Though this typology is useful for comparing and analysing different purity rituals and discourses, it is important to note that the three forms are frequently not well differentiated in the sources, and presumably in the minds of religious adherents.[1] They rather overlap and interact, creating a web of allusions and meaning. Although all three forms are represented in the three religions, the picture in Christianity is quite different from in Judaism and Islam. While in Judaism and Islam certain substances, bodily processes, or people are seen as intrinsically impure and therefore as the basis for circumstantial impurity rituals, Christian theologians nominally rejected the notion of intrinsic impurity as incompatible with that of a uniformly good creation, and with it

[1] For similar (though by no means identical) typologies in classical sources, see Maimonides, *Guide of the Perplexed* 3.47; Nawawi, as cited in Reid 2013: 170.

also rejected the possibility of circumstantial impurity and its purification. They therefore required sin to be at the basis of all impurity; impurity can only originate from the actions or thoughts of a being with free will, i.e. a person or a demon. On the other hand, while in Judaism and Islam the management of moral impurity remains mostly in the realm of personal religion or of the courts, Christianity created complex ritual and religious systems for the management of moral impurity.

As an alternative to a typology of causes, the field of purity and impurity may also be analysed according to the locus of holiness threatened by impurity and constructed through maintenance of purity. Three main options occur: a specific sacred space, time, or group inside the community; the community as a whole; and the individual. In the first option, the sacrality of spaces, times, objects, or groups is maintained and constructed by maintaining their purity and the purity of the people connected to them, through distancing from both circumstantial and offensive impurity. Examples are the historical Jerusalem Temple in Judaism (and associated sancta and priesthood), prayer and the ḥajj in Islam, and the Eucharist and priesthood in Christianity. Human life legitimately includes both profane and sacred moments and places, and purity rituals are those which separate the sacred from that which is not. For the second option, the community may also be seen as sacred, requiring purity rituals to maintain its borders and to purge it from impurities. This conception is present already in the Book of Leviticus as relating to the Israelite community, and is used to explain the dietary laws of Lev. 11; it was reiterated in the prophets and Ezra. In Christianity, it received significant emphasis by Paul's description of the community of believers as a temple and as a 'body of Christ' (1 Cor. 6: 19, 12: 12–27, Rom. 12: 5) and in the ritual of baptism safeguarding the entrance to the holy Christian community. In Islam, the idea of the purity of the community has a weaker presence, but still comes into play in the rhetoric of an original, pure Islam to which some movements such as the Wahhabis aspired to return. The third option is that the individual is seen as the sacred locus requiring safeguarding and distancing from pollution. This perspective leads to an ideal of perpetual purity, and is most commensurate with an ascetic ideology and practice, for which the individual body is the main staging ground of the struggle between good and evil. Though ascetic leanings are found already in early rabbinic literature (Diamond 2003; and see Balberg 2014), they are much more pronounced in early Christianity and especially the monastic movement, and here we find pervasive conceptions of individuals (or their moral faculties) as sacred and requiring protection or purification, especially from sin. In Islam, too, such ideas were frequent in currents of thought and practice which emphasized individual religious achievement.

A note on the scholarship: of the three Abrahamic religions, studies of purity and defilement have historically focused on Judaism. This was presumably a result of the importance of purity rules in the Hebrew scriptures, in the Mishnah, and in subsequent *halakha*. In Christian scholarship, purity and defilement were typically seen as a solely ritual matter, characteristic of the Old Testament rather than the New, and as quite irrelevant to the central message of Christianity. Purity was therefore rarely studied as a Christian topic. This situation has changed somewhat with the 'cultural turn' and the interest in the role of the body in Christian culture, but here too the focus has been more on sex and gender than on purity and defilement. The study of purity in Islam, for different reasons, has also been very limited until the past two decades (Maghen 1999).

The impurity of certain animals or foods, and their resulting prohibition for consumption, is a central feature of Jewish, Islamic, and to a lesser extent Christian custom, and also a common subject for interreligious discussion and polemic. This subject, however, is the focus of Freidenreich's comprehensive article in this volume, and therefore we shall relate to it only occasionally.

Major Sources and Domains of Impurity

a. Bodily Events

The Bible designates as impure various types of genital emissions (Lev. 15); giving birth (Lev. 12: 2–8); *ṣaraʿat*, a type of skin disease or fungus, commonly translated as leprosy (Lev. 13–14), and corpses or graves. The biblical laws governing the methods of contraction, contagion, and purification of these defilements are highly complex, and are further elaborated in the Qumran documents and in rabbinic literature. Defilements vary in severity: some require complex and lengthy purification rituals, with the polluted person banished from the Israelite camp (Num 5: 2–3), while others require only a single day's wait and a single washing in water. In general, contracting these defilements is not a sin; only contact with the sacred while defiled (Lev. 7: 20–1; 22: 1–7, Num. 9: 6–7) and in certain cases delaying purification (Lev. 17: 15–16; Num. 19: 13, 20) are considered sinful. All of these defilements are natural occurrences, and their contraction and subsequent purification are described as a routine part of Israelite worship.

Following the destruction of the Jerusalem Temple the relevance of most ritual purity rules for Jewish life waned, though there are narratives about certain individuals who continued to maintain ritual purity. To this day, ritual purity remains a practical issue in three main areas, in which defilement caused ritual results even without a temple. By far the most important of these for everyday life is menstruation (*niddah*), as the period of menstrual defilement corresponds with a period of prohibition of sexual contact or intimacy; the second and less significant is the prohibition of priests' contact with corpses. A third area is that of the washing of hands after sleep and before eating, which presupposes a slight degree of impurity. Nevertheless, discussions of all areas of ritual purity laws continued: the sixth and largest section of the Mishnah is dedicated to purity laws, and discussions of ritual purity continued in the Talmud and subsequent literature, though in a less organized fashion.

In legal Islamic sources, certain substances are viewed as impure, e.g. urine, faeces, blood, semen, pigs, dogs, carrion, or wine; if these adhere to a person, they must be removed and washed off in order to allow participation in sacred activities. Furthermore, certain human actions or events are defiling to the person, some in a major fashion, requiring an elaborate whole-body ablution (*ghusl*), and some minor, requiring a washing of head, hands, and feet (*wuḍū'*). Major defiling events are all genital: sexual intercourse, the emission of sperm, or menstruation, while minor defiling events are more diverse. In Islamic law, there is no essential problem with being in a state of pollution. However, as prayer cannot be performed in a state of defilement, in practice purification must be achieved within a short time. Purification is also required before touching (and for some authorities, reciting) the Quran, entering a mosque, fasting during Ramadan, and performing the central rites of the ḥajj.

In Christianity, bodily purity is constantly problematized but nevertheless frequently practised. On the background of the differentiation of earliest Christianity from its Jewish context, the Gospels (Mark 7, Matt. 15) relate that Jesus rejected the possibility that certain foods are impure, 'making all foods clean' (Mark 7: 19). Paul, too, states that food is categorically pure (Rom. 14: 14, 20), and a vision to Peter (Acts 11) conveys a similar message. Early Christian writers expanded this to a more general principle: impurity cannot be a natural status or the result of an involuntary bodily event; to create true impurity, conscious moral choice must be present. While this principle would appear to preclude impurity as a result of involuntary bodily events or of eating certain foods, in fact Christians did practise such purity rules in many cases, appealing to ascetic, demonic, or scriptural motivations.

i. Death

As in most of the ancient Near East and in ancient Greece, in the Hebrew Bible death is a major source of impurity. Contact with human corpses (Num. 11: 11–20) and certain animal carcasses (Lev. 5: 2–3, 11: 24–7) requires purification, the former through a week-long ritual including sprinkling with the ashes of a red cow, the latter by a shorter ritual. Purification is essential in order to enter sacred space or eat of sacrifices or tithes; to priests and the *nazir*, who must maintain a higher degree of holiness, the contraction of corpse impurity is categorically prohibited (21: 1–5, 22: 8, Num. 6: 6–7; cf. Ezek. 44: 15–31, Judg. 13: 14). Death impurity is contracted not only by contact but also by abiding in the same structure or under the same roof with a corpse. Rabbinic literature testifies to a trend beginning already in the late Second Temple period (first century CE) of circumscribing the ambit of death impurity by restrictive exegesis of the biblical laws (Noam 2008). With the destruction of the Temple, which essentially limited the consequences of death impurity to priests only, this trend became stronger. In the Talmuds (third–eighth century) we find attempts to permit defilement by corpses even to priests in certain cases. Nevertheless, orthodox Jewish priests (*kohanim*) maintain their distance from corpses and graves to this day.

Early Christianity did not devote much attention to the question of death impurity, and it was little disputed until the late fourth century. At this time, the spread of cult surrounding tombs of saints and martyrs meant that corpses, or at least some of them, were seen as sources of powerful holiness rather than impurity, an opposition explicitly made by several Christian writers (Chrysostom, *On St Babylas*; *Didascalia apostolorum* 26). The custom of burial near or inside churches, adjacent to the relics of the saints, created a closeness between the sacred and the dead totally antithetical to ideas of death impurity. Though some anti-Christian polemicists attempted to ridicule the cult of the saints by appealing to the disgustingness of corpses and bones, the issue was never central to inter-Abrahamic discourse.

Though in earliest Islam there are disputes about the question of corpse impurity, by the eighth century the dominant Sunni opinion was that the corpse itself must be washed and purified, but those touching it are not defiled, since 'a Muslim is not impure/defiling, dead or alive'. Shi'ites ruled that the corpse is intrinsically impure, and yet not contaminating to its handlers. In general, however, Islamic law is preoccupied more by impurity spreading from the living to the dead than vice versa (Halevi 2011: 71–5).

ii. Birth

According to Leviticus (12: 2–8) birth defiles the mother, requiring a minor sacrifice and a lengthy wait before entering sacred space. The sacrifice, and implicitly the impurity, is linked by some rabbinic sources to possible sins committed by the mother. The child, however, is not said to be impure, though some have explained circumcision on the eighth day to have a purificatory function, and the Gospel of Luke (2: 2) records a tradition for which the child was impure as well. Christian exegetes starting with Origen rejected the ritual understanding of this impurity, and read it as relating to an impurity adhering to all humans at birth, as an aspect of their corporeal nature or of Original Sin. This impurity could be managed only through baptism. Nevertheless, while in Judaism this impurity had little practical import after the destruction of the Temple, in Christianity the sacral dimensions of the Eucharist and the church prompted the development in the Middle Ages of abstinence of parturients from entering the church, marking the first entrance with a ritual known as churching, which had penitential and purificatory themes. In Islamic law, a woman who has given birth is defiled, but this is not a result of the birth of itself but rather because the blood emitted during birth is a genital discharge.

iii. Genital emissions

In the Bible (Lev. 15), genital emissions by both males and females are defiling, affecting the individual to whom they occur and other persons with whom they come in contact. Abnormal emissions resulting from illness create heavier pollution than normal ones such as menstruation or seminal emission in intercourse. Since a woman polluted by genital emissions was not only barred entrance to the Temple but also prohibited sexual contact, this impurity (especially that of menstruation or *niddah*) and the purification from it (by waiting a set number of days and washing in water) continued to be practised after the destruction of the Temple, and are observed to this day;

this is the main domain of impurity which has significant practical repercussions in contemporary Judaism. As it relates directly to women only, this led to a strong gender bias in the field of impurity (Koren 2011).

Christian authorities in late antiquity and the Middle Ages debated the question of the impurity of genital emissions, both male and female. Despite the repudiation of most Old Testament impurity laws, some Christian writers believed it self-evident that menstruation would bar a woman from participating in Eucharist or baptism, seeing these rituals as sacred activities parallel to temple worship; an opinion which was canonized in the eastern Orthodox tradition (Synek 2001; Taft 1998). This conception is somewhat different from the Judaic concept as it developed in late antiquity, where *niddah* impurity, at least for the dominant *halakhic* tradition, relates to the domestic sphere and does not require abstinence from religious worship. Other Christian writers, however, allowed menstruating women to participate in worship (Cohen 1991; Meens 2000; Marienberg 2003).

Seminal emissions were dealt with much more leniently. In Judaism vestiges of observance of their impurity appeared to have mostly died out in late antiquity, to be revived to some extent in mystical movements of the Middle Ages. In monastic Christianity, however, they were seen as one of the major dangers to the body of the monk or the cleric and linked to the work of demons, although many authorities argued that the emissions without sexual thoughts are not defiling (Brakke 1995; Leyser 1998).

iv. Sexual relations

The attitude towards sex is undoubtedly the major difference in purity perceptions between Christians on the one hand and Muslims and Jews on the other. Both the Jewish and the Islamic tradition are generally highly positive towards marriage, including sexual relations in marriage (though there are some exceptions to this). Sexual relations and their relationship to sacred practices and places could be managed through ritual rules of impurity, and had minimal moral implications, as long as they were practised as part of a legitimate marriage (Maghen 2005). Thus in the Bible sexual relations produce a minor impurity, which can be relatively easily purified. In the Christian tradition, however, sexual asceticism became a central part of Christian culture mostly thanks to monastic heritage. Sexual relations, even in marriage, were repeatedly cast as polluted and polluting, a stain that cannot be purified through ritual alone. The only totally pure option was virginity and celibacy, or, as a second-best option, chastity in marriage. In Christian literature, 'purity' was synonymous with 'chastity', and 'pollution' meant sexual pollution, and specifically sexual sin. The degree of a Christian's sexual abstinence became an index for his or her spiritual level, and thereby a social-religious index.

The impurity of sexual relations was linked with Adam and Eve's original sin and with human corporeality, a reflection of human sinfulness. In practical terms, this impurity meant that community members who had had sexual relations were called upon not to partake of the Eucharist for some time, even by authorities such as Gregory the Great, who was more lenient regarding other defilements (Meens 2000). The implications were most severe for the clergy; it was argued that as they should be perpetually ready for ministering, they should abstain from relations altogether. This provided the basis for calls for clerical celibacy in the church, which met with differing success through Christian history (Callam 1980; Hunter 2007).

b. Sin

Classic texts in the Abrahamic traditions frequently speak of sins as defiling or as disgusting. A basic function of such descriptions is to arouse strong negative emotions towards such acts and the person perpetrating them. In many cases, however, the use of such images goes further to suggest certain ways of understanding and managing sin which are equivalent to the management of bodily impurities: first, sin is contagious, influencing people and places beyond its perpetrator: once unleashed, it may work its evil automatically, harming even those who have no evil intentions. Second, it lingers on for some time after its performance, but may nevertheless be purified through the correct procedures. Third, it is inimical to the sacred, and thus is especially dangerous to those who see themselves as true believers, closer to God than the rest of humanity.

In the Hebrew Bible, some types of sins were seen to be so serious that they polluted not only the person involved but the sanctuary and/or the land as well. These sins, namely murder, sexual sins, and idolatry, could not in fact be expiated through ordinary ritual. Other sins—or perhaps the defilement they created—could be allayed through a purification sacrifice (*ḥaṭat*) and blood ritual at the sanctuary. The rituals and sacrifices of the Day of Atonement (Lev. 16) are said both to expiate for sin and to purify the sanctuary of impurity, and in the prophets, images of defilement and purification are commonly used for depicting Israel's sins and future restoration. The triad of idolatry, sexual sin, and murder return under various formulations in Second Temple literature as the most significant moral defilements.

Early Christians, who nominally rejected the possibility of bodily defilement lacking a moral aspect, focused on the defilement of sin as the only real and significant defilement. They therefore commonly read scriptural references to bodily defilement as relating symbolically to the defilement of sin. Furthermore, Christianity developed institutions and rituals through which sin could be purified and removed: baptism for those still outside the community, and penitence for those already inside it. While these rituals were conceived mainly as transforming the sinful persons themselves to reach a new spiritual state, they were also seen as a purification of the sins committed by the persons, requiring both repentance and faith as well as the performance of the required ritual in order that God send his grace (Stroumsa 1999). Christianity continued the scriptural and Jewish emphasis on bloodshed, idolatry, and sexual sin as the paradigmatic polluting sins, most dangerous to the divine presence in the community. To these we may add deceit, heresy, and disrespect for authority, sins which endangered social trust and structure.

The Quran, too, speaks of certain sinful behaviours, especially idolatry, unbelief, and associated sins, as impure or abominable (*rijs*: Q. 5: 90, 22: 30, 33: 33; see Freidenreich 2010: 14–19); ceasing from these behaviours is at times described as purification (see e.g. Q. 2: 125, 19: 13, 91: 9; *Ṣaḥīḥ Bukhārī* 1: 345, 8: 386). Nevertheless, the dominant object of purification in Islamic sources is certainly bodily defilement rather than moral, and the central objective of rituals is not described as purification from sin.

While sin as defilement and its removal as purification was a more frequent image in the Christian church than in Islamic and Jewish traditions, this is true mostly of the mainstream tradition as codified in *halakhah* and *fiqh*. Among mystical, ascetic, and philosophical groups and currents, as well as in penitential traditions, images of purification of the individual's soul and/or the heart from the defilement of sin are more common. Prayer, the study of religious texts, repentance, charity, and other pious acts are described as a purification of the individual from evil influences and experiences. In certain cases, purification may be the objective of an ascetic or mystical programme, intended to raise the individual closer to God (thus some Sufi traditions, Picken 2011). In these currents the performance of the standard bodily purity rituals as well as additional, supererogatory rituals for bodily purity (at times involving some degrees of sexual and alimentary abstinence) was seen as especially conducive to spiritual or moral purity. This was frequently based on an understanding of the body defiling as the soul and therefore of the suppression of the former as the purification of the latter (see *m. Sota* 9: 15, Reid 2013: 144–97). These common concepts of individual purification are at least partly attributable to the strong impact of Platonic thought on these strands of Judaism and Islam.[2]

An important perspective for understanding the character of purity in the Abrahamic traditions is the relationship between bodily impurity and sin impurity: to what extent is ritual purity conceived of also in terms of purification from sin? Klawans (2000: 75, 93) claimed that in Rabbinic Judaism the two realms are mostly 'compartmentalized', while in Qumran as well as in early Christianity they were 'merged'. In Christianity, the centrality of asceticism meant that bodily purity and purity of the heart or the soul were always seen as closely linked. The majority of scholars see the situation in Islam as opposite: generally speaking, ritual purity in Islam is not an expression of spiritual purity but rather a legal requirement for prayer (Maghen 2005; Reinhart 1990). Nevertheless, when looking away from legal writings to folklore and philosophy, the picture becomes more complicated with additional, spiritual meanings being given to the legal purity requirements. The situation in medieval and early modern Judaism is similar.

[2] e.g. Ibn el-Arabi, *Mysteries of Purity* (thirteenth century); *The Epistles of the Brethren of Purity* (tenth–eleventh century). For Plato on the purification of the soul from the influences and effects of the body in order to gain true virtue, salvation, and a good afterlife, see *Phaedo* 67–9.

c. Social Groups

Theorists have long observed that the human body and the rituals relating to it may be taken as a symbol for the social group. Purity rituals, which typically define, protect, and regulate the borders of the body, may therefore express and support the definition, regulation, and protection of society's borders (Mauss 1936; Douglas 1966). Indeed, this idea is expressed in a more functional fashion by many classical religious writers, starting with the Bible, who emphasize the role of purity laws in maintaining the identity of the religious community vis-à-vis external groups who threaten it or compete with it. In line with this conception, all three religions have developed conceptions of the impurity of foreigners, though with greatly differing emphases. The practical question of the impurity of foreigners naturally arises concerning the ritual of conversion and incorporation in the community, but more commonly as regards quotidian contacts and the cultural image of the foreigner.

Furthermore, purity rituals are frequently used to create a hierarchy inside a society, whether to set apart a religious, cultural, or gendered elite (Douglas 1970) or to degrade deviants, 'heretics', or opposition groups. This inner hierarchizing function was also present in all three Abrahamic religions, though the degree of its formalization differed.

i. Foreigners

In attributions of impurity to foreigners, there is a spectrum in all Abrahamic religions between the understanding that impurity is produced simply by the evil behaviour they supposedly adhere to (especially idolatry and sexual misdoing), and the understanding that foreigners are intrinsically impure. Another question, to some extent corresponding with the first, is the extent to which this impurity is ritual and therefore may be managed through ritual means, or is moral or spiritual only.

The Bible identifies Israel as a holy nation, set apart from other peoples both by divine election and by their (desired) behaviour. To achieve and maintain this status, Israel is called to remain pure in its dietary customs and in the abomination of bloodshed, sexual impurity, and idolatry, all of which, according to the Bible, were practised by its enemies, the Canaanites and Egyptians. This implies that these nations are impure, due to their behaviour if not intrinsically. The usage of purity imagery to enforce separatism became more urgent with the notion found in Ezra (chs 9–10) and reiterated in later Second Temple sources that intermarriage defiles the holy seed of Israel (Hayes 2002). The rabbis sought to integrate the ill-defined impurity of Gentiles into the general ritual purity system by stating that they defile 'like a *zavah* (a woman with irregular genital emission)' (*b. Shab.* 83b), a comparison probably used for its disgust factor. More significant than this ruling in maintaining the aura of Gentile defilement were the dietary laws as well as the rules of kosher wine (*yein nesekh*); although these are not predicated on the assumption that Gentiles are impure, they make common eating difficult if not impossible.

Similarly, throughout history Christians frequently used the language of disgust, commonly gendered, to denigrate non-Christians, both Jews and Gentiles, to weaken their appeal, and to justify their oppression (Cuffel 2007). The discourse of pollution joins that of demonization in the demarcation of Christians from outsiders. Entrance into the Christian community through baptism is described not only as an act of faith, a renewed birth in which all sins are removed, but also as the rejection of Satan and protection from polluted demons that accompany non-Christians, attracted by their sins and assisting them (Kelly 1985). Although at first this language was directed mostly at pagans, whose gods were equated to demons, with the demise of the Graeco-Roman cults its main object became Jews, Muslims, and heretics.

We have seen that the Quran uses defilement language to describe idolatry as well as idolaters, associated with Satan's influence, and in this it was similar to Judaism and Christianity. As opposed to Christianity, however, Islam had a complex ritual purity mechanism with which it managed impurity; thus the question of foreigners' impurity could potentially be expressed through a ritual system, and not remain only on the level of image and rhetoric. In practice, however, this option was only partly utilized: in general, while Shīʿah Islam practised ritual purification after contact with foreigners or idolaters, Sunnis did not (see Maghen 2007; Freidenreich in this volume).

ii. Hierarchy, elites, heretics, and deviants

Purity practice and language serve to enhance the power of social-religious groups and to create internal hierarchies. First, purity rules can be used to create, maintain, and justify institutional hierarchies and religious elites, such as a priesthood of which stricter purity rules are demanded. In this case the requirements of purity go together with enhanced rights of access to sacred space, rights of conducting religious ceremonies, and rights to tithes or taxes from the laity. In parallel, such elites may malign competing groups by casting them as heretics and deviants, describing them through language of defilement and disgust. Second, purity discourse may also serve the opposite function: an upstart group which wishes to gain power may represent itself as purer than the rest of society and/or the elite and thus justify its ascendancy; these claims may be supported by actual purity practices. Historically, in times of social strife, both scenarios occurred simultaneously, with various groups describing themselves as pure and their opponents as defiled.

The Bible requires priests and the *nazir* to adhere to more rigorous purity rules than the rest of Israel. However, the separation of priests from non-priests is not a main objective of the biblical purity rules, which referred much more frequently to Israel as a whole, and was hardly relevant in later Jewish history. Purity rules for Jews thus served more for the othering of non-Jews rather than of competing Jewish groups. Nevertheless, some exceptions may be found. Late Second Temple Judaism witnessed a general trend towards an expansion of the ritual purity rules to contexts outside of the Temple and its personnel. As a result, the degree of maintenance of ritual purity in daily life was now used as an index for piety and social prestige, with groups such as the Qumran sect or the Pharisees (and, for some interpretations, the Jesus movement as well) proving their superiority over other Jewish groups by adherence to more rigorous or morally significant purity rules (Baumgarten 1997: 81–113). Medieval and early modern Jewish groups, such as the Qara'aites and the Ḥasidei Ashkenaz, also emphasized their adherence to purity rules, as did more isolated magicians or mystics (Swartz 1994). However, this could cut both ways, as some groups differentiated themselves by emphasizing their leniency in purity issues relative to others (for an excellent discussion in an early Christian context, see Brakke 1995).

This function of purity as an instrument for social power was especially prominent in Christianity. In the first centuries of Christianity, certain Christian groups cast themselves as purer than others due to their adherence to more rigorous ascetic regimes or unbending stance in face of persecution (e.g. the groups described in 1 Tim. 5 and Titus 1; the Nag Hammadi *Testimony of Truth*; the Montanist movement in Asia Minor; and the North African Donatists). Competing, perhaps more powerful groups countered that their rejection of central authority made these groups polluted rather than pure. The history of Christianity is punctuated by the emergence of reform movements, in which groups called for a return to the original purity of the Christian church (the medieval Cathars ('pure ones') and the early modern Puritans are cases in point; see Lansing 2001). Central authorities reacted by demonizing heretics as polluted groups which defile the pure and virginal church by their disgusting beliefs and behaviours, instigated by Satan and his minions. On a more static level, the priesthood and the monastic movements demonstrated their superiority over the laity through their sexual purity, whether in total celibacy or in greater abstinence. Indeed, in many cases there was competition between the clergy and the monastics, with the latter appealing to their asceticism to enhance their status.

In Islam, the main purity rules are equally binding on all believers and are therefore a force for religious homogeneity rather than hierarchy. At the same time, Islamic ascetic and reform movements, whether medieval or modern, commonly used purity discourse to bring their point home (for a modern example, see Gauvain 2012).

d. The Demonic

Impurity in the Hebrew Bible is rarely linked to the realm of spirits, good or evil. An understanding that demons cause or accompany impurity first surfaces distinctively in the Gospel narratives on Jesus' exorcism of 'impure spirits' (Wahlen 2004), though the precise nature of their impurity, generally linked to disease and madness, is unclear. More significant was the identification of the pagan gods as demons and the resulting demonization of idolatry (LXX Ps. 95: 5; 1 Cor. 10: 20–1), as well as the casting of demons as instigators of other sins, especially of sexual nature, by Hellenistic Jews and early Christians. Demons could thus be identified as the quasi-material carriers of the impurity of sin, providing early Christians with a vehicle for conceptualizing defilement, contagion, and purification as physical processes with a strong moral dimension.

Demons played star roles in Christian descriptions of struggle between good and evil, whether intra-personal (as in monastic literature, e.g. Athanasius' *Life of Anthony*), social, interreligious, or cosmic (Origen, *On First Principles* 1.5, 8). These diverse roles, and the association of demons with the impurity of sin and corporeality, at times expressed in bodily pollution (e.g. in seminal emissions, an idea present also in the medieval Kabbalah) continued into medieval Christianity (Elliott 2011).

In Islam and Judaism the dominant legal discourse of impurity was not closely linked to demons; ritual impurity was a result of natural bodily processes, and therefore did not require demonic explanation. There are a good number of exceptions to this rule, however: defecation, which requires purification, is linked to demonic activity in Islam, and *wuḍū'* purification is said to drive away demons (Katz 2002: 13, Gauvain 2012: 68); a much-discussed Jewish text explains the method of purification from death defilement by analogy to healing by expulsion of demons (*Pesiqta De Rav Kahanna* 4.7, though the text itself has its doubts about this analogy).

Interactions, Influences, and Comparisons

Though Islamic sources of defilement, rituals of purification, and general attitude towards ritual purity bear many resemblances to the corresponding Jewish ritual purity system, they are by no means simply adaptations of the Jewish rites. For example, while the human corpse is perhaps the source of strongest defilement in Jewish law, most Muslim authorities do not recognize human corpses as defiled or defiling. In the Bible impurity is contagious, passing from person to person, while in Islamic law it only affects the person first in contact with it. In general, while in Judaism impurity appears to have a tangible/physical existence, in Islam it is cast as a legal construct. For example, though menstruation is defiling, if a woman has an ongoing emission of blood due to illness she may nevertheless pray, since otherwise she will not be able to pray at all. Many scholars have seen this as the expression of a tendency to leniency in Islamic ritual law, at times explicitly opposed to supposed Jewish rigorousness. However, the opposite is also true: in Islam daily prayer can only be performed when pure, while in Judaism the consensus (arrived at after some deliberation) is that impurity does not normally prevent prayer. Therefore, defilement necessarily has greater significance in the day to day religious life of Muslims than of Jews. Indeed, this can be seen in the placement of the chapter on *ṭaharah* (purity) at the very beginning of Islamic legal tracts.

Christian ritual purity practices have a rather different flavour from those of Judaism and Islam; they were shaped by several factors, somewhat at odds with one another. As a religion which created sacred spaces (churches), times (festivals), people (saints), and objects (relics and the Eucharist), ritual purity was essential for determining and marking off hierarchies of sacrality. Furthermore, the focus on the human body in Christian theologies of incarnation and resurrection and the correspondence between the body of the individual Christian, of the community, and of Christ meant that attitudes towards the body were central for Christian practice and society. At the same time, the theological importance of the body and the insistence that the person is a combination of body and soul meant that for Christians, bodily ritual practices had to have an explicit moral or spiritual dimension. Thus, while ritual purity rules certainly exist in Christianity, they are typically overlaid with moral language and/or symbolism.

To these internal dynamics we may add interactions with Jewish and Graeco-Roman traditions in the formative first centuries of Christianity, which led to much theoretical discussion of the ideas and practices of impurity. Already in the Gospels Jewish purity rituals are criticized, though there is much scholarly debate concerning the precise extent of this criticism: did it entail total rejection of such rituals or a more traditional critique of external practice lacking in true meaning. By the third century, in any case, Jewish dietary laws were almost unanimously rejected by Christians, and this rejection was cast as an opposition to the idea and practice of ritual purity in general. Since all animals were created by the good God, asked Christian theologians, how could some of them be pure and others impure? Following the Gospels, most Christian writing on the subject concerned the Jewish dietary laws rather than other Jewish purity rules. Nevertheless, issues such as death defilement, leprosy, or genital emissions were also treated to a similar argument: purity and defilement are—or should be—products of the heart or mind of the person, relating to vices and virtues, and not of the body or its actions. A conception of purity in which the vagaries of the body are treated without direct recourse to moral semantics was non-comprehensible and unacceptable for Christians.

Despite this legacy of anti-Judaism and anti-ritualism, however, Christians actually did hold to many purity rules similar to the Jewish ones. The prohibition on food offered to idols and on blood, and their perception as defiled, was common through most of the first millennium, and additional dietary rules were found in many communities. Menstruation and seminal emissions were considered impure and precluding participation in the Eucharist as early as the third century.

Additional aspects of Christianity's attitude towards purity are found in the rituals of baptism and the Eucharist. To a greater extent than Jewish or Muslim rituals, the sacraments of Catholic and Orthodox Christian denominations have a strong sacral dimension: they are performed in sacred space and by a priesthood; the wine and bread of the Eucharist, as well as the water and oil used in baptism, are seen as sacred and blessed by the Holy Spirit, and in the case of the former, as the body of Christ. This sacrality leads to purity requirements for participating and especially for officiating in these rituals. These requirements include not only sexual abstinence prior to performing the ritual, but also (in the case of baptism) exorcisms of demonic spirits preceding baptism, or demands of purity from circumstantial defilements such as menstruation or seminal pollutions. Furthermore, both baptism and Eucharist are perceived not only as holy but also as purifying from sin, i.e. as rituals in which God purifies the adherents from their sins. Such a dimension of purification from sins is less central in mainstream Jewish and Muslim rituals, though it features in the more mystical traditions.

The Abrahamic religions are not alone in their purity and defilement discourse: though each religious tradition is of course unique, the functions and phenomenology of the purity discourses and practices of many religions are broadly similar to those described above. Nevertheless, there are some characteristics of the Abrahamic religions which lead to particular problematics and dynamics in the development of their purity discourses.

The very idea of impurity indicates that some created things are essentially incompatible with the sacred sphere, and indicates that value ascription may derive not only from the actions of humans as moral agents but also simply exists as part of creation. For dualist theologies impurity is simple to explain: its source is some totally evil sphere or creator. For monotheistic schemes, however, there is at times a tension between the fundamental belief in a single and good creator and the independence of impurity. The Abrahamic religions utilized two main avenues to accommodate impurity in the monotheistic programme: either it is not evil, but rather a temporary result accompanying bodily processes (as in the dominant Jewish and Muslim ritual purity traditions); or it is indeed evil, but derives from sin—moral decisions made by free-willed agents, whether human or demonic (producing moral impurity in all three religions). These explanations, however, were never totally successful. The first is difficult to square with the perception both in Islam and in Judaism that certain substances or animals are naturally and inherently impure; the second, with the fact that not all types of impurity, even in Christianity, can be directly linked to a sin. Furthermore, dualist mythologies if not mythogonies are found in the Abrahamic religions, and then we encounter terms such as 'powers of impurity', when impurity is closely associated with evil spiritual beings. Although these powers are formally subordinate to the Creator, in fact they function as largely independent agents.

Another problematic is the status of the human body. In all three religions, the body is the focus of a spectrum of views and practices, between conceptions of the perfected human body as *imago dei* and of the body as a husk, obstacle, or prison for the soul. Ritual purity rules in Islam and Judaism cohere with a view of the body as perfectible, at least temporarily; though it is always susceptible to defilement, the body can be purified so as to approach sacred places or be compatible for worship (though the picture is certainly complicated by the conception that most impurities derive from the body itself; see Katz 2002: 164–86, 207–9). In both religions, however, ascetic and mystic currents saw the usual purity rules as capable of refining the body only up to a point, beyond which more rigorous purity practices may be required; even these cannot totally purify the embodied person. In Christianity the lack of ordered ritual purity practices meant that ascetic currents, along with their purity discourse, were more dominant, and that options for temporary bodily purification, though recognized (e.g. purification as allowing access to the Eucharist), were less central in the purity discourse, which centred on more radical purification through asceticism, baptism, or penitence. Furthermore, accepted doctrines of Original Sin informed a view of the body as inherently flawed and fallen, only partly purifiable through the rituals of the church (Beatrice 1978). Nevertheless, ascetic practices could be conceived not only as a total rejection of the defiled body in favour of the soul, but also as its refinement in order to gain an exalted, angelic, pure body (Miller 1994). The bodies of Jesus and of the 'immaculate' Virgin provided models for such pure and purified bodies (Stroumsa 1990; Foskett 2002).

Despite, and perhaps because of, the similarities between the purity discourse and practices of the three religions, they themselves were frequently the focus of polemic, reciprocal differentiation, and stereotyping. Both Christians and Muslims characterized Jewish purity practice as harsh and inhumane, as opposed to their own practices which are more lenient and reasonable. Patristic and later Christian writers worked to create an image of Jewish purity practice as ritualistic, arbitrary, and external, not corresponding to moral and spiritual truths. The identification of Judaism with purity practices, especially of food (*kashrut*), in turn served to reinforce an image of Judaism itself as a religion obsessed with technical bodily purity, rather than religious truths and morals. At the same time, some writers identified purity practices as a universal feature of human religion, essential for honouring the divine and setting apart the sacred.

References

Balberg, M. 2014. *Purity, Body, and Self in Early Rabbinic Literature*. Berkeley: University of California Press.

Baumgarten, A. I. 1997. *The Flourishing of Jewish Sects in the Maccabean Era: An Interpretation*. Leiden: Brill.

Beatrice, F. 1978. *Tradux peccati: alle fonti della dottrina agostiana del peccato originale*. Milano: Vita e Pensiero.

Brakke, D. 1995. 'The Problematization of Nocturnal Emissions in Early Christian Syria, Egypt, and Gaul'. *Journal of Early Christian Studies* 3 (4): 419–60.

Callam, D. 1980. 'Clerical Continence in the Fourth Century: Three Papal Decretals'. *Theological Studies* 41 (1): 3–50.

Cohen, S. J. D. 1991. 'Menstruants and the Sacred in Judaism and Christianity'. In S. B. Pomeroy, ed., *Women's History and Ancient History*. Chapel Hill, NC: University of North Carolina Press, 273–99.

Cuffel, A. 2007. *Gendering Disgust in Medieval Religious Polemic*. Notre Dame, IN: University of Notre Dame Press.

Diamond, E. 2003. *Holy Men and Hunger Artists: Fasting and Asceticism in Rabbinic Culture*. Oxford: Oxford University Press.

Douglas, M. 1966. *Purity and Danger: An Analysis of Concepts of Pollution and Taboo*. London: Routledge.

Douglas, M. 1970. *Natural Symbols: Explorations in Cosmology*. London: Routledge.

Elliott, D. 2011. *Fallen Bodies: Pollution, Sexuality, and Demonology in the Middle Ages*. Philadelphia: University of Pennsylvania Press.

Foskett, M. F. 2002. *A Virgin Conceived: Mary and Classical Representations of Virginity*. Bloomington: Indiana University Press.

Freidenreich, D. M. 2010. 'Holiness and Impurity in the Torah and the Quran: Differences within a Common Typology'. *Comparative Islamic Studies* 6 (1–2): 5–22.

Freidenreich, D. M. 2011. *Foreigners and their Food: Constructing Otherness in Jewish, Christian, and Islamic Law*. Berkeley: University of California Press.

Gauvain, R. 2012. *Salafi Ritual Purity: In the Presence of God*. London: Routledge.

Haidt, J. et al. 1997. 'Body, Psyche, and Culture: The Relationship between Disgust and Morality'. *Psychology & Developing Societies* 9 (1): 107–31.

Halevi, L. 2011. *Muhammad's Grave: Death Rites and the Making of Islamic Society*. New York: Columbia University Press.

Hayes, C. 2002. *Gentile Impurities and Jewish Identities: Intermarriage and Conversion from the Bible to the Talmud*. Oxford: Oxford University Press.

Hayes, C. 2007. 'Purity and Impurity, Ritual'. In *Encyclopedia Judaica*. Detroit: Macmillan.

Hunter, D. G. 2007. *Marriage, Celibacy, and Heresy in Ancient Christianity: The Jovinianist Controversy*. Oxford: Oxford University Press.

Katz, M. H. 2002. *Body of Text: The Emergence of the Sunni Law of Ritual Purity*. Albany, NY: State University of New York Press.

Kazen, T. 2002. *Jesus and Purity Halakhah: Was Jesus Indifferent to Impurity?* Stockholm: Almqvist & Wiksell.

Kelly, H. A. 1985. *The Devil at Baptism: Ritual, Theology, and Drama*. Ithaca, NY: Cornell University Press.

Klawans, J. 2000. *Impurity and Sin in Ancient Judaism*. New York: Oxford University Press.

Koren, S. F. 2011. *Forsaken: The Menstruant in Medieval Jewish Mysticism*. Waltham, MA: UPNE.

Lansing, C. 2001. *Power & Purity: Cathar Heresy in Medieval Italy*. Oxford: Oxford University Press.

Lemos, T. M. 2013. 'Where There is Dirt, is There System? Revisiting Biblical Purity Constructions'. *Journal for the Study of the Old Testament* 37 (3): 265–94.

Leyser, C. 1998. 'Masculinity in Flux: Nocturnal Emission and the Limits of Celibacy in the Early Middle Ages'. In D. Hadley, ed., *Masculinity in Medieval Europe*. London: Longmans, 103–19.

Maghen, Z. 1999. 'Much Ado about Wuḍū''. *Der Islam* 76 (2): 205–52.

Maghen, Z. 2005. *Virtues of the Flesh: Passion and Purity in Early Islamic Jurisprudence*. Leiden: Brill.

Maghen, Z. 2007. '"They Shall Not Draw Nigh": The Access of Unbelievers to Sacred Space in Islamic and Jewish Law'. *Journal of Arabic and Islamic Studies* 7: 103–31.

Marienberg, E. 2003. *Niddah: lorsque les juifs conceptualisent la menstruation*. Paris: Belles lettres.

Mauss, M. 1936. 'Les techniques du corps'. In *Sociologie et anthropologie*. Paris: PUF.

Meens, M. 2000. '"A Relic of Superstition": Bodily Impurity and the Church from Gregory the Great to the Twelfth Century Decretists'. In M. Poorthuis and J. Schwartz, eds, *Purity and Holiness: The Heritage of Leviticus*. Leiden: Brill, 281–93.

Miller, P. C. 1994. 'Desert Asceticism and "The Body from Nowhere"'. *Journal of Early Christian Studies* 2: 137–53.

Noam, V. 2008. 'The Dual Strategy of Rabbinic Purity Legislation'. *Journal for the Study of Judaism* 39 (4–5): 471–512.

Picken, G. 2011. *Spiritual Purification in Islam: The Life and Works of Al-Muhasibi*. London: Routledge.

Reid, M. H. 2013. *Law and Piety in Medieval Islam*. Cambridge: Cambridge University Press.
Reinhart, A. K. 1990. 'Impurity/No Danger'. *History of Religions* 30 (1): 1–24.
Rozin, P., Haidt, J., and McCauley, C. 2008. 'Disgust'. In M. Lewis, J. M. Haviland-Jones, and L. F. Barrett, eds, *Handbook of Emotions*. 3rd edn. New York: Guilford, 757–76.
Stroumsa, G. G. 1990. '"Caro Salutis Cardo": Shaping the Person in Early Christian Thought'. *History of Religions* 30 (1): 25–50.
Stroumsa, G. G. 1999. 'Purification and its Discontents: Mani's Rejection of Baptism'. In J. Assman and G. G. Stroumsa, eds, *Transformations of the Inner Self in Ancient Religions*. Leiden: Brill, 405–20.
Swartz, M. D. 1994. '"Like the Ministering Angels": Ritual and Purity in Early Jewish Mysticism and Magic'. *AJS Review* 19 (2): 135–67.
Synek, E. 2001. 'Zur Rezeption Alttestamentlicher Reinheitsvorschriften ins Orthodoxe Kirchenrecht'. *Kanon* 16: 25–70.
Taft, R. F. 1998. 'Women at Church in Byzantium: Where, When—And Why?' *Dumbarton Oaks Papers* 52: 27–87.
Valeri, V. 2000. *The Forest of Taboos: Morality, Hunting, and Identity among the Huaulu of the Moluccas*. Madison: University of Wisconsin Press.
Wahlen, C. 2004. *Jesus and the Impurity of Spirits in the Synoptic Gospels*. Tübingen: Mohr Siebeck.

CHAPTER 25

DIETARY LAW

DAVID M. FREIDENREICH

IF the term *Abrahamic* has any substantive meaning when applied to Judaism, Christianity, and Islam, it emphasizes certain affinities among these religious traditions while downplaying both other affinities and also the distinctions among these traditions. One could, after all, reasonably refer to these three religions as *Near Eastern*, a label that highlights their emergence and development within a common geographical and cultural region. Until recently, it was customary within academia to define these religions as *western*, a term that is not only broadly geographical but also and more significantly a nod to the profound influence of the Greek philosophical tradition on intellectual life within all three communities. A relatively new trend is to examine Judaism, Christianity, and Islam as *Mediterranean* religions, an approach that highlights the impact of that region's distinctive network of commercial, cultural, and intellectual exchange, especially during the Middle Ages. Alternatively, one can choose to emphasize criteria that exclude one tradition or another, such as a claim of affinity with biblical Israel (excluding Islam), a radically monotheist theology (excluding Christianity), or universal and missionary aspirations (excluding Judaism).

The term *Abrahamic* calls to mind two interrelated sets of affinities. The first is reverence for Abraham and, more broadly, for the myths, heroes, concepts, values, and norms found within the Hebrew Bible. As such, *Abrahamic* serves as a more generic substitute for *Judaeo-Christian*, another term that emphasizes the shared scriptural heritage of distinct religions. The second affinity highlighted by the term *Abrahamic* is a claim to descent, biological or spiritual, from Abraham. This affinity, which implies a familial relationship between Jews, Christians, and Muslims, probably accounts for the rise in popularity of *Abrahamic* among those who seek to overcome hostilities between members of the Judaeo-Christian traditions and contemporary Muslims. Unlike the geographic monikers mentioned above, *Abrahamic* bears a valence that can inspire present-day Jews, Christians, and Muslims to work toward a more harmonious future.

Examination of Jewish, Christian, and Islamic dietary law affords a valuable opportunity to assess the utility of the term *Abrahamic* in the academic study of pre-modern sources from these three religions. The assessment that follows proceeds along two tracks. It first probes the degree to which their common biblical heritage accounts for food restrictions central to Judaism, Christianity, and Islam. These traditions do share a number of food practices in common with one another and with those found in the Hebrew Bible, but the differences are arguably more profound than the similarities. Indeed, all three traditions depart in significant ways from biblical dietary norms, both because each tradition reveres its own distinctive scripture and because of interpretations and innovations that developed after the biblical period. This chapter then assesses the utility of the term *Abrahamic* by examining the ways in which food restrictions reflect traditional approaches to conceptualizing the relationships between Judaism, Christianity, and Islam. Jewish, Christian, and Islamic laws regarding food associated with members of other religions demonstrate that the pre-modern authorities who speak for these three traditions do not see themselves or their counterparts within an Abrahamic paradigm.

The first half of this chapter examines the fate of the Hebrew Bible's dietary laws within the Abrahamic religions. It addresses in turn three aspects of biblical dietary law: the prohibition against consuming the meat of certain animal species, the prohibition against consuming meat whose blood was not drained, and the prohibition against boiling a young goat in its mother's milk. We will also consider Islam's prohibition of alcohol, despite the fact that this prohibition is not rooted in biblical dietary law. Rigorous adherence to the biblicism implicit in the Abrahamic paradigm, after all, would result in the failure to address an important aspect of Islamic food practices. As we will see, such rigour would also do an injustice to important aspects of Jewish and Christian practices. A focus on common origins alone obscures the divergent ways in which all three Abrahamic religions understand and apply biblical material within their own communities.

The second half of this chapter explores Jewish, Christian, and Islamic norms regarding the food of members of other religions, with particular attention to the conceptions of foreign religions implicit in these norms. Most prominent among these norms is the prohibition against food associated with idolatry. Jewish, Christian, and Islamic authorities alike apply this prohibition and others not only to the food of pagans but also to one another's food. Pre-modern religious authorities employ a variety of distinct paradigms for conceptualizing the relationships between Judaism, Christianity, and Islam, and for evaluating the reverence by religious foreigners for biblical norms. These paradigms, which clash with the logic of familial relationship that underlies the contemporary concept of Abrahamic religions, bolster particular worldviews that promote the supremacy of one's own religious tradition at the expense of its peers. The diversity and ideological baggage of these pre-modern approaches to relating Judaism, Christianity, and Islam render them unsuitable for use within the academy. Ironically, the value of the term *Abrahamic* for contemporary scholarship rests precisely in its incongruity with the paradigms traditionally employed by Jews, Christians, and Muslims themselves. The more one focuses on the meaning of the term, however, the less useful it becomes.

Biblical Dietary Law within the Abrahamic Religions

Laws Governing Particular Animal Species

The most widely familiar of the Hebrew Bible's dietary laws, from antiquity to the present day, are those that address the permissibility of eating meat from various types of animal species. Land animals must have split hoofs and chew their cud, characteristics that ensure the animal is a herbivore and exclude such species as pigs and camels. Water animals must have fins and scales: thus, most kinds of fish are permitted but not other forms of seafood. The Torah also addresses the permissibility of eating various types of birds and insects (Lev. 11: 1–23, 41–2; Deut. 14: 3–20; see Milgrom 1991: 718–36). These regulations constitute the core of Jewish dietary law to the present day. Christian and Islamic authorities, in contrast, do not believe that members of their communities ought to observe the Hebrew Bible's strictures regarding forbidden animal species even though they regard these laws as divine in origin. These understandings result from reading the dietary laws of the Torah within the framework of the Christian Bible or the Quran. To speak of an Abrahamic scriptural heritage uniting Judaism, Christianity, and Islam is overly simplistic: members of these religions revere three distinct scriptures and therefore understand the shared content of these scriptures in different ways.

Consider the evolution of attitudes toward biblical dietary laws within the earliest history of Christianity. Jews at the time of Jesus commonly regarded adherence to biblical dietary laws as a primary marker of Jewish identity and, indeed, as a litmus test: Jews alone followed these laws, and those Jews who wilfully rejected them were deemed apostates (Barclay 1998: 91–2). Jesus and his disciples, all Jews, adhered to biblical dietary laws as well, and some of these disciples believed that non-Jews wishing to join the community of Christ ought to become Jews and observe biblical law in its entirety. Paul and other communal leaders, however, exempted Gentile believers from this obligation; indeed, Paul explicitly permitted Gentile believers to eat all kinds of food (Rom. 14: 2–3, 14; see Barclay 1996). Paul's letters contain no instructions regarding whether Jewish believers in Christ should continue to adhere to biblical dietary laws, but circumstantial evidence strongly suggests that he approved of such behaviour. As scholars now recognize, Paul took for granted that observant Jews have a place within the nascent Christian community, and biblical dietary laws were a core component of Jewish practice. Whereas other Jewish writers of his era seized upon biblical dietary practices as a marker of one's Jewishness, however, Paul believed that adherence to these norms or lack thereof should in no way affect one's status as a believer in Christ.

Within a few generations, those who spoke for the church regularly disparaged abstention from the meat of specific animal species, like pork. They interpreted the Old Testament's dietary norms through the lens of post-Pauline verses in the New Testament, such as the report that Jesus 'declared all foods pure' (Mark 7: 19; see Räisänen

1982), and various statements pseudonymously ascribed to Paul, including 'for the pure all things are pure' (Titus 1: 15) and 'everything created by God is good' (1 Tim. 4: 4). The second-century *Letter to Barnabas*, for example, explains that Moses' teachings about food were intended solely to convey spiritual lessons about morality, 'but because of their fleshly desires [the Jews] received his words as if he were actually speaking about food' (10.9). Church fathers were not the first to offer moralistic allegorical interpretations of biblical dietary laws (see e.g. the second-century BCE *Letter of Aristeas*), but they were the first to claim that these laws should not be followed literally. These authorities understood adherence to biblical dietary laws, by Jews and others who followed so-called 'Jewish' practices, as reflecting a failure to understand not only the significance of Christ but also of God's original revelation to Moses. These failures, after all, are deeply intertwined: only through the lens of the New Testament (Christians assert) can one can truly understand the meaning of the Hebrew Bible itself. The Jewish and Christian Bibles contain many of the same words, but those words convey very different messages because of the scriptural contexts in which they are read.

The Quran understands biblical laws forbidding the consumption of certain animal species literally, as do Jewish interpreters. The Torah describes these laws as a manifestation of Israel's holiness (e.g. Lev. 11: 45). The Quran, in contrast, portrays them as punishments for the transgressions of the Children of Israel (Q. 4: 160, 6: 146, 16: 116; similar portrayals also appear in early Christian sources, e.g. Aphrahat, *Demonstration* 15.3, dated 344 CE). As such, there is no reason for non-Jews to adhere to biblical dietary law by abstaining from such foods as camel meat. Muslims need only abstain from pork, which is forbidden within the Quran itself (Q. 2: 173, 5: 3, 6: 145, 16: 115), and from particular species enumerated in *ḥadīth* and in the literature of the various legal schools (Cook 1986). Notice that whereas Jews and Christians claim the mantle of biblical Israel and regard themselves as faithfully adhering to biblical dietary law (either literally or spiritually), Muslims do neither. Instead, they reject both the ultimate authority of the Bible and the belief that Israel constitutes a uniquely holy or particularly pious nation (Freidenreich 2010b: 5–12).

The Quran and subsequent Sunni works portray Islamic dietary law as a golden mean between the unfounded practices of polytheists and the burdensome obligations with which God punished the Jews. These sources employ rhetoric about biblical dietary law to emphasize both the authenticity of God's revelation to Moses and the fact that this revelation has been superseded (Freidenreich 2011: 131–43, 184–90). This rhetoric also highlights the leniency of God's final revelation relative to prior versions. Indeed, Islamic descriptions of biblical dietary law, based on an interpretation of quranic verses rather than on the Hebrew Bible itself, are more restrictive than those found in the Bible or subsequent Jewish practice (Maghen 2006: 146–60). Jews, along with the dietary norms imputed to them, function as a negative foil against which to define not only Christian identity but Islamic identity as well. The scriptural frameworks distinctive to each of these traditions result in understandings of biblical dietary law self-consciously at odds with those espoused within a sister Abrahamic religion.

Christian and Islamic scriptures contain passages that shape the manner in which laws forbidding consumption of various animal species are understood. The absence of these passages from the Jewish Bible, however, does not imply that Jews necessarily understand biblical dietary law in the same manner as biblical Israelites. After all, the precise meaning of these laws is sometimes ambiguous. How, for example, should one apply the biblical injunctions forbidding consumption of specific species of birds, listed without any explanation (Lev. 11: 13–19; Deut. 14: 12–18)? Rabbinic authorities derive categorical principles from the Torah's list and then apply these principles to determine the status of unmentioned species (*Mishnah Ḥullin* 3.6). Karaite authorities, in contrast, hold that neither the identity of the forbidden birds nor the rationale underlying these prohibitions can be ascertained with certainty. Karaites therefore permit only those birds whose consumption is explicitly approved within other biblical texts (Frank 2004: 39–61). This difference, which helped to distinguish rabbinic and Karaite Jews one from the other during the Middle Ages, highlights the role of tradition-specific interpretation within all scriptural religions.

Interpretation results not only from ambiguity within scripture itself but also from the changing context in which scripture is read. Over the centuries, Jews have developed a variety of justifications for adherence to these laws that augment the rationale found in the Bible itself: 'I the LORD am your God who has set you apart from other peoples. So you shall set apart the pure animal from the impure, the impure bird from the pure . . . You shall be holy to Me' (Lev. 20: 24–6). One finds, for example, portrayals of biblical law as conveying moral lessons (e.g. *Letter to Aristeas* 128–71) or promoting a healthy diet (e.g. Maimonides, *Guide of the Perplexed* 3.48). Both of these interpretations reflect the influence of Greek thought on post-biblical Judaism.

Portrayals of biblical dietary laws as setting Jews apart from all other people in their morality or physical health complement the Torah's own claim that these laws set Israel apart as uniquely holy and Godlike in their behaviour. (Notice that these binary conceptions of Jews and non-Jews leave no room for distinguishing Christians and Muslims from adherents of non-Abrahamic religions.) In other cases, however, the interpretations and practices espoused within Abrahamic religions on account of post-biblical developments depart radically from or even directly contradict the dietary norms established within biblical literature. This dynamic can be seen with respect to the Latin Christian practice of consuming blood, the Jewish injunction to separate meat from dairy, and the Islamic prohibition of wine and other alcohol.

The Blood Taboo

Ingesting blood ranks among the foremost taboos within the Hebrew Bible. This prohibition, which refers primarily to eating meat from which blood was not drained rather than to drinking liquid blood, is the only law in the Torah that explicitly applies not only to Israelites but to all of humanity (Gen. 9: 3–6; Lev. 17: 10–14; cf. Deut. 12: 16,

23–5). Underlying the importance ascribed to this rule is the concept that blood constitutes the seat of life itself: just as humans must not take the life of fellow human beings, they also must not ingest the life of the animals that God has allowed them to kill (Milgrom 1991: 704–13).

The universality of the Hebrew Bible's blood prohibition probably accounts for the declaration by leaders of the nascent Christian community that even Gentile believers in Christ must abstain both from blood and from the meat of strangled animals (Acts 15: 28). The prohibition of these foodstuffs also figures prominently in the Quran (Q. 2: 173, 5: 3, 6: 145, 16: 115). Rabbinic law preserves the blood taboo as well and lists consumption of bloody meat—albeit solely from a living animal—among the norms binding upon all humankind (Novak 1983: 239–54).

Jewish, Christian, and Islamic sources also attest to the requirement that slaughter be performed by means of slitting the throat with a sharp knife so as to ensure that the animal's blood drains out. The norms of butchery employed within these communities, including those of eastern Christians (Barhebraeus, *Nomocanon*, ch. 35, composed *c.*1264–86), were in fact similar enough that many Sunni authorities regarded them as functionally equivalent (Freidenreich 2011: 142, 197–203). The close similarities in the mechanics of slaughter enjoined by all three traditions as well as in the Semitic terminology used to describe these mechanics suggest that religious authorities drew upon a common Near Eastern method of animal slaughter. This method may well have been employed in biblical times as well, but it is never mandated in the Hebrew Bible; the diffusion of this practice within the Abrahamic religions, therefore, is not directly related to their shared reverence for biblical norms.

The fate of the blood taboo within the Latin Christian tradition attests dramatically to the difference between Abrahamic food practices and those enjoined within biblical literature. Despite the fact that the Hebrew Bible regards consumption of blood as morally equivalent to murder and adultery (e.g. Ezek. 33: 25–6), and despite the reiteration of the blood taboo within the New Testament itself, western Christians ultimately came to regard this prohibition as no longer binding. This transformation was instigated in the late fourth century by Augustine, who asserted that the Apostolic Decree (Acts 15: 28) only forbade consumption of blood and meat containing blood as a temporary measure intended to bridge the gap between Jewish and Gentile members of the nascent Christian community. Augustine, seeking to counter claims that the Bible supports the restrictive food practices endorsed by Manichaeans, instead privileged Jesus' teaching, 'It is not what enters your mouth that defiles but what comes out of it' (Matt. 15: 11; cf. Mark 7: 15). True Christians, Augustine taught, follow Christ by consuming anything nutritious (*Answer to Faustus* 32.13). Although many in the West continued to follow the Apostolic Decree's blood prohibition for some time, by the twelfth century Augustine's interpretation was universally accepted among Catholics (and, later, Protestants). During the transitional period, proponents of the Augustinian position labelled those who continued to follow traditional Christian dietary practices as 'Judaizers' (e.g. Vega 1941).

The history of the blood taboo in the Latin West offers a clear example of the way in which Christian authorities sometimes depart radically from biblical norms in response to post-biblical developments, even as they affirm their reverence for scripture by using proof texts to justify these departures. This dynamic, also attested in Judaism and Islam, reflects the nature of scripture not merely as a point of origin but, more fundamentally, as 'a relation between a people and a text' (Smith 1993: 18). In its orientation toward the shared biblical roots of Judaism, Christianity, and Islam, the Abrahamic paradigm is liable to draw attention away from the evolving meaning of biblical sources as understood within three distinct interpretative traditions.

Not Mixing Meat and Dairy

'You shall not boil a kid in its mother's milk,' the Hebrew Bible declares on three occasions (Exod. 23: 19, 34: 26; Deut. 14: 21). None of these passages provides a rationale for this prohibition against a specific manner of cooking the meat of young goats; among the most plausible explanations are the promotion of humanitarian values and the separation of life-giving forces from processes associated with death (Haran 1979; Milgrom 1991: 737–42). This prohibition finds no expression in Christian or Islamic food norms. Rabbinic Judaism, however, employs this set of verses to justify an extensive and unprecedented set of laws separating meat from dairy (Kraemer 2007). Not only is it forbidden for Jews to cook the meat of an animal in the milk of its own mother, or even in milk from the same species, Jews also may not consume any kind of meat with any kind of dairy (e.g. chicken and cheese). Rabbinic law, moreover, requires that pots, dishes, and utensils used with meat may not be used with dairy and imposes a waiting period between the consumption of meat and the consumption of dairy. The biblical Abraham, who served both milk and meat to his guests (Gen. 18: 8), would be flummoxed by these unfamiliar regulations. David C. Kraemer (2007: 46) aptly describes the separation of meat and dairy not as the outcome of scriptural exegesis but rather as 'a new Jewish eating practice, one invented by the early rabbis and elaborated, slowly and variously, by generations of their disciples'. This new practice bolsters the distinction between Jews and non-Jews made manifest through Jewish adherence to biblical dietary law while also serving to distinguish followers of the rabbis from other Jews; both of these distinctions play prominent roles within rabbinic discourse about food and identity (Rosenblum 2010). Indeed, rabbinic Jews who wished to drive a wedge between themselves and the Karaites sought a ban of excommunication 'against the eaters of meat with milk' (Rustow 2008: 209).

Of all Jewish dietary norms, those regarding the mixture of meat and dairy arguably have the greatest impact on the daily life of rabbinic Jews. Nevertheless, references to this practice are rare in Christian and Islamic rhetoric about Jews. This rhetoric focuses on what Jeremy Cohen dubs 'hermeneutical Jews', a construct derived not from social interaction with actual Jews but rather from theologically oriented engagement with sacred texts, especially the Bible. Jews function within Christian and Islamic discourse alike as 'living letters of scripture', to use the words of Bernard of Clairvaux (Cohen 1999: 2). Neither the Bible nor the Quran addresses the anti-mixture practices of the Jews, so Christians and Muslims ignore these practices as well. As we saw with respect to Latin Christian norms regarding blood, however, biblical texts alone do not encapsulate the fullness of the dietary practices observed by members of the Abrahamic religions. This dynamic, evident in rabbinic strictures regarding meat and dairy, is even more readily apparent with respect to Islam's prohibition against consuming alcohol.

Wine and Other Alcohol

Biblical literature takes for granted that wine played an important role in both cultic rituals and everyday life in ancient Israel (Broshi 1984). Priests may not consume wine or other alcoholic beverages while serving in the shrine, apparently because it is liable to impair their ability to perform their duties (Lev. 10: 8–11). Nazirites, who vow to observe restrictions similar to yet more onerous than those imposed on priests, may not consume alcohol or any grape product (Num. 6: 3–4). Ordinary Israelites and off-duty priests, however, are free to enjoy alcohol. Wine, moreover, is regularly offered in libation on the altar in the context of various sacrificial rites. Non-legal biblical literature portrays wine as a regular part of the diet, a source of joy, and a gift of God (e.g. Ps. 104: 15).

The ritual function of wine persists within Christianity through the use of wine in the Eucharistic sacrifice, although the centrality of wine in the ritual was not a given in early Christian communities with ascetic tendencies (McGowan 1999). Wine also plays an important role within rabbinic Judaism through its use as a physical anchor for the performance of abstract actions, such as the sanctification of holidays or the pronouncement of wedding blessings. (On Jewish and Christian concern about wine offered in libation to idols, see the next section.) The importance of wine within Judaism and Christianity reflects its centrality in the diet and culture of the Graeco-Roman world: wine, along with bread and olive oil, was a dietary staple in the Mediterranean region and a key component in civilized dining (Smith 2003: 28–31).

The status of wine within the Islamic tradition is quite different, owing both to the different cultural milieu in which Islam emerged and its distinctive scriptural canon. Although the Quran describes the intoxicants derived from grapes and dates positively (16: 67), it also warns that the harm of wine outweighs its benefits (2: 219), forbids praying while intoxicated (4: 43), and describes wine as a Satanic abomination from which believers should abstain (5: 90–1). *Ḥadīth* collections, meanwhile, are consistent in their condemnations of alcohol (Kueny 2001). Classical exegetes explain that God's revelations on the subject of wine grew more restrictive over time, with the absolute prohibition last and therefore uniquely authoritative (McAuliffe 1984: 159–67). The scope of this prohibition also grew over time, ultimately encompassing not only wine but also other alcoholic beverages and foodstuffs containing alcohol, even in quantities that do not result in intoxication (Haider 2013). Similarly, the prohibition applies not just to consuming alcohol but also to producing or selling it or even, according to some authorities, patronizing an establishment in which others are consuming alcohol. The joys of wine, according to the Islamic tradition, are reserved for heaven alone (McAuliffe 1984: 167–73). If the term *Abrahamic* refers to reverence for myths, heroes, concepts, values, and norms found within the Hebrew Bible, there is nothing Abrahamic about this important aspect of Islamic dietary law.

All three Abrahamic religions display a reverence of sorts for the dietary laws found within the Hebrew Bible. Nevertheless, the food restrictions endorsed by Jewish, Christian, and Islamic authorities differ both one from another and each, in various ways, from the evident meaning of the biblical text itself. These authorities, moreover, highlight such differences as a means of bolstering their own tradition's distinctiveness and disparaging adherents of other traditions. Attention to these divergences enriches our understanding of the evolution that has occurred within Jewish, Christian, and Islamic food practices. To the extent that the Abrahamic paradigm is employed as a means of grouping these traditions together for the purpose of assessing their differences as well as their similarities, it serves a useful function. The paradigm becomes problematic, however, if its orientation toward a point of common origin draws attention away from the different contexts in which each tradition interprets biblical source material, from elements of these traditions that originate outside the Bible, or from the manner in which each tradition differentiates itself from others.

The Food of Foreigners within the Abrahamic Religions

The term *Abrahamic* suggests not only a relationship with the content of the Hebrew Bible but also a sense of kinship that binds Jews, Christians, and Muslims one to another through their common biological or spiritual ancestor. Such a notion, although popular and arguably beneficial in contemporary society, finds little support in the traditional sources of Judaism, Christianity, or Islam. The authorities who spoke for these religions in pre-modern times rarely employed the Abrahamic paradigm when describing the relationships among these traditions, and when they did make reference to Abraham it was to claim the patriarch for themselves alone (Hughes 2012: 34–46). As regulations governing the food of religious foreigners attest, these authorities often did not place the Abrahamic religions within a single category at all. The methods of classification they employed, we will see, emphasize characteristics unrelated to Abrahamic ancestry and serve to reinforce ideas particular to each tradition's approach to claiming superiority over foreigners. (The subject matter surveyed in the present section is addressed in greater detail in Freidenreich 2011.)

Food Offered to Idols

All three Abrahamic religions—but not the Hebrew Bible itself—portray Abraham as an uncompromising monotheistic opponent of idolatry (see the chapter by Reuven Firestone in this volume). Similarly, all three religions strongly prohibit the consumption of food offered in idolatrous sacrifices, even though no such prohibition appears within the text of the Hebrew Bible. The Torah forbids Israelites from offering sacrifices to beings other than God and warns that eating food sacrificed by foreigners will lead Israelites down the path toward idolatry. The condemnation of eating such food, however, first appears in works from the final centuries before the common era. The authors of these works lived in a Hellenistic society in which Jews were invited, encouraged, and on rare occasions required to participate in Graeco-Roman cultic practices. Because these authors understood the consumption of food offered to idols as a paradigmatic expression of apostasy from monotheism (e.g. 2 Macc. 6: 9), they established a severe and unprecedented prohibition against such behaviour. This prohibition manifests itself initially in narratives about heroic figures, much as the stark contrast between monotheism and idolatry finds its expression in new stories about Abraham. The rabbis later expressed this norm through an elaborate set of laws whose stated purpose is to ensure that Jews avoid any sort of engagement with food offered to idols (see further below).

The prohibition against food offered to idols is foundational not only within the Jewish tradition but also within Christianity and Islam. Indeed, the New Testament and Quran alike employ this prohibition as a primary marker of the difference between those who belong to their communities of believers and the broader polytheistic societies from which these communities distinguish themselves. As Paul taught his disciples, 'You cannot partake of the table of the Lord and the table of demons' (1 Cor. 10: 21; cf. Acts 15: 28). Abstention from food offered to idols continued to be a hallmark of Christian practice throughout the period in which Christians lived under pagan rule (Cheung 1999: 165–295), but the practical significance of this taboo receded with the Christianization of the Roman Empire.

The Quran forbids consumption of all meat over which a name other than God's was invoked (Q. 2: 173, 5: 3, 6: 145, 16: 115; cf. the inverse formulation of 6: 121, which forbids meat over which God's name was not invoked). Subsequent works of Islamic law, however, devote little attention to food offered to idols as a practical concern. Rather, these sources address the applicability of this quranic prohibition to the food of Jews and Christians, in the process reflecting distinctly Sunni or Shiʿi conceptions of the relationship between Islam on the one hand and Judaism and Christianity on the other. As we will see, Christian and Jewish authorities also applied prohibitions against food offered to idols to adherents of fellow Abrahamic religions.

Islamic Authorities on the Food of Jews and Christians

On the authority of Quran 5: 5, 'The food of those who were given the Book is permitted to you,' Sunni authorities permit eating meat prepared by Jewish and Christian butchers but forbid meat prepared by other non-Muslims. Sunnis employ this distinction, along with a parallel distinction regarding the marriageability of non-Muslim women, to highlight the affinity between Muslims and People of the Book. The relatively elevated status among non-Muslims that Sunni authorities ascribe to Jews and Christians is the closest pre-modern approximation to the contemporary notion of Abrahamic religions, albeit one that coexists with and reinforces Islamic claims to theological and social superiority over all non-Muslims. According to Sunnis, Islam's affinity with Judaism and Christianity rests not on Abrahamic descent or even on adherence to the monotheism associated with Abraham but rather on the fact that Jews and Christians 'were given the Book', i.e. the Torah or the Gospels. Muslims regard these works as authentic scriptures that point toward the ultimate revelation of the Quran, so respect for People of the Book on account of these scriptures serves to bolster Sunni truth claims.

Sunnis hold that Jews and Christians merit special treatment because of their reverence for an authentic divine revelation, regardless of the fact that they reject God's final revelation and espouse flawed theologies. In particular, Sunni authorities believe that Christians do not conform to Islamic standards of monotheism. This concern underlies debates over whether Christian invocations of Christ run afoul of the quranic prohibition against meat over which a name other than God's was invoked. Nevertheless, Sunni authorities uniformly endorse the general permissibility of Christian meat and, more broadly, all Jewish or Christian foods that do not directly contradict quranic norms. As we noted above with respect to portrayals of Jewish food practices, Sunni authorities apply distinctly Islamic norms when assessing the food of Jews and Christians rather than granting authority to Jewish or Christian norms in their own right: these non-Muslims are not only People of the Book, they are also 'living letters' of Islamic scriptures (Freidenreich 2010a).

Shiʿi authorities also address 'hermeneutical' Jews and Christians but take a very different stance regarding the food of these foreigners and, more fundamentally, the status of Judaism and Christianity. Beginning in the tenth century, works of Shiʿi law pronounce an absolute ban on meat prepared by Jewish and Christian butchers, whether because these non-Muslims invoke a being other than God (e.g. Christ), fail to invoke God, or are incapable of invoking God properly on account of their erroneous beliefs. Concurrently, Shiʿi authorities develop the notion that Jews and Christians are impure and transmit impurity to moist foodstuffs. Shiʿis therefore forbid consumption of most foods associated with Jews and Christians. This prohibition reflects the Shiʿi notion that, contrary to Sunni claims, there is no significant affinity between Muslims and recipients of prior revelations because the latter reject the truth about God and the divine will, found only within the teachings of Shiʿi Islam

(Freidenreich 2011b). In this worldview, which reinforces the exclusivist claims of Shiʿi theology, Judaism and Christianity are no better than Zoroastrianism or idolatry.

In order to accommodate their restrictive policies regarding Jewish and Christian food, Shiʿis offer an exceedingly narrow interpretation of the verse 'The food of those who were given the Book is permitted to you' (Q. 5: 5). Early Shiʿis, like their Sunni counterparts, understood this verse as referring to the meat of Jewish and Christian butchers, an interpretation supported by the verse's literary context. Later Shiʿi authorities, however, asserted that the verse refers exclusively to dry, unprocessed produce such as grains and greens, foods that are not susceptible to contracting impurity. ʿAlī b. al-Ḥusayn al-Sharīf al-Murtaḍā (d. 1044 CE) formulated what became the classic justification for Shiʿi norms governing Jewish and Christian food. Jews and Christians, he declared, are equivalent to polytheists on account of their flawed theologies and are therefore incapable of performing a valid invocation of God when slaughtering an animal. The Quran, moreover, declares that 'the polytheists are impure' (Q. 9: 28), attesting to the literal state intrinsic to those who reject Islamic beliefs. Just as the quranic permission of Jewish and Christian food surely does not encompass the pork of Christians, it similarly excludes impure foods and meat over which no proper invocation was made (Freidenreich 2011b: 75–8). Notice the way in which al-Murtaḍā, like Augustine on the subject of the blood taboo, employs scripture itself to justify a radical departure from that scripture's evident meaning. Notice as well al-Murtaḍā's binary division of humanity into Muslims and polytheists, one that leaves no room for ascribing significance to Jews and Christians as adherents of authentic divine revelations or as descendants of Abraham.

Christian Authorities on the Food of Jews and Muslims

Islamic authorities regard Jewish and Christian reverence for authentic scriptures positively and, through the medium of laws about food, debate whether this reverence suffices to place People of the Book in the same broadly defined camp as Muslims themselves. Christian discourse about the food of Jews, in contrast, reflects a much more negative assessment of Jewish adherence to the Old Testament. As we have seen, Christian authorities regarded observance of biblical dietary law as a sign of the Jews' rejection of Christ and, more generally, their failure to understand the true meaning of scripture. These authorities also feared that Jews, because they base their practices on the Bible, are better able than others to lead unwitting Christians astray. For these reasons, canonical laws and papal edicts from the fourth to the nineteenth centuries forbade Christians to share meals with Jews. Some ecclesiastical authorities, apparently responding to rhetoric that associates Jews and demons, also applied to Jewish food the prohibition against food offered to idols. Tellingly, these authorities permitted Christians to consume non-idolatrous food associated with other non-Christians, in part because pagans and Christians alike eat all kinds of food without making the distinctions mandated by biblical dietary law (Freidenreich 2008: 47–58).

Pre-modern Christian teachings portray Jews as the antithesis of good Christians and therefore enjoin Christians to behave in a manner opposite that of the Jews. Thus, the consumption of foods prohibited in the Hebrew Bible, especially pork, came to constitute a powerful expression of Christian identity. Consider, for example, the following verse from an eighteenth-century Burgundian song:

> While the Jewish law
> Prohibits lard as heretical
> The same is not so in Christian lands.
> Let us eat fresh pork, Let us eat!
> The more we enjoy the piglet
> The better Catholics we become. (Fabre-Vassas 1997: 247)

The shared scriptural heritage of Judaism and Christianity constitutes within traditional Christian literature grounds for avoidance and hostility, not warm sentiments of affinity.

Even though medieval Latin Christian scholars respected the claims of Muslims to be descendants of Abraham, they did not regard Islam as Abrahamic but rather, in many cases, as idolatrous. Indeed, discussions regarding the food of Muslims within medieval Latin canon law uniformly presume that Muslims are pagans and often warn missionaries not to consume the food that Muslims sacrifice to their idols. Although Latin canon lawyers initially deemed other Muslim foods fit for consumption, by analogy to the food of pagans, consensus ultimately swung toward a general prohibition against sharing meals with Muslims. This shift occurred during the late twelfth century in response to the fact that Muslims, like Jews, draw distinctions between permitted and forbidden foods (Freidenreich 2008: 58–70). Discovery of this commonality, which canonists ascribed to the pernicious influence of the Jews, contributed to the ultimate equation within Latin canon law of the legal status of Jews and Muslims (Freidenreich 2011c). Eastern Christian authorities, in contrast, were fully aware that Islam is not idolatrous; several regarded Muslims and their food as superior to other non-Christians, particularly Jews. Even in the West, where Christians associated Muslims with Jews in various ways, Judaism generally retained its status as the primary antithesis of Christianity.

Neither Abrahamic pedigree nor reverence for the Hebrew Bible constitutes grounds for positive portrayals of Judaism or Islam within pre-modern Christian thought. Quite the contrary, Christians highlighted the differences between themselves and others who claimed Abrahamic descent, with food playing an important role in this process. Jewish authorities also dismissed the significance of common ancestry and scriptural heritage, albeit in a different way than their Christian counterparts.

Jewish Authorities on the Food of Christians and Muslims

Unlike their Christian and Islamic counterparts, rabbinic authorities continued to discuss the practical implications of food offered in idolatrous sacrifices long after the decline of Graeco-Roman paganism. This discourse reflects both the rabbinic penchant for the systematic application of legal norms and the wilful interpretation of Gentile practices in light of rabbinic categories rather than those employed by non-Jews themselves. Thus, the founders of rabbinic Judaism (first–third centuries CE) taught that Jews may neither consume nor benefit in other manners from any wine made or even touched by a Gentile, out of concern that the Gentile employed that wine in an idolatrous libation. By extension, Jews also may not consume foods that Gentiles might have prepared using wine or wine vinegar and must take precautions when making, storing, and transporting their own wine to prevent Gentiles from accessing it. These prohibitions, inspired in part by the prominent place of wine libations within Graeco-Roman culture, received their fullest expression in Talmudic literature produced within Christian and Zoroastrian societies in which libational activity was not in fact a part of daily life. Nevertheless, Talmudic rabbis and most of their medieval successors persisted in regarding non-Jews, Christians and Muslims included, as an undifferentiated mass of idolatrous Gentiles whose actual beliefs and practices merit no attention.

Limited exceptions to this generalization can be found within rabbinic literature produced in the Islamic world. Authorities from ninth- to eleventh-century Babylonia (Iraq) relaxed the prohibition against deriving benefit from Jewish wine touched by Muslims on the grounds that Muslims do not offer wine libations as part of their purportedly idolatrous worship. Moses Maimonides (d. 1204) went further, justifying this relaxation of Talmudic laws on the grounds that Muslims are not idolaters at all (*Mishneh Torah, Hil. Ma'akhalot Asurot* 10.7–8; see Freidenreich 2012b: 151–6). In another context, namely the commandment of circumcision, Maimonides even ascribes normative significance to the fact that Muslims are descendants of Abraham (*Hil. Melakhim* 10.7–8; see Kasher 1995). This, however, is the farthest any pre-modern rabbinic authority goes in embracing Abrahamic descent as a meaningful criterion for classifying religious communities, and Maimonides himself affirms the classical rabbinic assertion that descendants of Ishmael do not qualify as being of 'Abraham's seed' (*Hil. Nedarim* 9.21–2). Maimonides, moreover, pointedly defines Christians as idolaters irrespective of their reverence for the Bible. Maimonides also emphasizes the constraints of the elevated status he ascribes to Islam: even though Jews may benefit from wine touched by Muslims, they still may not drink such wine. His respect for Islamic monotheism notwithstanding, Maimonides did not espouse an Abrahamic paradigm for conceptualizing the relationship between Jews, Christians, and Muslims.

Rabbis active in the Islamic world ascribed a limited degree of normative significance to Islamic beliefs and practices when determining the legal status of wine associated with Muslims. The same cannot be said regarding rabbis active in medieval Christian Europe. These authorities, who draw no distinctions among different types of Gentiles, sidestep the question of whether Christianity is idolatrous by redefining the purpose of the prohibition against Gentile wine. Rather than protecting Jews from inadvertent association with idolatry, this prohibition comes to be understood as preventing the kind of social intimacy that might result in mixed marriages (Soloveitchik 2003:

137–40). This rationale also appears within the Babylonian Talmud as a justification for prohibitions against bread baked by Gentiles (Freidenreich 2012a) and certain types of shared meals with Gentiles. Medieval authorities explained traditional prohibitions against foods cooked by Gentiles in light of concern about mixed marriages as well. In addition to restrictions designed to limit social interaction, rabbinic law also contains regulations forbidding Gentile foods that are likely to contain non-kosher ingredients. All of these rules apply equally regardless of whether the Gentile in question is Christian, Muslim, pagan, or otherwise. Indeed, rabbinic discourse about the food of Gentiles reinforces a binary worldview that draws no distinctions among non-Jews, irrespective of their beliefs, scriptural commitments, or descent. This worldview bolsters the traditional conception of the Jewish people as uniquely significant.

We saw in the first half of this chapter that the conception of a common scripture at the foundation of all three Abrahamic traditions is overly simplistic and therefore misleading. None of the pre-modern sources surveyed in the second half of the chapter express the sense of kinship among Jews, Christians, and Muslims implied by the term *Abrahamic* either. Indeed, with the exception of Sunnis, these authorities do not even place Judaism, Christianity, and Islam within a single category. These religions may all anathematize idolatry, but that does not prevent their members from asserting that adherents of other Abrahamic traditions are themselves idolaters or functional equivalents. The Sunni conception of People of the Book, moreover, differs fundamentally from the contemporary notion of Abrahamic religions because it is situated within a hierarchical framework and serves to bolster Sunni claims to supersession and superiority.

In short, this survey of Jewish, Christian, and Islamic dietary law has found no recognition within pre-modern sources of the biblical or familial affinities implied by the contemporary term *Abrahamic*. This does not mean, however, that the term itself is necessarily inappropriate when employed by historians of religion. Pre-modern Jews, Christians, and Muslims, after all, did not employ a common method of classifying humanity that scholars might draw upon instead of using contemporary paradigms. The Sunni conception of People of the Book, for example, found no traction even among Jewish and Christian jurists who internalized other aspects of Islamic theology and law (Freidenreich 2012b: 156–60). This and other pre-modern conceptions, moreover, further confessional goals at odds with those associated with the academic study of religion.

We have seen that much can be learned through the juxtaposition of Judaism, Christianity, and Islam. The term *Abrahamic* offers a convenient label for this juxtaposition even though the substantive meaning associated with this term does not resonate with pre-modern sources. Indeed, because the concept of Abrahamic religions does not derive from these sources, use of this concept offers the opportunity to reflect critically on the conceptions that underlie both traditional and contemporary approaches to describing the relationship between self and other. The term *Abrahamic* is useful precisely because it does not conform to pre-modern sources, so long as the scholars who employ it do not presume that these sources acknowledge the scriptural or familial affinities implied by this term.

References

Barclay, J. M. G. 1996. 'Do We Undermine the Law? A Study of Romans 14: 1–15: 6'. In J. D. G. Dunn, ed., *Paul and the Mosaic Law*. Tübingen: Mohr, 287–308.

Barclay, J. M. G. 1998. 'Who was Considered an Apostate in the Jewish Diaspora?' In G. N. Stanton and G. G. Stroumsa, eds, *Tolerance and Intolerance in Early Judaism and Christianity*. Cambridge: Cambridge University Press, 80–98.

Broshi, M. 1984. 'Wine in Ancient Palestine: Introductory Notes'. *Israel Museum Journal*, 3: 21–42.

Cheung, A. T. 1999. *Idol Food in Corinth: Jewish Background and Pauline Legacy*. Sheffield: Sheffield Academic Press.

Cohen, J. 1999. *Living Letters of the Law: Ideas of the Jew in Medieval Christianity*. Berkeley: University of California Press.

Cook, M. 1986. 'Early Islamic Dietary Law'. *Jerusalem Studies in Arabic and Islam*, 7: 217–77.

Fabre-Vassas, C. 1997. *The Singular Beast: Jews, Christians, and the Pig*, trans. C. Volk. New York: Columbia University Press.

Frank, D. 2004. *Search Scripture Well: Karaite Exegetes and the Origins of Jewish Bible Commentary in the Islamic East*. Leiden: Brill.

Freidenreich, D. M. 2008. 'Sharing Meals with Non-Christians in Canon Law Commentaries, circa 1160–1260: A Case Study in Legal Development'. *Medieval Encounters* 14: 41–77.

Freidenreich, D. M. 2010a. 'Five Questions about Non-Muslim Meat: Toward a New Appreciation of Ibn Qayyim al-Ǧawziyyah's Contribution to Islamic Law'. In C. Bori and L. Holtzman, eds, *Re-evaluating Ibn Qayyim al-Ǧawziyyah's Literary Stature: Religious and Historical Issues. Oriente moderno* 90: 85–104.

Freidenreich, D. M. 2010b. 'Holiness and Impurity in the Torah and the Quran: Differences within a Common Typology'. *Comparative Islamic Studies* 6 (1–2): 5–22.

Freidenreich, D. M. 2011a. *Foreigners and their Food: Constructing Otherness in Jewish, Christian, and Islamic Law*. Berkeley: University of California Press.

Freidenreich, D. M. 2011b. 'The Implications of Unbelief: Tracing the Emergence of Distinctively Shiʿi Notions Regarding the Food and Impurity of Non-Muslims'. *Islamic Law and Society* 18: 53–84.

Freidenreich, D. M. 2011c. 'Muslims in Western Canon Law, 1000–1500'. In D. Thomas et al., eds, *Christian–Muslim Relations: A Bibliographic History*, vol. 3. Leiden: Brill, 41–68.

Freidenreich, D. M. 2012a. 'Contextualizing Bread: An Analysis of Talmudic Discourse in Light of Christian and Islamic Counterparts'. *Journal of the American Academy of Religion* 80: 411–33.

Freidenreich, D. M. 2012b. 'Fusion Cooking in an Islamic Milieu: Jewish and Christian Jurists on Food Associated with Foreigners'. In D. M. Freidenreich and M. Goldstein, eds, *Beyond Religious Borders: Interaction and Intellectual Exchange in the Medieval Islamic World*. Philadelphia: University of Pennsylvania Press, 144–60.

Haider, N. 2013. 'Contesting Intoxication: Early Juristic Debates over the Lawfulness of Alcoholic Beverages'. *Islamic Law and Society* 20 (1–2): 48–89.

Haran, M. 1979. 'Seething a Kid in its Mother's Milk'. *Journal of Jewish Studies* 30: 23–35.

Hughes, A. 2012. *Abrahamic Religions: On the Uses and Abuses of History*. New York: Oxford University Press.

Kasher, H. 1995. 'Maimonides' View of Circumcision as a Factor Uniting the Jewish and Muslim Communities'. In R. L. Nettler, ed., *Medieval and Modern Perspectives on Muslim-Jewish Relations*. Luxembourg: Harwood, 103–8.

Kraemer, D. C. 2007. *Jewish Eating and Identity through the Ages*. London: Routledge.

Kueny, K. 2001. *The Rhetoric of Sobriety: Wine in Early Islam*. Albany, NY: State University of New York Press.

McAuliffe, J. D. 1984. 'The Wines of Earth and Paradise: Qurʾānic Proscriptions and Promises'. In R. M. Savory and D. A. Agius, eds, *Logos Islamikos: Studia Islamica in honorem Georgii Michaelis Wickens*. Toronto: Pontifical Institute of Mediaeval Studies: 159–74.

McGowan, A. 1999. *Ascetic Eucharists: Food and Drink in Early Christian Ritual Meals*. Oxford: Clarendon Press.

Maghen, Z. 2006. *After Hardship Cometh Ease: The Jews as Backdrop for Muslim Moderation*. Berlin: De Gruyter.

Milgrom, J. 1991. *Leviticus 1–16: A New Translation with Introduction and Commentary*. Anchor Bible. New York: Doubleday.

Novak, D. 1983. *The Image of the Non-Jew in Judaism: An Historical and Constructive Study of the Noahide Laws*. New York: E. Mellen.

Räisänen, H. 1982. 'Jesus and the Food Laws: Reflections on Mark 7.15'. *Journal for the Study of the New Testament* 16: 79–100.

Rosenblum, J. D. 2010. *Food and Identity in Early Rabbinic Judaism*. Cambridge: Cambridge University Press.

Rustow, M. 2008. *Heresy and the Politics of Community: The Jews of the Fatimid Caliphate*. Ithaca, NY: Cornell University Press.

Smith, D. E. 2003. *From Symposium to Eucharist: The Banquet in the Early Christian World*. Minneapolis: Fortress.

Smith, W. C. 1993. *What is Scripture? A Comparative Approach*. London: SCM.

Soloveitchik, H. 2003. *Yeinam: Saḥar be-yeinam shel goyim ʿal gilgulah shel halakhah be-ʿolam ha-maʿaseh*. Tel Aviv: ʿAlma.

Vega, A. C. 1941. 'Una herejia judaizante del siglo VIII en España'. *La ciudad de Dios* 153: 57–100.

CHAPTER 26

LIFE-CYCLE RITES OF PASSAGE

HARVEY E. GOLDBERG

A systematic concern with the life cycle of individuals, as an organizing theme in itself, was not part of the Abrahamic religions during their formative stages.[1] The emergence of this focus is a recent development in research. This is not to say that the events surrounding birth, marriage, and death were unimportant or went unnoticed. They were omnipresent and also served as vehicles for central religious ideas and symbols. But the sequential life course of individuals was not a prominent axis along which major religious categorization and discourse took shape.

Brief examples may be given from each religion. The commandments in the Hebrew Bible, addressed to both the collective and to individuals, came to be called *miẓvot* (sg. *miẓvah*). This term was also applied to some rituals ordained later in rabbinical culture. Within the life progression of Jews, male circumcision is the only ritual that appears as a commandment in the Pentateuch. Marriage is often mentioned in the Hebrew Bible (*Tanakh*), but a set of prescribed marriage rites does not appear, even though norm-setting rabbinic literature later used the Tanakh as a source of proof texts. The bar mitzvah, the Jewish coming-of-age ceremony, first emerged only in the late Middle Ages in Europe. Circumcision, bar mitzvah, and marriage, discussed in terms of rabbinic law (*halakhah*), each appear under a different *halakhic* subcategory established in the fourteenth-century code called *Arbaʿah Ṭurim* (Four Columns), which still forms a basic framework for discussing rabbinic law and elaborating it.

Christianity crystallized its central ritual mode in the sacraments. The notion implies an external visible gesture—by a person ordained to do so—that is a sign of divine grace imparted to individuals. Some sacraments are characteristic of different life stages, and Catholicism came to formulate Seven Sacraments. The concept is also central to other forms of ancient Christianity, even with their doctrinal and ritual

[1] Thanks are due to Wasfi Kailani, David Satran, and Gillian Feeley-Harnik for the opportunity of discussing some of the issues in this chapter.

differences (Markschies 1999). Protestant denominations, however, limited or abandoned the notion of sacrament. It is possible to view the liturgical calendar of Christianity as built around the life-progression of Christ, but this does not provide the historical key to understanding the sacraments. The notion and practice of the first sacrament, baptism—an act of purification by water—was present from the beginning but not inherently linked to childhood. Originally, it was the mode by which people converted to Christianity; more people became Christian in this manner than by being brought up and educated in the religion. Regular infant baptism emerged in the early Middle Ages and its status as a Catholic sacrament was established later in the medieval period. Marriage became a sacrament in the sixteenth century, and other Catholic sacraments—Penance and ordination into a Holy Order—are not formally linked to a stage in life.

In Islam, the foundational text—the Quran—is centred on a single individual, Muhammad, who is the source of authority because of the divine revelations he received. Traditions relating to the pronouncements and deeds of Muhammad emerged in succeeding generations and constitute the *ḥadīth*. Also appearing after Muhammad's life was the formulation of Islam and the quranic message as coalescing in five 'Pillars' (*arkān*), the first of which—the *shahāda*—was declaring belief in a singular Allah and that Muhammad was his prophet. The other *arkān* form major axes providing direction and guidance for daily life. The range of actions by Muslims that relate to quranic and post-quranic sources are comprehended by another fivefold categorization: deeds that are obligatory (*farḍ*), recommended, indifferent, reprehensible, or forbidden. The juridical literature discussing these is the *fiqh*; Frederick Denny notes (1985: 64) that '*fiqh* books always begin with ritual duties by considering the four "Pillars"' that follow upon the *shahāda*. One practice universally accepted by Muslims, and discussed in *fiqh* while not mentioned in the Quran, is male circumcision. Because no canonical source specifies the details of its practice, there exists significant variation within the Muslim world as to when it is carried out, from seven days until close to puberty and even close to marriage. The only obligatory act included in the five Pillars with a loose connection to a life stage is the pilgrimage to Mecca. Often Muslims who attained the economic ability to do so would fulfil this once in their lifetime, during their later years. With the ease of modern travel, ḥajj is now often performed earlier in life, and sometimes more than once.

Given the diffuse nature of the subject, the present chapter outlining an approach to the systematic examination of life-cycle rituals in Abrahamic religions will consist of several dimensions. It first identifies challenges presented by the emergence of the notion of 'ritual', in which the observation of actual practice is a significant component in the context of disciplines that have given primacy to the study of texts and to philological methods. A further conceptual dilemma discussed is the conceptual 'location' of life-cycle rituals, which frequently are embedded in multidimensional social milieux and include strands of meaning that are relevant both to the individual and the collective. Interaction among the three Abrahamic traditions presents other hurdles to mount in formulating productive conceptual paths. These have to be negotiated both from a historical-diachronic perspective and through comparisons in which historical documentation and the results of more recent ethnography are placed side by side. One part of this chapter considers the former emphasis, with the comparative-analytic perspective highlighted in the subsequent section. A concluding discussion will show how life-cycle events can be critical indicators of contemporary cultural and socio-political processes, even as they reflect an augmented sense and recognition of the single self.

Texts, the Study of Rituals, and Life-Cycle Events

From the point of view of modern academic scholarship, the category of 'ritual' in general was not a major theme in the study of Abrahamic religions, and reflected various biases when it was applied. Ritual, as a fairly recent analytic category, did receive emphasis in the disciplines of anthropology, which focused on 'tribal' societies that came into European purview beginning in the sixteenth century, and folklore, whose subject originally was the rural members of European society. Various early modern theories linking the newly discovered inhabitants of the New World to the Israelites, or Jews of antiquity, may be connected to the discovery among them of rituals and taboos that brought to mind some of the rules in the Pentateuch. The very concept of 'ritual', applied to non-utilitarian symbolic gestures in a variety of societies, may have a Eurocentric bias, anchored in developments such as the Reformation (Asad 1993: 55–79). Before the Reformation, the notion of ritual was more specifically linked to monastic life within Catholicism. Andrew Buckser (2008: 414) has noted that anthropological studies of Christian societies and ritual have mostly been trained on Catholic communities rather than on Protestant ones, as if the latter were more 'normal' or 'rational', rather than symbolic. Scholarship on Islam relevant to ritual has privileged texts that outline religious obligations rather than accounts of ritual action. Islam's decentralized structure of authority and its broad geographic spread, often led to the non-productive question of what is 'really Islamic'. Apart from a few works of elaborate description such as Edward Lane's *Manners and Customs of the Modern Egyptians* (1954 [1860]), or Edward Westermarck's *Ritual and Belief in Morocco* (1926), studies that provide ample accounts of actual ritual behaviour have been relatively rare until recent decades. There still exists an unclear and uneasy relationship between ethnography and textualized approaches to ritual, even when carried out by anthropologists (Hammoudi 2009).

Another set of questions, based on partial similarities in practice and in terminology, enquires into historical precedent and influence. Jewish practice served as a reference point for Christianity, and both these religions were potential background factors for Islam. Also, once they began to flourish, the latter religions could react upon the ideas and praxis of the earlier ones. The identification of Jewish precedents for Islamic ritual behaviour and prayer constitutes one attempt along these lines. While some important historical questions are involved, a focus that only looks at origins, and ignores practice and meaning as they evolve, misses the emergent and dynamic side of rituals in a new religious milieu. Descriptions and discussions of the ritual behaviour of Jews also were coloured by normative notions. Christian Hebraists in early modern Europe, who paid attention to contemporary Jewish communities, at times did not distinguish between what they observed in synagogues and what appeared in Jewish texts (Deutsch 2001). Within Judaism arose a category of religious sanctioned custom, *minhag*, which incorporated religious practice not strictly derived from earlier *halakhic* rules. Only recently have there been attempts to formulate *halakhah* in terms of a general approach to ritual (Gruenwald 2003; Swartz 2011).

The absence of an explicit focus on ritual is also evident with regard to life-cycle transitions and events. These are often interwoven with the major concepts and practices in Abrahamic religions, but the nature of the connection has varied greatly over time and place. The links between textual-based principles and local life-cycle practices are loose, contingent, and at times problematic. Highlighting the individual and his or her whole life trajectory as a systematic locus of discourse on rituals is a feature of modernity and more recently, postmodernity. It has been abetted by the notion of *rites de passage* introduced by Arnold Van Gennep into scholarly literature in 1909 (Van Gennep 1960), which has passed into popular understanding, but is still a developing topic that presents challenges to both conceptualization and empirical research.

The gap between sanctified texts and actual practices linked to life-cycle events has several types of implications. Some are parallel in the three Abrahamic religions while others reflect variation in structures of authority in the different traditions. A basic source of tension is the historical spread of these religions to new regions and the concomitant encounter with pre-existing customs and beliefs. Where these appeared to run counter to accepted religious ideas and behaviour, the formal reactions to them have reflected a range of positions that include overlooking variance, reinterpreting existing practices in terms of religiously acceptable norms, or direct attempts to extirpate practices that are deemed deviant.

For example, the Jewish custom of breaking a glass as part of a marriage ceremony is first documented in twelfth-century Europe. Jacob Lauterbach (1925) suggested that the practice had existed long before, but rabbis refrained from writing about it because of its link to ideas and gestures regarding demons. It became a matter of explicit discussion once an explanation arose (mourning for the destroyed Temple in Jerusalem) that linked it to normative tradition. Within Catholicism, in the eighteenth century, a debate arose as to how to understand rites of ancestor worship in Chinese culture. Jesuit missionaries argued that they were social ceremonies and hence not at odds with Catholic doctrine and thus did not have to be abandoned. Dominicans took the position that there was a direct clash between the practice and established doctrine. Islamic societies today differ widely in the form of celebration for the same rite according to their relation to the Salafiyya movement. Countries that are less influenced by Salafi ideology, like Indonesia or Morocco, are more characterized by long and elaborate celebrations for circumcision or for naming a child than are the Gulf states, which are strongly affected by Salafism. Within all historical settings, the outcome of preaching and pressure by religious authorities has not always corresponded with their original intentions.

The scholarly study of rites of passage from the perspective of modern disciplines has also suffered from the gap between rites as normative prescriptions and the availability of data on concrete examples of observance. The Abrahamic religions are viewed as growing out of foundational texts, and textual-philological study became the major method of charting their development. This relegated direct observation, or even historical records, of actual practice to a secondary status for several reasons. First, the nineteenth-century paradigm of scholarship that privileged viewing human matters in terms of history and evolution viewed the tracing of origins as a major key to understanding religion. Statements that were normative and formative were assumed to be more significant than evidence or hints of everyday practice. Second, as indicated, the spread of Christianity and Islam to regions far beyond their original settings made the task of comprehending the range of variation in practice so immense, that focusing on the kernel of rituals, as they were discussed in authoritative texts, was an understandable default option. A corollary was the attitude that information gained from 'ordinary' followers of a religious tradition was secondary, and might reflect 'external' influences, in comparison to the writings and insights of literati. Third, as the scholarly principles that shaped anthropology and folklore studies in the nineteenth and twentieth centuries took shape, a perspective emerged that customs and rituals were better understood through new theoretical lenses, rather than by following explanations offered by 'native' practitioners. This was articulated, among others, by William Robertson Smith (1914: 16–18) in his studies of ancient Israel and Islam that drew upon the anthropology of his day, by Franz Boas (1916: 229–30) in his work on native North American groups that left no literary storehouse, and is implicit in the theoretical emphasis of Van Gennep (1960) on the classification of rites in his discussion of rites of passage based mostly on materials from what he calls 'semi-civilized' societies. Van Gennep did, however, also relate to rituals within Christianity, Islam, and Judaism. More recently, anthropology began consider 'native exegesis' as an important source of insights.

Only in the mid-twentieth century did there emerge a cumulative thrust, attempting to link ritual practices observed by anthropologists in agricultural villages or small towns to the central textual-based features of world religions. Robert Redfield, who conducted fieldwork in several locales in Mexico, formulated the notion of a 'Great Tradition' in comparison to a 'Little Tradition' in order to analyse the way that Catholicism was expressed concretely in specific settings, including communities in which aspects of pre-Columbian culture and religion were still vibrant. One of his studies, in a village where daily communication was in a Mayan language (Redfield and Rojas 1962), describes how the formal name of a child, announced at baptism, was taken from a calendar hanging in a local church, which provided saints' names corresponding to dates of birth. Often, however, that name was not used in everyday interaction. An analysis of a funeral in Java by Clifford Geertz (1973: 142–69) provided a detailed example of how Islam was interwoven with local traditions in Indonesia. Other researchers in Islamic settings provided analyses that emphasized the distinction between Islamic and non-Islamic traditions. On the other hand, Nadia Abu-Zahra (1997) has argued that often these studies do not grasp the extent to which textually based Islam has penetrated the consciousness and ritual practices of unschooled members of Muslim societies, including women. The demographic upheavals that changed the face of world Jewry in the nineteenth and twentieth centuries meant that no parallel ethnographic field studies took place in functioning 'traditional' Jewish communities. However, by the end of the twentieth century, anthropological perspectives appeared in research into cultural history (*mentalités*). Two studies of Ashkenazi Jewry, one relating to the Middle Ages (Marcus 1996) and the second to the early modern period (Goldberg 1996), illustrate this with regard to rituals marking initiation into schooling in the first case, and illness, death, burial, and mourning in the second.

Locating Life-Cycle Events

Utilizing the 'life cycle' as a criterion for delineating or classifying rites presents challenges in terms of ritual contexts within specific traditions, and also from the perspective of comparative analysis. Taking the biological life trajectory as a starting point provides only partial guidelines. Van Gennep (1960: 3) was aware that 'man's life resembles nature', and that individuals and societies do not 'stand independent' from natural periodicity. Yet he highlighted extensive variation within human societies even as he argued that basic structural principles repeated themselves. Van Gennep likewise recognized that certain concrete acts or ritual sequences could be rites of passage from one point of view, while serving other social purposes as well. Therefore strict rubrics and classification are only partially helpful, and a broad horizon of ritual activities must be purveyed in seeking to identify life-cycle rituals.

For example, the Abrahamic religions do not stress birth itself as a focus of ritual activity, while there is every reason to assume that the activities of mothers, attending relatives and neighbours, and midwives were peppered with ritual gestures in historic societies (Patai 1983; Granqvist 1947). The Tanakh dictates the obligatory act of male circumcision eight days after birth. While not appearing in the biblical text as part of the prescription, circumcision also became the occasion for naming a child, and the first historically identifiable incident appears in the New Testament (Luke 1: 59). The baptism of infants (male and female) became widely established in Christianity, but the original kernel of the ritual had to do with the conversion of adults. In Islam, according to some *ḥadīths*, on the first day after birth, the *adhān* (call to prayer) is to be whispered into the newborn's right ear as the first sound it hears and the *ṣalat iqāma* (a second call that initiates prayer) is recited in the left ear. Local practice of this custom varied in detail, and may have been perceived locally as an act that wards off evil (Lane 1954: 53), but indicates, as in the other religions, a stress on early initiation of the individual into a collective and a tradition, beyond the process of birth itself.

Consequently the cumulative inculcation of a religious culture, in itself, becomes a factor shaping the life cycle. Teaching Jewish male children to master the text of the Hebrew Bible has taken place since antiquity, while the bar mitzvah ceremony, marking the culmination of early education and the adult obligation to fulfil the commandments from the age of 13 (see below), crystallized in the Middle Ages in Europe and consequently has spread elsewhere. Confirmation, in Christianity, became designated as a sacrament in Catholicism, and initially was to follow soon upon baptism. Even though the earlier sacrament was defined as a transformative and irreversible event, with time Confirmation was shifted to later years and associated with a more mature and conscious engagement of the individual with the presence of the Holy Spirit. In some Protestant denominations, where confirmation is not viewed as a sacrament, it may signal adult incorporation into a congregation. In several Islamic settings in Asia there are rituals to accompany a male child when he first begins to learn to recite the Quran, while no precise age is specified. One *ḥadīth* recommends the age of 7 years for children—both boys and girls—to begin fasting a few days during Ramadan, and extending the number of days until they observe the full fast at adulthood. From a comparative perspective, the emergence of a formal bar mitzvah transition at a precisely defined age represents the coalescence of textual exegesis with a social-historical process that may provide an analytic model for historical developments in other traditions (Weinstein 1994; Marcus 1996: 119–26).

The identification of a 'life cycle' may thus emerge through a focus on other aspects of ritual life. A central Jewish prayer sanctifying God—the *qaddish*—that appears repetitively in the liturgy has become firmly associated with memorializing departed relatives even though there is no mention of death in it. In another realm, the minor festival of *Lag Baʿomer*—thirty-three days after Passover—is the occasion, for some ultraorthodox Ashkenazim, of giving a 3-year-old boy his first haircut and introducing him to the study of Torah (Bilu 2003). Both the springtime custom of Easter eggs which is assigned formal symbolism linked to Christ's resurrection, and the autumn celebration of Halloween—the eve of All Saints' Day, have evolved to shape practices appropriate to children which, in some settings, take on features of a rite of passage (Rogers 2002: 37–8). In Tunisia, community rituals and prayers that are suffused with Islamic content and which are aimed at ending drought, designate specific and distinct roles both to young boys studying in a quranic school and to young girls who engage in gestures of supplication, some of which may pre-date Islam. Along with the main purpose of this cycle of rain-rituals, Abu-Zahra (1997: 27–32) perceives rites of passage embedded within them.

The intertwining of individual experiences and collective symbols, and, indeed, the mobilization of the former to the benefit of the latter, has been discerned in different forms in the three Abrahamic religions. Pardes (2000) has analysed the account of the emergence of the 'nation' in ancient Israel, in terms of the growth and maturity of an individual, passing through ritual phases. As noted, it is possible to view the Christian liturgical calendar as built around the life-trajectory of Jesus. The accumulative traditions in *ḥadith*, adding many details of practice not made explicit in the Quran, may be viewed as comprising an authoritative ritual biography of Muhammad. These long-accepted modes of common practice and shared symbolization mitigate the valorization of individual experience vis-à-vis prescribed authority and received tradition.

For the most part, the modern study of ritual has taken social units as a starting point, but understanding group processes always brings up the place of individuals, and the enquiry into private behaviour and experience inevitably leads to a consideration of shared activities and meaning. While the collective significance and impact of rituals in terms of time and space often appears as a distinct topic from that of ritual and the single body (normally conceived as a 'private' realm in western terms), all three factors are co-extant 'environments' within which ritual action flows and leaves an imprint, yielding dialogic interfaces between group and individual processes. For example, a focus on the individual human organism cannot be fully separated from mate-selection and reproduction which insert persons into wider social matrices. At the same time, each of these three 'environments' has its own rhythm that may have links to the other two, but never thoroughly overlap with them. There thus appear a variety of partial connections within rituals between the individual and the social in terms of both functionality and cultural meaning, in which frameworks of time and space interlock with the progression of individual life events.

In the Book of Exodus (ch. 12), the month in which the events establishing Passover take place is explicitly designated as the beginning of the Hebrew year. In the same textual field, participation in the Paschal sacrifice is made dependent on a male having undergone circumcision. Here, as in the verses ordaining circumcision in Genesis 17, the possibility of 'outsider' individual adults joining the Israelite collective is envisioned, even while the overall narrative underlines familial and 'national' continuity. The Gospels are deeply sensitive to the significance of Passover, while taking its ritual symbols in new directions (including some opposite to the older ones), and thus provide a performative basis for a religious system that challenged family ties and stressed individual faith (Feeley-Harnik 1994). Some have viewed developments within Christianity in late antiquity as shifting the locus of holiness from place to person (Swartz 2011: 297). This did not fully eliminate elements of place from the schemata of holiness, as seen in the symbolic centrality of 'Rome', Crusades to the Holy Land, or pilgrimages to the shrines of saints. The first of Islam's five Pillars, the confession of faith—*shahāda*—underlines personal commitment, while two other Pillars—prayer (*ṣalāt*) and ḥajj to Mecca—are oriented toward, and give shape to, both place and time (Denny 1985: 71–4). The Ramadan fast is calendar dependent as well, and also demands discipline over the body. Talal Asad (1993: 125–57) has stressed discipline in regard to rites of monastic life characterizing medieval Christianity, while mystical ritual regimes in all the Abrahamic religions contribute to the sacralization of individual persons. While imbuing selected persons with special religious virtuosity and sometimes social power, one long-term implication of mystical traditions may be the emergence of models for the valuation of all individuals, as Turner and Turner (1978) have argued with reference to Christian pilgrimage (see Goldberg 1990b regarding Judaism).

Interaction among Traditions

The image of a single individual—Abraham—stands at the genealogical apex of the three religions. The narrative surrounding him in the Tanakh feeds into later developments in all of them, both in terms of Abraham's special relationship with God and with regard to central rituals. Viewing the traditions together does not reveal easily defined lines of influence, but rather overlapping streams of significance including meanings that are at times directly opposed to one another. The figure of Abraham is thus shared and constitutes a platform for continuity, but is also a taking-off point of contention. Genesis 17 ordains circumcision for Abraham and for his descendants while linking this 'sign' to a promise of biological continuity. Reproduction within the family became a basic mechanism of continuity within rabbinic Judaism, while early Christianity turned to the incorporation of Gentiles as a major mode of recruitment. The downplaying of circumcision in Paul and subsequent sources goes hand in hand with this emphasis, as exemplified in Galatians 3: 7 and elsewhere, claiming that faith includes a person within the 'children of Abraham'. The close Tanakhic connection between circumcision and the Passover sacrifice (Exod. 12: 48; Josh. 5) is similarly relegated to a background position within Christianity, in comparison to the foregrounding of the image of Jesus as a Paschal lamb. Another 'Old Testament' trope of Jesus' crucifixion, carried forward with perhaps less emphasis, is Abraham's near-sacrifice of Isaac insofar as even its non-occurrence may foreshadow a father bringing about the death of his son. When comparing the evolution of Jewish and Christian traditions, it might be noted that Abraham's 'binding' of Isaac is not central to Passover symbolism, but is a repeated theme at the other pole of the Jewish liturgical year: the New Year Convocation and the Day of Atonement in the autumn.

Abraham—Ibrāhīm in Arabic—also may be viewed as the first Muslim. The Quran portrays him as establishing monotheistic worship in connection with the Kaʿba in Mecca and later tradition assigns a significant role to ʾIsmāʿīl in this regard. From this perspective, Muhammad may be perceived as restoring aspects of Allah's earlier revelation that had waned in impact or had been distorted. As stated, circumcision is taken for granted among Muslims, and considered 'recommended' in several schools, even though not mentioned in the Quran, while other aspects of the traditions surrounding Ibrāhīm, in relation to ʾIsmāʿīl, are assigned different highlighting vis-à-vis Judaism. It is has been widely accepted among Muslims that Ibrāhīm's almost-sacrificed son was ʾIsmāʿīl rather than Isaac (Lane 1954: 95), but early sources are unclear on the matter (Paret 1990). This varying and unclear genealogical perspective notwithstanding, another significant Islamic tradition is Ibrāhīm's connection to Hagar/Hājar, ʾIsmāʿīl's mother, in particular the account of her banishment to the desert (Gen. 16; Hagar does not appear in the Quran). Islam views the barren place that the mother and son reached, where divine intervention saved ʾIsmāʿīl from death, as the future location of the ḥajj. This quranic portrayal and later elaboration not only links Ibrāhīm to the Pillar of pilgrimage to Mecca, but provides a narrative matrix for the prime spatial axis of routine rituals: daily prayer, the direction for placing the head of a corpse during burial, and (according to widespread practice), the direction faced when slaughtering a beast. More recently, the attention tradition pays to Hagar has provided a model and stimulus for female participants in the ḥajj (Hammoudi 2009).

The overlapping of traditions, and the effort to mark distinction vis-à-vis the other religion while relating to ancient sources, is not only a matter of the early stages in the Abrahamic religions but may be viewed as an ongoing process, taking myriad shapes in different historical circumstances. A ceremony of childhood initiation into the study of Torah, among Ashkenazi Jews in the Middle Ages, appears in pictorial representation that suggests that the 'imbibing' of Torah was viewed in polemic counterpoint to the image of infant Jesus sucking at the breast of Mary (Marcus 1996: 91–4). A more recent instance of interaction is provided by a Muslim in twentieth-century Libya describing the local practice of circumcision and indicating that there are different customs as to when it is performed. Demonstrating some general familiarity with Jewish life but also a lack of precision, he states that some Muslims circumcise on the fortieth day, but that most, in order to be distinguished from the Jews, do so from the second to the seventh year (Goldberg 1990a: 91). His Tripolitan dialect echoes the Islamic principle of *khālifūhum*—do not act as do the people of the Book (Vajda 1960). One concrete context of mutual contact between groups on ritual occasions is supplied by an account of Jewish weddings in Jerba, Tunisia, in recent times, where Muslim guests might be present at festivities in the course of the preparatory days of celebration, but were absent during the culminating evening in which a rabbi guides the steps of the formal marriage and musicians play traditional hymns (Valensi 1989). There are also occasional references to rural settings where a Jewish circumciser (*mohel*) might be called upon to carry out the procedure on Muslim children (Marx 1966). The Emancipation of Jews in Europe created new social circumstances and cultural contexts. Historically, Christian baptism, applied to men and women, was a rite that stood in stark contrast to the Jewish circumcision of males. Yet some Jews in modern France adopted the term *baptême* as a translation of the circumcision. In German-speaking regions, early in the nineteenth century, there was a direct borrowing of the notion of 'confirmation' from Catholicism to develop a synagogue ritual attuned to the eve of adulthood, in distinction from the by-then conventional bar mitzvah at the age of 13.

More often than not, we lack precise micro-historical or ethnographic information that demonstrates the processes of cultural interaction, which might entail borrowing, reinterpretation, intentional distancing of practice, or misrecognizing ritual influence. It is therefore frequently a matter of speculation whether similarities, or structured differences, reflect adherence to ancient norms, the impact of the environment, independent cultural innovation, or some combination of these factors. Rather than treating these as firmly distinct categories in each historical instance, the following discussion will identify several issues relevant to the shaping and performance of life-cycle rituals, offering examples from the three Abrahamic religions that may be instructive to compare, and even be mutually illuminating, without seeking to determine historical primacy or direction of influence. The working assumption is that the grasp of process must take an important analytic place alongside attempts to reach definite historical assignation.

Lines of Comparative Analysis

Ritual actions, whether brief and low-keyed or prolonged and dramatic, need to be seen in terms of the flow of life as they are experienced in particular cultural matrices. The Babylonian Talmud (*Brakhot* 58b) mandates a blessing—*Blessed be the reviver of the dead*—that is appropriate to recite when meeting a person whom one has not seen for over a year. In both Europe and the Middle East, traditional Jews incorporated the blessing into the flow of normal speech. Ethnographic evidence from a Muslim Arab village near Bethlehem in the twentieth century shows a range of standard responses to what Hilma Granqvist calls the 'glad tidings of return' (1947: 83–5). These include the invoking of known proverbs and/or the composition of songs of welcome by women. There are also dramatic life situations that engender parallel responses in diverse historical settings. Granqvist (1947: 65–6) describes how in the case of a woman experiencing stalled labour, those assisting her went to the home of a woman who had made the ḥajj and brought back a rosary from Mecca. Borrowing the set of beads, they placed them around the neck of the struggling parturient woman and the gesture had an immediate calming effect. Such an act perhaps is popular, rather than textually based, but also constitutes part of conventional practice, and may be compared with a custom noted among Jews in Italy, of placing a Torah Scroll in the hands of a woman experiencing difficult childbirth (Adelman 1991: 146).

Not only crises, but expected life-transitions within mundane realms may be attached to rituals rooted in religious culture. As noted, the regularization of bar mitzvah ceremonies at the precise age of 13 occurred late in medieval Europe. As its practice began to spread within the Jewish world, the age for marking it at first remained variable; a boy capable of praying publicly and reciting a lesson might celebrate the occasion earlier. In Morocco in recent times, among the verses sung by women on these occasions, some reflected that the young person would now begin working and contribute to the family. This may be placed in the context of Granqvist's observation in Artas near Bethlehem (1947: 130–2), that when asked about the age of a boy women did not name a year but would state the work activity in which he was engaged at the time. The integration of bar mitzvah into Moroccan practice cannot be separated from prevalent conceptions of life's course.

This perspective applies to gender as well as to age. Stanley Brandes (1980: 187–8) argues that taken-for-granted notions of masculinity may resist forms of standard ritual expression. In an Andalusian village, he found that men participated in Catholic Communion much less than women, both throughout the year and on life-cycle occasions. He suggests that the act of kneeling, linked to both the raising of the wafer-host by a priest and its ingestion by the individual communicant, was perceived as undergoing feminization, and was avoided by men as much as they could. The history of Jewish circumcision also provides examples of the interaction of gender with ingrained perceptions of public space. The movement of the ceremony from the home to the synagogue in the Middle Ages appears to have squelched the presence of women from certain active roles within it (Baumgarten 2004: 86–9).

Another topic that straddles everyday common-sense notions and ritual perceptions is that of 'purity'. A strict theological point of view may seek to define it in precise ritual terms, or apply it as a metaphor to an inner condition of a specific organ (like 'the heart'), while in quotidian reality it commonly overlaps with culturally shared notions of cleanliness and dirt (Douglas 1996). Judaism, based on biblical laws (mainly in Leviticus), developed elaborate categories and rules relating to purity/defilement, in particular with relationship to the Tabernacle in the desert (and by extension, the Temple in Jerusalem) and its paraphernalia. Two sources of biblical impurity relate directly to life-cycle processes, death and features of the reproductive process: menstrual flow, childbirth, and the emission of semen. Many rules, while preserved in rabbinic texts, became 'dead letters' in terms of practice after Temple worship ceased, but purity in relation to sexual activity and genital flow continued as a focus of concern. At times popular understanding among Jews exceeded rabbinic requirements (Cohen 1999). In some places, women felt that they should not enter a synagogue while menstruating, or should refrain from preparing unleavened Passover bread, even though rabbis declared that there was no such prohibition (Goldberg 2003: 119). The elaborate rabbinic system was not reproduced in the succeeding Abrahamic cultures, even as another set of detailed rules evolved in Islam. Regarding Christianity, there is evidence of historical continuity on a 'common-sense' level. In the third Christian century, Peter Brown notes, a 'bishop of Alexandria could assume that no Christian women would approach the Eucharist during her period' (Brown 1988: 146), even though other Christian authors sought to 'persuade both men and women to pay no attention to the disqualifications contained in the Jewish laws of purity' (ibid.). Popular notions of impurity due to childbirth may have persisted in the practice of the 'churching of women', wherein a new mother visited a church to receive a blessing from a priest about forty days after giving birth (cf. Lev. 12: 2–8). This was not an obligatory act, even though at times explained in terms of biblical texts (including Luke 2: 22), and the details and frequency of its practice have varied considerably. To unravel it historically would require attention to commonly held local notions along with canonical directives.

A picture of detailed rules and distinctions pertaining to purity in daily life emerges in the work of Granqvist among Muslim villagers (1947; 1965). One norm explained to her, for example, was that a woman who is impure may visit a woman who is in labour, but should not be there after the child is born (Granqvist 1947: 87). Another is that an impure woman entering a room where a corpse has been ritually washed, defiles it. The possibility of impurity is ubiquitous, and direct enquiries about it appear routinely. 'Are you pure or impure?' is asked of a woman in labour by a midwife entering the room (1947: 61), or of a man about to slaughter an animal or chicken (1965: 33). The practices and beliefs articulated by her female interlocutors, or viewed by Granqvist directly, were not presented on the basis of textual authority but as accepted practice, while her own formulation of a general principle is that: 'a ritually unclean person should not come into touch with a holy thing' (1965: 32). Thus, both impure men (after sexual intercourse), and women (for whom menstruation and childbirth defile as well as intercourse) should not fast or enter a place of prayer. At the same time, prohibitions linked to impurity apply to 'many actions in daily life which non-Muslims would consider profane... ploughing, [or] portioning wheat on the threshing floor' (Granqvist 1965: 33). The latter observation may be understood in terms of the sanctity attached to threshing floors since antiquity in the Near East, beyond the specifics of any authoritative textual directives. In addition, notions of purity seem 'naturally' to adhere to food as substance which transverses the boundaries of the body (Douglas 1970). Along with rules of prohibition and permission, foods also take on positive spiritual meanings in life-cycle events, such as representation of the departed (e.g. Danforth 1982: 56, 105–6).

Contemporary Developments: Some Examples

Many of the analytical questions raised continue to be relevant even as contemporary external conditions have dramatically altered the configuration of factors impinging upon the trajectories of individual lives. In terms of the emergence of 'modernity' in the West, and the growing valorization of the individual, it is now clear that even with a degree of 'sanctity' attributed to the judgements and emotions of single persons in today's world, there is no unitary form to these developments as they appear within diverse socio-political frameworks and ritual routines. The traditional form of establishing a marriage in Judaism exemplifies such variation.

The ancient rabbinic formulation for a man to 'take' a wife assumes that he acquires exclusive rights over her sexual activities, and utters a public statement to that effect, while the woman agrees to this transaction by silently accepting an item of monetary value (a ring). The ceremony entails no parallel gesture or statement concerning her rights vis-à-vis the new husband. The political and legal situation in contemporary Israel makes Orthodox procedure the only manner in which a Jewish 'religious' marriage is sanctioned by the state, but both secular Israelis and Modern

Orthodox women who have internalized some feminist assumptions have expressed reservations about traditional wedding ritual and have taken steps seeking to challenge or modify it. Among the former, there is a growing trend of couples travelling abroad and marrying in a civil procedure, and later having an unofficial traditional ceremony at home that includes gestures of equality like each member of the couple giving the other a ring. In some Modern Orthodox circles, women have begun to pressure amenable rabbis, who are sensitive to current developments, to find modifications of marriage ritual that do not contravene *halakhah* (Koren 2005). In both cases, these choices place this life-cycle ritual at the centre of attention and contention, and in the latter instance also reflect the growing access of women to the classic texts of rabbinic culture.

A different configuration of feminist engagement with normative scholarly traditions has been analysed by Saba Mahmood (2005) regarding the Mosque Movement in Egypt, through which women, who in the past had minimal direct contact with literate Muslim culture, became engaged in Islamic revival. While not focusing extensively on specific rituals, the importance of the body in the movement appears as 'a site of moral training and cultivation' (p. 139), and has implications for various life milestones. In discussions with mentors in the mosque, many mothers raised questions—with their daughters in mind—about premarital sexual activity. Another practical dilemma was: 'at what age should girls be veiled in public?' Some mothers wished daughters to begin at an age that collided with the ban of the Ministry of Education on veils in school. Mahmood's account also questions some of the liberal assumptions of feminism, by explicating a contemporary movement that empowers individuals but 'does not endorse a privatized notion of religion' (p. 47) and ritual life.

Rituals related to death, burial, and mourning in Oaxaca, Mexico (Norget 2006), illustrate another pattern of responses linking received customs to changing conditions. The celebration of *Dia de Muertos* is a clear historical example of pre-Columbian rituals becoming absorbed into acceptable Catholic forms: in this case the consecutive holy days of All Saints' Day and All Souls' Day. In general, ancient rituals related to death continue to provide an avenue for the public expression of ongoing socially valued and emotional involvement of the living with the dead. Women are critical and central actors in performing these rites (that are interspersed among standard Catholic practices), not by moving into spheres previously closed to them by canonical authority, but precisely by their being specialists in older ritual forms that are sensuous, fluid, and non-codified (Norget 2006: 147). These popular forms, both persisting and continually evolving in non-elite segments of Mexican society, provide a glimpse into the sense of self of the participants, and into the moral vision that sustains them in marginality and poverty.

It clearly is not productive to seek lines of connection among these cases in any conventional 'historical' sense, but might it be useful to look for 'family resemblances' in the way that the three religions process the search, by everyday adherents, to situate life trajectories in the context of venerable traditions?

References

Abu-Zahra, N. 1997. *The Pure and the Powerful: Studies in Contemporary Muslim Society*. London: Ithaca Press.

Adelman, H. 1991. 'Italian Jewish Women'. In J. Baskin, ed., *Jewish Women in Historical Perspective*. Detroit: Wayne State University Press, 135–58.

Asad, T. 1993. *Genealogies of Religion: Discipline and Reasons of Power in Christianity and Islam*. Baltimore: Johns Hopkins University Press.

Baumgarten, E. 2004. *Mothers and Children: Jewish Family Life in Medieval Europe*. Princeton: Princeton University Press.

Bilu, Y. 2003. 'From Milah ("Circumcision") to Milah ("Word"): Male Identity and Rituals of Childhood in the Jewish Ultraorthodox Community'. *Ethos* 32: 172–203.

Boas, F. 1916. *The Mind of Primitive Man*. New York: Macmillan.

Brandes, S. 1980. *Metaphors of Masculinity: Sex and Status in Andalusian Folklore*. Philadelphia: University of Pennsylvania Press.

Brown, P. L. 1988. *The Body and Society, Men, Women, and Sexual Renunciation in Early Christianity*. New York: Columbia University Press.

Buckser, A. 2008. 'Protestantism'. In R. Scupin, ed., *Religion and Culture: An Anthropological Focus*. Upper Saddle River, NJ: Pearson Prentice Hall, 402–29.

Cohen, S. J. D. 1999. 'Purity, Piety, and Polemic: Medieval Rabbinic Denunciations of "Incorrect" Purification Practices'. In R. R. Wasserfall, ed., *Women and Water: Menstruation in Jewish Life and Law*. Hanover, NH: University Press of New England, 82–100.

Danforth, L. M. 1982. *The Death Rituals of Rural Greece*. Princeton: Princeton University Press.

Denny, F. M. 1985. 'Islamic Ritual: Perspectives and Theories'. In R. C. Martin, ed., *Approaches to Islam in Religious Studies*. Tucson: University of Arizona Press, 63–77.

Deutsch, Y. 2001. '"A View of the Jewish Religion": Conceptions of Jewish Practice and Ritual in Early Modern Europe'. *Archiv für Religionsgeschichte* 2: 273–95.

Douglas, M. 1970. *Natural Symbols: Explorations in Cosmology*. London: Barrie & Rockliff.

Douglas, M. 1996 [1966]. *Purity and Danger: An Analysis of Concepts of Pollution and Taboo*. New York: Praeger.

Feeley-Harnik, G. 1994. *The Lord's Table: The Meaning of Food in Early Judaism and Christianity*. Washington, DC: Smithsonian Institution Press.

Geertz, C. 1973. 'Ritual and Social Change: A Javanese Example'. In *The Interpretation of Cultures*. New York: Basic Books, 142–69.

Goldberg, H. E. 1990a. *Jewish Life in Muslim Libya: Rivals and Relatives*. Chicago: University of Chicago Press.

Goldberg, H. E. 1990b. 'The Zohar in Southern Morocco: A Study in the Ethnography of Texts'. *History of Religions* 29: 233–58.

Goldberg, H. E. 2003. *Jewish Passages: Cycles of Jewish Life*. Berkeley: University of California Press.

Goldberg, S.-A. 1996. *Crossing the Jabbok: Illness and Death in Ashkenazi Judaism in Sixteenth-through-Nineteenth-Century Prague*, trans. C. Cosman. Berkeley: University of California Press.

Granqvist, H. 1947. *Birth and Childhood among Arabs: Studies in a Muhammadan Village in Palestine*. Helsingfors: Soderström Förlagsaktiebolag.

Granqvist, H. 1965. *Muslim Death and Burial: Arab Customs and Traditions Studied in a Village in Jordan*. Helsinki- Helsingfors: Commentationes Humanarum Litterarum 34.1.

Gruenwald, I. 2003. *Rituals and Ritual Theory in Ancient Israel.* Leiden: Brill.

Hammoudi, A. 2009. 'Textualism and Anthropology: On the Ethnographic Encounter, or an Experience in the Hajj'. In J. Borneman and A. Hammoudi, eds, *Being There: The Fieldwork Encounter and the Making of Truth.* Berkeley: University of California Press, 25–54.

Koren, I. 2005. 'The Bride's Voice: Religious Women Challenge the Wedding Ritual'. *Nashim* 10: 29–52.

Lane, E. W. 1954 [1860]. *Manners and Customs of the Modern Egyptians.* London: Dent & Sons.

Lauterbach, J. 1925. 'The Ceremony of Breaking a Glass at Weddings'. *Hebrew Union College Annual* 2: 351–80.

Mahmood, S. 2005. *The Politics of Piety: Islamic Revival and the Feminist Subject.* Princeton: Princeton University Press.

Marcus, I. G. 1996. *Rituals of Childhood: Jewish Acculturation in Medieval Europe.* New Haven: Yale University Press.

Markschies, I. 1999. *Between Two Worlds: Structure of Earliest Christianity,* trans. John Bowden. London: SCM Press.

Marx, E. 1966. 'Ḥagigot brit milah bein beduei ha-negev'. *Ha-mizraḥ he-ḥadash* 16: 166–75.

Norget, K. 2006. *Days of Death, Days of Life: Ritual in the Popular Culture of Oaxaca.* New York: Columbia University Press.

Pardes, I. 2000. *The Biography of Ancient Israel: National Narratives in the Bible.* Berkeley: University of California Press.

Paret, R. 1990. 'Ismā`il'. In *Encyclopaedia of Islam.* 2nd edn. Leiden: Brill, IV. 184–5.

Patai, R. 1983. *On Jewish Folklore.* Detroit: Wayne State University Press.

Redfield, R. and Rojas, A. V. 1962. *Chan Kom: A Maya Village,* abridged edn. Chicago: University of Chicago Press.

Rogers, N. 2002. *Halloween: From Pagan Ritual to Party Night.* New York: Oxford University Press.

Smith, W. R. 1914. *Lectures on the Religion of the Semites: The Fundamental Institutions.* London: Black.

Swartz, M. D. 2011. 'Judaism and the Idea of Ancient Ritual Theory'. In R. Boustan, O. Kosansky, and M. Rustow, eds, *Jewish Studies at the Crossroads of Anthropology and History: Authority, Diaspora, Tradition.* Philadelphia: University of Pennsylvania Press, 294–317.

Turner, V. and Turner, E. 1978. *Image and Pilgrimage in Christian Culture: Anthropological Perspectives.* New York: Columbia University Press.

Vajda, G. 1960. 'Ahl al-Kitāb'. In *Encyclopaedia of Islam.* 2nd edn. Leiden: Brill, I. 264–6.

Valensi, L. 1989. 'Religious Orthodoxy or Local Tradition: Marriage Celebration in Southern Tunisia'. In M. R. Cohen and A. L. Udovitch, eds, *Jews among Arabs: Contacts and Boundaries.* Princeton: Darwin Press, 65–84.

Van Gennep, A. 1960 [1909]. *The Rites of Passage.* Chicago: University of Chicago Press.

Weinstein, R. 1994. 'Rites of Passage in Sixteenth-Century Italy: The Bar-Mitzvah Ceremony and its Sociological Implications'. *Italia* 1: 77–98.

Westermarck, E. 1926. *Ritual and Belief in Morocco.* London: Macmillan.

CHAPTER 27

THE CULT OF SAINTS AND PILGRIMAGE

YOUSEF MERI

THIS chapter offers a broad overview of two interrelated phenomena: the cult of saints and pilgrimage among Jews, Christians, and Muslims, with a focus on the Middle East, the cradle of the three Abrahamic religions.[1]

The Cave of the Patriarchs (Heb. *Meʿarat ha-Makhpela*, Arab. *Al-Ḥaram al-Ibrāhīmī* [The Sanctuary of Abraham]) in Hebron, the burial place of Abraham, Isaac, Jacob, and their wives, is an important pilgrimage site, especially for Muslims and Jews. Yet, the sanctity of this holy place was violated when in 1994 a Jewish settler murdered worshippers at the shrine, a heinous act that was condemned by leaders of the Abrahamic faiths. Violence at shrines has always been antithetical to the pre-Islamic and Islamic idea of the *ḥaram*, an inviolable or sacred precinct.[2] In the biblical context King Josiah desecrates tombs and sacred places (2 Kings 23). Yet this was the exception and not the rule. In the Bible and post-biblical literature the Temple and by extension all of Jerusalem was regarded as holy. Sacred sites were treated with deference in contrast to the Hebron massacre or the persistent settler attacks against mosques and churches.

By contrast, in the history of the Hebron shrine under Islamic rule, no acts of violence were recorded against Muslim or Jewish worshippers. Like Jerusalem, Hebron today is a symbol of what has gone wrong with the practice of the Abrahamic religions—the ascendancy of militancy and the application of the contentious notion of 'sovereignty'.[3] Yet violence at holy places occurred under various historical

[1] I would like to express my utmost appreciation to the editors for their helpful comments and suggestions and especially thank Guy Stroumsa for his patience and understanding.

[2] In ancient civilizations as well as in the Abrahamic faiths, approaching sacred space requires believers to perform certain rituals. For a discussion of the word *ḥaram* and its use, see Serjeant 2005. For an understanding of the sacred as it relates to pilgrimage topography see Meri 2002: ch. 1.

[3] Israeli scholars have argued over the controversial idea of vertical sovereignty over the Ḥaram al-Sharīf (Noble Sanctuary) or Temple Mount in Jerusalem. That is to say that anything above the

circumstances, including political instability, war, ideology and the theft of money and property. In 1009 the Fāṭimid Ismāʿīlī Shīʿi ruler al-Ḥākim bi-Amr Allāh (r. 996–1021 CE), who was believed to be insane, ordered the destruction of the church of the Holy Sepulchre in Jerusalem and of churches and synagogues. The church was only rebuilt under his successor al-Ẓāhir (r. 1021–36 CE). During the First Crusade in 1099 CE, upon entering Jerusalem the crusaders murdered tens of thousands of Muslims and Jews and tortured priests of the eastern churches. Moreover, they set fire to synagogues, destroyed the shrines of saints, including the tomb of Abraham in Hebron, and ransacked the mosque of the caliph ʿUmar in Jerusalem.[4] Moreover, they launched attacks against Muslim shrines in Syria in 1124 and 1170. In 1124 Joscelin of Edessa set fire to a Muslim shrine outside Aleppo. In 1170 the crusaders attacked the Damascus countryside and destroyed shrines and mosques.[5] In 1492 the Reconquista resulted in the systematic destruction and conversion of non-Christian sacred places to churches. In contrast with the First Crusade and the Reconquista where violence against persons and holy places occurred on a large scale, under Muslim rule this was not the norm.

Today Israeli 'Sovereignty' is invoked in order to justify or negate political claims over the holy sites of Jerusalem and the West Bank. Attempts to impose secular law over the holy sites have failed largely because sites of such importance as the Ḥaram al-Sharīf or Temple Mount and the Cave of the Patriarchs defy legislation. They possess a sacred history along with sacred narratives of more than one religious tradition, a history that is largely ignored. Moreover, while it is possible to speak of sovereignty over holy sites shared by two or more faiths, the very notion distorts sacred history by relegating the divine to the realm of the secular. Alternatively the belief that 'Sovereignty belongs to God', which embodies the universal nature of all holy sites in Islam and Judaism, is understood by Jews and Muslims as a way of approaching the issue of control and access to holy sites. In the Bible it is said: 'The Lord shall reign for ever and ever' (Exod. 15: 18). The same idea is expressed in the Quran: 'Unto God belongs the sovereignty of the heavens and the earth and all this is therein, and it is He who has power over all things' (Q. 5: 120).

Acts of violence at major shrines venerated by two or more faiths in the Middle East and North Africa are the exception not the rule. Yet such incidents serve as a poignant reminder that the veneration of Abraham as of other holy persons has always held profound levels of meaning for Jewish and Muslim worshippers. Tension has always existed in the background among Jews, Christians, and Muslims throughout history. Yet with notable exceptions this did not prevent the veneration of holy persons and places. A more immediate danger to shrines and their devotees were the predations of brigands and tribes which occasionally resulted in shrines being looted.

Temple Mount is to remain under Islamic waqf administration and everything below under Israeli government control. For a discussion of the types of sovereignty in Israeli political and legal discourse, see Breger and Reiter 2010: 1–21.

[4] See for instance Amin Malouf 1989: 50–1.

[5] Meri 2001: 7.

Background

The nineteenth-century Jewish Orientalist Ignaz Goldziher was one of the first scholars to study the cult of saints and pilgrimage in Islam and its points of contact with Judaism and Christianity. In his *Muslim Studies*, Goldziher explores the origins of Muslim practices:

> There is an enormous gap between this concept held by early Islam and the position which the veneration and invocation of saints everywhere occupies shortly after the spread of the new religion. Within Islam as well, the believers sought to create, through the concept of saints, mediators between themselves and an omnipotent Godhead in order to satisfy the need which was served by the gods and masters of their old traditions . . . Here too applies what Karl Hase says of the cult of saints in general: that it 'satisfies within a monotheistic religion a polytheistic need to fill the enormous gap between men and their god, and that it originated on the soil of the old pantheon'. (Goldziher 1967–71: II. 259)

In Goldziher's view Islam renders the pre-Islamic elements of saint veneration into an 'Abrahamic' form (Goldziher 1967–71: II. 298). The same logic can be applied to other more complex ritual forms such as pilgrimage. While the issue of origins remains a central paradigm in the study of the relationship of Islam to Judaism and Christianity in many areas where points of contact existed between the Abrahamic religions, a more fluid model has been proposed by Jacques Waardenburg (2002) who differentiates between 'popular' practices such as saint veneration and pilgrimage to holy places and normative and official forms of Islam. In Judaism the veneration of saints existed at the margins of Orthodoxy (Cohn 1987). Yet, from the eighth and ninth centuries under Islamic rule the cult of the prophets and patriarchs found diverse expressions in such places as Iraq where Jews from across the Mediterranean and the Islamic world visited the shrines of Ezekiel and Ezra (Meri 2002: 229–38; Meri 2012: 22–5), Greater Syria (Elijah),[6] Palestine (e.g. Isaac, Leah, Rachael, and Abraham),[7] and Iran (Daniel, Esther). Jewish communal leaders in the Middle Ages, such as Moses Maimonides (d. 1204), often condoned or acquiesced to the veneration of holy persons and pilgrimage to their tombs, though like their Muslim counterparts they at times criticized the impious behaviour displayed at holy places (Meri 2002: 215, 236). Indeed the veneration of the Talmudic sages and local saints and pilgrimage to their shrines was a more widespread phenomenon than previously believed (Meri 2002: ch. 4; for the modern era, see Kosansky 2010). In the modern era Morocco and Tunisia remain major centres of Jewish pilgrimage among North African Jews (Kosansky 2010).

[6] Multiple shrines dedicated to Elijah existed throughout Greater Syria and Mesopotamia, see Meri 2002: ch. 3, esp. pp. 224–9; Meri 1999b.

[7] The same is true of the Jewish veneration of the Talmudic sages in Palestine. The cult of the sages became institutionalized during the later Middle Ages, particularly from the sixteenth century, with the influence of Safed Kabbalah. See, for instance, Fenton 2000.

Late antique notions of holiness and sanctity provided fertile ground for the interaction of Judaism and Christianity and the emergence of Islam. Christian shrines dotted the landscape of Greater Syria (includes present-day Syria, Palestine/Israel, Jordan, and Lebanon) and Iraq. Christian shrines like the Shrine of the Virgin at Ṣaydnāyā outside Damascus were for centuries revered by Christians and visited by local Muslims seeking cures (Meri 2002: 210–12). Yet this interaction of traditions should not merely be regarded as one of Christian and Jewish influence on Islam. Indeed commonalities exist in saint veneration historically. An equally important consideration is the mystical dimensions of the Abrahamic religions, particularly of medieval Islamic mysticism or Sufism, which contributed in large part to the spread of the veneration of holy persons and pilgrimage during the Middle Ages. In the Islamic context Sufis, ascetics, and others compiled pilgrimage guides that included the burial places of scriptural personages and other varieties of holy persons. With the spread of the Sufi orders in thirteenth-century Cairo and Damascus, pious visitations to tombs and shrines of the Family, Companions, and Followers of the prophet Muhammad and Sufi shaykhs became routinized. The pilgrimage places of Damascus associated with scriptural figures such as Cain and Abel, Moses and Elijah occupied pride of place in medieval Hebrew and Arabic pilgrimage and travel accounts.[8]

Proposing a methodological framework for the interaction of the three Abrahamic faiths as suggested by the present volume's theme is both useful and challenging. The paradigm of 'Abrahamic Religions' invites one to look at holy persons and places held in common by the three faiths rather than their significance in each of the traditions. This chapter will highlight a number of key aspects of pilgrimage and saint veneration and discuss the extent to which these phenomena may be considered 'Abrahamic' and how we may understand them in the light of this paradigm.

Echoing Goldziher, Francis Peters in his study of *The Children of Abraham* (2006: 113) argues that the veneration of saints was 'not an entirely natural development in Islam' and that it 'placed an almost infinite gulf between a transcendent Allah and his creation here below'. Similarly Peter Brown in his seminal work on the Cult of Saints (1981: 10) has characterized the phenomenon of saint veneration in Islam as existing at the periphery. However, the veneration of saints and making pilgrimage to tombs and shrines were ubiquitous to the medieval Islamic landscape as they were to the medieval Christian experience (Meri 1999a). Within an Abrahamic context, saint veneration in the Middle Ages does not merely carry with it the baggage of late antique traditions. Rather a particular dynamic existed among the faiths from the perspective of the believer which explains the veneration of holy persons. No single factor can explain the rise of the veneration of the martyrs in Christianity, the Talmudic sages in Judaism, and the Companions and Followers of the prophet Muhammad and other classes of saints in Islam. The act of veneration in Islam does not necessitate visiting tombs and shrines, but rather in the first instance reading and reciting scripture, sacred, or

[8] See Meri 2002: chs 3 and 4.

edificatory texts (such as those dedicated to praise of the excellent qualities (Arab. *faḍāʾil*) and miracles of righteous individuals) concerning a holy person or place. In Christianity this includes reading and reciting liturgical texts, in Judaism, reading texts (scripture and poetry) attesting to the miraculous virtues of the patriarchs and the Talmudic sages. In all traditions devotees routinely recounted the heroic deeds and exploits of holy persons, particularly on holy days or special festivals.

Saints

A few words about the cult of saints in each of the three traditions is in order. By the cult of saints we mean the veneration of holy persons in general, including but not limited to the prophets and patriarchs, martyrs, the righteous, pious sages, and Sufi saints (Meri 2002; Meri 1999a). Such designations are not mutually exclusive. We will not focus on how saints are designated in each of the traditions as this would require discussions of Sufism, mysticism, and early Christian ideas of sainthood and would take us far from the objective of looking at the Abrahamic context of the cult of saints and pilgrimage.[9] The fundamental concept of the cult of saints in late antique Christianity is that the martyrs who were persecuted for their faith became loci of veneration.[10] The martyrs and other saints like the apostles were imitators of Christ. In Christianity, the saints came to be venerated in the liturgical calendar.[11] Church fathers like Augustine (d. 430), the Bishop of Hippo in present-day Algeria, declared the importance of the martyrs to the Christian faith:

> It is true that Christians pay religious honour to the memory of the martyrs, both to excite us to imitate them and to obtain a share in their merits, and the assistance of their prayers. But we build altars not to any martyr, but to the God of martyrs, although it is to the memory of the martyrs. No one officiating at the altar in the saints' burying-place ever says, We bring an offering to thee, O Peter! or O Paul! or O Cyprian! The offering is made to God, who gave the crown of martyrdom, while it is in memory of those thus crowned. The emotion is increased by the associations of the place, and love is excited both towards those who are our examples, and towards him by whose help we may follow such examples. We regard the martyrs with the same affectionate intimacy that we feel towards holy men of God in this life, when we know that their hearts are prepared to endure the same suffering for the truth of the gospel. There is more devotion in our feeling towards the martyrs, because we know that their conflict is over; and we can speak with greater

[9] On the theme in Sufism see Radtke and O'Kane 1996. References to sainthood in other traditions may be found throughout this chapter.

[10] See for instance Peter Brown (1981: 1), who refers to the shrines of saints representing the 'joining of Heaven and Earth'.

[11] About saints in eastern Christianity, see Synek 2007: 439–49 and Youssef 2007: 450–7.

> confidence in praise of those already victors in heaven, than of those still combating here. What is properly divine worship, which the Greeks call latria, and for which there is no word in Latin, both in doctrine and in practice, we give only to God.[12]

Other church fathers like Cyril of Jerusalem (d. 386) mention the efficacy of prayer to the patriarchs, prophets, and apostles:

> Then we commemorate also those who have fallen asleep before us, first Patriarchs, Prophets, Apostles, Martyrs, that at their prayers and intercessions God would receive our petition. Then on behalf also of the Holy Fathers and Bishops who have fallen asleep before us, and in a word of all who in past years have fallen asleep among us, believing that it will be a very great benefit to the souls, for whom the supplication is put up, while that holy and most awful sacrifice is set forth.[13]

The church fathers cautioned against worshipping saints, instead encouraging their veneration and seeking their intercession. In the late antique context, Peter Brown's magisterial study of *The Cult of the Saints: Its Rise and Function in Latin Christianity* (1981) brilliantly captures the dynamic of the veneration of the dead and the various catalysts and motivations for the veneration of the special dead. One of the major differences between Christianity on the one hand and Islam and Judaism on the other is the absence in the latter of a cult centred on touching human remains, which both traditions maintain were inviolable. The trade in corporeal relics became widespread in the medieval European context, though relics were handled and transferred in late antiquity. Yet within the Islamic world of the eighth century onwards, the veneration of the holy dead assumed various forms.

While the Mediterranean of late antiquity provided fertile ground for the emergence of living and dead holy persons in the Christian tradition to whose tombs and shrines devotees made pilgrimage, this phenomenon manifested itself in diverse and highly complex ways across the medieval Islamic world (Meri 1999a). In Judaism the Talmudic sages became foci of veneration because of their exemplary piety and learning. Yet as Robert L. Cohn (1987) has shown Jewish saintly individuals were the exception, not the norm. Jewish traditions concerning the veneration of the holy dead were consolidated long after the death of the Talmudic sages. As early as the ninth century, the Jewish veneration of saints took root in Palestine. Textual evidence suggests that their veneration became popular from the twelfth century. Within an Islamic environment the Christian and especially the Jewish veneration of holy persons at shrines took on peculiar characteristics associated with an Arabo-Islamic culture. At the commemoration of a holy person, whether a prophet or Talmudic sage, scripture and the Talmud were invoked and their miracles recounted. Later sages' cults were centred on notable mystical and Kabbalistic figures.

[12] Augustine against Faustus, 20: 21, NPNF1, IV. 262, <http://www.ccel.org/ccel/schaff/npnf104.iv.ix.xxii.html>.

[13] The Catechetical Lectures, NPNF2, XXVII. 154, <http://www.ccel.org/ccel/schaff/npnf207.ii.xxvii.html>.

Defining the Saint

Saints defy definition because they embody different characteristics, some that are universally recognized within a tradition and others that are shared between two or more traditions. The lack of a precise definition does not preclude the formulation of one. When collectively referring to the Abrahamic faiths, the word saint (Lat. *sanctus*) may be employed in a context which does not merely suggest a Christian holy person. While the Christian understanding of a saint has largely defined how the veneration of saints and their relics along with pilgrimage are understood in academic discourse, I have previously argued for a shift toward a more fluid paradigm which recognizes the complex nature of other traditions (Meri 1999a; Meri 2002: ch. 2). Thus, in addition to the qualities of exemplary piety and learning mentioned above, it may be said that a saint is a person who possesses *baraka* (blessing), a God-given quality to the righteous of all the Abrahamic traditions (Meri 1999c).

In Christianity the earliest saints were the martyrs who were persecuted by the Romans. In medieval Europe, the saint came to be recognized through a more formal process of identification, namely through beatification and canonization by the church. In eastern Christianity, the icons of saints became central to the veneration of saints, while in western Christendom, the body of the saint became central to the cult. In the case of the multiple shrines throughout the Middle East dedicated to the prophets and patriarchs, the body was not always present and many an oratory was established as a result of a dream or vision as in the case of the prophet Elijah and his Islamic counterpart al-Khaḍir (Meri 1999b).

In Judaism and Islam the display of relics or physical remains of the saint was never central to the act of venerating the saint (Meri 2010). In fact Jewish and Islamic traditions emphasize the inviolability of the body. Thus, in an Abrahamic sense, a saint is a person who acquires through the grace of God a measure of sanctity in their lifetime or after death regardless of their official designation in edificatory, exegetical, literary, or historical sources. In the Middle East and North Africa holy persons came to be identified as such through their acts of exemplary piety and learning, their charismatic or thaumaturgic gifts in their lifetimes and posthumously.

All three Abrahamic religions acknowledge the universality of the prophets and patriarchs, though Jews do not acknowledge Jesus as the Messiah and Jews and Christians do not recognize Muhammad as a prophet within their traditions. The central figures of Moses in Judaism, Jesus in Christianity and Muhammad in Islam are essential to understanding how the believers articulate their experiences vis-à-vis the performance of ritual and the creation of centres of devotion. In Christianity the saints sought to imitate Jesus in their acts of piety and devotion. The pilgrimage to Jesus' reputed tomb is attested in late antiquity by Jerome and Egeria among others.[14] The

[14] An excellent website documenting Egeria's travels is to be found at: <http://www.egeriaproject.net/about_egeria.aspx>.

purported tomb of Christ in the church of the Holy Sepulchre in Jerusalem was empty, yet the process of discovery was somehow an essential part of his veneration among Holy Land pilgrims. The veneration of a holy person is not always bound to a specific location as in the case of Moses whose tomb according to biblical tradition is unknown. However, this does not prevent Muslims from seeking to rediscover the location of Moses' tomb near Jericho and Damascus, and Jewish travellers from visiting the Jericho shrine.[15] Muslims to this day make a pious visitation, or a lesser pilgrimage, to the tomb of the prophet Muhammad. However, this did not constitute canonical pilgrimage as does pilgrimage to Mecca.

Varieties of Saints

Jews, Christians, and Muslims venerated different types of holy persons, the greatest varieties being in late antique Christianity and medieval Islam. As mentioned earlier, saints possessed exemplary piety and learning, sometimes one or both. Indeed, some led an ascetic lifestyle and renounced the worldly life, while others were said to have performed miracles. Some saints were shared among traditions like the prophets and patriarchs while others were officially acknowledged only within a given tradition. Yet in Islam others like the *muwallah* (lit. the one enamoured of God) were considered by theologians to be heterodox, insane, and in a state of ritual impurity (Meri 2002: 61, 91–9, 100, 117, 119).

The most important category of holy person shared by the three monotheistic faiths is the prophets and patriarchs. Throughout the Middle Ages the shrines of the prophet Elijah and his Islamic counterpart al-Khaḍir were the most important centres of devotion among Muslims, Jews, and Christians throughout historic Syria and Iraq (Meri 2002: ch. 3; Meri 1999b).

In Judaism the veneration of the Talmudic sages occupied an important place after the veneration of the prophets and patriarchs. Those frequently mentioned in historical and literary accounts include Ḥoni the Circle Drawer and his descendants, who were efficacious for producing rain in their lifetimes and posthumously (Meri 2002: 64).

Apart from the prophets and patriarchs whose authority derives from God and whose veneration is normally associated with their mention in scripture, in Islam the process of recognizing the sainthood (here read state of holiness) of an individual was through popular acclimation. Muslim authors produced hagiographical biographies and other works about the better-known saints that attested to their acts of piety and charity as well as the lesser miracles (*karāmāt*) they worked (Meri 2002: ch. 2; Meri 1999a).

15 To this day Muslims visit his tomb near Jericho. For the medieval context see Sadan 1981. For a more recent discussion with a focus on the early Ottoman period, see Cohen 2006. For a more comprehensive overview see al-ʿAsalī 1990.

Medieval Hebrew travel accounts frequently contain references to the *avot* (the ancestors), the *ẓaddiqim* (the righteous), *ḥaṣidim* (the pious), and the *qdoshim* (the holy ones). From the seventeenth and eighteenth centuries, the veneration of Jewish saints in North Africa became common, down to the twentieth century, particularly in Morocco and Tunisia.

In the Christian context as mentioned above in the accounts of the church fathers, saints included the martyrs, the apostles, church fathers, to which may be added other male and female clergy, anchorites, and ascetics who were posthumously recognized as saints.

In the Islamic context, Shīʿis venerate the twelve imams, the prophet Muhammad's male descendants through his cousin and son-in-law ʿAlī b. Abī Ṭālib (d. 661) and his descendants through his son Ḥusayn, who was martyred at Karbalāʾ in 680. The earliest extant pilgrimage manuals focus on the veneration of ʿAlī, his son Ḥusayn (d. 680) and the fifth and sixth imams Muḥammad al-Bāqir (d. 733) and Jaʿfar al-Ṣādiq (d. 765). The earliest guides are essentially a compilation of traditions attributed to them.

In the modern context, the varieties of saints includes *marabouts*, or pious individuals, commonly referred to as *awliyāʾ* (friends of God), *ṣāliḥūn* (pious persons), or *ṣiddīqūn* (righteous persons).[16] Many of these saints are venerated within the context of the Sufi orders.

Pilgrimage: Introduction

Jerusalem and Mecca are not only the two archetypal pilgrimage cities; they are cities of Abraham and Abrahamic cities. The sacred topography of the Middle East consists of intertwined spaces and places which believers associate with events from sacred history such as from the lives of the prophets and patriarchs and other holy persons. Worshippers perpetuated the memory of these places by offering prayers, supplications, and sacrifices among other rituals.

In Judaism, following the destruction of the Second Temple in Jerusalem in 70 CE, pilgrimage ceased to be obligatory for adult males. Synagogues emerged as centres not only of worship but also for pilgrimage and the veneration of holy persons. One of the earliest preserved examples of the veneration of holy persons in the Middle East is from the Dura Europos synagogue in Syria, which contained murals of the prophets and patriarchs at which pilgrims made supplications (Meri 1999b: 239–40), the synagogues of Moses at Dammuh in Egypt (Meri 2002: 222–4) and the various synagogues of Elijah throughout Syria and Iraq (Meri 1999b; Meri 2002: chs 3–4). Medieval Hebrew and Judaeo-Arabic accounts routinely mention that Jews visited pilgrimage places during

[16] In Islam the categories are not mutually exclusive and are fairly extensive. For discussion, see Meri 2002: ch. 2 and Meri 1999a.

the high holy days, especially on Passover, the Festival of Weeks, and Sukkot. After Saladin's conquest of Jerusalem in 1187 Jews were once again permitted to take up residence in Jerusalem and visit the Western Wall.

In late antiquity, church fathers such as St Jerome urged pilgrimage to Jerusalem as did subsequently the Byzantine emperors and their families who led by example. The fourth century marked a revival of pilgrimage interest in holy places. The Byzantines patronized Christian pilgrimage sites and encouraged pilgrimage to Jerusalem. The Emperor Constantine had the tomb of Jesus consecrated in 326 CE.

Only in Islam is pilgrimage ritual so intimately connected with Abraham and the intended sacrifice of his son Ishmael. Pilgrims re-enact the Farewell Pilgrimage of the prophet Muhammad whose rituals they believe Abraham and Ishmael began. In Islamic sacred history, Abraham and Ishmael raise up the foundations of the Kaʿba (Q. 2: 127). Muslim pilgrims re-enact the rituals attributed to Abraham, including sacrificing livestock to commemorate the intended sacrifice. In Quran 22: 26, God commands Abraham to purify the house for those who circumambulate it: 'And when We settled for Abraham the place of the House: "Thou shall not associate with Me anything. And do thou purify My House for those that shall go about it and those that stand, for those that bow and prostrate themselves."'

Other forms of pilgrimage such as *ziyāra* (Arab.; a visitation, pious visitation), while not explicitly Abrahamic, may be seen as illustrating the intersection of texts and rituals of saint veneration. Ziyāra is the act of pilgrimage or pious visitation to any holy place in Islam. As discussed later the word was used by Jews and Christians in the medieval Islamic world. Christian Arabic texts also mention that Christians would travel to Jerusalem in order to derive blessings from the holy sites.[17] In the Islamic context it refers to non-canonical pilgrimage, that is pilgrimage other than the ḥajj and ʿumra to Mecca. The pilgrimage to Jerusalem is an example of *ziyāra* which appears in the *ḥadīth* traditions of the prophet Muhammad and in travel and pilgrimage accounts. The prophet Muhammad is believed to have ascended to Heaven from Jerusalem on his miraculous night journey mentioned in Quran 17: 1. As he ascended the heavens he encountered the various prophets and patriarchs.

In the medieval Islamic world Muslims as well as Jews and Christians venerated Abraham, who was known by the Arabic name of Ibrāhīm. Abraham is a saint, that is a holy person in the general sense of the word, and in Islam he is referred to as a Friend of God (al-khalīl).

Aleppo (Arab. Ḥalab), whose name may derive from the Arabic word for milk, is a pilgrimage city that Muslim historians connect to Abraham based upon popular traditions of Abraham milking his flocks there and distributing the milk to the poor. A shrine of Abraham was found near the Jews' quarter. Yet the shrines of other prophets and patriarchs throughout Syria and the Middle East, particularly Ezekiel, Elijah, Moses, Ezra, and Daniel, were popular among medieval Jews.

[17] Zayyāt 1982: 111.

The Arabic language became the lingua franca among Jews, Christians, and Muslims throughout the Islamic world from the seventh century. It provided a common vocabulary to refer to pilgrimage. Jews used the word *ḥogeg* (a word related to the Arabic *ḥajj*) as they made pilgrimage to their holy places. They also used such words as *baraka* (blessings) to refer to the divinely inspired quality possessed by righteous individuals. In this light pilgrimage was an Abrahamic phenomenon (Meri 2002: ch. 4).[18]

Holiness

The Jewish conception of holiness was rooted in the Land of Israel. After the destruction of the Second Temple in 70 CE synagogues became metonymies for the Temple, wherein the liturgies of the holy days were performed, though Jews no longer offered up sacrifices. In Christianity, the holiness of places associated with Jesus, the martyrs, and the apostles became part of Christian sacred history.

Accessing the holy required the enactment of various rituals such as donning a garment, saying prayers, and making supplications, the act of remembering the holy person and remembering God and the Hereafter. Jews, Christians, and Muslims identified holiness through similar means (Meri 2002: ch. 1 and throughout). Jewish, Christian, and Muslim devotees of saints had similar spiritual needs which they sought to fulfil, such as approaching God and seeking intercession, as well as worldly needs, such as bestowing a child, good health, and wealth. Nevertheless, each Abrahamic tradition had its own particular prayers and supplications which included verses from scripture and Arabic supplications requesting in prayer that God through the shrine's inmate (not all shrines were associated with physical remains particularly in medieval Islam) fulfil spiritual or physical needs, heal the visitor, and provide relief from adversity. Whenever they condoned visiting holy places, Muslim theologians maintained that prayer should be made to God directly on behalf of the dead and that seeking the direct intercession of holy persons was tantamount to the major sin of associating other deities with God (Meri 2002: 126–40).

Defining Pilgrimage

Pilgrimage is any sacred journey to a sacred or holy site that may be venerated in one or more traditions. Any definition of pilgrimage and saints must take into account both the general and local characteristics of what constitutes a saint and pilgrimage.

[18] Also see Zayyāt 1982: 112, where the text has '[The monk] sought blessings (*tabāraka*) from the holy sites [of Nazareth]'.

By general we mean that which is universal to the Abrahamic faiths (e.g. common places of pilgrimage, the essential forms of pilgrimage etiquette, and fundamental rituals) and by local that which is associated with a given tradition, e.g. a pilgrimage site recognized locally or regionally, but which does not necessarily have any official status within a faith, such as the grave of a medieval saint. Scholarship which seeks to understand both phenomena has historically focused on the origins of one tradition or another within a distinctly Christian or Judaeo-Christian framework.[19] While it is not our intention to entirely reject this limited traditional approach, this has created a false standard by which to define scholarship on the Jewish and Islamic traditions, which in turn negates the unique qualities and characteristics of both these traditions, or at least subsumes them to a dominant paradigm. Furthermore it has the potential to marginalize the beliefs of a given religion.

Studies of origins abound, yet they do not impart a real sense of these phenomena within a genuinely Abrahamic framework. Herein we shall strive to create such a framework which not only recognizes the universal qualities and attributes of the respective traditions but also examines their peculiar characteristics.

The origins of pilgrimage and the veneration of saints are to be found in the ancient Near East, the cradle to the three Abrahamic faiths. Ultimately it is the sacred centre, which historians of religion such as Mircea Eliade (1958: 367–87) saw as sites in which the sacred manifests itself and encompasses the landscape around it. While on one level one may regard shrines as fulfilling a basic desire, such a perspective offers a limited understanding of the Abrahamic context. By contrast to primitive pilgrimage places, Abrahamic pilgrimage places are centres vested with scriptural authority dedicated to exemplary figures from the monotheist past, endowed with divine blessings by virtue of their association with such figures, and often translatable and made intelligible to devotees of other monotheistic faiths through the public display of ritual at or surrounding it.

Both the veneration of saints and pilgrimage are often regarded as 'popular religion'.[20] Popular should not merely be understood as the practice and custom of the common people. In fact we find Jews, Christians, and Muslims from all walks of life undertaking pilgrimage to holy places and venerating saints. The term 'popular religion' is useful for categorizing certain religious phenomena.[21] In the Near Eastern Christian and Jewish contexts, saint veneration emerged as a central aspect of popular religiosity. By popular we specifically mean normative practice among Jews and Christians.

[19] For a discussion of possible influences, see the work of the Hungarian Orientalist Ignaz Goldziher 1967–71: I. 209–38, II. 255–341; Goldziher 1911.

[20] For a discussion of popular culture and popular religion, see Meri 2002: conclusion; Vrijhof and Waardenburg 1979: 9. For an expanded and updated discussion see also Waardenburg 1979: 2002: 85–111. Also for the medieval Islamic context see Yehoshua Frenkel 2008: 195–225.

[21] Especially useful in this regard is Waardenburg 1978.

Shrines of Abraham

Shrines dedicated to Abraham existed throughout the Middle East. The best-known shrine of Abraham today is the Cave of the Patriarchs in Hebron which Jewish, Christian, and Muslim pilgrimage and travel accounts routinely mention. One of the earliest pilgrimage accounts that mentions holy places associated with Abraham is Egeria's fifth-century itinerary, in which she visits the House of Abraham in Harran:

> Then, after three days spent there, it was necessary for me to go still farther, to Charrae, as it is now called. In holy Scripture it is called Charran, where holy Abraham dwelt, as it is written in Genesis when the Lord said unto Abram: Get thee out of thy country, and from thy father's house, and go to Charran and the rest . . . He took us at once to the church, which is without the city on the spot where stood the house of holy Abraham; it stands on the same foundations, and it is made of the same stone, as the holy bishop said. When we had come to the church, prayer was made, the passage from Genesis was read, one psalm was said, and after a second prayer the bishop blessed us and we came out. (Egeria 1919: 36)

The twelfth-century Muslim traveller and ascetic ʿAlī b. Abī Bakr al-Harawī (d. 1215 CE) mentions multiple shrines dedicated to Abraham throughout Greater Syria, Palestine, Lebanon, Egypt, and Iraq. In one instance he mentions a church in the Valley of Kidron in Palestine which was a Christian pilgrimage place (Harawī 2004: 74). In 1192 al-Harawī visited the Cave of the Patriarchs after first visiting it while Hebron was under crusader rule. He mentions the account of a scholar who visited some years earlier:

> [The scholar] al-Ādamī sought to visit Hebron and became friends with the place's custodian, who was a Byzantine. He sought to gain his favor with a gift and requested to descend to the grotto. He promised him [that he could do so] when the pilgrimage traffic ceased in the winter. When the people stopped coming, [the custodian] took him to a tile that he uplifted and took a light and both of them descended approximately seventy steps and came to a large spacious grotto where the wind blew. It contained a slab upon which was Abraham the Friend covered in a green garment and the wind was playing with his white hair. (Harawī 2004: 30–1)[22]

Other shrines dedicated to Abraham were to be found at the Citadel of Aleppo where one of Saladin's son's al-Malik al-Muʾayyad Najm al-Dīn Masʿūd was buried (Harawī 2004: 12 and n. 1).

[22] One of the most detailed accounts of the shrine is Mujīr al-Dīn al-Ḥanbalī's (d. 1522 CE) Al-Uns al-Jalīl bi-Taʾrīkh al-Quds wal-Khalīl which incorporates earlier Muslim traditions about the Cave of the Patriarchs and its founding.

Common Pilgrimage Sites

Common pilgrimage sites were an integral part of the medieval landscape. They were not claimed exclusively by a particular religious community. Access to them was not forbidden to devotees of various faiths.

In twelfth-century Aleppo we find a telling example of a common pilgrimage site and the rituals performed there:

> [Aleppo] contains a rock visible at the Jew's Gate on the road to which votive offerings are made (*yundharu lahu al-nudhūr*) and upon which rosewater and sweet fragrances are sprinkled. Muslims, Jews, and Christians hold it in regard. It is said that beneath it is the tomb of one of the prophets . . . or saints (*awliyāʾ*) . . . (Harawī 2004: 12)

As significant an Abrahamic cult was that of the prophet Ezekiel (Arab. Ḥizqīl), which became a leading centre of pilgrimage throughout the Islamic world from Egypt and North Africa to Syria and Palestine. Jews visited the shrine during the High Holy Days, at the New Year and the Day of Atonement. On the Day of Atonement, they read from a Torah scroll believed to be in Ezekiel's handwriting, while a lamp burned day and night over the tomb. Benjamin of Tudela, writing in the twelfth century, states: 'The light thereof has been kept burning from the day that he [lit] it himself, and they continually renew the wick thereof, and replenish the oil unto the present day.' Regular vows of oil from devotees ensured that the place would glow with the light of holiness.

Rabbi Petaḥiyah of Regensburg reports that 'Whoever wishes to go to a distant land deposits his purse, or any valuables, with Ezekiel, saying: "Our Lord Ezekiel, take charge of this valuable for me until I return, and let nobody take it but its heir". And many purses with money lie there rotting because they lay there many years. There were books there, and a worthless person wished to carry away one of the books, but could not, for pain and blindness seized him; therefore everyone fears Ezekiel.'

Before entering Ezekiel's shrine, and quite possibly others, devotees removed their shoes, as was the custom up until the early twentieth century. Muslims remove their shoes before entering mosques. At Ezekiel's shrine as elsewhere, devotees pronounced formulas before depositing their possessions for safekeeping. Ezekiel's presence was perceived by devotees and those who violated the sanctuary's sanctity.

The shrine of Ezekiel was always an object of edification and continuous pilgrimage for the Jewish inhabitants of Iraq and Iran and their Muslim neighbours. The earliest mention of Muslims making pilgrimage there is from the twelfth century at least. Benjamin reports that prominent Muslims (*bnei gdolei Yishmaʿel*) went there to pray because of their profound respect (*ḥiba*) for the prophet Ezekiel. They also venerated Ezra the scribe and prayed at his tomb in Basra. 'They love the Jews on that account.' Jews lived at peace with their Muslim neighbours and both Jewish and Muslim servants served at the shrine.

Muslims also sought the saint's protection before undertaking long journeys. Petaḥiyah mentions that 'Every [Muslim] who makes Pilgrimage [and visits] the tomb of [Muḥammad] makes his way over to the tomb of Ezekiel . . .'

We find other interesting accounts such as that of an Egyptian Jew writing *c.*1371 visiting the shrine of Aaron at Petra who goes so far as to praise the Muslims who visit the shrine:

> In Petra inside the cave of Aaron the Priest the Holy of the Lord . . . the inner cave is sealed. Great miracles were produced many times. Many come to bow down (*l'hishtaḥavot*) and prostrate themselves. The Gentiles [i.e. the Muslims] maintain the place in great purity and for the honour of the Prophet (Aaron) . . . They respect and conduct the Jews and allow them to enter and prostrate themselves and pray there. May the Lord answer their prayers and our prayers and those of His nation Israel. Amen.[23]

One of the most extraordinary examples from the Middle Ages of the three faiths coming together is of the shrine of a Muslim saint Shaykh Arslān (d. *c.*550/1155) who fought against the Crusades through prayer and supplication and spiritual exercises. The shrine remains popular among Muslims down to this day outside Bāb Ṭūma or Thomas's Gate. Jews, Christians, and Zoroastrians visited the tomb of Shaykh Arslān. Since Arslān was a patron saint of sorts, it was natural that monotheists would come together to venerate him. Furthermore, the shrine appealed to a common Damascene identity rooted in mysticism which may have attracted broad segments of the population, including Jews, Christians, and Zoroastrians, who otherwise would not have necessarily visited the shrine. The occasion of the saint's *mawlid* or birth would have been another central occasion. It is also likely that it was a place of congregation for Damascenes at times of popular festivals.

According to one late medieval account:

> The people of [Greater Syria] believe in [Shaykh Arslān] greatly and allege that he possessed the power to manage nature (*walāyat al-taṣarruf*) after his death as he did in life, that his tomb is efficacious for the fulfilment of supplication (*qabruhu mustajāb*), that the four religious communities—Muslims, Jews, Christians, and Zoroastrians believe in him (*ya'taqidūnahu*) and go to him with votive offerings (*nadhr*), such as oil, candles, dirhams and dinars for the sake of getting near [to God] (*'alā sabīl al-qurba*), and whoever seeks him at an occasion of great importance or severe affliction and seeks the intercession (*tawassala*) of God the Exalted through him, his need is fulfilled (*quḍiyat ḥājatuhu*).
>
> They compete among themselves in serving [his tomb], attaching themselves closely to his shrine and seek honour through its upkeep and bring Sultanic decrees for taking charge of his tomb. One person is removed from office and another appointed who is in turn replaced by another person. Scarcely had one person settled in place for a whole year than he was removed and another appointed in his stead. This is an indication of the high value of Shaykh Arslān. May God requite us

[23] Ilan 1997: 135.

and the Muslims with his blessings in the world and the Hereafter. (Meri 2002: 209–10)

It is likely that Jewish, Christian, and Zoroastrian attraction to Shaykh Arslān was due to adherents of faiths other than Islam being attracted to and adhering to a Sufi order which was founded after his death.

More than any other religious phenomena the cult of saints and pilgrimage illustrate a dynamic quality of the confluence of popular ideas and practices as well as individuals and communities coming together at certain times to venerate holy persons.

Memory

Ultimately, the veneration of holy persons and pilgrimage is rooted in the memory of the holy person by the individual and the nation. *Memoria* is at the heart of the veneration of holy persons. Medieval Jews, Christians, and Muslims sought to perpetuate the memories of the holy persons, places, and objects in a number of ways. First, medieval scholars and travellers composed texts which edified the deeds of holy persons. The prophets are memorialized in scripture and saints in the Talmud, liturgical texts, and hagiographical accounts. Written texts as well as oral accounts in the case of modern saints such as the Jewish and Muslim saints of North Africa perpetuate their memory for eternity. The Sīra or Biography of the prophet enumerates various miracles attributed to him in his life. A number of these miracles are associated with the signs of prophethood. Hagiographical traditions mention that at Muhammad's birth a brilliant light emanated from his mother's womb and illuminated the lands of Syria.[24]

In medieval Damascus such texts proliferated at the times of the Crusades but had their origins in the early Islamic period. In the Jewish communities of the Middle East and North Africa, hagiographical traditions did not exist as such. Rather, we find pilgrimage and travel accounts and inventory lists of shrines such as those found in the Cairo Geniza, a cache of medieval documents rediscovered in the nineteenth century in Fusṭāṭ, which enumerate the miracles of the patriarchs and the Talmudic sages (Meri 2002: ch. 4). Two of the most important works in this regard are the itineraries of Benjamin of Tudela and Petaḥiyah of Regensburg.

Second, rulers and the elite contributed to constructing tangible repositories of memory by constructing shrines. In so doing they not only perpetuated the memory of a holy person but their own legacy. This may be regarded as a form of memory common to all faiths. Yet in the medieval Islamic world, one finds that the endowment and construction of shrines was an activity associated with the Muslim ruling class and elite.

[24] e.g. Ibn Kathīr 1998: I. 147, where the prophet's mother has a vision of herself while she bore the prophet of 'a light coming forth from her that lit up the castles of Syria'.

Conclusion

The notion of sovereignty over holy places is antithetical to the universal principles of saint veneration embodied in the Abrahamic faiths. Abrahamic faiths are repositories of collective memory, memories of holy persons and places, and events from scripture and the sacred past. At the heart of the veneration of saints and pilgrimage is belief in the prophets and patriarchs, as exemplars of piety and learning. The exemplary behaviour of the prophets, including that of Jesus (for Christians and Muslims),[25] was emulated by the Jewish sages, the Christian martyrs, Muslim saints (*awliyāʾ*), and others. Reflecting on the meaning of the cult of saints and pilgrimage within the Abrahamic religions requires an appreciation for the role that Abraham played in propagating the monotheistic message of devotion to the One God. Ultimately Abraham's legacy manifested itself in shrines and other holy places and spaces, many dedicated to him, throughout the Islamic world. In historic Syria, the cradle of the monotheistic faiths, the pilgrimage places associated with the prophets and other holy persons are being threatened. In 2013 the Synagogue of Elijah at Jobar outside Damascus suffered extensive damage after shelling by Syrian government forces. While the secular regime has in the past protected Jewish and Christian holy places in order to guarantee its survival and project itself as a defender of minorities, it and its allies have waged a war targeting and destroying Sunni Muslim shrines and mosques and have employed the imminent threat to a historic shrine of Sitt Zaynab, the prophet Muhammad's granddaughter, as a rallying call to perpetuate the war. In marked contrast, the Abrahamic legacy of the veneration of holy persons serves to inspire Jews, Christians, and Muslims throughout the Middle East and North Africa.

Postscript

In 2014 and 2015 ISIS systematically destroyed numerous Christian and Muslim shrines in Iraq and Syria, including the shrines in Mosul of the prophet Jonah (Nabī Yūnus), Seth, son of Adam, and the shrine of St George (Nabī Jirjīs), the fourth-century Christian monastery and shrine of St Benham and St Sarah, as well as other Sunni and Shi'i shrines.

References

al-ʿAsalī, K. 1990. *Mawsim al-Nabī Mūsā fī Filasṭīn: Taʾrīkh al-Mawsim wal-Maqām*. Amman: Dār al-Karmil.

Breger, M. and Reiter, Y., eds. 2010. *Holy Places in the Israeli-Palestinian Conflict: Confrontation and Co-existence*. London and New York: Routledge.

[25] Muslims regard Jesus as the Messiah and a prophet and messenger (i.e. a bearer of a Revelation), and believe that he was taken up by God to Heaven.

Brown, P. 1981. *The Cult of the Saints: Its Rise and Function in Latin Christianity*. Chicago: University of Chicago Press.

Cohen, A. 2006. 'Al-Nabi Musa: An Ottoman Festival (*mawsim*) Resurrected?' In A. Ayalon and D. Wasserstein, eds, *Mamluks and Ottomans: Studies in Honour of Michael Winter*. London, New York: Routledge, 34–44.

Cohn, R. 1987. 'Sainthood on the Periphery: The Case of Judaism'. In J. S. Hawley, ed., *Saints and Virtues*. Berkeley: University of California Press, 87–108.

Egeria. 1919. *The Pilgrimage of Etheria*, ed. and trans. M. L. McClure and C. L. Feltoe. London: Society for Promoting Christian Knowledge.

Eliade, M. 1958. *Patterns in Comparative Religion*. London, New York: Sheed & Ward.

Fenton, P. B. 2000. 'Influences soufies sur le développement de la Qabbale à Safed: le cas de la visitation des tombes'. In P. B. Fenton and R. Goetschel, eds, *Expérience et écriture mystiques dans les religions du livre: actes d'un colloque international tenu par le Centre d'études juives, Université de Paris IV-Sorbonne, 1994*. Leiden: Brill, 163–90.

Frenkel, Y. 2008. 'Popular Culture (Islam, Early and Middle Periods)'. *Religion Compass* 2 (2): 195–225.

Goldziher, I. 1911. 'The Cult of Saints in Islam'. *Moslem World* 1 (1): 302–12.

Goldziher, I. 1967–71. *Muslim Studies*, ed. S. M. Stern, trans. C. R. Barber and S. M. Stern. Chicago: Aldine.

al-Harawī, ʿAlī b. Abī Bakr. 2004. *A Lonely Wayfarer's Guide to Pilgrimage: ʿAlī ibn Abī Bakr al-Harawī's Kitāb al-Ishārāt ilā Maʿrifat al-Ziyārāt*, ed. J. W. Meri, with critical introduction and Arabic text. Princeton: Darwin Press.

Ibn Kathīr. 1998. *The Life of the Prophet Muḥammad*, trans. T. Le Gassick. Reading: Garnet Publishing, Ltd.

Ilan, Z. 1997. *Qivrei Ẓaddiqim be-Ereẓ Yisraʾel*. Jerusalem: Kanah.

Kosansky, O. 2010. 'Pilgrimages and Pilgrimage Rituals, Saints' Tombs in the Modern Period'. In N. A. Stillman, ed., *Encyclopedia of Jews in the Islamic World*, 5 vols. Leiden: Brill, IV. 60–5.

Malouf, A. 1989. *The Crusades through Arab Eyes*. New York: Schocken.

Meri, J. W. 1999a. 'The Etiquette of Devotion in the Islamic Cult of Saints'. In J. Howard-Johnston and P. A. Hayward, eds, *The Cult of Saints in Late Antiquity and the Middle Ages: Essays on the Contribution of Peter Brown*. Oxford: Oxford University Press, 263–86.

Meri, J. W. 1999b. 'Re-appropriating Sacred Space: Medieval Jews and Muslims Seeking Elijah and al-Khadir'. *Medieval Encounters* 5: 237–64.

Meri, J. W. 1999c. 'Aspects of Baraka (Blessings) and Ritual Devotion among Medieval Muslims and Jews'. *Medieval Encounters* 5: 46–69.

Meri, J. W. 2001. 'A Late Medieval Syrian Pilgrimage Guide: Ibn al-Hawrānī's *Al-Ishārāt ilā Amakin al-Ziyārāt* (Guide to Pilgrimage Places)'. *Medieval Encounters: Jewish, Christian and Muslim Culture in Confluence and Dialogue* 7: 3–78.

Meri, J. W. 2002. *The Cult of Saints among Muslims and Jews in Medieval Syria*. Oxford: Oxford University Press.

Meri, J. W. 2010. 'Relics of Piety and Power in Medieval Islam'. *Past and Present* 206 Suppl. 5: 97–120.

Meri, J. W. 2012. 'Pilgrimage to the Prophet Ezekiel's Shrine in Iraq: A Symbol of Muslim–Jewish Relations'. *Perspectives* 12: 22–5.

Peters, F. E. 2006. *The Children of Abraham: Judaism, Christianity, Islam*, 2nd rev. edn. Princeton: Princeton University Press.

Radtke, B. and O'Kane, B. 1996. *The Concept of Sainthood in Early Islamic Mysticism*. Richmond: Curzon Press.
Sadan, J. 1981. 'Le Tombeau de Moïse à Jéricho et à Damas'. *Revue des études islamiques* 49: 59–99.
Serjeant, R. B. 2005. 'Ḥaram and Ḥawṭah'. In L. Jones, ed., *Encyclopedia of Religion*. 2nd edn. Detroit: Macmillan, 3776–8.
Synek, E. 2007. 'Syriac Hagiography'. In K. Parry, ed., *The Blackwell Companion to Eastern Christianity*. Oxford: Blackwell, 439–49.
Vrijhof, P. H. and Waardenburg, J. 1979. *Official and Popular Religion: Analysis of a Theme for Religious Studies*. The Hague: Mouton.
Waardenburg, J. 1978. 'Official and Popular Religion in Islam'. *Social Compass* 25: 315–41.
Waardenburg, J. 2002. *Islam: Historical, Social and Political Perspectives*. Berlin: DeGruyter.
Youssef, Y. N. 2007. 'Coptic Hagiography'. In K. Parry, ed., *The Blackwell Companion to Eastern Christianity*. Oxford: Blackwell Publishing.
Zayyāt, Ḥ. 1982. *Khabāyā al-Zawāyā min Taʾrīkh Ṣaydnāyā*. Damascus.

CHAPTER 28

RELIGIONS OF LOVE

Judaism, Christianity, Islam

DAVID NIRENBERG AND LEONARDO CAPEZZONE

IN *Seven Pillars of Wisdom*, T. E. Lawrence ('Lawrence of Arabia') describes the interruption of his bath in Wadi Rumm (southern Jordan):

> a grey-bearded, ragged man with a hewn face of great power and weariness, came slowly along the path till opposite the spring: and there he let himself down with a sigh upon my clothes spread out over a rock beside the path. . . . He heard me and leaned forward, peering with rheumy eyes. . . . After a long stare, he seemed content, and closed his eyes groaning, 'The love is from God; and of God; and towards God.' His low-spoken words were caught by some trick distinctly in my water pool. They stopped me suddenly. I had believed Semites unable to use love as a link between themselves and God. (Lawrence 1926/1985: 364–6)

Lawrence's narrative is of transformative revelation. But for us, the anecdote is more useful for what it reveals about the world the author came from. For his 'Semitic' prejudices flowed within a stream of Christian thought—secularized into the philosophies and sciences of European modernity—that articulated the failings of Judaism and Islam (as well as of Jews and Muslims), in terms of handicaps in spheres of love.

The history of this articulation is very long. The earliest Christian writings already attempt to distance salvific forms of loving relation to the world and its creator from the alleged practices of Jews and pagans. In the Sermon on the Mount, for example, Matthew's Jesus presents his teachings in contrast with those that had come before:

> Ye have heard that it hath been said, Thou shalt love thy neighbour, and hate thine enemy. But I say unto you, Love your enemies, bless them that curse you, do good to them that hate you, and pray for them which despitefully use you, and persecute you. (5: 43–4)

The Gospel authors surely knew that the injunction to love one's neighbour is nowhere joined to the hatred of enemies in the Decalogue or the Pentateuch. The Gospels' misrepresentation of the teachings on love of Jesus' predecessors and rivals (most notably the Pharisees) was rather part of a sectarian strategy through which Jesus' teachings were presented as the perfection and fulfilment of a flawed law that came before. (A sectarian strategy that, in John, does take the form of a stress upon the love of one's 'friends' and brothers within the sectarian community, rather than one's 'enemies' outside of it: John 13: 34–5; 15: 9–13; 1 John 3: 14, 4: 12.)

Over time the utility of this strategy, sometimes combined with classical stereotypes of Jewish misanthropy, produced a powerful theological discourse about the supersession of a loveless Judaism by a loving Christianity. That discourse was not overturned by modernity, so much as put to new kinds of work. When Spinoza, for example, launched his revolutionary criticism of priestly political power in the *Theologico-Political Treatise* (= *TTP*) of 1670, he did so by suggesting that the basis of this power was in the bad laws of the Old Testament, bad (among other reasons) because they instructed the Hebrews to love only themselves and hate all others. Spinoza's choice of proof-text is striking: '[i]t was for this reason that they were told: "Love thy neighbor and hate thine enemy"' (*TTP* 216/iii.233, citing Matt. 5: 43).

We should stress that 'Jewish' lovelessness was not only a charge against Jews. St Paul, for example, used the verb 'to Judaize' in one of the earliest Christian writings (Gal. 2: 14) in order to criticize St Peter for urging what he deemed to be an inappropriate attachment to the ritual laws of Judaism upon Gentile followers of Jesus. 'Judaizing' was here a Christian error: the error of placing (as the Jews had allegedly done in rejecting Jesus) excessive attention on earthly signs rather than on the divine signification of those signs. Such inappropriate love came to be thought of as 'Judaizing' the Christian. Some 1,600 years after Paul, the English poet George Herbert put the point bluntly in his poem 'Self-Condemnation' (of 1633): 'He that doth love, and love amisse, | This worlds delights before true Christian joy, | Hath made a Jewish choice . . . | And is a Judas-Jew' (Herbert 1991: 160–1).

Nevertheless, for all that love could discriminate among Christians, it drew an even sharper line between religions. Blaise Pascal provided a lapidary version of the logic in his *Pensées* of 1670: 'Carnal Jews are half-way between Christians and pagans. Pagans do not know God and only love earthly things; Christians know the true God and do not love earthly things. Jews and pagans love the same possessions, Jews and Christians know the same God' (Pascal 1995: 85). Within this comparative scheme, improper love is the common characteristic of the condemned, whether they know God (like the Jews) or not (like the pagans).

Pascal did not mention Muslims and Islam, a faith and people sometimes classed by Christians among those who 'know the same God', sometimes among those who do not (i.e. as pagans), but in both cases charged with inadequate love. The standard criticisms appear already in the earliest Christian writers about Islam in the seventh century and are still sometimes repeated today: (1) Islam is a religion of fear and violence, not of love; and (2) when Muslims love, they love the flesh, not the divine: even the vision of Paradise offered by their (false) prophet is merely one of carnal lusts writ large (Kaegi 1969; Lamoreaux 1996; Tolan 2002; Nirenberg 2009).

How best to intervene in this long polemic about the relative lovingness of the Abrahamic faiths? We might begin by stressing that love is not a necessary prerequisite for religion. God's love of humanity, humanity's love of god, man's love for man: theogonies, cosmologies, theodicies, and ethics have existed without one or any of these. For an example we need look no further than Aristotle's cosmos, moved by love for an 'unmoved mover' who does not—because incorporeal, unchanging, and unmovable—love anything in return (Aristotle, *Metaphysics* 1072a27). If we have come to think of these loves as the foundation of religion (see e.g. the recent *Encyclopedia of Love in World Religions* (Greenberg 2007)), it is in part because of the work done by love in the history of the three 'Abrahamic' religions. Judaism, Christianity, and Islam have all used love to imagine, contest, and represent relations both proper and improper between and among created beings and divine creator. And all three religions (in their myriad flavours and sects) have also used love to imagine their relation to each other (as well as to other religions), and to represent the stakes in their competing claims to truth.

We cannot map, in our brief compass, the work done by love in these three faiths. Instead, we will focus on the faiths criticized within the Christian tradition as relatively loveless—that is, Judaism (beginning with the Hebrew Bible) and Islam. Along the way, we will pay special attention to those moments in which the different religious traditions formulated their claims to love in interaction (real or imagined) with each other. For we wish to insist that although claims of love animate many Abrahamic ethical, social, and onto-theological ideals, the same claims—articulated in terms of the other's lack of love, or of false love versus true—underpin many of the sectarian dynamics and discriminations through which religious communities distinguished themselves from one another.

Judaism Biblical and Rabbinic

Unlike Aristotle, the compilers of the Hebrew Bible had little trouble imagining God's love, whether for creation in general or for a particular person or people. In the words of Deuteronomy's Moses (7: 7–8), 'the Lord did not set His heart upon you, nor choose you, because you were more numerous than any people, but because the Lord loved you, and because He would keep the oath which He swore unto your fathers.' Or as Hosea's God puts it, 'I led them with cords of human kindness, with ties of love. To them I was like one who lifts a little child to the cheek, and I bent down to feed them' (Hos. 11: 4). The Hebrew word for love used here is *ahava*, which approximately subsumes the meaning of the Greek words *agape* ('true love' or love of God), *philía* (love between friends, love of wisdom), and *storgē* (familial love) (Thomas 1939; Moran 1963).

In the Hebrew Bible, *ahava* is used not only for God's love of his people and that people's love of God (as in 'love God with all your heart', Deut. 6: 5) but also of the people's love of each other. 'Do not seek revenge or hold a grudge, but love your neighbour as yourself' (Lev. 19: 18). The imperative form of the verb (*ve-ahavta*), used elsewhere in the Pentateuch only with reference to man's love of God, is in this chapter extended into a command to love one's *re'a*, an uncommon word in the Pentateuch, and one whose semantic field is therefore difficult to define, but meaning 'other', 'companion', 'friend', and translated 'neighbour' by Tyndale and *King James*. A few verses later, the command is extended further: as you love yourself, love the foreigner (*ger*) residing in the land (Lev. 19: 34).

In these verses love of self is presented as the proper basis and measure for love of others. These verses came to seem to many later commentators, from Rabbi Hillel (*b. Shabbat* 31a) and Jesus (e.g. Matt. 22: 39) in the first century to Hermann Cohen in the early twentieth, as the foundations of the Hebrew Bible's ethical stance toward all humanity (Hirshman 2004). We will return to the future of these verses. But first we should note that *ahava* is only one of several words for love in the Hebrew Bible. *Ḥesed*, for example, often translated as 'loving kindness', denotes love of the stronger for the weaker (including that of God for creation). 'I show', says God, 'loving kindness unto the thousandth generation of those who love me [*ohavai*] and keep my commandments' (Exod. 20: 5). In God's loving kindness toward his creation, some of the authors of the Hebrew Bible seem to have seen an ethical foundation just as central as love of neighbour. Micah, for example, summarizes all of the commandments as 'just this: to do justice, to love kindness [*ḥesed*], and to walk humbly with your God' (6: 8). (See generally Harvey 1976.)

Even passionate love—the love of lover and beloved, or husband and wife—is used in the Hebrew Bible to represent the relationship between God and his follower, whether individual or collective. The Song of Songs provides a famous and sustained example, one that rabbinic exegetes would much later extend and apply to the relationship between God and Israel in every time and place (Wolfson 2003). Thus the classical commentators, from the early Song of Songs Rabbah to the eleventh-century Rabbi Shlomo ben Yitzhak (Rashi), explained that Solomon (traditionally understood as the author of the Song), foreseeing the exiles of Israel, wrote a love song in order to represent the relationship between God and Israel in that Diasporic future. The song would remind Israel of her earlier marriage to God (cf. Hos. 2: 9), of her betrayal of that love (cf. Lev. 26: 40), and of her lover's ongoing suffering (cf. Isa. 63: 9), thereby recalling her to her divine spouse (cf. Hos. 2: 4).

As this medieval exegesis makes clear, passionate love could represent the ideal relationship between God and people, but it could also—in its negative form as adultery and infidelity—serve as a powerful metaphor for an individual or a people's straying from that ideal. Even Solomon, for all his inspired knowledge of divine love, was led away from God by inappropriate erotic interests, which, according to the Hebrew Bible, took the form of 1,000 women (1 Kgs 11).

Erotic passion, loving kindness, love: the differences between these affections will become important in all three religions. Within a biblical context, however, those differences should not be exaggerated. God, in Jeremiah 2: 2, remembers 'the loving-kindness [*ḥesed*] of your youth, the love [*ahava*] of your betrothal, how you followed me in the desert . . .'. In such a passage, the multiple Hebrew forms of love stand in indistinguishable proximity, expressing the relation between God and Israel. We can still see a similar proximity in the first centuries of the Common Era, when the Talmud treats 'loving kindness' as a commandment just as all-encompassing as love of neighbour: just as in loving kindness God took the time to make 'garments of skin' for Adam and Eve before expelling them from Paradise (Gen. 3: 21), so it is incumbent upon each of us to clothe the poor (*b. Sotah* 14a).

As these examples make clear, each of these loves, regardless of its specific vocabulary, could (and did) serve as the foundation of a system of ethical and even legal obligation. (On the use of *be'ahava*—'with love'—in Talmudic and gaonic formularies for sales contracts see Muffs 1992: 122–3.) This may seem odd to some modern philosophers, brought up on the secularized Christian conviction that love and law are inimical, and that the ethical cannot be imposed but must be self-legislated. (Recall, for example, Hegel's critique of Kant's 'categorical imperative'.) Late antique and medieval Jewish thinkers, less committed to Protestant axioms, did not assume an essential conflict between love and law, though they did explore some potential tensions in the command to love. Thus the thirteenth-century rabbi Moses ben Nachman (Nachmanides) commented on Lev. 19: 18: 'A human heart cannot undertake to love one's other as oneself. Did not Rabbi Akiva himself teach "your own life takes precedence over the life of another"? (*b. Bava Metzia* 62a). What the mitzvah commands is that one weigh the concerns of another as carefully as one weighs one's own' (Goodman 2008: 3–30, here 13).

Though medieval Jewish thinkers did not worry much about a conflict between love and law, they were quite concerned (particularly the more Aristotelian among them) about the possible incommensurability between love and divinity. In much ancient philosophy, love was thought to result from imperfection or lack. The imperfect loves the perfect, but the Perfect One, lacking nothing, does not, cannot, love the imperfect. This position was problematic for Jewish philosophers working within a scriptural tradition that attributed such an important place to God's love. For example Moses ben Maimon (Maimonides), who was both the greatest systematizer of rabbinic law and the greatest Jewish Aristotelian of the twelfth century, had no difficulty speaking of our human *ahavah* (Arabic: *mahabbah*) for God (Lamm 1995; Vajda 1957). In fact it is the love of God that provides the ultimate stimulus for the study of scripture and law. Students start with baser motivations, but the highest goal is to move (as he puts it in the introduction to his commentary on *Mishna Sanhedrin* ch. 10, also known as *Ḥelek*) from serving for the promise of reward to serving purely for the love of God. He quotes here the words of an early rabbinic commentary, *Sifrei on Deut.* 11: 13: 'Should you be tempted to say "I will study Torah in order to become rich, or in order to be called Rabbi, or in order to receive a reward in the world to come," Scripture says "to love the lord your God": whatever you do, it is only out of love'. (Compare this teaching of the early rabbis to the polemic in Matt. 23.)

But for all his emphasis on human love, Maimonides was (with rare exceptions) unwilling to speak of divine *ahavah* toward us, since this would be to attribute a bodily passion to an incorporeal God. Similarly when it came to speaking of erotic love (Greek *éros*, Hebrew *ḥesheq*, Arabic *ʿishq*), he attributed to humans a passionate (intellectual) love for God (*Guide* 3.51), but did not attribute to God a passionate love toward us. In good Aristotelian fashion, the only form of love that Maimonides attributes to God is *ḥesed*, the loving kindness of the strong for the weak. He cites Psalms 89: 3: 'The world is built on loving kindness' (*Guide* 3.53).

Maimonides seems to have understood biblical suggestions of God's love as heuristic anthropomorphisms, meant to help the weaker in knowledge and faith, but that should not mislead the wise. Other Jewish rationalists were much more willing to put God's love at the centre of creation. Following the Muslim philosopher Avicenna's view that God has a 'passionate love' (Arab. *ʿishq*) for creation, Levi ben Gershon (Gersonides, 1288–1344) suggested that Gen. 2: 2 should not be understood as 'And God *concluded* (*va-yekhal*) his work on the seventh day', since God had in fact concluded his work on the sixth day. Instead the passage should be understood 'And God loved (*ḥesheq*, cognate of Arab. *ʿishq*) his work on the seventh day' (Gersonides 1866: 7.2; his commentaries on the Song of Songs and on Gen. 2: 2 are also relevant here). A little more than a generation later Ḥasdai Crescas (*c.*1340–1410/11) suggested, contra Plato, Aristotle, and Maimonides, that God's creation is itself the paradigm of love. For Crescas, love and perfection go hand in hand, and God is not only the ultimate object of love, but also the ultimate lover (Harvey 1998: 108–9).

Jewish mysticism, too, produced a powerful discourse of love between and among humanity and divinity, a discourse saturated with erotic vocabulary of love, and even ascribing feminine and masculine 'attributes' (*sfirot*) to the godhead. The medieval Kabbalists of the Castilian and the Catalan schools understood the divine as itself caught up in a process of separation and reunification, of alienation, yearning, and recuperation, and often they represented the history of that process in terms drawn from human spheres of love and the erotic (Scholem 1946: 225; Idel 1989; Idel 2009; Wolfson 1994; Wolfson 1995). The same was true of relations between human and divine. In *Iggeret ha-Qodesh* (The Holy Letter), for example, Nachmanides or one of his students undertook to show how knowledge of and union with God is achieved through 'proper sexual intercourse'. The project was explicitly posed as a philosophical polemic, here taking aim at Maimonides and Aristotle: 'The matter is not as Rabbi Moses of blessed memory said in his *Guide of the Perplexed*. He was incorrect in praising Aristotle for stating that the sense of touch is shameful for us. Heaven forbid! The matter is not like the Greek said' (Nachmanides 1976: 42; Mopsik 1986; Mopsik 2005).

Such texts make clear that 'philosophical Judaism' had many streams. In some of these streams love and even marital intercourse remained a powerful way to imagine the overcoming of the gap between God and creation: so powerful, in fact, that soul and body, god and matter, might even become one flesh in nuptial union. In this sense, we can say (anachronistically) that love provided these strands of Judaism with a dialectical power capable of overcoming the stark gap between the created and mutable on the one hand, and on the other the eternal and divine. Thus in his *Shnei Luḥot ha-Brit* (two tablets of the covenant), the early seventeenth-century rabbi Isaiah ben Abraham Halevi Horowitz (also known by acronym as the Shlah) could write: 'In one respect, the body and the soul are both equal: i.e., both are spiritual, as was the first man before the fall and as he will be in the future.... Even earthly matter becomes spiritual again and both will have the same value. This is the goal: [that the body and the soul] are eternal...' (Mopsik 2005: 72).

Islam Early and Classical

Islam, like Judaism, had many ways of thinking about the roles of love in the relationship between and among God and creation. We might begin with the nature of revelation itself. Islamic classical theology understood the Quran as God's word made book, an intermediate space between the transcendent God and his creature, a space in which the disclosure of God's will unfolds through qualities of act (as distinguished from qualities of essence, that is, from God's uncreated eternal 'meanings', *ma'nā*) (Gimaret 1990; Frank 1999). One of these temporal qualities of action in relation to created being is God's infinite mercy (*raḥma*). The twofold concept of *al-raḥmān al-raḥīm* encompasses the whole range of divine grace and benevolence offered to the human understanding. Indeed God's revelation to Muhammad is itself an act of divine mercy in history: 'It is only as a mercy that We sent you to all people' (Q. 21: 107).

Love is another quality with which God acts within history. Indeed if we take seriously the classical Islamic idea that the quranic revelation should be understood in terms of the historical context of its revelation, the manifestation of the concept of love undergoes a marked evolution (Rippin 2001; Dammen McAuliffe 2003a; Hawting 2003). The classical method of Quran interpretation—as established by Ṭabarī in the tenth century—depends upon the identification of historical causes, or occasions, for the revelation of individual verses (*asbāb al-nuzūl*) (Rippin 1988). In the specific case of the vocabulary of love—*ḥubb*, or *maḥabba* (in its general meaning of love) and *wadd*, or *mawadda* (loving affection, friendship)—we can distinguish between its use in the (earlier) Meccan revelations and in the Medinan, revealed after Muhammad's establishment of a polity.

In the Meccan revelations, terms of love appear as relevant features of the relational system between God, human beings, and the community of believers: one of the names of God, for example, is *al-wadūd*. Whether such names indicate God's attributes or essences has long been a subject of debate in Islam. We might want to infer from the name *wadūd* that loving affection is part of the nature of God and is therefore infinite. But at the very least we can say—adhering to the position of the classical theologians that we can know only the will and not the nature of God—that loving affection is one of the manifold manifestations of God's will in the created world.

The Meccan revelations are marked by apocalyptic tension, and it is within this tension that Muhammad exhorts his hearers to 'ask forgiveness from your Lord and turn to Him in repentance: my Lord is merciful and most loving' (Q. 11: 90). Conversion to a God who 'is the Most Forgiving, the Most Loving' (85: 14) emerges here as the human's (loving?) response to God's love. This response, in turn, is the first step toward a collective love expressed in terms of a mutual affection between believers, mediated through the figure of the prophet: 'Say (Muhammad), "I ask you no reward for this, only the affection due to kin (*al-mawadda fī'l-qurbā*)"' (42: 23).

This is not the only form of social or 'inter-subjective' love in the Meccan suras. The semantic field of *mawadda* extends as well to the expression of marital love: 'Another of His signs is that He created spouses from among yourselves for you to live with in tranquility: He ordained love and kindness between you. There truly are signs in this for those who reflect' (30: 21). Likewise, God's affection for justice and righteousness begins to be affirmed, as in 19: 96 ('But the Lord of Mercy will give love (*waddan*) to those who believe and do righteous deeds', echoing God's special tenderness for Moses: 'I showered you with My love (*maḥabbatan*) and planned that you should be reared under My watchful eye' (20: 39). Over time, this specific orientation of God's love toward justice will be repeatedly declared, shifting the semantic emphasis from *wadd* to *ḥubb*. To give but an example among many others: 'But if you [Muhammad] do judge between them, judge justly: God loves (*yuḥibbu*) the just' (5: 42). It is worth noting (given the future of the issue in the history of philosophy) that in the quranic lexicon of love, the multiple significations of the word *ḥubb* and its derivatives clearly include passionate and erotic dimension of human love, as in the Sura *Joseph*: 'Some women of the city said, "The governor's wife is trying to seduce her slave! Love for him consumes her heart (*qad shaghafa-hā ḥubban*)!"' (12: 30).

In the Medinan suras the social, religiously oriented function of love as a sentiment that ties and binds each Muslim to another and the entire community of believers to God is most fully attested. All the verses in which a vocabulary of love is used in order to represent socio-political bonds are Medinese: that is, their revelation to Muhammad is associated with the establishment of the first Muslim community, and with the accompanying transformation of collective values (such as the rise of spiritual brotherhood alongside the old kinship bonds).

Within this new community of converts, love becomes (much as it had been for earlier Christian and Jewish sectarian communities) a relational representation of an ethic of living in spiritual solidarity within a structured social body enjoined to the good. It is in this context, for example, that charity (the giving to others of worldly benefits that one loves for oneself) becomes a manifestation of the believer's proper loving orientation toward God, as for example in 2: 177: 'The truly good are those who believe in God and the Last Day, in the angels, the Scripture, and the prophets: who give away some of their wealth, however much they cherished it (*'alā ḥubbi-hi*),[1] to their relatives, to orphans, the needy, travelers and beggars, and to liberate those in bondage, those who keep up the prayer and pay the prescribed alms'; or in 76: 8–9: 'They give food to the poor, the orphan, and the captive, though they love it themselves, saying: We feed you for the sake of God alone, We seek neither recompense nor thanks from you.'

Love, in the Medinese revelations, becomes one of the foundations of the believers' covenant (*mithāq*) with God (7: 172) (Nuwya 1970: 46), as in 5: 54 'You who believe, if any of you go back on your faith, God will soon replace you with a people He loves (*qawm yuḥibbu-hum*) and who love Him (*yuḥibbūna-hu*).' This covenant is transferable to the prophet as well, who is told to proclaim: 'Say: "If you love God, follow me, and God will love you and forgive you your sins; God is most forgiving, most merciful"' (3: 31). In fact, the Medinese revelations often refer, whether implicitly or explicitly, to an almost transitive affection between God and Muhammad, between Muhammad and his community of believers, and between *mu'minīn/muslimīn* and the prophet, as for example in the following verses: 'God and His angels bless the Prophet—so, you who believe, bless him too and give him greeting of peace' (33: 56).

The exemplarity of the prophet could sustain a discourse of *imitatio propheti* capable of framing a communitarian identity in which love (*ḥubb*) for the prophet is a condition of faith and a political expression of loyalty. This potential was thoroughly developed in the prophetic tradition (*Sunna*) (Wensinck 1936: I. 406–10), in which the humanity of the prophet is often used to translate God's transcendent mercy and kindness into an immanent moral and behavioural norm that provides the community with an ethical system. When dealing with the political meaning of love in their works on ethics, Muslim philosophers—from al-Fārābī to Miskawayh to Nāṣir al-Dīn al-Ṭūsī—will mirror this political discourse of love, evidently taking inspiration from it, although translating it into philosophical terms (Miskawayh 1969: 211–32; Nāṣir al-Dīn al-Ṭūsī 1981: 275–80). Al-Fārābī provides a good example of this attempt to maintain an ethical convergence between ancient philosophy and the modernity of revelation, for example, when he writes about the legislator's duty to keep love alive among the citizens of a city ruled by a common law (al-Fārābī 1952: 21; *concordiam* is the Latin preferred by F. Gabrieli to translate the Arabic *maḥabba* with which al-Fārābī rendered platonic *philia*).

But let us remain, for the moment, with the Medinan revelations in order to explore one more political aspect of quranic love: God's love for his community can imply as well a demand for solidarity against external threats. 'God truly loves (*yuḥibbu*) those who fight in solid lines for His cause, like a well-compacted wall' (61: 4). Such passages—which we can understand historically, if we like, as the product of a sectarian community's logic of solidarity marked by alliances, partnership, and enmities—might strike some modern commentators as out of place in a 'religion of love'. We should remember, however, that our sense of what religions of love should look like is

[1] So M. A. S. Abdel Haleem's translation, from which we quote here; Yusuf Ali's renowned translation renders this passage 'out of love for Him'.

conditioned by a distinctly modern and secularized interpretation of the Christian injunction to 'love your enemy'. Historically, all three Abrahamic scriptural traditions have been quite capable of imagining violent enmity as a necessary corollary of 'love of neighbour'. Think, for example, of Luke 19: 27: 'But those mine enemies, which would not that I should reign over them, bring hither, and slay them before me.'

Quran and *Sīra* (Muhammad's biography) varied in their sense of how the adherents of Muhammad's prophetic predecessors should be classed within the friend–enemy distinction. These ambivalent attitudes towards Christians and Jews are often thought to reflect a historical context of actual encounters between Muhammad and representatives of these communities. However that may be, the Quran renders them in prophetic idiom, as at 5: 82: 'You (Muhammad) are sure to find that the most hostile to the believers are the Jews and those who associate other deities with God; you are sure to find that the closest in affection (*mawadda*) to the believers are those who say, "we are Christians", for there are among them people devoted to learning and ascetics. Those people are not given to arrogance.'

Certainly there are many quranic passages like this one that proclaim differences between the Abrahamic faiths, and even those that insist on separation, such as Quran 5: 51 which states that Muslim must not take Jews and Christians as 'close allies or leaders'. Nevertheless, Jews as well as Christians were included within the boundaries of the first umma as stipulated in the so-called Constitution of Medina, thereby establishing what we might call a socio-political precedent for the development of the quranic idea of People of the Scriptures (*ahl al-kitāb*), with all its historically realized potential for permitting and legitimizing religiously plural societies in Islam.

We might give the last quranic word here to sura 60 (*al-Mumtaḥana*, or 'Women Tested'), revealed (according to Islamic tradition) after the Ḥudaybiya truce between Muhammad and his Medinan followers, and their Quraish opponents in the city of Mecca. The keyword in this sura, dedicated to establishing both a criterion for and a limit to enmity, is *mawadda*. The sura begins with hostility declaring in 60: 1: 'You who believe, do not take My enemies and yours as your allies, showing them friendship . . .' But this enmity is limited by an awareness of the potential for peace, mutually respectful justice, and even love: 'God may still bring about affection between you and your present enemies—God is all powerful, God is most forgiving and merciful—and He does not forbid you to deal kindly and justly with anyone who has not fought you for your faith and driven you out of your houses: God loves (*yuḥibbu*) the just' (60: 7).

Quranic exegesis quickly set to the interpretative work of expanding God's love for humankind. According to tradition, Muhammad himself began this work, as the Quran's first exegete, in the *ḥadīth qudsī*, the collection of his sayings that is separated because of its divine inspiration from the canonical corpora of *ḥadīth* literature. Interpretation of the prophet's words—and criticism of their chains of transmission—was ceaselessly practised in order to put the prophetic texts to living work, producing (among many other things) a long and multi-disciplinary history of debate about love.

We could point to countless examples, among the earliest, the female mystic Rabīʿa (d. 801), whose exegesis gave women access to a transcendental knowledge of God through a de-historicized reading of Quran 5: 54 ('. . . a people He loves (*qawmyuḥibbu-hum*) and who love Him (*yuḥibbūna-hu*)') that stressed the precedence of God's love over human love for God (Schimmel 1975). We will, however, focus on just two notable thinkers, Ibn Dāwūd al-Iṣfahānī (d. 883) and Ibn 'Arabī (d. 1240), both of them representatives of literalist approaches to the Quran.

Ibn Dāwūd, the leader of the *ẓāhirī* juridical school in Baghdad, played a foundational role in the development of Arabic courtly love theory, insisting on the dignity of human love, both spiritualizing it and distinguishing it from mystical love. His school flourished at a time when love was becoming a convergence point of the main trends in an urbanizing Islamic culture newly conversant with Greek terms. It was at this time, for example, that Aristophanes' myth of the divided androgyne (the only fragmentary witness of Plato's *Symposion* in Arabic: Gutas 1988) entered the Arab cultural horizon. Ibn Dāwūd, 'the first of the Arabic writers on love theory (whose work we have) to quote the opinions of Greek thinkers' (Giffen 1971: 12; Raven 1989), was very much alive to all of these currents.

He felt (and expressed in his poetry: al-Iṣfahānī 1985: 20–1) the crucial importance of love as existing in human nature as created by God, but as a literalist, he also felt the limits to interpretation imposed by the Quran. His juridical response was to place love outside of the Law. He invoked the prophet's authority, quoting a celebrated (and also much criticized) *ḥadīth* according to which someone who loves, conceals his love in chastity, and dies from love, dies as a martyr (Bell 1979; Gruendler 2004).

This development could be considered a turning point in a quest for a subjective concept of spiritual love imagined as a gendered duality of Lover and Beloved, under the sign of desire. It is analogous to the striking passage, after the tenth century, from *ḥubb* (love in a general sense) to *ʿishq* (passionate, extreme love) (Lumbard 2007) in the mystical lexicon of love. In Avicenna's *Treatise on Love* (*ʿishq*), we see the achievement of a sublimation into mysticism of cultures of love coming from intellectual debates in many different fields: medicine, philosophy, jurisprudence, and literature (Avicenna 1945; von Grunebaum 1952; Rundgren 1978–9; Bell 1986). God has here become, in a most un-Aristotelian fashion, both the lover and the beloved. (Avicenna 1956: 369; al-Farabi 1985: 86–9, and for the influence upon Judaism of this development in Islamic philosophy, see above.)

The gendered nature of lover and beloved (conceived by Rabīʿa even before this philosophical turn) provides one way of thinking about the remarkable presence of women in Islamic mysticism, seeing in the role mysticism assigns women as subjects of desire a clue to the disruptive potential in mystical discourse. The mystical/philosophical (male) treatment of love, which borrows its most powerful metaphors of salvific knowledge from the language of courtly love, introduces the possibility (not to say the necessity) of a feminine element in the worldly manifestation of God's wisdom and beauty (think of Ibn 'Arabī's Niẓām, or in the Christian West, Dante's 'donne ch'avete intelletto d'amore') (Corbin 1995; Schimmel 1975). This possibility does not, however, prevent the establishment of an implicitly male gendered order in such discourses of love, even one that represents women's bodies as an obstacle to the attainment of knowledge, and excludes women from the possibility of a spiritualized subjectivity or a relation of love with the transcendent Beloved.

Our second example, Ibn 'Arabī, belonged like Ibn Dāwūd to the literalist juridical school, and shared the singular *ẓāhirī* sensitivity to issues of profane love (as did Ibn Ḥazm, author of *The Neck of the Dove*). Again like Ibn Dāwūd, his hermeneutical approach was based on a range of *ḥadīth* not unanimously recognized as authentic. For example, the long chapter 178 of his *Futūḥāt al-makkiyya* introduces a *ḥadīth qudsī* explicitly defined as unestablished by transmission: 'I was a hidden treasure and was not known; I loved (*aḥbabtu*) to be known, therefore I created the creation and made Myself know to them so that they came to know me' (Ibn 'Arabī 1911: II. 399; Chittick 1995; Addas 2002). Ibn 'Arabī juxtaposes these words to Quran 5: 54 and 51: 56 in order to suggest that God created the world out of desire, including his desire to be loved. Such a concept of God might seem far from orthodox tenets, according to which love and longing for the beloved are qualities that God, the self-sufficient, could not possess. But such a position, with all of its potential antinomianism, is implicit in Ibn 'Arabī's definition of *his* Islam as 'the religion of love' (*dīn al-ḥubb*), a definition that culminated in the mysticism of the Persian Jalāl al-Dīn al-Rūmī (Chittick 1983). One way to understand the relationships implicit in this definition between a loving and a legal knowledge of God was offered by another Persian mystic, 'Ayn al-Quḍāt al-Hamadānī (executed in 526/1132), who explicitly used the Islamic notion of *madhhab* (a juridical school) to define the mystical path: 'The lovers ... do not follow the religion (*madhhab*) of Shāfi'ī or Abū Ḥanīfa or anyone else. They follow the religion of love and religion of God (*madhhab-i 'ishq wa-madhhab-i Khudā*)' (al-Hamadānī 1961: 114).

Polemics of Love

Just as all three Abrahamic traditions make claims on God's love, all three also make claims about the love of others. Perhaps already in the early Israelite context, we might want to see in the Decalogue's assertions about the murderous cruelty of Ba'al worshippers a sectarian strategy of representation whereby one's lovingness is established through negative contrast. But contrast need not equal exclusion. In the Hebrew Bible God loves not only the Jewish people (for example, Deut. 7: 7–8), but others as well: 'The Lord is good to all and His tender mercies are over all his works' (Ps. 145: 9). God acts in the world for the benefit of many peoples, including Israel: 'Have not I brought up Israel out of the land of Egypt, and the Philistines from Caphtor, and the Syrians from Kir?' (Amos 9: 7). Even at the end of the world, at least according to Isaiah's visions, there are competing versions of God's love. At times, the prophet tells us that all the nations will be saved, at times, that all but Israel will be destroyed. Very different visions of the future, to be sure, but among them the possibility that God's love extends to all.

This possibility persists in rabbinic Judaism. When Maimonides, for example, explicates the biblical commandments to know and love God in his Foundations of the Torah (*Mishneh Torah*, 1–4), he does not mention Israel. According to him, the commandment is addressed to the human being, with no distinction between Jew and non-Jew. Almost four centuries later, in his *Dialoghi d'amore* (Abrabanel 1535), Judah Abrabanel/Leon Hebreo draws on philosophical and Kabbalistic themes (as well as many other materials) in order to present love as a universal cosmological principle, orienting the relations of all things and persons in heaven and earth.

Christianity, too, has found ways to include non-Christians in its community of love. But what is more important for our topic here is the roles that Christian arguments about the insufficiencies of Jewish and Muslim love have played in the development of western thought about these religions (and hence, in the development of disciplines such as the history and philosophy of religion). There is of course a great deal of historical variation in these roles, but there are also important continuities. In the case of Judaism, the long history of complex interaction between classical and Christian motifs of Jewish misanthropy and lovelessness creates a formal continuity between, for example, G. W. F. Hegel's remark about Abraham's decision to follow God's instruction and leave his homeland—'Love alone was beyond his power'—and the condemnations of Abraham that Philo of Alexandria had attempted to rebut almost 2,000 years earlier (Hegel 1948: 185–7).

Similarly in the case of Islam, the long tradition of Christian thought has reproduced and transformed its initial polemical onto-theological commitments about Islamic love in accordance with its evolving historical experience. Thus the earliest Quran translations into Latin (like the one produced, with accompanying commentary, at the request of Peter the Venerable in 1140) were designed to demonstrate the depraved fleshiness of the prophet's passions and teachings (d'Alverny 1947–8; Kritzcek 1964; Burman 2007). The old idea of Muslim lust was here demonstrated through a new Christian attention to the Quran as a religious text, and deployed in a new direction: that of articulating a sharper difference between an emerging 'Christendom' and Islam (Nirenberg 2009). Islam's supposed love of the flesh was posed in seemingly intractable antithesis to the Christian love of God so eloquently preached by Bernard of Clairvaux (in works like *De amore Dei*) and other Latin Christians: an antithesis so stark that it could even justify the Christian killing of Muslims in crusade as an 'act of love' (Riley-Smith 1980).

If today many in the West perceive Islam as puritanical and sex-phobic, the medieval Christian understanding was in some sense the reverse: every kind of lust, from polygamy to homosexuality, was licit to Muslims both in this world and the next. In this sense Christian medieval polemics against Islam were focused not so much on the lack of love in Islam's spiritual and ethical values, but on the type of love—carnal and passionate, which is to say, profane—that Christians understood as characteristic of Islam and enjoined by its law.

We have already given one example—justification for crusade and mission—of the cultural work done by this polemic. We could give many more, for the charge of Muslim lust was a powerful tool through which Christian cultures could proclaim their distance from Islam on any number of fronts. One of these, worth mentioning because so well studied, was in the poetic field of the love lyric, a field tilled with precocious genius in Arabic, and one whose sensuous fruits threatened Christian cultivators—themselves aware of the reputation of their Muslim predecessors—with the charge of excessively carnal love.

Christian poetry addressed these 'anxieties of influence' (Menocal 1987) by stigmatizing the love culture of the Arabs. Thus Petrarch, himself a founding father of the Christian sonnet, condemned with one gesture both Arabic science and Arabic poetry to the realm of carnality: 'As to Arab physicians, you know them very well. As to their poets, I know them: nothing more feeble, more spineless, more lewd. What can I say more, hardly someone will convince me that something good could come from Arabia' (*Seniles* 16.2, in Petrarca 1987: 888) (Petrarch's knowledge of Arabic poetry presumably came from the few excerpts in the Latin translation to Averroes' *Commentary* to Aristotle's *Poetics* (cf. Bodenham 1982; Mancini 2003).)

We could continue tracing this western criticism of Islamic love poetry from the Middle Ages through A. W. von Schlegel (according to whom Islam was precocious in its poetics, but too 'cruel' to know anything of love) and G. W. F. Hegel (who presented Goethe as the heir of a poetic tradition that Islam, because merely a 'frenzied fanaticism of faith', had proven unable to sustain) to the 'Orientalist' critics of the nineteenth and twentieth centuries. But these are projects for another day. Here we simply want to conclude by reminding ourselves that these polemics of love did not lose their power in Lawrence's bath. It is certainly true that the decades after the Second World War spoke much less (in the West) of Judaism's loveless distance from Christianity, and much more (again in the West) of 'Judaeo-Christian civilization'.

In the case of Islam, however, echoes of lovelessness continued to resonate in some modern scholarship. Perhaps not many scholars today would posit the lack of an adequate doctrine of divine love in the Quran (e.g. Sweetman 1947: 48, criticized by Lewisohn 2008: 163). But scholarly approaches to quranic ethics (e.g. Izutsu 1966; Fakhry 1991) usually neglect the considerable space the Islamic sacred book devotes to love between God and the believers, and ignore what we take to be the important work done by love at the intersection of ethics and spirituality in the historical development of Islamic discourse.

The problem becomes more acute the more apologetic the genre. Perhaps the most striking example in recent memory was Pope Benedict XVI's invocation of love in his Regensburg Address of 2006, which invited Islam to an ecumenical dialogue at the 'banquet of love', but at the same time presented Islam as a fanaticism of faith, incapable of love, and hence of dialogue (Nirenberg 2008). Such arguments may seem convincing to those brought up (wittingly or unwittingly) in certain traditions of Christian and western thought, but can only lead to an impasse in any attempt at real interreligious dialogue. Attempts at dialogue would be better based, we maintain, on comparative research into the theologies of love produced by the three 'Abrahamic' monotheisms, research that requires our reassessment of the historical development of the interpretative frames of their scriptures (cf. Dammen McAuliffe 2003b). But such reassessment must take place in the awareness that the historical development of love in the theological and exegetical agendas of Judaism and Islam has often taken place (and often takes place today) within contexts of confrontation with Christian categories of love, categories that sometimes aspire to hegemony (e.g. Cumming 2010). If we wish to understand the many roles of love in the Abrahamic faiths, we must bring the same critical eye we apply to charges of Jewish and Muslim lovelessness to these Christian claims of love.

References

Abrabanel. 1535. *Dialoghi d'Amore*. Rome: Antonio Bladod'Assola.

Addas, C. 2002. 'The Experience and Doctrine of Love in Ibn 'Arabī'. *Journal of the Muhyiddin Ibn 'Arabi Society* 32: 25–44.

Avicenna. 1945. *A Treatise on Love by Ibn Sīnā*, trans. by E. L. Fakhenheim. *Medieval Studies* 7: 208–28.

Avicenna. 1956. *al-Ilāhiyyāt al-Shifā'*. Cairo: Matba'a al-Amiriyya.

Bell, J. N. 1979. *Love Theory in Later Hanbalite Islam*. Albany, NY: State University of New York Press.

Bell, J. N. 1986. 'Avicenna's Treatise on Love and Nonphilosophical Muslim Tradition'. *Der Islam* 63: 73–89.

Bodenham, C. H. L. 1982. 'Petrarch and the Poetry of the Arabs'. *Romanische Forschungen* 94: 167–78.

Burman, T. E. 2007. *Reading the Qur'ān in Latin Christendom, 1140–1560*. Philadelphia: University of Pennsylvania Press.

Chittick, W. C. 1983. *The Sufi Path of Love: The Spiritual Teachings of Rumi*. New York: State University of New York.

Chittick, W. C. 1995. 'The Divine Roots of Human Love'. *Journal of the Muhyiddin Ibn 'Arabi Society* 17: 55–78.

Corbin, H. 1995. *L'Imagination créatrice dans le soufisme d'Ibn Arabî*. Paris: Aubier.

Cumming, J. L. 2010. 'Understanding the Meaning of Love: Eternal or Temporal? Self-Giving or Gift-Giving?' In M. Volf et al., eds, *A Common Word: Muslims and Christians on Loving God and Neighbor*. Cambridge: Eerdmans, 145–52.

d'Alverny, M. T. 1947–8. 'Deux traductions latines du Coran au moyen âge'. *Archives d'histoire doctrinale et littéraire du moyenâge* 22–3: 69–131.

Dammen McAuliffe, J. 2003a. 'An Introduction to Medieval Interpretation of the Qur'ān'. In Dammen McAuliffe et al. 2003: 311–19.

Dammen McAuliffe, J. 2003b. 'Preface'. In Dammen McAuliffe et al. 2003: v–viii.

Dammen McAuliffe, J. et al., eds. 2003. *With Reverence for the Word: Medieval Scriptural Exegesis in Judaism, Christianity, and Islam*. Oxford: Oxford University Press.

Fakhry, M. 1991. *Ethical Theories in Islam*. Leiden: Brill.

al-Fārābī. 1952. *Compendium Legum Platonis*, ed. and trans. F. Gabrieli. London: Warburg Institute.
al-Fārābī. 1985. 'On the Perfect State', ed. and trans. R. Walzer. Oxford: Clarendon Press.
Frank, R. M. 1999. 'The Ashʿarite Ontology: I. Primary Entities'. *Arabic Sciences and Philosophy* 9: 169–231.
Gersonides. 1866. *Milḥamot ha-Shem*. Leipzig: Karl Lorck.
Giffen, L. A. 1971. *Theory of Profane Love among the Arabs. The Development of a Genre.* New York-London: New York University Press-London University Press.
Gimaret, D. 1990. *La Doctrine d'al-Ashʿarī*. Paris: Cerf.
Goodman, L. 2008. *Love Thy Neighbor as Thyself.* Oxford: Oxford University Press.
Greenberg, Y. 2007. *Encyclopedia of Love in World Religions*, 2 vols. New York: ABC-CLIO.
Gruendler, B. 2004. '"Pardon Those Who Love Passionately". A Theologian's Endorsement of *Shahādat al-ʿIshq*'. In F. Pannewick, ed., *Martyrdom in Literature: Visions of Death and Meaningful Suffering in Europe and the Middle East from Antiquity to Modernity.* Wiesbaden: Reichert Verlag, 189–236.
Von Grunebaum, G. E. 1952. 'Avicenna's *Risāla fī'l-ʿishq* and Courtly Love'. *Journal of Near Eastern Studies* 9: 233–8.
Gutas, D. 1988. 'Plato's *Symposion* in the Arabic Tradition'. *Oriens* 31: 36–60.
al-Hamadānī 'Ayn al-Qudāt. 1961. *Al-Tamhīdāt*, ed. 'Afif 'Uṣayran. Teheran: Teheran University Press.
Harvey, W. Z. 1976. 'Love: The Beginning and the End of the Torah'. *Tradition* 15: 5–22.
Harvey, W. Z. 1998. *Physics and Metaphysics in Hasdai Crescas*. Amsterdam: Gieben.
Hawting, G. 2003. 'Qur'ānic Exegesis and History'. In Dammen McAuliffe et al. 2003: 408–21.
Hegel, G. W. F. 1948. *Early Theological Writings*, ed. T. J. Knox. Chicago: University of Chicago Press.
Herbert, G. 1991. *The Complete English Poems*, ed. J. Tobin. London: Penguin.
Hirshman, M. 2004. 'Love Thy Companion as Thyself: Musings on its Usage in Tannaitic Literature and the Sermon on the Mount'. In J. Malino, ed., *Judaism and Modernity.* Aldershot: Ashgate Publishing, 228–33.
Ibn 'Arabī. 1911. *Al-Futūḥāt al-makkiyya*. Beirut: Dār al-ṣādir, s.d. (1968 = ed. Cairo 1911).
Idel, M. 1989. 'Sexual Metaphors in Praxis and the Kabbalah'. In D. Kraemer, ed., *The Jewish Family*. New York: Oxford University Press, 197–225.
Idel, M. 2009. *Kabbalah and Eros*. New Haven: Yale University Press.
al-Iṣfahānī (Ibn Dāwūd). 1985. *Kitāb al-zahra*, ed. I. al-Sāmarrā'ī. 2 vols. al-Urdun: Maktabat al-Manār.
Izutsu, T. 1966. *Ethico-Religious Concepts in the Qur'an*. Montreal: McGill University Press.
Kaegi, W. 1969. 'Initial Byzantine Reactions to the Arab Conquest'. *Church History* 38: 139–49.
Kritzcek, J. 1964. *Peter the Venerable and Islam*. Princeton: Princeton University Press.
Lamm, N. 1995. 'Maimonides on the Love of God'. *Maimonidean Studies* 3: 131–42.
Lamoreaux, J. 1996. 'Early Christian Responses to Islam'. In J. Tolan, ed., *Medieval Christian Perceptions of Islam: A Book of Essays*. New York: Garland, 3–31.
Lawrence, T. E. 1926/1985. *The Seven Pillars of Wisdom: A Triumph*. New York: Penguin.
Lewisohn, L. 2008. 'Divine Love in Islam'. In Greenberg 2007: 163–6.
Lumbard, J. E. B. 2007. 'From *ḥubb* to *'ishq*: The Development of Love in Early Sufism'. *Journal of Islamic Studies* 18: 345–85.
Maimonides. 1961. *The Guide of the Perplexed*, trans. S. Pines. Chicago: Chicago University Press.

Mancini, M. 2003. 'Petrarca e la poetica degli Arabi'. In P. Bagni-M. Pistoso, eds, *Poetica medievale tra Oriente e Occidente*. Rome: Carocci, 211–22.
Menocal, M. R. 1987. *The Arabic Role in Medieval Literary History: A Forgotten Heritage*. Philadelphia: Pennsylvania University Press.
Miskawayh. 1969. *Traité d'éthique*, trans. with introd. and notes M. Arkoun. Damascus: Institut Français de Damas.
Mopsik, C. 1986. *Lettre sur la sainteté*. Étude préliminaire, traduction et commentaire, suivi d'une étude de Moshé Idel. Lagrasse: Verdier.
Mopsik, C. 2005. *Sex of the Soul: Vicissitudes of Sexual Difference in Kabbalah*. Los Angeles: Cherub Press.
Moran, W. L. 1963. 'The Ancient Near Eastern Background to the Love of God in Deuteronomy'. *Catholic Biblical Quarterly* 25: 77–87.
Muffs, Y. 1992. *Love & Joy: Law, Language and Religion in Ancient Israel*. New York: Jewish Theological Seminary.
Nachmanides. 1976. *The Holy Letter: A Study in Medieval Sexual Morality Ascribed to Nahmanides*. New York: Ktav Publishing.
Nirenberg, D. 2008. 'Islam and the West: Two Dialectical Fantasies'. *Journal of Religion in Europe* 1: 1–33.
Nirenberg, D. 2009. 'Christendom and Islam'. In M. Rubin and W. Simons, eds, *The Cambridge History of Christianity: Christianity in Western Europe c.1100–c.1500*. Cambridge: Cambridge University Press, 149–69.
Nuwya, P. 1970. *Exégèse coranique et language mystique*. Beirut: Dar al-Mashreq.
Pascal, B. 1995. *Pensées* (1670). Oxford: Oxford University Press.
Petrarca, F. 1987. *Invective contra medicum*. In A. Bufano, ed., *Operelatine*. Torino: UTET.
[*The*] *Qur'an*. 2005. Trans. M. A. S. Abdel Haleem. Oxford: Oxford University Press.
Raven, W. 1989. *Ibn-Dâwûd al-Isbahânî and his Kitâb al-Zahra*. Dissertation. Leiden, Amsterdam.
Riley-Smith, J. 1980. 'Crusading as an Act of Love'. *History* 65: 177–92.
Rippin, A. 1988. 'The Function of the *asbāb al-nuzūl* in Qur'ānic Exegesis'. *Bulletin of the School of Oriental and African Studies* 51: 1–20.
Rippin, A. 2001. 'Literary Analysis of Qur'ān, Tafsīr and Sīra: The Methodologies of John Wansbrough'. In R. C. Martin, ed., *Approaches to Islam in Religious Studies*. Oxford: Oneworld, 151–63.
Rundgren, F. 1978–9. 'Avicenna on Love: Studies on the *Risāla fi Māhiyat al-'išq*'. *Orientalia Suecana* 27–8: 42–62.
Schimmel, A. 1975. *Mystical Dimensions of Islam*. Chapel Hill, NC: University of North Carolina Press.
Scholem, G. 1946. *Major Trends in Jewish Mysticism*, rev. edn. New York: Schocken Books.
Sweetman, J. W. 1947. *Islam and Christian Theology: A Study of the Interpretation of the Theological Ideas in the Two Religions*. London: Lutterworth Press.
Thomas, D. W. 1939. 'The Root אהב "Love" in Hebrew'. *Zeitschrift für Alttestamentlische Wissenschaft* 57, n.s. 16: 57–64.
Tolan, J. 2002. *Saracens: Islam in the Medieval European Imagination*. New York: Columbia University Press.
al-Ṭūsī, Nāṣir al-Dīn. 1981. *Akhlāq-i Nāṣirī*, ed. M. Mīnowī. Teheran: Intishārāt-i Khwārazmī.
Vajda, G. 1957. *L'Amour de Dieu dans la théologie juive du Moyen âge*. Paris: Vrin.
Wensinck, A. J. 1936. *Concordances et indices de la tradition musulmane*. Leiden: Brill.

Wolfson, E. 1994. 'Woman: The Feminine as Other in Theosophic Kabbalah. Some Philosophical Observations on the Divine Androgyne'. In L. Silberstein and R. Cohn, eds, *The Other in Jewish Thought and History: Constructions of Jewish Identity and Culture*. New York: NYU Press.
Wolfson, E. 1995. *Circle in the Square: Studies in the use of Gender in Kabbalistic Symbolism*. Albany: SUNY Press.
Wolfson, E. 2003. 'Asceticism and Eroticism in Medieval Jewish Philosophical and Mystical Exegesis of the *Song of Songs*'. In Dammen McAuliffe et al. 2003: 92–118.

CHAPTER 29

RELIGION AND POLITICS IN THE AGE OF FUNDAMENTALISMS

MALISE RUTHVEN

FUNDAMENTALISM is a problematic term when applied to religions other than Protestant Christianity. It was first minted in the 1920s in the specific context of a conservative theological reaction to the hermeneutics of 'higher criticism', whereby received understandings of the Bible, including its provenance, authorship, and content, were coming under critical scrutiny from textual scholars. Despite the sectarian context of its origins, 'fundamentalism' has been applied progressively in both scholarly and media usage to non-Christian traditions. These include Judaism and Islam, as well as Mormonism, Hinduism, Sikhism, and Buddhism. In recent years the term has become so widespread that it has acquired non-religious usages as well: critics of the World Bank and International Monetary Fund have accused these institutions of 'market fundamentalism'. In polemical exchanges within parties as different as Scottish nationalists and German 'greens', factions least disposed to compromise over issues such as power-sharing or nuclear energy face accusations of 'fundamentalism'. And while the term—outside of its original Protestant matrix—has generally acquired the pejorative connotations of absolutism, dogmatic intransigence, and intellectual inflexibility, at least one modern scholar, Ernest Gellner, has turned negativity on its head by choosing to describe himself, oxymoronically perhaps, as an 'Enlightenment Rationalist Fundamentalist' (Gellner 1992: 80).

Despite its sectarian provenance, the rapidity with which the term has been applied to religious attitudes in other traditions both within and outside the Abrahamic group of religions suggests that there are certain 'family resemblances' existing between styles of militant religiosity that transcend confessional boundaries. The concept of 'family resemblances' was explained by the philosopher Ludwig Wittgenstein through the example of games, such as board-games, card-games, ball-games, Olympic Games, and so forth. Instead of assuming that all must have a single, defining feature because of the common name applied to them, Wittgenstein suggested that games should be examined for similarities and relationships. Such an examination, he argued, would reveal a complicated network of similarities overlapping and crisscrossing: sometimes overall similarities, sometimes similarities of detail such as one finds in different members of the same family, in which build, facial features, colour of eyes, gait, temperament, and so forth overlap and crisscross in similar ways (Kenny 1994: 48–9).

'Family resemblances' relevant to our subject that may be shared across the traditional boundaries separating the three Abrahamic families of Judaism, Christianity, and Islam may be briefly summarized to include:

- A reactive defensiveness towards modernity stemming from the perception that a traditional worldview based on religion is under threat from secular trends and values
- Adherence to the text of scripture, with emphasis on its plain or obvious meanings
- Selectivity in the uses of scripture or tradition. Since texts such as the Bible and the Quran are too vast and complex to be defended in their entirety, fundamentalists tend to use 'proof-texting'—taking certain passages out of context—to justify particular arguments or courses of action
- Drawing boundaries between righteous and unrighteous, 'saved and unsaved', and anathematizing the latter
- Belief that laws decreed by God have precedence over those of men
- An obsession with purity, especially sexual purity, proper conduct between men and women, and rejection/denunciation of homosexuality, especially between consenting males
- The adoption of 'traditional' or reinvented dress codes and facial displays such as beards for men and lengthy dresses with head coverings for women as markers of religious commitment and group identity
- Recourse to violence in the event of actual, anticipated, or perceived threats, with violence sometimes linked to ideas of religious sacrifice
- Concern with a coming apocalypse, with the expectation of a transformed religious and political order.

These generalizations need to be treated with caution: none of them necessarily applies 'across the board'. With regard to selectivity, for example, the choices made by 'fundamentalists' may vary considerably and may or may not be textually anchored. Churches in rural parts of the American south, where worshippers handle dangerous reptiles such as rattlesnakes and copperheads to prove they are saved, indulge in proof-texting by focusing on a single verse from Mark's Gospel, 'They shall take up serpents: and if they drink any deadly thing, it shall not hurt them . . . ' (Mark 16: 18; see Ruthven 1989: 278–83). However, Muslim 'fundamentalists' who insist on veiling for women and strict sexual segregation in school classrooms may be less beholden to scripture, given the ambiguity of the Quran's references to veiling. Rather, their actions derive from an invented tradition entailing a trade-off between an approved modern project—female education—and an idea of sexual propriety, which makes an important concession to modernism by abandoning traditional strictures limiting social contacts between unrelated males and females. For Mormons the term 'fundamentalist' is usually attached to polygamous groups who reject the suspension of plural marriage in 1890 by Church President Wilford Woodruff, under US congressional pressure. Curiously the term is not applied to traditionalists within the Utah church who take issue with revisionists over the more significant and 'fundamental' question of the Book of Mormon's authorship. Whereas traditionalists hold to the view that the Book of Mormon was 'translated' from golden tablets by the church's founding prophet Joseph Smith using a pair of magical spectacles, revisionists argue that he composed the text himself.

Generally speaking the uses of 'fundamentalism' are highly eclectic and lacking in analytic rigour. The subject is therefore best approached diachronically in the context of individual traditions. All 'fundamentalist' movements make significant concessions to the modernist forces they profess to oppose. All of them operate under historical conditions that define, and limit, the contexts in which they occur. Despite some family resemblances, fundamentalisms are not really '-isms' at all.

1. Fundamentalist Trajectories

American Original

In 1910 the brothers Milton and Lyman Stewart, Californian oil magnates, sponsored a series of pamphlets for free distribution to pastors, missionaries, and Christian educationists in the English-speaking world. Entitled *The Fundamentals: A Testimony of Truth*, the tracts, written by leading conservative American and British theologians, were intended to arrest the erosion of what the Stewart brothers and their editors believed to be fundamental to Christian belief. The issues that concerned them included challenges to the inerrancy of the Bible and the authenticity of its putative authorship (with scholars doubting that five books had been authored by Moses himself or that the New Testament Gospels had been written by Matthew, Mark, Luke, and John rather than the multiple authorships suggested by 'higher critical' studies); the direct creation of the world and humanity *ex nihilo* by God (now being challenged by Darwinian theories of evolution by natural selection); the truth of the miracles and other supernatural events described in the Bible, such as the sun standing still or Jesus walking on water; the virgin birth of Jesus, his crucifixion, and bodily resurrection; the doctrine of substitutionary atonement (according to which Christ died to redeem the sins of humanity); and his imminent messianic return, to judge and rule over the world.

The belief in the imminent messianic return of Christ to rule the world concerns the End Time prophecies contained in the Old Testament books of Ezekiel and Daniel, and the Revelation of St John, the last book of the New Testament. Such a belief was held by leading editors and contributors such as Cyrus Ignatius Scofield, editor of the Scofield Reference Bible, and Reuben Torrey as well as the Stewart brothers. They drew on an influential tradition of prophecy interpretation and speculation developed by John Nelson Darby (1800–82) an Anglo-Irish evangelist who left the official Anglican church to become one of the founders of the Plymouth Brethren.

Darby is an exotically influential figure, the architect of the peculiar theology known as premillennial dispensationalism. Although he was not the first theologian to introduce the 'dispensationalist' idea that salvation history is divided into different divinely ordained 'dispensations' or epochs, he worked these ideas into a uniquely structured and highly organized system that would prove attractive to Protestants in the nineteenth and twentieth centuries, especially in the United States. According to Darby, following the dispensations revealed in the Bible, the last of which ended with Jesus' crucifixion, the present age, or the 'Church Age', will begin with the Rapture, when all the believers will rise to meet Christ in the air. For those 'left-behind'—people who have chosen not to become born-again Christians—the sequence of events outlined in the apocalyptic books of the Bible will unfold with disconcerting rapidity, starting with the seven-year rule of Antichrist and the Apostate church and the Tribulation, ending in the Battle of Armageddon and the return of Christ as the ruler of the Millennium. In a critical departure from centuries of mainstream Christian writings derived from Paul and Augustine that saw the church as the New Israel (as well as from Protestant variants that assigned this role to England or America), Darby assigned a special End-Time role to the Jews, allowing for two distinctive tracks in the scheme of salvation, one for Jews, and one for Gentiles, before the two tracks would merge in the ultimate eschaton. In the near future God's chosen people would return to their ancient homeland and rebuild the Temple. Thereafter, following a period of terrible persecution during the reign of Antichrist, the surviving remnant—the 144,000 righteous Jews—would finally embrace the Messiah. Premillennialists expect these events to unfold very soon. They see it as their duty to save as many people as possible from the coming catastrophe when sinners will perish horribly and the saved will be physically 'raptured' into the presence of Christ.

Up to three million copies of *The Fundamentals* were distributed on both sides of the Atlantic, and in 1919 some 6,000 conservative Christians gathered for the inaugural meeting of the World Christian Fundamentals Association in Philadelphia. The *-ist* was added in 1920 by Curtis Lee Laws, a conservative Baptist editor. He defined fundamentalists as those prepared to 'do battle royal for the Fundamentals'. Initially the Fundamentalists—who were happy to describe themselves as such—conducted their battles inside various Protestant denominations by seeking to take greater control of Baptist, Methodist, Presbyterian, Congregationalist, and Episcopalian churches and congregations. Although the liberal theologies arising from higher critical studies remained in their sights, an important target for their campaign was the teaching of evolutionary theory in American public schools. Prior to the Second World War the greatest of the battles royal in America's culture wars was the Monkey Trial in Dayton, Tennessee, in which John Scopes, a high-school teacher, was indicted—and convicted—for breaking a state law banning the teaching of evolution. The clash between Scope's lawyer, Clarence Darrow, and the prosecuting attorney William Jennings Bryan, a former secretary of state and presidential candidate (famously captured as fictionalized drama in Stanley Kramer's 1960 movie *Inherit the Wind*) became a landmark event in American cultural history. By manipulating literalist interpretations of the Bible approved of by conservatives, Darrow inflicted a rhetorical defeat on Bryan, who died five days after the trial, an apparently broken man. In the massive media treatment surrounding the trial, Bryan's moral concerns disappeared from view: a Democrat and populist, he believed that the German militarism leading to the First World War had been a by-product of Darwin's theories of natural selection combined with Friedrich Nietzsche's ideas about the Death of God and the human will to power. Given the way that ideas of social Darwinism were subsequently used by Hitler and the Nazis, he deserves more credit than he has been given.

Although anti-evolution laws remained on the statute books of several states, for the American public at large fundamentalism was generally discredited and its exponents seen as being out of touch with modern thinking. In mainstream academies, seminaries, and denominations, liberal theology with its acceptance of evolutionary theory swept the board until the late 1970s. Despite its exclusion from the religious and cultural mainstream, however, the half-century 1930–80 saw a steady institutional growth, with numerous (mainly Baptist) churches seceding from national denominations. The outcome was an impressive infrastructure of pastoral networks, parachurch organizations, and megachurches, schools, and colleges linked to book and magazine publishing, with radio, television, and direct-mail operations, building on older institutions such as Chicago's famous Moody Bible Institute dating back to the great nineteenth-century revival movements. Factors energizing this movement included student radicalism, the rise of anti-Vietnam war protests, sexual freedoms following the introduction of oral contraception, changing views of gender relations, and open discussion about homosexuality (Bruce 2000: 70).

The emergence of fundamentalism as a force underpinning the New Christian Right (NCR) was also a consequence of economic factors such as the shift in manufacturing wealth from the northern 'rustbelt' cities to the increasingly affluent south, where fundamentalist beliefs such as premillennialism had become entrenched in the aftermath of the Civil War. Increasing affluence, not to mention worldliness, led to significant if unacknowledged shifts in what might be called the secularization of fundamentalist discourse. A crucial step was the politicization of Protestant fundamentalism—that is to say, its engagement with the wider world by forming strategic alliances with groups such as conservative Jews, Mormons, and Catholics who would previously have been considered heretical or out of bounds. Significantly, three of the leading figures in NCR's formation were two Catholics, Richard Viguerie and Paul Weyrich, and a Jew, Howard Phillips (Bruce 2000: 70).

The presence of prominent Catholics in this campaign raises the theoretical question as to whether 'Catholic fundamentalism' can be said to exist alongside the Protestant original. A defining feature of Catholicism, in contrast to the cult of the text in

Protestant, Islamic, and Jewish traditions, is that loyalty to the church as the 'body of Christ' is as important as adherence to scripture (Coleman 1992: 7). In contrast to the more loosely textured systems of religious leadership in Protestant and Jewish traditions and the majority Sunni tradition in Islam, Catholic ultras or 'integralists' are constrained against open religious dissent by 'papal fundamentalism'. As papal legitimists they are reliant on Vatican bureaucrats to defend their positions. If the papal vessel turns in a direction they dislike—as when Pius XII gave his approval to modern biblical scholarship, or after the liberal reforms of Vatican II (1962–5)—integralists are for the most part forced to toe the 'party line', resorting to 'tortured rhetoric' in order to claim that they represent the authentic spirit and letter of the papal reforms (Coleman 1992: 86). Where Protestant, Jewish, and Sunni fundamentalists tend to divide into competing and often mutually hostile camps, Catholic discipline tends to keep religious disputation inside church walls. Almost everywhere Catholics practise contraception in defiance of official church teachings. Those who publicly refuse to accept changes in doctrine—such as the followers of Archbishop Lefebvre, who refused to recognize popes after Pius XII—are rare exceptions.

The ecumenicism of the newly politicized Christian right in the USA was not without teething problems. In 1980 Bailey Smith, President of the Southern Baptist Convention, caused a storm in the national media with his candid proclamation that 'God Almighty does not hear the prayer of the Jew' (Bloom 1992: 226).

Smith's, however, was the voice of the past. With the emergence of figures such as the televangelist Jerry Falwell (leader of the Moral Majority) and his smoothly professional television presenter colleague Pat Robertson as major players on the national media scene, with millions of regular viewers, political expediency trumped theological rigour. Secluded in their distinctive institutions, fundamentalists could make little impact on the wider social scene. Allied to believers of like persuasion politically—though not theologically—they could make their voices heard on issues such as opposition to abortion (framed as the foetus's 'right to life') and a proposed constitutional amendment granting equal rights for women (ERA). Although ERA passed both houses of Congress in 1972 it failed to acquire the requisite number of ratifications by state legislatures before the expiry of a final deadline mandated by Congress in June 1982. Its most prominent opponent was a Catholic lawyer, Phyllis Schlafly, who mobilized an anti-ERA movement in a coalition comprising southern whites, Evangelical Christians, Mormons, Orthodox Jews, and Roman Catholics. These were bussed in large numbers to Washington and state capitals in order to oppose the required ratifications (several of which were rescinded). Religious conservatives from all these traditions have also joined in opposing moves to grant social approval to homosexual relationships or to legalize them via civil partnerships or 'gay marriage'.

Bruce suggests that the greatest political success of the Christian Right was its contribution to the victory of Ronald Reagan in the 1980 presidential election (Coleman 1992: 72). This is hard to determine absolutely, however, as Reagan's victory meant the defeat of the incumbent, Jimmy Carter, after the final weeks of his presidency were marred in a bungled attempt by US special forces to secure the release of

American hostages held in the Iranian embassy in Tehran. After winning power Reagan did little to satisfy his fundamentalist supporters, and during his two terms of office they found it increasingly difficult to raise funds. Under conservative pressures some modifications were made to *Roe v. Wade*, the Federal law permitting abortions, but even these modest achievements must be attributed to the broader coalition of the NCR rather than to fundamentalist activists alone. As Bruce points out, the requirements of activism in a complex rule-based democracy such as the United States means that fundamentalists must choose between religious purity ('only born-again Bible believers are saved') and political pragmatism which requires them to mobilize with other groups around more broadly framed Judaeo-Christian or even secular conservative values (Coleman 1992: 80–4).

2. Judaeo-Christian Linkages

The application of the term 'fundamentalism' to ultra-orthodox Jewish movements is problematic because it fails to distinguish between separatists, some of whom do not even recognize the state of Israel, and militant religious nationalists who establish settlements in Palestinian lands in defiance of international law and UN resolutions. Both tendencies, however, are rooted in radical notions of Jewish distinctiveness. The ultra-orthodox Ḥaredim ('fearful ones'), said to constitute some 13 per cent of Israel's Jewish population (Shahak and Mezvinsky 2004: 8), are strict traditionalists who seek to perpetuate the legacy of the pre-Enlightenment East European *shtetels* by Talmudic study and wearing distinctive black coats and fur-brimmed hats of the eighteenth-century Polish nobility. Paradoxically, some of those who live in Israel reject the state's legitimacy. They avoid singing the *Hatikva* (the anthem of Israel and Zionist organizations) and are exempted from military service. They eschew the female voice which they regard as an invitation to lust. Ḥaredi opposition to Zionism is religious and Judaeo-centric: it is not driven (like liberal or leftist opposition to Israeli policies) by secular principles of universal human rights. It is based, rather, on ancient Talmudic strictures stating that Jews should not rebel against non-Jews and must not emigrate to Palestine en masse before the coming of the Messiah (Shahak and Mezvinsky 2004: 18).

Prior to the pogroms of the late nineteenth century and the rise of Nazism in the twentieth, a majority of orthodox rabbis held similar views. When political Zionists began transforming the messianic promise of redemption into a practical programme in the late nineteenth century, most orthodox rabbis were appalled. The yearning for Zion, they argued, was a spiritual longing, to be assuaged only at the eschaton or end of days, when the Messiah would come and restore the land of Israel to its rightful owners. To turn this religious vision into a political reality was both foolish and blasphemous. Some rabbis went so far as to excommunicate the Zionists. However perilous the situation facing Jewish communities in Europe, especially those under Russian rule, the Zionist solution was unacceptable. If the Zionists had their way Jewish life would be directed away from religious observance and the study of holy texts towards a political project outside the control of the rabbis.

The impact of the Nazi extermination programme, which brought many orthodox Holocaust survivors to Palestine, along with the foundation of Israel in 1948, undermined orthodox resistance to the Zionist project. In Palestine Rabbi Abraham Kook, chief rabbi during much of the era of the British Mandate (1920–48), rationalized orthodox support for secular Zionism by arguing that, unbeknownst to themselves, the secular Zionist 'atheists' might be carrying forward the project of redemption. His son Rabbi Ẓvi Yehudah Kook founded the first political party of religious Zionists, the National Religious Party (NRP), which often holds the balance of power in Israeli parliamentary coalitions. In the 1960s he established a set of yeshiva seminaries in which orthodox Jews were, exceptionally, allowed to combine their religious studies with military service. After the June 1967 war in which Israel occupied East Jerusalem and the West Bank territory formerly controlled by Jordan, Rabbi Kook Jr stated:

> I tell you explicitly that the Torah forbids us to surrender even one inch of our liberated land. There are no conquests here and we are not occupying foreign lands; we are returning to our home, to the inheritance of our ancestors. There is no Arab land here, only the inheritance of our God . . . (Pichnick 1967; Ruthven 2004: 160)

Gush Emunim, the principal settler movement, founded by members of the National Religious Party in 1974, explicitly describes its aim as being 'the redemption of the Land of Israel in our time'. This was to be achieved by allowing Jews to settle anywhere in the occupied territories, and by political campaigning. Gush Emunim members saw themselves as reviving ancient Israel. They named their settlements after ancient biblical towns and their children after Old Testament heroes. As one of their leaders, Rabbi Moshe Levinger, put it, the land conquered in 1967 had been returned to its rightful owners as promised to their biblical ancestors by God. Gush Emunim deliberately breached Israeli government rules banning settlements near Arab towns. Another of their leaders, Rabbi Bin-Nun, declared:

> Jewish immigration to Israel and settlement are beyond the law. The settlers' movement comes out of the Zionist constitution and no law can stop it. For those to whom the Bible and the religious prescripts are beyond the law there is no need to say anything further. (Abramov 1985)

To the charge that they were acting in contravention to the will of the people expressed through their elected government, another Gush Emunim rabbi replied:

> For us what really matters is not democracy, but the Kingdom of Israel. Democracy is a sacred idea for the Greeks, not for us Jews. (*Nekudah* 1985; Ruthven 2004: 161)

The notion that there is a divine mandate that justifies Jewish settlement in all parts of Palestine, regardless of international limitations, is far from being confined to followers of the Jewish faith. Christian evangelicals such as Gary Bauer, the late Jerry Falwell, Ralph Reed, and Pat Robertson have been among Israel's most vociferous supporters in the USA. They are following a tradition dating back to the early twentieth century, when early supporters of Zionism, including the British Foreign Secretary Arthur Balfour and Prime Minister David Lloyd George, lent critical Great Power support for the establishment of a Jewish homeland in post-Ottoman Palestine. Premillennialists in the tradition of John Nelson Darby believe that the return of the Jewish people to the land promised by God to Abraham is the prerequisite for the second coming of Christ, and that any impediment to this process (such as the 'two-state solution' envisaging the establishment of a Palestinian sovereign state alongside Israel) could interfere with God's plans. In January 1998 when Israeli Prime Minister Benjamin Netanyahu was coming under pressure from the Clinton administration to make concessions to the newly formed Palestinian National Authority, he infuriated the White House by visiting Falwell before seeing the US President. Falwell lost no time in announcing his public support for the Israeli leader:

> There are about 200,000 evangelical pastors in America, and we're asking them all through e-mail, faxes, letters, telephone, to go into their pulpits and use their influence in support of the state of Israel and the Prime Minister. (Goodstein 1998)

By the same logic militant settlers such as Rabbi Benny Elon, leader of the Emunim faction within Gush Emunim, have found it expedient to request financial help from Christian supporters in the USA. According to Shahak and Mezvinsky (2004: 74–5):

> Elon and his associates succeeded in acquiring some of this requested funding. As Jewish fundamentalists who abominate non-Jews, they forged a spiritual alliance with Christians who believe that supporting Jewish fundamentalism is necessary to support the second coming of Jesus. This alliance has become a significant factor in both US and Middle Eastern politics.

The continued stalling of the peace process between Israelis and Palestinians should not be attributed exclusively to Jewish fundamentalists and their Christian Zionist allies. There are other significant factors such as divisions within the Palestinian national movement (divided between the more secular al-Fatah movement in the West Bank territories and the Islamist Hamas movement based in Gaza) as well as the broader instabilities arising from civil war in Syria and the geopolitical rivalry between Iran and Saudi Arabia and their respective Russian and US allies. But in discussions about the influence of the 'Jewish lobby' on US policy, the influence of Christian Zionism is often overlooked. There are many more evangelical Christians in the USA who hold premillennialist views than there are Jews, whose attitudes towards Israeli policies are in any case no longer monolithically supportive. One indicator of this vast premillennial constituency is the phenomenal commercial success of books, such as Hal Lindsay's *Late Great Planet Earth* (1970) and the *Left Behind* series of novels by Tim LaHaye and Jerry B. Jenkins, with sales running into many millions (Didion 2003; Ruthven 2012).

3. Islamic Problematic

The term 'Islamic fundamentalism' with its echoes of militancy and terror had become part of the modern vocabulary even before the hijacked airline attacks on New York and Washington in September 2001. Its first recorded use—to my knowledge—occurs in a letter written by Sir Reader Bullard, British Minister in Jeddah in May 1937, in which he states that the country's ruler King Abdul Aziz al-Sa'ud (known as Ibn Saud) has 'been coming out strong as a fundamentalist' by condemning women who mix with men 'under the cloak of progress' (Hodgkin 1993: 167–8). Bruce Lawrence, however, suggests that the term was coined by the distinguished British orientalist H. A. R. Gibb in his book *Mohammedanism* (later retitled *Islam*), the first edition of which appeared in 1953. Gibb used the term with reference to Jamāl al-Dīn al-Afghānī, the Iranian-born activist and reformer who represented himself as a Sunni of Turkish-Afghan origin to conceal his Shiʿite origins (Lawrence 1989: 272 n. 10). These conflicting provenances for the use of the 'F-word' regarding Islam exposes the problematic of applying a concept derived from a cultivated, even sophisticated, debate about textual origins intrinsic to Protestant Christianity to the much more fractured discourses and debates of the contemporary Islamic world. Generally speaking, issues of textual authenticity surrounding the Quran, raised by scholars such as the late John Wansbrough, Günter Lüling, Volker Popp, and others working in western universities, have not surfaced in the public discourses of Islamic countries. Most observant Muslims, not just those described as Islamists or fundamentalists, regard the Quran as the literal word of God as dictated to Muhammad through the agency of the angel Gabriel (Jibreel). For conservative Muslim scholars as for more radical Islamist militants, approaches to the Quran that regard the language of revelation as a human construct reflecting the knowledge and prejudices of its time may be under way and are certain to arouse hostility. The Egyptian academic Nasr Abū Zaid, who ventured to use modern critical methods in his analysis of the Quran's language, was forced into exile after militants had him declared an apostate by Egyptian courts. However, while the attitude of Abū Zaid's critics certainly corresponds to that of Protestant biblical literalists, it would be wrong to see the issue of textual inerrancy or theological liberalism as being the primary causes around which those Muslims described as 'fundamentalists' tend to rally. If all Muslims are 'quranic fundamentalists', the term loses any descriptive power in distinguishing between militants and moderates, conservatives and liberals. Issues of orthopraxy such as male–female segregation, institutional observance of the Ramadan fast, women's deportment, and female rights generally—plus considerations of 'respect' for the tradition and its founder—are much more salient issues in the current climate.

The designation of Ibn Saud and Afghānī as Islamic 'fundamentalists' by two well-informed observers is nevertheless interesting, as in many regards they are polar opposites. Ibn Saud's warriors who conquered the Hijaz in the 1920s, ousting the incumbent Hashemite rulers, may be described as 'fundamentalist' in a way that exhibits some resemblances to the Protestant variety. As followers of Muhammad ibn Abd al-Wahhab, the eighteenth-century Arabian Hanbalite reformer, they sought a return to the seventh-century scriptural 'roots' of Islam unsupplemented by the accumulated customs, doctrines, and traditions of subsequent centuries. Unlike other reformers, who looked to the prophet's message for social justice as well as moral correctness, ibn ʿAbd al-Wahhab's strictures were exclusively religious. Proclaiming the call of *tawhid*—the absolute unity of God—he denounced devotional practices such as praying at the tombs of saints or the imams of the prophet's family as forms of idolatry or *shirk*. Violently opposed to Sufism in all its manifestations, he was equally opposed to Shiʿism. Inspired by his teachings, the Nejdi tribesmen who created the first Saudi state attacked and desecrated the Shiʿi shrines of Najaf and Karbala in Iraq in 1803. True worship of God, according to ibn ʿAbd al-Wahhab, meant that rituals other than the strictest forms of *ṣalat* (ritual prayer), fasting, and pilgrimage to Mecca amounted to *kufr* (disbelief). Anyone observing them was an infidel to be shunned, denounced, or even killed (Dalal 2013: 115).

Afghānī was a very different type of figure. Born in Asabad near Hamadan, he concealed his Persian Shiʿite origins to avoid arousing the hostility of his mainly Sunni audiences. A polemicist and political activist, his driving motive was opposition to British imperialism, which he saw as posing a greater threat to Muslim civilization than the Russian version, despite the Russian advances in Inner Asia. The 'Islam' he sought to defend was a civilization based on faith, and independent sovereignty. Far from being a textual literalist he scandalized the conservative Ottoman *ʿulamā* by describing prophecy as a 'craft' that he equated with philosophy. In his celebrated rejoinder to a lecture by Ernest Renan attacking Islam as being hostile to science, he strongly criticized the 'Muslim religion' as currently practised, for its stifling of free thought and progress (Keddie 1972). *The Strongest Link* (*al-ʿUrwa al-wuthqa*)—the periodical he published in Paris with his disciple Muhammad ʿAbduh—was the leading reformist journal of its time. As well as attacking Britain and supporting the pan-Islamic claims of the Ottoman Sultan Abdul Hamid, the journal focused on the social teachings of Islam rather than its theological aspects. Afghānī's disciple and collaborator Muhammad ʿAbduh (1849–1905) is widely seen as the Sunni world's most influential reformist thinker. Far from being 'fundamentalist', his thought is relatively progressive and liberal. Where conservatives tended to reject any suggestion that the divine prescriptions revealed in the Quran and the prophet's teachings were subject to reason, ʿAbduh argued that actions may be distinguished as 'beautiful or ugly according to the idea of their utility or harmfulness', a distinction that 'can be discovered by human reason and the senses without the aid of revelation' (Safran 1961: 67).

Far from challenging the basic premises of the Enlightenment, a family resemblance shared by many Jewish and Christian 'fundamentalists', the movement launched by Afghānī and ʿAbduh in the 1870s, known as the Salafiyya, after the 'pious ancestors' or Prophet's Companions, absorbed the spirit of modernism to the point where ʿAbduh broke with Afghānī and chose to collaborate with the British power in Egypt in order to further his reformist agenda.

In the course of time, however, the Salafism associated with Afghānī and ʿAbduh, as well as ʿAbduh's more conservative disciple Rashid Rida (editor of the influential periodical *al-Manar* in the early decades of the twentieth century), became associated with the much more conservative Wahhabi movement, as Islamic modernism (like its Christian and Jewish equivalents) became absorbed into the intellectual mainstream. Today Salafism, in all its variants, is often conflated with Wahhabism. Although the two are not identical the family resemblances are obvious, and it is this conservative current in Islam that is most deserving of the 'fundamentalist' label, sharing as it does some of the features to be found in both Christian and Jewish varieties. As Roel Meijer (2009a: 4) points out, Salafists are not only scripturalist, returning to the textual sources of Islam in the Quran and the *ḥadīth*. They are literalist in their imitation of the styles of dress, beards, and so forth they believe to have characterized the first generation of Muslims. 'Muslims had to behave exactly like the pious forefathers whose deeds and thoughts were found in the sources of Islam.'

Like many ultra-orthodox Jews they eschew any social contacts with outsiders. As with the case of Jewish fundamentalism, their political attitudes range from quietist disengagement from the mainstream 'Gentile' or 'infidel' society, to efforts to enact revolutionary change.

At the quietist end of the spectrum are those Salafists who argue that the project of bringing society back to correct Islamic values and behaviour cannot be achieved on the basis of state power, as advocated by the Muslim Brotherhood and other branches of the Islamist movement. An influential exponent of this position is the Kuwaiti-born writer ʿAbd al-Rahman ʿAbd al-Khaliq who argues:

> The leaders of the reform movements and Islamic missions do not appreciate the enormity of the real burden in the road to establishing an Islamic society. They imagine that its establishment could happen overnight and through the efforts of 100, or 200, or 1000, or 2000 people. And they don't bear in mind that the matter (i.e. task) has become greater than this and needs a long struggle and a lot of patience and long years of moral rearing and education. (Salomon 2009: 150–1 n. 16)

Gradualist Salafism based on conversion of other Muslims is particularly appealing to immigrants to Europe who inhabit the *banlieux* or fringes of its cities. As Mohamed-Ali Adraoui (2009: 366–7) explains:

> The appeal of Salafi Puritanism lies in its ability to provide a way of not only opting out of society but of creating an alternative, superior community based on the unity of God (*tawḥīd*). It can justify the Salafi Puritanism alienation from society while submitting oneself only to God and fighting all forms of religious heterodoxy. In contrast to the often deplorable situations of its followers, Salafism empowers these 'dropouts' by providing them with a transcendental dimension, a holy identity and the belief that they are chosen . . . Muslims looking for existential answers are attracted by the 'absolute Islam' that Salafism provides. This has led to a revolution in their lives. Instead of being passive 'followers' they have become active 'models' for others. Where before the migrant lived on the fringe of society . . . as a Salafi he

> now stands at the centre of the world and embodies a sacred history . . . Their own community has replaced the alien French nation and Islam has supplanted the antagonistic West.

In the West, however, the adoption of Salafism, especially by young women, may be as much a lifestyle choice representing an accommodation with the wider society than resistance to it. A shrewd observer of 'globalized Islam', Olivier Roy, objects to the notion that the behaviour of young Muslims in the *banlieux* of Paris or other large French cities should be defined in terms of religion.

> Islam is . . . turned into an essence, as though it has become the invariant that determines attitudes in very different contexts . . . The macho attitudes of young men in the *banlieus*, regrettably similar in very different contexts (from Los Angeles to Moscow), is attributed to Islam. Adolescents' intentions to assert themselves by wearing provocative clothing is a banality in secondary schools, but the affair of the veil has been experienced as the penetration of the school system by Islamism. A girl wearing a veil wants simultaneously to assert herself as an individual, escape from the social constraint of her milieu by adopting a sign that grants her both value and autonomy, make herself noticed, affirm a form of authenticity, and on and on. There is very clearly an 'Islam of the young' made up of a complex mixture of generational conflict, a search for authenticity going beyond the parents' generation, and an affirmation of identity *and* protest. (Roy 2007: 88)

At the other end of the spectrum are the Salafists who insist that however pious their behaviour, Muslims living in non-Muslim lands will be contaminated. Thus the Saudi scholar Sāliḥ ibn Fawzān al-Fawzan (b. 1935) argues that Muslims living in non-Muslim countries should emigrate to the Islamic world because 'settling in the countries of the unbelievers will lead to forming loyalty [to them]' (Wagemakers 2009: 89–90). Some Salafist scholars have taken the idea even further, adopting the Wahhabi practice of declaring Muslims they regard as being in error to be infidels, a prerequisite for waging jihad or holy war against them.

As in Judaism the Islamic fundamentalist movement is highly fissiparous, with Salafists readily pronouncing *takfīr* (declaration of infidelity) against other Muslims. The practice of *takfīr* is entirely contrary to the classical view that anyone who accepts the *shahāda* (the declaration of belief in one God and Muhammad his prophet) may be considered a Muslim. The principle of 'loyalty and disavowal' (*wala*ʾ *wa-l-bara*ʾ) was taken to its radical conclusion by Abū Muḥmmad al-Maqdisī who pronounced *takfīr* on the Saudi state for its close relations with the West, thus legitimizing jihad against its rulers on the basis of its own Wahhabi/Salafist reasoning (Meijer 2009a: 11). Such a ruling sets an important precedent for the legal rulings Osama bin Laden obtained for his jihad against the country of his birth and the 'far enemy' backing it.

Wahhabis, and indeed many Salafists, are strongly hostile to Shiʿism, a fact that must complicate efforts to include Khomeinism and Wahhabism under the same 'fundamentalist' umbrella. Shiʿism, the minority tradition in Islam, resembles Catholicism in seeking to balance adherence to scripture with an emphasis on religious leadership.

Although there is no overarching authority comparable to the pope, senior Shiʿi clerics emerge from a rigorous and a complex process of induction that balances theological study with pastoral acclaim. During the nineteenth century the Shiʿi *ʿulamā* divided into two major schools, the *uṣūlis* and *akhbāris*. The *uṣūlis* (derived from the Arabic word for root, sometimes used to denote 'fundamentalism' in Islamic languages) believed in independent *ijtihād*, or reasoning in the interpretation of texts, while their *akhbāri* rivals relied exclusively on earlier authorities.

Though described in the western media as a 'fundamentalist', the leader of the 1979 revolution in Iran, Ayatollah Khomeini, belonged to the *uṣūli* school and was a specialist in Sufism and Islamic Gnosticism. Though presenting himself as an upholder of Islamic tradition, he was a radical innovator in Shiʿi religious and political thought who, despite his frequent denunciations of Marxism, incorporated a good deal of Marxist thinking into his discourse. To regard Khomeini as a 'fundamentalist' comparable to Salafists in Arabia or Sudan is a serious distortion, which makes it difficult to penetrate the political and religious rivalries now afflicting Muslim societies.

Nevertheless the radical Shiʿite movement that emerged with the Khomeinist movement in Iran and beyond its boundaries during the 1970s has important family resemblances with other movements, most notably Protestant premillennialism. In Twelver Shiʿism—the majority sect in the minority tradition of Islam—the messiah is twelfth in the line of imams or spiritual leaders—descended from Muhammad's cousin and son-in-law ʿAli, whom the Shiʿa believe was cheated of the succession after the prophet's death in 632 CE. In the majority version the last of these twelve imams 'disappeared' in 876; in the populist imaginings he is hiding in a cave in Samarra in Iraq awaiting his triumphant Return. Shiʿite devotion centres on the fate of the second imam, ʿAli's son Ḥussein, who was massacred with his band of loyalist followers on the field of Karbala (in modern Iraq) by the forces of the Umayyad caliph Yazid in 680.

Since the dispossession of the prophet's family in the earliest Muslim civil wars, Shiʿism has for more than thirteen centuries followed a trajectory that oscillates between revolutionary activism and quietist disengagement. In this respect it bears a strong family resemblance to orthodox Judaism, with its oscillations between quietist disengagement from the political life of Israel and the 'realized eschatology' of Gush Emunim, who see themselves as enacting redemption on the plane of current history. In the early Muslim era ʿAli's loyalists (his *Shiʿa* or partisans) instigated numerous revolts that challenged and sometimes toppled the military-tribal complexes holding power in the wake of the great Arab conquests. Many of these revolts were conducted in the name of the Mahdī (messiah) or *Qāim* (resurrector), an eschatological figure with more than a passing resemblance to the avenging Christ of the Book of Revelation (who incidentally, was much admired by the millennialist Adolf Hitler) (Landes 2011: 355).

The most enduring revolt was the movement of Turkic tribes that brought the Safavid dynasty to power in Iran in 1501, making Shiʿism the state religion and creating a fusion of Persian and Shiʿa identities. Significant dimensions of the Shiʿia story mesh with pre-Islamic Iranian and Zoroastrian myths. The cult of Ḥussein's martyrdom, celebrated in passion plays and ritual flagellations, evokes the theme of mourning for the murder of the hero Iraj—a primordial representation of Iran—and the martyrdom of Prince Suyush in the national epic the *Shahnama*. Zoroastrianism in its reformed Zurvanite version, the state religion of the pre-Islamic Persian Empire, conveyed a vision of a coming millennium or 'making wonderful' to be brought about by the Saoshyant, the 'future benefactor', who would resurrect the dead and restore the world to rights after an era of tribulation during which the forces of evil would temporarily prevail (Cohn 1993: 100).

Having ridden to power on a wave of messianic expectations, the Safavids succeeded in defusing its revolutionary dynamic. In the imam's absence the Shīʿah *ʿulamā*—religious scholars—exercise spiritual authority on his behalf, lending them an authority and status superior to that of their Sunni counterparts. An estate within the realm, they were the direct recipients of religious dues, amassing considerable wealth as trustees of religious foundations. In the clergy–state equilibrium that followed the Safavid settlement the Hidden Imam was safely relegated to an ever-receding future, with speculations about the Return dismissed as unorthodox, even heretical. The process of eschatological deferment neatly parallels that which occurred in orthodox Christianity after it became the state religion of Rome. St Augustine dematerialized the millennial hopes that kept the earliest Christians in constant expectation of Christ's return by teaching that the church was itself the promised kingdom. The millennial reign of Christ envisioned in the Book of Revelation was merely a metaphor for the prosperous destiny of the church till the end of time. In similar fashion orthodox rabbis would inveigh against Jewish yearnings for the restoration of the physical kingdom of Israel as an impious pre-emption of the messiah's divinely appointed destiny.

However, millennial aspirations, when linked to persecutions and social discontents, are liable to escape from the grip of religious establishments, especially when current orthodoxies—as in all the Abrahamic traditions—can be represented as a betrayal of pristine origins. In all the traditions the eschatological currency retains its convertibility: the promise of Kingdom Come undergoes a shift towards constructing the Kingdom Now. That vital shift (which in the American context represents a transition from premillennial pessimism to post-millennial optimism) may involve a subtle, and unacknowledged, 'de-supernaturalization' of the apocalyptic scenario. The project of making the world ready for the messiah's coming by improving society's order is a Promethean one that in practical terms leaves God—or his supernatural appointee—out of the picture. As Abbas Amanat (2009: 23) explains:

> in a millennial momentum, common to all apocalyptic trends, a crucial shift occurs from dormant aspiration to keen ambition. This turning point invariably pertains to crossing a psychological barrier, one which divides adherence to the established belief system from an experience of rebirth and in turn discovering a communal identity with like-minded individuals.

In Iran this transition was overseen and manipulated by Khomeini, a sophisticated theologian and consummate political operator. The culture fostered by the *madrasas* (religious seminaries) under the Pahlavis and their Qajar predecessors had been strong in rhetorical skills, but theologically pusillanimous. Its hallmark had become 'a fetishistic avoidance and frowning defiance of anything new, novel and unfamiliar' that appeared to threaten the *'ulamās*' power or influence. The establishment kept the lid on the apocalyptic movements including Shaykhism and Babism that surfaced during the nineteenth century in response to social dislocations and modernist influences resulting from western encroachments. The law was interpreted, not in terms of the broad ethical principles governing social interactions as enacted by government, or even in the context of their own theological and legal discourses. Instead the Shiʿite scholars of Khomeini's generation continued to focus obsessively on issues with the potential to nullify the efficacy of prayers, such as ritual pollution and sexual intercourse.

In *Purity and Danger*, her masterly study of pollution fears, the anthropologist Mary Douglas suggests that the pollution rules that define or draw boundaries around many religious activities are actually substitutes for morality, for in contrast to moral rules, they are unequivocal.

> They do not depend on intention or a nice balancing of rights and duties. The only material question is whether a forbidden contact has taken place or not. If pollution dangers were placed strategically along the crucial points in the moral code, they could theoretically reinforce it. However, such a strategic distribution of pollution rules is impossible, since the moral code by its nature can never be reduced to something simple, hard and fast. (Douglas 1984: 130)

Pollution taboos maintain the condition of purity, but as Douglas suggests purity can be a deadening concept. It 'is the enemy of change, ambiguity and compromise' (Douglas 1984: 162). The greatest problem with purity lies in its opposite: the notion that infidels, aliens, and in most cases women are unclean. What might be called the process of 'othering' enemies may also be effected through rhetorical tropes, gradually transformed into fixed assumptions. As the neuroscientist Susan Greenfield explains, 'disgust is a biological defence against things that harm the body. It has nothing to do with anger or fighting something. It's preserving your body against contamination.'

Janet Afary has described the inhibiting effects born of the 'dangers threatening the body' affecting young women, as well as the traumatic effects of unveiling to which women were exposed under the modernizing reforms of the Pahlavis:

> Unveiling and also modern clothing for women exposed believers to ritual pollution and possible damnation in the afterlife—contributing mightily to antagonism toward gender reforms on the part of the old middle classes. (2009: 26)

The consequence was a society living under what the philosopher Daryush Shayegan (1992) has called a condition of 'cultural schizophrenia': as Afary explains with regard to the *bazaaris* or traditional urban trading classes in Iran,

> modernity instituted a double life for pious Muslims. Outwardly they behaved as modern citizens of the state, ignoring religious hierarchies and engaging not just in business and trade with women and non-Muslims, as they had always done, but

> also mingled socially, shaking hands and sharing tea or meals with them. Inwardly, many *bazaaris* harboured a constant sense of anxiety since they continued to believe that a pious Shiʿi Muslim who ignored the proper rituals of purification after encounters with *najes* (polluted) individuals had 'nullified' his prayers and supplications to God and the Imams. (Afary 2009: 150)

One can read the Islamic revolution that erupted in Iran in 1979, in part, as a response to ritual pollution, a reaction against personal defilement.

The dialectic between millennial activism and what might be called 'Augustinian' deferment persists in Iran, where the constitutional issues take theological forms. In contesting the authority of the Ayatollah ʿAli Khamanei, Khomeini's successor as the Supreme Leader, the former President Mahmoud Ahmadinejad infuriated the traditionalist clerics by claiming that ordinary believers can have direct access to the Hidden Imam without clerical intermediaries. His approach was seen as an attempt to promote the office of the Iranian presidency at the expense of the clerical establishment and to boost the electoral prospects of his preferred successor as president, his chief of staff Esfandiar Rahim Mashaei, whose daughter is married to Ahmadinejad's son (Erdbrink 2013).

The concept of 'fundamentalism' obscures the complexity of Iranian politics where issues are fought in the contested arenas of religion and state under the competing sovereignties of God and the people. Similar issues arise in the case of Egypt and Tunisia where the reformist Muslim Brotherhood won electoral victories in the upheavals following the 2011 'Arab spring'. In the ongoing Syrian civil war, Salafist groups such as Jabhat al-Nuṣra (the 'Victory Front') and ISIS (the so-called 'Islamic State') were making gains at the expense of more secular-oriented opposition groups. In the confusion of war, militias in zones outside of government control, such as parts of 'free Hama', were reported to be establishing committees for 'enjoining virtue and repressing vice' modelled on similar militias in Saudi Arabia. The dynamic sustaining these movements was increasingly driven by sectarian demonization of Syria's minority Nuṣayrī, a Shiʿa sect—also known as ʿAlawites—that had dominated Syria's ruling Baʿath party since 1970. In the wider Islamic context the rivalry between Saudi Arabia, allied to the United States, and Iran, supported internationally by Russia and China, contributed to the military stalemate in Syria, with a rising toll of dead and wounded.

Conclusion: Religious Absolutisms after the Death of God

Fundamentalist movements attract followers who appear to believe that the worldview in which they were brought up, which they inherited from their forebears, is threatened under modern conditions. As Anthony Giddens reminds us, modernity is not so much characterized by faith in 'science' (which as Karl Popper famously pointed out, always rests on shifting sands), but on trust in such anonymous abstract systems as the international banking system (responsible for a series of catastrophic failures) or the impersonal interactions between specialists such as the engineers, mechanics, pilots, air traffic controllers, and even financiers that keep aeroplanes flying. Trust in abstract systems provides for the reliability of day to day living, but by its very nature cannot supply the mutuality or intimacy of personal trust (Giddens 1990: 112–13). In modern versions of the Abrahamic traditions, 'God'—conceived as a supernatural being upholding the universe and capable of defying the laws of nature—may be 'dead' as related in Nietzsche's celebrated fable. But he can nevertheless be experienced (as a 'delusion' or otherwise) as a source of personal trust. The processes of secularization, integral to modernity, removed the divine from the natural order, but not from individual psyches of peoples whose individual or group identities were configured around centuries of cultural programming that included religious beliefs. As Martin Marty suggests, 'most people who live in a traditional culture do not know they are traditionalists' (Marty 1992: 18). Tradition in this sense consists in not being aware that how one behaves or what one believes is 'traditional', because alternative ways of thinking or living are not taken into consideration. At their broadest, fundamentalisms in religious traditions arise at the point where traditionalism becomes self-consciously reactive.

The Dutch sociologist Hans Mol sees the 'sacralization of identity' as a phenomenon that 'produces immunity against persuasions similar to the biological immunization process'. 'Sacralization', he argues, 'is the inevitable process that safeguards identity when it is endangered by the disadvantages of the infinite adaptability of symbol-systems' (Mol 1976: 5). In Mol's formulation, the process of sacralization is Janus-faced in that it can either obstruct or legitimize change. Mol's view of sacralization is much more fluid and flexible than that of Émile Durkheim, who made an absolute distinction between the sacred and the profane. This is a complex area of enquiry that cannot be fully addressed here. However, few social scientists would deny that group identities are socially constructed and interactive, or that they are often, if not invariably, formed in contradistinction to a concept of 'the other'.

'Fundamentalism' originated in the United States as a sectarian Protestant response to advances in liberal theology. As explained above, the plurality of American churches allied to the 'wall of separation' between church and state limits the capacity of fundamentalists to influence policy without active engagement with other groups. Forming coalitions across sectarian boundaries may increase fundamentalist influence on policy—as in the case of the defeat of ERA—but at the expense of theological absolutism. To that extent fundamentalist involvement in the political process must be self-defeating. Conflicts arising from environmental or political causes such as the civil war in Syria, with its devastating human cost, contests over power and resources, as in Israel and Nigeria, or the resistance of tribal people vis-à-vis the state, as in Pakistan, Yemen, or Somalia, become increasingly intractable when the legitimacy of a central authority is contested on religious grounds. As Mark Juergensmeyer (2013: 21) has commented:

> What makes religious violence particularly savage and relentless is that its perpetrators have placed images of divine struggle—cosmic war—in the service of worldly political battles. Acts of religious terror serve not only as tactics in a political struggle, but also as evocations of a much larger spiritual confrontation.

Conflicts over power and resources produce victims, and victimhood has its own revengeful dynamic. The religious component that serves the sense of victimhood—or anticipated victimhood—relates less to theological issues of belief in a deity or deities, than to the manner in which religious teachings are transmitted by means of highly routinized ritual processes. As Harvey Whitehouse (2004: 67) observes,

> many routinized religions are successful at holding on to their followers through a variety of mechanisms, including supernatural sanctions (such as eternal damnation) and, more positively, incentives (such as eternal life and salvation.) Of course, the power of these mechanisms depends on people believing the religious teachings. In order for people to believe in a set of doctrines, these doctrines have to be cast in a highly persuasive fashion... Routinized religions tend to be associated with highly developed forms of rhetoric and logically integrated theology founded on absolute propositions that cannot be falsified. All of this is commonly illustrated by poignant narratives that can easily be related to personal experience

The sense of victimhood, cultivated but also repressed, can become a powerful revolutionary force. However, it can also be highly destructive, especially when violence is directed towards an alienated 'other', where the mirror neurons in the brain that engender empathy are suppressed or overtaken by notions of disgust. Atrocities committed in the course of religious conflicts—such as beheadings that are deliberately filmed and posted on the internet—serve to dehumanize the perceived 'enemies of God'. This enhances the process of 'demonization', sanctified in religious courses, that loosens moral constraints on violence. The 'religionization' of conflict consequent upon the 'death of God' ups the ante on human depravity. In the mid-twentieth century Nazis made efforts to conceal their atrocities. Warriors in the cosmically enhanced apocalyptic conflicts of the twenty-first celebrate them as proofs of power.

The persistence of religious conflict within and beyond the Abrahamic family of religions in the twenty-first century is not so much about differences of belief as about manifestations of customs or social habits that are the outcome of those beliefs. Theological differences—about God, or the Holy Virgin, the Real Presence, the divine mission of Muhammad, the docetic Christology of the Quran, the inheritance of ʿAli ibn Abi Talib, or the martyrdom of the Imam Ḥussein—are not sufficient causes for humans to indulge in murderous behaviour towards their neighbours or 'intimate enemies'. Religious conflicts, between Catholics and Protestants, Sunnis and Shiʿas, Hindus and Muslims, are better seen as 'turf wars' between parties over resources and rights and the less tangible, but not of itself theological, issue of human 'respect'. Threats were made against the life of Salman Rushdie, author of *The Satanic Verses*, and Kurt Westermaark, the Danish cartoonist who depicted Muhammad with a bomb-shaped turban, not because they may or may not be 'non-believers', but because they were deemed to have insulted Muslims by violating two of their sacred icons: the aniconic image of the prophet and the integrity of the inerrant Quran. One could even extend this notion to the 11 September attacks on America—which were motivated, in part, by Bin Laden's accusation that holy Islamic soil was being violated by the presence of infidel US troops.

The defence of the sacred can be expressed territorially, iconically, or even sartorially—as when the idea of the sacred is configured around women's apparel, because sexuality is deemed to have mystical overtones. But it is too simplistic to argue that conflicts arising from clashes over the contested symbols that represent the sacred are motivated by matters of belief in the face of 'secularization'. A more plausible explanation lies in the way that sacred symbols become the bearers of both personal and group identities. 'Fundamentalism' is a modern phenomenon constructed out of ancient materials. Its components are symbolic systems, which once sustained individual or group identities, and find themselves challenged by the 'other'. In that sense it is a response to the crisis brought about by a new awareness of difference in a globalized world. As Clifford Geertz (quoted in Marty 1992: 5) once put it in plain language: 'From now on no one will leave anyone else alone.'

References

Abramov, S. 1985. *Ha'aretz*, 30 May.

Adraoui, M.-A. 2009. 'Salafism in France: Ideology, Practices and Contradictions'. In Meijer 2009b: 364–83.

Afary, J. 2009. *Sexual Politics in Modern Iran*. Cambridge, MA: Harvard University Press.

Amanat, A. 2009. *Apocalyptic Islam and Iranian Shiʿism*. London: Tauris.

Bloom, H. 1992. *The American Religion: The Emergence of the Post-Christian Nation*. New York: Simon & Schuster.

Bruce, S. 2000. *Fundamentalism*. Cambridge: Polity Press.

Cohn, N. 1993. *Cosmos, Chaos and the World to Come: The Ancient Roots of Apocalyptic Faith*. New Haven: Yale University Press.

Coleman, J. A. 1992. 'Catholic Integralism as a Fundamentalism'. In L. Kaplan, ed., *Fundamentalism in Comparative Perspective*. Amherst, MA: University of Massachusetts Press.

Dalal, A. 2013. *New Cambridge History of Islam*. Vol. VI. Cambridge: Cambridge University Press.

Didion, J. 2003. 'Mr. Bush and the Divine'. *New York Review of Books* 50: 17 (6 November).

Douglas, M. 1984. *Purity and Danger: An Analysis of the Concepts of Pollution and Taboo*. London: Routledge.

Erdbrink, T. 2013. *New York Times*, 4 March.

Gellner, E. 1992. *Postmodernism, Reason and Religion*. London: Routledge.

Giddens, A. 1990. *The Consequences of Modernity*. Stanford, CA: Stanford University Press.

Goodstein, L. 1998. 'Falwell Offers to Mobilize Churches to Oppose Israeli Pullback'. *New York Times*, 21 Jan.

Harlow, J. 1988. *Machzor for Rosh Hashanah and Yom Kippur*. New York: United Synagogue of Conservative Judaism.

Hodgkin, E. C., ed. 1993. *Two Kings in Arabia—Sir Reader Bullard's Letters from Jeddah.* Reading: Ithaca Press.

Juergensmeyer, M. 2013. 'Religious Roots of Violence'. In K. Almqvist and L. Belfrage, eds, *Roots of Violence.* Stockholm: Axel and Margaret Ax:son Johnson Foundation.

Keddie, N. R. 1972. *Sayyid Jamal ad-Din al-Afghani: A Political Biography.* Berkeley: University of California Press.

Kenny, A. 1994. *The Wittgenstein Reader.* 9th edn. Oxford: Blackwell.

Landes, R. 2011. *Heaven on Earth: The Varieties of the Millennial Experience.* New York: Oxford University Press.

Lawrence, B. B. 1989. *Defenders of God.* San Francisco: Harper & Row.

Marty, M. E. 1992. 'The Fundamentals of Fundamentalism'. In L. Kaplan, ed., *Fundamentalism in Comparative Perspective.* Amherst, MA: University of Massachusetts Press.

Meijer, R. 2009a. 'Introduction'. In Meijer 2009b: 1–32.

Meijer, R., ed. 2009b. *Global Salafism: Islam's New Religious Movement.* London: Hurst.

Mol, H. 1976. *Identity and the Sacred: A Sketch for a New Social-Scientific Theory of Religion.* Oxford: Oxford University Press.

Nekudah. 1985. Issue 73, October.

Pichnick, A. 1967. *Year by Year 5728.* Jerusalem.

Roy, O. 2007. *Secularism Confronts Islam*, trans. George Holoch. New York: Columbia University Press.

Ruthven, M. 1989. *The Divine Supermarket.* London: Chatto & Windus.

Ruthven, M. 2004. *Fundamentalism: The Search for Meaning.* Oxford: Oxford University Press.

Ruthven, M. 2015. 'The Apocalyptic Social Imaginary'. In E. Tonning et al., eds, *Modernism, Christianity and Apocalypse.* Leiden: Brill.

Safran, N. 1961. *Egypt in Search of Political Community.* Cambridge, MA: Harvard University Press.

Salomon, N. 2009. 'The Salafi Critique of Islamism'. In Meijer 2009b: 143–68.

Shahak, I. and Mezvinsky, N. 2004. *Jewish Fundamentalism in Israel.* 2nd edn. London: Pluto Press.

Shayegan, D. 1992. *Cultural Schizophrenia: Islamic Societies Confronting the West*, trans. John Howe. London: Saqi Books.

Wagemakers, J. 2009. 'Transformation of a Radical Concept'. In Meijer 2009b: 81–106.

Whitehouse, H. 2004. *Modes of Religiosity: A Cognitive Theory of Religious Transmission.* Lanham, MD: Rowman & Littlefield Publishers.

PART VI

EPILOGUES

CHAPTER 30

JEWISH AND OTHER ABRAHAMIC PHILOSOPHIC ARGUMENTS FOR ABRAHAMIC STUDIES

PETER OCHS

In its classical self-description, the people Israel is a people set apart but also one obliged to serve as a light to the nations. While these apparently contradictory characterizations do not define the mission or religion of the Jewish people, they are, nonetheless, suggestive portraits that raise a compelling question for this volume of essays. The question is: how might contemporary Jews honour this dual role, as a people apart and for the others? One answer is: by contributing, for one, to inter-Abrahamic engagements, including the academic project of Abrahamic studies.

In this chapter, I shall argue that some of the primary methods of scriptural study that distinguish rabbinic Judaism among the Abrahamic traditions (approaches to *midrash*) could also serve as a significant prototype for one as yet underappreciated dimension of inter-Abrahamic studies (what I will label *reparative enquiry*). I shall argue, furthermore, that work on inter-Abrahamic logics of reparative enquiry might, in turn, challenge contemporary philosophers both to help refine such logics *and to deploy them*. I shall suggest, finally, that these two arguments provide warrants for the work of Abrahamic studies in the Academy.

A Vocabulary for this Chapter

In this chapter, I employ the term 'Abrahamic' in a collective, not a distributive sense. That is, I use the term, not in the sense that there is a natural class of traditions called Abrahamic (since I do not believe there is), but in the sense that warranted readings of distinctly Jewish and also Christian and also Muslim traditions of scriptural reading and interpretation can be collected into a set (named 'Abrahamic studies') and that warranted and interesting observations can be made about relations among or characteristics of the members of that set. In previous writings on some of the linguistic markers of inter-Abrahamic conflict, I have introduced a distinction between two different contexts of language use: what I dub 'language in times of peace', and 'language in times of conflict, disruption, and radical social change'. In this chapter, I argue that these different contexts lend themselves to two different genres of academic enquiry and that serious errors result when the wrong genre is applied to the wrong context of language use.

Language in times of peace. I have used this phrase metaphorically, to refer to the way everyday communication works when the underlying language system is relatively undisturbed (so that the language itself is 'at peace', whether or not it is a time of societal conflict). At such times, the paradigm for language use is dinnertime conversation among close friends or family members. Here, if you ask your table mates to 'please pass the salt', they won't pass you the pepper and they won't stop to ask what you really mean. In times like this, the order of language use seems to correspond to the order of the world: language is 'natural language'. *Language in times of non-peace.* I have used this phrase to refer to the way both everyday and specialized forms of communication work when *a society's language system is undergoing radical change.* At such times, the rules of conventional systems of language are no longer reliable. These rules may hold in individual cases of communication, but they may also fail: for example, because events are observed that no longer correspond to the vocabulary or even syntax of a given system of natural language; because traumatized or exiled individuals may forget conventional language conventions; or because language communities may be enslaved or uprooted and absorbed into other communities, so that different vocabularies and rules of syntax are hybridized in various ways. In such settings, a given order of language may no longer correspond to the order of the observed world.

Different enquiries for different times. Writing about strategies for peacebuilding in times of conflict, I have suggested that, in the modern Academy, enquiries framed for 'times of peace'—times when language conventions are reliable—tend to display comparably ordered languages of analysis. But what enquiries are appropriate to times of 'non-peace': when—for example, in Muslim, Jewish, or Christian studies—the texts or societies or peoples being studied communicate by way of languages that are in distress, disrupted, suffering radical change? I have written that enquiries appropriate for conventional language use tend not to be appropriate for contexts of radical distress; enquiries appropriate for such times are themselves capable of continual adjustment in relation to their continually changing subject matter. I label these 'reparative enquiries', which I claim are guided by rules of observation, analysis, and repair that operate in close relationship with their subject of study.

Two kinds of enquiry for Abrahamic studies. This marvellous volume of essays offers a fitting context for both testing and expanding this model of 'two types of enquiry for two contexts of language use'. The essays also suggest a somewhat different analytic vocabulary for testing the model. I shall therefore reintroduce this model in the following terms:

- *Normal enquiry*. Following Sinai's lead in Chapter 12,[1] I shall employ this version of the Kuhnian term 'normal science' to refer to 'enquiry appropriate to contexts of conventional language use' (substituting 'conventional' for 'peacetime').
- *Reparative enquiry*.[2] Rather than adopt Kuhn's notion of 'revolutionary science', I will retain this term because I am making a somewhat different claim: that 'normal enquiry' is interrupted by disruptions and changes in natural language use and not only in the practices of specialized science.

Orders of enquiry in this chapter. In order to conduct the work of this chapter, I shall refer to different 'orders of enquiry', drawing on a medieval practice (for example, in Aquinas) of distinguishing 'first-order judgements' about what one observes or wants to do from 'second-order judgements' about the character of these primary judgements. I shall refer to enquiries that tend to draw first- or second-order judgements as first- or second-order enquiries. Some theologies, for example, offer first-order judgements about what someone should do on this earth; others offer second-order judgements about, for example, 'prescriptive discourses'. But I shall add a third term, 'third-order enquiries', for enquiries that tend to offer judgements *about* second-order enquiries. For example, I would classify George Lindbeck's *The Nature of Doctrine* as a third-order enquiry because it reviews and reclassifies Church doctrines as expressions of second, rather than first-order enquiry. In these terms, normal enquiry could include one, two, or three orders, but most scholars of normal enquiry refer only to two. Reparative enquiry is necessarily a third-order enquiry, since it claims to begin with reflections on disruptions in the language systems that enable both first- and second-order enquiries.

Illustrations from this volume: As I read them, most of the essays in this volume practise Abrahamic studies as a genre of normal comparative enquiry: comparing certain features of Muslim, Christian, and Jewish traditions or sub-traditions. The essays in this genre succeed because none of the authors tries to stretch the domain of normal enquiry to cover cases of linguistic distress.

A few authors name dimensions of Abrahamic studies that address contexts of conflict among the traditions and of reparative modes of enquiry in response. Silverstein, for example, describes how communities in conflict may summon the name of Abraham as a potentially unifying figure. In the terms I am using, Silverstein is referring to reparative enquiries as they may emerge among the communities

[1] Utilizing analytical categories coined by the historian of science Thomas Kuhn, one might characterize the works of Spinoza and Simon as marking an exegetical shift of 'paradigm' followed by a period of 'normal science'.

[2] Nicholas Adams (2006, 2008) coined this term to capture what we both meant by the corrective character of pragmatic reasoning.

themselves: employing the name 'Abraham' in a way that is, in fact, non-conventional, since it refers at once to the tradition-specific, conventional Abraham *and* to the one who might defuse some conflict among these traditions at some time (Silverstein in this volume, pp. 37–43). Silk devotes comparable attention to the performative force of enquiry in both academic and traditional circles of study: for example, in the way that scholars may attend to 'Abrahamic traditions' inclusively, in order to ameliorate some perceived conditions of interreligious conflict (Silk in this volume, pp. 80–4).[3]

Three authors introduce the genre of enquiry to which my chapter belongs: third-order reflection on the methods and presuppositions of a given field of academic science. Examining the history of academic Abrahamic studies, Stroumsa opens the questions I want to ask about both the epistemic assumptions and performative purposes of various practices of comparative Abrahamic studies. Illustrating a good bit of what I mean by 'reparative enquiry', Stroumsa uses Kuhnian terms to name the difference between conventions:

> We can detect . . . some paradigm shifts in systems of knowledge and on the reconstruction of central cognitive structures, throughout the trajectory of modern scholarship on religion. . . . It should be obvious, I repeat, that such fields are never innocent productions of knowledge. They are ultimately related to the construction of the self through the understanding of the other, in particular when they deal directly with religious identities. (Stroumsa in this volume, p. 62)

Surveying medieval approaches to the study of religious multiplicity, Weltecke extends this kind of methodological analysis, constructing a broad typological scheme for classifying and illustrating the various ways that scholars and believers have sought to account for the plurality of religions (Weltecke in this volume, pp. 192–202). I offer a different, but I hope complementary typology of contemporary approaches to Abrahamic studies as cases of either normal or reparative enquiry. This typology frames my central arguments. Ford is a long-term co-worker in the effort to develop Abrahamic models of reparative enquiry. His chapter begins with the assumption that scholars of Abrahamic studies will need to promote both normal and reparative enquiries.[4] He then undertakes the kind of work we too rarely perform in the Academy: third-order reflection on the best institutional contexts for nurturing both of these genres of enquiry, side by side (Ford in this volume, pp. 580–95).

[3] Also pertinent to this approach are Stoyanov's study of religious dualisms and Ruthven's study of fundamentalism.

[4] Ford's writings have for decades explored the reparative dimensions of inter-human, interreligious, and divine–human relations. See, for example, Ford 2007 for detailed studies of responses to 'the cry' in Scripture (what I would label scripture's reparative reasoning), including the cries of Job and the cries of Jesus on the cross. His writings on 'wisdom' in interreligious relations and in the university identify the virtues of facing, listening, hearing, caring, and rejoicing that are foundational for reparative work; and they identify the pitfalls of reducing reparative enquiry to the terms of normal enquiry (see also Ford 2006, 2009).

Arguments

(1) There are two different contexts for what, most broadly, may be termed 'tradition studies', including Abrahamic studies, as well as other studies of scriptural or religious traditions.

(a) Tradition studies for times when the subject society's language system is relatively undisturbed.

At such times, the prototype for language use is what I earlier dubbed 'dinnertime conversation', where the rules of communication and the criteria for meaning and for truth or falsity are comparable to what Ludwig Wittgenstein set out in his *Tractatus logico-philosophicus. The first rule is that the order of language corresponds, for all practical purposes, to the order of the world. This 'at-homeness' of language in the world warrants a second rule: that claims about the world can be tested, when necessary, by a propositional logic.* According to this logic, testable claims are delivered by way of individual judgements that predicate some familiar qualities of some identifiable entities in the worlds of thought or experience. The 'at-homeness' of language also warrants a third rule: that to see if a claim is publicly verifiable, one needs to verify only its semantics (the publicly recognizable meaning of its key terms) and not its material elements or its pragmatics (the consequences of its being asserted in a particular time and place). When guided by these rules, tradition studies tend to be composed as types of *normal enquiry* that generate third-person descriptions of states of affairs within various domains, such as religious documents, redaction and reception histories, ritual practices, and systems of belief. Meaning is assumed to be specific to various systems of natural language, some of them civilization-wide, others specific to local social groups or associations. The fifth rule is ontological: that, since language corresponds reasonably well to the world, authors of normal enquiries can assume, until there is evidence otherwise, that their enquiries display verifiable knowledge of the worlds they are examining. The fifth rule implies a sixth: that, until there is evidence to the contrary, readers may assume that these authors' knowledge claims provide readers with comparable knowledge of the *actual* worlds to which those claims refer. In other words, these enquiries provide 'objective knowledge': or knowledge whose validity is independent of the conditions and methods of enquiry.

(b) Tradition studies for times of conflict or disruption, when a society's language system is undergoing radical change.

At such times, the rules of conventional systems of natural language are no longer reliable. These rules may hold in individual cases of communication, but they may also fail: for example, because events are observed that no longer correspond to the semantics of a given system of natural language; because traumatized or exiled individuals may forget conventional semantics or syntax; or because language communities may be uprooted and absorbed into other communities, so that different vocabularies and rules of syntax are hybridized. In such settings, a given order of language may no longer correspond to the order of the observed world; conventional rules of propositional logic may no longer be reliable; semantic rules may appear to vary in each new context for social interaction; realist ontologies and epistemologies that draw clear subject/object distinctions will most likely generate false claims. At such times, scholars can no longer predict if and when they can rely on their skills of discerning rules of meaning within conventional systems of natural language. They can no longer assume that their customary practices of normal enquiry apply equally everywhere.

(2) How is it possible to locate rules of enquiry that apply when the rules of normal enquiry are no longer reliable? As students of Plato, Aristotle, or Kant would readily tell you, the answer to this question cannot come from normal enquiry, but only from an enquiry capable of disclosing, examining, and potentially revising the presuppositions of normal enquiry (what Kant called its transcendental conditions). But who is prepared to conduct such an enquiry? Or, having conducted it, who is capable of getting anyone to listen to the results? The best name and location for this enquiry is philosophy, when identified as a discipline of both analytic and reparative third-order reflection.

(3) There are two contexts for conducting philosophic enquiry.

(a) Philosophy as third-order, normal enquiry, when a society's language system is relatively undisturbed.

A significant proportion of writings in contemporary analytic philosophy, for example, examine natural language systems as relatively stable sources of evidence about rules of logic, ethics, aesthetics, and so on. Such stability warrants efforts by such philosophers to repair errors that arise within the academy when scholars make second-order claims that either misrepresent natural language semantics or flaunt its rules of logic.

(b) Philosophy for times of conflict or disruption, when a society's language system is undergoing radical change.

At such times, the rules of conventional systems of natural language are no longer reliable, so that philosophers lose their warrant for conducting third-order normal enquiry.[5]

Philosophical Enquiry in Times of Conflict and Change

(4) What models of philosophic enquiry are appropriate for times marked by conflict, disruption, or radical social change? There are two surprisingly complementary models:

[5] I recognize that this claim would be rejected by, for example, some schools of analytic philosophy as well as of phenomenology, who may claim to have access to transcendental disciplines of enquiry (like Kant's) that are not affected by disruptions in societal or civilizational orders. Such claims appear to me to be foundationalist and not readily defended against the genres of postmodern criticism that, for example, are illustrated in this volume's chapter by Anidjar.

one derived from quantum physics and one derived from Abrahamic traditions of scriptural interpretation. These are complementary sources, as well, of pragmatism as a practice of philosophic, reparative enquiry.

Jewish, Christian, and Muslim studies are most often prosecuted today as if they were designed only for contexts appropriate to normal enquiry. They tend to examine their objects of study as if each belonged to a coherent language system with respect to which most propositional claims could be measured as clearly true or false. In the face of such contexts, practitioners of these modes of enquiry tend, more often than the academic guilds acknowledge, to understate the vagueness and indeterminacy of their data and observations and to overstate the reliability and generality of their conclusions. Some practitioners may, as an alternative, acknowledge the inadequacy of their data and observations, but attribute this to the unavailability of scientifically verifiable information. On the evidence of both contemporary quantum science and the long history of Abrahamic scriptural studies, I would argue that, in many of these cases, verifiable information is indeed available, but it is visible only to methods of enquiry fashioned specifically for times of radical linguistic change.

(a) Quantum physics as a science of disorderly systems

Quantum physics emerged in the late nineteenth century as a practice of enquiry that would enable scientists to make truth-functional claims about the behaviour of subatomic particles that could not be directly observed. Today, introductory college textbooks in physics often introduce quantum science as the single most general characterization of the field as a whole; and some science writers refer to quantum theory as the most general account of the natural sciences as a whole. For our purposes, the significance of quantum science is not that the behaviour of subatomic particles somehow gives us better insight into the behaviour of scriptural traditions in times of disorder. The significance is that the disciplines of enquiry that made quantum theory possible were available in other forms long before they were applied to the accounts of subatomic behaviour. I have argued elsewhere that these disciplines are visible in rabbinic and some patristic approaches to scriptural interpretation and that these approaches are among the sources of the philosophic discipline Charles Peirce labelled 'pragmatism'.[6]

As Warner Heisenberg, one of the founding theorists of quantum science, wrote in the early twentieth century: Charles Peirce's logic of science somehow anticipated quantum theory forty to fifty years earlier. I mention this because Peirce offered his proto-quantum studies (for example his 'logic of relatives', 'semeiotic', and system of 'existential graphs') to correct errors in the logic of laboratory science that he believed stemmed from his contemporaries' fixation on a single, mechanical model of the

[6] See Ochs 2009 and Markus 1972. Complementary claims have been made about Origen, Clement, and Gregory of Nyssa. I anticipate that complementary claims will be identified, as well, in the early traditions of quranic *tafsir* and legal interpretation. For intimations, see, *inter alia*, Ahmed 2012.

behaviour of the universe. Peirce complained that the natural sciences of his day tended to extend only to fields of enquiry and mathematical frameworks that were appropriate to the study of phenomena that fell within the ken of everyday human experience and language use (and thus within the ken of normal enquiry). Peirce introduced his 'pragmatic method' as a means of resolving the interminable debates that arise when enquirers offer equally inadequate, competing accounts of phenomena that fall outside that ken: as, for example, objectivist vs. subjectivist efforts to offer competing, clear, and distinct judgements about behaviours undergoing radical change (Peirce 1878). His method offered logical guidelines and strategies for reformulating one's tools of measurement when changing conditions render previously reliable tools unreliable. Inheriting the objectivist models of scientific measurement that dominated nineteenth-century philosophy and logic of science, Peirce may first have observed such changing conditions as exceptions to the reach of these objectivist tools (Peirce 1868, 1905), for example, when he found these tools inadequate to the task of mapping geodesic phenomena, or force fields, or human perceptions of continuous sound or melody. He discovered that, rather than falling outside the reach of science, such phenomena could be mapped and measured successfully with other tools: if, for example, he employed statistical and other practices of probabilistic or stochastic mapping and reasoning.

Stated in terms of the Bayesian models popular today (cf. Lipton 2004), Peirce discovered that phenomena that appear chaotic when examined one datum at a time may be mapped as statistically predictable functions or waves or fields when observed macroscopically as sets of enormous numbers of individual events. He discovered, in other words, that objectivist models of science overstate not only the universality of observed laws but also the discreteness of the bits of data that purportedly displayed such laws. As he extended his new field of enquiry, Peirce discovered something more: he could map the laws of normal enquiry as special cases of more general probabilistic functions. He found that it was scientifically more efficient to treat all phenomena as if they were observed in conditions of disorder and change and then to define the data of normal enquiry as the way phenomena appear within certain highly defined conditions of experience or observation. In this way, he made another 'Copernican turn', claiming that Newton's mechanical laws define the laws of the universe only as they appear within the limited frames of measurement that characterize everyday human experience. These frames are not illusory, only limited. Peirce's conclusion implies that, within the broader frame of statistical models, what normal enquirers consider 'individual entities' in the world no longer function as passive objects of enquiry. They are now to be observed as relational aspects and relative functions, waves, or fields.

When referring to phenomena of literature and communication, Peirce restated his statistical logic of relations as what he called a 'semeiotic': a non-binary logic of signs and symbols. In the terms of this semeiotic (which scholars of logic and linguistics now distinguish sharply from the binary 'semiology' of de Saussure[7]), claims are not truth-

[7] For a readable introduction, see Sheriff 1989.

functional when they are presented as ways of predicating certain discrete characteristics of certain individuals in the world ('X is Y'). They are truth-functional only when they display the context of measurement (or what Peirce called the 'interpretant') with respect to which a certain set of possible relations (the predicate of a judgement) is displayed in a certain space-time or event (the subject of a judgement): mapped, for example, as 'xMy' or 'y is observable at x with respect to measurement M', or 'x is a sign of y for M'.

I have reviewed all of this material about Peirce, because his semeiotic may function like a quantum logic for scholars in Abrahamic studies (or the humanities more broadly): providing a means of mapping phenomena that remain invisible to the tools of normal enquiry. If, as I argue, Abrahamic studies should include studies of Muslim, Jewish, and Christian scriptural traditions in contexts of disruption and radical social change, then Peirce's semeiotic—or cognate models of statistical measurement—should play some role in Abrahamic studies. To strengthen this claim, I shall add another argument: that Peirce's semeiotic and proto-quantum logic derive from an Abrahamic scriptural semeiotic.

(b) Abrahamic scriptural sources of semeiotic (and comparable quantum logics)

I refer here to 'Abrahamic' in a collective, not distributive sense. That is, I use the term, not in the sense that there is a natural class of traditions called Abrahamic (since I do not believe there is), but in the sense that sources of semeiotic can be located in warranted readings of distinctly Jewish and also Christian and also Muslim traditions of scriptural reading and interpretation. I do not, furthermore, presume that these traditions necessarily generate semeiotic or quantum models of reasoning: the semeiotic model precludes necessaritarian claims. I argue only that, among other ways of reading, there are also logically and rationally warranted ways of reading each of these traditions as displaying semeiotic or quantum-like models of reasoning. I will sample evidence here only from one reading of rabbinic scriptural traditions, with a complementary note about Augustinian directions in scriptural semeiotic. I anticipate that scholars could offer many more comparable readings from each of the three Abrahamic scriptural traditions.

(bi) A rabbinic scriptural semeiotic

I summarize here an argument I have offered elsewhere in several places: that, for at least one direction in contemporary Jewish studies—'Textual Reasoning (TR)'—hermeneutical reflection on the classical rabbinic practice of *midrash* is an effective source of models for conducting Jewish reparative reasoning in contexts of conflict, disruption, and radical change. In the following, I identify a single line of hermeneutical reflection that uncovers what I call five rules for a practice of rabbinic reparative reasoning. Each rule reflects a reading offered by some contemporary rabbinic scholar, but the effort to name and collect these into an ordered series is my own.

(1) Narratives of conflict, destruction, and radical social change contribute significantly to the biblical record and reappear frequently as means of intra-biblical commentary. For TR, these narratives illustrate the first rule of rabbinic reparative reasoning: 'Bear witness to events of destruction in the history of the people Israel. Narrate these events and reflect on these narratives regularly.'

Consider for example these prototypical narratives of distress:

- Miẓrayim, Bondage in Egypt:

> The Israelites groaned in their bondage and cried out and their cry for help because of their bondage went up to God. (Exod. 2)

- Chorban: First Destruction:

> I reared up children and brought them up, but they have rebelled against me . . . The Lord's anger burns against his people. (Isa. 1).
>
> How solitary sits the city, once so full of people.
> Bitterly she weeps at night, tears are upon her cheeks . . .
> Jerusalem has become unclean (Lam. 1).

Consider how the Bible regularly rereads these narratives, for example:

> Why should you harden your hearts as the Egyptians and Pharaoh hardened their hearts? (1 Sam. 6: 6)
>
> For thus says the Lord of hosts, the God of Israel: I have put an iron yoke on the neck of all these nations so that they may serve King Nebuchadnezzar of Babylon, and they shall indeed serve him; I have even given him the wild animals. (Jer. 28: 14)

(2) For a certain genre of inner-biblical interpretation, narratives of distress are reread as signs both of destruction and of the possibility of future redemption (*geulah*). For TR, this rereading illustrates the second rule of reparative reasoning: 'Pray that a Redeemer will come. Read the memory of your own loss as also a sign of a future redemption.'

- Miẓrayim:

> The Lord continued, 'I have marked well the plight of My people in Egypt and have heeded their outcry because of their taskmasters. . . . I will send you.' Moses said, 'Who am I that I should go?' . . . He said, '*ehyeh ʿimach*, I will be with you.' . . . 'Thus shall you say to the Israelites, *ehyeh* sent me to you.' (Exod. 3)

- Chorban, First Destruction:

> But you, Israel, My servant, Jacob, whom I have chosen, Seed of Abraham my friend—You whom I drew from the ends of the earth . . . I have put My spirit in him, He shall teach the true way to the nations . . . Who formed you, O Israel: Fear not, for I will redeem you. . . . You are Mine. (Isa. 41–3)

> Ezra opened the scroll in the sight of all the people, for he was above the people; as he opened it, the people stood up. Ezra blessed the Lord, the great God, and all the people answered, Amen, Amen, with hands upraised. Then they bowed their heads.... Jeshua, Bani... and the Levites explained the Teaching to the people, while the people stood in their places. They read from the scroll of the Teaching of God, translating it and giving the sense; so they understood the reading. (Neh. 8: 4–8)

In these intra-scriptural rereadings of both distress and redemption, one biblical pericope may function in a way that is comparable to a second-order reflection on another pericope: Isa. 1 and Lam. 1, for example, as reading the record of past punishments as sources of prophecy concerning future punishment (Fishbane 1985: 446–9, 458n[8]); or Isa. 41–3 as rereading past punishments as marks of prefilled punishment and therefore future redemption (Fishbane 1985: 469); or Isa. 29: 25 as rereading Exod. 3: 10 is anticipating a very different time when YHVH will also call Egypt 'My people' (Fishbane 1985: 368); or Neh. 8: 4–8 as evidence of the work of intra-biblical reflection itself ('they read from the scroll, ... giving the sense,' Fishbane 1985: 83). The overall lesson is that intra-biblical commentary already introduces patterns of potentially third-order reflection, through which changing contexts of language use are read as occasions for new rules of meaning.

(3) For a major genre of rabbinic literature, the biblical memory of both destruction and redemption anticipates cycles of post-biblical Jewish history. For TR, the third rule of reparative reasoning is that destruction is and will be one recurring context of Jewish life (what I call the context of conflict, disruption, and radical social change) and that meantime (non-final) redemption will be another.

- Rabbinic narratives of distress: Chorban, Second Destruction:

> When Rabbi Joshua looked at the Temple in ruins one day, he burst into tears. 'Alas for us! The place which atoned for the sins of all the people Israel lies in ruins!' Then Rabbi Yohannan ben Zakkai spoke to him these words of comfort: 'Be not grieved, my son. There is another way of gaining ritual atonement: ... through deeds of loving-kindness.' (*Avot de Rabbi Natan* 11a, cited in Harlow 1988: 615)
>
> It was decreed for Israel that they study words of Torah in distress, in enslavement, in wandering and in uncertainty, suffering for lack of food. (*Midrash Eliayahu Rabbah* 21)

- Rabbinic narratives of redemption after the Chorban:

> All Israel has a place in the world to come, as it is written, 'Your people shall all be righteous, they shall possess the land forever; there are a shoot of My planting, the work of My hands in whom I shall be glorified' (Is. 60). Moses received Torah from Sinai and transmitted it to Joshua, and Joshua to the elders, the elders to the prophets, the prophets to the members of the Great Assembly... Simeon the Just

[8] Fishbane also notes how the *ekah* ('alas!') of Lam. 1 rereads the *ekah* of Isa. 1: 21.

> was one of the last members of the Great Assembly. He used to teach: The world rests on three things: on Torah, on service to God, and on acts of loving kindness. (*m Avot (Ethics of the Fathers)* 1)
>
> [A midrash] must not deprive a scriptural text of its plain sense (*'eyn mikra yotse mide peshuto'*: *b Shabbat* 63a).

Mishnaic reflection, and later Talmudic re-reflection, on the Destruction of the Second Temple constitute the prototype for rabbinic reparative reasoning[9]. I find it useful to read these reflections as anticipating the following four stages of reparative enquiry: (a) *Perceptions of stark contradiction between conventional readings (the 'plain sense') of Israel's covenant according to the biblical text and reports about the empirical realities of Israel's life in times of destruction and exile*: displayed, for example, in Joshua's words, 'Alas! The place which atoned for the sins of all the people Israel lies in ruin!' (b) *Radical rereadings of the interpreted meaning of the biblical text* (for example, 'There is another way of gaining ritual atonement:... through deeds of loving-kindness') so as to reassure a given community of its enduring covenant (for example, 'Be not grieved' and 'All Israel has a place in the world to come'), while at the same time revising its reading habits and reorienting its behaviour (for example, by engaging in atoning 'deeds of loving-kindness suggested'). (c) *Significantly revised practices and institutions of Jewish religious life, including revisions of law and theology and of the structures of authority and learning: all attentive to the new worldly realities* ('Moses received Torah from Sinai and transmitted it to Joshua, and Joshua to the elders, the elders to the prophets, the prophets to the members of the Great Assembly... ': the Mishnah signals the emergence of several new practices and institutions: chief among them the rabbinic sages as recipients of Moses' oral Torah, of much of the work of the scribal priesthood and much more). (d) *Procedures for testing and, when necessary, revising these new revisions* (for example, the injunction '[A midrash] must not deprive a scriptural text of its plain sense,' suggests that the plain sense remains the arbiter of future scriptural interpretations: interpretations speak to needs of their day; the plain sense speaks eternally).

(4) For this major genre of rabbinic literature, the narrative and historical cycle of destruction and redemption signifies the hermeneutical rule of rabbinic midrash: that the plain sense (*peshat*) of the people Israel's narrative memory will never be superseded, but that it will also cyclically contradict the plain sense of the people's social history, and that this contradiction will be repaired only

[9] Daniel Weiss observes that my pragmatic typology appears contradictory, since I argue for both the medieval distinction between plain and interpreted sense and David Halivni's account of early rabbinic exegesis, which differs sharply from the medieval account. My response is that I begin with Halivni's account of the rabbinic distinction between initial readings mamash ('akin to what we call plain meaning': Halivni, 76) and additional readings that disclose 'applied' meanings. I extend this mild distinction into an explicit, pragmatic rule that, I believe, captures the primary hermeneutical practice of contemporary 'textual reasoners': inspired, at once by classic rabbinic midrash and those medieval hermeneuts who honoured both the textual authority of peshat and the performative guidance, or at times authority, of derash.

through prayerful scriptural interpretation (midrash) composed anew by scholar-sages in each generation and context of the people's history. For TR, the fourth rule of reparative reasoning is that, for times without radical disruption, contradiction may be a mark of human error, to be corrected and erased by more carefully following the rules of normal enquiry; but that, for times of radical disruption, contradiction may mark the work that needs to be done to repair the rules of enquiry themselves.

- David Halivni: A survivor and Talmudist's midrash of distress:

> The sword and the book came down from heaven tied to each other. Said the Almighty, 'If you keep what is written in this book, you will be spared this sword; if not, you will be consumed by it'. (*Midrash Rabbah Deuteronomy* 4: 2). We clung to the book, yet were consumed by the sword. (Halivni 1998)

- David Halivni: A survivor and Talmudist's rabbinic hermeneutic after the Shoah:

> The horrendous Divine abandonment that took place during the years of the Shoah marked the nadir of a long, gradual process that may have already begun with the Golden Calf. To paraphrase a Talmudic saying, 'If the Tablets were not broken, the Torah would not have been forgotten.' 'If they would not have abandoned God by worshipping the Golden Calf, God would not have abandoned us in the years to follow.' But He did abandon us, and His absence has affected all aspects of Jewish spiritual life, including the way we interpret the Torah. (Halivni 2007: 124)

A Talmudic prodigy as a boy in Sighet, Halivni was brought from town to town to recite Talmud. He was interned at Auschwitz and other camps during the Shoah and suffered the loss of his entire family. After the Shoah, he became an academic Talmudic scholar. I spent some years interviewing him to discern how the immeasurable disruption of his world might have left its mark on his practice of Torah study. I read these two citations as illustrating three of these marks: (a) that he did not abandon the institutions of rabbinic Judaism into which he was socialized (he did not depart, one might say, from the plain sense of his textual tradition); (b) but he focused his scholarly attention on the profound contradictions between the reparative hopes of rabbinic midrash and the reality he captured in the phrases 'We clung to the book, yet were consumed by the sword' and 'He did abandon us'; (c) as a result, he revised his practices of Talmudic enquiry: in my reading, his scholarship moved from normal to reparative enquiry.

- Halivni writes:

> I have often used the term *tikkun hamikra* or 'repairing Scripture' to describe the task of those who have accepted some of the conclusions reached by methods of historical criticism as applied to the study of Bible and Talmud. These scholars are cognizant of inconsistencies, repetitions, and irregularities within the text of sacred Scripture. And yet, while accepting the critical approach to Scripture, they still believe in Torat Moshe: the revelation of both the Written and Oral Laws at Mount Sinai. They attribute the corruption of the text to human error, a consequence of the

> 'Sins of Israel', *chate'u yisrael* (a phrase I adapt from the Babylonian Talmud, Sanhedrin 21a) . . .
>
> I apply the expression *tikkun hamikra* to the entire Torah because I consider the need for tikkun to be pervasive. I contend that the Written Torah was 'maculated' through a process of forgetfulness and neglect that I call chate'u yisrael and that it is therefore in need of a general restoration in order to 'reinstate its glory as in the days of old' . . .
>
> My use of the expression *tikkun hamikra* is most similar to the Lurianic notion of repairing what was broken in the beginning. In my reading, Scripture needs restoration because its text has suffered maculation since its inception. . . . As the sages lament, 'If only the first Tablets had not been broken, then Israel would not have forgotten the Torah' ('Eruvin 54a). It remains our obligation to engage actively in the ongoing project of restoring this maculated text, investigating its defects, and making every effort to discover anew the words of the Living God as they were originally revealed at Sinai . . .
>
> If the text of the Written Torah, Scripture, is marred by maculation, the text of the Talmud is marred by forced interpretation, dochok: the effort to cover over, or rationalize, the maculations of received texts rather than seeking to repair or at least acknowledge them. This defect of the Talmud inhibits our capacity to study *torat emet*, the Torah as it was given. First of all, the forced interpretations introduce a kind of reasoning that is foreign to the texts they seek to explain. Second, by covering over defects in the received texts, these interpretations prevent us from seeing those defects and, thereby, from taking on, let alone fulfilling, the obligatory work of repairing them. Since we belong, still, to the generations of those whose life in Torah is defined by how we read Talmud, the Talmud's forced interpretations remain an obstacle to our living lives of Torah. I therefore extend the obligation of *tikkun hamikra* to the work of restoring the original texts of the Tannaim, the authors of the Mishnah, and restoring the correct reasonings of the Amoraim, the authors of the Gemara. This has been my lifelong work in *Mekorot Umasorot.*

Mekorot Umasorot ('Sources and Traditions'), Halivni's (1968) voluminous, critical commentary on the Babylonian Talmud, is highly respected by contemporary rabbinic scholars because it displays extraordinary erudition in the redaction and reception history of the Talmud. While his personal, theological accounts of why he undertook this critical commentary tend to remain in the margins of contemporary academic interest, I cite them here because I believe they demonstrate two enduring features of the rabbinic scholarly tradition: (a) it maintains both normal and reparative enquiries, each appropriate to its context; (b) even when the times demand it, reparative enquiry will tend to be dismissed or openly rejected by contemporaries who practise normal enquiry. Unless it becomes repressive, this dismissal is not inappropriate, since it protects a scholarly community against errant projects of repair. One proof of appropriate reparative enquiry is its capacity, over time, to convince its opponents.

(4) Jewish philosophy today tends for the most part to promote its work as normal enquiry. Most writings in academic Jewish philosophy examine the writings of previous Jewish philosophers in the manner of Jewish intellectual history. This practice tends to

apply, as well, to recent writings on the set of post-Kantian Jewish philosophers who saw their own work as reparative enquiry (Hermann Cohen, Martin Buber, Franz Rosenzweig, Emmanuel Levinas). This is unfortunate. While the Academy will continue to be well served by philosophic scholarship that addresses fairly well ordered language systems, contemporary Jewish civilization is animated by sharply disordered systems of language, many in competition one with the other and many undergoing radical change.

Without abandoning its attention to more conventional discourses, Jewish philosophy carries an additional and perhaps greater responsibility in times like these. Because they have direct access to both the reparative hermeneutics of rabbinic Judaism and the logical tools of western philosophy, Jewish philosophers have the capacity to craft potentially powerful instruments of reparative reasoning. I believe that, in times like these, this capacity carries the moral obligation we might associate with lifeboat ethics, except that in this case the philosopher has little to lose by helping. By way of illustration, philosophic reflection on cases of reparative reasoning like Halivni's will generate models of reasoning that may, when tested on specific occasions of disruption, prove to be of reparative use. Without normal rules of enquiry, what method of modelling should one use? Here, Kuhn's approach is instructive: new paradigms of science both build on and experimentally revise the older ones. But what guides the experimentation? The secret of reparative enquiry is that certain kinds of guessing—hypothesis making or 'abduction'—actually work and that reparative traditions like rabbinic Judaism record and transmit long histories of successful and unsuccessful examples and methods of guesswork. Then why add philosophy to the mix? Because philosophy names a discipline for modelling modes of reasoning. What philosophic method is indigenous to rabbinic Judaism? Questions about 'indigenous authenticity' often betray efforts to extend patterns of normal enquiry to cover conditions of disruption as well: valorizing 'what is indigenous' may mask an effort to protect conventional rules of enquiry from revision.[10] The well-remembered Jewish philosophers, from Philo to Levinas, have all devoted portions of their work to reparative enquiry and have all drawn the techniques of modelling from any sources they found useful.

Here are samples of how I might, strictly for illustrative purposes in this chapter, try to model the rules of reparative enquiry I observe in Halivni's writings. I have previously explored this exercise with the writings of other rabbinic scholars, as well. I shall have succeeded in these exercises if better-qualified readers see that they can do this better:

- *Peshat and derash.* For TR, Halivni's account of *peshat/derash* suggests an epistemological as well as hermeneutical distinction (Halivni 1991, Ochs 2002). To distinguish between plain and interpreted senses of scripture is to announce that some conventional system of language has been interrupted and that, for the reparative enquiry appropriate to this transitional time, words of scripture will

[10] When examined by way of third-order enquiries, conventional rules (such as those that inform contemporary programmes in any field of Jewish, Muslim, or Christian studies) may display 'non-indigenous' origins, where the point of origin was an occasion of reparative enquiry.

signify performative meanings that are not evident in what is now called the 'plain sense'. The plain sense is not superseded, but for this transitional time, it lacks performative meaning.

- *Dochok* (forced meaning). To promote normal enquiry at such a transitional time, scholars must either ignore the interruption and the contradictory claims that accompany it, or else construct theories to justify conventional meanings. In his study of the Talmud, Halivni labels such efforts 'forced meaning', or efforts to 'cover over, or rationalize, the maculations of received texts rather than seeking to repair or at least acknowledge them'. He considers these 'obstacle[s] to our living lives of Torah' and devotes his work to removing them. For TR, 'forced meaning' is an appropriate term of opprobrium for any effort to generalize the domain of a normal enquiry beyond the system of language that informs it or to promote the claims of normal enquiry as adequate, as well, to times of disruption. One example of forced meaning would be an effort to discount the place of reparative reasoning in the texts of great figures in the history of Jewish philosophy.
- *Tikkun hamikra* (an effort to 'repair Scripture'). For TR, Scripture is the prototype for any elemental display (or 'revelation') of civilizational norms and linguistic rules; Halivni's *tikkun hamikra* is therefore a prototype for any form of reparative reasoning (or effort to repair elemental norms and rules).
- And so on.

This section has, I trust, illustrated how Jewish philosophers might frame rules of reparative enquiry that could, per hypothesis, be reshaped and tested for use outside of Jewish studies. Since these rules are derived from practices of rabbinic scriptural interpretation, I trust this section has also illustrated how at least one of the Abrahamic scriptural traditions might generate rules of reparative enquiry. But what evidence do we have of a scripturally based practice of reparative reasoning outside of rabbinic Judaism? In the next section, I close by sampling an argument that I have offered in detail elsewhere (Ochs 2009): that Augustine introduced a scripturally based semiotic model of reparative reasoning that anticipated Charles Peirce's pragmatic model. This is an important argument, because it illustrates how analogous modes of reparative reasoning can be identified through philosophic readings of both classic rabbinic midrash and patristic scriptural interpretation.[11] The argument is important, as well, because it locates a prototype for Peirce's proto-quantum logic in a genre of Abrahamic scriptural studies. The argument would offer a strong warrant for reading quantum science as complementing a scriptural practice of reparative reasoning.

(bii) An Augustinian Scriptural Semeiotic

The immediate object of Peirce's critique was what he considered the faulty inductive logic of John Stuart Mill, but Peirce traced Mill's errors to modern philosophy's turn to

[11] It would be good in the future to test for analogues in philosophic readings of classic quranic commentary.

a species of foundationalism Peirce labelled 'intuitionism', or 'Cartesianism'.[12] For Peirce readers, including Wittgenstein, 'foundationalism' refers to the effort to locate truth claims independent of inherited traditions of practice, on the basis of which one could construct entire systems of belief and practice. Peirce argued that most efforts of this kind are grounded in an 'intuitionism': the belief that such truth claims come in the form of self-legitimizing intuitions.[13] Peirce's critique is that the arguments of intuitionism are circular: immune from any criticism, self-legitimizing intuitions constitute mere assertions, not truth claims. Peirce's mature critique of Cartesianism begins with a claim that anticipates the distinction I introduced earlier between peacetime and non-peacetime contexts of philosophic enquiry. Peirce argued that there are at least two different classes of truth claims: (a) *constative* claims[14] and (b) *reparative* or *contested* claims. *Constative claims* are *conventional* in that they state a matter of fact with respect to an implicit set of non-contested conventions or rules of meaning: because these rules are assumed, these claims are often presented as if they were self-evident. Emerging when conventions of meaning are subject to disruption and radical change, *reparative claims* are offered to recommend ways of modifying aspects of these conventions. These claims are sufficiently clear to call a community's attention to certain disruptions in their conventions of meaning; but they must remain partially unclear, since it is the community's task now to investigate what has happened to them and decide how best to respond.

Peirce's critique of Cartesianism is not a critique of any constative claim but a critique of the Cartesian tendency to treat reparative claims as if they were constative claims and, therefore, self-evident. In the terms of this chapter, Cartesianism treats reparative enquiry as if its concerns were already met by a normal enquiry; in the terms of a rabbinic reparative reasoning, it imposes 'forced meanings'. But what would tempt thinkers like Descartes to misrepresent reparative recommendations as self-evident claims? Without space here to connect the genealogical dots from Descartes to Scholastic and earlier medieval sources, I shall merely report on conclusions I have presented elsewhere: that Augustine is among the founders of a more inclusive 'Cartesian' tradition that includes both Descartes-like intuitionists and those, like

[12] Since this turn was displayed prototypically, but by no means exclusively, in the works of René Descartes.

[13] In his early *Journal of Speculative Philosophy* papers of 1868–9, Charles Peirce identified Cartesianism with intuitionism, the assumption that there is a 'cognition not determined by a previous cognition of the same object, and therefore so determined by something out of consciousness' (Peirce 5.213).

[14] 'Constative' claims are declarative utterances, asserted as either true or false. These are distinguished from claims made through some performance (rather than direct utterance) and from utterances that do not assert any matter of truth-or-falsity. Constative claims, include both 'common sense or everyday' claims and 'specialized or scientific' claims. Common-sense or everyday claims are made with respect to sub-communities of natural language use. Specialized or scientific claims are offered to sub-communities of enquirers who share an argot constructed not for the sake of furthering specific projects of enquiry that do not replace or substitute for everyday discourses. The truth or falsity of a constative claim is judged with respect to the coherence of the claim with a given set of semantic and illocutionary conventions and the correspondence of the claim with what listeners would expect to perceive or cognize as the object or referent of the claim if it were true.

Augustine and Peirce, whose work displays both the temptations to intuitionism and a means of repairing the temptations.

Augustine worked within a broader Hellenistic/Mediterranean civilization that drew its epistemic rules from several sources, of which the most influential were Hellenic and scriptural models of reasoning and action. But these two models are not easily mediated: individual thinkers who try to mediate them are likely to find themselves drawn instead into an irremediable inner dialectic. That is at least how I read Augustine's *Confessions*: the inner story of one who sought, on his own, to tame this dialectic but found himself infected by it instead, leaving him with a 'restlessness' that was relieved only when he was shown how Hellenic and scriptural models can find rest in each other's company. On this reading, Augustine's 'place of rest' would be a practice of reparative reasoning that both demonstrates the Bible's reasonableness and articulates its *ratio.*[15]

In this reading of Augustine, restlessness and rest anticipate the pragmatist's journey of reparative enquiry. 'Restlessness' marks the epistemic dialectic that results when methods of normal enquiry are errantly adopted as methods of reparative enquiry. 'Rest' marks the wisdom and inner peace that accompanies a triple discovery: that the source of restlessness is now to be found within and not without (from one perspective, it appears as an inner dialectic between two poles of normal enquiry: 'objectivism' and 'internalism'); that the source of rest now lies within as well (his redeeming word); and that the dialect is not quieted until one receives his word, alone, as its mediator.[16] In this

[15] My thanks to Thomas Higgins (Ph.D. University of Virginia 2005) for this insight into the *Confessions.*

[16] Three epistemic tendencies are internal to Augustine's process of reparative reasoning:

1. *Objectivism: a tendency to read certain external signs as indices (or direct indications of the existence) of the real.* (a) *Biblical objectivism*: a tendency to categorize the Bible as a direct description of the life of God on earth. This tendency appears in dialectical opposition to another one: (b) *Logical objectivism*: a tendency to categorize formal systems of logic as direct descriptions of the elemental characteristics of being itself as the real.
2. *Internalism: a tendency to perceive certain modes of consciousness as icons (or images) of being (as the real).* Internalism appears, overall, in dialectical opposition to Objectivism. (a) *Biblical internalism*: a tendency to identify one's reception of the Bible with an icon of the divine presence. This is a foundationalist tendency that appears in dialectical opposition to another one: (b) *Logical internalism*: a tendency to identify the cogito with the internalized character of the real, or being itself. This is an intuitionist tendency.
3. *Mediatory or reparative rationality: a reparative tendency to participate in certain semiotic processes as means of redeeming sin and (non-identically) imitating the actions of God in this world.*
   a) *Confessional Rationality*: A capacity, in the face of Scripture's witness, to recognize and acknowledge marks of sinfulness in one's own habitus. This is a capacity to recognize as a part one's objectivism a capacity to misrepresent the real and to recognize as a part of one's internalism a capacity to mistake oneself for an unclouded image of the divine. But the dialectic of objectivism and internalism, alone, is what initiates the process of reparative reasoning.
   b) *Transformative Rationality*: A capacity for radical habit-change. This is a capacity, by way of Scripture's witness, to recognize and internalize rules of askesis and, thereby, to transform objectivism and internalism into tendencies for confessional and transformative rationality.
   c) *Trinitarian Rationality*: A capacity to engage intimately with the divine life and, through this engagement, to participate in God's love of and repair of the world. God alone is mediator and redeemer, and no representation or agent substitutes for God in this work.

reading, 'receiving his word' is not a matter of conation alone, but of logos received through a certain discipline of semeiotic as well as of devotional reading (Markus 1972).[17]

Like all pragmatists in the Cartesian tradition, Augustine's reparative reasoning arises first as a means of repairing his own inner dialectic. In the movement of his writings, from *De doct.* to *De conf.* to *De trin.*, one can therefore trace the gradual resolution of the dialectic from *within* his reparative reasoning. And that, one might say, is the secret of the thing: the Cartesian dialectic arises only within an unacknowledged early stage of reparative reasoning. The opposing sides, for example objectivism or internalism, are divided, misplaced, and misidentified dimensions of reparative activity. No wonder, then, that for Augustine and all the Cartesian pragmatists to follow, a sign of distress (disruption or conflict) is also a sign that one's Redeemer lives: the distress has always been a dimension of repair already under way.

Conclusion

By way of conclusion, I shall articulate one as yet unspoken theme of this chapter: 'Abrahamic studies: how to respond to critics, supporters, and curious onlookers.' Collected together my responses have been:

1. For scholars dedicated to academic studies as strictly normal enquiry, 'Abrahamic studies' names a curriculum that collects together individual studies of Jewish, Christian, and Muslim traditions of belief, practice, and social history. Such scholarship also gives space to comparative studies that refrain from imposing any overarching interpretative scheme that would occlude the distinctiveness of each individual study. This approach to Abrahamic studies contributes at once to current academic practices of Islamic, Christian, and Jewish studies *and* all of the additional approaches mentioned below.
2. For scholars concerned to contribute to reparative enquiry, Abrahamic studies names an academic response to perceived conditions of radical disruption and conflict among the Abrahamic traditions today and between such traditions and the secular West. The contemporary academy offers few models for conducting this kind of enquiry, while quantum science reflects a more distant analogue. Charles Peirce's pragmatic semeiotic offers a model closer to the methods and subject matters of Muslim, Christian, and Jewish studies. But the best resources for this kind of study rest within the Abrahamic scriptural traditions themselves. Tapping those resources would enable scholars of Abrahamic studies to

[17] On this reading, Stoic logic offered Augustine the most mature expression of Hellenic logical enquiry; *De. doct.* shows Augustine at work transforming Stoic logic into the triadic semiotic that, alone, can diagram the mediatory movement of intra-scriptural rationality; and *De trin.* displays Augustine's semeiotic in its most mature expression.

contribute models of reparative reasoning that may be of use in all areas of enquiry in the Academy.

3. For scholars drawn to the study of relations among Abrahamic communities and traditions, Abrahamic studies names enquiry that addresses epistemic and behavioural spaces in-between and to varying degrees outside of finite and ordered systems of language use. Such scholars should recognize that the contemporary academy offers limited models for this kind of study. They should be wary of foundationalist models that purport to provide conceptually clear guidelines for examining extra-linguistic patterns of behaviour and belief. Their best strategy may be to begin with models of enquiry designed for contexts of conflict change (outlined in response #2) and adjust these models as needed to the specific contexts of their inter-Abrahamic studies.
4. Critics of Abrahamic studies may have one cautionary lesson to offer: that there is no natural class of 'Abrahamic religions' or 'Abrahamic Scriptures' and that scholars of Abrahamic studies should therefore be wary of reifying such entities. Beyond that lesson, critics should themselves be wary of overgeneralizing the domain of appropriately objectivist studies of Muslim, Christian, Jewish scriptural traditions. Critics should therefore be wary of ignoring the lessons of quantum science, pragmatic semeiotic, and the reparative enquiries that are nurtured by the scriptural traditions themselves: that models of strictly normal enquiry do not succeed when applied to the study of language systems in times of radical conflict, disruption, and change. Programmes in Abrahamic studies should provide environments in which both objectivist/subjectivist and reparative enquiries are nurtured and refined for use in their appropriate contexts.

References

Adams, N. 2006. 'Making Deep Reasonings Public'. *Modern Theology* 22 (3): 385–401.

Adams, N. 2008. 'Reparative Reasoning'. *Modern Theology* 24 (3): 447–57.

Ahmed, R. 2012. *Narratives of Islamic Legal Theory*. London: Oxford University Press.

Augustine. 1958. *On Christian Doctrine*. Upper Saddle River, NJ: Prentice Hall.

Augustine. 1998. *Confessions*. Oxford: Oxford University Press.

Augustine. 2012. *On the Trinity*. New York: New City Press.

Fishbane, M. 1985. *Biblical Interpretation in Ancient Israel*. Oxford: Oxford University Press.

Ford, D. 2006. 'An Interfaith Wisdom: Scriptural Reasoning between Jews, Christians and Muslims'. *The Promise of Scriptural Reasoning*. Oxford: Blackwell, 1–22.

Ford, D. 2007. *Christian Wisdom: Desiring God and Learning in Love*. Cambridge: Cambridge University Press.

Ford, D. 2009. 'Theology and Religious Studies for a Multifaith and Secular Society'. In D. Bird and S. Smith, eds, *Theology and Religious Studies in Higher Education: Global Perspectives*. London: Continuum, 231–43.

Halivni, D. 1968–. *Mekorot Umasorot* ('Sources and Traditions'). 9 vols. Jerusalem and Tel Aviv: Assorted publishers.

Halivni, D. 1991. *Peshat and Derash: Plain and Applied Meaning in Rabbinic Exegesis.* Oxford: Oxford University Press.

Halivni, D. 1998. *The Book and the Sword: A Life of Learning in the Shadow of Destruction.* New York: Farrar, Straus & Giroux.

Halivni, D. 2007. *Breaking the Tablets: Jewish Theology after the Shoah*, ed. P. Ochs. Boulder: Rowman & Littlefield Publishers.

Heisenberg, W. 1958. *Physics and Philosophy: The Revolution in Modern Science.* New York: Harper & Row.

Heisenberg, W. 1979. *Philosophical Problems of Quantum Physics.* 2nd edn. Woodbridge, CT: Ox Bow Press.

Kuhn, T. 1962/1996. *The Structure of Scientific Revolutions.* 3rd edn. Chicago: University of Chicago Press.

Lindbeck, G. 1984. *The Nature of Doctrine: Religion and Theology in a Postliberal Age.* Louisville, KY: Westminster John Knox.

Lipton, P. 1991/2004. *Inference to the Best Explanation.* 2nd edn. London: Routledge.

Markus, R. 1972. 'St. Augustine on Signs'. In R. A. Markus, *Augustine.* Garden City, NY: Anchor Books, 61–91.

Ochs, P. 2002. *Textual Reasonings: Jewish Philosophy and Text Study at the End of the 20th Century.* Grand Rapids, MI: William Eerdmanns.

Ochs, P. 2009. 'Reparative Reasoning: From Peirce's Pragmatism to Augustine's Scriptural Semiotic'. *Modern Theology* 25 (2): 187–215.

Peirce, C. 1868. 'Grounds of Validity of the Laws of Logic'. *Journal of Speculative Philosophy* 2: 193–208.

Peirce, C. 1878. 'How to Make our Ideas Clear'. *Popular Science Monthly* 12: 286–302.

Peirce, C. 1905. 'What Pragmatism Is'. *The Monist* 15: 161–81.

Sheriff, J. 1989. *The Fate of Meaning: Charles Peirce, Structuralism, and Literature.* Princeton: Princeton University Press.

Wittgenstein, L. 1921/2001. *Tractatus logico-philosophicus.* London: Routledge Classics.

CHAPTER 31

CHRISTIAN PERSPECTIVES

Settings, Theology, Practices, and Challenges

DAVID F. FORD

THE *Oxford Handbook of the Abrahamic Religions* is a complex multi-disciplinary composition engaging its subject from many angles. In the light of the *Handbook*, this Epilogue attempts to look to the future by asking: in which institutional settings, along which lines of theological and other thinking and imagining, through which practices, and in which practical directions specifically Christian perspectives on the Abrahamic religions might best be developed in the twenty-first century. It no more assumes a single agreed Christian perspective to be possible than the *Handbook* assumes a single disciplinary perspective. Rather, this Epilogue has four concerns.

The first is to enquire into the 'where' of the institutional settings within which Christian perspectives on the Abrahamic religions can be best worked out. After considering the main settings represented in the *Handbook*, the conclusion will be that, whilst a diversity of settings is healthy and desirable, as regards developing Christian perspectives on the Abrahamic faiths, the balance of advantage lies with those places where Christian and other theologies can be studied and developed critically and constructively alongside, and in dialogue with, a full range of other academic disciplines that engage with the religions. These 'theology and religious studies' or 'religion and theology' academic settings are, it is argued, the optimal ones, not only for furthering academic Christian thought about Christianity and other traditions, but also for others (whether religious or not) who are engaged in analogous enterprises. Such settings, usually located within universities, at their best enable the types of disciplined study, conversation, critique, constructive thinking, and debate among diverse participants that are needed by pluralist twenty-first-century societies which are complexly and simultaneously both multi-religious and 'multi-secular'.

The second concern is for well-educated, critical, and constructive academic Christian thought, in theology and other disciplines. If Christian thought is to engage well with its own and other traditions, what is required of it? This leads to identifying four elements at the heart of contemporary Christian theology: retrieval of the past (scriptures, traditions, history of many types); engagement with God, church, and world; rigorous, thoughtful, and imaginative thinking in many fields; and communication in many genres, modes, and media. With regard to the Abrahamic traditions, each of these needs to be pursued in dialogue with Judaism and Islam, and especially with those Jews and Muslims who are concerned academically with analogous elements in their own traditions.

The third concern is for the practices that can help such Abrahamic dialogue be as fruitful as possible. Thorough scholarship in many fields, as exemplified in this *Handbook*, is assumed; so too are other staples of wise dialogical practice, such as diverse conversations, mutual hospitality, cooperation in many activities and spheres of society, and joint projects for the good of humanity. The main focus here is on Scriptural Reasoning, a practice that has historical analogies but has largely developed in the late twentieth and early twenty-first centuries, originating in 'theology and religious studies' academic settings, and spreading into other educational and non-academic contexts. It is seen as a paradigm case of engagement among the Abrahamic traditions that is not dependent on a particular construal of 'Abrahamic' (it could accommodate the full range of suggestions in this *Handbook*) and can embrace both religious and academic diversity.

The fourth concern is for the wider public sphere beyond both the academy and the religious traditions. In each of the Abrahamic religions the God who has created and sustains all things and all people, and who has love and compassion for all, is worshipped. Within this horizon, what might be the main challenges of the twenty-first century? Five are identified as the most urgent: increasing religious literacy; the wise formation of those who carry leadership and other major responsibilities in each tradition; justice and compassion for those who are poor, oppressed, sick, elderly, disabled, or otherwise vulnerable; peace and reconciliation amidst many conflicts and divisions; and care for our planet—its ecosystems, its climate, air, soil, and water, its many forms of life, culture, beauty, and civilization.

Settings

The contributors to this *Handbook* are unevenly divided among the types of academic institutional setting in which religions are studied today.

The majority are based in 'study of religion' or 'religious studies' settings in colleges and universities in Europe, North America, or Israel. These are places where such modern academic disciplines as history (intellectual, cultural, political, scientific, economic, legal, and more), archaeology, the natural, human, and social sciences, phenomenology of religion, philology, textual, literary, and aesthetic studies, medicine, law, politics, ethics, hermeneutics, and philosophy are brought to bear on the religions of the world.

A small minority of the *Handbook*'s contributors work in places where the central focus is on one religion in its thought and practice—in Christian terms this is often called a theological college, seminary, Bible college, or theology department.

A larger minority are based in institutions where there are 'theology and religious studies' or 'religion and theology' settings (all three of the Epilogues, for example, are written from such). Here, study of the theologies and practices of one or more traditions can be pursued, critically and constructively as well as historically, together with the study of religions through a range of other disciplines.

There are many variations on these three basic types, and in each country different formative influences, pressures, and conflicts have led to the current institutional arrangements. This is not the place for detailed description or analysis, but I want to make a constructive proposal for the future of the field along broad lines that can be analogously applied to many settings.

The proposal, whose rationale and main elements have been described in greater detail elsewhere,[1] takes for granted the value of the three types, sees limitations in each, and advocates a paradigm that is nearer to the third as the one that, with special regard for the Abrahamic religions, can best serve universities, societies, and religious traditions in the twenty-first century. This is not to advocate that all settings should conform to this, but rather that in their development all should, in ways outlined below, pay attention to this inclusive paradigm.

The study of religion, or the religious studies approach (hereafter called religious studies), has the obvious strengths of each of its disciplines, and the added attractiveness of the possibility of cross-disciplinarity. Its limitations are largely self-imposed, due to the properly limited aims of each discipline. The main exclusion is of theology in the sense of an academic discipline through which a particular tradition seeks to articulate, debate, and develop further its wisdom, meaning, truth, norms, and practice.

There is no unanimity among those in religious studies about how to regard their relationship to theology in this sense. They range from a very negative view, seeing their field as having its origins in liberation from the domination by theology of the study of religions in universities, and regarding theology as having very dubious academic credentials, to a very positive view (the one taken by this Epilogue) of theology as a complementary discipline with which there can be fruitful interaction. The latter position sees it as appropriate for the field of religion to be somewhat analogous to economics, which has its historical, analytical, theoretical, and statistical side but also has applied and normative sides (for example, in applied economics and in business schools), in which there can be various constructive and contentious proposals about how to understand and run economies and businesses, about what policies governments should pursue, and about what ethics and values are to be

[1] Ford 2013b; Ford 2011; Ford 2010; Ford 2007b; Ford, Quash, and Soskice 2005. These also include relevant bibliography.

preferred. The living religions likewise can benefit from academically mediated normative discourse alongside other academic studies.

If the strengths of academic theology are as suggested in the previous paragraph—studying, debating, and developing the wisdom, meaning, truth, norms, and practices of a particular tradition—its possible limitations are most evident where it is pursued in settings where it is out of touch with other disciplines and where the theology of one tradition is not in conversation with theologies of other traditions. If Christian theology is about God and all reality in relation to God, the horizon within which Christian theological thinking should be conducted embraces all fields of knowledge, understanding, and practice. This is greatly facilitated if those fields are represented in the same institution. But worldwide, by far the majority of institutions where Christian theology is pursued have a solely Christian allegiance (the same is true of the theology or religious thought of other religious traditions too). This is appropriate: for example, the theological higher educational, scholarly, and research needs of a billion or so Roman Catholics are largely met within Catholic colleges, seminaries, and universities; likewise those who teach and lead the hundreds of millions of Evangelical and Pentecostal Christians mostly receive their theological education and develop their academic thinking in Bible colleges, seminaries, and (increasingly) universities that owe allegiance to their own traditions. Such institutions are essential to the educational needs of their traditions, and are always likely to make up the great majority of places where their theology, doctrine, and ethics are studied, debated, and worked out further. But their limitations, or challenges, with regard both to the broad horizon of theological thought and to engagement with the Abrahamic religions, are evident. Most are not universities with a full range of academic disciplines with which theological thought can be in dialogue; and even when this is the case in tradition-specific universities (which are multiplying in some parts of the world) these rarely have full collegiality with the theological thinkers of other religious traditions.

There are various ways of addressing these challenges. The options (all of which are becoming more common) include: seminaries developing associations with universities, and tradition-specific elements complemented by university courses in a range of academic religious studies disciplines and by courses in the theologies of other traditions; or the seminaries of different traditions (both within and beyond Christianity) linking up with one another through shared courses, staff or student exchanges and collaborations; or teachers from other faith traditions being added to the staff of a seminary or tradition-specific university.

Such arrangements are always likely to be the most common ways for Christian institutions to create spaces in which their staff and students engage with Judaism and Islam alongside and in dialogue with Christianity. But there are other settings in which Christian engagement with and perspectives on the Abrahamic religions can be worked out: those where theologies of different traditions and the disciplines of religious studies are combined in a university context. These university 'theology and religious studies' or 'religion and theology' settings too have been multiplying in recent decades. Sometimes they result from a tradition-specific university becoming more pluralist within itself (e.g. the University of Notre Dame), sometimes from a non-religious foundation developing its tradition-specific theological staffing and curriculum alongside religious studies (e.g. the University of Virginia), and often from a long period of gradual evolution. In the United Kingdom the study of theology and religion has gradually become the norm. The national organization representing the study and teaching of theology and religious studies in higher education has since 2013 been called 'Theology and Religious Studies UK' (TRS UK). It concerns itself with promoting and supporting (as it states in the TRS UK constitution): 'all academic disciplines concerned with the significance and meaning of religion and religions, incorporating fields of study such as theology, divinity and religious studies, in addition to sub-fields applying different theories and methods to the study of religions, such as the sociology or psychology of religion.'

The UK universities represented by two of the Epilogues in this *Handbook* exemplify the trend. In the University of Oxford a lengthy process that developed its department from Christian theology into theology and religious studies (including a professorship in Abrahamic Religions) culminated in a change of name to the 'Faculty of Theology and Religion' in 2012; complementing this, various other faculties and institutes also contribute to the field. The University of Cambridge's Faculty of Divinity changed the names of its degree courses from 'theology' to 'theology and religious studies' in 1979, and since then has added more posts and courses in other faiths and their theologies (including a professorship in Abrahamic Faiths) alongside Christian theology.[2] Some other western universities, such as Aberdeen, Chicago, Duke, Durham, Edinburgh, Exeter, the Free University of Amsterdam, Harvard, Heidelberg, Kings College London, Leuven, Lund, McGill, Toronto, Tübingen, and Yale, have worked out their own ways of seeking to do justice both to the multi-disciplinary study of the religions and tradition-engaged, academically mediated theological thinking. Others have stayed committed to either religious studies or theology, and in some countries, such as France, universities are not permitted by the state to include theology.

Where the main direction of development in the UK has been towards departments of theology and religious studies, the difficulty from a Christian standpoint (matched by analogous difficulties experienced by those of other traditions) has often been that of maintaining in-depth distinctively Christian theological thinking, teaching, and research in the new context. In response to this, current developments in some German universities stand out as an alternative to those in most other countries. During the nineteenth and twentieth centuries Germany had what was probably the world's

[2] It is worth noting that, in most cases in the UK where there has been a shift in nomenclature it has been one of bringing 'religion' into a 'theology' department rather than the other way around. That is to say, the UK story is often one—as described in the case of Cambridge in Ford 2007a: 345–7—of increasing breadth and diversity of engagement within a Faculty or Department, growing from, rather than leaving behind, a historic concern with Christian theology. So, bringing in 'religious studies' is not about creating a new 'neutral' space, but 'embodying a negotiated and still developing settlement' (Ford 2007a: 347), bound up with the complex histories of all the disciplines involved, and responsive to the likewise complex and continually negotiated settlements of wider social life in the contemporary era.

leading tradition of academic, university-based Protestant and Catholic theology. It is now complementing that strongly Christian tradition with Islamic theology through setting up posts and departments in selected universities, such as Tübingen. These allow for tradition-specific, academically mediated Islamic thought to be accommodated alongside Christian theology. It has been a controversial innovation that is still in the experimental phase, with much ongoing debate about it.

That German innovation and the growth of theology and religious studies in other countries can be seen as ways in which higher education has tried to respond to increasing religious pluralism. Without any implication that either religion-specific theology or non-theological religious studies are unacceptable, there has been a growing recognition that in a pluralist society there is also a need for spaces where those of all faiths and none can come together to learn, teach, research, discuss, and debate questions relating to the religions. Moreover, attempts to limit the pursuit of such questions—for example, ruling out the exploration of controversial doctrinal, ethical, and political issues by students or academics seeking to offer critical or constructive responses to them in tradition-related ways—may be seen as arbitrary or in the service of a particular religious or secular ideology. There are vigorous disputes around these matters, but in principle they are no different from analogous ongoing debates in other fields where the inseparability of normative discourse from academic enquiry is recognized.

If, as I propose, the 'ideal type' of academically mediated engagement with the religions in the universities of pluralist societies is that of theology and religious studies, this would suggest certain guidelines for those with institutional responsibility to bear in mind as they work out policies and take decisions. The intention of the guidelines is to offer maxims that might enable each type of setting (theology, religious studies, theology and religious studies) to be more open to the others and to interaction for the good of each tradition and the wider society.[3]

- *Develop rich descriptions of the field, both historical and contemporary, using the field's academic disciplines to do so, and seeking to identify the strengths and limitations of each type.*
- *Develop rationales for the field, not just in general terms, but also in diverse Jewish, Christian, Muslim, Hindu, Buddhist, secular, and other terms. Then bring the rationales into dialogue with each other and build departments and institutions that can be justified and nourished by more than one tradition.*
- *Whatever the nature of the settlement in one's own setting, make the case for it being open in both directions, both towards theology and towards religious studies, and being supportive of an overall diverse 'ecology' of the field.*

[3] These are adapted from ch. 8, 'New Theology and Religious Studies: Shaping, Teaching and Funding a Field' in Ford 2011, where the points are further developed.

- *Hold together trans-generational responsibilities towards universities, religious communities, and societies, and build forms of collegiality around each responsibility.*
- *Seek the good of the whole field of theology and religious studies, and put intellectual and political energy into debates about its future in order to help it become 'mutual ground' (rather than 'neutral ground') for those of many religions and none.*
- *Have a global vision for the field, commensurate with the global presence of the religions, and embody this not only in the curriculum but also, whenever possible, in the teaching staff and student body, in institutional alliances and in responsibilities undertaken.*

From a Christian perspective, these allow both for distinctively Christian settings and for places where there can be collegiality and theological engagement with those of other faiths and none. With regard to the Abrahamic religions, the built-in specificity allows for both bilateral and trilateral engagements and studies, such as the practice of Scriptural Reasoning, which will be discussed further below.

One further extremely important dimension of academically mediated theology and religion has already been introduced in the assumption that the horizon of Christian thought is as broad and all-embracing as God and all reality in relation to God, and therefore has implications for all academic fields. This means that, besides a 'focused' concentration on the religions in specialist departments of theology, religious studies, or theology and religious studies, there is also required a 'distributed' engagement of Christian thought across other fields. Christian thought is far more than Christian theology. Most Christian thought in universities is not done in departments of theology, religious studies, or theology and religious studies, but by Christians in the other departments. As regards the Abrahamic religions, here too it is likely that there is much to be learnt through study, enquiry, conversation, and debate with Jews and Muslims who are facing analogous issues about how, for example, their faith and practice relate to history, philosophy, media studies, education, the social, human or natural sciences, music, or medicine.

It matters a great deal whether the institutional ethos of a university is open to such learning and debate. In the twentieth century in particular the ethos of many universities was 'default secularist', in the sense that a non-religious or anti-religious worldview was taken for granted. It was often hard for university-educated secular scholars and thinkers to imagine that those committed within religious traditions could be as intelligently rational, scientific, or scholarly as themselves. The new public prominence of the religions since the end of the twentieth century has led both to sharpened polemics against religion in many regions (since the prominence has often come about through religious involvement in conflict and violence) and also to a wider recognition that the world today is neither simply 'secular', nor developing in one direction from being 'religious' to 'secular', but that it is complexly and simultaneously both multi-religious and 'multi-secular', and that there are many forms of twenty-first-century modernity, some more secular and some more religious, with many hybrids. Within universities, one challenge to Jews, Christians, and Muslims is to think through and articulate academically mediated forms of their faith and practice. That leads to the second concern.

THEOLOGY

The Christian scriptures encourage readers to seek wisdom and truth, to love God with all their heart, soul, mind, and strength, to meditate on God's word and God's creation, to be able to give an account of their faith, to mature in their understanding, and to do much else that involves thought and imagination. Developing Christian perspectives on their own and with the other Abrahamic religions therefore calls for wise and imaginative thinking by Christians in all spheres of life. I am mainly focusing on the sphere of academic life as represented in universities.

In societies so pervasively shaped by information, knowledge, and learning universities have become crucial to the future of our world: they educate most of those in positions of major responsibility in contemporary societies; they generate, directly or indirectly, much of the scientific and technological knowledge and know-how on which societies depend; they are the home of disciplines that enable society to understand itself better; and they are one of the main channels for the transmission of the sciences, arts, and humanities. In this context the importance of religion mediated academically through theology and religious studies is considerable, and it has been reflected in a global increase in religiously affiliated academic institutions and in the burgeoning academic engagement with the religions through many disciplines.

How might academically mediated Christian perspectives on Christianity, Judaism, and Islam best be generated in the twenty-first century? This is first of all a question about Christian theology proper, in the sense of explicitly Christian interpretation of scriptures, traditions, history, and experience, and Christian thinking about God, creation, sin, providence, Jesus Christ, the Holy Spirit, the church, ethics, politics, the future, and related themes. It is also a question about the thinking Christians do, informed consciously or not by such theological thinking, relating to the whole range of disciplines and practices embraced in modern universities.

A first point to make is that the past century has been exceptionally generative of Christian theologies and other Christian thought. My own main education in this has been through editing three editions of a basic textbook on Christian theology since 1918, through which I have come to the conclusion that it has in some ways been a uniquely fruitful period in the history of Christian thought (Ford and Muers 2005). There has been an impressive array of reappropriations of past theologies; there has been fresh thinking and theological renewal within the major Christian traditions, such as Roman Catholicism, Orthodoxy, Anglicanism, diverse strands of Protestantism, and

Pentecostalism; many new voices have contributed to theology to an unprecedented extent, including those of women, and those of diverse regions, races, sexual orientations, cultures, and classes; theology has been related to the full range of academic disciplines, literature, the arts, theatre, and film, and there have been vigorous debates about the challenges of western modernity.

A second point is that that abundance of theological discourses and perspectives has been the context in which Judaism and Islam have also been thought about by Christians. To ask about Christian perspectives on them is to open up many of the deepest and most difficult questions of theology and practice: the character of divine revelation, God as Trinity, the authority and interpretation of scriptures, incarnation, law, justice, love and compassion, sin and evil, supersessionism, usury, violence, and many more. Each question calls for rereading scriptures and traditions, engagement with God, church, and world, discernment of contemporary contexts and developments, rigorous and imaginative thinking, and appropriate articulation and dissemination in many genres, modes, and media (Ford 2011). But in addition, if justice is to be done to Judaism and Islam as actually understood and practised today, each of those activities needs to be performed in dialogue, preferably long term, with Jews and Muslims. That is perhaps the most difficult task of all, and one way of attempting it, Scriptural Reasoning, will be the main topic of the next section on practices.

A third point is that Judaism and Islam unsettle even the category of 'theology' as understood in Christianity. It could be argued that neither Judaism nor Islam has anything that is straightforwardly equivalent to Christian theology. Any Christian perspective on them will therefore find itself thinking in strange categories, entering into very different intellectual and imaginative worlds, and tentatively exploring how one might even know whether one agrees or disagrees on a topic. Like the previous point, this too leads to recognizing that long-term conversation accompanied by study is vital.

Overall, attempts to understand and assess Judaism and Islam from Christian perspectives commonly lead to the realization that, while texts and other carriers of meaning such as art, architecture, and liturgies are important, the most significant carriers of meaning are Jews and Muslims themselves, and the depth and complexity of religious traditions are such that worthwhile conversation with them takes a great deal of time: again, long-term practices are required.

Practices

Which practices might best help generate Christian perspectives that could do justice to the three Abrahamic faiths? I take for granted the full range of scholarly work that is seen in this *Handbook*, together with all the academic practices that involves. I also assume specifically Christian theological work in many settings, together with all that requires in terms of scholarship, prayer and worship, life in church and world, critical and constructive thought, imagination, discussion and debate, and creative communication.

Yet adequate Christian perspectives on the Abrahamic faiths today cannot simply be taken over from the chapters of this *Handbook* or from other scholarly exercises, essential though these are. Nor can Christian thinkers adequately work out just among themselves their understanding of Judaism and Islam. Scholarly practices and in-house theological enquiry and debate need to go together with engagement among Jews, Christians, and Muslims. One reason why settings where religious studies and theology come together are so important for our pluralist world is that they facilitate the working out of Jewish, Christian, and Muslim perspectives in dialogue with each other. The further question is: which practices can enable this dialogue to be more fruitful?

Interreligious dialogical practices are flourishing in the early twenty-first century. Mutual hospitality is perhaps the most fundamental of all, and is open to endless variation in a multitude of contexts, from next-door neighbours to representatives of national or international bodies. It is often at the heart of the best conversations across religious differences, and these too are endlessly diverse, occurring in all spheres of society. A great number of centres, organizations, and networks now bring people of different faiths together, and social and other media have added to the range of interactions. The 'face to face' of conversation is often most fruitful when accompanied by the 'side by side' of collaboration in practical projects, on which more will be said under 'Tasks' below.

My focus here will be on one practice, that of Scriptural Reasoning (Ford and Clemson 2013; Higton and Muers 2012; Ford and Pecknold 2006). Its roots were in Textual Reasoning (Ochs and Levene 2002), a practice that began in the early 1990s through a gathering of North American Jewish text scholars and philosophers who met as a fringe group at the American Academy of Religion. They studied and argued around Talmud and texts by Jewish philosophers such as Hermann Cohen, Emmanuel Levinas, and Franz Rosenzweig. They brought together contemporary issues with a variety of forms of rabbinic Judaism, using textual exegesis, hermeneutics, phenomenology, ethics, and theology.

A basic concern of Textual Reasoning was how to be Jewish in the aftermath of the Shoah and within the powerful structures of modernity. In this, several key concerns came together.

The first concern of the group was to reread their classic texts, especially Tanakh and Talmud, in the aftermath of the trauma. Just as, during and after the exile in Babylon and the destruction of the First Temple, there was large-scale editing, reworking, and prophetic reinterpretation of the tradition, and after the fall of the Second Temple in 70 CE rabbinic Judaism was developed, so after the Shoah the Textual Reasoners discerned a similar imperative to reread, argue, rethink, and reimagine.

The second concern was to rethink western modernity. The Shoah was conceived and carried out by a western nation that prided itself on its modern science, technology, industry, business, education and research universities, culture, bureaucracy, philosophy, and theology. It might in its aftermath be tempting simply to reject modernity and try to be pre-modern or anti-modern. Many forms of religion attempt this. For Textual Reasoning the challenge was to combine a critical and constructive approach to modernity with rabbinic wisdom.

The third concern of Textual Reasoning was to engage with others who were following analogous paths in different religious traditions, especially Judaism's younger siblings, Christianity and Islam. It made sense that much could be learned and shared with others who were trying to reread their own scriptures and pre-modern classics while also coping with the complexities and challenges of modernity.

There was also a fourth concern related especially to the academic setting of North America. They were reacting against what they saw as the atomization of the different disciplines of Jewish studies, the unwarranted competition among these disciplines, and the isolation of many Jewish academics within the Jewish religious communities, a world that they perceived to have in many ways turned inward and away from modernity and its challenges. They wished to complement a view of Jewish philosophy as a subset of Jewish intellectual history with a view of it as engaged both with Judaism's evolving commentarial tradition and with the immediate conditions of Jewish life in our epoch (including intellectual life across all disciplines, such as mathematics, logic, and the sciences). In his Epilogue to this *Handbook*, Peter Ochs gives a fuller account of Textual Reasoning as it relates both to Jewish Studies and to studies of the Abrahamic religions.

Scriptural Reasoning began when some Christian academics from the UK and the USA joined with members of Textual Reasoning, and soon after with Muslim academics. Scriptural Reasoning's central practice is studying and discussing together texts from Tanakh, Bible, and Quran in small groups. It spread first in academic settings in North America and the UK, and then to other parts of the world. It has also spread beyond the academy to local congregations in synagogues, churches, and mosques, to civic settings, to schools, prisons, hospitals, reconciliation and peacemaking initiatives, and religious leadership programmes. There have also been variations, for example: studying scriptural texts alongside texts from commentary traditions; studying Abrahamic scriptures alongside texts from Asian religious traditions (especially in Minzu University's Institute for Comparative Scripture and Interreligious Dialogue in Beijing); and other sessions using logic, music, poetry, and liturgy.

From a Christian perspective it is striking that the leading concerns of Textual Reasoning (as noted above and in Ochs's Epilogue) have analogies in contemporary Christian traditions. For example, one of the twentieth century's major religious events, the Second Vatican Council of the Roman Catholic church, has at its core three practices: *ressourcement* (going back to the deepest sources of the tradition); *aggiornamento* (engaging with the modern world and bringing the church up to date, including taking into account the full range of academic disciplines); and *conversazione* (conversation, not only within the Catholic church but across its boundaries with other churches, other religions, and secular people and worldviews) (Ford 2013a).

This, indeed, might be seen as a Christian form of the common sense of many non-extremist religious groups in our world: they want to be true to their roots and core identity, hence the renewed engagement with scriptures and traditions; they do not want simply to assimilate to modernity or simply to reject it, so must constantly discern what to accept, what to oppose, and what to work on in order to transform it for the better; and they recognize that in a plural, interconnected world it makes sense to be in communication and even collaboration with people of other traditions, especially those with shared roots.

A crucial further element in both Textual Reasoning and Scriptural Reasoning is their mode of discussion inspired by the rabbinic practice of *havruta* (or *chevrutah*). Its features include being a learner and a teacher simultaneously, reading the text aloud, constantly revisiting it to test ideas, listening attentively to fellow readers, being willing to probe, challenge, and argue for and against interpretations, not needing to come to a consensus, taking risks in offering interpretations, developing shared norms for how to conduct sessions, and becoming more self-aware about one's own presuppositions (Holzer and Kent 2013: 219–20).

Peter Ochs, who was more responsible for the development of Textual Reasoning and Scriptural Reasoning than anyone else, describes as follows the basic practice of formational Scriptural Reasoning:

> Formational Scriptural Reasoning refers to the simplest practice of Scriptural Reasoning: symbolized by study around a small table, with three or more chairs, one small selection from each of the three Abrahamic scriptural canons, and three or more persons of any age eager to enter into a conversational fellowship with one another and, as it were, with these three text selections. This practice is the basis for all training in Scriptural Reasoning and it is also what we might call the 'mode of welcome' that initiates all Scriptural Reasoning-related encounters. (Ochs 2013: 207)

He goes on to describe some of the features of this practice, giving special emphasis to three.

First, studying together texts that participants feel most deeply about he sees as a 'hearth-to-hearth' engagement, each sharing from the place of warmth at the heart of their tradition, and in this way generating a mutual appreciation and feeling that often leads into friendship. A sense of collegiality without consensus on some very important matters is a characteristic of Scriptural Reasoning. 'Hearth-to-hearth' relationships enable participants not only to find areas of agreement but also to improve the quality of their long-term disagreements, which is essential to realistic Abrahamic interaction.

Second, this study can '*open unexpected levels of textual and hermeneutical discovery*' (Ochs 2013). There have in fact been very few settings in the history of Judaism, Christianity, and Islam where members of the three traditions have been able to meet face to face (especially without one or other being in a position of dominance) and study texts from their scriptures or commentary traditions. So a session of Scriptural Reasoning may well be the first occasion in history on which the particular texts on the table have been explored in this way. It is not surprising, therefore, that fresh insights can be generated, especially when participants bring together diverse religious formations, linguistic skills, reading habits, contemporary contexts, imaginative resources, practical interests, and academic trainings.

Ochs emphasizes that there is no need to make any normative claim for the readings that result—to make such a claim would require going through the usual processes that each tradition has for assessing new interpretations. It is enough that, as in personal reading of these rich texts, deeper engagement with the texts can happen, with fresh illumination. Each of the three traditions recognizes the desirability of exploring interpretations that may never become normative parts of the tradition but may yet have value in a specific context or engagement. In Jewish interpretation, for example, midrash can mean an interpretation that does not claim to be the plain sense of the text in its original context but attempts to interpret it in relation to other texts, different circumstances, or new issues. Such improvisation on texts is inevitable if they are ongoing parts of a living tradition that is continually facing the questions that are raised by new encounters, events, cultures, medical and other scientific discoveries, and so on. Giving sermons, teaching the next generation, and working out in changed circumstances what to reject, what to accept, and how to transform what is only partly acceptable: these are among the main settings for improvisation in each of the traditions and their subdivisions. Of course, how these are gone about varies enormously, but each can be enriched by learning from the others, and often key insights can be sparked by engaging with those who are very different, and with whom one continues to disagree.

The third feature of Scriptural Reasoning mentioned by Ochs is its reparative potential (see also his Epilogue in this volume). Studying together can help address conflicts, divisions, and disagreements. As Steven Kepnes, another founder of both Textual Reasoning and Scriptural Reasoning, argues in his influential 'A Handbook for Scriptural Reasoning', there is a 'scriptural sense that the human world is broken, in exile, off the straight path, filled with corruption, sickness, war and genocide. Scriptural Reasoning practitioners come together out of a sense of impoverishment, suffering, and conflict to seek resources for healing' (Kepnes 2006: 28). But as Jews, Christians, and Muslims they come together convinced that their own tradition is not only part of the problem (which it is) but also does have resources for healing and repair, and that these are enhanced if they share them together. This is especially relevant to the tasks to be considered in the next section.

Participants from each of the three religions, and from each of the traditions within each of the three, are free to come up with their own rationales for taking part in Scriptural Reasoning, and these do not have to agree with each other. There can be diverse and even conflicting reasons for engaging in the same practice. There does not have to be prior agreement on how the three scriptures are to be regarded, or on how to interpret them: this is a practice in which differences on such matters can be part of the conversation, with no consensus expected. Perhaps the most helpful Christian introduction to and exploration of Scriptural Reasoning have been given from two perspectives, Quaker and Anglican (Higton and Muers

2012), and a variety of Catholic understandings of it have been offered elsewhere (Ford and Clemson 2013).

Perhaps the most distinctive overall characteristic of Scriptural Reasoning is what I have described elsewhere (Ford 2013a) as its ability, at its best, to enable multiple deepening: one is enabled to go deeper into the scriptures of one's own tradition and of the traditions of the other Abrahamic religions; to go deeper into the common good of our world, including but going beyond these three religions; to go deeper into disagreements as well as agreements; and to deepen the quality of collegiality and community among those who share the first four deepenings. All this above all takes time, and the two decades of Scriptural Reasoning are, one suspects, only a taster for what might be possible as scriptures that carry with them centuries of recitation, reading, and interpretation are brought into conversation with each other.

Finally, it is no accident that the academic practice of Scriptural Reasoning has been especially associated with places where theology and religious studies go together, such as the Universities of Virginia and Cambridge. It is a practice that welcomes the whole range of religious studies disciplines, but, by its living engagement between members of three religions,[4] and by its freedom to engage with questions of truth and practice, it also crosses the usual religious studies boundaries. In doing so it enters the field of theology or critical and constructive religious thought, while also challenging that field to be open to considering theologies (or their analogues) within more than one tradition. It is a long-term practice within the field of theology and religious studies that symbolizes the *raison d'être* of the field.

Tasks

As Tariq Ramadan and Peter Ochs argue in their Epilogues, concern for the wider public sphere beyond both the academy and the religious traditions is also essential to each of the Abrahamic religions. The traditions may vary in their ways of identifying God as creator and sustainer of all things and all people, understanding how God expresses love and compassion for all, and fulfilling responsibilities towards all creation; but they agree on the need to discern such ways. Perhaps the greatest challenge facing them now is how to collaborate with each other and with those of other religions and none in order to serve the common good of humanity and the whole of creation.

What might the agenda be? I would identify five tasks as the most important, each large enough to require many initiatives, and each controversial enough to require spaces for conversation, debate, and deliberation among all concerned.

One is the need for a broad religious literacy. The problem-centred way of putting this is that in a plural world, in which the religions are directly involved in many

[4] It is not necessarily confined to members of these traditions, and participants have been from outside them, sometimes with no particular religious affiliation.

tensions, divisions, and conflicts, it is dangerous to have societies in which, with regard to the religions, there is ignorance, misunderstanding, prejudice, stereotyping, distortion, and misrepresentation of many sorts, all reinforced by a lamentable quality of public conversation about religion. The required response to the problem is multi-faceted: it involves schools, universities, media, and every major sphere of life where religion is relevant—which is every major sphere of life. There are many initiatives in this expanding field, ranging from efforts to improve the ways universities and schools relate to the religions and their members (including the quality of religious education) or raising the awareness of healthcare professionals about religious matters connected with their work, to programmes in spheres such as politics, the media, the civil service, business, the arts, and culture. These are not a luxury for pluralist societies, which need broad public understanding that includes religious literacy.

Yet religion is not just a problem. It is one of the strongest motivators of billions of people; it is a key to understanding a good deal of the past and the present; it leads into fascinating questions of meaning, truth, beauty, goodness and how to live well; and it shapes visions, ideals, acts of compassion, vocations of dedicated service, works of art, music, and architecture, and the values and beliefs that individuals, families, and whole communities live by. Religious literacy is about appreciating all that too. Not to appreciate it is to miss out on something that is not only important but also enriching and gripping. It is the combination of the richness and the problems that frequently leads beyond religious literacy into something deeper, such as the types of practice discussed in the previous section.

A second task is also educational: the formation of those who carry leadership and other major responsibilities (both specifically religious and in other areas) in each tradition. The logic of this Epilogue is that such formation should if possible include time spent together with those of other traditions in study, conversation, and activity. This should not be confined to initial formation: often the capacity and recognition of the need for engagement with those with analogous callings in other traditions only develops gradually through years of experience.

A third task centres on justice and compassion for those who are poor, oppressed, sick, elderly, disabled, refugees, or otherwise vulnerable. There may be more signs of hope in this sphere than any other, yet overall the global picture is still discouraging. A major issue is how to regard the systemic and institutional dimensions of this task: how financial, economic, political, educational, and legal systems work for or against vulnerable groups, and what the responsibilities of the religions are in such areas.

A fourth task is facing the conflicts and divisions of our world. Again, there are many signs of hope in the overlapping areas of peacemaking, peacebuilding, reconciliation, mediation, arbitration, and the resolution or transformation or stabilization of conflicts; but the overall situation is not encouraging. A large number of conflicts have a religious dimension, and this leads some to write off religion. It leads others to mobilize the resources of the religious traditions for peace, and there is a growing recognition, even among non-religious leaders and agencies, that unless this happens the prospects for peace in many conflicts are considerably lessened. There is immense scope for such mobilization, not only through the initiatives of leaders and authorities, but also through grassroots movements and through alliances of religious and non-religious networks, groups, and organizations. The other forms of Abrahamic engagement are, rightly, likely to be judged above all by their contributions to peace.

Finally, there is the increasingly urgent need to appreciate and care better for our planet. Food, eating, and drinking are perhaps the most obvious symbolic and practical focus of this, being interwoven with daily life and ritual, local and global community, fasting and feasting, justice and compassion, nature and culture, air, soil and water, science and technology, ethics and politics, conservation and sustainability (Wirzba 2011). Each of the other four tasks has long-term practical effects here in the ways human civilization relates to creation. Mobilization of the religions for ecological responsibility has hardly begun. This is a practical imperative, and also an imaginative, intellectual, and comprehensively spiritual one. The beauty and wonder of creation, its forms, marvels, intricacy, and capacity to evoke thanks, praise, and blessing are intrinsic to the Abrahamic religions, and can also be a bond between them and many other traditions, both secular and religious.

Conclusion

This Epilogue has concluded with a challenging agenda of tasks, placing the Abrahamic religions in the broadest contemporary context. It has also reflected upon the spheres of scholarship and thought that have helped to generate this *Handbook*. It has made some specific proposals about where and how Christian perspectives on the Abrahamic religions might best be developed in the twenty-first century. The optimal settings are, it is argued, where theologies (or analogous discourses) of a variety of religious traditions can be pursued in conversation with each other and also with the full range of other academic disciplines that contribute to the study of religions. In such settings, Christian theologies dealing with the Abrahamic religions can be worked out through retrieval of scriptures, traditions, and histories, engagement with God, church, and world, rigorous and imaginative thinking, and many modes of expression, all informed both by dialogue with Jews, Muslims, and others and also by contributions from relevant academic disciplines. Among the many practices that can contribute to such dialogue, special attention has been paid to Scriptural Reasoning, in which study and discussion of the scriptures and interpretative traditions of the three religions takes place. The embracing goal is one that all three Abrahamic religions, together with most other religions and philosophies, desire: a habitable wisdom for our time.

REFERENCES

Ford, D. F. 2007a. *Christian Wisdom: Desiring God and Learning in Love.* Cambridge: Cambridge University Press.

Ford, D. F. 2007b. *Shaping Theology: Engagements in a Religious and Secular World.* Oxford: Blackwell.

Ford, D. F. 2010. 'Theology'. In J. R. Hinnells, ed., *The Routledge Companion to the Study of Religion.* 2nd edn. Abingdon: Routledge, 93–110.

Ford, D. F. 2011. *The Future of Christian Theology.* Malden, MA: Wiley-Blackwell.

Ford, D. F. 2013a. 'Scriptural Reasoning and the Legacy of Vatican II: Their Mutual Engagement and Significance'. In Ford and Clemson 2013: 93–119.

Ford, D. F. 2013b. *Theology: A Very Short Introduction.* 2nd edn. Oxford: Oxford University Press.

Ford, D. F. and Clemson, F., eds. 2013. *Interreligious Reading after Vatican II: Scriptural Reasoning, Comparative Theology and Receptive Ecumenism.* Malden, MA: Wiley-Blackwell.

Ford, D. F. with Muers, R. 2005. *The Modern Theologians: An Introduction to Christian Theology since 1918.* 3rd edn. Malden, MA: Blackwell.

Ford, D. F. and Pecknold, C. C., eds. 2006. *The Promise of Scriptural Reasoning.* Malden, MA: Blackwell.

Ford, D. F., Quash, B., and Soskice, J. M., eds. 2005. *Fields of Faith: Theology and Religious Studies for the Twenty-first Century.* Cambridge: Cambridge University Press.

Higton, M. and Muers, R. 2012. *The Text in Play: Experiments in Reading Scripture.* Eugene, OR: Cascade.

Holzer, E. and Kent, O. 2013. *A Philosophy of Havruta: Understanding and Teaching the Art of Text Study in Pairs.* Boston: Academic Studies Press.

Kepnes, S. 2006. 'A Handbook for Scriptural Reasoning'. In Ford and Pecknold 2006: 23–39.

Ochs, P. 2013. 'Re-socializing Scholars of Religious, Theological, and Theo-Philosophical Inquiry'. In Ford and Clemson 2013: 201–19.

Ochs, P. and Levene, N., eds. 2002. *Textual Reasonings: Jewish Philosophy and Text Study at the End of the Twentieth Century.* London: SCM Press.

Wirzba, N. 2011. *Food and Faith: A Theology of Eating.* Cambridge: Cambridge University Press.

CHAPTER 32

ISLAMIC PERSPECTIVES

TARIQ RAMADAN

Introduction

The concept of the 'Abrahamic religions' is in some ways a relatively recent concept. Indeed it was really only during the nineteenth century that the subject began to appear within academia and the 'religious studies'. The French Christian theologian Louis Massignon (1883–1962) referred to Abrahamic religion in his articles and books, where he was considering ways in which such a concept might be best explained and understood. Yet from an Islamic perspective the concept appears to have a much longer history and indeed there is some intimation of the very meaning of Abrahamic religions in the Islamic scriptural sources. There are a number of verses in the Quran referring to 'people of the Book' (*ahl al-kitāb*)[1] with the common concept of revelation (*kitab* in Arabic); and the common trunk of three monotheistic religions. Muslims therefore believe that each monotheistic religion received its guidance directly through revelations from the same one God. The Islamic tradition also maintains that the three monotheistic traditions have the same 'father' Abraham; indeed there is a specific quote in the Quran pertaining to this affiliation:

> It is the religion (*millat*: cult, religious community) of your father Abraham. It is He who has named you Muslims, both before and in this (Revelation). (22: 78)

From the Islamic perspective it is entirely understandable that the earliest-formed monotheistic religion, Judaism, would not acknowledge the two subsequent monotheistic religions (Christianity and Islam) as the truth because the receipt of God's revelations through the three different historical periods is a sequential process. Similarly the final monotheistic religion can acknowledge the previous two monotheistic religions as they are recognized as being early parts in the sequence of God's entire revelation, which becomes complete with Islam, according to Muslims.

[1] Twenty-nine verses in the Quran refer to the notion of *ahl al-kitāb* such as 2: 105, 109.

This understanding from the most recent of the three monotheistic religions is critical in enabling the acknowledgement of a common trunk between all three religions, that is to say, there is one God who revealed guidance and reference for humankind in a chronological order, following Abraham, first to Jews through Moses, then to Christians through the teachings and example of Jesus of Nazareth, and finally to Muslims, through Muhammad. From an Islamic perspective, there were separate periods of revelation from the same one God, received and recorded as a book specific to each particular religion—Jews following the teachings in the Torah, Christians, the Bible and Muslims, the Quran.

In the Islamic tradition, the reference to Abraham as the 'father' of Judaism, Christianity, and Islam is fundamental for it enables the three religions to be linked together in a logical sequence and for Muhammad to be acknowledged as the 'Last Messenger' of the overall umbrella of the 'Abrahamic religions'. Thus, from an Islamic perspective, the concept of Abrahamic religions is not only an acceptable notion but also a necessary one so as to situate Islam within the context of a wider framework.

With such an intertwined history and complex relationship, these commonalities based on the oneness of God, the revelations, and Abraham as a central figure, are essential towards facilitating dialogue between the three monotheistic traditions, and are crucial to the success of helping to bring believers of all three traditions together to explore and consider ways to jointly address both classical theological questions and contemporary challenges.

Having acknowledged the importance of identifying commonalities, it is equally necessary to acquire a deep understanding and acceptance of the differences between the three monotheistic religions. Several of the chapters in this volume also refer to some such differences. There are, for example, differences surrounding the very figure of Abraham himself who is not understood in the same way within each of the monotheistic religions in terms of his role, affiliation, and the specific legacy which he left for each of the Jewish, Christian, and Islamic traditions. Thus whilst it is important to acknowledge a common trunk, it is equally critical to recognize that there are different interpretations and understandings between the traditions and also different expectations in terms of the relationship of the specific religion with Abraham. Yet by understanding the general essence of the three respective traditions the possibility exists to build a dialogue and develop an acceptable, clear relationship or framework between the three, from commonality to differences and from specific rituals to common objectives.

It is important to start by exposing the way Islam and Muslims should look, upstream, at this diversity of religion and its consequences. With this in mind, the ensuing discussion will consider the different steps towards understanding the aforementioned common trunk, then proceed to outline the differences that become evident by examining the respective religions more closely. The third part addresses the relationship between the three respective traditions and their scriptural sources whereby, from the Islamic tradition, the Abrahamic religions are principally based upon the understanding that Jews, Christians, and Muslims are 'people of the book', *ahl al-kitāb*. This part emphasizes the importance of the relationship to the scriptures—the history, discerning what is immutable and what is changeable, analysing the divine project and the role of the human agency. The fourth part will explore the sense of the community which other contributions to this volume have also raised, in terms of having a sense of belonging—how to reconcile singularity within the community, the universality of principles, the human family as 'one family', and the overall shared sacred history of the Abrahamic religions based on the diversity of various messengers. The fifth section will consider education and the transmission or dissemination of the three religions, and once again, following the way that this particular point has been raised elsewhere in this volume, explore both the transmission of knowledge of the religions and the transmission of faith, spirituality, and behaviour as a contemporary challenge. This in itself will act as an introduction to other contemporary issues that need to be addressed which are covered in the sixth section. That is to say, looking at the role of religion within secular societies and reflecting upon what the role of religion could be with respect to 'having' and 'being' and today's consumerist society; and the question of environment and issues pertaining to applied ethics, from medicine, food, arts, media, economics, politics, and so on. These are all contemporary issues, common challenges that need to be addressed. Finally the issue of violence will be considered. This is both a historical and contemporary issue, and certainly relevant for inclusion within this volume. The conclusion will profess to the consequent necessity for continual dialogue so as to facilitate the understanding of one another's references and viewpoints. Such dialogue must be efficient and realistic, one that has genuine impact on reality and it should not only be that of the specialists within academia but include the discourse of ordinary citizens, from scholars to practitioners on the ground, regular people who are striving to be faithful to their religious principles in their daily lives.

Dealing with (a Necessary) Diversity

According to Muslims, the last Revelation teaches them to recognize all the books of the prophets who had gone before. They all have the same purpose, to remind human beings of the presence of the Creator and the finiteness of life on earth. The Islamic tradition's concept of humankind emerged through this teaching: after forgiving Adam his sin, God told men:

> A guidance will certainly come to you from me. Those who follow my guidance will have nothing to fear and will not grieve. (Q. 2: 38)

This guidance is the series of Revelations that came throughout human history, each one to confirm, complete, and correct the preceding ones. So individuals, innocent and free, have to make their choices (either to accept or to reject the Revelation). There will necessarily be diversity among people, and so these three seemingly similar verses contain teachings that augment and complete each other:

> Had God so willed, He would have united them [human beings] in guidance, so do not be among the ignorant. (6: 35)
>
> If your Lord had so willed, everyone on earth would have believed. Is it for you to compel people to be believers? (10: 99)
>
> If God had willed, He would have made you one community but things are as they are to test you in what He has given you. So compete with each other in doing good. (5: 48)

The first verse instructs human beings that diversity is willed by the Transcendent, the second makes clear that, in the name of that will, compulsion in matters of religion is forbidden,[2] and the Revelation teaches that the purpose of these differences is to test us in order for us to discover what we are going to do with what has been revealed to us. The last commandment is to use these differences to 'compete in doing good'.

Diversity of religions, nations, and peoples is a test because it requires that we learn to manage difference, which is in itself essential:

> If God did not enable some men to keep back others, the world would be corrupt. But God is the One who gives grace to the worlds. (2: 251)
>
> If God did not enable some men to keep back others, hermitages, synagogues, chapels and mosques where the name of God is often called upon, would have been demolished. (22: 40)

These two verses give complementary information that is of prime importance. If there were no differences between people, if power were in the hands of one group alone (one nation, one race, or one religion), the earth would be corrupt because human beings need others to limit their impulsive desire for expansion and domination. The latter verse is more precise with regard to our present discussion, referring to places of worship and suggesting that if there is to be a diversity of religions, the purpose is to safeguard them all. The fact that the list of places begins with hermitages, synagogues, and chapels before referring to mosques shows recognition of all these places of worship and their inviolability and, of course, respect for those who pray there. Thus, just as diversity is the source of our test, the balance of power is a requirement for our destiny.

Difference might naturally lead to conflict. Therefore the responsibility of humankind is to make use of difference by establishing a relationship based on excelling one another in doing good. It is vital that the balance of power is based not on a tension born of rejection or mutual ignorance but fundamentally on knowledge:

> O people, we have created you from a male and a female, we have divided you into nations and tribes so that you might know one another. (49: 13)

[2] The Quran confirms this in a clear general rule: 'No compulsion in religion' (2: 256).

Knowing the other is a process that is unavoidable if fear of difference is to be overcome and mutual respect is to be attained. So human beings live a test that is necessary for their nature but that they can, and must, master by making the effort to know and recognize those who are not of their tribe, their country, their race, or their religion.[3] Dialogue, particularly interreligious dialogue, is indispensable: Abrahamic monotheism is by essence a tradition, a cycle, and cannot be embodied in one single religion.

Commonalities

Common concerns and challenges in relation to specific theological and legal issues are evident among the three Abrahamic religions. The identification of commonalities as a first step is critical in terms of helping to identify common challenges. The most important common thread running through the Abrahamic religions is the reference to one God and the 'oneness' of God. The Jewish and Islamic traditions are closer in this respect than the Christian tradition, whose belief in the Trinity (God the Father, the Son, and the Holy Spirit) is problematic for the Jewish and Islamic traditions, yet the notion of the 'oneness' of God and the belief that one God revealed to humanity the message for salvation, through scriptural sources and revelations, is shared by all three of the Abrahamic religions, acknowledging Abraham as the central reference. Thus the second commonality is this relationship between one God and humanity, a relationship based upon revelations being given to humanity from God through time and the mutual acknowledgement that scriptural sources are essential in being able to understand God's will, God's message, and God's expectation of humanity. Indeed, from the Islamic perspective, as mentioned previously in the Introduction, there are numerous verses in the Quran referring to the concept of Abrahamic religions, with references to 'the religions of the Book' and 'the people of the Book' and as a consequence, Muslims recognize Jews and Christians as being such people although Jews and Christians do not necessarily always share the same understanding. Muslims argue that this is because Jews and Christians are the receivers of the two earlier periods of God's revelation and it is quite normal for earlier versions to have difficulty in accepting the legitimacy of latterly established religions, as mentioned already in this chapter. Having said that, Richard Bulliet mentions in his chapter on 'Islamo-Christian Civilization' in Part II of this volume the notion that at least one of the Christian Gospels (Barnabas 97: 10) includes an explicit 'prediction' directly from God about the coming of Muhammad. This is a disputed interpretation, obviously, and has been mentioned repeatedly by many Muslim scholars and commentators.

[3] Read and understood globally, these quranic references bring together all the dimensions of 'difference' among human beings: tribe, nation, race, religion.

The third common feature is the acknowledgment by all three Abrahamic religions of a path which when followed can lead believers closer towards God, one that is based on rituals—prayers that are qualified; deeds that are considered lawful or unlawful, obligations, and prohibitions; and ethical values to be respected. Particular rituals are specific to each of the religions and contribute towards defining their differences within the commonality of the path towards God. Indeed the Islamic tradition, through numerous verses of the Quran, anticipates this understanding of differences between the religions, such as the verse mentioned earlier about diversity being God's will. Added to this is the understanding that to every single religious community God gave methodology and praxis and this methodology is based on the fundamentals of that religion, with rituals, particular ways of praying, and forming one's own individual relationship with God.

> For every one (religion) we appoint a way (*shirʿatan*) and a methodology (*minhājā*). (5: 48)

From an Islamic perspective, it is acknowledged that whilst believers of the three religions follow a specific path according to their particular Abrahamic religion, the fact that there are such differences within this common feature of rituals is critical towards affirming their own belief in Islam and being faithful to their understanding of God's complete revelation.

Not to reduce the Abrahamic religions to the commonality of a set of respective rituals, the last important common feature concerns values and ethical concerns such as the understanding of human behaviour beyond rituals, beyond any legal framework, and beyond even the Abrahamic religions per se. This is a common concept relating to controlling oneself; managing the limits of right and wrong; the dignity of human beings; what it truly means to be a human being; and the notion of family and society. These dimensions are of great significance to all three of the Abrahamic religions—directing human behaviour, distinguishing right behaviour from wrong behaviour, good from evil, just from the unjust. A common set of ethical values and concerns are connected to the central common concern of salvation.

So four key commonalities that, notwithstanding the diversity in the rituals, values, path, and scriptural sources, can be considered together within an overarching commonality of the essence of God's revelation and thus give rise to this common trunk of the Abrahamic reference.[4]

Challenges

Common challenges also exist between the Abrahamic traditions. One of the first, and more critical, challenges is the status of the scriptures and how exactly believers should

[4] These aspects are highlighted in Dirks 2004.

read and apply them. Of course, in Judaism there is a long-standing tradition of reading the scriptural sources, the Torah (and of course the Talmud), and striving to understand what needs to be contextualized and what is immutable; whether the text is a human product or whether this comes directly from God; the meaning of revelation; how to read the scriptural sources within history and using different levels of a linguistic approach in terms of semantics, grammar, and even the morphology of the words. The same questions exist in the Christian tradition with there being extensive discourse about the text in terms of both the historical and scientific approaches. That is to say, for a long period of time the Christian text was originally perceived as also coming directly from God then it was accepted as being a product of humans, having been gradually transformed and diversified throughout history. Thus it is imperative that the text be considered within a historical context and any interpretation needs to take into account differing contexts and cultures. From an Islamic perspective, the majority position is that the religious book, the Quran, is the very word of God, having been received by the Last Messenger, Muhammad over a period of twenty-three years and dictated verbatim from memory by Muhammad to local scribes of his day (since he himself could not write). Notwithstanding that the Quran is the direct word of God, it remains critical for Muslims to acknowledge that there can be diversity and interpretation of its verses and thus the challenge for Muslims is to consider how to interpret the text in the light of the history. God's word was revealed over a twenty-three-year period and the relationship between the text and context will naturally produce many interpretations. This is an important, necessary acknowledgement within the Islamic tradition which some currents or trends of Islam have difficulty accepting (for instance the literalists), that so as to be completely truthful to God's will, it is critical to consider context and the interpretation by the reader of the text as much as to consider the direct meaning of text (in its specific context). Furthermore, beyond the challenge of interpretation within any given time (the historical context) is the question of cultures and how to identify any cultural projection connected to the texts. Once again this is a common challenge for all three of the Abrahamic religions, the need to identify within the texts any cultural and geographical influences and to highlight the cultural projections through the historical interpretations. Indeed is it even possible to differentiate between the principles and any cultural and geographical stimuli that might have influenced the original interpretation of these principles and their consequent implementation? A crucial question per se (see Ramadan 2009).

These poignant examples illustrate how the three Abrahamic religions share common challenges in terms of their scriptural sources whereby all follow a scriptural source and all face the challenges of diversity of scriptural interpretations and tensions existing between the text and the context (history, culture, geography, and even the sciences).

This leads on to the third common challenge in terms of the scriptural text, differentiating between what is immutable and what is changeable, and all three of the Abrahamic religions are considering this together. Immutable principles relate to the 'oneness' of God; the very essence of the theological framework; and the rituals, prohibitions, and obligations, and then there is the need to identify what is changeable—using the text relative to the context and in accordance to the ultimate goals intended by that particular part of the text. Such tensions between recognizing and accepting what is immutable and what is changeable and any consequent interpretation and action are present throughout many contemporary ethical issues, for example in bioethics, medicine, culture, gender, and social behaviour. These are questions which are once again common to all three traditions.

The last point concerning common challenges is the tension between how to define the divine project for human beings and the agency in setting the understanding, or how to translate this divine project within our human history. Again this is an essential point worthy of some reflection. Some dogmatic minds or literalists consider that the human agency contribution of the divine project should be reduced to almost nothing, such that humans have no real part to play and their function is simply to follow the literal meanings. Yet one could argue that this falls short of God's intentions and what is really needed is to have an understanding of the divine project as it is understood when reading the scriptural sources, the Torah, Bible, or the Quran such that the role of the human agency is in itself of significance. For many believers, within all three of the traditions, there is no understanding of the divine project without human agency and this tension is at the heart of the respective understanding of faithfulness.

Community

When it comes to the sense of the religious community, in the Islamic tradition there is the notion of belonging to the umma, the 'religious community' or, as I would say myself, the community of principles and spirituality. Sometimes this notion is understood within the confines of very narrow terms—a community of people sharing the same faith and values but very much a closed community based on a very strict belonging to Islam. Similar situations exist in the Jewish and Christian traditions. Yet what is it that specifically defines a Jew or a Christian? Is it with reference to a spiritual dimension, is it about belonging to a specific culture or race, what does 'belonging' mean, how is the belonging to a specific religious community defined? What exactly makes a Jew a Jew, a Christian a Christian, a Muslim a Muslim? Such questions are at the starting point of this sense of community, this sense of belonging.

Not only is it important to reflect upon particular criteria used to identify who belongs to a particular community, it is also about communities nurturing that sense of belonging. So there exists a definition of community, a sense of belonging that becomes more exclusive to some people, those who are accepted or recognized as being members of a religious community. This is something which is much more open and acknowledges the fact that a community of principles is wider and more inclusive than a community of believers which is defined only through their belonging to a specific religion.

Such questions and reflections exist in all three Abrahamic religions in relation to who are the people who are defining and building the respective community. The sense of belonging also includes how, as a Jew, Christian, or Muslim, one nurtures the fact that not only are you a Jew, Christian, or Muslim, but you also belong to a human or a religious community, and/or a community of principles. This introduces the third challenge faced by all three religions, that is to say how to move from the singularity of belonging to a religious community to the universality of the principles with humanity. Here there is tension everywhere and this is related ultimately to a potential understanding of salvation—which of us shall be saved (from the Islamic perspective this refers to the Day of Judgement) (Khalil 2013). Thus the singularity of belonging to a religious community versus the universality of the principles that are shared and promoted among all three of the Abrahamic religions is a challenge that needs to be faced when it comes to reconciling one's religion with how to live in a pluralistic society, with a plurality of communities and how best to live together with others in respect and mutual understanding, not to reject 'the other' yet also not to go as far as syncretism and accepting that there are differences between us. An important observation when it comes to the notion of community—mutual respect in the light of the respective salvation theories.

The last point which goes beyond the tension between singularity and universality is looking at how to define the human family. Discourse from all the Abrahamic religions supports this notion of a 'human family' and that everyone belongs to it. This human family is also a family that was shaped through a sacred history, one based upon belief in God's revelations to Abraham, Moses, Jesus, and Muhammad, among others. Having said that, the human family has a synchronic tangible reality, being part of the human family which is shaped through the diachronic understanding that there is a sacred history. That is to say for Jews, the first Messengers and first period of Revelations is the truth; for Christians, that Jesus of Nazareth's example is the truth; and for Muslims, the Last Messenger, the final period of revelations is the truth. Thus each tradition believes that theirs is the ultimate goal of the sacred history. Through history, communities are being shaped and through history one can achieve a specific understanding of truth beyond this belonging to a human family. Sharing universal values and being able to interact positively and engage with people of other traditions is especially important in the discussions of this volume, which is exploring the interface between the three Abrahamic religions.

Education

In our contemporary world one of the big questions asked today throughout all three Abrahamic religions is how to transmit, how to educate new generations in the light of the scriptural sources, the revelations, and the messages of these revelations. The question of transmission (how to transmit not only the rules but also the spirit, not only the spirit but also the spiritual meaning of believing in God) is a very difficult discussion in contemporary societies where such great emphasis and value is placed on efficiency and having more than ethics and being. Accomplishment is often valued in terms of material benefit and profit, more than being human, understanding and having a sense of responsibility and solidarity. In a world where understanding our rights is being so much encouraged, all three Abrahamic religions cultivate a sense of responsibility and duty and this is where knowledge is so important.

How can more people attain religious knowledge and how can the religious teachings be best transmitted when there is so much religious illiteracy? This is a common concern, not only in the quest to know more about our respective religions but also to seek further knowledge of others, religious knowledge of the diversity among the religions and spiritualities. How can religious literacy best be attained and its transmission increased within our societies? This is an essential goal for there can be no living together, even between the three Abrahamic religions, without knowledge of both one's own religion and mutual knowledge of each other's. From the Islamic perspective, this is alluded to in one of the verses of the Quran, quoted earlier:

> . . . We have created you from male and female and made you tribes and nations that you may know one another . . .

There is a second important point relating to education. Religious education is also about teaching the rules, prohibitions, and limits. Today a discourse has developed about spirituality and faith, and whilst the most important focus is certainly about being spiritual and having faith, the religious education has become focused on the rituals and rules, reducing the religion to practices and protective regulations (certainly from an Islamic perspective, but similar trends are apparent in Judaism and Christianity). It is as if today 'religion' is deemed to be based on rituals and 'spirituality' is becoming defined as only a kind of a feeling of experiencing faith towards God. In the three traditions, there is similar concern about religious education and, in a world where rules and limitations are not very much in fashion, how should religious education be administered, what should it include? Educating only about the protective rules, regulations, and rituals may not necessarily be the best way and instead it could be better to encourage within the education process a focus on open spirituality and a deeper understanding of the faith. These are common discussions both within religious communities but also, transversally, across the board.

Of course the last stage in relation to education is behaviour, how to translate this knowledge into a behaviour. Certainly all the Abrahamic religions refer to the spiritual dimension of believing in God, the place of rituals in educating the being, and lastly the role of behaviour so as to change our world for the better. Within our society this behaviour is the public side of a private belief. In our secular societies it is an important topic of discussion, how to educate in the best possible way when the private side of this spiritual experience is encompassed by the rituals, and the rules and behaviour are the conveyance of our spiritual experience within the public sphere. Thus the question of how best to educate new generations towards achieving this is critical. There are some who consider that the only way to meet this challenge is to create privately funded religious schools away from the public state school system. However some caution is necessary here because sometimes such schools can be so insular as they aim to protect their students so much from the surrounding society and its influences, that it is not always possible to reconcile the teachings and principles of the respected revelation with the reality of today's world or to successfully nurture their students towards becoming adults who are able to live contentedly and contribute positively towards the pluralistic societies in which we live today.

Contemporary Issues

Here again the concept of the Abrahamic religions is important and contributes to the understanding that, in our contemporary societies, there are issues and concerns that are experienced and shared by all three, and beyond with atheists and agnostics. Often believers, from within their respective religion, think that they are the only ones facing a particular contemporary challenge. Where there is interfaith dialogue, it concerns the principles of their particular religion and such dialogue does not often broach any admittance to particular contemporary challenges. Yet in fact this is an area where the three Abrahamic religions could assist one another.

One such challenge is exploring the role that religion can have within secular society, the contribution that religion could make. Within the context of secularity, it is certainly acceptable for believers of religion to agree to separating the state from religion and to acknowledge the fact that within the private sphere, religion is important, but it is also crucial to engage in discourse regarding what part religion should play within the public sphere, now and in the future. Should religious signs disappear? Some secularists are quite dogmatic as they are calling for the end of the visibility of religion.[5] Yet such a proposition supports a very problematic understanding of secularism and all three Abrahamic religions need to proactively address this notion and enter into the debate. To accept secularity advocating a public sphere where it is possible for everyone to live together does not mean to accept any subsequent ending of the visibility of religion or for religious traditions to cease to have any positive and constructive role within our societies.

There is another—deeper—challenge which relates to how to cope with living in today's consumerist society. As mentioned earlier, it seems that there is an increasing celebration of the trend of having, much more so than being. This is where all religious traditions are striving to promote practices which can liberate us from this dependency, addiction, and consumerism; freedom from our consumer society which serves to

[5] Jean Baubérot (2012) speaks about a specific type of 'secular fundamentalism'.

generate a sense of perpetual, meaningless dependence. The challenge for the Abrahamic religions is therefore how to educate, how to best support societies towards this improvement: how to promote the joy of finding contentment in being, intimate peace, to celebrate values and to find contentment in the essence of the respective faiths. Such a challenge is connected to the previous discussions of education.

One of the great challenges of our time is of course environment. All three Abrahamic traditions, Judaism, Christianity, and Islam, have a very deep understanding of an obligation in terms of the need to respect the environment. This is because our environment is viewed as the very creation of God and, with this in mind, believers accept a responsibility towards looking after it and with this acknowledgement comes the need to formulate how to fulfil such a duty (Gottlieb 2011). Yet unfortunately all too often the religious traditions are far from being involved in discussions relating specifically to the environment or, when there is involvement, the religious participants of the discourse rely on the scriptural sources to provide some very deep theoretical and spiritual meaning rather than advice and recommendations as to what could be put into practice. It is sometimes as if environment is considered a secondary issue in religious terms. Yet this is a critical challenge which would certainly benefit from increased input from all religious voices, and given the overall theme of this volume there is no doubt that the voices of the Abrahamic traditions can come together to encourage participation in practical terms and urge that 'If you believe in God, if you respect God's creation, then you need to respect the environment, treat and care for it with responsibility and wisdom'.

This leads on to another practical challenge about dealing with science, the contemporary sciences, and new technologies. Applied ethics exists within some religious traditions but what is really needed is for Protestant applied ethics, Catholic applied ethics, Jewish applied ethics, Islamic applied ethics, and beyond, to all come together and to contribute to the discourse in bioethics, in medicine, indeed in any human behaviour or activity where the concept of ethics is present. The contribution of the Abrahamic religions together is not to prevent science from progressing or to inhibit the adding of knowledge to knowledge, rather to enable humankind to be more aware of the cause, of ethics, and to generate ends that are dignified in terms of respecting and preserving human dignity and preserving rather than destroying nature or indeed human beings. The Abrahamic religions can contribute together towards encouraging humankind to respect the very essence of what it means to be a human being and to ask the important questions that are being generated by these new realms of sciences. The examples of the relatively recent progress in cloning techniques and the implications in relation to changing creation spring immediately to mind.

The last issue that is in fact affecting everyone worldwide, not only the Abrahamic religions, relates to violence. For in the name of these religions, in the name of what believers accept as the truth, innocent people are being killed. No one can deny that actions, atrocities even, have been committed throughout history in the name of the Abrahamic religions that are simply unacceptable in human rights terms and in relation to human dignity. Antony Black touches upon this in his chapter on 'Political

Thought' in Part IV of this volume. So this is imperative to address: what is the relationship between the Abrahamic religions, dogmatism, and violence. Such issues need to be tackled from many different dimensions, not only from an Islamic perspective, where certainly it appears there is much focus today with regard to this topic. The situation is threefold—historical, contemporary, and evolutionary—a necessary discussion in terms of the concept of just war (Hashmi 2012), whether violence is always illegitimate or when it could be legitimate, and, if it is legitimate, how and when might there be something pertaining to legitimate resistance. What are the conditions and how can violence be defined? These are vital discussions to facilitate a new understanding for the future.

Shared Involvement

Dialogue is not enough. Even if it is rigorous, even if it is necessary to give time to knowing, trusting, and respecting each other, even if we should take on ourselves the widest possible responsibility to report back, it is only one stage or one aspect of the encounter among the various religious traditions. In western societies, it is urgent that we commit ourselves to joint action. In dialogue, we soon realize that we hold a great number of convictions and values in common, as we mentioned. We understand very quickly that we are facing the same difficulties and challenges. But we very rarely move outside these circles of reflection. Together we say 'God' awareness, spirituality, responsibility, ethics, solidarity, yet we live and experience each one on our own, the problems of education, transmission of spirituality, individualism, consumerism, and moral bankruptcy. In philosophical terms, we could say that we know one another in words but not in action. My own experience of twenty-five years of joint action in South America, Africa, and Asia has convinced me not only that this path is necessary but that it is the only way to eventually change minds and build mutual respect and trust.

In the West, there are many shared challenges. How can we pass on to our children the sense of the divine, for the monotheistic faiths, or of spiritual practice, for example? In a society that pushes people to own, how are we to form individuals whose awareness of being enlightens and guides their mastery of possession? Again, how are we to explain morality and boundaries, to pass on principles of life that do not confuse liberty with carelessness and that consider neither fashion nor quantity of possessions as the measure of goodness? All the Abrahamic and spiritual traditions are experiencing these difficulties, yet there are few examples of shared commitment to proposing alternatives. And there is so much to do—working together, as parents and as citizens, so that schools will provide more courses on the religions; suggesting ways of providing educational modules outside the school structures to teach the general population about the religions—their fundamental beliefs, particular topics, and social realities. Such modules need to be planned together in partnership rather than only inviting a partner from other religions to give a course as part of a programme that we have compiled for and by ourselves.

Acts of solidarity take place from within each religious family, but the examples of shared initiatives are rare. People sometimes invite others, but do not act in collaboration. One of the best testimonies that a religious Abrahamic tradition can give of itself lies in acts of solidarity between its adherents and others. To defend the dignity of the latter, to strive so that our societies do not produce indignity, to work together to support marginalized and neglected people, will certainly help us know one another better but it will, above all, make known the essential message that shines at the heart of the Abrahamic traditions: never neglect your brother in humanity and learn to love him, or at least to serve him.

More broadly, we have to act together so that the body of values that forms the basis of our ethics is not relegated to such a private and secluded sphere that it becomes inoperative and socially dead. Our philosophies of life must continue to inspire our civil commitment, with all due respect to the supporters of a postmodernism whose aim seems to be to deny any legitimacy to all reference to a universal ethic. There is a need to find together a civil role, inspired by common convictions, in which religions will work to demand that the rights of all be respected, that discriminations be outlawed, that dignity be protected, and that economic efficiency cease to be the measure of what is right. Differentiating between public and private space does not mean that women and men of faith, or women and men of conscience, have to shrink to the point of disappearance and fear to express themselves publicly in the name of what they believe. When a society has gone so far as to disqualify, in public debate, faith and what it inspires, the odds are that its system is founded only on materialism and ruled only by materialist logic—the self-centred accumulation of goods and profit.

The faithful of Abrahamic religions must dare to express their faith, its demands, and its ethics, to involve themselves as citizens in order to make known their human concerns, their care for justice and dignity, their ethical standards, their fears as consumers and media-consumers, their hopes as mothers and fathers—to commit themselves to do the best possible, together, to reform what might be. All religious traditions have a social message that invites the faithful to work together on a practical level. We are still far from this. In spite of thousands of dialogue circles and meetings, Abrahamic traditions still seem to know one another very little and to be very lacking in trust. Perhaps methods must be reconsidered and a mutual demand needs to be formulated: to behave in such a way that actions, as much as possible, mirror words, and then to act together.

Conclusion

Many commonalities, valued diversities, and countless challenges. With this in mind, further dialogue and proactivity are an absolute necessity and this in itself is an important challenge! Dialogue between the Abrahamic traditions among scholars who are familiar with one another's work and far from ordinary people is not the way forward. From specialists to academia to ordinary people it is essential to push and to understand our commonalities, our relationships to the scriptures, our belonging to the communities and to our challenges when in the field of education and contemporary issues. This is where more involvement is critical, engagement of many more people, at all levels and crossing all borders, trans-culturally and trans-nationally. Acknowledgement that intra-community dialogue within the religious traditions is also important on the theological basis or even cultural (because the experiences of Christians living in South America may be different from the experiences of Christians living in Africa or in the West, likewise there will be differences between the Jewish and Muslim communities in different parts of the world). Thus trans-intra-community dialogue and inter-community dialogue have a role to take into account the diversity of trends within each of the Abrahamic religions and also between the Abrahamic religions altogether.

In terms of the aforementioned contemporary issues, not only is it necessary to acquire a very deep understanding of the Abrahamic religions, but also not to exclude other religions and to consider, in a similar approach to this discourse, commonalities and common challenges, and to be involved with Hindus, Buddhists, Confucianists, and so on. It is also to have the courage not to accept the notion that we are living in a world where ideology does not exist. The Abrahamic religions should come with an assertive, ethical courage to propose that some ways of behaviour are not acceptable; there should be regulations; there are rules that can be beneficial if followed correctly; and values that can be celebrated altogether. Such courage means also to face all the human activities, from education to science and technology, economy, and politics. This is where the Abrahamic religions can be an influential contribution rather than being quite timid and overly concerned for anything that could be said about God and religion, or being anxious not to be perceived as backward to such an extent that our voice cannot be heard amongst the contemporary clamour. It might be that conserving values and promoting universal shared values is the common proposal by the 'Abrahamic religions', a resolution, perhaps, towards addressing the common challenges of today and the future tomorrow.

References

Baubérot, J. 2012. *La Laïcité falsifiée*. Paris: La Découverte.

Dirks, J. F. 2004. *The Abrahamic Faiths: Judaism, Christianity, and Islam Similarities and Contrasts*. Beltsville, MD: Amana Publication.

Gottlieb, R. S. 2011. *Engaging Voices: Tales of Morality and Meaning in an Age of Global Warming*. Waco, TX: Baylor University Press.

Hashmi, S. H. 2012. *Just Wars, Holy Wars, and Jihads: Christian, Jewish, and Muslim Encounters and Exchanges*. New York: Oxford University Press.

Khalil, M. H., ed. 2013. 'Salvation: The Known and the Unknown'. In *Between Heaven and Hell: Islam, Salvation, and the Fate of Others*. New York: Oxford University Press, ix–xiii.

Ramadan, T. 2009. *Radical Reform: Islamic Ethics and Liberation*. Oxford: Oxford University Press.

Index